BATHS

ROUGH GUIDE

KT-445-812

BOOK OF

Playlists

There are more than two hundred and fifty Rough Guide
travel, phrasebook and music titles, covering destinations from
Amsterdam to Zimbabwe, languages from Czech to Vietnamese,
and musics from World to Opera and Jazz.

To find out more about Rough Guides,
and to check out our coverage of more than
10,000 destinations, find us on the Web at:

Credits

Text editors: Peter Buckley, Duncan Clark, Mark Ellingham, Matt Milton, Joe Staines, Greg Ward

Layout/design: Peter Buckley, Duncan Clark, Henry Iles

Proofreading: Susannah Wight

Production: Julia Bovis

Series Editor: Mark Ellingham

Publishing Information

This first edition published October 2005 by
Rough Guides Ltd, 80 Strand, London WC2R 0RL
345 Hudson St, 4th Floor, New York 10014, USA
Email: mail@roughguides.com

Distributed by the Penguin Group:

Penguin Books Ltd, 80 Strand, London WC2R 0RL
Penguin Putnam, Inc., 375 Hudson Street, NY 10014, USA
Penguin Group (Australia), 250 Camberwell Road, Camberwell, Victoria 3124, Australia
Penguin Books Canada Ltd, 10 Alcorn Avenue, Toronto, Ontario, Canada M4V 1E4
Penguin Group (New Zealand), Cnr Rosedale and Airborne Roads, Albany, Auckland, New Zealand

Printed in Italy by LegoPrint S.p.A.

Typeset in Helvetica Neue and Myriad Pro
416 pages

A catalogue record for this book is available from the British Library

ISBN 13: 978-1-84353-603-1
ISBN 10: 1-84353-603-X

1 3 5 7 9 8 6 4 2

THE
ROUGH GUIDE
BOOK OF

Playlists

Edited by
Mark Ellingham

Contributing editors
Nigel Williamson & Al Spicer

ROUGH
GUIDES

Contributors

This book took shape in discussions at Rough Guide's music HQ between all the editors – Mark Ellingham, Duncan Clark, Peter Buckley, Matt Milton, Joe Staines, Andrew Lockett and Daniel Crewe – along with old lags Al Spicer and Greg Ward. Nigel Williamson ran with the project and, as well as writing scores of lists, garnered most of the guest entries.

The book wouldn't have made it to press without their contributions, nor those of Essi Berelian, Lloyd Bradley, Peter Shapiro, Richie Unterberger, David Honigmann, Andrew Rosenberg (and his crew), Garth Cartwright, Ed Wright, Chris Ingham, Ian Cranna, Jon Lusk and Toby Manning, each of whom wrote great and multiple entries.

Thanks also to all the musicians who said yes, and to the writers Nick Hornby, Ed Smith, Mark Ellen, Barry Miles, Ian Anderson, Charlie Gillett, Simon Broughton and Tony Wheeler (we signed him from Lonely Planet on a close season free transfer) for generously responding to email pleadings. Here's the full roll call.

WRITER CONTRIBUTORS

Ian Anderson
Dave Atkinson
Richard Baker
Frank Barrett
Steve Birt
Lloyd Bradley
Peter Buckley
Tom Bullough
Garth Cartwright
Duncan Clark
Chris Coe
Rachel Coldicutt
Geoff Colquitt
Ian Cranna
Daniel Crewe
Nat Defriend
John Duhigg
Martin Dunford
Nick Edwards
Mark Ellen
Mark Ellingham
Lisa-Jane Ellis
Jan Fairley
Neil Foxlee
Ben Garfield
Simon Garfield
Charlie Gillett
Pete Hogan
David Honigmann
Nick Hornby
Colin Irwin
Butch Lazorchak
Andrew Lockett
Jon Lusk
Toby Manning
Dan May
Gavin McNamara
Phil Meadley
Barry Miles

MUSICIAN CONTRIBUTORS

Carl Barat
Peter Blegvad
Dennis Bovell
Billy Bragg
Peter Buck
Tim Burgess
Eric Clapton
Elvis Costello
Dani Filth
Hugh Hopper
Dr John
Bert Jansch
Marianne Faithfull
David Gray
Al Green
Emmylou Harris
David Harrington
Robyn Hitchcock
Jazzy B

Stephen Malkmus
Phil Manzanera
Mariza
Danny McNamara
Moby
Sinead O'Connor
Andrew Loog Oldham
Robert Plant
Keith Richards
Mykaell S Riley
Michael Stipe
Richard Thompson
KT Tunstall
Tom Waits
James Walsh
Lucinda Williams
Brian Wilson
Robert Wyatt

Matt Milton
Greg Neale
Chris Nickson
Werner Pieper
Tim Pollard
Alastair Rolfe
Andrew Rosenberg
Madelyn Rosenberg
Rough Trade, Portobello
Greg Salter
Seb Secker-walker
Peter Shapiro
Paul Simpson

Hunter Slaton
Ed Smith
AnneLise Sorensen
Sue Steward
Mike Symons
Jean Trouillet
Richie Unterberger
Greg Ward
Alex Webb
Tony Wheeler
Rowland White
Nigel Williamson
Ed Wright

"There's always the possibility that you're going to come across a record that transforms your life. And it happens weekly. It's like a leaf on the stream. There are little currents and eddies and sticks lying in the water that nudge you in a slightly different direction. And then you break loose and carry on down the current. There's nothing that actually stops you and lifts you out of the water and puts you on the bank but there are diversions and distractions and alarums and excursions which is what makes life interesting really. Not in a Roman Emperor kind of way where you have an *excess* of stimulation – I forget which Emperor it was that used to have animal skins thrown over him and then scamper into an arena and claw the testicles off naked slaves with his bare hands, not quite *that* level – but a little excitement here and there. And music provides that. It's fantastic."

JOHN PEEL

Introduction

You're reading this book, so you know the deal. Albums aren't everything anymore. Sure, they're a handy format for symphonies and concertos, but when it comes to rock, soul, pop, reggae, hip-hop, jazz, world music – the terrain of this book – it's individual tracks that matter. It's all about assembling those tracks for yourself, or for your friends, in **playlists**.

You can do anything with a playlist. Historic overviews of artists, restrospectives of a micro-genre that passed everyone else by, lists of the greatest soul songs ever, classic hip-hop, or prog rock that stands the test of time. Or something more flip, like the weirdest covers ever recorded, or songs about the moon, or rain, or stars, or chickens and insects, or jelly, or getting drunk.

That's what this book is all about. Not the drunk thing, especially, though we do have lists for drinking songs (and sex, and drugs, and most conceivable forms of of rock'n'roll). But this is a book about enthusiasms, obsessions and sharing. It's a collection of playlists that will burst into life as you download the tracks, reflecting a fantastic depth of knowledge from a myriad of contributors, who have scrutinized their iPods or MP3 players and set out their stores.

Most of these contributors are professional music writers, but there are some first timers, too, who got to hear about the project and sent in their ideas. And, it's a pleasure to be able to say that the book is chock-full of playlists from legends such as Tom Waits, Keith Richards and Robert Plant. In these pages you'll find the songs that turned Eric Clapton on to blues, the tracks that move Al Green or Emmylou Harris.

But as the cliché goes, this is a book that needs no introduction. Just get browsing – and start downloading. And if you think we've got it all wrong, let us know. There's a second edition of this book planned, and we'll be changing things around, adding more artists, genres and quirks. To see what we're up to, check roughguides.com/playlists – where you will also find a useful guide to the best sites for downloading music, posted from our companion book, *The Rough Guide to iPods and Digital Music*.

Meantime, see what you think of this lot…

Mark Ellingham, Editor

ABBA

You didn't have to hear an ABBA song twice to get it: they hit you square in the heart and the head first time.

❶ KNOWING ME, KNOWING YOU from **ARRIVAL**
The synths and acoustic guitars are crisp and clean as the snow in the video, but there's nothing cold about that climactic whisper ("baaad days"). Alan Partridge notwithstanding, still the stuff of goosebumps.

❷ SOS from **ABBA**
ABBA in excelsis: coat-grabbingly immediate piano riff, plaintive verse suddenly gives way to instantly anthemic chorus.

❸ THE WINNER TAKES IT ALL from **SUPER TROUPER**
Agnetha's accent rarely sounded thicker, yet this somehow adds to the emotional impact of another great breakup ballad that had poignant parallels in real life.

❹ THE NAME OF THE GAME from **ABBA THE ALBUM**
Even The Fugees' pillaging of the riff has done the song no harm: curiously complex for something so immediate, simultaneously fragile, forlorn, hopeful and happy.

❺ DANCING QUEEN from **ARRIVAL**
Frida famously burst into tears when she first heard the backing track for this song: rightly so, rarely has disco exuberance had such an undercurrent of melancholy.

❻ MAMMA MIA from **ABBA**
Only consummate pop craftsmen understand the glory of the glockenspiel, which takes equal billing to the girls' glorious voices here.

❼ MONEY MONEY MONEY from **ARRIVAL**
Pounding, piano-fuelled paean to 70s excess. Wonderfully disingenuous use of English slang too: "I bet he wouldn't fancy me." Yeah, right!

❽ WATERLOO from **WATERLOO**
Where it all started: this 1974 Eurovision winner may be lyrically daft, but it's musically deft, reeling you in with hook after hook after hook.
Toby Manning

Acid Jazz

Take a dash of acid house, a slice of jazz-funk, sprinkle with lounge – and you have a musical movement. The DJ Gilles Peterson came up with the name acid jazz and for a while in the 1990s it ruled.

❶ LONG TIME GONE GALLIANO from **THE PLOT THICKENS**
Acid jazz at its most inventive on an urbanized version of David Crosby's song from the first CS&N album.

❷ STONED WOMAN MOTHER EARTH from **STONED WOMAN**
Funky, Hammond-led title track from the debut album from Matt Deighton's band.

❸ MIDNIGHT AT THE OASIS BRAND NEW HEAVIES from **BROTHER SISTER**
Great, jazzy vocal from N'Dea Davenport on a reinvention of the old Maria Muldaur song.

❹ VIRTUAL INSANITY JAMIROQUAI from **TRAVELLING WITHOUT MOVING**
A simple groove and clever, complex arrangement on a track from the most commercially successful band to earn – and then transcend – the acid jazz tag.

⑤ SO WHAT RONNY JORDAN from **THE ANTIDOTE**
The Miles Davis classic reworked with a modern groove by the British guitarist, with Arnie Somejee on superb acoustic bass.

⑥ LOUNGIN' JAZZMATAZZ from **JAZZMATAZZ VOLUME ONE**
An experimental fusion of hip-hop and doctored jazz-funk beats courtesy of Guru of Gang Starr and jazz veteran Donald Byrd.

⑦ SKIRT ALERT CORDUROY from **DAD MAN CAT**
Swinging but playful organ-led grooves from the post-modern Booker T & The MGs.

⑧ STARSKY AND HUTCH THEME JAMES TAYLOR QUARTET from **WAIT A MINUTE**
One of the key records that kicked off the Acid Jazz movement in the late 80s, complete with ex-James Brown horn section.

Nigel Williamson

AC/DC

Australia's finest – the smutty schoolboys who went on forever. Scroll that volume wheel all the way round to 11...

❶ WHOLE LOTTA ROSIE from **LET THERE BE ROCK**
A song of ballsy brilliance – loose, raw and very, very fast. Just listen to Angus shredding his fingers on the solo.

❷ DOWN PAYMENT BLUES from **POWERAGE**
One of the all time great rock'n'roll penury lyrics from Bon Scott. He's so poor he can't even feed his cat!

❸ OVERDOSE from **LET THERE BE ROCK**
Who said things ever had to be perfect? Angus fumbles the intro and creates timeless magic.

❹ JAILBREAK from **DIRTY DEEDS DONE DIRT CHEAP (AUSSIE RELEASE)**
Featuring the most immaculate mid-song pause – and a top riff to boot.

⑤ DIRTY DEEDS DONE DIRT CHEAP from **DIRTY DEEDS DONE DIRT CHEAP**
Bon Scott at his menacing best, over a riff built to smash concrete.

⑥ RIFF RAFF from **IF YOU WANT BLOOD...**
If the hum of juiced-up amps at the start doesn't hook you then you must be deaf or dead. The best live album opener. Ever.

⑦ ROCK'N'ROLL AIN'T NOISE POLLUTION from **BACK IN BLACK**
A spot-on, two-finger salute to the band's detractors as new boy Brian Johnson sleazes through the song like he'd been in for years.

⑧ FOR THOSE ABOUT TO ROCK (WE SALUTE YOU) from **FOR THOSE ABOUT TO ROCK...**
Amazing solos and great big feckin' cannons at the end! What more do you need?

Essi Berelian

Adam & The Ants

The sweaty, leather clad champions of Art-Punk sleaze who grew into dandy highwaymen, and blossomed as kings of the wild frontier. Adam and his Ants always had designs on your underwear.

❶ STAND AND DELIVER from **PRINCE CHARMING**
Adam's campest, most hook-laden hit lays out the Ants' plan to rob you blind and spend the money on flash clothing. Perfect pop, heavy on the drums and drama queen guitar riffs.

❷ KINGS OF THE WILD FRONTIER from **KINGS OF THE WILD FRONTIER**
More of the same, all pomp and swagger, plus a neat line-dance that you can use to clear the floor at wedding parties this day.

❸ STRIP from **THE VERY BEST OF**
All tease and swagger as Adam bumps and grinds his 80s magnificence in your face like... well, like some overly made-up stripper.

❹ DEUTSCHER GIRLS from THE VERY BEST OF
Vintage Ant music looked back to the Weimar decadence glorified in *Cabaret*, then added a dash of Nazi-chic and shiny shiny leather. This is the result, a tango about masochism.

❺ WONDERFUL from THE VERY BEST OF
No-nonsense love ballad crooned by a mature and oh-so-experienced Ant whose days as a pirate highwayman have eased into decadent middle age. If Tom Jones recorded it, they could both retire on the profits.

❻ WHIP IN MY VALISE
from DIRK WEARS WHITE SOX
The Ants play dungeon master to Adam's master of debauch. Great title, painful puns ("who taught you to torture, who taught ya?").

❼ PHYSICAL (YOU'RE SO)
from KINGS OF THE WILD FRONTIER
Sounding as if the gag has just been ripped from between his jaws, Adam gasps through a tune so sleazy it could be in a nudie show.

❽ CLEOPATRA from DIRK WEARS WHITE SOX
According to the Ants, history's best stories were the dirty ones. This is gleeful dirty sex, celebrated by Adam trying to get rid of that scary rictus glare of lust.

Al Spicer

Ryan Adams

Erratic, unpredictable and at times infuriating – but at his best Ryan Adams is clearly touched by genius.

❶ COME PICK ME UP from HEARTBREAKER
"Fuck me up, steal my records, screw all my friends" – the highlight of his first and most potent solo album to date.

❷ OH MY SWEET CAROLINA from HEARTBREAKER
On the road and homesick with suitably aching backing vocals from Emmylou Harris.

❸ TO BE YOUNG (IS TO BE SAD, IS TO BE HIGH) from HEARTBREAKER
Sure it sounds like Subterranean Homesick Blues. But then Dylan borrowed *his* song from Chuck Berry's Too Much Monkey Business…

❹ NEW YORK, NEW YORK from GOLD
Ryan lifts the opening riff of Pinball Wizard but takes it somewhere all his own on an exuberant hymn to the Big Apple.

❺ WHEN THE STARS GO BLUE from GOLD
Deliciously cracked vocals and a tune to die for on one of Gold's more reflective moments.

❻ MAGNOLIA MOUNTAIN from COLD ROSES
Whiskeytown-sounding opener from 2005 album that marked a major return to form.

Nigel Williamson

Aerosmith

Big, bad-ass rockers in the 70s, Aerosmith went off the rails then returned as one of the slickest mega-bands of the MTV era and beyond.

❶ DREAM ON from AEROSMITH
A ballad devoid of schmaltz. The build-up is masterful and singer Steven Tyler sounds suitably frayed at the edges.

❷ DUDE (LOOKS LIKE A LADY) from PERMANENT VACATION
MTV loved this one. This lady-boy identity crisis is both funny and irritatingly catchy, plus Joe Perry delivers one hell of a twangy guitar solo.

❸ HANGMAN JURY from PERMANENT VACATION
A tale of drunken murder and retribution down in the bayou. You can almost smell the stale hooch and stagnant swamp water.

❹ LAST CHILD from ROCKS
A streetwise and funky riff bounces off some of Tyler's sassiest vocals. And a great guitar solo.

5 MAMA KIN from **AEROSMITH**

A salutary lesson for would-be sleazesters everywhere. This is how you write great gutter-level rockers with balls.

6 RAG DOLL from **PERMANENT VACATION**

Smokin' slide guitar and Technicolor New Orleans brass collide with a monster drum track. This sounds simply immense.

7 RATS IN THE CELLAR from **ROCKS**

When they hit the gas there's no stopping them. Tyler's schizophrenic vocals ricochet all over the place and the honking blues harp just adds to the chaos.

8 SWEET EMOTION from **TOYS IN THE ATTIC**

A Vocoder classic. Weird wobbly voices make the intro sound like a descent into some sort of erotic nightmare. Great riff too.

Essi Berelian

Africa calling

A playlist for a whole continent? Tall order, mad idea, etc. Still, here are 10 tracks that wear the classic tag with some ease.

1 PATA PAPA

MIRIAM MAKEBA from **THE VERY BEST OF**

They call her "Mama Africa" and her biggest hit really does transcend its South African town-ship origins to create a joyous soundtrack for the entire continent.

2 SOUL MAKOSSA

MANU DIBANGO from **SOUL MAKOSSA**

Africa doesn't get much funkier than this crossover hit from the Cameroonian veteran.

3 LADY FELA KUTI from **THE BLACK PRESIDENT**

Classic Afrobeat from Nigeria's late, legendary rebel. The man who invented the whole genre.

4 MONIE

KANDA BONGO MAN from **THE VERY BEST OF**

A prime slice of Congolese soukous from one of its most ebullient performers.

5 BIRIMA YOUSSOU N'DOUR from **JOKO**

His biggest hit in the West was Seven Seconds, but back home in Senegal this is his best-loved anthem.

6 LASIDAN ALI FARKA TOURE from **TALKING TIMBUKTU**

One of the finest guitarists in Africa, the Malian here teams up with Ry Cooder.

7 DIDI KHALED from **KHALED**

A thrilling international hit for Algeria's "king of raï" in the early 90s.

8 TEKERE SALIF KEITA from **FOLON – THE PAST**

The golden voice of Mali at his imperious best…

9 SHUMBA THOMAS MAPFUMO from **THE BEST OF**

Mapfumo created the soundtrack for Zimbabwe's independence struggle with hits like this.

10 YEKE YEKE MORY KANTÉ from **THE BEST OF**

Monster 80s dancefloor hit from the singer from Guinea and one of the records that first put African music on a global stage.

Nigel Williamson

Alice Cooper

Matching pop sensibility with house-of-horror theatrics and heavy metal thunder, Alice spat in the face of the love'n'peace generation… and his spirit spawned bastard child Marilyn Manson.

1 HALO OF FLIES from **KILLER**

Alice as modern day Rasputin. And below the schlock is serious music – mad monk dance moves and an extremely tight rhythm section.

2 DESPERADO from **KILLER**

Alice as gunslinger-for-hire. He's a killer. He's a clown. His shots are clean. His shots are final.

3 SCHOOL'S OUT from **SCHOOL'S OUT**

Alice as school leaver drunkenly marching

towards the Principal's office. Was there ever anything more pure delinquent rock'n'roll?

❹ ELECTED from **BILLION DOLLAR BABIES**
Alice as demented politician, egomania laid bare. Fabulous tune, too.

❺ NO MORE MR NICE GUY
from **BILLION DOLLAR BABIES**
Alice plays… Alice. Only tongue in cheek, of course.

❻ ONLY WOMEN BLEED from **WELCOME TO MY NIGHTMARE**
Alice sings sensitive ballad shock. And it was a #1 hit for Julie Covington.

Chris Coe

Alt-Country

Known by many names, this bastard, rebellious mini-genre channels a world where Nashville doesn't exist and Hank Williams had no progeny.

❶ NO DEPRESSION UNCLE TUPELO from **NO DEPRESSION**
According to many, the song that started it all, an updated-for-latter-times (at least by implication) Carter Family classic from the 1930s.

❷ WINDFALL SON VOLT from **TRACE**
Rising from Uncle Tupelo's ashes, Jay Farrar's Son Volt was soon eclipsed by Wilco – but not before releasing this alt-country classic.

❸ EMMA RICHARD BUCKNER from **BLOOMED**
One of many character study gems by the oft-overlooked Buckner, delivered in his gloriously deep, sorrowful trademark drawl.

❹ HIGHWAY PATROLMAN BRUCE SPRINGSTEEN from **NEBRASKA**
Though technically Nebraska predates alt-country, the album shares its spirit; this tale of two brothers is its heartbreaking highlight.

❺ SUNKEN WALTZ CALEXICO from **FEAST OF WIRE**
Too Southwest'for some, Calexico mines a rich end-of-century Americana here, praying for rain "to cover the whole Western states".

❻ JOHN WALKER'S BLUES
STEVE EARLE from **JERUSALEM**
Written from the POV of the "American Taliban'" John Walker Lindh, Earle growls about being "Just an American boy, raised on MTV".

❼ OH MY SWEET CAROLINA
RYAN ADAMS from **HEARTBREAKER**
Adams was an alt-country darling before he got too big for his britches; you'll see why on this duet with the inimitable Emmylou Harris.

❽ PORTLAND, OREGON LORETTA LYNN & JACK WHITE from **VAN LEAR ROSE**
Timeless Loretta teams up with White Stripe Jack, hollering "Portland, Oregon and sloe gin fizz – if that ain't love then tell me what is".

❾ ATONEMENT LUCINDA WILLIAMS
from **WORLD WITHOUT TEARS**
Lucinda shows why she's on the outs with the Nashville establishment, howling fire and brimstone toward preachers and their flock.

❿ MISUNDERSTOOD WILCO from **BEING THERE**
Before Wilco got all art-rock, they turned in this furious milestone. Tweedy would like to thank you all for "nothing, nothing, nothing at all".

Hunter Slaton

The American Songbook (1)

"The fundamental things apply, as time goes by…" Here is the essential canon from the American Songbook: the great popular song composers of the 1930s and 40s, such as Cole Porter, George Gershwin, Jerome Kern, Harold Arlen, Rodgers & Hart.

❶ FOOLS RUSH IN BROOK BENTON from **BEST OF THE DEFINITIVE AMERICAN SONGBOOK, VOL 1**
Early rock'n'roll? Sounds like it. But this song, with lyrics by Johnny Mercer (co-founder of Capitol Records) and music by Rube Bloom, first appeared in 1940.

❷ SMOKE GETS IN YOUR EYES SARAH VAUGHAN from **AMERICAN SONGBOOK SERIES: JEROME KERN**
Written by Jerome Kern (music) and Otto Harbach (lyrics), this made its debut in the 1933 musical *Roberta*, which starred a pre-movies Bob Hope. The song "swept the dance-floors, radio stations, and glee clubs of the country," noted the *Herald Tribune*.

❸ I'VE GOT YOU UNDER MY SKIN PEGGY LEE from **AMERICAN SONGBOOK SERIES: COLE PORTER**
This evergreen favourite of Franks Sinatra and Valli was written by Cole Porter for *Born To Dance* (1936) where it's sung by a Broadway star pursuing a young sailor on shore leave.

❹ NIGHT AND DAY FRANK SINATRA from **BEST OF THE DEFINITIVE AMERICAN SONGBOOK, VOL 2**
Another by Cole Porter. The song was inspired by dancer-choreographer Nelson Barclift, with whom Porter had an intense affair. Written, appropriately enough, for the 1932 musical comedy *Gay Divorce*.

❺ I'LL BE SEEING YOU BING CROSBY from **BEST OF THE DEFINITIVE AMERICAN SONGBOOK, VOL 1**
Written by Sammy Fain and Irving Kahal for the 1938 Broadway production *Right This Way*, this classic has demonstrated considerably more staying power than the show, which lasted all of 14 performances.

❻ STORMY WEATHER LENA HORNE from **BEST OF THE DEFINITIVE AMERICAN SONGBOOK, VOL 2**
Harold Arlen wrote this for the 1933 Cotton Club Revue. And it sounded just as great half a century later in Derek Jarman's movie of Shakespeare's *Tempest*, where it is sung by the wonderful Elizabeth Welch.

❼ BLUE MOON MEL TORME from **BEST OF THE DEFINITIVE AMERICAN SONGBOOK, VOL 1**
It was third time lucky for this Richard Rodgers and Lorenz Hart song, composed for a Rita Hayworth project, but discarded, then re-worked as "The Bad In Every Man" (for Clark Gable movie *Manhattan Melodrama*) before at last emerging as "Blue Moon".

❽ OVER THE RAINBOW JUDY GARLAND from **AMERICAN SONGBOOK SERIES: HAROLD ARLEN**
You have to have this Harold Arlen song on your iPod. If you've got a heart. Everybody has covered it – Chet Baker notably on trumpet – but the original is essential.

❾ EMBRACEABLE YOU NAT KING COLE from **AMERICAN SONGBOOK SERIES: GEORGE GERSHWIN**
Gershwin wrote this as an instrumental for *An American in Paris* but it took flight with lyrics, becoming a #1 hit for Nat King Cole.

❿ MY FUNNY VALENTINE CHET BAKER from **BEST OF THE DEFINITIVE AMERICAN SONGBOOK, VOL 2**
Rodgers & Hart again: a gorgeous creation for the kids-in-showbiz musical, *Babes in Arms*, starring Judy Garland and Mickey Rooney.

Ian Cranna

The American Songbook (2)

The American Songbook has been an enduring gift, in every decade. Here are 10 fine revisitings from the 1960s on.

❶ THESE FOOLISH THINGS BRYAN FERRY from **THESE FOOLISH THINGS**
Ferry looked strangely menacing in Lounge Lizard gear, but this 1973 cover of a 1936 musical revue song started a new appreciation of standards.

❷ MY HEART STOOD STILL THE MAMAS & THE PAPAS from **THE MAMAS & THE PAPAS**
Were harmonies ever so thrilling? It's just 1.43 mins long but this 1966 rendition of a Rodgers & Hart song (from the musical *A Connecticut Yankee*) was the group's finest moment.

❸ HAPPY TALK CAPTAIN SENSIBLE single

An irresistible tune, the incontrovertible logic of "If you don't have a dream, how you gonna have a dream come true?", and the punk Captain's genial looning gave this classic from *South Pacific* (1949) new life back in 1982.

❹ I'M AN OLD COW HAND DAN HICKS & HIS HOT LICKS from RETURN TO HICKSVILLE

Johnny Mercer's witty dissection of a 1936-style cowboy (who learns his songs from the radio and drives in the range in his car) is perfect for Hicks' eccentric vision and acoustic swing. Beautifully delivered by Lickette Naomi Eisenberg.

❺ I GET A KICK OUT OF YOU GARY SHEARSTON from ONLY LOVE SURVIVES

An inspired, sweeping violin accompaniment helped send this memorable Cole Porter cover (by an otherwise unremarkable Australian singer-songwriter) up the UK charts in 1974.

❻ ANYTHING GOES HARPERS BIZARRE from ANYTHING GOES

This Cole Porter song might have been written for the Californian quintet's close harmonies, though some of his waspish wit does get lost.

❼ I ONLY HAVE EYES FOR YOU ART GARFUNKEL from GARFUNKEL

Beautiful song, beautifully sung. Originating in the 1934 musical *Dames*, this Harry Warren/Al Dubin composition launched Art's solo career with a worldwide #1 in 1975.

❽ SUMMERTIME BILLY STEWART from ONE MORE TIME: THE CHESS YEARS

R'n'B singer Stewart's unforgettable, Force-10 performance of this George Gershwin song (from *Porgy & Bess*) is full of soulful brrrs and chucks… guess nobody told him it's supposed to be a lullaby.

❾ MISS OTIS REGRETS KIRSTY MACCOLL from RED HOT & BLUE

Cole Porter again, the man who told Frank Sinatra to stop singing his songs unless he stuck to the tune. He'd have had no problem with Kirsty MacColl's melancholy treatment of his 1934 melody and black humour.

❿ IT NEVER ENTERED MY MIND PEGGY LEE from MISS WONDERFUL/DREAM STREET

An intriguing note to close on: were it not for the Rodgers & Hart writing credit (1940), you would swear that Ms Lee's 1952 reworking was a Pet Shop Boys' song. A classic of unanticipated loneliness and wistful regret.

Ian Cranna

Tori Amos

Tori Amos often appears to be out there with the fairies, but her gift for melody and a startlingly original line combined with her extraordinary voice has made her a Kate Bush for her generation.

❶ ME AND A GUN from LITTLE EARTHQUAKES

A harrowingly autobiographical tale of rape that is not for the squeamish.

❷ SILENT ALL THESE YEARS from LITTLE EARTHQUAKES

Has there ever been a more startling exploration of a dysfunctional relationship?

❸ CORNFLAKE GIRL from UNDER THE PINK

Some people thought this one *was* Kate Bush when they first heard this 1994 top ten hit.

❹ PAST THE MISSION from UNDER THE PINK

Featuring Nine Inch Nails' nihilist Trent Reznor and recorded in the house where Manson's mob murdered Sharon Tate. Was she trying to shock us, by any chance?

❺ LOSING MY RELIGION from THE SOUNDTRACK TO HIGHER LEARNING

She's made a secondary career out of quirky versions of other people's songs, culminating in the all-covers album *Strange Little Girl* in 2001. This extraordinary take on an REM song was recorded for the movie *Higher Learning*.

❻ PROFESSIONAL WIDOW from BOYS FOR PELE

A striking remix by Armand Van Helden gave Amos a British #1 single with this in 1997.

❼ DOWN BY THE SEASIDE from ENCONIUM: A TRIBUTE TO LED ZEPPELIN

Another cover, but this time as a duet with her teenage hero and the man who originally sang the song on Zep's *Physical Grafitti*, Mr Robert Plant.

❽ JAMAICA INN from THE BEEKEEPER

From her most recent 2005 album and inspired by Daphne Du Maurier's book of the same name, set in Cornwall where Amos now lives.

Nigel Williamson

Laurie Anderson

At her best, performance artist Lindsay Anderson makes the familiar strange again with a precise ear for a telling banality.

❶ FROM THE AIR from BIG SCIENCE

Whip-cracking drums and robotic saxophone lead into an in-flight announcement that morphs into a demented game of Simon Says: "Jump out of the plane. There is… no… pilot."

❷ O SUPERMAN (FOR MASSENET) from LIVE IN NEW YORK

Back in the 80s, we had hit singles which lasted for eight minutes and whose lyrics consisted largely of the repeated word "Ah". Tell the kids nowadays, and they won't believe you. This live version, just a week after 9/11, adds a new chill to "Here come the planes/They're American planes/Made in America".

❸ GRAVITY'S ANGEL from MISTER HEARTBREAK

Opens in near hysteria with a tintinnabulation of bells and keening, high-pitched singing, and then pays oblique homage to Thomas Pynchon's *Gravity's Rainbow*, or at least to that book's central parabola.

❹ KOKOKU from MISTER HEARTBREAK

Hypnotic Japanoiserie, patterned with wood-block and kayagum and parrot noises.

❺ BLUE LAGOON from MISTER HEARTBREAK

A sampled voice barks like a tropical frog amid quotations from *The Tempest* and *Moby Dick*. Melville remained an obsession: Anderson would later devote an entire show and album to the Great White Whale.

❻ LANGUAGE IS A VIRUS from UNITED STATES LIVE

One of the only moments when this eight-hour performance piece broke into something that resembled a song; short, sharp, funky and driven by the theories of William S Burroughs.

❼ STRANGE ANGELS from STRANGE ANGELS

Anderson's work is never actually pretty, but this is comes close, with a tinkling keyboard trill and swooning pedal steel. The lyrics were inspired by a conversation with Wim Wenders while he was working on *Wings Of Desire*.

❽ SAME TIME TOMORROW from TIGHTROPE

"Is time long? Or is it wide?" It sounds like an editorial from the heyday of *Wired* magazine.

David Honigmann

Animal magic

There's a whole world of exciting animals out there to sing about. This is just a small sampling from the kingdom.

❶ PIGGIES THE BEATLES from THE WHITE ALBUM

❷ PINK ELEPHANTS ON PARADE SUN RA AND HIS ORCHESTRA from STAY AWAKE

❸ TIGER MAN ELVIS PRESLEY from TIGER MAN

❹ EFFERVESCING ELEPHANT SYD BARRETT from BARRETT

❺ SEE YOU LATER ALLIGATOR BOBBY CHARLES from WALKING NEW ORLEANS

❻ HOLY COW LEE DORSEY from THE VERY BEST OF

❼ MONKEY MAN TOOTS & THE MAYTALS from MONKEY MAN

❽ THE MONKEY DAVE BARTHOLOMEW from THE MONKEY

⑨ MONKEY MAN
THE ROLLING STONES from LET IT BLEED

⑩ BRONTOSAURUS THE MOVE
from THE VERY BEST OF

Greg Ward

Anti-Flag

Pittsburgh's agit-punk outfit has been churning out politically charged sounds for a decade and has upped the ante since the Bush Führer's coup d'état. They can kick up a storm, too.

❶ DIE FOR YOUR GOVERNMENT from DIE FOR YOUR GOVERNMENT
Popular live chant-along with the right mixture of mangled chords and simple chorus: "Die for your country? That's shit!".

❷ RANK-N-FILE from THE TERROR STATE
The catchy harmonies and clipped guitars with rocket flashes definitely summon up early Clash as Justin Sane and co show their solidarity with the masses.

❸ YOU CAN KILL THE PROTESTER BUT YOU CAN'T KILL THE PROTEST from THE TERROR STATE
Another anthem for the disillusioned and disenfranchised as guitars and vocals race each other for the cause.

❹ STARS AND STRIPES
from UNDERGROUND NETWORK
A delicious loping bass underlies the chunky chords and chanted vocals in this high energy tirade against America's obsession with Old Glory.

❺ MIND THE G.A.T.T. from THE TERROR STATE
The band turn their anger on corporate globalization to a punk/reggae beat with a couple of brilliant pop hooks, all introduced by Mr Bush himself.

Nick Edwards

Aphex Twin

A one-man case for an independent Cornwall, Richard D James makes for some fantastically uneasy listening

❶ COME TO DADDY from COME TO DADDY EP
Play this at bedtime and you'll never be asked to babysit again. Loud, dirty, bad, scary music.

❷ WINDOWLICKER from WINDOWLICKER EP
Aphex get a bit funky. Exploring Hip-Hop beats, deconstructing them to their component parts and building them back up like a transformer robot, this instrumental packs more menace than a thousand lines of cheap rap boasts.

❸ CORNISH ACID from RICHARD D JAMES
You know, I think the secret of his inspiration might be in the title. Another madcap, high speed dash round Richard's neurones.

❹ MOUNT SAINT MICHEL MIX from DRUKQS
Includes pretty much all the effects, including police sirens and, somewhere deep deep down, the kitchen sink.

❺ VORDHOSBN from DRUKQS
Lovely delicious acidity, maddening beats and crazy rhythms.

❻ DIDGERIDOO (LIVE IN CORNWALL 1990)
from CLASSICS
It sounds like a didgeridoo at first, then before you know it, you're on your feet dancing, laughing wildly, screaming at the dawn and throwing your clenched fists high into the sky. You might need a sit down afterwards.

❼ FOUR from RICHARD D JAMES
Aphex drifts off into a dreamy, lost-concentration drum'n'breaks reverie before a voice from the real world drops in and calls us all suddenly back into pin sharp focus.

❽ XTAL from SELECTED AMBIENT WORKS 85–92
Aphex Twin's most beautiful chill out track.

Al Spicer

Arabesque

"Arabesque" refers to a heavily stylized type of Arabic decoration, or something that is "strangely mixed" or "fantastic". That sums up dance music's new-found love affair with contemporary Arabic music pretty much perfectly.

❶ EYE OF THE DUCK NATACHA ATLAS from MARRAKESH MISSION
An insistently funky mix of Jamaican Dancehall and Egyptian bellydance, featuring the ragga toasting of Princess Juliana.

❷ KALZOOM U-CEF FEATURING AMINA ANNABI from MARRAKESH MISSION
Amina covers the great Umm Kalthum, the Arab world's legendary singer, whilst U-Cef adds a powerful, string laden drum & bass backdrop.

❸ ALAOUI (DIGITAL BLED DANCE MIX) L'ORCHESTRE NATIONAL DE BARBÉS from FLYING CARPET BY CLAUDE CHALLE
An epic remix from Paris-based DJ Pedro of this French-Maghrebi outfit, creating a track that manages to encapsulate all the best elements of Westernised Arabic dance music.

❹ BEYROUTH ECOEUREE CLOTAIRE K from LEBANESE
A poignant tale of Beirut's war torn heart played out amidst hard hip-hop beats and scattered automatic weapon fire.

❺ CHICKY OOJAMI from BELLYDANCING BREAKBEATS
A supremely funky slice of Turkish break-beat featuring the rapping of Samir Bouchakara.

❻ SOUTANBI GNAWA NJOUM EXPERIENCE FEATURING AIWA from AIWA
The gutsiest slice of gnawa this side of the Rif Mountains, this hypnotic track sees the Iraqi brothers hooking up with hot new French-Moroccan collective.

Phil Meadley

Louis Armstrong

The first instrumental genius of jazz and the father of jazz singing, ladies and gentlemen: The Great Satchmo…

❶ HEEBIE JEEBIES from THE COMPLETE HOT FIVE AND HOT FIVE SEVEN RECORDINGS
A risky, joyful, note-perfect, wordless vocal chorus in 1926 heralds the birth of scat singing.

❷ POTATO HEAD BLUES from THE COMPLETE HOT FIVE AND HOT FIVE SEVEN RECORDINGS
Astonishingly intrepid trumpet playing from 1927, especially in the celebrated stop-time chorus.

❸ WEST END BLUES from THE COMPLETE HOT FIVE AND HOT FIVE SEVEN RECORDINGS
This 1928 track featured a solo trumpet fanfare whose daring virtuosity bewitched jazz fans and musicians for generations to come.

❹ WEATHER BIRD from THE COMPLETE HOT FIVE AND HOT FIVE SEVEN RECORDINGS
A veritable joust in 1928 between Armstrong and pianist Earl Hines in which there's no clear winner but much thrilling improvised music.

❺ TIGHT LIKE THIS from THE COMPLETE HOT FIVE AND HOT FIVE SEVEN RECORDINGS
Offbeat verbal exchanges between Louis and arranger Don Redman don't distract from Armstrong's powerful trumpet choruses on this 1928 track.

❻ MAHOGANY HALL STOMP from THE COMPLETE HOT FIVE AND HOT FIVE SEVEN RECORDINGS
Though already by 1929 settled into commercial routines somewhat removed from the New Orleans jazz feeling of his earlier work, this rollicking track is an exception.

❼ BLACK AND BLUE from LOUIS ARMSTRONG IN NEW YORK
Andy Razaf's modest cry for racial equality ("my only sin is in my skin") delivered to plaintive perfection by Louis in 1929.

⑧ ROCKIN' CHAIR from **COMPLETE LOUIS ARMSTRONG ON RCA**

An amusing, highly musical call-and-response vocal routine between Louis and the brilliantly laconic Jack Teagarden,.

⑨ HESITATING BLUES from **PLAYS W.C. HANDY**

A highlight of a great later-period album from 1954 in which Louis eschews commercial settings for a gutsy examination of classic material close to his roots.

⑩ THERE'S NO YOU from **LOUIS ARMSTRONG MEETS OSCAR PETERSON**

Accompanied only by guitarist Herb Ellis in 1957, Louis shows how affecting his cement mixer voice could be on a delicate pop melody.

Chris Ingham

The Associates

Singer and lyricist Billy MacKenzie and multi-instrumentalist Alan Rankine created intoxicating, epic, eclectic music.

① PARTY FEARS TWO from **SULK**

This four-minute melodrama possesses an instantly memorable keyboard hook and displays Billy's voice at the height of its power.

② SKIPPING from **SULK**

A vocal intro gallops into this compelling and mischievous track, with chords that bloom from unidentified instruments and a rare Sean Connery impersonation from Billy during the second chorus.

③ LOVE HANGOVER from **SULK**

Billy sprawls, stretches and soars through this Diana Ross cover, hitting impossible notes with langorous ease and complementing infectious guitar and drum rhythms.

④ A SEVERE BOUT OF CAREER INSECURITY from **RADIO 1 SESSIONS**

Deranged kitchen sink drama set to a loose but insistently energetic musical backdrop. The track has a thrown-together brilliance.

⑤ PAPER HOUSE from **AFFECTIONATE PUNCH (1982 REMIX)**

Piano arpeggios burst through fidgetting guitars, while Billy heads for an octave-straddling, goosebumps-inducing coda.

⑥ A GIRL NAMED PROPERTY from **FOURTH DRAWER DOWN**

Operatic, intensely emotional track of bleak beauty – and with a heart-stopping note.

Doug Hall

Awopbopaloobop alopbamboom

As Little Richard knew so well, if you can't think of the right words for a song, you can always make some up.

① BE-BOP-A-LULA GENE VINCENT from **BEST OF**

② DA DOO RON RON THE CRYSTALS from **THE VERY BEST OF**

③ DIDDY WAH DIDDY CAPTAIN BEEFHEART from **DIDDY WAH DIDDY EP**

④ DIGA DIGA DOO THE MILLS BROTHERS WITH DUKE ELLINGTON & HIS ORCHESTRA from **DUKE ELLINGTON & HIS ORCHESTRA 1932–33**

⑤ DOO WAH DIDDY MANFRED MANN from **MANFRED MANN'S EARTH BAND**

⑥ FA-FA-FA-FA-FA OTIS REDDING from **THE VERY BEST OF**

⑦ MAHNA MAHNA THE MUPPETS from **THE MUPPET SHOW: MUSIC, MAYHEM AND MORE**

⑧ OB-LA-DI, OB-LA-DA THE BEATLES from **THE WHITE ALBUM**

⑨ UM, UM, UM, UM, UM, UM MAJOR LANCE from **THE BEST OF**

⑩ ZUNGGUZUNGGUGUZUNGGUZENG YELLOWMAN from **ZUNGGUZUNGGUGUZUNGGUZENG**

Greg Ward

Kevin Ayers

He was Bryan Ferry with cool, Noel Coward on acid. Yet in an age that liked its big rock numbers, fame steadfastly eluded Kevin Ayers, the cultish hippie, with his songs of hedonistic, psychedelic whimsy. He's worth rediscovery, not least to hear the guitar work from a young Mike Oldfield.

❶ THE LADY RACHEL from **JOY OF A TOY**
Ah, 1968: shades of the time, when earnest Pre-Raphaelite young men invested would-be lovers with such titles. But this was a lovely song, on Ayers' first solo album, and would become one of his live standards.

❷ MAY I from **SHOOTING AT THE MOON**
A sensuous crooner that opened an unusually experimental and jazz-fuelled album. A seductive version in French appeared on the *Odd Ditties* album.

❸ THE OYSTER AND THE FLYING FISH from **SHOOTING AT THE MOON**
A duet with Bridget St John, with peculiar folk overtones, this comes from a gentler age, but retains heaps of charm.

❹ WHATEVERSHEBRINGSWESING from **WHATEVERSHEBRINGSWESING**
Mike Oldfield's staggeringly beautiful guitar solo is a delight to behold.

❺ STRANGER IN BLUE SUEDE SHOES from **WHATEVERSHEBRINGSWESING**
A ramshackle slice of wit on the joys of herbal indulgence, when it seemed revolutionary.

❻ DIDN'T FEEL LONELY TILL I THOUGHT OF YOU from **THE CONFESSIONS OF DR DREAM**
A last bid for stardom, the *Dr Dream* album stands up nicely, and nowhere better than this song with its doo-wop chorus, swaggering lyrics, and Ollie Halsall's virtuoso guitar break.

Greg Neale

Bacharach & David

Burt Bacharach and Hal David – one of the great songwriting partnerships – met working at the Paramount Music Company in New York's legendary Brill Building. There are numerous Bacharach/David anthologies, and you get a whole raft on classic Dionne Warwick compilations.

❶ DO YOU KNOW THE WAY TO SAN JOSÉ DIONNE WARWICK
Dionne Warwick – the greatest of all Bacharach/David interpreters – sings this so light it almost floats away on the melody.

❷ CASINO ROYALE HERB ALPERT & THE TIJUANA BRASS
The main hook is built around glorious bright parping stabs of brass, and the maracas half way through are simply sublime.

❸ TRAINS AND BOATS AND PLANES FOUNTAINS OF WAYNE
The NYC popsters make this track entirely their own, with a cool acoustic treatment. It never made sense before but here (on the band's Out of States rarities CD) it is a miniature classic.

❹ I SAY A LITTLE PRAYER ARETHA FRANKLIN
Aretha made this her's, positively smouldering with soul over a cool Motown-style vibe.

❺ THE LOOK OF LOVE DUSTY SPRINGFIELD
Delivered in a smokey, jazz bar style, Dusty really sounds smitten, and her crystalline vocals contrast beautifully with the understated sax solo.

❻ (THE MAN WHO SHOT) LIBERTY VALANCE GENE PITNEY
Romance, heroism and a deadly Wild West showdown – this concise melodrama has it all.

❼ (THEY LONG TO BE) CLOSE TO YOU THE CARPENTERS
Just why do birds suddenly appear? The Carpenters' immaculate explanation is so sweet it could make your teeth fall out.

❽ TWENTY FOUR HOURS FROM TULSA GENE PITNEY
Pitney was perfect for this bitter tale of infidelity set to a mariachi-style arrangement.

❾ WALK ON BY DIONNE WARWICK
Another classic tale of heartbreak, this is arguably Dionne's finest song: pure emotion, with its message of fragile defiance perfectly set against the smooth piano and trumpet hooks.

❿ WHAT'S NEW PUSSYCAT? TOM JONES
The swaggering bar room piano is genius and Jones' fruity, love-addled bellow one of the iconic pop performances of the 60s.

Essi Berelian

Badly Drawn Boy

Singer-songwriter Damon Gough, aka Badly Drawn Boy, is both bouncy and bittersweet – an inspired choice for a man to soundtrack the movie of Nick Hornby's About A Boy.

❶ THE SHINING
from THE HOUR OF BEWILDERBEAST
The horns portray the sun rising mentioned in the lyrics and the strings are persuasive. One of the great album openers.

❷ A PEAK YOU REACH from **ABOUT A BOY**
Energetic keyboards and percussion – all the
sounds you need when driving.

❸ SOMETHING TO TALK ABOUT
from **ABOUT A BOY**
A beautifully constructed song that manages
to swing along tightly.

❹ SILENT SIGH from **ABOUT A BOY**
A tune driven by a piano riff and a solid beat
that is crying out for football montage.

❺ HAVE YOU FED THE FISH?
from **HAVE YOU FED THE FISH?**
The chorus/title line finally makes sense, before
the bounciest of riffs kicks in.

❻ YOU WERE RIGHT from **HAVE YOU FED THE FISH?**
BDB at his story-telling best, observing songs
are only "the soundtrack to a life".

❼ ANOTHER DEVIL DIES
from **ONE PLUS ONE IS ONE**
After the quiet piano opening, the passion is
overwhelming and almost out of control.

❽ YEAR OF THE RAT from **ONE PLUS ONE IS ONE**
A song that knows just how anthemic it is. Its
choral sound makes it even more showcase.

Daniel Crewe

Chet Baker

**The coolest trumpeter and jazz crooner of
them all.**

❶ MY FUNNY VALENTINE from **THE COMPLETE
GERRY MULLIGAN QUARTET WITH CHET BAKER**
Achingly lonely version of the Rodgers and
Hart classic which established Baker as the
most popular trumpeter of his generation.

❷ WALKIN' SHOES from **THE COMPLETE GERRY
MULLIGAN QUARTET WITH CHET BAKER**
Archetypical west coast wizardry from the
trend-setting piano-less Mulligan Quartet, with

Gerry and Chet weaving contrapuntal magic.

❸ MAID IN MEXICO from **CHET BAKER QUARTET
WITH RUSS FREEMAN**
Enchanting Latin ditty which changes gear into
steaming 4/4, from the first Baker quartet in
1953, featuring pianist/composer Freeman.

❹ BUT NOT FOR ME from **CHET BAKER SINGS**
The first cut on Chet's famous 1954 10-inch
album revealing his unique vocal gifts; soft,
smooth and pretty as a lady.

❺ SAD WALK from **CHET BAKER IN PARIS**
An alluring Bob Zieff mood piece featuring
Chet's short-lived 1955 quartet which included
pianist Dick Twardzik who died of an overdose
days after this session.

❻ I'VE NEVER BEEN IN LOVE BEFORE
from **CHET BAKER SINGS**
A highlight of Chet's second all-vocal session
from 1956, this *Guys And Dolls* ballad has never
sounded so wistful and innocent, and Baker's
trumpet solo is heartbreaking.

❼ DO IT THE HARD WAY from **CHET BAKER SINGS
IT COULD HAPPEN TO YOU**
An obscure Rodgers and Hart throwaway is
subjected to Chet's polite and immaculate scat.

❽ E.S.P. from **ONCE UPON A SUMMERTIME**
A surprisingly muscular and inventive
approach to Wayne Shorter's elliptical tune
from an excellent 1977 album.

❾ I WAITED FOR YOU
from **THE TOUCH OF YOUR LIPS**
From the scores of European albums made in
his last decade, the 1979 trio with Neils
Pederson (bass) and Doug Raney (guitar) in
Denmark stands out for sheer beauty and
musicality.

❿ ALMOST BLUE from **THE FILM LET'S GET LOST**
Written with Baker in mind by fan Elvis
Costello, Chet unsurprisingly manages to make
perfect sense of this peculiar, brooding song in
1982.

Chris Ingham

Robyn Hitchcock's
The Band

Psychedelic songsmith **ROBYN HITCHCOCK** (see his own playlist) has been called the human jukebox for his ability to play any song, any style. For this book, he sent in an entry for The Band:

"In Levon Helm, Richard Manuel and Rick Danko, Robbie Robertson had three great character actors to sing his songs. Garth Hudson was the alchemist who found melodies on keyboards and horn that hadn't ever been found before. Though Levon contends that the songs were not Robertson's as much as Robbie claims, no one could accuse Robbie of overplaying."

❶ CALEDONIA MISSION
from **MUSIC FROM BIG PINK**
A meandering, autumnal verse leads into a funky chorus that is peppered with Richard's gleeful piano, scurrying around like a squirrel.

❷ UP ON CRIPPLE CREEK from **THE BAND**
Levon sang the libido tracks, mostly, and here he puffs up like an Arkansas toad in anticipation of Bessie down in Lake Charles, Louisiana.

❸ WHISPERING PINES from **THE BAND**
Richard's eerie lonesome melody foreshadows his own suicide in a motel in 1983. Robbie's lyrics evoke a very desolate coast.

❹ W.S. WALCOTT MEDICINE SHOW
from **STAGE FRIGHT**
By contrast, Levon leads the boys through a leering carnival groove with no regrets at all.

Garth's saxophone is so buoyant, everything a horn break should be and usually isn't.

❺ CHEST FEVER from **MUSIC FROM BIG PINK**
A murky song about some Scandinavians getting excited in a dairy that was preceded live by Garth's keyboard opus "The Genetic Method".

❻ KING HARVEST from **THE BAND**
Ray Bradbury meets Flannery O'Connor under a big orange moon while the weather holds its breath. "My horse Jethro, well he went mad" sings Rick, and you know it did.

❼ IT MAKES NO DIFFERENCE from **SOUTHERN CROSS**
Rick was the goofiest but also the most poignant of The Band's three vocalists. A requiem for a still-bleeding relationship, Rick sings this in straight pain – no accusation, all hurt.

❽ THE SHAPE I'M IN from **STAGE FRIGHT**
Richard leads the band through a fun catalogue of woe. Garth's shapes on the keyboard are a good example of how you hear only the sound he makes, not the instrument that he's playing.

❾ DON'T DO IT from **THE LAST WALTZ**
Not written by The Band, but the last thing played by them at *The Last Waltz*, it's punctuated by Robbie's terse, flaming guitar and is one of their most rockin' recordings.

❿ ALL LA GLORY from **STAGE FRIGHT**
Levon sings this lullaby so sweet and unsentimental, all honey and no sacharine, falling leaves at bed-time and a painkiller tomorrow. Another masterful solo from Garth on some unfathomable instrument.

Syd Barrett

Original lead singer, lead guitarist, and principal songwriter of Pink Floyd, Syd's deviously playful acid visions remain pinnacles of psychedelic rock, even if the ragged drug casualty solo work that followed his 1968 exit from the Floyd wasn't quite all the stuff of legend.

❶ SEE EMILY PLAY PINK FLOYD from **RELICS**
Swooping slide guitar, exotic organ, and a definitive lyrical portrait of a flower child.

❷ ARNOLD LAYNE PINK FLOYD from **RELICS**
Pink Floyd's debut 45 was this whimsically unsettling tale of a suburban pervert: "Arnold Layne, don't do it ay-gayne!"

❸ ASTRONOMY DOMINE PINK FLOYD
from **PIPER AT THE GATES OF DAWN**
Pink Floyd's journey to the heart of the sun starts with this pulsating space rocker, the scat vocals descending like asteroids hurtling through the cosmos.

❹ LUCIFER SAM PINK FLOYD
from **PIPER AT THE GATES OF DAWN**
Early Barrett/Floyd at their most devilish, propelled by surf-music-from-hell guitar twang and edgy intimations of the occult and maybe Syd's own oncoming madness.

❺ FLAMING PINK FLOYD
from **PIPER AT THE GATES OF DAWN**
Barrett's Floyd at their most ingratiatingly childish, making interstellar travel sound easy.

❻ MATILDA MOTHER PINK FLOYD
from **PIPER AT THE GATES OF DAWN**
Another catchy, otherworldly Barrett fairy tale– or is it, with that evil mother leaving the singer/ child eternally waiting for the story's end?

❼ BIKE PINK FLOYD
from **PIPER AT THE GATES OF DAWN**
A Lewis Carroll-like dive into childhood fantasies, utterly subverted by the frightening climax of discordant crashes and incessantly clacking ducks.

❽ GOLDEN HAIR from **THE MADCAP LAUGHS**
Enchanting adaptation of James Joyce's poem, its lingering, almost lethargic sensuality evoking temptation whose fulfillment lies permanently just out of reach.

❾ MILKY WAY from **OPEL**
Solo Syd was at his bounciest and most hap-hazardly likable on this street-busker-as-space-cowboy outtake.

❿ WOULDN'T YOU MISS ME (DARK GLOBE)
from **OPEL**
A plaintive folky dirge on the surface, a moving bemoaning of loss of identity underneath. Yes, we did miss you, Syd…

Richie Unterberger

Hey Bartender!

You may not remember the words in the morning, but you can't beat a good drinking song last thing at night. Here's a romp through the past six decades.

❶ WHAT'S THE USE OF GETTING SOBER (WHEN YOU GONNA GET DRUNK AGAIN)?
LOUIS JORDAN

❷ DRINKIN' WINE, SPO-DEE-O-DEE
STICKS MCGHEE

❸ ONE SCOTCH, ONE BOURBON, ONE BEER
AMOS MILBURN

❹ HEY BARTENDER FLOYD DIXON & HIS BAND

❺ ALABAMA SONG (WHISKEY BAR)
THE DOORS

❻ DRUNKARD PSALM PRINCE BUSTER

❼ DOWN WHERE THE DRUNKARDS ROLL
RICHARD & LINDA THOMPSON

❽ DELIRIUM TREMENS CHRISTY MOORE

⑨ WHISKEY IN THE JAR
THE POGUES & THE DUBLINERS

⑩ TOO DRUNK TO FUCK NOUVELLE VAGUE

Greg Ward

The Beach Boys

The Beach Boys produced the most gorgeously sung, melodically sophisticated 60s California Dream pop, before the dream turned to nightmare with the crash of leader Brian Wilson's psyche.

❶ I GET AROUND FROM ALL SUMMER LONG
Dizzying vocal harmonies, chugging guitar and organ, and an unabashed celebration of the 60s Southern Californian teenage lifestyle.

❷ GOOD VIBRATIONS from SMILEY SMILE
An early zenith of psychedelic pop, with an ebullient love song of great sexy tenderness under its unworldly Theremin chords and exquisitely layered production.

❸ DON'T WORRY BABY from SHUT DOWN VOL 2
Some of the finest lead falsetto-group harmony blends in all of rock'n'roll, and one of the first hints of Brian Wilson's depthless vulnerability.

❹ GOD ONLY KNOWS from PET SOUNDS
A love song that becomes a hymn to the deity of Love itself, courtesy of its heavenly orchestral production.

❺ SURFIN' U.S.A. from SURFIN' U.S.A.
Chuck Berry gets dressed up in multi-part harmony and goes to the beach on the greatest vocal surf hit of all.

Brian Wilson's
Tributes

The two great geniuses of 60s American pop music were Beach Boys' mastermind BRIAN WILSON and Phil Spector – and here the former pays generous tribute to the latter with no fewer than five of his "wall-of-sound" productions in his all-time top ten.

❶ BE MY BABY THE RONETTES from BEST OF

❷ YOU'VE LOST THAT LOVIN' FEELIN' THE RIGHTEOUS BROTHERS from BEST OF

❸ RIVER DEEP MOUNTAIN HIGH IKE & TINA TURNER from RIVER DEEP MOUNTAIN HIGH

❹ DA DOO RON RON THE CRYSTALS from BEST OF

❺ WALKING IN THE RAIN THE RONETTES from BEST OF

❻ (I CAN'T GET NO) SATISFACTION THE ROLLING STONES from BIG HITS (HIGH TIDE...)

❼ HEY JUDE THE BEATLES from MAGICAL MYSTERY TOUR

❽ THE LONG AND WINDING ROAD THE BEATLES from LET IT BE

❾ WHAT A FOOL BELIEVES THE DOOBIE BROTHERS from MINUTE BY MINUTE

❿ REALLY WANNA KNOW YOU GARY WRIGHT from THE RIGHT PLACE

6 THE WARMTH OF THE SUN from **SHUT DOWN VOL 2**

An overlooked early ballad with one of the group's most supremely seductive melodies, blurring together melancholy and golden optimism as one.

7 CAROLINE, NO from **PET SOUNDS**

Yes, it's an ode to lost innocence (and lost long hair) – but has heartbreak ever been so pretty?

8 DON'T TALK PUT YOUR HEAD ON MY SHOULDER from **PET SOUNDS**

The spookiest piece of rock-cum-chamber music from Pet Sounds, the simulated heartbeats echoing like an oncoming visitation from Kingdom Come.

9 SURFER GIRL from **SURFER GIRL**

Later Beach Boys love songs might have gotten more sophisticated in both production and lyric, but few were as suffused with lovely longing.

10 YOU STILL BELIEVE IN ME from **PET SOUNDS**

Like a choirboy ensemble grown adult, the Boys offer a beautifully harmonized sermon that beams with optimism and redemption.

Richie Unterberger

Beastie Boys

From thrashy teenage punks to 80s bad boys to darlings of glossy style magazines, the Beastie Boys' path has been a chequered one. But they've always been extremely good at shouting over the top of loud drums.

1 EGG RAID ON MOJO from **SOME OLD BULLSHIT**

The embryonic Beasties (with a token Beastie Girl on bass) sound just like any other bunch of kids who like Minor Threat and Black Flag: Beasties punk rock at its most authentic.

2 FIGHT FOR YOUR RIGHT TO PARTY from **LICENSE TO ILL**

Spoilt rich kids have rarely sounded so feral as on this snotty, spotty pyschodrama: a Lord Of The Flies for 80s American teenagers.

3 POSSE IN EFFECT from **LICENSE TO ILL**

Ridiculously incoherent boasting over impassive drum machines that sound like fridge-freezers being slammed together incessantly.

4 BRASS MONKEY from **LICENSE TO ILL**

A cheerleading chant, with empty liquor bottles instead of pom-poms, champions the boys' favourite tipple.

5 EGG MAN from **PAUL'S BOUTIQUE**

The Beasties at their most poetic and political: a celebration of the humanist levelling of having egg on your face. A rework of an early punk track, it's an unlikely paean to "eggalitarianism".

6 PASS THE MIC from **CHECK YOUR HEAD**

Contains the laziest rhyme in rap history ("rehearsal" rhymed with "rehearsal"), but its titanic drums, excoriating scratching and looped guitar feedback seize the day.

7 ILL COMMUNICATION from **ILL COMMUNICATION**

A seasick electronic tone provides the bassline, nudging a jazz piano off-kilter, whilst guest rapper Q-Tip and the boys talk about nothing in particular with quirky finesse.

8 BODY MOVING from **HELLO NASTY**

Cacophonously messy steel drums and Mix Master Mike's octopoid cuts make for an ear-catching Beasties party invitation.

9 ELECTRIFY from **HELLO NASTY**

Throbbing cables of electro psychedelia pullulate virally. Positively radioactive.

10 THE BROUHAHA from **TO THE FIVE BOROUGHS**

A concise synth loop that's as cute as a riff by Yellow Magic Orchestra daintily supports the now (marginally) more mature trio, determined to grow old disgracefully.

Matt Milton

The Beatles

The Lennon/McCartney songbook is the greatest achievement in pop history. But not every song for which Paul and John share the credits was a genuine collaboration. Here are ten that were.

❶ I SAW HER STANDING THERE
from PLEASE PLEASE ME
Composed in 1963 in the front room of the McCartney family home in Forthlin Road, Liverpool – and with a bassline nabbed from Chuck Berry's Talkin' 'Bout You – this was The Beatles at their Cavern-rocking best.

❷ I WANT TO HOLD YOUR HAND from PAST MASTERS 1
Like From Me To You and She Loves You before it, this – The Beatles' first US #1 and the very essence of their apparently innocent charm – was written by John and Paul together in a hotel room on tour.

❸ I'LL GET YOU from PAST MASTERS 1
Slight but winning B-side of She Loves You, knocked out to a 1963 formula. McCartney was particularly pleased with the "faggy" way the boys sing "oh yeah, oh yeah".

❹ THIS BOY from PAST MASTERS 1
Delicious three-part harmony feature on the B-side of "I Want To Hold Your Hand".

❺ EIGHT DAYS A WEEK from BEATLES FOR SALE
On the way to a 1964 writing session with John, Paul heard his driver use this phrase about his own work schedule whereupon the Lennon-McCartney song factory turned it into one more love ditty.

❻ DRIVE MY CAR from RUBBER SOUL
After a slow writing session in 1965, Paul and John eventually got onto such a roll with this tongue-in-cheek faux soul song, they even thought "beep-beep, beep-beep, yeah" a good idea. It was.

❼ WITH A LITTLE HELP FROM MY FRIENDS
from SGT PEPPER'S LONELY HEARTS CLUB BAND
A little something for Ringo to sing – one of the lesser tracks on their 1967 magnum opus album but with ground-breaking Greek chorus questions in the backing vocals and notably resourceful basswork.

❽ A DAY IN THE LIFE from SGT PEPPER'S LONELY HEARTS CLUB BAND
After hitting on the idea of inserting a song of Paul's into the middle of one of John's, they finished their magnificently stoned masterwork together.

❾ YOU KNOW MY NAME (LOOK UP THE NUMBER) from PAST MASTERS 2
The B-side of Let It Be, this Goons-esque collage of daft voices and jazzy pastiche was hardly The Beatles' finest hour, but in a period when John and Paul were barely talking, at least they could still have a little fun.

❿ I'VE GOT A FEELING from LET IT BE
In which a Lennon half-song ("Everybody had a good year") is bolted onto a McCartney half-song (I've Got A Feeling) making little sense but a good vehicle to deliver a fabulous Apple rooftop performance in January 1969.

Chris Ingham

Beatle John

Ten "Lennon/McCartney" compositions that were actually penned by John...

❶ I SHOULD HAVE KNOWN BETTER
from A HARD DAY'S NIGHT
A chiming, harmonica-driven rocker from the 1964 album dominated by Lennon, memorably performed in the *Hard Day's Night* movie in the luggage compartment of a train.

❷ YOU'VE GOT TO HIDE YOUR LOVE AWAY
from HELP!
Lennon goes Dylan in 1965, complete with cap, truculently strummed acoustic guitar and this enchantingly opaque folk waltz.

❸ NOWHERE MAN from **RUBBER SOUL**

Banks of vocal harmonies, Harrison's glistening Rickenbacker chords and the retrospectively unmistakeable sound of an unhappily-married Beatle.

❹ TOMORROW NEVER KNOWS from **REVOLVER**

Inspired by *The Tibetan Book Of The Dead*, as quoted by acid guru Timothy Leary, this 1966 melange of drones, backward tapes and thunderous drumming is a virtual psychedelic revolution.

❺ SHE SAID SHE SAID from **REVOLVER**

A scything, splashing acid rock peak for the band, with Lennon stumbling onto death and childhood amid resplendent guitars and dizzying beat shifts.

❻ STRAWBERRY FIELDS FOREVER
from **BEATLES 1967–1970**

Two entirely different versions of Lennon's deliciously hallucinatory reminiscence spliced together by producer George Martin into one glorious, multi-hued slab of Beatlemusic.

❼ ALL YOU NEED IS LOVE
from **BEATLES 1967–1970**

Though casually elliptical in the verses, the timelessly uplifting chorus ensures this 1967 hippie anthem will endure for years to come.

❽ I AM THE WALRUS
from **MAGICAL MYSTERY TOUR**

Somewhere between Lennon at his sly, free-association best and a writhing pit of nasty nonsense, "Walrus" is stunning psychedelia.

❾ JULIA from **THE BEATLES "WHITE" ALBUM**

A delicate, ruminative, finger-picking ballad in which Lennon blends a paean to his mother Julia with a reverie for new love Yoko.

❿ COME TOGETHER from **ABBEY ROAD**

Leary, Dylan and Chuck Berry influences can be detected but this beautifully performed swamp-rock is Beatlemusic of the ultra-Lennon variety.

Chris Ingham

Beatle Paul

…and another ten Fabs classics written by Mr. McCartney.

❶ ALL MY LOVING from **WITH THE BEATLES**

With furious triplets under a sunnily ascending scale of a melody, McCartney's pop classic was the first Beatles tune the US saw played on the initial Ed Sullivan appearance in February 1964.

❷ CAN'T BUY ME LOVE from **A HARD DAY'S NIGHT**

Paul injected a little blues into this song written in George V Hotel in Paris in January 1964 and nabbed the A-side of The Beatles' next single, to Lennon's chagrin.

❸ EVERY LITTLE THING from **BEATLES FOR SALE**

Written in Paul's bedroom at 57 Wimpole St, where he lived with the family of his girlfriend Jane Asher, this melodic attempt at a single ended up being a 1964 album track sung by John, a rare instance in The Beatles of the composer relinquishing lead vocal duties.

❹ I'M DOWN from **PAST MASTERS 1**

In an effort to supplant Long Tall Sally as his Little Richard-style live feature, McCartney fashioned this throat-tearing rocker and climaxed the Beatles' 1965 Shea Stadium set.

❺ YESTERDAY from **HELP!**

This mature and elegant ballad apparently arrived fully formed as McCartney awoke one morning in 1965 and following the Paul-plus-string-quartet "Beatles" recording went on to be one of the most covered songs in pop history.

❻ YOU WON'T SEE ME from **RUBBER SOUL**

Another Wimpole Street missive, petulantly composed after a row with Jane Asher, this is a great album track – never performed live by the Beatles or McCartney.

❼ FOR NO ONE from **REVOLVER**

A chilly, blank-eyed vignette about a once-intimate couple drifting apart which perhaps betrays more about McCartney's inner life in

1966 than his work is usually credited with.

❽ WHEN I'M SIXTY-FOUR
from SGT PEPPER'S LONELY HEARTS CLUB BAND

Paul was 16 when he came up with the tune in Liverpool and 24 when he revived it for Sgt Pepper, turning it – with George Martin's help – into archetypal rootie-tootie Macca.

❾ FOOL ON THE HILL
from MAGICAL MYSTERY TOUR

Mysterious meditation on an inscrutable spiritual leader of the same general size and build as the Maharishi. Also features one of the great recorder solos in pop.

❿ HEY JUDE from BEATLES 1967–1970

A special blend of personal encouragement and universal celebration, Hey Jude was written for Lennon's son Julian, though John thought it was a message to him and Yoko while McCartney realized later it was about himself and Linda.

Chris Ingham

Beatles covers

The Fabs' best songs didn't always make for great cover versions (sit down please, The Massed Band of the Grenadier Guards…) but just occasionally it all came together.

❶ A DAY IN THE LIFE EUGENE CHADBOURNE from DOWNTOWN DOES THE BEATLES: LIVE AT THE KNITTING FACTORY

The iconoclastic guitarist/singer troubadour lets fragments of For No One and I'll Follow The Sun bleed into his skewed version of A Day In The Life in which he sings about "10,000 holes in Margaret Thatcher".

❷ WITH A LITTLE HELP FROM MY FRIENDS JOE COCKER from WITH A LITTLE HELP FROM MY FRIENDS

A remarkable reinvention, as Ringo's bouncy mum's-and-dad's pop turns into heavy 6/8 rock with gospel overtones. With justice, this is the

track, sung at Woodstock, that made Cocker's career.

❸ RAIN THE LONDON JAZZ FOUR from TAKE A NEW LOOK AT THE BEATLES

The B-side of 1966 single "Paperback Writer" is coolly reharmonized by the obscure MJQ soundalike combo led by pianist Mike McNaught in 1967, from one of the best Beatle covers albums ever.

❹ DAY TRIPPER OTIS REDDING from THE OTIS REDDING DICTIONARY OF SOUL

A stomping, relentless 1966 reimagining of the Fabs' 1965 single with soul screamer Redding on searing form.

❺ I WANT YOU (SHE'S SO HEAVY) BOOKER T AND THE MGS from MCLEMORE AVENUE

Lennon's cry of sexual dependency is given the cool-hot Stax treatment with guitarist Steve Cropper really chewing on the blues licks and Booker T lashing out some sharp organ work.

❻ DRIVE MY CAR BOBBY MCFERRIN from SIMPLE PLEASURES

Elastic-voiced McFerrin manages to sing bass-line, melody, lyric and percussion parts in one vocal pass. Has to be heard to be believed.

❼ REVOLUTION GRANDADDY from I AM SAM

This Sean Penn movie had a neat hook: a character obsessed by Beatles songs. Cue the soundtrack album, whose delights include Rufus Wainwright doing Across the Universe and this very cool take from California band Grandaddy.

❽ ONE AFTER 909 LAIBACH from LET IT BE

Growling, industrial reading of the Quarrymen-era rocker by provocative Slovenian collective, taken from their 1988 album in which they mangle the whole of The Beatles' *Let It Be* to fascinating effect.

❾ ELEANOR RIGBY STANLEY JORDAN from MAGIC TOUCH

"All the lonely people" get an impressive seven-minute workout from innovative fret-tapping jazz guitarist Jordan in 1984.

⑩ BLUE JAY WAY BUDDHA PEST from **DOWNTOWN DOES THE BEATLES: LIVE AT THE KNITTING FACTORY**
Covers connoisseurs must hear this: a whispered vocal, a cello carrying the tune, thrash punk interludes and a free jazz attitude make for a startling Fabs-inspired experience.

Chris Ingham

Bebop classics

In the mid-1940s, a new breed of jazz virtuosi emerged – a fleet-of-finger crew with a penchant for substitute chords and intricate melodies. Put your hands together for the Beboppers.

① HOT HOUSE DIZZY GILLESPIE from **THE DIZZY GILLESPIE STORY**
A slippery Tadd Dameron theme based on the chords of Cole Porter's What Is This Thing Called Love? is given its inaugural outing by Dizzy's All-Stars (including Charlie Parker) in 1945.

② KOKO CHARLIE PARKER from **THE COMPLETE CHARLIE PARKER ON SAVOY**
The theme of Ray Noble's Cherokee is dropped, Bird cuts loose over the chords and creates an improvised classic in 1945.

③ INDIANA BUD POWELL from **TEMPUS FUGUE-IT**
The king of bop piano at his clear-thinking best, a sparkling trio performance of the 1917 warhorse from 1947.

④ OW! DIZZY GILLESPIE AND HIS ORCHESTRA from **THE DIZZY GILLESPIE STORY**
Dizzy's bebop big band didn't last long but produced some classic cuts like this I Got Rhythm variation in 1947.

⑤ MILESTONES MILES DAVIS from **EARLY MILES**
A cool alternative to Gillespie's fiery trumpet style on this thoughtful, measured performance by Miles Davis in 1947, making his first appearance as leader.

⑥ DONNA LEE CLAUDE THORNHILL from **BEBOP SPOKEN HERE**
Excellent big-band realization of Miles Davis's labyrinthine bop theme, set to the chords of Indiana and a clear forerunner to Miles's *Birth Of The Cool* nonet sessions of 1948–49.

⑦ NOSTALGIA FATS NAVARRO from **THE FATS NAVARRO STORY**
The trumpeting stylistic bridge between Gillespie and Clifford Brown, Fats is faultless and incisive on his 1947 variation on the changes to the 1931 standard Out Of Nowhere.

⑧ BONE-O-LOGY J. J. JOHNSON from **BEBOP SPOKEN HERE**
The first trombone virtuoso of bebop on his original variation of Sir Charles Thompson's Robbin's Nest in 1947, JJ makes his double time, 16th-note runs sound as easy as turning on a tap.

⑨ EPISTROPHY THELONIOUS MONK from **THE COMPLETE THELONIOUS MONK ON BLUE NOTE**
From a unique pianist/composer, this is extraordinarily original music from 1949 with its roots in bop harmony but with an eccentric swing all of it own.

⑩ TWISTED WARDELL GRAY from **THE WARDELL GRAY STORY**
A vivid 1949 blues from the ill-fated tenor saxophonist, with a riffy, weaving solo sufficiently melodic for singer Annie Ross to put lyrics to in her famous vocalese.

Chris Ingham

Beck

Lurching onto the scene with a beat-up guitar, a tote bag full o'songs, two turntables and a microphone, Beck Hansen singlehandedly gave focus to the term "Slacker" as applied to his generation of peers and that particularly American musical genre. He made it cool for indie kids to dance, for anglo kids to pick up some hispanic groove and invented the line, "MTV makes me want to smoke crack". Love the Beck.

❶ LOSER from MELLOW GOLD
Mixing up a meaty stew of delta blues, the kind of Spanish you never find in textbooks, hip-hop and psychedelia, this is the track with the refrain "I'm a loser baby, so why don't you kill me" that a million unfairly treated teenagers have retired to their rooms to play.

❷ NITEMARE HIPPY GIRL from MELLOW GOLD
Anybody who's spent a deal of time on the underground side of things will know this woman. Her male counterpart, it must be said, is equally irritating, but Beck didn"t write a song about him.

❸ DEVIL'S HAIRCUT from ODELAY
Equal parts rap and sub-Dylan nonsense rambling giving the man a chance to concentrate on his dance moves. Beck sure can get down!

❹ NEW POLLUTION from ODELAY
Beck's most confidently weird surefire chart success, this blends trippy keyboard and guitar lines with a rock-hard precision tooled set of beats that will drag your funky bones out to the dancefloor.

❺ NOBODY'S FAULT BUT MY OWN from MUTATIONS
Mid-period Beck moved away from the relentless beats of his hip-hop roots and focused instead on his folkie, country influences, while he grew up a little and sorted out his soul in the wake of a broken romance. Tragic, but totally irresistible.

❻ WE LIVE AGAIN from MUTATIONS
Sorrowful, thoughtful and with every word weighed in advance, Beck dives deep into the universal soul.

❼ SEXX LAWS from MIDNITE VULTURES
Putting the fun and the funk back into his music can't have been that easy, but he makes it appear a cinch. Performing this track in the

full heat of a Glastonbury summer afternoon, wearing a tweed suit and smoking a briar pipe, Beck bumped and ground his way across stage, winning swathes of the audience with every swivel of his hips.

❽ DEBRA from MIDNITE VULTURES
The whole *Midnite Vultures* album, looked at in the right light, can be seen as a tribute to Prince in his sex-elf majesty. Debra is not only magnificently Beck, it's superbly Prince at the same time.

❾ E-PRO from GUERO
Back in the studio with his old sparring team The Dust brothers at the production desk, Beck put together *Guero*, a stunning 21st-century creation, with E-Pro one of its standout cuts.

❿ BLACK TAMBOURINE from GUERO
Layering different sounds, and instrumentation with a gentle touch, Beck whips up a frothy piece of patisserie, just to show he can. Sounds blend seamlessly from strings, to keyboards, to slide guitar.

Al Spicer

Chuck Berry

Though he's best known as the pioneer of the rock'n'roll guitar riff, Chuck Berry also deserves to be remembered as rock's first great songwriter, thanks to his intricate, deft and often very funny lyrics. All of these tracks feature on several Greatest Hits compilations, as well as such desirable items as *The Chess Box*.

❶ JOHNNY B. GOODE from THE CHESS BOX
The saga of the Louisiana country boy who could play the guitar just like ringing a bell. There are few better songs to teach yourself rock'n'roll.

❷ BROWN EYED HANDSOME MAN from THE CHESS BOX
Some see this song as a searing indictment of

racial prejudice; others simply think Chuck's wordplay has never been cleverer.

❸ BACK IN THE USA from THE CHESS BOX

A consummate, idealized vision of what it was like to live in the US in the rock'n'rolling 50s; the perfect companion piece to The Beatles' Back In The USSR, which it inspired.

❹ ROCK AND ROLL MUSIC from THE CHESS BOX

All the joy and release of the rock'n'roll rebellion, crammed into two and a half minutes.

❺ NO PARTICULAR PLACE TO GO from THE CHESS BOX

From the man for whom automobile was a three-letter word – S-E-X – this is the best car song of the lot. Can you imagine the way that he felt, when he couldn't unfasten his safety belt?

❻ TOO MUCH MONKEY BUSINESS from THE CHESS BOX

An exhilarating outpouring of youthful nihilism, in which Chuck dismisses everything as more bother than it's worth.

❼ MEMPHIS from THE CHESS BOX

Chuck's story-telling may be a little leaden, and the twist might make you wince, but the beat is just too damn catchy for that to matter.

❽ YOU NEVER CAN TELL from THE CHESS BOX

Perhaps Chuck's loveliest song; a tender, witty, swinging meditation on the passing of time.

❾ PROMISED LAND from THE CHESS BOX

Chuck wrote this one in prison with an atlas on his knees; it's hardly surprising that his yearning for freedom, as represented by sunny California, should be so palpable.

❿ SWEET LITTLE SIXTEEN from THE CHESS BOX

In which one of the major archetypes of rock'n'roll – the wide-eyed teenage ingenue – springs fully-fledged from Chuck's lascivious imagination.

Greg Ward

The Bevis Frond

For nearly twenty years, Nick Saloman has been crafting some of the best neo-psychedelia around as the Bevis Frond, with the help of such cohorts as Ade Shaw (ex-Hawkwind) and Andy Ward (ex-Camel).

❶ STAIN ON THE SUN from NEW RIVER HEAD

This slow, meandering, majestic and unbearably moving tale of a failing relationship climaxes in a weeping guitar solo that leaves us all wondering who put the bullet hole in the holy Roman flag.

❷ LIGHTS ARE CHANGING from TRIPTYCH

Only the Almighty knows why this wasn't #1 for weeks. Oh, it was never a single. Phenomenally catchy psych pop.

❸ LONDON STONE from LONDON STONE

Powerful and eloquent lament for the destruction of the environment in Nick's native East London. Enough to simultaneously warm and chill the cockles of any Cockney's heart.

❹ ONCE MORE from INNER MARSHLAND

Not many tracks open with Harry H Corbett moaning about Sooty and Sweep and culminate in a Hendrix-style guitar fest via a gentle British folk interlude.

❺ HE'D BE A DIAMOND from NEW RIVER HEAD

This strum-along singalong ditty has been covered by Teenage Fanclub as well as Mary Lou Lord. The line about "an unpaid analyst who shags" used to crack them up in concert.

❻ SPLENDID ISOLATION from MIASMA

Nick Saloman emerged from years of splendid isolation into magnificent obscurity with his debut album, the highly psychedelic *Miasma*. This song set his power pop benchmark very high.

Nick Edwards

Bhangra/Asian underground

British Asians have created a dynamic music scene that for the most part exists indepedent of the mainstream. Bhangra has roots in Punjabi folk and Hindi pop, but in its current incarnation, and that of the Asian Underground, owes as much to dance music of all persuasions.

❶ KORI PMC from **DHOL JAGEERO DA**
Gidda track that slows down and speeds up intermittently sending clubbers into a frenzy.

❷ MERA LAUNG GAWACHA BALLY SAGOO from **STAR CRAZY 1**
Sung by Rama with rap from Cheshire Cat, this bhangramiffin classic translates as "I've lost my nose-ring".

❸ KE HAI BARI SANGEETA PYAR from **FLOWER IN THE WIND**
Sangeeta's biggest song to date with lyrics by Preet Nihal and music by Kuljit Bhamra. She sings in Hindi instead of the Punjabi customary in bhangra music.

❹ FLIGHT IC 408 STATE OF BENGAL from **ANOKHA-SOUNDZ OF THE ASIAN UNDERGROUND**
Massive drum'n'bass tune with swirling sitars and frenetic tabla beats themed around a flight from Bangaldesh

❺ NEELA TRICKBABY from **HANGIN' AROUND**
Compelling, hypnotic instrumental East-West concoction.

❻ BOR BOR PARTNERS IN RHYME from **REPLAY**
Bouncy bhangra at its best.

❼ FINGERS JOI from **ONE AND ONE IS ONE**
Trancey techno with sitar and a house vibe featuring the Voice of Shusheela Raman.

❽ NACHANGEH SARI RAATH TAZ from **SLAVE TO THE FUSION**
Pop-house Hindi number with a Latin American edge

DJ Ritu

Big-band jazz

Ten Big Band numbers from the heart of the Swing era, 1934–42. You'll find them on countless compilations.

❶ STOMPIN' AT THE SAVOY CHICK WEBB'S SAVOY ORCHESTRA
The Savoy Orchestra, led by hunchback drummer Webb and featuring the arranging of Edgar Sampson (who co-wrote this swing classic with Benny Goodman), swung as hard as any band of the period. "Stompin'" from 1934 was their biggest hit.

❷ WALKIN' AND SWINGIN' ANDY KIRK AND HIS CLOUDS OF JOYS
Neat, intricate arranging and composing from band pianist Mary Lou Williams for Andy Kirk's Kansas City heroes in 1936.

❸ ONE O'CLOCK JUMP COUNT BASIE
From the same town in the same period, Basie's outfit featured simpler, more straightforwardly swinging arrangements better to feature – on this jazz-blues staple – the two contrasting tenor stars, Herschel Evans and Lester Young.

❹ DON'T BE THAT WAY BENNY GOODMAN
This ingenious 1938 lick is one of the great anthems of the swing era and one of its biggest hits from its biggest star, the thrilling clarinettist and crowned King Of Swing.

❺ IN THE MOOD GLENN MILLER
The most famous swing theme of all was played by what considered a "sweet" band, but its infectious syncopations and compelling dynamics make the 1939 recording of Andy Razaf and Ed Garland's riff an imperishable classic.

⑥ T'AIN'T WHAT YOU DO (IT'S THE WAY THAT YOU DO IT) JIMMIE LUNCEFORD

Lunceford's orchestra is considered by many to be the great band of the era with its exciting arrangements by Sy Oliver and audience-pleasing swing-pop like this 1939 hit (which was a hit again in 1982 for the Fun Boy Three.)

⑦ AT THE WOODCHOPPER'S BALL WOODY HERMAN AND HIS ORCHESTRA

Herman's outfit was billed as "The Band That Plays The Blues" and this breakthrough 1939 hit proved it; by no means the subtlest record of the era but replete with raw excitement.

⑧ TAKE THE 'A' TRAIN DUKE ELLINGTON

Ellington's compositional prowess set him rather apart from the Swing craze but this memorably dissonant swinger from 1941 – actually composed by Billy Strayhorn – did his popularity no harm at all and became the Ellington Orchestra theme tune for the rest of its existence.

⑨ DRUM BOOGIE GENE KRUPA

A charismatic drumming star with Benny Goodman, Krupa scored a huge hit with his own band in 1941 on this rockin' novelty featuring manic drums, shouts of "boogie" from the band and a fine vocal by Irene Day.

⑩ FLYING HOME LIONEL HAMPTON

Another former star of the Goodman outfit, vibraphonist Hampton specialized in swing music as roaring exhilaration, like this 1942 hit which builds a delirious momentum.

Chris Ingham

Birdsong

Avian songs that fly.

① HIGH-FLYING BIRD JUDY HENSKE from HIGH-FLYING BIRD

② BIRD OF PARADISE SNOWY WHITE from WHITE FLAMES

③ RHYADER CAMEL from THE SNOW GOOSE

④ SONGBIRD FLEETWOOD MAC from RUMOURS

⑤ YELLOW BIRD HUBERT SMITH from BERMUDA IS ANOTHER WORLD

⑥ THE LITTLEST BIRDS (SING THE PRETTIEST SONGS) THE BE-GOOD TANYAS from BLUE HORSE

⑦ NTYILO NTYILO THE SKYLARKS from THE BEST OF MIRIAM MAKEBA AND THE SKYLARKS

⑧ EAGLE ABBA from ABBA THE ALBUM

⑨ LES TROIS BEAUX OISEAUX DE PARADIS LINDA THOMPSON from ONE CLEAR MOMENT

⑩ THREE LITTLE BIRDS BOB MARLEY from SONGS OF FREEDOM

David Honigmann

Björk

Since her separation from crazed Icelandic indie outfit Sugarcubes, this pint-sized vocal gymnast has gone from strength to strength, consistently roping in top producers for her work and crafting album after album of stunning and ground-breaking music.

① VENUS AS A BOY from DEBUT

The lush strings and off-kilter beats gave a few clues of the genius and oddness that would soon follow.

② COME TO ME from DEBUT

Björk's larynx doesn't jump through any hoops, but it's still one stunning cut.

③ PLAY DEAD from DEBUT

With rousing horns and strings, this could almost be a Bond theme – awesome.

④ MOUTH'S CRADLE from MEDULLA

A deeply elegant arrangement of bleeps, choruses and processed voice samples – dislocated listening not to be missed.

❺ ALL IS FULL OF LOVE from **HOMOGENIC**
This is angelic music at its best – a cacophony of atmospherics, beats and love.

❻ HYPERBALLAD from **TELEGRAM**
It was a great song the first time around, this reworked version features the radical strings of the Brodsky Quartet.

❼ PAGAN POETRY from **VESPERTINE**
A confusion of denticulated beats and melodies wash and splash around Björk's vocal musings – glorious and euphoric.

❽ IT'S OH SO QUIET from **POST**
This is pure pop, as Bjork creates a swing number all her own. Quirky, happy, almost silly – more fun than a sack of kittens in a wool factory.

❾ IN THE MUSICALS from **SELMA SONGS**
A stupendous track with balls (literally). The whole album is great, inspired by the Björk-starring movie *Dancer In The Dark*.

❿ GRATITUDE from **DRAWING RESTRAINT 9**
This soundtrack's opening cut is the most accessible of a wonderful, largely instrumental, clutch; it features the vocal twangs of Will Oldham.

Peter Buckley

Black Sabbath/ Ozzy Osbourne

Monolithically heavy Sabbath were core progenitors of modern metal, and, of course, frontman Ozzy Osbourne has rollocked his way to ever greater stardom.

BLACK SABBATH

❶ BLACK SABBATH from **BLACK SABBATH**
Thunder rolls, a distant bell tolls and a titanic doom-laden riff grinds into life. Scarily brilliant.

❷ KILLING YOURSELF TO LIVE from **SABBATH BLOODY SABBATH**
Slickly produced, Sabbath rarely sounded quite so focused. Great solos, terrific drumming and a storming vocal performance.

❸ PARANOID from **PARANOID**
Written in just a few minutes as the legend goes, this is one of the most famous and enduring metal tunes ever.

❹ PLANET CARAVAN from **PARANOID**
Not a distorted guitar within earshot as Sabbath bring it down several notches for this spacey and oddly mellow drift through the cosmos.

❺ SUPERNAUT from **VOL 4**
A looser, more rock'n'roll feel to Tony Iommi's guitar here, and one hell of a sizzling solo.

❻ SWEET LEAF from **MASTER OF REALITY**
First a hacking cough then a sledgehammer riff and Ozzy's voice wreathed in cool herbal smoke. An awesome doper's anthem.

❼ SYMPTOM OF THE UNIVERSE from **SABOTAGE**
Basic and brutal there's no messing about here – until the crazy, inspired jazz'n'blues acoustic breakdown at the end.

❽ WAR PIGS from **PARANOID**
The scream of air raid sirens welcomes you to the hell of war. Ozzy rails against the destruction and madness in this timeless classic.

OZZIE OSBOURNE

❾ MR CROWLEY from **BLIZZARD OF OZZ**
Just listen to that immense cathedral organ intro. How can you go wrong with a song about arch Satanist Aleister Crowley?

❿ SUICIDE SOLUTION from **BLIZZARD OF OZZ**
In which Ozzy gets serious about the booze as guitarist Randy Rhoads creates a stunning monster riff.

Essi Berelian

Blaxploitation

Cheaply-made, nastily violent and gratuitously sexy – the blaxploitation films of the 1970s were, hopefully, all of that. But the back story was one of black pride and that was celebrated with soundtracks that opened up new areas of creativity and personnel to bring the very best out of some of the era's soul music talent.

❶ PURSUIT OF THE PIMPMOBILE ISAAC HAYES from **TRUCK TURNER**

Screaming tyres, flying hub caps, scattering pedestrians and acres of crushed velvet… hammering hi hat, hyperactive wah-wah guitar, assassin squad brass and a sumptuous string section. It's all here in this white-walled '74 Cadillac of a tune.

❷ SLICK WILLIE HUTCH from **THE MACK**

A relatively small scale piece of work that keeps the horns at arms length, but maintains a smoke and mirrors-type trickery as paranoid bongos supercharge the basic rhythms.

❸ MAIN THEME BARRY WHITE from **TOGETHER BROTHERS**

Big sounds from the big man as a full orchestra slugs it out with a tight funk rhythm section to create a springboard for all manner of musical strutting and showing-off.

❹ ACROSS 110TH STREET BOBBY WOMACK from **ACROSS 110TH STREET**

A superb balance of menace and desperation, manifesting itself in the plaintiveness of Bobbie Womack's vocals, brilliantly captures the tension that was shot through the film itself, as well as this classic soundtrack.

❺ SEE THE LIGHT EARTH WIND & FIRE from **THAT'S THE WAY OF THE WORLD**

An expectedly positive offering from EWF, with beautifully harmonizing vocals and bubbling, percussion-laced rhythms prove it weren't all doom and gloom in "the hood".

❻ CAFÉ REGIO'S ISAAC HAYES from **SHAFT**

Of course, any blaxploitaion film worth its 'fro had sex to go with the violence, and this is lazy, Sunday morning, guitar-led, flute-flavoured orchestral smoooove of the highest order.

❼ T PLAYS IT COOL MARVIN GAYE from **TROUBLE MAN**

With the drums up front in the mix and endlessly-layered electric pianos, moogs and ARPs, this is as tough as it is cool and cleverly jazzy. The entirely self-written and produced soundtrack was always Gaye's favourite among his own albums.

❽ THE BOSS JAMES BROWN from **BLACK CAESAR**

Tight, taut and totally James Brown, an ascending spiral of funk that escalates from scratch guitar into a JB extravaganza that hovers on the edge of overwhelming.

❾ FREDDIE'S DEAD CURTIS MAYFIELD from **SUPERFLY**

Thematically turning the perceived blaxploitation ethic on its head, but doing so with a simmeringly complex exercise in orchestral funk that keeps the latter firmly in control.

❿ TIME IS TIGHT BOOKER T & THE MGS from **UPTIGHT**

Blaxploitation before the word was invented (1968), this elegant funk is timeless and probably the most unrelenting interplay between and Hammond organ and a bass guitar ever to grace a groove.

Lloyd Bradley

Blondie

Blondie was a band, and a damn good one: they blended pure songwriting craft with a fistful of punk attitude and they had, in Debbie Harry, one of the all-time great frontwomen.

❶ RIP HER TO SHREDS from **BLONDIE**
Their first calling card: catchy, nasty and

wrapped up in a sharp-and-shiny package. The song made for a great advert, too

❷ NO IMAGINATION from **PLASTIC LETTERS**
The gems on Blondie's second album are hidden away. This one is sass on legs.

❸ HANGING ON THE TELEPHONE from **PARALLEL LINES**
A ringing tone – and then Harry comes slamming into the song, daring the band to keep up. Has any album ever started better?

❹ SUNDAY GIRL from **PARALLEL LINES**
One of the best Blondie homages to Brill-Building Girl-Group pop. Also in French.

❺ FADE AWAY AND RADIATE from **PARALLEL LINES**
Spooky guitar lines, loads of shimmering reverb, an air of unspecified and impossibly cool threat.

❻ ATOMIC from **EAT TO THE BEAT**
Futuristic and classic at the same time: the riff is unforgettable, and when the band come back in after the break it just keeps growing.

❼ CALL ME (FULL VERSION) from **AMERICAN GIGOLO SOUNDTRACK**
If you are going to have any truck with this smash-hit Giorgio Moroder collaboration, you want the full eight-minutes-and-then-some heavy breathing version. Anything shorter would be premature.

❽ RAPTURE from **AUTOAMERICAN**
A pure distillation of New York, 1980, with its proto-rap and references to Fab Five Freddy.

❾ ISLAND OF LOST SOULS from **THE HUNTER**
Blondie's take on ska classic The Tide Is High may have outworn its welcome but this second stab at Caribbean summer fun still sounds like a good time.

❿ MARIA from **NO EXIT**
As if they had never been away.

David Honigmann

The colour blue

The colour of the sky, of the sea, of the night, of sadness, of seductive clothing… it even has a whole genre named after it.

❶ BLUE SKIES ELLA FITZGERALD from **THE JOHNNY MERCER SONGBOOK**

❷ BLUE MOON THE COWBOY JUNKIES from **THE TRINITY SESSIONS**

❸ TANGLED UP IN BLUE BOB DYLAN from **BLOOD ON THE TRACKS**

❹ BLUE JONI MITCHELL from **BLUE**

❺ SKY BLUE PETER GABRIEL from **UP**

❻ BLUE NILE ALICE COLTRANE from **PTAH, THE EL DAOUD**

❼ AFRICAN SKY BLUE JULUKA from **AFRICAN LITANY**

❽ COOL BLUE EURYTHMICS from **TOUCH**

❾ BLUE SUEDE SHOES ELVIS PRESLEY from **ELVIS '56**

❿ BLUE VELVET BOBBY VINTON from **GREATEST HITS**

Essi Berelian

Bluegrass

While mainstream country music was embracing trends like honky-tonk, Bill Monroe & His Blue Grass Boys steadfastly clung to the "high lonesome" sound of old-time Appalachian string bands. Modernizing it with lightning-speed picking, the group gave birth to bluegrass.

❶ BLUE MOON OF KENTUCKY BILL MONROE & HIS BLUE GRASS BOYS from **THE ESSENTIAL, 1945–1949**
The song that started it all, Monroe's big hit inspired Elvis Presley (though you can't really waltz to the king's version).

❷ THE WHITE DOVE THE STANLEY BROTHERS from **THE COMPLETE COLUMBIA STANLEY BROTHERS**
The epitome of "high lonesome".

❸ FOGGY MOUNTAIN BREAKDOWN LESTER FLATT, EARL SCRUGGS & THE FOGGY MOUNTAIN BOYS from '**TIS SWEET TO BE REMEMBERED**
A breakdown so fast and furious even city slickers will break out their rebel yells.

❹ YOU DON'T KNOW MY MIND JIMMY MARTIN from **YOU DON'T KNOW MY MIND 1956–66**
The self-styled "King of Bluegrass" mixes in some honky-tonk.

❺ I WONDER HOW THE OLD FOLKS ARE AT HOME MAC WISEMAN from '**TIS SWEET TO BE REMEMBERED**
A model lesson in how the banjo and fiddle elevate nostalgia above greeting card sentimentality.

❻ RANK STRANGER THE STANLEY BROTHERS from **RIDIN' THAT MIDNIGHT TRAIN**
The definitive bluegrass hymn, and indeed sung at Bill Monroe's funeral. It has the perfect mingling of Carter's emotional lead and Ralph's ethereal tenor.

❼ LONG BLACK VEIL HAZEL DICKENS & ALICE GERRARD from **WHO'S THAT KNOCKIN'**
The first ladies of bluegrass deliver what may be the finest interpretation of this classic of American song.

❽ GET DOWN ON YOUR KNEES AND PRAY THE DEL MCCOURY BAND from **THE FAMILY**
On this goose-bump-raising track there are no instruments, only voices that climb and twist and bend, with McCoury's high tenor reaching forever skyward.

❾ WILL THE CIRCLE BE UNBROKEN NITTY GRITTY DIRT BAND from **WILL THE CIRCLE BE UNBROKEN**
Maybelle Carter, Jimmy Martin, Roy Acuff, Merle Travis and other old school country and bluegrass artists reach out to the unwashed hippies from California.

❿ DUELING BANJOS ERIC WEISSBERG & STEVE MANDELL from **DELIVERANCE ORIGINAL SOUNDTRACK**
Even if it wasn't in Deliverance, this would have been an instant classic.

Peter Shapiro/Madelyn Rosenberg

Blue Öyster Cult

Too clever by half to be heavy-metallers (though not too clever to deploy a Heavy Metal umlaut), the Cult's list of listenable songs (in descending order of merit) goes nowhere near 11. But these ones are the biz, especially on their live albums (SOME ENCHANTED EVENING and EXTRATERRESTRIAL LIVE).

❶ DON'T FEAR THE REAPER from **AGENTS OF FORTUNE**
The one Öyster Cult song everyone can hum: call-and-response comic death cutlery with a circular riff that won't let go.

❷ VETERAN OF THE PSYCHIC WARS from **EXTRATERRESTRIAL LIVE**
This Michael Moorcock-penned tale of Forever War ends in a lengthy inferno of guitar soloing, after which you too will feel like the veteran of a thousand wars.

❸ TAKE ME AWAY from **THE REVOLUTION BY NIGHT**
A relatively late and little regarded song, but tight and hard and heavy as they come. It is, of course, about UFO abductions.

❹ ASTRONOMY from **SOME ENCHANTED EVENING**
In the studio, the opening is underpowered and meandering; live, it achieves real menace.

❺ GODZILLA from **SPECTRES**
Fabulously rhymes "There goes Tokyo" with "Oh no". Exactly.

❼ BLACK BLADE from **EXTRATERRESTRIAL LIVE**
More Moorcock: the Elric of Melnibone saga handily condensed.

Essi Berelian

Blues standards

Perhaps more than any other genre of popular music, the blues depends on a received canon of much-covered classic songs. Here are ten of the greatest blues standards of all time, in their definitive, original versions.

❶ STACK O'LEE MISSISSIPPI JOHN HURT (1928)

❷ KEY TO THE HIGHWAY BIG BILL BROONZY (1938)

❸ THEY CALL IT STORMY MONDAY (BUT TUESDAY'S JUST AS BAD) T-BONE WALKER (1947)

❹ CRAWLIN' KING SNAKE JOHN LEE HOOKER (1949)

❺ DUST MY BROOM ELMORE JAMES WITH SONNY BOY WILLIAMSON (1951)

❻ BRIGHT LIGHTS, BIG CITY JIMMY REED (1956)

❼ NEED YOUR LOVE SO BAD LITTLE WILLIE JOHN (1956)

❽ DEATH DON'T HAVE NO MERCY REV GARY DAVIS (1960)

❾ YOU GOTTA MOVE MISSISSIPPI FRED MCDOWELL (1964)

❿ BORN UNDER A BAD SIGN ALBERT KING (1966)

Greg Ward

Blues ain't dead

And nearly 100 years after the first bluesmen allegedly sold their souls to the devil for fame, here are some tracks that show the blues ain't dead nor even endangered.

❶ DEATH LETTER I JOHNNY FARMER WITH ORGANIZED NOIZE from NEW BEATS FROM THE DELTA
A dance beat with samples, it's been done again since but never with as much feeling for this original.

❷ MISSISSIPPI KKKROSSROADS CHRIS THOMAS KING from DIRTY SOUTH HIP-HOP BLUES
A new version of the crossroads myth, with a redneck lawman in the role of the devil.

❸ BLUESMAN ON THE RUN NUBLUES from DREAMS OF A BLUES MAN
The spirit of the wandering wronged musician oozes from this track.

❹ WHO DO YOU LOVE? THE JESUS AND MARY CHAIN from BARBED WIRE KISSES
An odd choice at first glance, but a cover that has all the swagger and menace left out of other versions.

❺ REVELATIONS CHRIS THOMAS KING from DIRTY SOUTH HIP-HOP BLUES
Mixing Son House's John The Revelator with Robert Johnson's If I had Possession Over Judgement Day to fine apocalyptic effect.

❻ RIDE ON (FIGHT ON) LITTLE AXE from THE WOLF THAT HOUSE BUILT
The magnificent Skip Mcdonald mixes dub textures with blues guitar on this slice of history.

❼ IT'S BAD YOU KNOW R L BURNSIDE from COME ON IN
Contemporary blues on the Fat Possum label, this is the excellent Burnside with remixed beats behind him.

❽ DARK AS THE NIGHT, COLD AS THE GROUND LITTLE AXE from HARD GRIND
An old tune remade in the Little Axe manner.

❾ ST. JAMES SNAKEFARM from SONGS FROM MY FUNERAL
An eerie and moving version of an old standard, the very sparse arrangement adding to the mood of the piece.

⑩ DEATH LETTER II JOHNNY FARMER AND ORGANIZED NOIZE WITH PREECHER from NEW BEATS FROM THE DELTA

A rerun of the first track, but now with a rap about death and vengeance that shows how the old blues and new rap worlds are linked.

Steve Birt

Stolen Blues

Ten rock'n'roll behemoths – which were all firmly stolen property. For these original blues versions, check out any number of classic blues compilations.

❶ THAT'S ALL RIGHT ARTHUR "BIG BOY" CRUDUP

A great version, but you'll probably know it better as Elvis Presley's first single.

❷ MYSTERY TRAIN LITTLE JUNIOR PARKER

Another early Elvis single. His producer Sam Phillips had actually cut the song a couple of years earlier with a black act.

❸ CROSSROADS ROBERT JOHNSON

A staple for Eric Clapton and Cream, whose first album also included songs by Howlin' Wolf and Muddy Waters.

❹ GOOD MORNING LITTLE SCHOOL GIRL SONNY BOY WILLIAMSON

Later covered by the Yardbirds, Van Morrison and countless others.

❺ LITTLE RED ROOSTER HOWLIN' WOLF

A 1964 hit for The Rolling Stones, originally written by Willie Dixon in Chicago for Chester Burnett (aka Howlin' Wolf).

❻ CRAWLING KING SNAKE JOHN LEE HOOKER

Hooker learned the song from Big Joe Williams and recorded it in 1949. Some 22 years later it appeared on The Doors' album, *LA Woman*.

❼ BABY PLEASE DON'T GO BIG JOE WILLIAMS

But she did, all the way to Belfast to give Van Morrison and Them one of their early hits.

❽ KEY TO THE HIGHWAY BIG BILL BROONZY

Big Bill played it on an acoustic guitar. Then it turned up with Eric Clapton and Duane Allman's twin electric guitars on Derek and the Dominos' *Layla and Other Assorted Love Songs*.

❾ I CAN'T QUIT YOU BABY OTIS RUSH

Written by Willie Dixon for Otis Rush and featured on the debut album by Led Zeppelin.

⑩ TROUBLE SO HARD VERA HALL

When Vera Hall was recorded singing this in Alabama by Alan and John Lomax in the late 1930s, nobody could have guessed it would turn up 60 years later as Natural Blues on Moby's multi-platinum album, *Play*.

Nigel Williamson

Blur

There's No Other Way or Chemical World? Beetlebum or Tender? This playlist favours the early material leading up to the golden era of Britpop.

❶ I KNOW (EXTENDED) from SHE'S SO HIGH SINGLE

Before they were famous: this bouncy psychedelic classic was a B-side to the first single and could – should? – have been a hit.

❷ SING from LEISURE

An early sign of the band's depth, with a pounding drum and persuasive riff that leaves space to do some of the work yourself.

❸ THERE'S NO OTHER WAY from LEISURE

After Sing come four of the best opening bars in indie history. Awesome, classic guitar pop, and their first Top Ten hit.

❹ FOR TOMORROW from MODERN LIFE IS RUBBISH

A darker piece that opens their great but hard-to-make second album with strings, London life and perhaps Blur's finest Kinksy la-la-las.

Damon Albarn's
World grooves

"When I travel I find there's so much great music out there that isn't widely available outside the country where it was made," DAMON ALBARN says. "That's why we set up our own label, just to get some of it out there." The Blur/Gorillaz singer Damon Albarn, has become a fervent champion of world music in recent years and in 2002 co-founded the Honest Jon's label, which has since released recordings from Mali, Nigeria, Cuba, Trinidad and elsewhere. His current personal playlist contains several Nigerian funk tracks as he is presently in the studio finishing up an album of original songs he started recording in Lagos in 2004 with ex-Fela Kuti drummer Tony Allen.

❶ DENI KELENBE KOKO (LONELY GIRL BY THE RIVERSIDE) LOBI TRAORE GROUP from LOBI TRAORE GROUP

❷ OMELEBELE DR VICTOR OLAIYA from LAGOS CHOP UP

❸ PROFESSIONAL SUPER BANTOUS SUPER NEGRO BANTOUS from LAGOS ALL-ROUTES

❹ CALPYSO BLUES MONA BAPTISITE from LONDON IS THE PLACE FOR ME VOL 2

❺ CHOCOLATE EN C7 CHOCOLATE from SON CUBANO

❻ EL HOB KEDA OUM KALTHOUM from EL HOB KEDA

❼ EYA KA JO JIMMY SOLANKE AND THE JUNKERS from THE SHRINE PRESENTS AFROBEAT

❽ THE OLD ARK'S A-MOVERIN' ALPHABETICAL FOUR MOVERIN from COMPLETED RECORDED WORKS 1938–43

❾ SHAKE SUGAREE ELIZABETH COTTEN from SHAKE SUGAREE SMITHSONIAN FOLKWAYS

❿ MANKUNTO MAULA MEHR ALI AND SHEER ALI QAAWAALI from SACRED VOICES: SUFI PASSION

❺ STARSHAPED from MODERN LIFE IS RUBBISH
Worth playing just for the angelic call-and-answer vocals. Great oboe too.

❻ TO THE END from PARKLIFE
A hit romantic ballad, made with Laetitia Sadier from Stereolab, which is in a different class – in many ways – from the rest of the album. The *version Francaise* B-side is even better.

❼ CLOVER OVER DOVER from PARKLIFE
Ok, so the title's not up to much, but listen to the opening bars and drum fill and you'll be swept into its atmosphere.

❽ THIS IS A LOW from PARKLIFE
Blur's best downbeat song: beautifully constructed, with wailing guitars.

❾ THE UNIVERSAL from THE GREAT ESCAPE
The highlight of a disappointing album, with the "it really, really, really could happen" line, warning that future life might be rubbish, still making it potentially inspirational.

❿ BEETLEBUM from BLUR
A gentle love song that shows the influence of American indie rock. No chords in the album notes now.

Daniel Crewe

The name's Bond…

The world's most famous spy also has some of the world's best theme tunes. A life in espionage never sounded so good.

❶ A VIEW TO A KILL DURAN DURAN
The lyrics are nonsensical but the collision of Duran Duran's poppy funk and more traditional Bond-esque orchestra make this far superior to the film.

❷ DIAMONDS ARE FOREVER SHIRLEY BASSEY
Second only to her own performance on *Goldfinger*, Shirley Bassey's voice drips ice cold avarice with every note.

❸ FROM RUSSIA WITH LOVE MATT MUNRO
Super smooth crooner Matt Munro brings a touch of romance to this deadly cold war thriller.

❹ GOLDFINGER SHIRLEY BASSEY
Sensual, chilling and passionate all at once, our Shirl's golden tonsils make this possibly the most famous Bond theme ever.

❺ JAMES BOND THEME MONTY NORMAN
Monty Norman's twangy and suspenseful original is a modern classic recognized as the soundtrack to espionage, mayhem and romance the world over.

❻ LIVE AND LET DIE PAUL McCARTNEY
Macca with unusual attitude, sounding positively mean. One of the rockiest Bond themes in the canon so far.

❼ MR KISS KISS BANG BANG SHIRLEY BASSEY from **THE BEST OF JAMES BOND 30TH ANNIVERSARY EDITION**
Almost the theme to what eventually became *Thunderball*, Dionne Warwick recorded a version but Shirley just pips her on this.

❽ ON HER MAJESTY'S SECRET SERVICE THE PROPELLERHEADS from **SHAKEN AND STIRRED**
John Barry's moody instrumental original is a classic but this beefy, funky version is a seriously groovy mini epic in its own right.

❾ THE MAN WITH THE GOLDEN GUN LULU
A mediocre Roger Moore effort with a brilliant theme. How Lulu kept a straight face delivering the cheeky double entendres we'll never know.

❿ YOU ONLY LIVE TWICE NANCY SINATRA
Achingly beautiful strings and a subtle oriental atmosphere provide Nancy Sinatra's smoky vocals with a gorgeous backdrop.

Essi Berelian

Book I read

Do rockers read books? Indie ones obviously do, and write about 'em, too.

❶ READ IT IN BOOKS ECHO AND THE BUNNYMEN from **CROCODILES**
"I've seen in your eyes/I've read it in books/ Who wants love/Without the looks."

❷ BOOK I READ TALKING HEADS from **TALKING HEADS '77**
"I'm embarrassed to admit it hit the soft spot in my heart /When I found out you wrote the book I read."

❸ BOOKS ABOUT UFOS HUSKER DÜ from **NEW DAY RISING**
"Walking down a sunny street to the library/ Checking out the latest books on outer space."

❹ ADULT BOOKS X from **WILD GIFT**
"Like Adult books/I don't understand/ Jackie Susann meant it that way."

❺ WRAPPED UP IN BOOKS BELLE AND SEBASTIAN from **DEAR CATASTROPHE WAITRESS**
"Our aspirations, are wrapped up in books Our inclinations are hidden in looks".

❻ EVERYDAY I WRITE THE BOOK ELVIS COSTELLO from PUNCH THE CLOCK
"You said you'd stand by me in the middle of Chapter Three/But you were up to your old tricks in Chapters Four, Five and Six."

❼ THE DANGLING CONVERSATION SIMON AND GARFUNKEL from PARSLEY, SAGE, ROSEMARY AND THYME
"And you read your Emily Dickinson/ And I my Robert Frost."

❽ PAPERBACK WRITER THE BEATLES from REVOLVER
"Dear Sir or Madam, will you read my book?/ It took me years to write, will you take a look?"

❾ I AM THE SUB LIBRARIAN PIANO MAGIC from LOW BIRTH WEIGHT
"A steady diet of Brautigan, 'Tapestry' on the walkman/Paranormal ill-health from dusting off the top shelf."

Butch Lazorchak

Cool bossa

Bossa Nova will always mean lift music to some, but to its fans the genre has produced some of the most laid-back, melting small-hours music ever made – sweet moments of serenity in a noisy world. Some of the very coolest…

❶ LIGIA JOÃO GILBERTO & STAN GETZ from THE BEST OF TWO WORLDS
Singer and guitarist Gilberto – Bossa Nova's originator – in a 1976 reunion with the master saxophonist, on one of Jobim's most achingly gentle songs.

❷ BOM SINAL CELSO FONSECA from NATURAL
It can still be done. Fonseca glides through a modern bossa without a hair out of place.

❸ ELA E CARIOCA VINICIUS CANTUARIA from VINICIUS
A contemporary, left-field take on Jobim's classic paean to a Rio beauty.

❹ MARIA/LINDA FLOR MARIA BETHANIA & JOÃO GILBERTO from 25 ANOS
A pair of old-school Brazilian ballads, caressed into life by two masters of the style.

❺ SAMBA DO AVAIO LEILA PINHEIRO from THE STORY OF BOSSA NOVA
Another Jobim warhorse, about looking at Rio from a plane, given a treatment as soft and lush as a club class seat.

❻ CORAÇÃO VAGABUNDO JOÃO GILBERTO from JOÃO: VOZ E VIOLÃO
Singing and playing as if he's trying not to wake the baby next door, Gilberto gives a great reading of Caetano's lament for the waywardness of the heart.

❼ APARECIDA IVAN LINS & TERENCE BLANCHARD from THE HEART SPEAKS
Blanchard's muted jazz trumpet tiptoes through one of Lins' greatest compositions.

❽ MALAGA JOÃO GILBERTO from JOÃO
Forsaking Portuguese for Italian – but with an accent so thick the difference is almost academic – Gilberto's vocal is cushioned by wonderful, swooning strings.

❾ COISA MAIS LINDA CAETANO VELOSO from CAETANO, THE DEFINITIVE COLLECTION
Caetano sings this tender declaration of love as if he's whispering in her ear.

❿ CORCOVADO JOÃO GILBERTO from O AMOR, O SORRISO E A FLOR
Well, this Jobim song had to be in – though this is the first version, without the lisping Astrid Gilberto. At 1'58", a perfect miniature, arguably never bettered in Gilberto's career.

Alex Webb

David Bowie

Approaching the end of four decades in the music business, the Dame of Rock has a back catalogue of classic tunes to live and die for – and maybe it's time to forget that he also recorded The Laughing Gnome. This is a list that ties itself in knots by taking just one cut from any one album (and we don't want to be too obvious, do we?).

❶ QUEEN BITCH from **HUNKY DORY**
Camp, New York and trashy, yet revealing a touching insecurity, this is early Bowie at his creative peak, a three-minute drama, with not a word out of place, set to an angry tantrum of a riff delivered like a slap to the face.

❷ SOUL LOVE from **THE RISE AND FALL OF ZIGGY STARDUST & THE SPIDERS FROM MARS**
Ziggy's eleven songs are all but perfect. Starman and Suffragette City tend to do service as Best in Show, but this is a gem, and presaged future directions.

❸ CANDIDATE from **DIAMOND DOGS**
A slow building seduction from the Grand Dame of decadent stardom in his part man/part beast phase, offering to show you the all time great rock'n'roll night out – a spot of dinner and some weird sex with Bowie, buy some drugs, watch a band and jump in the river holding hands. Perfect.

❹ WILD IS THE WIND from **STATION TO STATION**
Bowie pulls out all the stops for this most passionate of love songs, treading the thin line between intensity and melodrama with consummate skill.

❺ HEROES from **HEROES**
Take Fripp's epic guitar, add Bowie's gently burning vocal and you get a piece that swells so big that they couldn't film it even in wide screen. The greatest song he's ever written.

❻ BREAKING GLASS from **LOW**
Drug induced madness, paranoia, shame,

defiance and regret, and there are only four lines of lyrics! Deep dark beats and downright menacing guitar turn this into an episode from the darker side of glam rock.

❼ BOYS KEEP SWINGING from **LODGER**
Swaggering, boastful but cool, sharp and confident. Who needs to be aggressive when you look this good? Bowie came from a stylish, mod background and this track looks back to the glory days of 60s British pop with horn flourishes, a searing guitar line and trad bassline straight outta Carnaby Street.

❽ BLUE JEAN from **TONIGHT**
Gorgeous meaningless pop from a newly sober artist at his very best. David keeps the operatics to a minimum, stays cool, sharp and focused throughout, backed by a tight, soul-informed band. Get up and dance!

❾ HALLO SPACEBOY (PET SHOP BOYS REMIX) from **THE HALLO SPACEBOY CD SINGLE**
When Bowie met the Pet Shop Boys the sparks flew… sparks of genius, of course. With The Pet Shop contributing expertise, familiarity with the equipment and an arch, camp sensibility to challenge that of Bowie, all sides were on their mettle. Magic.

❿ I'M AFRAID OF AMERICANS (TRENT REZNOR MIX) from **BEST OF**
And who isn't, Dave? Especially Americans like that Mr Reznor. A good piece of late period paranoia with Bowie at his most urchin-like and Reznor chewing up the control board and ladling on the effects. Another meeting of egos, another draw with honour on both sides.

Al Spicer

Boy George/ Culture Club

Flamboyant, camp, witty and blessed with a gorgeous voice, Boy George cut some sublime pop with Culture Club before an intermittently successful solo career.

❶ DO YOU REALLY WANT TO HURT ME from **KISSING TO BE CLEVER**

This loping, reggae-inflected tune topped the UK charts and made the Boy a thrillingly unlikely household name, not to mention an icon for small girls.

❷ TIME (CLOCK OF MY HEART) from **KISSING TO BE CLEVER**

A heart stopping vocal from George as he waxes soulfully on CC's second huge hit.

❸ CHURCH OF THE POISON MIND from **KISSING TO BE CLEVER**

Faux Motown with wailing gospel-flavoured backing vocals. Where's the church, George?

❹ I'LL TUMBLE 4 YA from **KISSING TO BE CLEVER**

Infectious, uptempo playground pop – who would have thought that a portly, cross dresser would become a kids favourite?

❺ KARMA CHAMELEON from **COLOUR BY NUMBERS**

Number 1 on both sides of the Atlantic and much else of the world – this is CC at the peak of their pop powers.

❻ MISS ME BLIND from **COLOUR BY NUMBERS**

Funky dancefloor workout number with George warning an estranged boyfriend that he's gonna miss him.

❼ THE WAR SONG from **FROM LUXURY TO HEARTACHE**

"War is stupid and people are stupid" sings George on perhaps the silliest protest song ever. Catchy tho'.

❽ EVERYTHING I OWN from **GREATEST MOMENTS**

George goes solo and repents for heroin addiction with a lilting reggae take on the David Gates ballad.

❾ THE CRYING GAME from **GREATEST MOMENTS**

The Dave Berry tune became the theme tune to Neil Jordan's film. When George sings "I know all there is to know about the crying game" you believe him.

❿ EVIL IS SO CIVILISED from **CHEAPNESS AND BEAUTY**

George rages against homophobic murders backed by a cracking glam rock band

Garth Cartwright

Billy Bragg

A career of mixing pop and politics makes Billy Bragg easy to caricature. But his Barking manner hides a keen ear for cant and a punning lyrical gift easily the equal of Costello or Ray Davies.

❶ A NEW ENGLAND from **LIFE'S A RIOT WITH SPY VERSUS SPY**

This was Bragg's debut, with the acoustic wallop of a busker echoing off the tiled wall of a Central Line underpass. Everything he does well is wrapped up here: despite the insistence that he isn't looking for a New England, just another girl, it is clear that he wants both.

❷ BETWEEN THE WARS from **BETWEEN THE WARS**

What comes on like 1930s nostalgia turns out to be 1980s foreboding. Now as dated as a nineteenth century union ballad, its plea for moderation as the heart of the nation remains sweetly affecting.

❸ WORLD TURNED UPSIDE DOWN from **BETWEEN THE WARS**

Leon Rosselson's tribute to Gerald Winstanley and the Diggers (and obliquely to the Marxist historian Christopher Hill), and their occupation of St George's Hill in Surrey in 1649 fits perfectly into the Bragg songbook.

❹ A13 TRUNK ROAD TO THE SEA from **PEEL SESSIONS**

As a musical parodist, Bragg is a rarity, inasmuch as he writes parodies that can be listened to more than once. This Essex take on "Route 66" makes the end of the road in Southend (via Grays Thurrock, Basildon and Leigh-on-Sea) sound almost tempting.

Billy Bragg's
Busking Tunes

" I did a bit of busking in London in the early 1980s, sometimes earning as much as fifteen quid a day. Of the many songs I busked, these were my favourites. Occasionally I play one or two during my soundcheck, just to keep my hand in…"

❶ ME AND BOBBY MCGEE KRIS KRISTOFFERSON from THE BEST OF KRIS KRISTOFFERSON
Any busker worth their salt should be able to play this, a classic of the genre. Contains the frequently mis-heard lyric "Somewhere miscellaneous Lord, I let her slip away…"

❷ BRING IT ON HOME TO ME SAM COOKE from THE BEST OF SAM COOKE
I always found a little Sam Cooke helped things along, be it Wonderful World, A Change is Gonna Come or this beauty.

❸ LOVE HAS NO PRIDE BONNIE RAITT from GIVE IT UP
Complex chord changes, but they really wring the heartbreak out of a lyric that must rank amongst the greatest sad songs ever sung.

❹ CATCH THE WIND DONOVAN from WHAT'S BIN DID AND WHAT'S BIN HID
A song that just rolls gently along, drawing the listener in so that by the time they get to where you are playing their hand is already in their pocket…

❺ EARLY MORNING RAIN GORDON LIGHTFOOT from LIGHTFOOT!
Easy to play, great to sing. Buskers should always do a couple of rambling songs, to give passers-by the impression that they are travelling round the world with nothing but their musical talent to support them, even if they are just travelling in from Acton Town where they live with their Mum and Dad.

❻ THE MOUNTAINS OF MOURNE DON MCLEAN from PLAYIN' FAVOURITES
It's always good to have an unashamedly sentimental song in your repertoire. This was mine, written in 1896 by Percy French, an Irishman who also wrote Abdul Abulbul Amir.

❼ THAT'S ENTERTAINMENT THE JAM from DIG THE NEW BREED
This was my nod to contemporary taste – the only Jam song you can play convincingly on an acoustic guitar.

❽ SPANISH IS THE LOVING TONGUE BOB DYLAN from DYLAN
Dylan wrote quite a few busker's standards, but not this one which is based on a poem by a guy named Badger Clarke.

❾ YOU DON'T MISS YOUR WATER OTIS REDDING from OTIS BLUE
The definitive William Bell classic…

❿ CAN'T HELP FALLING IN LOVE ELVIS PRESLEY from THE HOLLYWOOD HITS
"Wise men say only fools rush in…" There was something about Elvis ballads that just kept the small change coming, and this one was my *piece de resistance*. Sung full-throated on my favourite pitch, the long subway that runs from South Kensington tube station to the Science Museum, I found the tiled walls of the tunnel greatly assisted my attempts to summon up some of its overwrought grandeur.

❺ LEVI STUBBS' TEARS from **TALKING WITH THE TAXMAN ABOUT POETRY**

A tiny domestic drama: the central character's only comfort is her Four Tops tape. And just before the end, over Bragg's percussive guitar, Dave Woodhead's fluegelhorn floats as fragile as an angel.

❻ WAITING FOR THE GREAT LEAP FORWARDS from **WORKERS' PLAYTIME**

Rueful political songs are few and far between, and this is one of the finest: in the wake of Labour's third election defeat of 1987, Bragg looks back on a career of mixing pop and politics and wonders what the use is, before rousing himself and his audience through a singalong chorus of slogans, half ridiculous and half defiant.

❼ RUMOURS OF WAR from **DON'T TRY THIS AT HOME**

By the early 90s there was a New World Order, and Cold War certainties dissolved into turbulence in the Balkans and the Gulf. Rumours of War deals subtly with domestic denial of clouds on foreign horizons. June Tabor, uncharacteristically, later murdered it with over-emotion; Bragg lets it speak for itself.

❽ A PICT SONG from **WILLIAM BLOKE**

Bragg became increasingly obsessed with notions of Englishness, and how it can be rescued from nationalism. And so, inevitably, he comes up against Rudyard Kipling, another populist with an uneasy relationship with Empire. Bragg sets Kipling's verse to abrasive guitar that harks back to his earliest work.

❾ ALL YOU FASCISTS BOUND TO LOSE from **MERMAID AVENUE TOUR OFFICIAL BOOTLEG**

None too subtle, this lyric of Woody Guthrie's: Bragg and the Blokes give it a rousing chorus that falls just the right side of embarrassing.

❿ ENGLAND HALF ENGLISH from **ENGLAND HALF ENGLISH**

Still celebrating the new England, one that mingles and mixes cultures as it has done throughout the centuries. The musical mixing is in the hands of a band directed by the great ex-Mustapha, Ben Mandelson.

David Honigmann

Brazil classics

The country covering half of South America produces more than its fair share of music, which is almost always instantly recognizable as Brazilian. After all, this is the culture which gave the world both samba and bossa nova. See also BOSSA and SAMBA playlists.

❶ ADEUS BATUCADA **CARMEN MIRANDA** from **IMPERATRIZ DO SAMBA**

Though best known for wearing a fruit head-dress during her Hollywood career of the 1940s, this 1935 hit (also covered by Virgínia Rodrigues, among others) shows why Miranda was the original "Empress of Samba".

❷ DESAFINADO **JOÃO GILBERTO** from **JOÃO VOZ E VIOLÃO**

Originally recorded by Gilberto in 1957 – when it was hailed as the first bossa nova – this remake from 2000 shows him still to be a master of timing.

❸ THE GIRL FROM IPANEMA **ASTRID GILBERTO** from **THE GENIUS OF ASTRUD GILBERTO**

By singing slightly off-key, the daughter of João Gilberto (also on this 1963 recording) ensured enduring listenability; as millions made subconscious corrections, she made millions.

❹ MAS QUE NADA **JORGE BEN JOR** from **THE DEFINITIVE COLLECTION**

A worldwide hit which many will know (even if they don't know its name) for its unforgettable chorus. Also a hit for Sergio Mendes, though this is the superior original.

❺ CRICKETS SING FOR ANA MARIA MARCOS VALLE from **BRAZILICA (VARIOUS ARTISTS)**
A jumpy little English language samba-pop number from 1968, by a singer-songwriter who is still making good records.

❻ CHICLETE COM BANANA GILBERTO GIL from **THE EARLY YEARS**
A defiant musical manifesto from this pioneer of the tropicalia movement, now Culture Minister for Brazil's socialist government.

❼ LONDON, LONDON CAETANO VELOSO from **THE DEFINITIVE COLLECTION**
Another tropicalista, Veloso penned one of his most memorable tunes while in exile from Brazil's military government. Depictions of homesickness don't come much more soulful.

❽ ROMARIA ELIS REGINA from **LITTLE PEPPER: THE DEFINITIVE COLLECTION**
The late lamented diva lived fast and died young, leaving behind a trail of wonderful interpretations. This intensely spiritual 1977 recording lives up to its title ("Pilgrimage").

❾ MARIA, MARIA MILTON NASCIMENTO from **CLUBE DA ESQUINA 2**
This exhilarating love song from Nascimento's seminal late 70s masterpiece always gets the crowds going at his gigs.

❿ RITMO NUMBER ONE PAULINHO DA COSTA from **BATUCADA THE SOUND OF THE FAVELAS**
Absolutely everything you can do with percussion instruments in eight and a half minutes of glorious, driving samba. Who needs melody?.

Jon Lusk

Brit-Blues

By the mid-1960s, most of the great American blues performers couldn't get arrested in their homeland. But they found an enthusiastic young audience in Britain where the blues enjoyed a boom and inspired the likes of Eric Clapton,

Jimmy Page and The Rolling Stones. Quite what qualified middle-class white boys from the English suburbs to play the music of sharecroppers from the Mississippi Delta has never been fully explained. But there's no doubt that they played it with a genuine conviction and passion.

❶ I'D RATHER GO BLIND CHICKEN SHACK from **CHICKEN SHACK: THE COLLECTION**
Singer Christine Perfect (later McVie) lived up to her then name on the Etta James song.

❷ I'M GOING HOME TEN YEARS AFTER from **WOODSTOCK**
A highlight of the Woodstock festival, movie and soundtrack album which saw Alvin Lee crowned the fastest guitarist in the West.

❸ NEED YOUR LOVE SO BAD FLEETWOOD MAC from **THE BEST OF FLEETWOOD MAC**
Peter Green's guitar plus strings equals blues heaven.

❹ SPOONFUL CREAM from **FRESH CREAM**
Willie Dixon gets the power trio treatment, copped by Clapton from Buddy Guy's band.

❺ RAMBLIN' ON MY MIND JOHN MAYALL'S BLUESBREAKERS (WITH ERIC CLAPTON) from **BLUESBREAKERS WITH ERIC CLAPTON**
Robert Johnson cover from the only album "God" ever made with the Godfather.

❻ TRAIN TO NOWHERE SAVOY BROWN from **BLUE MATTER**
A train to nowhere arguably carrying coals to Newcastle from the one British blues band to enjoy more success in America than at home.

❼ GOIN' DOWN SLOW FREE from **TONS OF SOBS**
They were alright then, back in the days when their debut album made them the toughest British blues combo of them all.

❽ MESSIN' WITH THE KID RORY GALLAGHER from **LIVE IN EUROPE/STAGE STRUCK**
Not really British as he came from across the

Irish Sea but he sure had those white boy blues.

⑨ BOYFRIEND BLUES JO-ANN KELLY from **BLUES AND GOSPEL**
The British Bonnie Raitt, who turned down the chance to sing with both Canned Heat and Johnny Winter.

⑩ DEAR JILL BLODWYN PIG from **A HEAD RINGS OUT**
Perhaps the best British slide guitar solo ever from ex-Jethro Tull guitarist Mick Abrahams.

Nigel Williamson

Britpop

When Blur, Oasis et al arrived in the early 90s, British pop music became a national obsession. For a time it seemed that even the attentions of Prime Minister (and student rock singer) Tony Blair couldn't kill it. A decade on, it seems very much like history, but these ten numbers, released 1993–95, remain live and kicking.

① PARKLIFE BLUR from **PARKLIFE**
The Colchester group's third album provided a quintessentially English snapshot, with this jaunty Phil Daniels-enhanced song.

② LIVE FOREVER OASIS from **DEFNITELY MAYBE**
The first Oasis song to break the UK Top 10, in 1994, Live Forever displayed the burgeoning songcraft of Noel Gallagher. His brother's unrefined vocals neatly juxtapose the gentle melody, and there's a triumphant guitar solo.

③ CONNECTION ELASTICA from **ELASTICA**
A moody three-quarters-female band with a sharp attitude and a sound that wore its influences on its sleeve. Debts to The Stranglers, Wire and Blondie were obvious, but this is still a tightly-wound pop-punk gem.

④ ALRIGHT SUPERGRASS from **I SHOULD COCO**
A summertime singalong anthem that thrust the hairy Oxford trio into the big league, Alright throbbed with teenage exuberance and showed a keen ear for lustrous melodies.

⑤ I CAN'T IMAGINE THE WORLD WITHOUT ME ECHOBELLY from **EVERYBODY'S GOT ONE**
This single's playful title was taken rather too seriously by the music press, and although some comparisons with Morrissey stood up, Echobelly made their own impression through provocative lyrics, chunky tunes and Sonya Madan's distinctive intonation.

⑥ COMMON PEOPLE PULP from **DIFFERENT CLASS**
Jarvis Cocker's Sheffield smoothies had been making music for years before their popularity rocketed in the Britpop era. A bouncy ode to class pretension, Common People matched sharp, witty lyrics with disco-friendliness.

⑦ INBETWEENER SLEEPER from **SMART**
Buoyant, husky vocals were Louise Wener's speciality, coupled with a sassy, cynical take on suburbia. Bright, chiming guitars and a shout-out chorus brought this effort deserved attention.

⑧ FOR THE DEAD GENE from **OLYMPIAN**
A spoonful of The Jam and a wink to The Faces enhanced the Morrissey-like intonation of singer Martin Rossiter on the Watford band's debut single. Graceful and sophisticated, it was a welcome antidote to the boorish rivalries of their contemporary Britpoppers.

⑨ SO YOUNG SUEDE from **SUEDE**
Bowie-esque glamour, Bernard Butler's exhilarating guitar and Anderson's trademark wailing captivated an army of devotees. So Young covers the themes that would come to be known as Suede's stock-in-trade: sex, drugs and alienated youth.

⑩ SPEAKEASY SHED SEVEN from **CHANGE GIVER**
These next-big-things from York enjoyed moderate success at home and were great live performers, led by the rubber-limbed Rick Witter. Top-notch riffs and strident but smooth vocals show off the Sheddies' best qualities.

Ed Wright

Carl Barat's
Libertine raves

The Libertines, the London-based band CARL BARAT formed with Pete Doherty, achieved notoriety for their in-fighting and drug abuse. Yet the intoxicating, grimy anthems of their self-titled 2004 album proved it was more than hype and that they were one of the most exciting new bands in many a year. Then it all went horribly wrong as the band split amid lurid tabloid headlines. At the time of writing, Carl Barat was preparing to release his first solo album. Here's what he rates.

❶ OH YOU PRETTY THINGS DAVID BOWIE from HUNKY DORY

❷ HURRICANE BOB DYLAN from DESIRE

❸ PERSONALITY CRISIS NEW YORK DOLLS from NEW YORK DOLLS

❹ REMOTE CONTROL THE CLASH from THE CLASH

❺ EATON RIFLES THE JAM from SETTING SONS

❻ NO MORE HEROES THE STRANGLERS from NO MORE HEROES

❼ TOO MUCH TOO YOUNG THE SPECIALS from THE SPECIALS

❽ BIG MOUTH STRIKES AGAIN THE SMITHS from BIG MOUTH STRIKES AGAIN

❾ SORTED FOR E'S AND WHIZ PULP from DIFFERENT CLASS

❿ FIT BUT YOU KNOW IT THE STREETS from A GRAND DON'T COME FOR FREE

Britpop (again!)

Britpop is back. Home-grown acts are again dominating the UK airwaves and denting the US, loading credible songs with bold influences, underscored by their youthful energy and teasing wit.

❶ I PREDICT A RIOT KAISER CHIEFS from EMPLOYMENT
Fun power-poppers who mix in enough influences to build a pub quiz around, the Chiefs know how to make foot-tapping tunes. Here, the Clash are revisited to catchy effect.

❷ PROCESSED BEATS KASABIAN from KASABIAN
Manchester c.1990 pulsates through the synthy rock rhythms of this Leicester outfit. The Happy Mondays' swagger fuses with the rippling riffs of the Stone Roses on this psych-edelic dancefloor-filler.

❸ HELICOPTER BLOC PARTY from SILENT ALARM
A political, post-punk vibe permeates the East London quartet's music, as edgy riffs support Kele Okereke's impassioned delivery. From an angry howl to a weary sigh, his voice fleshes out the already charged lyrics.

❹ YOU GOT THE STYLE ATHLETE from VEHICLES & ANIMALS
Deptford's indie hopefuls pull out a hook-laden summer ditty with a funky, feel-good melody and chorus that you'll be humming for the rest of the day.

❺ MEANTIME THE FUTUREHEADS from THE FUTUREHEADS
New-wave art-rockers effortlessly meld jittery guitars and boptastic rhythms, recalling

vintage XTC and the Jam. Topped off by the Wearsiders' untempered vocal harmonies, it's a refreshing, soulful concoction.

❻ CAN'T STAND ME NOW THE LIBERTINES from THE LIBERTINES

Frontmen Carl Barat and Pete Doherty serialized their turbulent friendship through dynamic, emotionally charged songwriting. Few Libertines tracks surpass the instant impact of this poppy yet poignant cat-and-mouse duet.

❼ UP ALL NIGHT RAZORLIGHT from UP ALL NIGHT

Jagger-a-like singer Johnny Borrell opens with gentle introspection then pulls out the bombast and bravado for some all-out rock'n'roll on the title track from the Londoners' debut LP.

❽ SOMEWHERE ONLY WE KNOW KEANE from HOPES AND FEARS

Graduates of the Coldplay school of bedroom poetry, Keane favour a delicate piano-led craft to scale those emotional highs. Tom Chaplin's crisp, chorister-esque vocals evoke Thom Yorke's distinctive falsetto.

❾ TAKE ME OUT FRANZ FERDINAND from FRANZ FERDINAND

Pouts and posing aside, the natty Glaswegians weld an appetizer of garage rock and a funky pop main, bridging the two with an ominous drumbeat and irrepressible guitar hook. A modern classic.

❿ APPLY SOME PRESSURE MAXÏMO PARK from A CERTAIN TRIGGER

Hard-hitting verses boosted by chunky guitars and vocalist Paul Smith's Geordie inflections slow down to a more reflective, extended middle-eight. Conviction and raw punk-rock energy whirl throughout.

Ed Wright

Brit-reggae

British reggae never quite managed to sound "authentically" Jamaican – and was
all the better for it. **The musical environment West Indians experienced growing up in the UK meant these acts were much more aware of a pop mainstream, imported US soul and rock. Hence lovers' rock, interesting instrumentation and Steel Pulse.**

❶ WARRIOR CHARGE ASWAD

A militant roots reggae track like no other, that could only have been made in Britain and succeeds in sounding positive, obnoxious, celebratory and scary all at the same time.

❷ HARD TIME STYLE PABLO GAD

When this double-time hi-stepping rocker came out in 1979 nobody guessed it was British, but then we were having too much fun singing along with the chorus: "When I was a yout I used to burn collie weed in Rizla/Now I am a man I jus' a burn collie weed in a chalwa…"

❸ SIX ONE PENNY MISTY IN ROOTS

Gently rocking roots that sums up UK reggae in its clever approach to pop-friendly sounds and easy-access melodies but with a bass and drum balance that leaves you no doubt what it is.

❹ MUSIC IN THE AIR MATUMBI

Matumbi were always the cleverest, most musically literate and stylistically open of the British reggae bands, and this is them at their cool, creeping best.

❺ NATTY ROCKERS TRADITION

Taken from the dub tracks of their big hit Moving On, it is pretty basic bass, drum, spinning echo and a few rising piano chords, but their tricky, cascading approach to the mix gives it real class.

❻ SOME GUYS HAVE ALL THE LUCK (EXTENDED MIX) MAXI PRIEST

British reggae taken to its logical conclusion, as Maxi manages to be totally TOTP-friendly, but retains all the deep roots feeling he needs to keep it on the right side of the riddim police.

b

⑦ LOVE MARCUS BLACK HARMONY

A cruelly under-appreciated reggae band who were usually rocking dancefloors with their smoooove lovers rock, but here they apply the same easy rocking action to deep roots lyrics.

⑧ SILLY GAMES JANET KAY

This best-known, best-loved lovers' rock tune has all its pop reggae ducks in a row: slow skanking beat, pop-oriented melody, strong bassline and a teenage girl singing about the problems of her love life.

⑨ HIGHER RANKING 4TH STREET ORCHESTRA

Circular, escalating dub track, by Matumbi under an assumed name, that manages to turn in on itself two or three times and still come out sounding upful.

⑩ HANDSWORTH REVOLUTION STEEL PULSE

Shimmering, superbly crafted, intricate song that would be a standout track in any genre from rock to pop to soul, but it's reggae and it raised the bar for anybody who came after…

Lloyd Bradley

Mykaell S Riley's
Philharmonia

MYKAELL S RILEY was a founder member of Steel Pulse, and co-wrote their definitive *Handsworth Revolution* album. Today, based in London, he runs The Reggae Philarmonic Orchestra, lectures in music at the University of Westminster and composes TV and film music.

❶ HANGING ON A STRING LOOSE ENDS from THE BEST OF LOOSE ENDS

Great 80s British R&B that we have not seen the likes of since.

❷ HANDSWORTH REVOLUTION STEEL PULSE from HANDSWORTH REVOLUTION

The revolution has taken place but little has changed.

❸ THE TIDE IS HIGH THE PARAGONS from THE TREASURE ISLE STORY

Demonstrates the resilience of a great song: Blondie… Atomic Kitten… as the lyric says, it's number one.

❹ GHOST TOWN THE SPECIALS from THE SPECIALS SINGLES

Great social commentary from the Midlands.

❺ MOVE ON UP CURTIS MAYFIELD from MOVE ON UP

Classic 70s soul, and for the world's black population the message remains the same.

❻ WALK ON BY ISAAC HAYES from HOT BUTTERED SOUL

Powerfully mellow version of a timeless classic, by the original walrus of love.

❼ SKIN DEEP DUKE ELLINGTON from SKIN DEEP

An exciting expression of individual feeling and musicianship – especially if you like drum solos.

❽ COCONUT ROCK THE SKATALITES from STUDIO ONE SCORCHER INSTRUMENTALS

Ska meets jazz in a big band Jamaican swing style.

❾ LONG TALL SALLY SALLY LITTLE RICHARD from LONG TALL SALLY

Rock'n'Roll comes in many forms but not much better than this.

❿ THERE'S NOTHING LIKE THIS OMAR from THERE'S NOTHING LIKE THIS

Classic British soul, which demonstrates we can deliver – if only in small doses.

Broken-hearted

Breaking-up is by a long chalk the most written about subject in popular music. Let's hear it for dark nights of the soul.

❶ MOST OF THE TIME BOB DYLAN from **OH MERCY**
He made the greatest break-up album of all time with *Blood On The Tracks*. But this song combines emotional desolation with a wonderfully knowing self-delusion: "I can survive, I can endure and I don't even think about her… most of the time."

❷ YOU'VE LOST THAT LOVIN' FEELING
RIGHTEOUS BROTHERS from **YOU'VE LOST THAT LOVIN' FEELING**
That heart-stopping moment when you're still head-over-heels and it suddenly dawns that the object of adoration no longer feels quite the same way…

❸ HERE COME THOSE TEARS AGAIN JACKSON BROWNE from **THE PRETENDER**
Just when you thought you were getting over the betrayal, she walks back in as if nothing had ever happened. Do you slam the door in her face or lick her all over like a grateful puppy?

❹ IT'S TOO LATE CAROLE KING from **TAPESTRY**
"Stayed in bed all morning just to pass the time…" Stop moping and pull yourself together, woman.

❺ STOP! IN THE NAME OF LOVE THE SUPREMES from **GREATEST HITS**
Holland, Dozier and Holland seemed to turn out classic teenage tear-jerkers every week at Motown's height. For the Supremes alone they penned Where Did Our Love Go, My World Is Empty Without You and You Keep Me Hangin' On among others. But perhaps best of all was this 1965 pleading, needing piece of pop perfection.

❻ NOTHING COMPARES TO YOU SINEAD O'CONNOR from **I DO NOT WANT WHAT I HAVEN'T GOT**
Prince wrote it but it was Sinead who recorded the most heartbreaking version, accompanied by a marvellous video with a tear rolling down her cheek which she insists to this day was real.

❼ YESTERDAY THE BEATLES from **HELP!**
The most covered song of all time, although it loses some of its emotional resonance when you remember that before he came up with the finished lyric, McCartney's guide vocal for the tune was built around the phrase "scrambled eggs".

❽ OH LONESOME ME NEIL YOUNG from **AFTER THE GOLDRUSH**
Written by Don Gibson, but Neil's version tops the original for squeezing every last ounce of self-pity out of the morose lyric.

❾ AIN'T NO SUNSHINE BILL WITHERS from **JUST AS I AM**
A song whose end-of-the-world heartache even survived being covered by the 13-year-old Michael Jackson.

❿ LINGER THE CRANBERRIES from **EVERYBODY ELSE IS DOING IT SO WHY CAN'T WE?**
Seldom has the sound of a broken heart sounded so gorgeous.

Nigel Williamson

James Brown

The mighty main man with the master plan, the way cool boss with the real hot sauce, the hardest working man in show business, Mr Dynamite: James Brown has more nicknames and honorifics than any other musician, but these are the ten records that made him Godfather of Soul.

❶ PLEASE PLEASE PLEASE from **STAR TIME**
Before rewriting every rule about the role of rhythm in Western music, Brown laid waste to the standard notion of a ballad singer – a feat perhaps even more important than his mutations of rhythm.

❷ I'LL GO CRAZY from LIVE AT THE APOLLO, 1962

One of the most brilliant performances of his incandescent career.

❸ PAPA'S GOT A BRAND NEW BAG from FOUNDATION OF FUNK: A BRAND NEW BAG 1964–1969

Reducing the gospel vocal tradition to falsetto shrieks and guttural roars and positing the bottom end as the be-all and end-all of music, this is Brown's most revolutionary record.

❹ I GOT YOU (I FEEL GOOD) from FOUNDATION OF FUNK: A BRAND NEW BAG 1964–1969

"I feeeeeeeeel nice…": one of the most glorious moments in pop history.

❺ IT'S A MAN'S MAN'S MAN'S WORLD from STAR TIME

Preposterous, grotesque, over-the-top: pure James Brown. One of the all-time great intros.

❻ COLD SWEAT from FOUNDATION OF FUNK: A BRAND NEW BAG 1964–1969

Brown uses his own voice like he uses the rest of the band – as a percussion instrument.

❼ GET UP (I FEEL LIKE BEING A) SEX MACHINE from STAR TIME

With almost nothing else but Jabo Starks' drums for company, the tension built up by Bootsy Collins' liquid bass and Catfish Collins' rawboned guitar is staggering.

❽ HOT PANTS (SHE'S GOTTA USE WHAT SHE'S GOT TO GET WHAT SHE WANTS) from HOT PANTS

Relishes the fact that it goes nowhere fast – it hits the groove from the get-go and stays there for nine minutes.

❾ THE PAYBACK from THE PAYBACK

A Tantric cut exploring the deepest regions of mantric wah-wah funk.

❿ GET UP OFFA THAT THING (RELEASE THE PRESSURE) from STAR TIME

Brown's last fast-and-furious record before The Original Disco Man was eclipsed by the genre he helped create.

Peter Shapiro

Bubblegum

There has been manufactured teen-pop in every post-War era. But bubblegum's golden era was launched by the invention of The Monkees (who soon transcended it) and reached its cartoonish peak in the late-60s before shading into glam-rock and Eurovision-pop in the early 70s. Here are five of the stickiest – yet chewable – songs from the period: as disposable pop singles, no albums are listed.

❶ LAST TRAIN TO CLARKSVILLE
THE MONKEES

They were the ultimate, manufactured pop group, but Tommy Boyce and Bobby Hart provided them with this uplifting song for their first hit which effortlessly swept aside the limitations of the genre.

❷ SUGAR SUGAR THE ARCHIES

The Archies, like The Monkees, were a Don Kirshner creation. But there was no chance of this bunch of cartoon characters turning serious on him.

❸ SIMON SAYS 1910 FRUITGUM COMPANY

An in-house creation from the "Super K" production team of Jerry Kasenetz and Jeff Katz (see also Nos 5 and 8) – and what could be more perfect for a bubblegum hit than adding a dance beat to a children's nursery rhyme?

❹ LOVE GROWS (WHERE MY ROSEMARY GOES) EDISON LIGHTHOUSE

Essentially a vehicle for session singer Tony Burrows, who went on to further bubblegum crimes with White Plains, Brotherhood Of Man and the Pipikins.

❺ GREEN TAMBOURINE LEMON PIPERS

The New York quartet added a psychedelic swirl to their bubblegum on this 1968 hit.

Nigel Williamson

Jeff Buckley

Buckley Jnr was the ultimate morbid romantic, the most yearning and wistful of singers. His early death sealed it all in an enigmatic, intangible aura.

❶ LOVER, YOU SHOULD HAVE COME OVER from **GRACE**
Buckley's best finds him in typically romantic/ morbid mood: funereal harmonium, rainy acoustic guitar and steadily building yearning.

❷ LAST GOODBYE from **GRACE**
Another heartbreaker – as the guitars, vocals and strings pile up, that climactic sound is Buckley's sink being unplumbed.

❸ EVERYBODY HERE WANTS YOU from **(SKETCHES FOR) MY SWEETHEART THE DRUNK**
Simpler now, leaner, with a soulful groove: a flood of gorgeous images building up to the moment his guitar appears to swoon at 3:14.

❹ MOJO PIN from **GRACE**
Opening Grace with a whimper which builds to a colossal bang: wave upon wave of guitar builds beneath an increasingly tortured vocal.

❺ MORNING THEFT from **SKETCHES FOR MY SWEETHEART THE DRUNK**
Lovely, stark, minor-key ballad hymning Jeff's brief romance with Cocteau Twin Liz Frazer.

❻ HALLELUJAH from **GRACE**
John Cale's rewrite of Leonard Cohen's Hallelujah is taken places neither could conceive via Buckley's elegy and eulogy.

❼ GRACE from **GRACE**
With emotions as convoluted as Gary Lucas's guitar part, there's plenty for those in search of portents: "I am not afraid to die" etc.

❽ FORGET HER from **GRACE (LEGACY EDITION)**
Replaced at the last minute by So Real, this is a power ballad effective enough to have interested Aerosmith.

❾ YARD OF BLONDE GIRLS from **(SKETCHES FOR) MY SWEETHEART THE DRUNK**
Buckley at his most direct, a chugging rocker that evokes summer, lazy sensuality and almost innocent sexuality.

❿ SHE IS FREE from **SONGS FOR NO ONE (JEFF BUCKLEY AND GARY LUCAS)**
Recently unearthed track from Buckley's early days in New York, the posthumous brass section lifts the song's soul elements into sunlit relief.

Toby Manning

Tim Buckley

One of the most expressive voices in popular music with a range than allegedly swooped and soared across five octaves, Buckley Snr was dead at 28. But he left a series of nine albums that spanned folk, psychedelia, jazz and blue-eyed soul.

❶ ONCE I WAS from **GOODBYE & HELLO**
The archetypal troubadour love song.

❷ PLEASANT STREET from **GOODBYE & HELLO**
Folk-rock meets emotional abandon.

❸ MORNING GLORY from **GOODBYE & HELLO**
Buckley as medieval minstrel…

❹ SONG TO THE SIREN from **STARSAILOR**
His best-known song, thanks to covers by This Mortal Coil and Robert Plant.

❺ DREAM LETTER from **HAPPY SAD**
Written about his estranged son – and answered by Jeff a quarter of a century later on with his song Dream Brother.

❻ BUZZIN' FLY from **HAPPY SAD**
Tim's voice at its most honeyed, supremely underpinned by Lee Underwood's guitar and David Friedman's vibraphone

7 MONTEREY from **STARSAILOR**
Demonic wails from his avant-garde masterpiece.

8 SWEET SURRENDER from **GREETINGS FROM LA**
From the x-rated, in-your-face album of pure lust that followed the experimental *Starsailor*.

9 MOVE WITH ME from **GREETINGS FROM LA**
"She was drinking alone, what a waste of sin…"

10 DOLPHINS from **SEFRONIA**
Moody, atmospheric cover of the Fred Neil song.

Nigel Williamson

Lord Buckley

Richard Myrle Buckley would have been 100 if he had lived to 5th April 2006. As it was, the funniest hip wiseman of all passed away in 1960. Still, he had already influenced everybody from Lenny Bruce to Bob Dylan, with his re-interpretations of classic works of history, literature and religion in "hip-semantic". He left a small but legendary legacy of recordings.

1 JONAH & THE WHALE from **HIS ROYAL HIPNESS**
The biblical tale: "Jonah, what's that you's smokin' in there?"

2 WILLIE THE SHAKE from **BUCKLEY'S BEST**
The Stratford bard's Marc Anthony funeral oration. "Hipsters, flipsters and fingerpoppin' daddies, knock me your lobes…"

3 THE GASSER from **BUCKLEY'S BEST**
The true story of Alvar Nunez Cabeza de Vaca in 1510, incorporating Ferdinand The 1st of Spain, Vasco Da Gama The Island Bumper and a parrot.

4 THE NAZZ from **BUCKLEY'S BEST**
Classic Buckley on J.C. and his miracles. "Nazz and his buddies were goofing off down the boulevard one day when they met this little cat with a bent frame…"

5 SCROOGE from **THE BAD RAPPING OF THE MARQUIS DE SADE**
Dickens in hip – the story of the three spooks.

6 THE BLACK CROSS from **LORD BUCKLEY IN CONCERT**
Not everything Buckley performed was full of mirth. Witness this stark tale of a Southern lynching proves.

Ian Anderson

Burning Spear

Winston Rodney, who borrowed the name Burning Spear from Kenyan leader Jomo Kenyatta, has been at the forefront of roots-reggae since his first extraordinary recordings for Studio One in the late 60s. With his soaring falsetto voice, direct yet deeply spiritual lyrics, and uncompromising vision, he's still a compelling live performer.

1 DOOR PEEPER from **SOUNDS FROM THE BURNING SPEAR**
The unsurpassable confidence of Burning Spear's 1969 Studio One debut is breathtaking, from its chanted acapella intro onwards.

2 CREATION REBEL from **SOUNDS FROM THE BURNING SPEAR FROM 1970**
Another eerily sparse and meditative chant from Spear's Studio One days.

3 MARCUS GARVEY from **MARCUS GARVEY**
This massive 1975 Jamaican hit became the title track of Spear's breakthrough Island album the following year.

4 SLAVERY DAYS from **MARCUS GARVEY**
A big hit in Jamaica, this 1975 song's refrain "Do you remember the days of slavery?" struck a deep chord.

⑤ MAN IN THE HILLS from **MAN IN THE HILLS**

Spear has always blended the personal with the politics, as in this 1976 exaltation of the joys of rural living.

⑥ SOCIAL LIVING from **SOCIAL LIVING**

With its simple message that "social living is the best", this represents Spear at his most anthemic.

⑦ HAIL HIM from **HAIL HIM**

The title track of Spear's last truly great album, from 1980, is an uplifting Rasta hymn.

⑧ COLUMBUS from **HAIL HIM**

An irresistible polemic, denouncing Christopher Columbus as a "damn blasted liar" for claiming to have discovered Jamaica.

Greg Ward

Kate Bush

With a supernatural vocal range and a penchant for weird songs and wacky videos, Kate Bush is one hell of an eccentric talent. And it was ever thus.

① ARMY DREAMERS from **NEVER FOR EVER**

A heartbreaking anti-war tune circling around a delicate mandolin melody. The vocals are almost childlike in their innocence.

② BREATHING from **NEVER FOR EVER**

Nuclear holocaust from the point of view of an unborn foetus; if this doesn't bring a lump to your throat something is definitely wrong.

③ CLOUDBUSTING from **HOUNDS OF LOVE**

Built around subtle, layered strings and a strangely martial rhythm this is one of Kate's finest mid 1980s moments.

④ IN THE WARM ROOM from **LIONHEART**

What carnal delights lie within the warm room? The single piano and intimate vocal are totally enchanting.

⑤ RUNNING UP THAT HILL from **HOUNDS OF LOVE**

A life-swapping deal with god is on the table complete with unmistakeable honking synths and a terrific drum track.

⑥ THE MAN WITH THE CHILD IN HIS EYES from **THE KICK INSIDE**

Even a love song isn't so straightforward for Kate Bush. One of her earliest songs, this is both romantic and just a little bit creepy.

⑦ THERE GOES A TENNER from **THE DREAMING**

Kate as Cockney safe cracker? Anything is possible. Jaunty pianos and parping synths give this odd little crime spree a cheeky spring in its step.

⑧ VIOLIN from **NEVER FOR EVER**

Kate goes rock with a completely bonkers vocal that seesaws violently from squeak to shriek. And the amazing scream towards the end is just inhuman.

⑨ WOW from **LIONHEART**

Who else could get so much mileage out of just three letters? One word stretched out into a hypnotic chorus.

⑩ WUTHERING HEIGHTS from **THE KICK INSIDE**

English literature turned into classic pop. Haunting, disturbing and utterly brilliant in its windswept, witchy delivery.

Essi Berelian

The Byrds

When The Byrds put a four-four beat to a Bob Dylan song, folk-rock was born. Then they embraced space-rock and country-rock. By the end of the 1960s, Roger McGuinn was the only original Byrd remaining and they were grounded soon after. But what a glorious flight it was while it lasted.

1 MR TAMBOURINE MAN from
MR TAMBOURINE MAN
The Byrds recorded more than a dozen further Dylan songs, but this was the jingle-jangle original that invented folk-rock and which they never bettered.

2 TURN! TURN! TURN! (TO EVERYTHING THERE IS A SEASON) from **TURN!TURN!TURN!**
The words come from the Bible. But accompanied by McGuinn's 12-string Rickenbacker and sung in a hipster drawl, you'd never have guessed.

3 SO YOU WANT TO BE A ROCK'N'ROLL STAR from **YOUNGER THAN YESTERDAY**
A sardonic commentary on the music industry given added power by Hugh Masekela's trumpet and the addition of real screams from a 1965 Byrds concert in Bournemouth.

4 EIGHT MILES HIGH from **FIFTH DIMENSION**
You can believe their claim that it was written about a Transatlantic jet flight, if you like. But to most of us it will always be one of the greatest drug songs ever recorded.

5 EVERYBODY'S BEEN BURNED from
YOUNGER THAN YESTERDAY
David Crosby's increasingly experimental compositions eventually led McGuinn and Chris Hillman to kick him out, but this ravishing song was a landmark in the group's growing sophistication.

6 WASN'T BORN TO FOLLOW from
THE NOTORIOUS BYRD BROTHERS
Carole King briefly replaces Dylan as the group's favourite songwriter.

7 HICKORY WIND from **SWEETHEART OF THE RODEO**
Gram Parsons' finest moment on the group's country-rock landmark. When he quit before the album's release many of his vocals were replaced. Fortunately, this one was left extant.

8 BALLAD OF EASY RIDER from **THE BALLAD OF EASY RIDER**
Dylan wrote half the lyric and then gave it to film director Dennis Hopper, saying "McGuinn will know what to do with it."

9 CHESTNUT MARE from **UNTITLED**
The line-up in which McGuinn was joined by Clarence White, Skip Battin and Gene Parsons, was perhaps the band's best-ever live incarnation. But they proved they could also cut it in the studio with this, co-written by McGuinn and Jacques Levy.

10 FOR FREE from **THE BYRDS**
An overlooked gem from the 1973 reunion album by the original line-up, with one of Crosby's finest vocals on Joni Mitchell's song.

Nigel Williamson

David Byrne

David Byrne's combination of cerebral art rock with a dance beat once led *Time* magazine to dub him a renaissance man for our times. The ex-Talking Head continues to aim at your head and your feet…

1 THE JEZEBEL SPIRIT WITH BRIAN ENO from **MY LIFE IN THE BUSH OF GHOSTS**
Electro-funk exorcism from groundbreaking sampling collaboration with Brian Eno.

2 INDEPENDENCE DAY from **REI MOMO**
Lurching , off-kilter Tex-Mex anthem that opened his Latin-loving masterpiece.

3 MAKE BELIEVE MAMBO from **REI MOMO**
Horn-driven salsa power juxtaposed with whimsical Walter Mitty fantasies.

4 NOW I'M YOUR MOM from **UH-OH**
Do the sex-change boogie.

⑤ CRASH from **DAVID BYRNE**
"I met my love at a funeral" may just be the most arresting opening line in popular song.

⑥ ANGELS from **DAVID BYRNE**
A strong echo of Once In A Lifetime meant Talking Heads fans thought this was his best song in years.

⑦ GATES OF PARADISE from **FEELINGS**
Who else would even think of mixing country and western and trip-hop?

⑧ U.B. JESUS from **LOOK INTO THE EYEBALL**
Disturbing and danceable at the same time.

⑨ LAZY (WITH X-PRESS 2) SINGLE
Improbable house music collaboration and a British #1 hit single a quarter of a century on from Psycho Killer.

⑩ EMPIRE from **GROWN BACKWARDS**
Mordant post-Iraq commentary complete with a lyrical spoof on The Times They Are A-Changin'.

Sue Steward

Cajun & zydeco

Cajun and zydeco are descended from the fiddle and accordion music of Arcadian settlers who landed in Louisiana's bayous whilst fleeing the English in Nova Scotia.

① **ALLONA A LAFAYETTE** JOSEPH & CLEOMA FALCON from **HARRY SMITH'S ANTHOLOGY OF AMERICAN FOLK MUSIC**
Tiny, guitar-picking Cleoma and her accordion-playing husband cut this, the first Cajun record, in 1928 and enjoyed an instant regional hit.

② **A BLUES DE LA PRISON** AMEDEE ARDOIN from **THE FIRST BLACK ZYDECO RECORDING ARTIST: HIS ORIGINAL RECORDINGS 1928-1938**
A pioneering black accordionist, Ardoin was viciously beaten by white racists at a concert (for accepting a white woman's handkerchief to wipe his brow), and died in 1941 in the Louisiana State Institution for the Mentally Ill.

③ **FAIS PAS CA** THE HACKBERRY RAMBLERS from **EARLY RECORDINGS 1935-1948**
The band lay down a good beat and yelp while Lennis Sonnier sings and swings. This legendary Cajun band formed in the 1930s and are still playing today.

④ **GRAND MAMOU** HARRY CHOATES from **THE FIDDLE KING OF CAJUN SWING**
The Cajun Hank Williams: played fast, lived hard, and died at 28.

⑤ **DYING IN MISERY** NATHAN ABSHIRE from **A CAJUN LEGEND: THE BEST OF NATHAN ABSHIRE**
The greatest Cajun accordionist, Abshire helped popularize Cajun music internationally. Here Dewey Balfa lends his plaintive voice.

⑥ **JOLE BLON** THE BALFA BROTHERS from **PLAYS TRADITIONAL CAJUN MUSIC, VOLS 1 & 2**
Dewey, Will and Rodney Balfa were Cajun music's greatest ever ambassadors, and they perform the Cajun anthem with great zest on their 1965 debut recording.

⑦ **BON TON ROULET (CLIFTON CHENIER)** from **ZYDECO DYNAMITE: THE CLIFTON CHENIER ANTHOLOGY**
The King of Zydeco. Gave the music a swinging groove and made many fine recordings between 1955 and 1987 including this swampy stomper. Classic black Creole music.

⑧ **WADE'S WALTZ (MICHAEL DOUCET)** from **BEAU SOLO**
Ambassador of Cajun music and culture both solo and with his band Beausoleil. Here he demonstrates deep Cajun fiddle.

⑨ **HEY NEGRESS (QUEEN IDA)** from **CAUGHT IN THE ACT**
The first lady of zydeco Ida sings and plays accordion and takes no prisoners. This traditional ballad is tough Louisiana blues.

⑩ **BOUGHT A RACOON** BUCKWHEAT ZYDECO from **BEST OF LOUISIANA ZYDECO**
Slick, funky and popular, BZ are lead by Stanley Dural Jnr who used to play in Clifton Chenier's band. Downhome humour permeates this good time number.

Garth Cartwright

John Cale

John Cale is one of rock's more enigmatic characters. A classically trained musician with an interest in minimalism, a Velvet Underground veteran, a songwriter and producer of some of the classic records of the 70s and 80s, his own work reveals a complex, intelligent and, deep down, romantic soul.

❶ CHICKENSHIT from SABOTAGE
Vicious, loud and terrifying, this is Cale dealing badly with success, stardom and the "godfather of punk" label stuck on him by a lazy music press.

❷ GUN from FEAR
Menacing guitar, evil-spirited drumbeat and a lyric that tells of a night lit up by drunken violence and emergency surgery that all ends in tears. Phil Manzanera and Eno add their own strains of distorted electro-nastiness to the mix and we sit transfixed through an eight-minute horrorshow

❸ ROSEGARDEN FUNERAL OF SORES from SABOTAGE
Nobody does long, drawn out, lugubrious tales of slowly building menace like John Cale, and this shows the man at his best.

❹ GUTS from SLOW DAZZLE
A drug-fuelled love/hate quandary in which our protagonist struggles to understand the actions of his partner. Kevin Ayers and Cale's wife Cindy had misbehaved together just before a concert, leading to the song's opening lyric; "The bugger in the short sleeves fucked my wife. Did it quick and split."

❺ DARLING I NEED YOU from SLOW DAZZLE
Part Two of the debacle. The drugs have worn off and the emotions are a little less raw. Cale's honesty is to be admired, but it's painful to listen to so close-up and personal.

❻ HEARTBREAK HOTEL from JUNE 1, 1974
Elvis might have recorded the best selling version of this song, but he never sounded even remotely heartbroken when performing it. John Cale, performing on the same stage as the above-mentioned Kevin Ayers, sounds like somebody's pulled his living heart out through his ribs and squeezed it in front of him.

❼ FEAR IS A MAN'S BEST FRIEND from FEAR
Beautiful piano and twiddly bass from the Welsh bard of rock'n'roll. It begins in Waiting For My Man narrative territory and expands into a rousing paranoiac chorus, part chapel-hymn part pub band boogie

❽ MAN WHO COULDN'T AFFORD TO ORGY from FEAR
A cuddly pop ballad, this song has hooks galore, sweetheart backing vocals and genuinely funny lyrics (complete with a delightful mispronunciation of "orgy" with a hard "g").

❾ TWILIGHT ZONE from HOBO SAPIENS
A classic Cale episode from a recording that's notable for its overall optimistic feel. Showcasing his familiar taste for tortured instrumentation moaning in pain behind a melody line of stately elegance, it shows there's a great deal of malice in the old wizard yet.

Al Spicer

Calypso & soca

Calypso has come far since the 1930s when the first calypso tents were raised in Port of Spain, Trinidad, to house contestants for the sharpest commentary on island life or world news. Harry Belafonte (from Jamaica, not Trini) made calypso an international hit with songs like Yellow Bird and Day-O, and suddenly every pop singer had a calypso lilt. By the 70s, calypso, promiscuous as every Caribbean style, made a formal alliance with soul and disco, to be reborn as soca.

❶ LONDON IS THE PLACE FOR ME LORD KITCHENER from LONDON IS THE PLACE FOR ME
Opening to a piano version of Big Ben chimes, this entrancing calypso jazz is led on clarinet and guitar, behind Kitch's witty observations of "the mother country'" which he reached in 1948.

❷ FREE UP CHRIS "TAMBU" HERBERT from
THE ROUGH GUIDE TO CALYPSO & SOCA
Bright, quintessential soca – brass upfront,
electric guitar mimicking steel drum melodies,
jigging jumpy rhythms and vocals from Tambu,
pioneer of 80s soca with Charlie's Roots.

❸ PHILLIP MY DEAR THE MIGHTY SPARROW from
THE ROUGH GUIDE TO CALYPSO & SOCA
Calypso's great lyricist-newscaster conjures
a raunchy conversation between the Queen
and Phillip about the intruder in her Palace
bedroom, as the brass adopts the air of a
military band.

❹ VOICES FROM THE GHETTO SINGING SANDRA
from THE ROUGH GUIDE TO CALYPSO & SOCA
One of calypso-soca's rare female singers,
Sandra documents Trinidadian ghetto life,
behind the carnival gloss. Backed by sweet
guitars and punchy trumpets.

❺ MAN PIABA HARRY BELAFONTE from THE BEST
OF HARRY BELAFONTE
Belafonte put calypso into the world's pop
charts in the 50s. Here, a poor, confused boy
wonders aloud about the Birds and Bees stories he's offered by adults.

❻ LORRAINE EXPLAINER from THIS IS SOCA MUSIC
Huge international hit in 82; brassy but sweet.
Every track on this Charlie Gillett compilation
is a treat.

❼ BURN DEM BLACK STALIN from THIS IS SOCA
References to Mussolini, the Fuhrer and the
KKK accompanied by sweet girls' chorus, salsa
brass and merengue saxes. A late 80s cocktail
by one of Trinidad's most radical lyricists.

**❽ ROUND AND ROUND (PABLO (FLORES)
MIX)** SPICE AND COMPANY single
Thumping, nostalgic drums, jangling cowbells,
shards of brass punctuating the beats, and a
Bajan line-dance caller instructing the dancers:
mad and irresistible.

❾ BILLS, INTERPOLATED AS BUSTED ARROW
from SOCA DANCE PARTY
The rule-breaking Arrow constantly redesigned

soca, and his unashamed un-PC tirade about
bills – "gas bill, alimony bill, girlfriend bill, children bill! Bills!" typically breaks the soca mould
with pealing zouk and soukous guitars.

❿ BAHIAN GYAL DAVID RUDDER &
CHARLIE'S ROOTS from THIS IS SOCA MUSIC 2
Imaginative, inventive, eclectic, Rudder shifts
emphasis from Trini to Bahia in Brazil, with this
sweet and jumpy samba/soca beaten out on
conga drums. A gorgeously languid smoocher.

Sue Steward

Glen Campbell

**Glen Campbell has been a singer,
composer, part-time Beach Boy and
country pop hitmaker as well as an actor,
golfer and hell-raiser. Thought of mainly
as a MOR favourite, his backlist offers a
surprisingly diverse range of styles.**

❶ WICHITA LINEMAN from WICHITA LINEMAN
Often praised as the greatest song of all time
by fans of Jimmy Webb. Check out the great
version by Johnny Cash on *American IV: The
Man Comes Around*.

❷ BY THE TIME I GET TO PHOENIX from BY THE
TIME I GET TO PHOENIX
This was a huge hit thanks to its bittersweet
lyrics and lush orchestration. Famously covered
by both Nick Cave and Frank Sinatra.

❸ GALVESTON from GALVESTON
A thinly disguised anti-war epic, this was written in the Vietnam era.

❹ GUESS I'M DUMB from THE CAPITOL YEARS
1965–77
Beach Boy Brian Wilson wrote this one for Glen
as a thank you for standing in for him while
he was ill.

❺ GENTLE ON MY MIND from GENTLE ON MY MIND
An oft-covered John Hartford song, this
became Glen's first hit single.

❻ RHINESTONE COWBOY from **RHINESTONE COWBOY**

After several years in the wilderness for Glen this track became a US #1 single. It's great.

❼ ALL I HAVE TO DO IS DREAM from **THE CAPITAL YEARS 1965–77**

Glen recorded plenty of duets with Bobbie Gentry on TV shows and albums. All are worth checking out but this one's a cracker.

❽ SOUTHERN NIGHTS from **SOUTHERN NIGHTS**

Glen's last proper hit single was funkier than almost all his other material, and mighty fine to boot.

Dave Atkinson

Can

At the tail end of the 1960s, the European response to the experimentalism of The Velvet Underground included an entire generation of German musicians making *cosmische-rock*. Can were the consummate Krautrockers, and their music is as entrancing now as when it was first released. It is both delightfully weird and unexpectedly beautiful.

❶ YOO DOO RIGHT from **MONSTER MOVIE**

A 20-minute masterwork, this was Can's response to the Velvet's epic-length Sister Ray. Its lyrics were loosely based on the intimate contents of a love letter. A monstrous jam of infinite variety, it features a short section when all the amps break down – through which singer Malcolm Mooney and the drumbeat press on oblivious.

❷ MOTHER UPDUFF from **UNLIMITED EDITION**

Far funnier than any of the Velvet's story-length outings, Upduff is a jazzy, rocky roller-coaster ride with lyrics about a couple who take granny on holiday.

❸ BLUE BAG from **UNLIMITED EDITION**

A deeply introspective, stoned exploration of what is of course the vital factor of a bag of salt'n'shake crisps, this track boasts pops, bangs and whistles and is psychedelia at its fun-loving best.

❹ FATHER CANNOT YELL from **MONSTER MOVIE**

Mooney yelps and barks a bad trip story of childbirth gone wrong over the classic "motorik" beat of Jaki Liebezeit. It has an old school groove from Holger Czukay, appropriately scary guitar attacks from Michael Karoli and a stomach-churning, low-end keyboard wobble from Irmin Schmidt.

❺ UPHILL from **DELAY**

This is Can at full power: a breathless Malcolm Mooney helms the space rock jam that Hawkwind never quite achieved.

❻ MUSHROOM from **TAGO MAGO**

Jaki Liebezeit's drum patterns are insanely great and have been endlessly sampled since. Damo Suzuki's vocal is pretty great, too – whatever it is he is singing about.

❼ GOMORRHA from **UNLIMITED EDITION**

This is the most beautiful, theatrical space rock ever, pierced by a meandering solo from Karoli.

❽ SHE BRINGS THE RAIN from **SOUNDTRACKS**

A lovely and, for Can, oddly conventional blues. Mooney delivers a simple poetic invocation: "she brings the rain, it feels like spring".

❾ DIZZY DIZZY from **SOON OVER BABALUMA**

Damo Suzuki had left, and Czukay took over vocals for this trancey, dubby opener, which bounces along like a kind of Germanic ska.

❿ PERSIAN LOVE from **HOLGER CZUKAY'S MOVIES**

Czukay played the radio as an instrument in the latter days of Can, switching the dials on stage. He developed this idea in his solo work, most memorably on this Iranian love song, embroidered upon with a gorgeous loop of guitar.

Al Spicer/Mark Ellingham

Secretly Canadian

Did you know some of the biggest names in American music actually came from north of the 49th parallel?

❶ HELPLESS NEIL YOUNG from DEJA VU
"There is a town in north Ontario/With dream comfort memory to spare/And in my mind I still need a place to go/All my changes were there."

❷ A CASE OF YOU JONI MITCHELL from BLUE
"On the back of a cartoon coaster in the blue TV screen light/I drew a map of Canada…"

❸ DEMOCRACY LEONARD COHEN from THE FUTURE
"Democracy is coming to the USA" sings Cohen – an expat Canadian's prayer.

❹ IF YOU COULD READ MY MIND GORDON LIGHTFOOT from IF YOU COULD READ MY MIND
He tried the American dream for a while, writing TV jingles in Hollywood, and hated it so much he fled back across the border to write songs like this instead.

❺ YOU OUGHTA KNOW ALANIS MORISSETTE from JAGGED LITTLE PILL
The line "Is she perverted like me?" appeared to confirm what many Americans had always suspected about their northern neighbours.

❻ FUMBLING TOWARDS ECSTASY SARAH McLACHLAN from FUMBLING TOWARDS ECSTASY
She left Nova Scotia to bring feminism to America via her femme-centric Lilith Fair tours.

❼ UNIVERSAL SOLDIER BUFFY SAINTE-MARIE from THE BEST OF
During the Lyndon Johnson years her name appeared on a White House list of those whose music "deserved to be suppressed" after she penned this peace movement anthem.

❽ CONSTANT CRAVING KD LANG from INGENUE
And she even made a covers album of songs by other Canadian writers called *Hymns Of The 49th Parallel*.

❾ THE NIGHT THEY DROVE OLD DIXIE DOWN THE BAND from THE BAND
It took a bunch of good ol' Canuck boys to really understand the American Civil War.

❿ SUMMER OF '69 BRYAN ADAMS from SO FAR SO GOOD
Whatever the song says, at the time Bryan was actually a nine-year-old boy growing up in Kingston, Ontario.

Nigel Williamson

Cape Verde

This arid, volcanic archipelago west of Senegal produces some of the most seductive music on the planet. Cesaria Evora – the "Barefoot Diva" – is by far the country's best-known export, but her work is just one strand of an exceptionally musical culture.

❶ PETIT PAYS CESARIA EVORA from ANTHOLOGY
On this yearning *morna*, Cesaria fondly lists the good things about her island home, backed by the gentle sway of her excellent acoustic band. Mesmerizing stuff.

❷ BOAS FESTAS LUIS MORAIS from THE SOUL OF CAPE VERDE
A sweetly soulful instrumental cut by the late saxophonist and composer, who was a revered and much loved figure of Cape Verdean music.

❸ TERRA LONGE BONGA from A VOZ DE OURO
The grand old man of Cape Verdean song interprets this B. Leza classic with enormous pathos, shadowed throughout by a sinuous clarinet solo.

❹ NOTE DE MINDELO TITINA from BETWEEN SEA AND SKY: A DREAM VOYAGE TO THE SOUL OF THE ISLES
A stark and tremulous performance of this

morna (also written by the great B.Leza) about the magic of the night on the island of Mindelo. Goosepimples guaranteed.

❺ DANÇA MA MI CRIOLA TITO PARIS from DANÇA MA MI CRIOLA
A very danceable *coladeira* by this well-respected singer, who runs the famed B.Leza club in Lisbon. A cool horn arrangement, fine gravelly vocals and a memorable tune.

❻ FALSO TESTEMUNHO MARIA ALICE from D'ZEMCONTRE
It's been on so many compilations it might as well be here; by far the most famous track by this Lisbon-based singer.

❼ CHICO MALANDRO ANA FIRMINO WITH TITO PARIS from PUTUMAYO PRESENTS CAPE VERDE
A slinky love song with strummed acoustic *cavaquinho* – a typical instrument of Cape Verdean music, which became the ukulele when Portuguese sailors took it to Hawaii.

❽ FUNDO BAXO GRUPO FERRO GAITA from THE ROUGH GUIDE TO CAPE VERDE
Ferro Gaita are a powerful live experience. Their speciality is the hard dance style called *funáná* – an accordion and percussion-based groove. This is a typical example.

❾ FLADU FA SIMENTERA from TR'ADICTIONAL
Lead singer Tété Alhinho gives an amazingly sensual performance and the arrangement is to die for. This one speeds up into a carnival blur of sound.

❿ VELOCIDADE CESARIA EVORA from VOZ D'AMOR
Another Luis Morais song, this time one of his upbeat, bouncy *coladeiras*.

Jon Lusk

Captain Beefheart

Mixing deep Delta blues and free-jazz with surreal, often punning lyrics sung in the most extraordinary voice you've ever heard, Captain Beefheart – aka Don Van Vliet – constructed an entire new musical universe. Like Jimi Hendrix, he took his art to such limits that there was literally nowhere left to go. In 1982 he retired to the Mojave Desert to paint, leaving behind these weird and wonderful creations.

❶ SURE NUFF 'N YES I DO from SAFE AS MILK
The opening track from the debut album: the first an astonished world heard of Don's magnificently mutant blues and his psychedelically warped band.

❷ ELECTRICITY from SAFE AS MILK
Buzzing theramin, the mighty Ry Cooder on slide guitar and the Captain's best feral bellow.

❸ AH FEEL LIKE AHCID from STRICTLY PERSONAL
Psychedelic blues at its most unsettling … you might want to think twice before tripping out to this scary soundtrack.

❹ ELLA GURU from TROUT MASK REPLICA
Almost a pop tune, then the guitars fracture, the sonic hurricane blows and Don delivers a bestial vocal – one of the best moments from his peerless masterpiece.

❺ MY HUMAN GETS ME BLUES from TROUT MASK REPLICA
Discordant, abrasive guitars, crazed time signatures and a rollercoaster ride of surrealist abandon – business as usual for the Captain, then.

❻ DACHAU BLUES from TROUT MASK REPLICA
Dark, convoluted visions of the atrocities of war with a vocal so intense you barely notice the music.

❼ NEON MEATE DREAM OF A OCTAFISH from TROUT MASK REPLICA
Neo-Beat poetry meets folk myth against a backing of mind-boggling musical complexity as the Captain gasps the sexual lyric with asthmatic excitement.

8 I LOVE YOU, YOU BIG DUMMY from **LICK MY DECALS OFF, BABY**
A more orthodox rock tune for once. But this is Beefheart, of course, so such descriptions are relative.

9 BIG EYED BEANS FROM VENUS from **CLEAR SPOT**
"Mr Zoot Horn Rollo, hit that long lunar note and let it float…" – an insight into the Beefheartian school of musical direction.

Nigel Williamson

Carter Family

Asked to name a song by country pioneers the Carter Family, many would scratch their heads. Yet they popularized some 300+ songs that have entered the collective consciousness of the US, and further afield. Tracks are available on various Carter Family compilations, the best being the single CD *An Introduction to The Carter Family* **and the five-CD box set** *The Carter Family: 1927-1934*.

1 WILL THE CIRCLE BE UNBROKEN
Theirs was the definitive version of the song that gave its name to the splendid biopic about the Carters made for American PBS television.

2 WABASH CANNONBALL
One of the first recordings of the folk standard, made in Atlanta in 1929, later covered by Roy Acuff and countless others.

3 WILDWOOD FLOWER
A 19th-century North American parlour song popularized by the Carters after they recorded it in 1928.

4 KEEP ON THE SUNNY SIDE
The theme song of their radio show, popular throughout the 1930s.

5 LITTLE DARLING PAL OF MINE
Maybelle Carter shines here on her self-converted steel guitar.

6 THE FOGGY MOUNTAIN TOP
This has been covered by everyone from bluegrass kings Flatt & Scruggs to Irish soulman Van Morrison.

7 NO DEPRESSION IN HEAVEN
The song that gave its name to the movement that became alt.country.

8 WORRIED MAN BLUES
Recorded in Memphis in 1930, with thrilling trio harmonies from Maybelle, Sara and A.P.

9 LONESOME VALLEY
More magnificent three-part harmonies from the same session that produced Worried Man Blues.

10 I'M THINKING TONIGHT OF MY BLUE EYES
If you wondered where Roy Acuff's Great Speckled Bird and Hank Thompson's The Wild Side Of Life came from, look no further than this tune they recorded in 1929.

Nigel Williamson

Johnny Cash

A rich and resonant baritone and an outlaw heart? It must be country music's one and only Man In Black…

1 A BOY NAMED SUE from **AT SAN QUENTIN**
A novelty song with a lopsided grin on its face. Who else could sing about losing a piece of his ear and make it sound both angry and funny?

2 FIELD OF DIAMONDS from **AMERICAN III: SOLITARY MAN**
Brimming with romantic longing this simple and deeply poetic song features June Carter Cash and, ahem, Sheryl Crow along for the ride.

❸ FOLSOM PRISON BLUES from AT FOLSOM PRISON

He shot a man in Memphis just to watch him die. A tale of murder and regret recorded in front of a real crowd of inmates. Simply electrifying.

❹ FLUSHED FROM THE BATHROOM OF YOUR HEART from AT FOLSOM PRISON

How many ways are there to say your woman thinks you're history? Cash does emotional pain with a wry smile.

❺ GOING TO MEMPHIS from MURDER

That chain gang sounds mighty mean even with the twangy guitar and honky tonk piano. You can almost taste the parched dust and misery.

❻ I WALK THE LINE from LOVE

A plain old-fashioned love song with a measured guitar refrain and Cash's charming leathery drawl centre stage. Unbeatable.

❼ JOE BEAN from EVERYBODY LOVES A NUT

The shadow of the gallows falls long and grim in this brief melodrama. Retribution doesn't come more ironic than this.

❽ MEAN EYED CAT from UNCHAINED

Our hero dares his woman to leave and wakes up to a Dear John letter. A rambunctious, driving little tune about doing the right thing.

❾ RING OF FIRE from RING OF FIRE

Those melodic stabs of Mexican brass and understated backing vocals are pure genius. Another passionate classic straight from the heart.

❿ SAN QUENTIN from AT SAN QUENTIN

You want pure rage? Just listen to Cash's venomous attack against the infamous prison in this definitive live performance.

Essi Berelian

Cat Power

Cat Power is the creative guise of one Chan Marshall, whose voice is at times gentle, at times brutal and bluesy. Her career has seen Cat Power turn from a wonderful, but standard, US indie trooper to a vehicle for some of the best songwriting of this young millenium.

❶ ICE WATER from MYRA LEE

Cat Power, the band, fall in line behind Chan as she sings with power and presence over lolloping guitar picking and distant drums.

❷ AMERICAN FLAG from MOON PIX

The reversed shuffle of a drum machine and oozing electric guitar *make* this cut – seductive and strange.

❸ SAY from MOON PIX

Stormclouds (and guitars) gather around an uplifting lyric of hope and confession.

❹ CROSS BONES STYLE from MOON PIX

The hypnotic guitar line plaits itself around a gallop of drums, while Chan sings a deep meandering harmony. Glorious.

❺ (I CAN'T GET NO) SATISFACTON from THE COVERS ALBUM

An intimate yet lazily-spun cover of the Stones classic. Chan makes it all her own.

❻ NUDE AS THE NEWS from WHAT WOULD THE COMMUNITY THINK

A rousing indie rocker with swathes of guitar and vocals that swell and crash like rolling waves.

❼ GOOD WOMAN from YOU ARE FREE

A song for when you know it's over. Chan's deep velvet voice is grazed by violin, a choir of children and, um, Eddie Vedder.

❽ WEREWOLF from YOU ARE FREE

The string arrangement is sublime and haunting, but not half as chilling as the vocals.

⑨ NAMES from **YOU ARE FREE**
A simple piano-and-voice pairing weaves stories of acquaintances long gone. One of the most moving songs you'll ever hear.

⑩ WILLIE DEADWILDER
from **SPEAKING FOR TREES**
It's 18 minutes long, and wonderful, with Chan sounding at her most relaxed and silky as she sings "even if it is too long, I don't care, I love to share".

Peter Buckley

Cats & dogs

Man's best friend and man's furriest friend; they may not get on with each other, but they've inspired many a musician to pick up his axe.

CANINE
❶ HOUND DOG ELVIS PRESLEY
❷ WALKING THE DOG RUFUS THOMAS
❸ I WANNA BE YOUR DOG IGGY POP
❹ I AIN'T GONNA BE YOUR DOG NO MORE HOWLIN' WOLF
❺ POLICE DOG BLUES BLIND BLAKE

FELINE
❶ THE CAT'S GOT THE MEASLES PAPA CHARLIE JACKSON
❷ CROSSEYED CAT MUDDY WATERS
❸ PUSSY CAT BLUES BO CARTER
❹ STRAY CAT BLUES THE ROLLING STONES

AND OF COURSE...
⑩ CAN YOUR PUSSY DO THE DOG ?
THE CRAMPS

Greg Ward

Nick Cave

Australia's greatest songwriter – simple as that. Styles come and go but Old Nick remains true to his art.

❶ THE MERCY SEAT from **TENDER PREY**
The intense thoughts of a man facing his imminent demise on the electric chair. Notably covered by Johnny Cash.

❷ THE WEEPING SONG from **THE GOOD SON**
A slow, heavy and very powerful duet between Nick and guitarist Blixa Bargeld.

❸ WHERE THE WILD ROSES GROW from **MURDER BALLADS**
A murder ballad gave Nick his only chart hit (with a little help from compatriot Kylie). Strange but oddly romantic.

❹ BY THE TIME I GET TO PHOENIX from **KICKING AGAINST THE PRICKS**
A warped rendition of the Jimmy Webb/Glen Campbell hit, from an album of covers.

❺ IN THE GHETTO from **FROM HER TO ETERNITY**
A cover of Elvis' hit – gloomy and dramatic, but what more could you hope for when Nick meets Elvis?

❻ STRAIGHT TO YOU from **HENRY'S DREAM**
A beautiful love song and, boy, can he write a beautiful love song…

❼ DO YOU LOVE ME? from **LET LOVE IN**
A huge rock number and a live favourite. Yes Nick, of course we all love you.

❽ INTO MY ARMS from **THE BOATMAN'S CALL**
The album from whence it came marked a turning point in style, demonstrated perfectly by its introspection and hope.

❾ THERE SHE GOES MY BEAUTIFUL WORLD from **ABATTOIR BLUES/LYRE OF ORPHEUS**
A gospel-infused rocker from what is perhaps his best album ever.

⓾ BREATHLESS from ABATTOIR BLUES/LYRE OF ORPHEUS

Fabulous poetry and one of the stand-out tracks from an amazing double album.

Dave Atkinson

Central Asia

The art of fine, virtuosic singing is integral to the music of central Asia, in which bards are still important and venerated.

❶ KELMADY MUNADJAT YULCHIEVA & ENSEMBLE SHAVKAT MIRZAEV from A HAUNTING VOICE

Munadjat unveils her beautiful voice slowly and subtly to the attentive listener, building up from a tranquil melancholy to culminate in a vibrant, expressive mood.

❷ EY ENCALAR ALIM QASIMOV & FERGANAH QASIMOVA from LOVE'S DEEP OCEAN

An energetic homage to Nusrat Fateh Ali Khan by Azerbaijan's foremost exponent of vocal art, and his skilful daughter. "Today is the day my soul parts from my body. Tears flow from my eyes like rain."

❸ DEVONAH SHAW DAVLATMAND from MUSIQUES SAVANTES ET POPULAIRES

This spiritual song uses a lovely swaying rhythm played on the setar, a long-necked lute. Davlatmand, from Tajikistan, is as profoundly rooted in the Sufi tradition as Munadjat Yulchieva.

❹ KÖGMEN SABIJLAR from THE SILK ROAD – A MUSICAL CARAVAN

Taken from an anthology which is a must have Khakas throat singing accompanied by horse head fiddle. Sabijlar revive the traditional music with stirring new compositions!

❺ PENJIGAH MUQAM OF ILI THE UYGHUR MUSICIANS FROM XINJIANG from MUSIC FROM THE OASIS TOWNS OF CENTRAL ASIA

Music from the far west of China. Playing music now affirms the Uyghur identity which is under permanent threat. A compact version of a *mugham* (suite) featuring fine singing and interaction from a large ensemble: "Let the dawn breeze carry my greeting to that girl who is slim like the poplar."

❻ GUL-I-ZARIM TURGUN ALIMATOV from OUZBEKISTAN: TURGUN ALIMATOV

He is the don on the plucked dutar and tanbur and the bowed tanbur or sato. On this one he delivers a highly dramatic duet with his son and pupil.

❼ GRANADINA YENGI YOL from DE SEVILLE À BOUKHARA

The project of Emmanuel Hossein During, son of the foremost connoisseur and researcher of Central Asian music Jean During, and young traditional musicians merges Spanish guitar play with local music. They are definitely exploring new paths (Yengi Yol).

❽ AN TUWRALI EL'MIYRA ZANABERGENOV from MUSIC from ALMATY

"Listeners, I wish to present you a tune. I don't shake my head simply because I sing a song. It is also quite embarrassing to open the mouth wide while singing." A song about the art of singing coming from the semi-classical tradition in Kazakhstan by a great female singer.

❾ BAYATY ASHKABAD from CITY OF LOVE

What a wonderful name for a city and for a band, too. These musicians merge regional traditions and instruments with the modern to find a new tone, a contemporary urban folklore.

❿ YOR-YOR SEVARA NAZARKHAN from YOL BOLSIN

Electronics from Western Hector Zazou and instrumental play and singing from Uzbek ensemble led by singer Sevara Nazarkhan work remarkably well on this one.

Jean Trouillet

Manu Chao

Manu Chao is a superstar in Europe, and just about the only "world music" figure who has got songs not in English across to a wide audience of English speakers. But language is irrelevant here: Manu mixes reggae, African music, Spanish and French roots, to create an addictive party cocktail. And he has recently spread fairy dust across the wonderful, bluesy Malian duo, Amadou & Mariam, producing their latest album.

MANU CHAO

❶ LUNA Y SOL from CLANDESTINO
After disbanding Mano Negra, the Franco-Spanish punk band, Manu went travelling in South America and the Caribbean and the 2m-selling *Clandestino* album was the result. A seductive mix of samples and influences: here it's the turn of Mexican horns. Wild and fun.

❷ BONGO BONG from CLANDESTINO
Ping-ping go the guitars, and Manu rolls the nonsense (in English) about being "King of the Bongo Bong".

❸ MINHA GALERA from CLANDESTINO
The sweetest, catchiest, contemporary-est bossa nova you could hope to hear. He could play this with a comb and toilet paper and bring the house down. Which he kinda does.

❹ WELCOME TO TIJUANA from CLANDESTINO
"Tekila, sexo y marihuana" – a daft, dubby assemblage of Latin sounds that goes down a storm in Manu's live shows.

❺ ME GUSTA TU from PROXIMA ESTACION ESPERANZA
A song that chugs along as Manu enunciates all he likes and keeps returning to the object of his affections: "Me gustas tu."

❻ DENIA from PROXIMA ESTACION ESPERANZA
It's the way he mixes things up: this is a delicate, upbeat number, sung in Arabic but unlike any Arab song.

❼ PROMISCUITY from RADIO BEMBA SOUNDS SYSTEM
There is no better festival headliner and this live record shows why: Manu and band embark on a mad whoop of Latin ska.

AMADOU & MARIAM

❽ LA REALITE from DIMANCHE A BAMAKO
An Amadou & Mariam blues-rocker transformed into a potential stadium winner, with a slice of Chao rhythm, a recurrent police siren, and audience invocations.

❾ TAXI BAMAKO from DIMANCHE A BAMAKO
Manu is very much at the controls on this gentle lilt of a track, sampling the sounds of a Malian taxi rank and children's song.

❿ SENEGAL FASTFOOD from DIMANCHE A BAMAKO
A Manu track in all but name, as he takes on lead vocals, namechecking all points West Africa, and joined by Amadou & Mariam for a catchy good-time chorus.

Mark Ellingham

Chapel Hill

For a time in the early 90s, Chapel Hill, NC, was touted as the "next Seattle" – a designation only slightly less hazardous than a singer-songwriter being tagged a "new Dylan". Chapel Hillians gracefully sidestepped the early attempts to delimit the town's sound to fresh-scrubbed indie punk, to create a diverse body of music.

❶ SLACK MOTHERFUCKER SUPERCHUNK from SUPERCHUNK
This widely misinterpreted song about a lazy co-worker became a slacker anthem at the dawn of the 90s.

❷ ROCK POST ROCK POLVO from SHAPES

Rock Post Rock is one of the highlights of the band's final album, where their angular guitars were finally successfully harnessed to a set of well-developed songs.

❸ WEB IN FRONT ARCHERS OF LOAF from ICKY METTLE

Often characterized as a scruffier version of Pavement, the Archers hit the jackpot the first time around with this bouncy singalong that kicked off their debut album from 1994.

❹ ANYTHING BUT LOVE SQUIRREL NUT ZIPPERS from ROASTED RIGHT

These musical archivists exploring the hot jazz sounds of the 20s and 30s turned out to be the most economically successful of all the bands from the scene.

❺ ROADSIDE WRECK SOUTHERN CULTURE ON THE SKIDS from TOO MUCH PORK FOR JUST ONE FORK

Roadside Wreck is an example of how the band incorporated the swampy blues of Slim Harpo and the rockabilly energy of Dale Hawkins into an edgy brew that counterbalanced their more lighthearted efforts.

❻ YOU'RE SOAKING IN IT PIPE from 6 DAYS TO BELLUS

Pipe shows were as much about audience participation (beer tossing) as they were about the band's relentless punk rock assault.

❼ THE TRAIN MOTOCASTER from ACID ROCK

Stadium-sized rock action from a Raleigh power trio who eventually signed to Interscope.

❽ SERVICE ENTRANCE FIASCO SPATULA from MEDIUM PLANERS AND MATCHERS

One of the first tracks to fully incorporate cellist Chris Eubank into their instrumental mix, this track moves fluidly from a scorched-earth guitarscape to a jaunty Eastern European hoedown and back again.

Butch Lazorchak

The Charlatans

You know what you're getting with the Charlies, so if you like it, you'll always be smiling.

❶ WHITE SHIRT from SOME FRIENDLY

Blunt, Burgess and Collins keep it bright, upbeat and simple, the highlight being a brief but great key change.

❷ THE ONLY ONE I KNOW from SOME FRIENDLY

You hear the opening to their second single and know you've got eight seconds to get to the dancefloor. One of the all-time indie greats.

❸ I DON'T WANT TO SEE THE SIGHTS from BETWEEN 10TH AND 11TH

The best of the band's ready-to-explode openers solicits with a dancy guitar hook.

❹ COME IN NUMBER 21 from UP TO OUR HIPS

Another album-opening classic, with the instruments seemingly talking, and the "ooh-ooh-ooh"s exploding all over.

❺ I NEVER WANT AN EASY LIFE IF ME AND HE WERE EVER TO GET THERE from UP TO OUR HIPS

All the ingredients of a classic Charlatans song, as well as a wicked descending bassline and screaming Burgess vocal.

❻ HOW HIGH from TELLIN' STORIES

The best of the Charlatans three-minute pop songs (well, 3.06), and one of their biggest successes. Here it's all in the solid, relentless vocals.

❼ HAPPEN TO DIE (LONG VERSION) from SONGS FROM THE OTHER SIDE

On this 1992 B-side to Tremelo Song the simple, flowing lyrics take a back seat to the driving force of an awesome bassline.

Daniel Crewe

Tim Burgess's
Play for Today

The singer with the Charlatans, the most enduring group to come out of the late-80s "Madchester" scene, TIM BURGESS sent us this list from somewhere deep in the the canyons of LA, where he now lives. He marked it with the words "Just for today".

❶ STRAIGHT TO HELL THE CLASH from COMBAT ROCK

❷ DANCE STANCE DEXY'S MIDNIGHT RUNNERS from THE BEST OF

❸ MAGIC CORNER BELITA WOODS from NORTHERN SOUL FEVER VOL 1

❹ WHO THE CAP FIT BOB MARLEY & THE WAILERS from RASTAMAN VIBRATION

❺ THEE MOST EXHALTED POTENTATE OF LOVE THE CRAMPS from SMELL OF FEMALE

❻ BUTTERBEAN B52'S from WHAMMY!

❼ SUNRISE NEW ORDER from LOW LIFE

❽ A HARD RAIN'S A-GONNA FALL BOB DYLAN from FREEWHEELIN' BOB DYLAN

❾ A SONG FOR YOU LEON RUSSELL from LEON RUSSELL

❿ GIMME SHELTER MERRY CLAYTON from GIMME SHELTER

Ray Charles

One of the founding fathers of soul music, mixing gospel, pop, blues and jazz with that immediately recognizable grainy, yearning voice.

❶ WHAT'D I SAY from ULTIMATE HITS COLLECTION
Rock'n'roll as a revival meeting, with that great circular keyboard line and orgiastic call-response vocals.

❷ HIT THE ROAD JACK from ULTIMATE HITS COLLECTION
Both the anvil-descending melody and brook-no-discussion backup female vocals make it clear this relationship is kaput, though Ray certainly pleads his case with wolfish charm.

❸ I GOT A WOMAN from ULTIMATE HITS COLLECTION
By setting a gospel melody to a sexy lyric and music that both swung and cooked, Charles also set the table for soul itself.

❹ I BELIEVE TO MY SOUL from THE BIRTH OF SOUL
Seems like Ray's reaching down into the soles of his shoes on this anguished vocal, set to pounding piano and one of his trademark minor-keyed melodies.

❺ UNCHAIN MY HEART from ULTIMATE HITS COLLECTION
Yet another tune that's at once grim but impossibly catchy, with suave and snazzy horns and backup female singing.

❻ I DON'T NEED NO DOCTOR from ANTHOLOGY
It was only 1966, but this wailing, urgent (and again minor-keyed) rocker was really about his last great moment on record.

❼ BUSTED from ULTIMATE HITS COLLECTION
Nothing's going Ray's way on this forceful jazzy number, sung as if he's honoring his misfortune with a bemused mock zest.

❽ ONE MINT JULEP from ULTIMATE HITS COLLECTION
Charles could play jazz too, as he did on this

exuberant horn-organ-duel 1961 hit single – instrumental save occasional way-hip spoken-shouted asides.

⑨ DON'T SET ME FREE from **ULTIMATE HITS COLLECTION**
Near-enslavement to passion was a common theme for Charles, here expelled with an almost get-it-over-with rush.

⑩ STICKS AND STONES from **ULTIMATE HITS COLLECTION**
Ray and his backup make being abused sound downright pleasurable, with an electric piano solo almost the equal of "What'd I Say"'s.

Richie Unterberger

Cheap Trick

Featuring the wildly talented and sartorially challenged guitarist Rick Nielsen, classy hard rock acts don't come funnier, edgier or more intelligent than this lot.

❶ CALIFORNIA MAN from **HEAVEN TONIGHT**
A top of the range Roy Wood tune given a transatlantic facelift. You want vintage rock'n'roll swagger? Just crank this one up.

❷ CLOCK STRIKES TEN from **IN COLOR**
Like Little Richard rocking out with Sweet, this is bubblegum pop packing some serious hard rock heat.

❸ COME ON, COME ON from **IN COLOR**
Is that Noddy Holder on backing vocals? Another formidably fine tune showcasing the Trick's British glam rock affinities.

❹ DREAM POLICE from **DREAM POLICE**
You've gotta love those violin-like keyboards and melodramatic mid section. Yet another cracking pop rocker from the band that makes it all sound so easy.

❺ ELO KIDDIES from **CHEAP TRICK**
A reference to The Electric Light Orchestra? With a cursory nod to the Brum sound, the pummelling drums belong to something Gary Glitter might have cooked up.

❻ GONNA RAISE HELL from **DREAM POLICE**
At over nine minutes, this is the heavy antithesis of the Trick's pop sensibilities. Nevertheless, it contains a great riff and a fist-banging, anthemic chorus.

❼ HE'S A WHORE from **CHEAP TRICK**
Ironic lyrics married to a melodic Beatlesy sensibility wrapped around a dark-hearted chorus that demands you shout along. '

❽ I WANT YOU TO WANT ME from **AT BUDOKAN**
In the studio this was cute. Live it sounds like a classic. Lush pop rock delivered to an audience willing to lap up every lovingly honed note.

❾ SURRENDER from **HEAVEN TONIGHT**
Clever, cutting lyrics, one of the band's best choruses, and everything underpinned by swirling keyboards and a terrific multilayered climax.

❿ WRONG ALL ALONG from **CHEAP TRICK**
Kicks off like an AC/DC style shuffle boogie before plunging headlong into a punchy and raucous stompalong.

Essi Berelian

80s Cheese

Nothing screams mid-80s like a sax solo, supple synth hook, sappy power ballad or film soundtrack from Kenny Loggins. Some things are so bad they're good.

❶ MANEATER DARYL HALL & JOHN OATES from **H2O**
The lyrics are beyond inane, but that "dum-dum-dum, dum-dum-de-dum" bassline is irresistible.

❷ CAN'T FIGHT THIS FEELING
REO−SPEEDWAGON from **WHEELS ARE TURNIN'**
So many words rhyme with "or"; REO pull out the rhyming dictionary to "fall upon your floor", "crash through your door", and discover whatever else might fit.

❸ TOTAL ECLIPSE OF THE HEART **BONNIE TYLER** from **FASTER THAN THE SPEED OF NIGHT**
Deliciously overdramatic, Tyler gives new meaning to the phrase "belt it out".

❹ AFRICA **TOTO** from **FOUR**
"I must do what's right/Sure as Kilimanjaro rises like Olympus above the Serengeti." If this isn't the best bit of pretentious rock poetry ever sung than it's surely close.

❺ MR ROBOTO **STYX** from **KILROY WAS HERE**
Hear a grown man sing "secret, secret, I've got a secret". But wait, is it in fact a robot singing that? The future never sounded less scary.

❻ SISTER CHRISTIAN **NIGHT RANGER** from **MIDNIGHT MADNESS**
The transition from tender piano ballad to revved-up, electrified rocker is so phony it makes you want to hear it over and over again.

❼ THE ONE THAT YOU LOVE **AIR SUPPLY** from **THE ONE THAT YOU LOVE**
The unabashed kings of schmaltzy love songs scale all sorts of epic heights – not least the chorus's use of the third person – on their most successful ballad.

❽ DON'T STOP BELIEVIN' **JOURNEY** from **ESCAPE**
The small town girl, the city boy – this is the kind of archetypal rock'n'roll fable that makes you want to head straight back to high school.

❾ DANGER ZONE **KENNY LOGGINS** from **TOP GUN SOUNDTRACK**
Someone so close to the middle of the road deserves a medal for chutzpah in claiming he'll "take you right into the Danger Zone." Still, it sort of rocks.

Andrew Rosenberg

The Chemical Brothers

Outstandingly chunky, heavyweight beats delivered by two of the least likely-looking funkmeisters ever. Ed and Tom Chemical met at university over a shared passion for old school hip-hop and started out as the Dust Brothers, a name borrowed from a successful US production team. When their own success moved into the same orbit as their heroes, a name change was in order.

❶ SUNSHINE UNDERGROUND from **SURRENDER**
Do not listen to this song while driving. It cranks itself up to an unbelievably fearsome pitch of excitement.

❷ IT BEGAN IN AFRICA from **COME WITH US**
Massive beats pay tribute to the root of all our dance music.

❸ BLOCK ROCKIN' BEATS from **DIG YOUR OWN HOLE**
Jack your body into the osteopathy clinic with this electro-based blast from the recent past.

❹ LEAVE HOME from **EXIT PLANET DUST**
Leave home with the Chemical Bros and you may find yourself arriving on another planet.

❺ FUCK UP BEATS from **EXIT PLANET DUST**
The track that the radio DJs never announce fully. One of the Chems' first compositions, its title is basically their motto.

❻ MUSIC: RESPONSE from **SURRENDER**
Robot vocals and a Kraftwerkian steady might lull you into a false sense of security. But halfway through it you'll find yourself on the dancefloor again.

❼ SONG TO THE SIREN (LIVE) from **EXIT PLANET DUST**
Beats of electro-mechanical passion provide a solid base for enticing, looped female vocals.

Then, with no warning, the trance kicks in and we're sailing ever closer to the rocks.

❽ INFLUENCED from **SURRENDER**
This features a perfect vocal sample from a consummate rock chick, somewhat partied out and perhaps, one dare say, a little under the influence herself.

❾ THE TEST from **COME WITH US**
Looking back to Ken Kesey and the "Acid tests" he carried out with the Grateful Dead, the beats will carry you away and keep you dancing way past bedtime.

Al Spicer

Neneh Cherry

Being Don Cherry's daughter gave Neneh a musical head start. Moving away from her punk-jazz roots, she became a feisty B-Girl in the late-80s before seating herself down on the comfy trip-hop sofa in the 90s.

❶ TAX SEX RIP, RIG & PANIC from **I AM COLD**
Chaotic, brittle disco, with Neneh and Andrea Oliver's mischievous taunts giving way to zippy, post-Cecil Taylor piano acrobatics.

❷ EPI EPI ARP WHOOSH! RIP, RIG & PANIC from **I AM COLD**
Puckish vocalese from Cherry and Oliver, toasting an Afro-Bristol gumbo that sounds like a squabble between Fela Kuti and McCoy Tyner.

❸ STORM THE REALITY ASYLUM RIP, RIG & PANIC from **I AM COLD**
Taking its title from one of William Burrough's revolutionary exhortations, this is an anarchic, sloganeering anthem with a touch of the showtune to it.

❹ THOSE ESKIMO WOMEN SPEAK FRANKLY RIP, RIG & PANIC from **GOD**
If Public Image Ltd had ever decided to write a playground skipping-rope song, it might have sounded as contrary as this.

❺ THE LONELIEST GIRL FLOAT UP CP from **KILL ME IN THE MORNING**
Swooning viola, a clicky drumbeat, and slightly reticent funk bass render Neneh's impassioned ballad all the sweeter: it's like hearing Rotary Connection in a bedsit.

❻ SEXY BUSHES FLOAT UP CP from **KILL ME IN THE MORNING**
Imagine Kate Bush being harangued by Frank Zappa to the mildewed parping of a horn section that smells of an 80s squat.

❼ BUFFALO STANCE NENEH CHERRY from **RAW LIKE SUSHI**
Ms Cherry restyles herself as "urban", via a few feisty put-downs, frothy hip-hop beats and the sort of perky but assertive keyboards that regularly soundtracked 80s cop show *Miami Vice*.

❽ MANCHILD NENEH CHERRY from **RAW LIKE SUSHI**
Apparently, it was playing with the "autochord" voicings on a cheap keyboard that led Neneh to one of the most imaginative string arrangements on a pop record since Prince's *Parade* album.

❾ TOGETHER NOW TRICKY from **NEARLY GOD**
Neneh's vocal verges a little too close to the histrionic, but Tricky's bruised and lolloping blues guitar riff keeps things grounded.

Matt Milton

Chic

In the late 70s and early 80s the sound of the Chic production team (guitarist Nile Rodgers and bassist Bernard Edwards) was the sleekest and most stylish in popular music.

❶ DANCE, DANCE, DANCE (YOWSAH, YOWSAH, YOWSAH) CHIC from **CHIC**
The first record that didn't remove sub-bass tones. Get up, dance, and feel the bottom end in your bowels.

❷ LE FREAK CHIC from *C'est Chic*
Maybe the archest, most ambiguous dance-craze disc ever.

❸ AT LAST I AM FREE CHIC from *C'EST CHIC*
Who says a dance band can't move you to tears?

❹ SATURDAY NORMA JEAN from *NORMA JEAN*
A cult disco classic that features one of Edwards' most outlandish basslines.

❺ LOST IN MUSIC SISTER SLEDGE from *WE ARE FAMILY*
An ode to the power of music so perfect that it drove Mark E. Smith to cover it with The Fall.

❻ GOOD TIMES CHIC from *RISQUÉ*
The greatest ever disco record, and one of the most influential records of the last 30 years.

❼ I'M COMING OUT DIANA ROSS from *DIANA*
Not since The Supremes' heyday has Ross sounded this good – or this coy.

❽ WHY CARLY SIMON from *SOUP FOR ONE*
Perhaps Chic's greatest feat – making Carly Simon listenable.

❾ LIKE A VIRGIN MADONNA from *LIKE A VIRGIN*
Rodgers' synthed-up Motown production turned Madonna into the biggest star ever.

❿ NOTORIOUS DURAN DURAN from *NOTORIOUS*
The boys from Birmingham finally got to work with their idol, but they were so awed that Rodgers ended up doing it all himself.

Peter Shapiro

Chicago blues

The electric blues of Chicago provided the inspiration for The Beatles, The Stones and countless other rock bands. Its best known stars, Muddy Waters and Howlin' Wolf, get their own playlists, but there's plenty of other music that's too good to miss – most but by no means all originally released on the legendary Chess label. Here's a quick chronological run-through.

❶ DON'T START ME TO TALKIN' SONNY BOY WILLIAMSON from *DOWN AND OUT BLUES*

❷ MY BABE LITTLE WALTER from *THE CHESS BLUES-ROCK SONGBOOK*

❸ WHO DO YOU LOVE? BO DIDDLEY from *HIS BEST: THE CHESS 50TH ANNIVERSARY COLLECTION*

❹ BABY WHAT YOU WANT ME TO DO JIMMY REED from *THE MASTERS*

❺ MY TIME AFTER AWHILE BUDDY GUY from *THE COMPLETE CHESS STUDIO RECORDINGS*

❻ GOOD MORNING SCHOOLGIRL JUNIOR WELLS from *HOODOO MAN BLUES*

❼ WANG DANG DOODLE KOKO TAYLOR from *WHAT IT TAKES*

❽ IN THE BASEMENT ETTA JAMES AND SUGAR PIE DESANTO from *THE SOUND OF THE CITY: CHICAGO*

❾ I DON'T WANT NO WOMAN MAGIC SAM from *WEST SIDE SOUL*

❿ GIVE ME BACK MY WIG HOUND DOG TAYLOR from *HOUND DOG TAYLOR AND THE HOUSEROCKERS*

Greg Ward

Chickens & insects

Or should that be poultry, insects and arachnids? Musicologists continue to come to blows over the precise definition of what remains one of pop music's biggest and most intriguing genres.

❶ CHICKEN CRAZY JOE TEX

❷ BEST DRESSED CHICKEN IN TOWN DR ALIMANTADO

❸ DO THE FUNKY CHICKEN RUFUS THOMAS

❹ LITTLE RED ROOSTER THE ROLLING STONES

❺ COLD TURKEY JOHN LENNON

❻ HEY THERE LITTLE INSECT JONATHAN RICHMAN AND THE MODERN LOVERS

❼ I GOT ANTS IN MY PANTS JAMES BROWN

❽ BORIS THE SPIDER THE WHO

❾ MOSQUITO SONG QUEENS OF THE STONE AGE

❿ I MAN A GRASSHOPPER PABLO MOSES

Greg Ward

Chill out

Or Ambient, as we once used to call it…

❶ A HUGE EVER-GROWING PULSATING BRAIN… THE ORB from ADVENTURES BEYOND THE ULTRAWORLD
Ambient music, for many people, started here, when sampled ocean noises and abstracted Minnie Riperton vocals hit the U.K. charts.

❷ 2/1 BRIAN ENO from AMBIENT 1: MUSIC FOR AIRPORTS
Twelve years before The Orb, in 1978, came this calm piano cum electronic effects tune.

❸ GYMNOPÉDIE NO. 1 ERIK SATIE from SARBAND: DANSE GOTHIQUE
Erik Satie wanted to create *musique d'ameublement*, music which is just there in your room, like a carpet or a settee. Here, one of his best-known piano pieces is played on medieval and Middle Eastern instruments.

❹ KALAVATI REMIXES SUNS OF ARQA from GIVE PEACE A DANCE VOL 2: THE AMBIENT COLLECTION
Indian bansuri flute sets the tone for a tune that lasts forever (well, 23 minutes).

❺ LITTLE FLUFFY CLOUDS THE ORB from THE ORB'S ADVENTURES BEYOND THE ULTRAWORLD
It all starts with the cry of a rooster over which

Rickie Lee Jones tells us: "When I lived in Arizona and the skies always had little fluffy clouds in them and there were lots of stars at night." Ambient made it to the dancefloors.

❻ DREAM TIME IN LAKE JACKSON KLF from CHILL OUT
Central Asian throat singing and synth drones langorously merge.

❼ THE THIRD CHAMBER PART 4 LOOP GURU from DUNIYA
It starts with a muezzin, then in comes some gamelan from Indonesia, a sample of Sheila Chandra's singing, birdsong, and electronics. All of which create a serene atmosphere.

❽ SPEEDLEARN (EMPATHYMIX) THE HIGHER INTELLIGENCE AGENCY from COLOURFORM
Masters of the Chill Out zones of numerous raves, The Agency really know how to tease a rhythmic progression from the ethereal atmospheres of their samplers.

Jean Trouillet

Chinn & Chapman

Loathed and despised by "real" rock fans, Nicky Chinn and Mike Chapman were the songwriting team behind a stream of bubblegum hits, from Sweet's Funny Funny in 1971 through to Toni Basil's Mickey in 1982, on Micky Most's RAK records. Here's six of the best, both originals and oddly cool revisitings.

❶ DEVIL GATE DRIVE SUZI QUATRO from GREATEST HITS
Holding the biggest bass guitar and wearing the tightest leather cat-suit, Suzi's possibly-kinky girl-next-door good looks had her teenage boy target market sewn up. She fronted a totally professional band and kicked ass in a way that girls in pop didn't do back then.

② BALLROOM BLITZ THE DAMNED from **MACHINE GUN ETIQUETTE**

Never a tune of shrinking virginal innocence, The Sweet's version of this was about a fight kicking off in a discotheque. Then The Damned, featuring the none-more-tasteless stylings of Captain Sensible and Dave Vanian, got their dirty punk rockers' hands on it.

③ BLOCKBUSTER THE SWEET from **THE VERY BEST OF**

The Sweet were macho enough under all that make-up to appeal to the young lads, and pretty enough for the girls to plaster their rooms with their photos. They never surpassed this invigorating shriek of glam nonsense.

④ ROCKET THE WEDDING PRESENT from **HIT PARADE**

Some reckon that Mud's original extracted the last drop of emotion from this ChinniChap masterpiece, but just give the Weddoes' version a spin for the full juice.

⑤ THE CAT CREPT IN MUD from **THE VERY BEST...**

Mud still exist, touring for eternity the windswept holiday camps of the UK, condemned to wear the same drapesuits and perform the same dance routine. This is a cheerful enough tune, though, to perform every night...

⑥ WIG WAM BAM THE YUMYUMS from **SWEET AS CANDY (COLD FRONT; 1997)**

The music masters from Østfold in Norway took this away from The Sweet – who recorded the original – and made it into a piece of tuneful, sunny perfection. Powerful pop, sugar coated and pumped with additives.

Al Spicer

Eric Clapton

The 60s graffiti called him God and few other guitarists save old rivals Jeff Beck and Jimmy Page can match his blistering solos when he gets in the mood; what is often overlooked is his talent as both a singer and songwriter.

① SUNSHINE OF YOUR LOVE CREAM from **DISRAELI GEARS**

The riff that launched a thousand bands. Heavy, man!

② WHITE ROOM CREAM from **WHEELS OF FIRE'**

Who isn't thrilled when that wah-wah kicks in?

③ CROSSROADS CREAM from **WHEELS OF FIRE'**

A radical reinterpretation of Robert Johnston that redefined how white men play the blues.

④ BADGE CREAM from **GOODBYE CREAM'**

A whiff of psychedelia about the lyrics (courtesy of George Harrison), and a sound that echoes the Byrds.

⑤ AFTER MIDNIGHT from **ERIC CLAPTON'**

A J.J. Cale song that he has reworked several times in his career, this best exemplifies Clapton's ability to make country rock sound almost funky.

⑥ LAYLA DEREK AND THE DOMINOS from **LAYLA AND OTHER ASSORTED LOVE SONGS**

A lovelorn plea to George Harrison's wife – and a major hit to boot.

⑦ WHILE MY GUITAR GENTLY WEEPS from **CONCERT FOR BANGLADESH'**

Clapton played on The Beatles' original and no-one makes a guitar weep like he does on this live performance from the 1970 charity gig.

⑧ GO BACK HOME STEPHEN STILLS from **STEPHEN STILLS'**

Clapton has often played his best as a special guest, and he is on fire on this bluesy number from Stephen Stills' first solo effort.

⑨ LET IT GROW from **461 OCEAN BOULEVARD**

A gentle ballad with an insistent refrain. Effortless emo for the 70s party set.

⑩ I SHOT THE SHERIFF from **CROSSROADS**

This spirited live version from 1974 shows that Clapton is able to weave his own guitar magic on the song without smothering it.

Chris Coe

Eric Clapton's
Blues roots

What was it about the blues that struck such a chord with a bunch of white kids growing up in suburban England in the 50s? "There was something about the solo bluesman and the knowledge that this guy was probably uneducated and on the bottom rung of the social ladder," ERIC CLAPTON recalls. "I grabbed at that and I had a built-in admiration for it but I still don't know why. I'd like to say it was something to do with my upbringing but it would be very hard to find a tangible cause…". Here are ten of those original inspirations.

❶ I LOVE THE WOMAN FREDDIE KING from BLUES GUITAR HERO

❷ KINDHEARTED WOMAN BLUES ROBERT JOHNSON from THE COMPLETE RECORDINGS

❸ HOBO BLUES JOHN LEE HOOKER from THE LEGENDARY MODERN RECORDINGS

❹ HAND IN HAND ELMORE JAMES from THE BEST OF ELMORE JAMES

❺ SPECIAL STREAM LINE BUKKA WHITE from MISSISSIPPI BLUES GIANT

❻ FRANKIE AND ALBERT MISSISSIPPI JOHN HURT from SATISFYING BLUES

❼ CHOCK HOUSE BLUES BLIND LEMON JEFFERSON from BLIND LEMON JEFFERSON

❽ ALABAMA WOMAN BLUES LEROY CARR from THE ESSENTIAL LEROY CARR

❾ STAESBORO BLUES BLIND WILLIE MCTELL from ATLANTA STRUT

❿ STRUTTIN' WITH SOME BARBECUE LOUIS ARMSTRONG AND THE HOT FIVE from THE BEST OF LOUIS ARMSTRONG AND THE HOT FIVE

The Clash

One of the seminal punk rock bands, The Clash wrote the book when it comes to sneering, teeth-bared rebellion. Then they went to America…

❶ LONDON'S BURNING from THE CLASH
This tells you everything you need to know about the boredom, street tension and frustration of late 70s Britain. Paramilitary beats, combat-strength guitar riffs and Joe's most tongue-flappingly lackadaisical vocals render this track essential.

❷ COMPLETE CONTROL from THE CLASH
The best ever "Fuck the record company!" song, full of artistic outrage and played by guys who are finally getting to grips with their instruments and gelling as a band.

❸ (WHITE MAN) IN HAMMERSMITH PALAIS from THE ESSENTIAL CLASH
A well-intentioned stab at UK pop reggae, a fine reminiscence of a great gig, and a bit of sniping at the boneheads. Marvellous.

❹ LONDON CALLING from LONDON CALLING
The title track stomp from their most accomplished album. Redolent of its time, with equal parts romance and menace, and as classic a slice of London life as anything by The Kinks.

❺ THE GUNS OF BRIXTON from LONDON CALLING
Our brave lads throw down the gauntlet on behalf of the capital's dispossessed youth.

71

6 RUDIE CAN'T FAIL from LONDON CALLING
White boy skanking of the highest order.
Strummer's never been in better voice.

7 LOST IN THE SUPERMARKET from LONDON CALLING
Mick Jones' most effective vocal outing. He
sounds completely knocked sideways by the
choice on offer at his local co-op.

8 IVAN MEETS G.I. JOE from SANDINISTA!
Electronic noises bleep away happily in the
background as the guys envisage World War III
as a computer game.

Al Spicer

Eddie Cochran

**Arguably the originator of the power chord
rock style, Cochran's rockabilly offered
some of the most joyous celebrations of
teenage fun of the late 50s. All selections
are from *Somethin' Else: The Fine Lookin'
Hits Of Eddie Cochran*.**

1 SUMMERTIME BLUES
The all-time disenfranchised teenage school-
boy anthem, its massively thick riff-chords
simmer with bottled-up frustration.

2 C'MON EVERYBODY
Party-party-party time on another thickly
chorded hit whose uplifting riff is almost as
good as the one on Summertime Blues.

3 SOMETHIN' ELSE
Rockabilly at its most cocksure, Cochran broad-
casting the charms of the babe he's got his eye
on with brash bravado.

4 NERVOUS BREAKDOWN
Stuttering rockabilly goofiness dominates this
relatively unknown gem.

5 WEEKEND
Another wholly unselfconscious celebration of
good times, from those distant days when the

weekend offered the only relief for youth with
energy to burn.

6 SITTIN' IN THE BALCONY
Eddie's in a smoochier mood than usual on this
rockaballad, the wholesome scenario dotted
by a slight suggestion of naughtiness.

Richie Unterberger

Cocteau Twins

**Robin Guthrie and Simon Raymonde
and vocalist Liz Fraser – collectively, the
Cocteau Twins – have, for the last two
decades, cultivated a unique blend of
ethereally expressive music, with vocals
that have reinvented the map. If an
emotion exists, there is – somewhere – a
Cocteau Twins moment for it.**

1 PANDORA from TREASURE
Liz's siren-like higher range blossoms out here,
as she dives headlong into verbal abstraction.

2 ICEBLINK LUCK from HEAVEN OR LAS VEGAS
Lush, indie-jangly guitars and driving drums
heralded a sharper, tighter sound for the
Cocteaus. Reverbs and echoes are stripped
back to reveal startlingly clear vocals.

3 SERPENTSKIRT from MILK AND KISSES
Stark, gothic guitars and snares intro a track
that waxes and wanes between bleak, whispering voids and swelling multi-vocal rivers. Then
just when you think it's all been said, the Twins
shift gear and fire another blissful tangent.

4 WHALES TAILS from VICTORIALAND
Fraser and Guthrie tumble on the arctic breeze,
snowflake-light, wafting between billowy
cumulonimbi and shimmering ice floes.

5 CICO BUFF from BLUE BELL KNOLL
One of the Cocteaus' most elegant pieces, with
Liz leisurely sliding up and down the scales
before a sublime guitar solo propels her up
and out into bursting choral incandescence.

6 THE SPANGLE MAKER from **THE PINK OPAQUE**
Throbbing bass and great whining feedback arcs, redolent of the Twins' punky debut, smooth out into anthemic grandeur.

7 THOSE EYES, THAT MOUTH from **LOVE'S EASY TEARS**
As with so many of the Cocteau's best tracks there is build and pay-off. The build here centres on pounding 3/4 guitar cycles spiralling round Fraser's full-pelt barks; the end pay-off is a tender wall-of-sound.

8 NEED-FIRE from **JUDGE DREDD SOUNDTRACK**
Liz turns to crushingly vulnerable child in one of the Cocteaus' most vocally spare tracks. Washes of guitar delays are carried along by a warm digital thump.

9 MUD AND DARK from **EVANGELINE**
Listen carefully and before your very ears will unfold the story of Echo and Narcissus, and the dangers of falling for an egotist.

10 GREAT SPANGLED FRITILLARY from **TINY DYNAMINE/ECHOES IN A SHALLOW BAY EP**
Liz duets her own unearthly yodelling across a morse code pattern of butterfly names. Undulating bass, kicking in midway, tugs you bodily into the disquieting soundjungle.

Link Hall

Leonard Cohen

Songs of Love and Hate, he called his best known album, and the laconic Cohen was for years seen as a byword for gloom. But his star has shone in recent years, with everyone from The Pixies to REM covering his songs.

1 FAMOUS BLUE RAINCOAT from **GREATEST HITS**
A bitter-sweet tale of a triangular love affair in which the cuckold detests then forgives his partner's seducer. Propelled by Paul Buckmaster's strings, this is Cohen's most iconic song, later wonderfully reworked by his backing singer Jennifer Warnes in her album of covers.

2 THE STRANGER SONG from **FIELD COMMANDER COHEN**
Compare and contrast with Billy Joel's take on the same personality type (The Stranger). Cohen's conversational depiction is full of self-knowledge, while Joel's feels like a simple minded pop song.

3 SEEMS SO LONG AGO, NANCY from **LIVE SONGS**
Suicide was never far from Cohen's early work and this meditation on a suicide victim, first released on *Songs From A Room*, is even more eerie and chilling live with the likes of Jennifer Warnes wailing in the background.

4 I CAN'T FORGET from **I'M YOUR MAN**
A lilting, lyrical, moving number – almost his answer to Kurt Weill's September Song – in which Len nostalgically confides "I can't forget… but I can't remember what".

5 FIRST, WE TAKE MANHATTAN from **I'M YOUR MAN**
In which the narrator has the energy left for a marvellously sinister laugh and a bid for world domination involving Manhattan and Berlin. Beautifully played, sardonically sung, compellingly daft, this is a minor masterpiece.

6 HEY THAT'S NO WAY TO SAY GOODBYE from **GREATEST HITS**
A rare outing for Cohen as love-struck fool, although even here the tender promise that "our steps will always rhyme" is undermined, as love runs aground on distances.

7 DRESS REHEARSAL RAG from **SONGS OF LOVE AND HATE**
After some of the bitterest self-reproach in his songbook, reinforced by an angry, beaten-up, backing, the singer just pulls back from slashing his wrists in a song which, for all the agony, is almost exhilarating.

8 BIRD ON THE WIRE from **SONGS FROM A ROOM**
Kris Kristofferson has promised to use the line about struggling to be free "like a drunk in a

midnight choir" as his epitaph. Listen to this often covered grandiloquent whimsy and it's easy to understand why

❾ CHELSEA HOTEL from GREATEST HITS
A wistful, self-lacerating, tuneful account of Cohen's brief fling with Janis Joplin in which he makes it perfectly clear that the blues chanteuse wasn't that nice to him and that, even dead, she doesn't prey on his mind very much.

❿ THE FUTURE from THE FUTURE
A hypnotic, low key, ode in which Cohen reveals that he has seen the future and it's murder. But then we'd expect no less.
Paul Simpson

Coldplay

On first appearance, you might have put money on Coldplay remaining a bit of a cult band, full of quiet songcraft. But with stadium status, celebrity status and PC status all secured, the sky seems not to be the limit for these lads. Here are three exemplary cuts from each of their three top-notch albums.

❶ YELLOW from PARACHUTES
Buckland's triumphant descending chords and Chris Martin's voice-just-breaking vocals helped make this the first hit single.

❷ TROUBLE from PARACHUTES
This song's worth goes well beyond its intro being borrowed for a myriad mobile ringtones. The sombre piano and lazy structure typify the band's forte at sweetly describing desperation.

❸ DON'T PANIC from PARACHUTES
The strummed opener ("We live in a beautiful world") sounds doomed with Martin's vocal counterpointed by some divine guitar picking.

❹ WARNING SIGN from A RUSH OF BLOOD TO THE HEAD
Soulsearching strings and keyboards enrich

the strummed simplicity of the song, and the line "When the truth is, I miss you" is genuine goosepimples territory.

❺ IN MY PLACE from A RUSH OF BLOOD TO THE HEAD
A gentle but piercing guitar riff sets the tone for the singer to lament being lost in his classic pained tunefulness.

❻ THE SCIENTIST from A RUSH OF BLOOD TO THE HEAD
Martin's majestic piano chords and more bleeding heart vocals raise this love song on high before the band weigh in to bring it gradually back to earth.

❼ TALK from X&Y
This plea to overcome alienation rides on a seething magma of bass and synthesiser while the haunting guitar bursts through like birds flying out of the mist.

❽ THE HARDEST PART from X&Y
Superbly crafted song with a series of sublime hooks to complement the wistful lyrics. Buckland's guitar flows like honey throughout.

❾ WHITE SHADOWS from X&Y
Quirky off-beat drums and sawing guitars almost remind us of Joy Division before Martin's shift into the melodic chorus remind us who we are listening to.
Nick Edwards

Colours

There isn't a colour in the rainbow that hasn't featured in a song title. Actually, come to that, there are an awful lot of song colours that don't feature in the rainbow at all.

❶ RED RED WINE UB40 from LABOUR OF LOVE
White wine just won't do to ease the pain of heartache for these Brummie reggae fans who took a shine to the classic Jamaican tune.

❷ ORANGE CRUSH R.E.M. from **GREEN**

'I've got my spine, I've got my Orange Crush,' sings Michael Stipe, in an askance reference to Agent Orange, the deadly nerve gas of the Vietnam war.

❸ YELLOW SUBMARINE THE BEATLES from **YELLOW SUBMARINE**

Why it was yellow and not some other colour is a mystery. So much so that the French, desperate for a rhyme, changed it to *vert*.

❹ GREEN GREEN GRASS OF HOME TOM JONES from **THE BEST OF TOM JONES**

From South Wales to New South Wales, farmers the world over use far too much fertiliser.

❺ BLUE JONI MITCHELL from **BLUE**

The title track of the Californian singer/songwriter's most iconic album.

❻ MOOD INDIGO NINA SIMONE from **NINA: THE ESSENTIAL NINA SIMONE**

What's bluer than blues? Ah, of course.

❼ PURPLE HAZE JIMI HENDRIX from **EXPERIENCE HENDRIX: THE BEST OF JIMI HENDRIX**

Not quite violet, but close enough. Love is the drug seems to be the basic message.

❽ CRIMSON AND CLOVER TOMMY JAMES & THE SHONDELLS from **ANTHOLOGY**

Double colours from the Pittsburgh band that brought you the original version of I Think We're Alone Now.

❾ WHITE LINES GRANDMASTER FLASH & MELLE MEL from **GREATEST HITS**

The anti-coke hip-hop smash backfired: many saw it as the best ever ad for charlie.

❿ BROWN SUGAR THE ROLLING STONES from **STICKY FINGERS**

Not one from the rainbow, granted, but it does feature one of pop music's most instantly recognizable riffs. A British band do America better than the Americans.

Jon Lusk

Coltrane on call

John Coltrane's place at the front of the stage in the Great Jazz Club In The Sky is safe, primarily as a result of his extraordinary feats as a bandleader (see overleaf). But every master was once a pupil, and Coltrane was given his first break as a relative unknown when he was picked in place of the great Sonny Rollins to be Miles Davis's tenor player. He was a fast learner, and graduated with honours.

❶ ROUND MIDNIGHT MILES DAVIS from **ROUND ABOUT MIDNIGHT**

Coltrane shows he can devote himself to a tune as well as improvise on it, supporting Miles's dry trumpet with deep, long notes.

❷ SALT PEANUTS MILES DAVIS from **STEAMIN' WITH THE MILES DAVIS QUINTET**

Coltrane and Davis do their cooler version of Bird 'n' Diz with this fast yet spacious track immortalized by the earlier duo.

❸ TRANE'S BLUES MILES DAVIS from **WORKIN' WITH THE MILES DAVIS QUINTET**

JC's unique style is already well in evidence in these sessions from 1956, and this blues provides an example of his early forays into composition.

❹ TENOR MADNESS SONNY ROLLINS from **TENOR MADNESS**

A fascinating opportunity to compare the two tenor giants of the day (Rollins being the better established). Much more anger is evident in Coltrane's playing.

❺ BLUES BY FIVE MILES DAVIS from **COOKIN' WITH THE MILES DAVIS QUINTET**

Coltrane's interpretation of the blues is clearly developing on this track as he seeks a middle way between Davis's "cool" and his own "fire".

Hugh Hopper picks
John Coltrane

HUGH HOPPER was, with Robert Wyatt, a founder member of the Canterbury group of musicians, who went on to form Soft Machine, Gong, Caravan, etc. He continues to record and play in many projects (see www.hughhopper.com) and cites Coltrane as his greatest jazz influence.

"John Coltrane came to prominence playing with Miles Davis – like so many other great musicians. But it was after he left Miles that he began to forge that totally dedicated music life. Surrounding himself with the energy of drummer Elvin Jones and the hypnotic piano of McCoy Tyner, he transcended jazz as it had been up to that time."

❶ AFRICA from AFRICA/BRASS
Two basses and McCoy Tyner chanting away, Coltrane wailing over Elvin Jones' jungle, Eric Dolphy's whooping brass arrangements.

❷ MR SYMS from COLTRANE PLAYS THE BLUES
A sad yet sweet mood. Coltrane just hints at a solo.

❸ TUNJI from COLTRANE
Absolutely pared-down modalism, with McCoy Tyner's hypnotic piano and Elvin's silky cymbals.

❹ SPIRITUAL from LIVE AT THE VILLAGE VANGUARD
The almost dirty sound of Eric Dolphy's bass clarinet alongside the classic Coltrane Quartet.

❺ CHASING THE TRANE from LIVE AT THE VILLAGE VANGUARD
Really a duet between Coltrane and Elvin. Total energy.

❻ SOUL EYES from COLTRANE IN A SOULFUL MOOD
Mal Waldron's ballad. Coltrane plays with deep soul and tenderness.

❼ DAHOMEY DANCE from OLÉ COLTRANE
Bassist Reggie Workman's ostinato octave riff started a whole new jazz feel.

❽ GREENSLEEVES from AFRICA/BRASS
One of the great 3/4-time epics that Coltrane loved to indulge in (alongside My Favourite Things and Inchworm). The rhythm section would work up a relentless steaming sound-scape for Coltrane's sax.

❾ TRANSITION from TRANSITION
Coltrane and Elvin's most extreme blast of pure energy. I can listen to this CD about once a year.

❿ BLUE TRAIN from BLUE TRAIN
Early Blue Note classic. Cooler than this you won't find.

❻ TRINKLE TINKLE THELONIOUS MONK from THELONIOUS MONK WITH JOHN COLTRANE
In some ways Coltrane seems more at home with Monk's disjointed and angular compositions than Miles; this track resulted from a short-lived though influential partnership.

❼ ON GREEN DOLPHIN STREET MILES DAVIS from '58 SESSIONS
From the first recordings by the sextet that would make the seminal A Kind of Blue, this warm, Bill Evans-inspired exposition features Coltrane and Cannonball Adderley sparring on saxes.

⑧ SID'S AHEAD MILES DAVIS from MILESTONES

Another blues, demonstrating the increasing confidence that would lead Coltrane to leave Miles Davis eighteen months later to form his own group. This is jazz soloing at its finest.

⑨ BLUE IN GREEN MILES DAVIS from KIND OF BLUE

One of Coltrane's most beautiful solos, perfectly constructed and demonstrating his ability to mould himself to another's vision.

⑩ ALL BLUES MILES DAVIS from KIND OF BLUE

On the greatest track on a great album, Coltrane –dark and brooding – and Cannonball – light and melodious – are in total harmony. Their different styles make a perfect whole.

Nat Defriend

Congolese

Congolese music – rumba, soukous, call it what you will – has been the core African dance sound for more than thirty years, influencing just about every other African pop style in existence.

❶ COOPERATION FRANCO & SAM MANGWANA From THE ROUGH GUIDE TO CONGOLESE SOUKOUS

From the first bars of the rousing guitar intro to the pure joy of the pair's vocal duelling, this is a bona fide classic.

❷ FRANCO & OK JAZZ MABELE from MABELE

A long, slow talking blues written by "le Poet" Simaro Lutumba and sung emotionally by Sam Mangwana.

❸ EL MANICERO BANTOUS DE LA CAPITALE from EL MANICERO

The all-time classic, Peanut Vendor, reprised here by two of Congo's finest saxophonsts and co-founders of this Brazzaville institution.

❹ L'UNION BISSO NA BISSO from RACINES

It's rap, but not as we know it. This mature, melodic and respectful track is a great intro to Passi's Parisian posse.

❺ SENTIMENT AWA ZAIKO LANGA LANGA from SENTIMENT AWA-ESSESSE

Fine melody, great harmonies and wild passion come together shortly before ZLL split acrimoniously.

❻ TWIST WITH THE DOCTEUR RYCO JAZZ from RUMBA'ROUND AFRICA

A Congolese take on 60s rockabilly which adds humour to the export rumba.

❼ CELIO CHOC STARS from LES MERVEILLES DU PASSÉ, CHOC STARS VOL 3

Sweet and soft, this marks the high spot for a formidable team of soukous crooners.

❽ LUFUA NDONGA KONONO NO1 from CONGOTRONICS

Smash-bang, low-tech urban reinventions of timeless ancestral music.

❾ MALI YA MUNGU MOSE FAN FAN from BAYEKELEYE

Gentle, introspective, semi-acoustic treatment of a typical Kikongo ballad by the one-time hard man of Congo guitar.

❿ SAMBA LITA BEMBO from KITA MATA ABC

Lita goes wild at the mic, while Stukas crank up the excitement level to fever pitch.

Graeme Ewens

Sam Cooke

The soul singer's soul singer, Cooke was the idol of everyone from Otis Redding to Aretha Franklin to Muhammad Ali and Rod Stewart. Selections #3–#10 are all Cooke compositions.

❶ ANY DAY NOW from SAM COOKE WITH THE SOUL STIRRERS

Cooke's consummate artistry and the intimacy of his approach take the listener close to heaven – just listen to how his voice roughens when he sings "sorrow".

② **WONDERFUL** from **SAM COOKE WITH THE SOUL STIRRERS**

This, the original, leaves its pop re-cut, Lovable, trailing in the dust, confirming that Cooke's gospel performances were his best.

③ **JESUS, WASH AWAY MY TROUBLES** from **SAM COOKE WITH THE SOUL STIRRERS**

Two minutes of aching, yearning beauty, simultaneously rough and smooth.

④ **NEARER TO THEE** from **THE GREAT 1955 SHRINE CONCERT**

Performing live in front of an ecstatic 6000-strong audience, Cooke and the Soul Stirrers strain every vocal chord in an epic eight-and-a half minute attempt to bring about the Second Coming through song. They nearly succeed.

⑤ **YOU SEND ME** from **PORTRAIT OF A LEGEND**

Melismatic magic. Cooke's transcendent voice and trademark yodel glides pure and free.

⑥ **WONDERFUL WORLD** from **PORTRAIT OF A LEGEND**

A pure pop masterpiece, and – perhaps – a coded plea for racial acceptance.

⑦ **TWISTING THE NIGHT AWAY** from **PORTRAIT OF A LEGEND**

The most memorable of Cooke's dance/party records, back when "gay" and "queen" signified very differently.

⑧ **THAT'S WHERE IT'S AT** from **PORTRAIT OF A LEGEND**

As gritty and soulful as Sam got on his studio recordings.

⑨ **BRING IT ON HOME TO ME** from **PORTRAIT OF A LEGEND**

Coming straight from the church, the call-and-response of Cooke and Lou Rawls' "yeah" is the icing on the cake of this oft-covered classic.

⑩ **A CHANGE IS GONNA COME** from **PORTRAIT OF A LEGEND**

Inspired by Dylan's Blowing In The Wind, Cooke's majestically orchestrated encapsulation of the black experience in pre-civil rights America became his musical epitaph after his shooting in a murky hotel incident.

Neil Foxlee

Julian Cope

Since dismantling Teardrop Explodes, Cope has gone from psyche-pop through 80s stadium rock into pagan krautrock. Here's a chronological way in.

① **KOLLY KIBBER'S BIRTHDAY** from **WORLD SHUT YOUR MOUTH**

Post-Teardrops psychedelia: a frantic drum machine, a Casiotone organ and Cope's non-sensically deep wordplay create an uptight urgency.

② **LUNATIC AND FIRE PISTOL** from **WORLD SHUT YOUR MOUTH**

His vocals have never been plummier, invoking village greens and gentleman soldiers on a breathless organ and oboe ballad.

③ **REYNARD THE FOX** from **FRIED**

Things get weirder – Julian morphs into a hunted fox on this glam-garage epic. This is Cope at his most lysergic, but also his most mysterious and compelling.

④ **WORLD SHUT YOUR MOUTH** from **SAINT JULIAN**

The self-deification now became unashamedly populist and found Cope in the charts wearing leather strides riding a killer riff.

⑤ **EAST EASY RIDER** from **PEGGY SUICIDE**

The best of an entire oeuvre of car songs by this eco-campaigner. Here he has baggy, rocky fun with his own contradictions.

⑥ **SAFE SURFER** from **PEGGY SUICIDE**

Like Neil Young jamming with the Spiders From Mars, this AIDS warning extracts the max from a one-line lyric and Michael Mooney's fantastically fried guitar.

❼ LAS VEGAS BASEMENT from PEGGY SUICIDE
Built around a cyclical bass riff as cavernous
and magical as the basement it hymns.

❽ UPWARDS AT 45ª from JEHOVAKILL
The angle is apparently of the penis on a pagan
symbol. Vocally Cope's never sounded so godly
as on this folk freakout from his challenging
but fun Krautrock period.

❾ TRY TRY TRY from 20 MOTHERS
A return to pop – and the charts – with this
jaunty, catchy ode to his mother.

❿ I WILL BE ABSORBED from CITIZEN CAIN'D
Not for the fainthearted, this is Cope at his
loosest, a 70s power trio jam positing death as
a reabsorbtion into nature.
Toby Manning

Elvis Costello

**His prolific, genre-hopping career has
delved into country, classical, jazz and R&B,
but to many he remains the prototypical
angry young man in glasses.**

❶ NO ACTION from THIS YEAR'S MODEL
A classic Elvis put-down – and extended pun –
snarled over a galloping riff and Pete Thomas's
manic drumming.

❷ BEYOND BELIEF from IMPERIAL BEDROOM
The fragmented lyrics, untraditional song
structure and vocals that seem to come from a
different direction each new line foreshadow a
taste for experimentation. Yet it still works as a
hook-filled pop song.

Elvis Costello's
Extreme restraint

**An inveterate list-maker, ELVIS COSTELLO
once published a list of his all-time
500 essential albums, with a key track
highlighted from each – and even then
he complained: "The minute this list goes
to press I will think of 20 records that I
left out…" Exercising extreme restraint,
here he plumps for 10 favourite African-
American records, drawn from jazz, blues
and classic soul.**

❶ LET'S DO IT (LET'S FALL IN LOVE) LOUIS
ARMSTRONG from BEST OF THE VERVE YEARS

**❷ I LOVE THE LIFE I LIVE (I LIVE THE LIFE
I LOVE)** MUDDY WATERS from THE ESSENTIAL
COLLECTION

❸ YESTERDAYS CLIFFORD BROWN from CLIFFORD
BROWN'S FINEST HOUR

❹ YOU AIN'T LIVIN' TILL YOU'RE LOVIN'
MARVIN GAYE from YOU'RE ALL I NEED [WITH TAMMI
TERRELL]

❺ DO RIGHT WOMAN, DO RIGHT MAN
ARETHA FRANKLIN from ATLANTIC RHYTHM & BLUES
VOL 6, 1965–1967

**❻ THE LOVE YOU SAVE (MAY BE YOUR
OWN)** JOE TEX from THE LOVE YOU SAVE

❼ BRING THE BOYS HOME FREDA PAYNE from
BAND OF GOLD: THE BEST OF FREDA PAYNE

❽ HIDDEN CHARMS HOWLIN' WOLF from CHESS
50TH ANNIVERSARY COLLECTION

❾ I'M A RAM AL GREEN from GETS NEXT TO YOU

❿ STEAL AWAY CHARLIE HADEN & HANK JONES
from STEAL AWAY

❸ KING HORSE from **GET HAPPY!**
Steve Nieve's cascading keyboards power and frame arguably the catchiest chorus of Elvis's career.

❹ I WANT YOU from **BLOOD AND CHOCOLATE**
Nearly seven minutes of tension, desperation and, ultimately, exhaustion, set to a spare, menacing guitar line.

❺ INVISIBLE MAN from **PUNCH THE CLOCK**
The horns add pep and sparkle to this supremely poppy confection, somewhat at odds with its narrator's struggles against a Big Brother-like world gone mad.

❻ POISONED ROSE from **KING OF AMERICA**
A big country ballad – with some typical Costello wordplay – that showcases the torch singer Elvis had been yearning to be from the start.

❼ (I DON'T WANT TO GO TO) CHELSEA from **THIS YEAR'S MODEL**
The thick bass rumble sounds like an invite to a fight, and Elvis's sneered vocals ("Capital punishment, she's last year's model") step up to meet the challenge.

❽ ACCIDENTS WILL HAPPEN from **ARMED FORCES**
His songwriting takes a leap in complexity, not to mention ambiguity; starting a song "Oh I just don't know where to begin" may still be his best joke yet.

❾ TOLEDO from **PAINTED FROM MEMORY**
Elvis goes lounge, effortlessly matching his tenor to a Bacharach melody, while damning an Ohio city in the process.

❿ COULDN'T CALL IT UNEXPECTED NO. 4 from **MIGHTY LIKE A ROSE**
A sweet, lilting melody that seems to have been rescued from a carnival junkyard. One of the highlights of a neglected album from 1991.

Andrew Rosenberg

Mary Coughlan

The Galway singer Mary Coughlan has done herself no commercial favours by being so hard to categorize: is this folk, or jazz, or blues, or all stations in-between? No matter: she has a voice so compelling that when she sings a song, you forget any other versions you've ever heard.

❶ DOUBLE CROSS from **TIRED AND EMOTIONAL**
"This is by an old ex-husband of mine", says Coughlan when she sings Double Cross live – and what a parting gift!

❷ I WANT TO BE SEDUCED from **TIRED AND EMOTIONAL**
Almost unaccompanied, Coughlan makes her intentions plain. Even the bass glissandos want in on the act.

❸ MY LAND IS TOO GREEN from **UNDER THE INFLUENCE**
This lulls you into a false sense of security by sounding like an old Irish ballad. Slowly the meaning creeps up on the hearer: this is an indictment of easy sentimentality and acquiescence in the face of sectarian violence.

❹ MOTHER'S LITTLE HELPER from **UNCERTAIN PLEASURES**
When Mick Jagger sang about what a drag it was getting old, he was play-acting. But Mary Coughlan knows all too well.

❺ MAGDALENE LAUNDRY from **SENTIMENTAL KILLER**
Coughlan isn't the only person to sing about the scandal of the Magdalene Laundries, where the fallen women of Ireland were pressed into service as launderers for Mother Church, but her defiant take is unforgettable.

❻ DAMN YOUR EYES from **LOVE FOR SALE**
This smouldering slow-burn blues uses her throaty growl to best effect, running from delicate precision to full-voiced wail.

❼ THAT FACE from **AFTER THE FALL**

Deceptively quiet piano ballads with a sting in the tail are a speciality in the Coughlan household: this Jimmy McCarthy-penned sleeper is one of her best.

❽ DETOUR AHEAD from **LONG HONEYMOON**

Greg Cohen was not the perfect producer for Coughlan on this album: he buried her voice under a morass of scratchy detail. But this song escaped free and clear, just piano and trumpet accompanying her down the road.

David Honigmann

Country Cheatin'

Love inspires good music, but the best stuff comes from good lovin' gone bad. Here are some country tunes in honor of that seven-year itch.

❶ WE'LL SWEEP OUT THE ASHES IN THE MORNING GRAM PARSONS WITH EMMYLOU HARRIS from **GRIEVOUS ANGEL**

Parsons' brief but influential career married rock with country. On this song, country remained a bachelor, and Parsons and Harris blend their voices in bittersweet harmony.

❷ JOLENE DOLLY PARTON from **THE ESSENTIAL DOLLY PARTON, VOL 2**

Desperation, Dolly's way. Her songwriting shines and her usual fresh-linen voice has bite on this track, one of her biggest hits.

❸ YOU AIN'T WOMAN ENOUGH LORETTA LYNN from **YOU AIN'T WOMAN ENOUGH**

A straight shooting, line-in-the-dirt song from the strong-voiced, strong-willed Lynn.

❹ FOOLIN' AROUND PATSY CLINE from **THE PATSY CLINE SHOWCASE WITH THE JORDANAIRES**

Cline belts out the part of the self-possessed cuckold in this Buck Owens tune while the legendary Jordanaires offering the finger-wagging backup.

❺ MOVE IT ON OVER HANK WILLIAMS from **GOLD**

When Williams moves into the doghouse, he brings a toothbrush. A warm and loose cheating song by the author of Your Cheatin' Heart, it was his first single to hit the Billboard charts for MGM.

❻ SNAKE IN THE HOUSE DEL McCOURY BAND from **COLD HARD FACTS**

The licks are hot, and the solos – each instrument gets one – are seamless. Jason Carter's fiddle slides through each verse and McCoury's voice is as high as the moon.

❼ FRANKIE AND JOHNNY JIMMIE ROGERS from **MY OLD PAL**

Recorded by everyone from Louis Armstrong and Duke Ellington to Elvis Presley and Doc Watson, this traditional ballad tells the tale of a woman who catches her true love in the act and then does him in. Rogers' version contains what others don't: his trademark yodel.

❽ DARK END OF THE STREET LINDA RONSTADT from **HEART LIKE A WHEEL**

The lyrics provide the time and the place; Ronstadt provides the voice, emotive, complicit and sultry. Just listening to it makes you feel like you're committing adultery.

❾ JACKSON JOHNNY CASH WITH JUNE CARTER from **AT FOLSOM PRISON**

One of the most upbeat and unapologetic of the cheating songs, perhaps because it's all threat and no follow through. Or perhaps because Johnny and June were so in love that we only hear the part about being married in a fever, and not the part about messin' around.

❿ DIM LIGHTS, THICK SMOKE (AND LOUD, LOUD MUSIC) MARTY STUART from **ONCE UPON A TIME**

Marty Stuart and company give a fiery, bluegrass treatment to Joe Maphis' honky-tonk classic about a faithful husband and his straying bride.

Madelyn Rosenberg

C

Brilliant covers

These interpretations go beyond mere homage, surpassing the originals for their style, innovation or just sheer audacity. See also Weird covers, under "W".

❶ MRS ROBINSON THE LEMONHEADS from **IT'S A SHAME ABOUT RAY**
Originally part of a UK-only EP, this rockin' version of Art & Paul's folk classic proved to be The Lemonheads' breakout hit.

❷ AT LAST I AM FREE ROBERT WYATT from **MID-EIGHTIES**
Okay, the Chic version is delightful. But Wyatt takes the song and does something extraordinary, slowing it beyond real, revealing the most poignant of lyrics.

❸ HURT JOHNNY CASH from **AMERICAN IV**
A hugely affecting rendition of the noisy Nine Inch Nails track, on which Cash leaves his vocal stamp, moulded from a lifetime's experience.

❹ NOTHING COMPARES 2 U SINÉAD O'CONNOR from **I DO NOT WANT WHAT I HAVEN'T GOT**
Written by Prince for The Family (part of his Paisley Park stable), O'Connor's definitive version of his tearjerking break-up song fully justified its global success.

❺ TAINTED LOVE SOFT CELL from **NON STOP EROTIC CABARET**
Marc Almond de-funks the 70s Gloria Jones track, excising the animated horns and the plunking basslines , but fills the void with posturing indignance and electro-histrionics.

❻ MS JACKSON THE VINES from **OUTTATHAWAY**
The Sydney band threw aside OutKast's R&B funk for acoustic guitar and Craig Nicholls' measured, elegiac delivery to create a moving modern rock ballad.

❼ ALL ALONG THE WATCHTOWER THE JIMI HENDRIX EXPERIENCE from **ELECTRIC LADYLAND**
Bob Dylan's original tale of revolution featured lyrics more arresting than the accompanying music, but when Hendrix dovetailed those words with equally dramatic instrumentation, the song was reborn as a rallying cry.

❽ SAILING STINA NORDENSTAM from **PEOPLE ARE STRANGE**
The Sutherland Bros/Rod Stewart schlock is stripped down to a few piano chords in this startling and affecting Stina reinvention.

❾ WONDERWALL RYAN ADAMS from **LOVE IS HELL**
This pared-down take on the Oasis hit needed only Adams' lilting vocals and an acoustic guitar to elevate it further. Noel Gallagher himself conceded after Adams' performance at a Manchester gig: "You can have that song, man, 'cos we could never quite get it right."

❿ MAD WORLD MICHAEL ANDREWS FEATURING GARY JULES from **DONNIE DARKO SOUNDTRACK**
Everyone who saw *Donnie Darko* adored the minimalist Tears for Fears cover that closed the movie. Andrews & Jules remodelled the song for a new generation, as far removed as possible from 80s synth stylings.

Ed Wright

Cowboy fantasies

Throughout the English speaking world, there's a peculiar and particular kind of guy who walks like he's wearing spurs and who stands at the bar like he's fixin' to draw on a mean hombre. Deep inside, he always wanted to be a cowboy. This is the soundtrack to his life.

❶ CHESTNUT MARE THE BYRDS from **UNTITLED/ UNISSUED**
The guy in this stoned country epic spends the whole of the song chasing after a horse with whom he plans to be friends for life. Whether the lyric "she'll be just like a wife" would get the green light these days is debatable but the piece still conjures up endless vistas.

❷ HORSE WITH NO NAME AMERICA from
THE DEFINITIVE AMERICA
Deliberate, monotone delivery of the verse lyrics evokes the unbroken scrub and dried out desert riverbeds crossed by our hero on his nameless horse. Nine days they rode out together and they didn't even exchange the most basic of social courtesies?

❸ RIDERS IN THE SKY MARTY ROBBINS from
THE BEST OF…
With its lyrics urging the traditionally godless cowpoke to mend his ways or else, this version of the spookiest of all cowboy songs turns on all the atmospheric tricks – echoing vocals, ringing guitar lines and fey backing calls of "Yippee-yi-yay, yippee-yi-yo".

❹ I'M SO LONESOME I COULD CRY COWBOY
JUNKIES from **THE TRINITY SESSION**
The CJs' superlative take on this old Hank Williams' classic manages to sound even more broken down and distraught than the original.

**❺ WHOOPEE TI YI YO – GET ALONG LITTLE
DOGIES** WOODY GUTHRIE from **THE VERY BEST OF…**
One of the wannabe cowboy's greatest singalong items, performed by one of the great folk artists of the 20th century.

❻ GAMBLER'S GUITAR RUSTY DRAPER from
GREATEST HITS OF…
Spend too long in the saddle and, like Rusty here, you'll start talking to your horse, to passing wildlife and to your 6-string buddy. The slightly deranged laughter that he affects between verses underlines the regret.

❼ NO MOTHER OR DAD LESTER FLATT & EARL
SCRUGGS from **A PROPER INTRODUCTION TO…**
A man shouldn't oughta ride the range without a heap of bluegrass a-loaded on his i-Pod, the more tear-jerking the better. Flatt and Scruggs get down to the eye-watering nitty gritty in this masterful story of orphans all alone.

❽ COWBOYS LIKE US GEORGE STRAIT from **LET
THERE BE ROCK**
Old-style waltz time number, dripping with fiddles and steel guitar flourishes. And even

though they're self-declared outlaws out on the run, George and his pals ride steel horses, probably manufactured by Harley.

❾ MY RIFLE, MY PONY AND ME DEAN MARTIN
from **THE VERY BEST OF… VOL 2**
Western guitars so clichéd you can hear the varnish peeling off them in embarrassment, and a lyric matched in cheesiness only by Dino's delivery of them, this is one of the all time great cowboy croon tunes.

❿ THE LAST COWBOY SONG JOHNNY CASH AND
WILLIE NELSON from **HIGHWAYMAN**
Sad as the death of your favourite horse, prime piece of cattle or even your wife, this is the kind of tune that has grown men complaining that the trail dust is making their eyes water.

Al Spicer

Credence Clearwater Revival

For a brief moment in the late 60s/early 70s, Credence were the biggest band in America, with their choogling, roots-based swamp rock coupled to the magnificent songwriting of John Fogarty (even if he did go on to write Status Quo's theme tune, Rockin' All over The World).

❶ SUSIE-Q from **CREDENCE CLEARWATER REVIVAL**
The 1957 Dale Hawkins hit became the definitive psychedelic, primal Credence stomp.

❷ PROUD MARY from **BAYOU COUNTRY**
John Fogarty came from California but few since Mark Twain have tapped more intuitively into the romantic imagery of the Old South.

❸ BORN ON THE BAYOU from **BAYOU COUNTRY**
Cajun queens and freight trains to New Orleans on the song that became their signature tune.

4 BAD MOON RISING from **GREEN RIVER**
Earthquakes and lightning, hurricanes a-blowing, rivers overflowing, and voices of rage and ruin. Fogarty conjures up a Biblical curse: concise, raw, rocking perfection.

5 DOWN ON THE CORNER from **WILLY AND THE POOR BOYS**
Perhaps the best song ever written about the sheer, funky joy of playing in a band.

6 FORTUNATE SON from **WILLY AND THE POOR BOYS**
It could have been a Springsteen song, as Fogarty shows who's really the boss when it comes to articulating life on the wrong-side-of-the-tracks.

7 I HEARD IT THROUGH THE GRAPEVINE from **COSMO'S FACTORY**
In stark contrast to Fogarty's two-and-a-half minute anthems, here are eleven glorious minutes of Credence's most epic choogling.

8 HAVE YOU EVER SEEN THE RAIN? from **PENDULUM**
That after six albums in two and a half years, Fogarty was *still* coming up with songs as strong as this was nothing less than astonishing.

9 HEY TONIGHT from **PENDULUM**
…as was the fact that this exuberant, life-enhancing gem only made the B-side of track nine above.

Nigel Williamson

Crosby, Stills, Nash (& Young)

They couldn't live together and they couldn't live apart. But there was something special when C, S, N and occasional Y stopped bickering for long enough to raise their voices in harmony. Neil Young's prolific solo career is dealt with elsewhere in this book, so most of these ten concentrate on CSN (together and solo), although old Shakey's Ohio simply couldn't be left out.

1 SUITE: JUDY BLUE EYES from **CROSBY, STILLS AND NASH**
Stephen Stills pours his heart out, after breaking up with Judy Collins, on the opening track of 1969's debut CSN album.

2 WOODEN SHIPS from **CROSBY, STILLS AND NASH**
Crosby's sci-fi tale of the aftermath of a nuclear holocaust ameliorated by some of CSN's sweetest harmonies.

3 MARRAKESH EXPRESS from **CROSBY, STILLS AND NASH**
Former Hollies-man Nash brings a breath of breezy pop fresh air to CSN's debut album.

4 DÉJÀ VU from **DÉJÀ VU**
Weird time signatures and dreamy harmonies combine magically on the Crosby-penned title track of the first CSN&Y album

5 CARRY ON from **DÉJÀ VU**
Captain Many Hands (as the multi-talented Stills was dubbed by his colleagues) at his life-affirming best.

6 COWBOY MOVIE from **IF I COULD ONLY REMEMBER MY NAME**
David Crosby's first solo album was a veritable West Coast jam session and included this brilliant Wild West allegory of the complicated relationships within CSN&Y.

7 PAGE 43 from **GRAHAM NASH/DAVID CROSBY**
Minus Stills and Young, a hidden gem of hippie philosophy from a 1972 duo album.

8 OHIO from **SO FAR**
Neil Young's angry reaction to the shooting of four protesting students at Kent State University was written one day, recorded the next and in stores a week later, giving CSNY an American Top 20 hit in summer 1970.

⑨ WOODSTOCK from **DEJA VU**
Joni Mitchell wrote Woodstock but as she wasn't actually there, it took CSN&Y (who were) to record the definitive version.

⑩ LOVE THE ONE YOU'RE WITH from **STEPHEN STILLS**
Not sure that Mrs Stills left waiting back at home would have approved the sentiment, but this was the highlight of Stills' first solo album and also heard to fine effect on the CSN&Y live album, *4 Way Street*.

Nigel Williamson

Cuban classics

For close on a century now, Cuba his given the world some of the best popular music going. Here are a few indelible gems from the Great Cuban Songbook.

① SON DE LA LOMA TRIO MATAMOROS from **CUBA: I AM TIME**
Miguel Matamoros has few equals in the history of Cuban song. You can almost hear the sugarcane rustling.

② YIRI YIRI BON BENY MORÉ from **BENY MORÉ: LA COLECCIÓN CUBANA**
The king of the mambo or "El Barbarito Del Ritmo" (the wild man of rhythm) sings this with such chutzpah, it feels like he's right there in front of you.

③ CUANDO SALI DE CUBA GUILLERMO PORTABALES from **EL CARRETERO**
So much aching nostalgia, patriotism and longing has seldom been invested in one song: "When I left Cuba, I left my life, my love.'" He went to live in Puerto Rico and was killed by a passing car after a gig.

④ BESAME MUCHO OMARA PORTUONDO from **OMARA PORTUONDO: LA COLECCIÓN CUBANA**
Cuba's evergreen diva does the business on this cabaret-style arrangement complete with dodgy electric guitar solo.

⑤ AL VAIVEN DE MI CARRETA ÑICO SAQUITO from **GOODBYE MR CAT**
An unforgettable nagging refrain on this surging guajira just burns itself into the brain. Born in 1901, Saquito was one of the most revered Cuban songwriters of the 20th century.

⑥ EL MANICERO (THE PEANUT VENDOR) ALBITA from **SON**
One of the most thoroughly covered Cuban songs ever (especially in West Africa) since Moisés Simon penned it in 1931. This Miami-based Cuban singer gives it her best shot.

⑦ SANTA BARBARA CELINA GONZÁLEZ from **SANTA BARBARA**
This feisty celebration of Chango – the West African god of thunder and lightning – from Cuba's Santería faith is easily the best-known song by this great Cuban icon.

⑧ GUAJIRA GUANTANAMIRA VIEJA TROVA SANTIAGUERA from **HOTEL ASTURIAS**
The now retired supergroup of veteran soneros from Santiago de Cuba did a highly original and atmospheric take on this infamous number composed by Joseito Fernandez in the 1930s. Everybody knows the tune!

⑨ TRES LINDAS CUBANAS RUBÉN GONZÁLEZ from **INTRODUCING...**
The much-loved late pianist who gained overdue international fame through his part in the Buena Vista Social Club is at his best on this elegant and swinging *danzón*. Sublime.

⑩ DOS GARDENIAS IBRAHIM FERRER from **BUENA VISTA SOCIAL CLUB**
A stellar version of this smoochy bolero, which catapulted the singer out of retirement.

Jon Lusk

The Cure

For almost thirty years Robert Smith and various cohorts have been churning out a unique brand of alternative pop. The

band's music has changed a great deal, and though many of Smith's biggest hits came from mid-period albums such as *Head On The Door* and *Kiss Me, Kiss Me, Kiss Me*, the real gems are to be found on sets from the group's early catalogue.

❶ 10.15 SATURDAY NIGHT from THREE IMAGINARY BOYS

A metronomic slice of claustrophobic punk – minimal and moody – and a great lyric.

❷ THREE IMAGINARY BOYS from THREE IMAGINARY BOYS

The Cure frequently closed their sets with a blinding, epic album title track and this is one of their best.

❸ KILLING AN ARAB from BOYS DON'T CRY

An early hit for the band, this nihilistic recontextualization of a scene from Albert Camus' *The Stranger* is an undisputed classic.

❹ FAITH from FAITH

One of their many stunning album epilogues, this time finding Smith at his most gloriously gloomy.

❺ PRIMARY from FAITH

The guitars chug like locomotives over a driving drum machine while Smith spits out the words of this great little single from 1981.

❻ AT NIGHT from SEVENTEEN SECONDS

The whole album, from 1980, is unmissable but this cut's frosty keyboard rumbles add venom to Smith's nocturnal phobias.

❼ A FOREST from SEVENTEEN SECONDS

It had to be here. This is the song that really put The Cure on the map and which became an immortal goth anthem.

❽ PLAY FOR TODAY from SEVENTEEN SECONDS

A great little song. Uncharacteristically chirpie for the period.

❾ ONE HUNDRED YEARS from PORNOGRAPHY

This track is a seething monster of dark imagery and densely layered sound – hard work, but worth it.

❿ PORNOGRAPHY from PORNOGRAPHY

Darker still, this album-closer is a majestic piece of music, its turmoil perhaps reflecting the fractured state of the band at the time.

Peter Buckley

Dance anthems

Taking you back to the old skool. This set of mood elevators will have you waving your arms in the air like you just don't care! Top one, Smiley t-shirts in da house! Sorted! Choooooooooooooooooooon!

Most of the singles below appear on countless house compilations.

❶ SWEET HARMONY (SAINTS & SINNERS MIX) LIQUID
Saints & Sinners mix of this heavenly soulful tune lays on even more maxi-diva vocals without taking anything from the dancing piano.

❷ GO SINGLE MOBY
Straight-edge 1994 dancefloor classic from a time when advertising deals were just a dream. This is a pure, head-clearing rush of a track.

❸ PROMISED LAND JOE SMOOTH from PROMISED LAND
Any mix of Joe Smooth's clubland triumph will do the trick. It's uplifting enough to get the straightest male strutting like a podium queen.

❹ BREAK 4 LOVE RAZE
Classic loved-up groove with soulful vocals and a melody that dances down from your fingertips to your knees, tickling all the way.

❺ PROFESSIONAL WIDOW SINGLE TORI AMOS (ARMAND VAN HELDEN MIX)
Armand's magic touch made Tori Amos, amazingly, a one-hit dancefloor wonder.

❻ (AMERICA) WHAT TIME IS LOVE THE KLF
Pre-millennial techno revision of their best-known hit throws everything including the kitchen sink in the mix – Volga Boatmen choruses, chants of "muu-muu" and more.

❼ DON'T YOU WANT ME FELIX
Delicious shivers of love-fear and paranoia turn into deep spine-massaging beats and skin-tingling keyboard riffs before the confidence-mashing vocal sets you to dance or die.

❽ INSOMNIA FAITHLESS
A hands aloft, blow your whistle, wide-eyed mood elevator of a track, sweetly reminiscent of those nights when we were all just too excited to sleep.

❾ I'M ALIVE STRETCH AND VERN
Cheesier than a double cheeseburger supreme with cheese sauce and extra cheese served on a cheesy bun, this is still a floor filler and will still one hundred percent mess with your head.

❿ FRENCH KISS LIL LOUIS & THE WORLD
One last rich slice of classic house for the big finish to get your funky self hot, sweaty and ready to pick up pneumonia as you wait in the taxi queue.

Al Spicer

Dancehall reggae

Practically all reggae gets played in a dancehall, but this, post-roots, late-1970s onwards material was made specifically for that purpose. That is to say there was never going to be too much to sit down and listen to and contemplate, and the subject matter was deliberately less spiritually and intellectually charged. Not that it was all sex and violence. The best ranks as the most exciting Jamaican music ever.

1 RING THE ALARM TENOR SAW from ORIGINAL STALAG 17–19

An urgent, pleading ode to the decline of sound systems due to police pressure and, by implication, the impending doom of the Jamaican music industry. But actually it's a pretty bouncy beat.

2 UNDER MI SLENG TENG WAYNE SMITH from SLENG TENG/PRINCE JAMMY'S COMPUTERIZED DUB

The first reggae track not to bother with a bassline, instead building itself up on a tiny Casio keyboard. It doesn't suffer in the slightest.

3 MR LOVER MAN SHABBA RANKS & MAXI PRIEST from MR MAXIMUM

The combination of the gruff-voiced Shabba and the sweetly-crooning Maxi Priest fitting round a suitably springy rhythm is a three-minute dancehall textbook.

4 GUNMAN MICHAEL PROPHET from GUNMAN

Jaunty condemnation of ghetto gunmen that, in structure, owes a great deal to roots reggae's traditional dub techniques, but does so with a deftly computerized punch.

5 HOW THE WEST WAS WON RANKING TOYAN from HOW THE WEST WAS WON

Real early dancehall, setting a righteous toast on top of a slowly-rocking rhythm so sparse you could drive a tractor around the gaps.

6 DISEASES MICHEGAN & SMILEY from DOWNPRESSION

Given the subject matter concerns Jah smiting the wicked with all manner of dreadful, deforming diseases, this is one of the most cheerful rhythms to come out of early dancehall.

7 ALMS HOUSE CAPLETON from THE BEST OF

Back to basics with a super-sparse backing track, but there's a lightness to Capleton's toasting that propels this track forward.

8 PRETTY LOOKS ISN'T ALL SANCHEZ from I CAN'T WAIT

Original dancehall had quite a tradition of updating classic rock steady rhythms, but Sanchez and later crooners updated whole songs. It works because his voice smoothes out any of the backing track's sharp edges.

9 IT'S GROWING GARNETT SILK from GOLD

One of modern Jamaican music's sweetest voices, that brought an increasingly longed-for tunefulness back into the dancehall, but managed not to lose the excitement.

10 DUPPY OR GUNMAN YELLOWMAN from DUPPY OR GUNMAN

You can't have a dancehall playlist without King Yellow in there somewhere, and, showing there was so much more to him than slackness, it's his playful sense of humour that drives this dubwise skit.

Lloyd Bradley

Miles Davis acoustic

It's taking nothing away from the "electric years" of Miles Davis to say that, for most of us fans, it's the acoustic albums we return to again and again. There's an intimacy in this work which never fails to reach across the decades – as in these few examples from the trumpeter's massive oeuvre.

1 BOPLICITY from BIRTH OF THE COOL

The most charming of all the gems from these 1949 sessions – Miles, at just 22, leading the nine-piece ensemble with his buttery trumpet, and announcing a new, "cool" aesthetic.

2 ROUND ABOUT MIDNIGHT from TALLEST TREES

Is this the greatest version of Thelonius Monk's much-recorded tune? Miles whispers eerily through the melody, setting up John Coltrane's menacing tenor for one of his classic solos.

3 I COULD WRITE A BOOK from RELAXIN'

Tossed off on the same day (in 1956) as the

track above, this is a candidate for most perfect jazz track ever: Miles' muted trumpet sketches a superbly poised solo before Philly Joe Jones' drums propel Coltrane into overdrive.

❹ **CHEZ LE PHOTOGRAPHE DU MOTEL** from L'ASCENSEUR POUR L'ECHAFAUD
The soundtrack to Louis Malle's thriller was recorded in one session while Miles and his group watched it on screen. It produced some of his most abstract and beautiful music.

❺ **SOMETHIN' ELSE** from SOMETHIN' ELSE
Miles's last date as sideman (1958), to the great altoist Cannonball Adderley, and he pulls out one of his greatest and fiercest blues solos.

❻ **MILESTONES** from MILESTONES
Childishly simple, and a modern jazz classic – one which, for the first time, eschewed continual chord changes in favour of looser "modes". Sidemen Adderley, Coltrane and pianist Red Garland all rise to the challenge.

❼ **GONE** from PORGY AND BESS
So many collaborations with arranger Gil Evans could make this list; this fast minor blues which Evans added to the Gershwin score shows Miles fusing melancholy and momentum.

❽ **BLUE IN GREEN** from KIND OF BLUE
All five tracks of this 1959 album are classics, but this ballad is the most affecting of them all – never did Miles sound so lonely, nor pianist Bill Evans so rhapsodic.

❾ **SOMEDAY MY PRINCE WILL COME** from SOMEDAY MY PRINCE WILL COME
Miles transmutes a Disney song into a mature lament, with great supporting solos from tenorists Hank Mobley and Coltrane.

❿ **ALL OF YOU** from MILES LIVE IN EUROPE
The 1963 live debut of the great quintet, with Herbie Hancock (23) and drummer Tony Williams (just 17), produced an uncompromising album, with this Cole Porter classic barely recognizable in Miles' inspired recomposition.

Alex Webb

Electric Miles

Even more radical a break with tradition than Bob Dylan going electric, Miles Davis plugging in and embracing the studio as a compositional tool was complete heresy to jazz orthodoxy. It also produced some of the most breathtaking and challenging music in recorded history.

❶ **IN A SILENT WAY/IT'S ABOUT THAT TIME** from IN A SILENT WAY
Constructed in the studio from vamps and grooves and solos, this is the record that launched jazz fusion in 1969.

❷ **BITCHES BREW** from BITCHES BREW
Distorted harmonics, huge blocky keyboards and a deep funk bottom make this 1970 track one of the most influential jazz recordings ever.

❸ **FUNKY TONK** from LIVE-EVIL
Davis' most fiery, most pulsating rhythmic experiment.

❹ **RIGHT OFF** from A TRIBUTE TO JACK JOHNSON
Davis, Herbie Hancock, guitarist John McLaughlin and bassist Michael Henderson channel Sly Stone into an unholy funk groove.

❺ **ON THE CORNER** from ON THE CORNER
McLaughlin is absolutely ferocious on this wah-wah monster, from 1972.

❻ **PRELUDE** from AGHARTA
With axe-slingers Reggie Lucas and Pete Cosey in tow, this 1976 combo may have been the greatest guitar band ever.

Peter Shapiro

De La Soul

De La Soul rewrote all the rules with their debut album, adding psychedelic colour to a stentorian hip-hop world.

1 THE MAGIC NUMBER from **3 FEET HIGH AND RISING**

Its distinctive opening riff quickly ushers in spritely, messy drums that seem to be so excited to be there they trip over themselves.

2 TREAD WATER from **3 FEET HIGH AND RISING**

The 60s backyard R&B sound that De La specialized in back then soundtracks the adventures of our three heroes as they swap lifestyle tips with Mr Squirrel, Mr Fish and Mr Monkey.

3 PLUG TUNIN' from **3 FEET HIGH AND RISING**

A honkin' horn riff, slowed down to an amenable sloth's pace, keeps a rendezvous with a naïve chorus of falsetto humming: the whole thing has a very cute, dayglo nostalgic vibe about it.

4 OODLES OF OS from **DE LA SOUL IS DEAD**

A rubbery double-bass descends repeatedly with a take-it-or-leave-it languor. "We're selling O's y'all", the trio inform us.

5 PEASE PORRIDGE from **DE LA SOUL IS DEAD**

A quirky, rattling tea-dance beat and explicit exhortations to tap-dance rub uneasily up against impatient, tetchy lyrics.

6 ITSOWEEZEE from **STAKES IS HIGH**

"I guess a diamond's just a rock with a name" muses Trugoy, pondering a failed love affair. A laidback electric piano shrugs philosophically. Eezee come, eezee go.

7 OOH from **ART OFFICIAL INTELLIGENCE: MOSAIC THUMP**

Listen past the squelchy moogs and you'll hear the same old see-saw rifferama that characterized De La's debut. The chorus has all the foolproof immediacy of an anthem and the drums are satisfyingly crunchy.

8 U CAN DO (LIFE) from **ART OFFICIAL INTELLIGENCE: MOSAIC THUMP**

Those synth sounds may be plain and unassuming, but they conceal a surprisingly subtle melody hiding down there in the low-end.

9 BIG BROTHER BEAT from **STAKES IS HIGH**

A gorgeous, murky bass riff is sprinkled with clipped techno bleeps: a welcoming carpet for guest rapper Mos Def. "We remain on your mind like skulls, not a golem" claim De La.

10 PATTI DUKE FROM **BUHLOONE MINDSTATE**

Knitting-needle jazz drums skipped along and, aided by a flute and a Gang Starr sample, De La convincingly tripped into the jazz-rap era.

Matt Milton

Death metal

With growling cookie-monster vocals and a predilection for thrashy gore this list is not for the squeamish.

1 BLACK SEEDS OF VENGEANCE NILE from **BLACK SEEDS OF VENGEANCE**

Death metal ancient Egyptian style. Ornate lyrics recount tales of terror from antiquity while the music swarms with the intensity of a desert storm.

2 BLINDED BY FEAR AT THE GATES from **SLAUGHTER OF THE SOUL**

A furious cut with flashes of tunefulness lurking beneath the aural violence.

3 CADAVERIC INCUBATOR OF ENDOPARASITES CARCASS from **SYMPHONIES OF SICKNESS**

Medical dictionaries and sick bags at the ready? A veritable soundtrack to an autopsy from these John Peel faves.

4 CURSE THE FLESH MORBID ANGEL from **HERETIC**

One from Deadly Time Changes R Us. A head-spinning amalgam of ultra-heavy mid-paced chuggery and lightning-fast kick-drum mayhem.

5 LIKE THIS WITH THE DEVIL ENTOMBED from **DCLXVI: TO RIDE, SHOOT STRAIGHT AND SPEAK THE TRUTH**

Grade A death'n'roll from the masters them-

Dani Filth's
Sanity checks

DANI FILTH is lead singer with British black metal band, Cradle Of Filth. He is possibly the only man to have been arrested at gunpoint in the Vatican for wearing a T-shirt boasting "I ♥ Satan". "These ten tracks", he says, "represent my sanity at the time of going to print. I had originally intended for the list to exceed ten thousand but I thought that would be a tad selfish in a book of this size. The songs listed have all poisoned my life in some way and given me avid, if not dangerous, inspiration."

❶ THE EVE OF THE WAR JEFF WAYNE from **THE WAR OF THE WORLDS**
Ever since hearing it as a child I have been in awe of this musical soundtrack. I know it sounds a little dated now (it's got bloody David Essex on it for chrissake!) but music should be a lot about creating nostalgia and the new film adaptation is just out.

❷ HALLOWED BE THY NAME IRON MAIDEN from **THE NUMBER OF THE BEAST**
Any Maiden song would do. I pick this because of its wending finality (it's about someone awaiting execution) and the sheer heart-rending melodic genius behind the guitar lines. Iron Maiden have a real talent for turning songs into stories. Which I like.

❸ THE IMPERIAL MARCH JOHN WILLIAMS from **THE EMPIRE STRIKES BACK SOUNDTRACK**
I have a passionate love of soundtracks and though I could name a few hundred greats, it is this song (Darth Vader's theme) that I want played at my funeral as my polished black casket is being loaded onto a Star Destroyer by a legion of crack imperial storm-troopers.

❹ GHOULS' NIGHT OUT THE MISFITS from **MISFITS**
The Misfits' punk greatness. They were the spirit of Halloween reincarnated as a band, and like the Ramones were full of two-minute hits.

❺ PAINKILLER JUDAS PRIEST from **PAINKILLER**
The ultimate heavy metal song. Full stop.

❻ POISON GIRL H.I.M. from **RAZORBLADE ROMANCE**
Wistful, romantic gothic rock that stirs the heart and is good to drive to – fast.

❼ RAINING BLOOD SLAYER from **REIGN IN BLOOD**
I distinctly remember my mother buying me this album, on request, for Christmas. Never equalled for savagery and atmosphere, the first riff is still the best announcement for the arrival of Satan's kingdom on earth.

❽ INTO THE INFINITY OF THOUGHTS EMPEROR from **IN THE NIGHTSIDE ECLIPSE**
The ultimate example of black metal. Forget production values and decrypting lyrical content, this is all about sonic weaponry and nocturnal ambience.

❾ SONNE RAMMSTEIN from **MUTTER**
A band full of soaring fire and flaming modern alchemy. This is morose, clinically industrial and, above all, symphonic – like some kind of Teutonic bio-mechanical musical chimera.

❿ SMACK MY BITCH UP/BREATHE THE PRODIGY from **THE FAT OF THE LAND**
I bought this album from Tesco as a way of putting my (then new) two and a half grand stereo through its paces. And what a way to deflower the virgin sub-woofers.

selves. Deadly thrash metal collides head-on with Motörhead.

6 PAIN THE BERZERKER from THE BERZERKER
Your worst nightmare turned into skin-flaying noise. Industrial strength percussion pushes the bpm meter well beyond meltdown.

7 SCORN IN FLAMES from COLONY
Essential melodic death-a-go-go. A gargantuan production sound coupled with complex riff harmonics and terrific widdling guitars.

8 ZOMBIE RITUAL from SCREAM BLOODY GORE BY DEATH
The clue is in the name. One of the most celebrated and influential extreme metal bands with a thrashy horror classic.

Essi Berelian

Deep Purple

With supernaturally talented Ritchie Blackmore on guitar, Purple were purveyors of classy, ear-bleeding heavy rock. Even without him, they cooked.

1 CHILD IN TIME from MADE IN JAPAN
A lengthy, hyper-indulgent version of a classic. It starts mellow enough but Gillan's awesome scream will send shivers through your soul.

2 DEMON'S EYE from FIREBALL
An ominous throbbing amplifier leads into a terrific heavy blues riff and Jon Lord delivers a cracking little keyboard solo.

3 HIGHWAY STAR from MACHINE HEAD
What an intro! That scream, those chugging riffs. This simply oozes rock'n'roll attitude and is, funnily enough, perfect for burning rubber.

4 SMOKE ON THE WATER from MACHINE HEAD
Inspiration to generations of rockers. A legend, pure and simple, featuring one of the best known riffs ever. Nuff said.

5 SPEED KING from IN ROCK
You'll swear you've blown your amp at the start cos it sure sounds like Blackmore's blown his. The definition of heavy rock.

6 STRANGE KIND OF WOMAN from MADE IN JAPAN
Is Gillan laughing halfway through? A great big swaggering rocker turned into a live epic with some wonderful instrumental excesses.

7 KNOCKING AT YOUR BACK DOOR from PERFECT STRANGERS
The 80s yielded some great material, not least this pumping effort with Gillan indulging in some typically smirk-inducing innuendo.

8 TED THE MECHANIC from PURPENDICULAR
Steve Morse replaced Blackmore years ago and Purple still rock very hard. Great, fret-shredding solos and Gillan never sounded better.

Essi Berelian

Depeche Mode

Quite simply, one of the great synth bands in the history of pop. They dominated the singles charts during the 1980s and early 90s and are still going strong.

1 BLASPHEMOUS RUMOURS from SOME GREAT REWARD
You want dark? How about midnight at the bottom of a mineshaft? Religion, attempted suicide and a car accident make for a bleak classic.

2 EVERYTHING COUNTS from CONSTRUCTION TIME AGAIN
It's a competitive world, indeed. The Mode boys clinically dissect the politics of greed helped by what sounds like a snake charmer.

3 HOME from ULTRA
Some sumptuously arranged strings almost take this (bizarrely) into Bond theme territory. Plush and soulful vocals from David Gahan too.

4 IT'S NO GOOD from ULTRA
This could have come from the soundtrack of a psycho-stalker thriller. Sounds like a love song until the lyrics sink in like a slow-acting poison.

5 MASTER AND SERVANT from 101
Less clinical than the studio version, the crowd here really sound like they're more than game for a little computerized domination and submission.

6 NEW LIFE from SPEAK & SPELL
Kraftwerk a-go-go! Sounds wonderfully naïve and youthful with loads of plinky-plonky synth noodling and a suitably robotic chorus.

7 PEOPLE ARE PEOPLE from SOME GREAT REWARD
A wonderful synth bassline, great clattering, metallic percussion and an instant chorus make this one of the band's finest tunes.

8 PERSONAL JESUS from VIOLATOR
Reach out and touch faith! Everything is great about this provocative gem, the intimate lyrics, the twangy riff and especially the bouncy rhythm track.

9 STRIPPED from 101
Sounds like the band were performing live in a steel foundry. Some seriously heavy clanging percussion give this a powerful industrial edge.

10 SWEETEST PERFECTION from VIOLATOR
This one will slither and creep up on you. The lyrics edge towards tormented obsession and the overload climax is beautifully orchestrated.

Essi Berelian

Detroit rockers

Maybe it's the noise of industry around them or all the fuel-injected cars or the mighty shadow of Motown, but rockers from the Motor City always turn out full-throttle, pedal-to-the-metal music.

1 JENNY TAKE A RIDE MITCH RYDER & THE DETROIT WHEELS from TAKE A RIDE
Rave-up mash-up of Chuck Willis' "CC Rider" and Little Richard's "Jenny Jenny" that was the birth of the Motor City's high energy rock tradition.

2 STORY OF MY LIFE UNRELATED SEGMENTS from WHERE YA GONNA GO
Some forty years later this remains the best garage record to be produced in Detroit.

3 I NEED YOU THE RATIONALS from THE RATIONALS
The link between the garage and The Stooges.

4 UP ALL NIGHT SRC from MILESTONES
An Ann Arbor classic that sounds like The Nazz, only a thousand times harder.

5 KICK OUT THE JAMS MC5 from KICK OUT THE JAMS
An unholy marriage of hippy and punk.

6 SUPER STUPID FUNKADELIC from MAGGOT BRAIN
George Clinton's troupe of merry pranksters bring it harder and faster than nearly anyone.

7 I GOT A RIGHT THE STOOGES from I GOT A RIGHT
They may have made more important records but none as fearsome as this.

8 CITY SLANG SONIC'S RENDEZVOUS BAND from CITY SLANG
High energy fury from veterans from the MC5, The Stooges and The Rationals.

9 WHAT I LIKE ABOUT YOU THE ROMANTICS from THE ROMANTICS
A great, great garage/power pop blast that would have sounded just as good in 1966 as it did in 1980.

10 FELL IN LOVE WITH A GIRL WHITE STRIPES from WHITE BLOOD CELLS
In which Jack White channels Iggy Stooge for 1:48.

Peter Shapiro

Dexys Midnight Runners

Passionate, intense, physically fit, disciplined and the tightest white soul band in decades, Dexys were marshalled by front man Kevin Rowland into shunning the very stimulants from which they took their name.

❶ GENO from **SEARCHING FOR THE YOUNG SOUL REBELS**
Check the lyrics, Kevin Rowland is a tough audience, a difficult man to impress even if you're Geno Washington. Then check the music – Dexys playing it just as hard, tight, fast and funky as The Ram Jam Band.

❷ THE CELTIC SOUL BROTHERS (MORE PLEASE THANK YOU) from **TOO-RYE-AY**
Exploding onto the stage of their pure passion soul revue show, Kevin and the gang flash all the floodlights and set off all the pyrotectnics.

❸ COME ON EILEEN from **TOO-RYE-AY**
The best sexual frustration song since the golden age of rock'n'roll. It stops dead, crawls back into slow life and pumps muscle up to a stomping climactic finish.

❹ JACKIE WILSON SAID (I'M IN HEAVEN WHEN YOU SMILE) from **TOO-RYE-AY**
One of the few men brave enough to attempt a Van Morrison cover, Kevin never quite succeeds in overshadowing the masterful soul musicians backing him up. Still good though.

❺ THERE THERE MY DEAR from **SEARCHING FOR THE YOUNG SOUL REBELS**
Sarcastic, bitchy, generally fantastic upbeat number with too many words crammed into the poor suffering musical spaces available.

❻ UNTIL I BELIEVE IN MY SOUL from **TOO-RYE-AY**
Soulful, melodramatic, shimmering, beautiful. With some fantastic horn work and the whole band at their pristine best, Kevin lets rip with his yodelling passionate spirit on display.

❼ MY NATIONAL PRIDE (FORMERLY KNOWLEDGE OF BEAUTY) from **DON'T STAND ME DOWN**
With Kevin at his uncompromising, ranting best and yet another total change of image, *Don't Stand Me Down* was destined to become a great lost album. A heart wrenching tune, too cruelly overlooked.

❽ I LOVE YOU (LISTEN TO THIS) from **DON'T STAND ME DOWN**
An absolute treat of a song. This is a desperate epic, sobbing and ebbing away with every throb of that vein at Kevin Rowland's temple.

Al Spicer

Dion

The Wanderer himself: Dion di Mucci. Or, in the words of Lou Reed, inducting him into The Rock'n'Roll Hall Of Fame in 1989: "Who could be hipper than Dion". Not a question, a statement.

❶ THE WANDERER from **DION & THE BELMONTS, LIVE AT THE MADISON SQUARE GARDEN 1972**
A classic Bronx-Brooklyn singalong, when The Wanderer & The Belmonts came back to perform their 1961 hit.

❷ PURPLE HAZE from **DION**
"We're going to the same place, different expression" – was Jimi's response to this 1968 folksy version of that acid-classic.

❸ THE TRUTH WILL SET YOU FREE from **INSIDE JOB**
Dion crossing over from Bronx-junkie to Catholic survivor, swapping junk for God in 1968.

❹ BORN TO BE WITH YOU from **DION: KING OF NEW YORK STREETS**
A perfect 76 wall-of-sound-production by fellow New Yorker Phil Spector.

Peter Shapiro's
Disco

PETER SHAPIRO is author of the acclaimed *Turn The Beat Around: The Secret History of Disco* (Faber, 2005). The book is, in his words, a trawl through the roots, development and excesses of "the music that taste forgot". It's an amazing story. Shapiro asserts that "although Disco may be the most maligned genre in human history, these are ten records no one should be ashamed of owning."

❶ LAW OF THE LAND THE TEMPTATIONS from MASTERPIECE
The relentless 4/4 beat marks this as most likely the first disco record.

❷ TEN PERCENT DOUBLE EXPOSURE from TEN PERCENT
The very first commercially available 12" single is also one of the very best thanks to a decadent mix by the great Walter Gibbons.

❸ DON'T LEAVE ME THIS WAY THELMA HOUSTON from ANY WAY YOU LIKE IT
Contains nearly every element of classic disco: the skipping hi-hats, the popping bassline, the slicing strings and the erotic, over-the-top, gospel-charged vocals.

❹ YOU MAKE ME FEEL (MIGHTY REAL) SYLVESTER from STEP II
With its synth licks, mechanized bassline and drum-machine beats, this was the genesis of

the disco sub-genre known as Hi-NRG, and one of the most glorious, uplifting records in the disco canon.

❺ WEEKEND PHREEK from DISCO CONNECTION (AUTHENTIC CLASSIC DISCO 1976–81)
A surging, percolating record that is all about dancefloor exorcism.

❻ I FEEL LOVE DONNA SUMMER from I REMEMBER YESTERDAY
The cocaine chill of the "Me Decade" in a nutshell.

❼ I WILL SURVIVE GLORIA GAYNOR from LOVE TRACKS
Moan and groan if you want, but ten million hen parties haven't managed to ruin what is the best disco record not made by Chic (who were so great they have their own playlist).

❽ DISCO CIRCUS MARTIN CIRCUS from MARTIN CIRCUS
Proof that daft European novelty records aren't necessarily the scourge of the earth.

❾ VERTIGO/RELIGHT MY FIRE DAN HARTMAN from RELIGHT MY FIRE
A record so good, not even Take That could mess it up.

❿ GO BANG #5 DINOSAUR L from 24->24 MUSIC
Crafted by the great disco maverick Arthur Russell, this is seven minutes of inspired dancefloor lunacy.

❺ NO ONE KNOWS from PRESENTING DION & THE BELMONTS
A teenage angst classic, telling of some heartbreakers he doowooped with the guys from Belmont Avenue. You can just see a young Brian Wilson humming along.

❻ BOOK OF DREAMS from DEJA NU
Dion cover of the Springsteen song. And he has the right: in one concert his backing singers included Lou Reed, Bruce Springsteen, Paul Simon and Billy Joel.

7 TURN ME LOOSE from **A TRIBUTE TO DOC POMUS**
Pomus wrote the song originally for Elvis, but then Fabian wrecked it. Dion wanted to do the song justice – and he did.

8 YOU MOVE ME from **LITTLE KINGS: LIVE IN NEW YORK**
"I love a good rock'n'roll song, you know, cars, girls, music," was Dion's comment on this recording, "There is a beauty in simplicity".

Werner Pieper

Divine Comedy

Neil Hannon's delicious and mischievous mix of big arrangements, gentle satire and Scott Walkerish crooning is utterly unique.

1 SOMETHING FOR THE WEEKEND from **CASANOVA**
The sleazy side of life, with a wonderfully dirty middle-aged chortle to get it going.

2 GENERATION SEX from **FIN DE SIÈCLE**
Jaunty satire of the sex-and-celebrity-obsessed generation.

3 NATIONAL EXPRESS from **FIN DE SIÈCLE**
Poking fun at cosily out-of-date UK institutions is one of Neil Hannon's favourite pastimes – and his delivery here, with its fantastically anachronistic backing vocals and characteristic croon, is perfectly judged.

4 SOMEONE from **A SHORT ALBUM ABOUT LOVE**
Brooding, big orchestration and Hannon's achingly emotional delivery make this the most dramatic song in the parade of dramatic songs that make up *A Short Album About Love*.

5 EVERYBODY KNOWS (EXCEPT YOU) from **A SHORT ALBUM ABOUT LOVE**
Neil Hannon at his most gentle on this straightforward love song. The words, arrangement and backing vocals are are glorious kitsch.

6 IN PURSUIT OF HAPPINESS from **A SHORT ALBUM ABOUT LOVE**
A great, lush, dramatic opener to the album, and it also, bizarrely, did time as a theme for BBC TV's *Tomorrow's World*.

7 COMMUTER LOVE from **FIN DE SIÈCLE**
Touching number about unrequited love on the morning train.

8 BECOMING MORE LIKE ALFIE from **CASANOVA**
Harking back to the risqué 1960s Michael Caine movie somehow perfectly encapsulates the Divine Comedy: saucy slap-and-tickle with a deeply serious underbelly.

Martin Dunford

Dizzee Rascal

The mouthy Dylan Mills graduated from pirate radio to become the UK grime scene's most charismatic voice.

1 FIX UP LOOK SHARP from **BOY IN DA CORNER**
Dizzee at his most hip-hop. Clangorously loud drums give Diz a hand telling us to pull our socks up.

2 LUCKY STAR BASEMENT JAXX from **LUCKY STAR**
Basement Jaxx throw everything but the kitchen sink onto this hysterically overwrought electro tune: plummy female vocals, cod-Asian fairground organs, Adam Ant-style "yee-hah!"s and, of course, guest rapper Dizzee's alarmingly dynamic chicken-like cadences.

3 OFF II WORK from **OFF II WORK**
Kicking off with some beautifully half-hearted whistling, this single is an irresistibly asthmatic off-key skank, with wheezing synth percussion and messy dub reggae snares. The most effervescent and carefree Dizzee's ever sounded (and on a song about work, too).

4 GET BY from **SHOWTIME**
A shadowy, wobbly bassline, a sibilant hi-hat, and an intermittent stagnant trickle of a syn-

thesizer clarion harden into the kind of slow, menacing dub Tricky used to make.

❺ KNOCK KNOCK from SHOWTIME
Dizzee turns the "Knock, knock" joke into a series of threats, while the music sounds as if the collected synths and drum machines of Jan Hammer, Ryuichi Sakamoto and Tangerine Dream are playing an aleatory string of their most tumescent noises.

Matt Milton

Dr Dre

From practically inventing West Coast electro-funk with World Class Wreckin' Cru to creating the blueprint for gangsta rap with NWA to birthing G-Funk as a solo artist, Dr Dre has started more mini-epochs in popular music than anyone this side of James Brown.

❶ CABBAGE PATCH WORLD CLASS WRECKIN' CRU from TURN OFF THE LIGHTS (BEFORE THE ATTITUDE)
For his first trick, Dre kick-starts the Cabbage Patch dance craze.

❷ HOUSE CALLS WORLD CLASS WRECKIN' CRU from TURN OFF THE LIGHTS (BEFORE THE ATTITUDE)
Proto-techno electro-funk from Dr Dre, "not your average gigolo".

❸ STRAIGHT OUTTA COMPTON NWA from STRAIGHT OUTTA COMPTON
Dre's drum machines knock you in the solar plexus like a gun butt.

❹ FUCK THE POLICE NWA from STRAIGHT OUTTA COMPTON
Dre is as unflinching as the rappers as they stare down the devil.

❺ ALWAYZ INTO SOMETHIN' NWA from EFIL4ZAGGIN
With its whining synth lick and rolling rhythm, this is the blueprint for G-Funk.

❻ DEEP COVER DR DRE from DEEP COVER
A beat more menacing and askew than anything trip-hop would come up with in five years of ripping it off.

❼ NUTHIN' BUT A G THANG DR DRE from THE CHRONIC
So effortlessly funky – the ultimate G-Funk anthem.

❽ CALIFORNIA LOVE 2PAC from ALL EYEZ ON ME
Bringing in Zapp's Roger Troutman to rock the Vocoder may have been the most inspired move of Dre's illustrious career.

❾ MY NAME IS EMINEM from THE SLIM SHADY LP
The kiddie park calliope keyboard and sing-song bassline helped propel Eminem towards superstardom.

❿ LET ME BLOW YA MIND EVE from SCORPION
The catchiest record Dre has made.

Peter Shapiro

Dr John

Over a long career, Mac Rebennack – aka Dr John – has played everything from R&B through psychedelic voodoo-rock to funk, jazz and swing, yet the spirit of everything he has done has remained rooted in the rich musical heritage of New Orleans.

❶ GRIS GRIS GUMBO YA-YA from GRIS GRIS
"They call me Dr John, known as the Night Tripper, got my bottle of gris gris in my hand…" Has rock'n'roll ever sounded more spooked?

❷ WALK ON GILDED SPLINTERS from GRIS GRIS
Forget Paul Weller's tame version. This is the real voodoo.

❸ RIGHT PLACE, WRONG TIME from IN THE RIGHT PLACE
Backed by The Meters and produced by Allen Toussaint, N'Awlins fonk at its rocking best.

4 SUCH A NIGHT from **THE LAST WALTZ**
The original was on the *In The Right Place* album but try this joyous live version backed by The Band at their farewell concert.

5 JUNKO PARTNER from **GUMBO**
A tribute to the music of New Orleans, the entire *Gumbo* album is a roots masterpiece but this syncopated take on a tune made famous by James Booker is a standout.

6 WHAT COMES AROUND (GOES AROUND) from **DESITIVELY BONAROO**
With Toussaint and The Meters back on board, this cut is even funkier – if that's possible – than anything on *Right Place, Wrong Time*.

7 GOIN' BACK TO NEW ORLEANS from **GOIN' BACK TO NEW ORLEANS**
A swinging, trumpet-driven tribute to the Crescent City featuring the Neville Brothers

on a tune written by Joe "Honeydripper" Liggins.

8 MAKIN' WHOOPEE from **IN A SENTIMENTAL MOOD**
A wonderfully brassy duet with Rickie Lee Jones that won a Grammy for best jazz vocal performance.

9 PARTY HELLFIRE from **IN ANUTHA ZONE**
In 1997, Parlophone decided to reinvent the good doctor by teaming him with the Britpop hordes. Against all the odds, the result was a great album that included this classic, featuring Paul Weller and Ocean Colour Scene.

10 I'M GONNA GO FISHIN' from **DUKE ELEGANT**
In the twilight of his career, Mac paid tribute to Ellington with an album of funk-fried versions of the Duke's tunes which showcased his own keyboard skills to thrilling effect.

Nigel Williamson

Dr John's
Big Easy

Since DR JOHN has been a New Orleans legend for half a century, it's hardly surprising that more than half of his list comes from the Crescent City.

1 PLEASE SEND ME SOMEONE TO LOVE PERCY MAYFIELD from **THE BEST OF PERCY MAYFIELD**

2 IN THE NIGHT PROFESSOR LONGHAIR from **FESS: THE PROFESSOR LONGHAIR ANTHOLOGY**

3 SOPHISTICATED CISSY THE METERS from **BEST OF THE METERS**

4 WILL THE CIRCLE BE UNBROKEN STAPLE SINGERS from **WILL THE CIRCLE BE UNBROKEN**

5 WHEN MY DREAMBOAT COMES HOME FATS DOMINO from **MY BLUE HEAVEN: THE BEST OF**

6 SWEET LITTLE ANGEL BB KING from **BEST OF BB KING**

7 SEVEN SPANISH ANGELS WILLIE NELSON & RAY CHARLES from **FRIENDSHIP**

8 TOUGH LOVER ETTA JAMES from **HICKORY DICKORY DOCK**

9 I WONDER LOUIS ARMSTRONG from **THE COMPLETE RCA VICTOR RECORDINGS**

10 MEET DE BOYS ON THE BATTLEFRONT WILD TCHOUPITOULAS from **WILD TCHOUPITOULAS**

The Doors

A psychedelic supernova of rock, blues, jazz, classical and Jim Morrison's transcendental poetry, The Doors are a genuine musical legend.

❶ LIGHT MY FIRE from **THE DOORS**
An obvious starter, but no other psychedelic rocker is as hypnotic as this 1967 American chart-topper, best heard in this extended LP version.

❷ RIDERS ON THE STORM from **L.A. WOMAN**
The hitchhiker's guide to hell, the hushed-and-damned atmosphere heightened by Jim Morrison overdubbing a whispered vocal on top of his singing.

❸ THE CRYSTAL SHIP from **THE DOORS**
A mesmerizing ballad of dream images melting in and out of focus, guided by Ray Manzarek's spellbinding blend of organ and piano.

❹ BREAK ON THROUGH (TO THE OTHER SIDE) from **THE DOORS**
A perfectly concise summary of Morrison's obsessions with breaking the barriers of ordinary experience, set to an explosive "bossa-nova meets Ray Charles" arrangement.

❺ L.A. WOMAN from **L.A. WOMAN**
Los Angeles's unofficial highway-cruising anthem, under which lies a cinéma vérité-like blues of the city's darker side.

❻ THE UNKNOWN SOLDIER from **WAITING FOR THE SUN**
The horrors of war, brought to life in the creepy bittersweetness of the verse, brutally killed in the mock-execution of the "instrumental" break.

❼ TAKE IT AS IT COMES from **THE DOORS**
Serene existentialism that soars like an arrow till the surprise dropout of everything save bass and drum near the end.

❽ HELLO, I LOVE YOU from **WAITING FOR THE SUN**
If it's a rip-off of the Kinks' All Day and All of the Night, at least it's a hell of a riff to rip off.

❾ PEOPLE ARE STRANGE from **STRANGE DAYS**
Bouncy dark carnival-saloon music strut, given an entirely different and disquieting dimension by the sober alienation of Morrison's words and voice.

❿ YOU'RE LOST LITTLE GIRL from **STRANGE DAYS**
Sex that's simultaneously dangerously threatening and irresistible: the supremely haunting, winding melody worthy of a horror flick.

Richie Unterberger

Nick Drake

The ultimate cult singer-songwriter, Nick Drake's idiosyncratic brand of reserved British folk-rock melancholy went virtually unheard in his brief lifetime – but that cult just grows and grows.

❶ HAZEY JANE II from **BRYTER LATER**
The surface prettiness of the motorway-cruising, brassy rock arrangement can't bury the uncertain doubt oozing from every pore of the lyrics and vocal.

❷ POOR BOY from **BRYTER LATER**
When the female backup singers on this languid soul-folk beauty croon "Oh poor boy, so sorry for himself," it's as close as Drake came to sly, self-deprecating wit.

❸ CELLO SONG from **FIVE LEAVES LEFT**
Marvellous fingerpicking guitar, haunting cello, and congas on an unclassifiable slice of autumnal brooding.

❹ AT THE CHIME OF A CITY CLOCK from **BRYTER LATER**
Great graceful string orchestration on this muted but chilling paean to urban loneliness. But is Drake reviling it or revelling in it?

⑤ SUNDAY from BRYTER LATER
Mixing folk-rock and baroque classical orchestration, *Bryter Later*'s closing instrumental says as much about fleeting hope and crushing disappointment as any of Drake's lyrics.

⑥ WAY TO BLUE from FIVE LEAVES LEFT
Not so much folk-rock as chamber folk, Drake's lilting regret accompanied only by Robert Kirby's sadness-soaked string arrangement.

⑦ I WAS MADE TO LOVE MAGIC from TIME OF NO REPLY
The finest delicately enunciated airy-fairy folk-rock song this side of Donovan who, incidentally, was probably more of an influence on Drake than many acknowledge.

⑧ STRANGE MEETING II from TIME OF NO REPLY
More Donovan influence on this posthumously released outtake, which boasts as captivating a minor-keyed melody as any of Drake's more renowned pieces.

⑨ ONE OF THESE THINGS FIRST from BRYTER LATER
He'd only just entered his 20, but Drake was already singing as though his life was a litany of missed opportunities.

⑩ NORTHERN SKY from BRYTER LATER
Amidst the repressed despair, a golden ray of hope strains toward the heavens on this effervescent, effortlessly engaging jazzy ballad.

Richie Unterberger

Drivetime

Songs in cars make a different kind of sense as your vehicle becomes a combination of walkman-on-wheels and leather-seated bedroom. But where you are makes a big difference. Drivetime in America summons up the intoxicating personal and sexual freedom of the open road. In the UK and Europe, it's about traffic jams, dodgy motors, and the ever-present risk of colliding with a ten-ton truck. Hence an extended list, split in two by continent.

ACROSS THE US

① NO PARTICULAR PLACE TO GO CHUCK BERRY from CHESS MASTERS
Riding around in his automobile, his baby beside him, Berry finds himself frustrated at his inability to unfasten her safety belt.

② PROMISED LAND JOHNNIE ALLAN from ANOTHER SATURDAY NIGHT
Johnnie Allan forgets one whole verse of Chuck Berry's classic, and you can hear his band members falling about behind him; and it's just perfect.

③ CAR WHEELS ON A GRAVEL ROAD LUCINDA WILLIAMS from CAR WHEELS ON A GRAVEL ROAD
The female Keith Richards hears the scrunch of tyres on gravel as both promise and threat.

④ FREEWAY OF LOVE ARETHA FRANKLIN from WHO'S ZOOMIN' WHO
Sharp and shiny pop-funk, as 1980s as a pillar-box-red G-reg Golf GTI.

⑤ WILLIN' LITTLE FEAT from LITTLE FEAT
Balladeering trucker takes the back roads so he won't get weighed.

⑥ PASSENGER IGGY POP from LUST FOR LIFE
Given how colossally stoned Iggy sounds, just be glad he isn't driving.

AND AROUND EUROPE

① DRIVING AWAY FROM HOME IT'S IMMATERIAL from LIFE'S HARD AND THEN YOU DIE
North-western one-hit wonders hymn the M62 If they're feeling ambitious, they might even make it to Glasgow.

② CARS AND GIRLS PREFAB SPROUT from FROM LANGLEY PARK TO MEMPHIS
A direct rebuke to Bruce Springsteen: some things, insist the fey rockers, mean much more than cars and girls.

❸ DRIVING IN MY CAR MADNESS from COMPLETE MADNESS

Nutty Boys buy a clunker from a North London Brazilian expat.

❹ STOLEN CAR BETH ORTON from CENTRAL RESERVATION

Folky electronica queen Beth Orton goes joyriding.

❺ AUTOBAHN KRAFTWERK from AUTOBAHN

The Dusseldorf robot-lovers at their most minimalist.

❻ THERE IS A LIGHT THAT NEVER GOES OUT THE SMITHS from THE QUEEN IS DEAD

Morrissey pleads with an unspecified lover to go out driving and to perish in a fiery collision; the way he puts it, it sounds not unattractive.

David Honigmann

Drug songs

"There's a hole in Daddy's arm where all the money goes". If only there was enough left over for the occasional CD, then we might have learned to avoid all this misery.

❶ WHITE LIGHT/WHITE HEAT VELVET UNDERGROUND from WHITE LIGHT/WHITE HEAT

The world's best song in praise of the world's best drugs; our old friends the central nervous system stimulants. All the fun of a seven-day weekend without having to deal with those awful dealers.

❷ MR PHARMACIST THE FALL from 458489 A SIDES

Following the punk rock belief of singing what you know about, Mark E Smith and The Fall carried out years of chemical research, one way and another, to prepare them spiritually and mentally for their own manic take on The Other Half's psychedelic garage rock triumph.

❸ TOO MUCH TO DREAM LAST NIGHT STIV BATORS from DISCONNECTED

Strangely poignant and fairly faithful version

of the Electric Prunes' original from the sadly missed Stiv (ex-Dead Boys), a man who genuinely did have too much last night every night.

❹ CHINESE ROCKS THE HEARTBREAKERS from L.A.M.F.

Penned by Dee Dee Ramone but initially turned down by his band, this song was credited to The Heartbreakers when they released it as a single. Although the royalties and hostility were eventually sorted out, there no beating the sense of "been there, done that, stole the T-shirt" in The Heartbreakers' definitive version.

❺ EBENEEZER GOODE THE SHAMEN from EBENEEZER GOODE

Deliriously "naughty naughty naughty", this is a chant'n'beats barely disguised tribute to the delights of an MDMA-assisted chemical smile. The accompanying video looked as if it was sponsored by the Ecstasy Marketing Board.

❻ I DON'T LIKE THE DRUGS (BUT THE DRUGS LIKE ME) MARILYN MANSON from MECHANICAL ANIMALS

Sexy tune – in a robotic, numb from the brain down kind of way – from Marilyn and the crew. But it sounds depressingly like the track was just one more damn thing to get out of the way before everyone could get back to powdering their noses in front of the mirror.

❼ PILLS THE NEW YORK DOLLS from THE NEW YORK DOLLS

"Taking this junk against my will"? Yeah, right. Any complaint about having to take drugs involuntarily is gonna sound a tad fake coming from the Big Apple's greatest ever set of fuck-ups. Still, a superb take on Bo Diddley's song.

❽ COMFORTABLY NUMB SCISSOR SISTERS – TIGA REMIX from THE REMIX! EP

Taking nothing from the sensitive Pink Floyd original but the lyrics, New York's Scissor Sisters updated this for the frantic pace and mind-boggling cocktails of today's music scene.

❾ COLD TURKEY PLASTIC ONO BAND from LIVE PEACE IN TORONTO

This live take of Lennon's withdrawal classic is rendered even more harrowing by the contribution of Yoko Ono (shut up in a bag on stage at the time).

❿ THE NEEDLE AND THE DAMAGE DONE NEIL YOUNG from **LIVE RUST**

On a good night, Neil can hush a stadium with this track, his own intensely personal contribution to the anti-heroin campaign. Then some pinhead yells "yeeeeeeeaaaahhh!" and the spell evaporates.

Al Spicer

Singing drummers

They don't just hit things you know.

❶ BACK OFF BOOGALOO RINGO STARR from **BLAST FROM YOUR PAST**

Ringo's rather groovy second solo single from 1971 on which he gets to moo about three notes with startling enthusiasm.

❷ HOTEL CALIFORNIA DON HENLEY from **HOTEL CALIFORNIA**

Henley's poignant vocal on The Eagles' 1976 epic of pessimistic LA soft rock helped the album become one of the biggest in history.

❸ THE NIGHT THEY DROVE OLD DIXIE DOWN LEVON HELM from **THE LAST WALTZ**

He had sung it on The Band's second album *The Band* in 1969 but Helm – vocalizing from behind his kit – performed Robbie Robertson's resonant tale of the US Civil War at the group's farewell concert in 1976 as though his life depended on it.

❹ SQUONK PHIL COLLINS from **TRICK OF THE TAIL**

With Genesis having trouble finding a replacement for Peter Gabriel, drummer Collins had a little go at this thunderous track and produced a soaring vocal; his fate was sealed.

❺ SILENCE IS GOLDEN DAVE MUNDEN from **CHIP, DAVE, ALAN AND RICK**

Just one of the lead vocalists in the harmony-laden Tremeloes but distinctive enough to take many a lead line on their various hits in the late 60s and early 70s.

❻ I'M NOT YOUR STEPPING STONE MICKEY DOLENZ from **MORE OF THE MONKEES**

He probably didn't play the galloping tom-tom part on the record, but he played it in later live performances and the sinister lead vocal on Tommy Boyce's manufactured garage classic is all Dolenz.

❼ WE'VE ONLY JUST BEGUN KAREN CARPENTER from **CLOSE TO YOU**

One of the great expressive pop voices of all time could also keep tidy time behind a kit but after initial Carpenters studio sessions usually left it to someone else.

❽ MOULDY OLD DOUGH NIGEL FLETCHER from **THE BEST OF LIEUTENANT PIGEON**

Not only was Fletcher responsible for co-writing the Lieutenant Pigeon 1972 novelty smash hit and the militaristic snare patter that drove the catchy beggar, he also got to growl "mouldy old dough" in the chorus at the same time.

Chris Ingham

Drum'n'bass

Drum'n'bass is too easily derided for being Heavy Metal's ugly, dance music cousin. These ten tracks show that there's loads of jazz, funk and pop sensibility lurking within the breaks. Dancefloor classics, one and all. They're all singles but available on compilations.

❶ INNER CITY LIFE GOLDIE/METALHEADZ

Metalheadz label owner and twisted graffiti artist applies visualization to the art of beat sculpture with engineer Rob Playford to create a soaring epic of soul and scope previously unheard in the genre.

❷ CIRCLES ADAM F

A clubland anthem that grew to a chart hit, still fresh whenever played. The art of sample had became skilful surgery in the hands of the producers by this time and here the 70s funk influence spins dizzying harmonies over synthetic beats to create futurejazz.

❸ PULP FICTION ALEX REECE

Simple yet deadly effective, Pulp Fiction's warping bassline and minimalist structure were like nothing before or since, shifting away from chopped breakbeats into two-step patterns.

❹ BROWN PAPER BAG RONI SIZE/REPRAZENT

Drum'n'bass shifted out of purely clubland mode into the live arena with the creation of Roni Size and his Full Cycle cohorts' Reprazent project. This track was a big part of it.

❺ SHAKE YOUR BODY SHY FX & T POWER

King of the party sound, Shy FX has a history of relatively few releases, but every one of them is essential. After a string of anthems, he hits his pinnacle (so far) with this, one of the most energetic singles ever to grace the UK Top 10.

❻ SUPER SHARP SHOOTER GANJA CREW

This is where it started for DJ Zinc, a prolific shapeshifter of an artist with a killer instinct for melody. The track intros at half-speed hip-hop tempo, before morphing into twisted drum'n'bass/jungle.

❼ MUSIC (I NEED YOU) LTJ BUKEM

The pioneer of melodic style drum & bass, Bukem opened the eyes of the Hardcore audience with this pivotal track.

❽ BODY ROCK SHIMON & ANDY C

Andy C, the biggest DJ in the drum'n'bass world, teams up with Shimon to rewrite the rules once again with this new take on the rhythmic DNA of the music's structure: a ludicrously springy bassline and triplet pattern beats, that won anthem status in the clubs.

❾ MUTANT REVISITED T POWER/DJ TRACE

Starting life as "Horny Mutant Jazz", a slower tempoed Scorcese-esque mindscape laden with lazy brass and scene setting vocal sam-

ples, T Power had his masterpiece twisted beyond recognition by DJ Trace – a pioneer of the subgenre Techstep. A classic to this day.

❿ LK DJ MARKY & XRS

Taking the drum'n'bass world by storm on his arrival in the UK from his native Brazil, DJ Marky and XRS created a sublime slice of music that brought a true breath of fresh air with its Latin guitar and skittering percussion.

Gavin McNamara/Paul Laidlaw

Dub

Popularized in Jamaica, dub is the technique of stretching, extending, remixing a record by dropping parts of the rhythm in and out of the mix, using EQ effects and altering the feel of the record with echo, delay and reverb. It is one of the most intoxicating sounds in music.

❶ SENSEMILLA KAYA DUB THE UPSETTERS from BLACKBOARD JUNGLE DUB

A union of titans: Lee Perry and King Tubby dub the heck out of the riddim of Bob Marley's Kaya.

❷ WATERGATE ROCK LARRY MARSHALL from I ADMIRE YOU IN DUB

King Tubby again remaking the track "with a flick of his musical wrists".

❸ RIVER NILE VERSION HERMAN CHIN LOY from AQUARIUS DUB

A quirky, offbeat version of Augustus Pablo's legendary East of the River Nile.

❹ SATIA KEITH HUDSON from PICK A DUB

Militant version of The Abyssinians' classic Satta Massa Gana.

❺ DUB FI GWAN KING TUBBY from DUB GONE CRAZY

Tubby takes a ride on Bunny Lee's fabled "flying cymbals".

❻ KING TUBBY MEETS ROCKERS UPTOWN
KING TUBBY/AUGUSTUS PABLO from KING TUBBY MEETS ROCKERS UPTOWN

Leagues deep, foggy, spacey – perhaps the pinnacle of dub.

❼ DREAD LION LEE "SCRATCH" PERRY & THE UPSETTERS from SUPER APE

Perry ditches the raw drum'n'bass sound in favour of layer upon layer of sound and effects.

❽ SATURDAY NIGHT STYLE MIKEY DREAD from AFRICAN ANTHEM

Derided by many purists as simple gimmickry, this is nevertheless a stunning sonic tour de force.

❾ CHAPTER THREE JOE GIBBS from AFRICAN DUB ALL MIGHTY CHAPTER THREE

Another dub dominated by sound effects rather than low end exploration but one that had a profound effect on the dancefloor.

❿ DOIN' THE BEST THAT I CAN BETTY LAVETTE from WEST END STORY VOLUME 2

Disco remix maestro Walter Gibbons shows what dub techniques can do for dance music.

Peter Shapiro

Dubstar

If popular music were a family, the underrated, underachieving Dubstar would probably be younger siblings to New Order, Pulp and Pet Shop Boys, with The Smiths their cousins. Their lyrics are funny, dark and tender, Steve Hillier's melodies are class, and Sarah Blackwood has one of the purest voices in British pop.

❶ BOW WOW NOW from STARS

The silly name belies a heartwrenching description of saying goodbye forever to your best friend.

❷ GHOST from GOODBYE

Daily routine can't mask a constant yearning for lost love. Again, Blackwood shows emotion can be expressed without gymnastics.

❸ POLESTAR from GOODBYE

Beautiful piano ballad. Newcastle has never sounded so poetic.

❹ SAY THE WORST THING FIRST from GOODBYE

Ugly truths are fearlessly confronted with sharp words, and producer Stephen Hague works his magic.

❺ STARS from DISGRACEFUL

The song that started it all off, with sliding bass, sparkling synths and Blackwood's melancholy northern-accented voice on top form.

❻ WHEN THE WORLD KNOWS YOUR NAME from MAKE IT BETTER

This heartbreaker is probably Dubstar's greatest moment. It's hard to stay composed when "the jukebox says our moment has arrived" and the chord change kicks in.

Rob Evers

Duets

Apart from opera and Broadway musicals, there aren't as many duets out there as you might imagine in the world of popular music. But these make you wish for more.

❶ I GOT U BABE SONNY & CHER from LOOK AT US

Romantic, bohemian and carefree, what pair of young lovers has not imagined this was written just for them?

❷ UNFORGETTABLE NAT KING COLE AND NATALIE COLE from UNFORGETTABLE

Some thought her duetting with her old man from beyond the grave was in bad taste. The five million who bought the album disagreed.

3 FAIRY TALE OF NEW YORK KIRSTY MacCOLL AND SHANE MacGOWAN from IF I SHOULD FALL FROM GRACE WITH GOD
Possibly the only cool Christmas song ever.

4 GIRL FROM THE NORTH COUNTRY BOB DYLAN AND JOHNNY CASH from NASHVILLE SKYLINE
The only track officially released from sessions for what remains one of the great lost albums of our time.

5 THIS ONE'S FROM THE HEART TOM WAITS AND CRYSTAL GAYLE from ONE FROM THE HEART
Beauty and the-beast – an improbable but inspired pairing.

6 ALL KINDS OF EVERYTHING SINEAD O'CONNOR AND TERRY HALL from COLLABORATIONS
You take a naff old Eurovision hit by Dana, an unhinged Irish diva and a grumpy bloke from The Specials and the result is genius.

7 HENRY LEE PJ HARVEY AND NICK CAVE from MURDER BALLADS
They both shared a dark side, which is what drew them together – and forced them apart.

8 JACKSON JOHNNY CASH AND JUNE CARTER CASH from JACKSON
George Jones and Tammy Wynette were the king and queen of country duets. But it's arguable whether they ever bettered this classic.

9 LOVE HURTS GRAM PARSONS AND EMMYLOU HARRIS from GRIEVOUS ANGEL
They were born to sing together and more than thirty years after his death, Emmylou is still the keeper of his flame.

10 AIN'T NO MOUNTAIN HIGH ENOUGH MARVIN GAYE & TAMMI TERRELL from UNITED
One of the most smouldering soul duets of all time.

Nigel Williamson

Duran Duran

Which one did you fancy? Two-Tone wedge-cut bassist John Taylor or singer Simon Le Bon? New Romantic froth rarely came better. The 1993 reunion was fun, too.

1 THE REFLEX from SEVEN AND THE RAGGED TIGER
The stuttering vocal intro lodges instantly in the brain instantly on this shamelessly polished, stadium-sized funk-pop.

2 THE CHAUFFEUR from RIO
A masterpiece of mood and atmosphere, charged with detached, voyeuristic sexual tension. Sing blue silver, indeed.

3 ORDINARY WORLD from THE WEDDING ALBUM
Mature songwriting ruled on this revivalist 1993 hit – Old Romanticism, if you will.

4 RIO from RIO
Ah, that video, the yacht, the supermodels, all that dayglo paint splashing around. A great Andy Taylor riff topped off with a suitably sultry sax solo. Effortless and chic.

5 GIRLS ON FILM from DURAN DURAN
Another great video, especially the X-rated late night version, and another pop classic. This is a perfect and preening hymn to a world of hedonistic decadence.

6 PLANET EARTH from DURAN DURAN
The epitome of New Romantic disco. The bouncing bassline demands you make a fool of yourself on the dancefloor.

7 ELECTRIC BARBARELLA from MEDAZZALAND
The 1997 album wasn't up to much but this single was terrific: a tale of fetishistic robot love that's creepy and addictive.

8 NEW MOON ON MONDAY from SEVEN AND THE RAGGED TIGER
Rhodes' keyboard flourishes *make* this track, with what can only be described as a sonic firework display in the middle.

⑨ LONELY IN YOUR NIGHTMARE from **RIO**
It sounds almost as if John Taylor is making his bass talk on this number, understated compared with the exuberant excesses of the band's big hits and all the better for it.

⑩ MY OWN WAY (SINGLE VERSION) from **RIO**
A brisk and sparkling funk gem decorated with splashy stabs of Technicolor disco strings missing from the album mix.

Essi Berelian

Ian Dury

Ian Dury's lyrics were poignant, confrontational and very funny. Combined with the Blockheads' funky music-hall style the result was a legend in British pop.

❶ HIT ME WITH YOUR RHYTHM STICK from **SEX & DRUGS & ROCK & ROLL – THE BEST OF**
Dury's having real fun with the lyrics and the joyously smooth disco vibes are simply terrific. Great sax and guitar solos too.

❷ MASH IT UP HARRY from **MR LOVE PANTS**
A brilliant latter day slice of Blockheads bravura with a cheeky, witty set of lyrics and a sublime swing to proceedings.

❸ MISCHIEF from **DO IT YOURSELF**
This sounds like an anarchist's manifesto set to a groovy rock track. Dury's soft almost understated delivery makes it all the funnier.

❹ REASONS TO BE CHEERFUL PART 3 from **SEX & DRUGS & ROCK & ROLL – THE BEST OF**
The NME dissed this as just a shopping list – but it's without doubt one of the best in pop history. Fantastic sax solo.

❺ SEX AND DRUGS AND ROCK AND ROLL from **SEX & DRUGS & ROCK & ROLL – THE BEST OF**
What else is there really? Dury talks complete sense here. Slinky ivory tinkling midway through, plus cool animal noises at the end.

❻ SPASTICUS AUTISTICUS from **LORD UPMINSTER**
Banned by the BBC, the frank and ironic lyrics will challenge your sensibilities but the relentlessly funky rhythms command you to dance.

❼ SWEET GENE VINCENT from **NEW BOOTS AND PANTIES!!**
Do you want to hear Dury doing sensitive instead of sweary? A wistful and nostalgic ballad opening leads to some good old fashioned rock'n'roll.

❽ THERE AIN'T HALF BEEN SOME CLEVER BASTARDS from **SEX & DRUGS & ROCK & ROLL – THE BEST OF**
Dury proves that swearing is big and clever. Where else would you find Noel Coward, Einstein and Van Gogh rubbing shoulders? Clever bastards one and all.

❾ UNEASY SUNNY DAY, HOTSY TOTSY from **DO IT YOURSELF**
Shut your gob! Up your bum! Dury's on a roll with this brisk trot of a political tune – if it doesn't make you laugh something's wrong.

❿ WAKE UP AND MAKE LOVE WITH ME from **NEW BOOTS AND PANTIES!!**
Great bassline, some fabulous Moog magic and some of Dury's most intimate, affectionate and funny lyrics.

Essi Berelian

Nigel Williamson on Bob Dylan

How do you deal with Dylan in a book of playlists? There really is no one to touch him in terms of essential catalogue: early acoustic Dylan, the electric rebel, the genius of rock's greatest album, *Blood on the Tracks*, and then the erratic deliverer, still reinventing himself, of the Never Ending Tour. NIGEL WILLIAMSON is a

contributing editor to this book and author of *The Rough Guide to Bob Dylan*. At his bidding, we have broken all rules and given Bob a mighty four-part überlist.

The protest years

When he arrived in Greenwich Village in early 1961, Dylan was a scruffy Woody Guthrie wannabe singing other people's songs. Within little more than a year, he'd become the foremost songwriter of his generation. Two years later he was ready to leave folk and protest behind and sail into new and uncharted waters. The times they were a-changin' and Bob was in one helluva hurry to stay ahead of them.

❶ BLOWING IN THE WIND from THE FREEWHEELIN' BOB DYLAN
How could you not start with this anthem? Yet oddly it was never a hit for Dylan, with Peter, Paul and Mary getting all the chart action.

❷ A HARD RAIN'S A GONNA FALL from THE FREEWHEELIN' BOB DYLAN
Inspired by the Cuban missile crisis, almost every line could have made a song in itself. Dylan said at the time he put them together because he didn't know if there'd be enough time left to write them all.

❸ DON'T THINK TWICE, IT'S ALL RIGHT from THE FREEWHEELIN' BOB DYLAN
He could write tender love songs, too, when he wasn't too busy putting the world to rights.

❹ MASTERS OF WAR from THE FREEWHEELIN' BOB DYLAN
The angriest, most potent protest song he ever wrote – and as relevant today as it was forty-something years ago.

❺ MIXED UP CONFUSON from BIOGRAPH
An early rocker recorded at the time of the *Freewheelin'* sessions that pointed the way to what was to happen when he went electric.

❻ THE TIMES THEY ARE A-CHANGIN' from NO DIRECTION HOME: THE SOUNDTRACK
Not the familiar studio version, but a jaw-dropping 1963 live performance featured in Martin Scorsese's splendid documentary.

❼ THE LONESOME DEATH OF HATTIE CARROLL from THE TIMES THEY ARE A CHANGIN'
Stunning storytelling on one of Bob's most effective protest songs. As objective as a newspaper report but with an emotional punch so strong it required no rhetorical flourishes.

❽ CHIMES OF FREEDOM from ANOTHER SIDE OF BOB DYLAN
For the countless, "accused, misused … the abandoned and forsaked" – Dylan at his most humane and universal. Critic Paul Williams reckoned it Bob's "Sermon On The Mount".

❾ TO RAMONA from ANOTHER SIDE OF BOB DYLAN
The best of the several songs inspired by the end of Dylan's relationship with Suze Rotolo. That was her on the cover of *Freewheelin'* and when she turned up in Scorsese's 2005 biopic she still looked like an angel.

❿ IT AIN'T ME BABE from ANOTHER SIDE OF BOB DYLAN
A farewell message to the folkies on his last all-acoustic album for almost thirty years.

Electric Messiah

Between 1965 and 1966, Dylan released the most audacious trilogy of rock albums ever made, a white-hot creative onslaught of breathtaking power and inventiveness. The folkies felt betrayed and booed him when he plugged in at Newport, backed by members of Paul Butterfield's blues band. Bloody but unbowed, his response was to recruit The Hawks (soon to become The Band) and launch a world tour.

❶ LIKE A ROLLING STONE from **LIVE 1966**

The infamous live version preceded by the shout of "Judas!". "I don't believe you. You're a liar", Dylan responds before turning to The Hawks and telling them to "Play fuckin' loud!" One of the most electrifying moments in rock'n'roll history.

❷ SUBTERRANEAN HOMESICK BLUES from **BRINGING IT ALL BACK HOME**

Chuck Berry meets Woody Guthrie.

❸ BALLAD OF A THIN MAN from **HIGHWAY 61 REVISITED**

Even Dylan has never sneered better than on this classic put-down.

❹ DESOLATION ROW from **HIGHWAY 61 REVISITED**

He may have gone rock'n'roll, but the poetry remained peerless and he could still name-check Ezra Pound *and* TS Eliot.

❺ VISIONS OF JOHANNA from **BLONDE ON BLONDE**

"Ain't it just like the night to play tricks when you're trying to be so quiet". Many will tell you this was his finest epic of all.

❻ SAD EYED LADY OF THE LOWLANDS from **BLONDE ON BLONDE**

The masterpiece that took up all of side four of Bob's 1966 double album.

❼ ONE OF US MUST KNOW (SOONER OR LATER) from **BLONDE ON BLONDE**

With Al Kooper's swirling organ, the epitome of what Dylan called "that wild mercury sound" and the first track recorded for *Blonde on Blonde*.

❽ POSITIVELY FOURTH STREET from **BIOGRAPH**

"You've got a lot of nerve to say you are my friend." Possibly the nastiest song ever written.

❾ CAN YOU PLEASE CRAWL OUT YOUR WINDOW from **BIOGRAPH**

Bob's third hit single in six months after Rolling Stone and Positively 4th Street.

❿ TELL ME, MOMMA from **LIVE 1966**

A brilliant song which Dylan tried recording for *Blonde on Blonde*. It officially saw the light of day on the live album from his 1966 tour, eventually released in 1998.

After the crash

After a motorcycle crash in the autumn of 1966, Dylan retreated to Woodstock. When he re-emerged with *John Wesley Harding* he sounded very different. His output over the next eight years was decidedly patchy. Yet it contained some fine songs, even before the release of 1975's *Blood On The Tracks*, one of his absolute masterpieces.

❶ THIS WHEEL'S ON FIRE from **THE BASEMENT TAPES**

A rare co-write with The Band's Rick Danko. The words may or may not refer to that famous motorcycle crash.

❷ I SHALL BE RELEASED from **THE BASEMENT TAPES**

Revenge, faith and acceptance – and a chorus that delivers salvation more convincingly than anything from his "born again" phase.

❸ ALL ALONG THE WATCHTOWER from **JOHN WESLEY HARDING**

Hendrix made the song his own and in concert Dylan follows the guitarist's super-charged arrangement. But the original has a stark and sombre beauty of its own.

❹ LAY LADY LAY from **NASHVILLE SKYLINE**

Believe it or not, the biggest hit single of his entire career…

❺ IF NOT FOR YOU from **NEW MORNING**

One of Dylan's simplest and most honest love songs, written for his wife Sara before it all went wrong (see #9, below).

❻ KNOCKING ON HEAVEN'S DOOR from **PAT GARRETT & BILLY THE KID**
It sounds like a hymn and it lifted the soundtrack of Sam Peckinpah's film to another level.

❼ FOREVER YOUNG from **PLANET WAVES**
Written for his youngest son Jakob, the only one of Dylan's children to follow him into the rock'n'roll life.

❽ TANGLED UP IN BLUE from **BLOOD ON THE TRACKS**
The opening track of the greatest break-up album ever written.

❾ IDIOT WIND from **BLOOD ON THE TRACKS**
"Peace and quiet's been avoiding me so long it seems like living hell". After ten years of marriage it was a very long way from "without your love I'd be nowhere at all" (see #5).

❿ SIMPLE TWIST OF FATE from **BLOOD ON THE TRACKS**
The softer side of the break-up – mournful, romantic and still hoping another twist might throw them back together again.

Bob ain't dead

You thought it was all over after *Blood On The Tracks*? Well it's not dark yet. In fact, it's not even getting there. Here are ten songs you need, from *Street Legal* onwards.

❶ HURRICANE from **DESIRE**
Hard on the heels of *Blood On The Tracks*, *Desire* got few plaudits. But for many it's an overlooked masterpiece and this song, with Dylan's voice counterpointed by Scarlet Rivera's violin, one of his great ever moments.

❷ CHANGING OF THE GUARDS from **STREET LEGAL**
A storming anger-charged momentum-laden anti-anthem. Like many of Bob's most rewarding songs, the precise meaning is wide open to interpretation.

❸ PRECIOUS ANGEL from **SLOW TRAIN COMING**
The most tender song from the first and best of the gospel albums (1979). Try those high notes yourself – they are not easy nor meant to be.

❹ BLIND WILLIE MCTELL from **THE BOOTLEG SERIES (VOL 3)**
A Deep South song from 1983 that would feel at home in any Dylan decade. Sin, the blues and one of Bob's most haunting tunes in honour of the legendary bluesman.

❺ JOKERMAN from **INFIDELS**
Lyrically a kind of Mr Tambourine Man for the 80s; musically just a nice cool breeze.

❻ BROWNSVILLE GIRL from **KNOCKED OUT LOADED**
Dylan goes to the movies in 1985. He's in the front row with soaring girlie chorus watching Gregory Peck. Or is it Gregory Peck?

❼ TWEETER AND THE MONKEY MAN from **TRAVELLING WILBURYS VOL 1**
A New Jersey crime thriller yarn with the poser: who is the monkey man? The vocalist – on *Blonde on Blonde* style form – is easier to suss on this 1988 outing.

❽ CAN'T WAIT from **TIME OUT OF MIND**
Dylan twanging and impatient – full of a taut energy rare in an otherwise magnificently resigned must-have album from 1997.

❾ NOT DARK YET from **TIME OUT OF MIND**
Dylan seems to foresee his death: "It's not dark yet, but it's getting there." Emmylou Harris reckoned it "the greatest song ever about growing old… it brings up things we didn't even know we were capable of feeling".

❿ THINGS HAVE CHANGED from **THE BEST OF BOB DYLAN (VOL 2)**
Dylan for the couldn't care less generation, used in the 1999 movie, *Wonder Boys*. Almost bouncy. The times had achanged again.

Nigel Williamson/Andrew Lockett

Dylan covers

They didn't necessarily *improve* on the originals, but all these interpretations added something fresh and new.

❶ MR TAMBOURINE MAN THE BYRDS from MR TAMBOURINE MAN

The rhythm was changed from 3/4 to 4/4, McGuinn added his jangling electric twelve-string, and folk-rock was born.

❷ WHEN I PAINT MY MASTERPIECE THE BAND from CAHOOTS

They'd backed him when he was being booed and they let him record *The Basement Tapes* at their house, so it was no surprise that they covered him better than most.

❸ THIS WHEEL'S ON FIRE JULIE DRISCOLL, BRIAN AUGER & THE TRINITY from A KIND OF LOVE IN

The spookiest version ever of one of Dylan's spookiest songs – later adopted as the theme of TV comedy *Absolutely Fabulous*.

❹ PERCY'S SONG FAIRPORT CONVENTION from UNHALFBRICKING

A heartbreaking vocal from the late Sandy Denny on a song Dylan himself didn't officially release until 16 years later.

❺ IT AIN'T ME BABE JOHNNY CASH from THE ESSENTIAL JOHNNY CASH

Well, he could sing anything and make it sound his own – even a Nine Inch Nails song.

❻ ALL ALONG THE WATCHTOWER JIMI HENDRIX EXPERIENCE from ELECTRIC LADYLAND

After this, the song was never the same again and even Dylan copied Hendrix's arrangement in concert.

❼ LIKE A ROLLING STONE SPIRIT from SPIRIT OF '76

The hardest jewel in the Dylan crown to cover, Randy California's band managed it by shrouding the song in a shimmering, ethereal beauty.

❽ CHIMES OF FREEDOM YOUSSOU N'DOUR from WOMMAT (THE GUIDE)

A protest anthem given an entirely new meaning in an African context.

❾ EVERY GRAIN OF SAND EMMYLOU HARRIS from WRECKING BALL

An almost spiritual version of one of Dylan's later masterpieces.

❿ MAGGIE'S FARM THE SPECIALS from THE SINGLES COLLECTION

It's 1981 and Thatcherism is in full cry, so you can guess which Maggie they didn't want to work for.

Nigel Williamson

Eagles & Doobies

LA country-flavoured rock dominated the US Top 40 throughout the 70s and, to a degree, still does: The Eagles' Greatest Hits is the biggest-selling album of all time.

❶ HOTEL CALIFORNIA THE EAGLES from HOTEL CALIFORNIA
Perhaps the most paranoid track about being a crazy rock star ever written. Should be declared California's state anthem.

❷ DESPERADO THE EAGLES from DESPERADO
Guaranteed to moisten eyes in biker bars across the US.

❸ TAKE IT EASY THE EAGLES from THE EAGLES
Co-written by Jackson Browne, this power ballad defined LA as the place for laidback dudes who, while getting high and rich, philosophized about life.

❹ TAKE IT TO THE LIMIT THE EAGLES from ONE OF THESE NIGHTS
Fine harmony vocals caress a very LA lyric, helping to build this slice of country rock into a man's-gotta-do-what-he's-gotta-do epic.

❺ LIFE IN THE FAST LANE THE EAGLES from HOTEL CALIFORNIA
Joe Walsh is snarling on guitar and the boys are telling how tough you gotta be to cope with all the women, drugs and fame. A record so macho it'll put hairs on your chest.

❻ BLACK WATER THE DOOBIE BROTHERS from WHAT WERE ONCE VICES ARE NOW HABITS
Country rock never had a tighter groove than this US #1 hit from 1974. As the chorus bubbles up you can't help being hooked.

❼ JESUS IS JUST ALRIGHT THE DOOBIE BROTHERS from TOULOUSE STREET
Jesus rock never really took off but this snappy, gospel-flavoured hit is a cool tribute to J Christ, man o' the people.

❽ TAKIN' IT TO THE STREETS THE DOOBIE BROTHERS from TAKIN' IT TO THE STREETS
For white boys, The Doobies were pretty funky, especially on this track, to which ex-Steely Dan vocalist Michael McDonald brings an R&B flavour.

❾ LISTEN TO THE MUSIC THE DOOBIE BROTHERS from TOULOUSE STREET
An annoyingly infectious early 70s tune. Lots of "whoo whoos" that today go down well in karaoke clubs.

❿ WHAT A FOOL BELIEVES THE DOOBIE BROTHERS from MINUTE BY MINUTE
Classic slice of blue-eyed soul that topped charts internationally.

Garth Cartwright

Steve Earle

Drugs, divorce, jail – Steve Earle's motto seems to be that you can't sing about it if you haven't lived it. Here are ten of his most uncompromising positions.

❶ GUITAR TOWN from GUITAR TOWN
Not so much an anthem as a manifesto: "Gotta keep rockin' while I still can/I gotta two pack habit and a motel tan/But when my boots hit the boards I'm a brand new man/With my back to the riser, I make my stand."

❷ COPPERHEAD ROAD from COPPERHEAD ROAD
Magnificent twang-infested hard-rock on a

knock-'em-dead tale of hillbilly bootleggers turned 'Nam vet drug-runners.

❸ THE DEVIL'S RIGHT HAND from
COPPERHEAD ROAD
The original country outlaw Waylon Jennings covered it – but this is still the definitive renegade version.

❹ JOHNNY COME LATELY from
COPPERHEAD ROAD
Backed by The Pogues with predictably rowdy and rousing results.

❺ GOODBYE from **TRAIN A-COMIN'**
One of Earle's tenderest lost-love songs, written for his first album after his release from jail (and then brilliantly covered by Emmylou Harris).

❻ CHRISTMAS IN WASHINGTON from
EL CORAZON
"Come back Woody Guthrie, come back to us now…" If he did, he'd probably be Steve Earle.

❼ ELLIS UNIT ONE from **DEAD MAN WALKING SOUNDTRACK**
Written for Tim Robbins' death-row movie – "even Jesus couldn't save me, though I know he did his best…"

❽ THE MOUNTAIN from **THE MOUNTAIN**
The best track from an album recorded with the Del McCoury Band. Bluegrass hadn't sounded this *edgy* in decades.

❾ OVER YONDER (JONATHAN'S SONG) from
TRANSCENDENTAL BLUES
An even more unflinching treatment of the same subject as Ellis Unit One, made more personal by being about Jonathan Wayne Nobles, whom Earle befriended and then watched die in the electric chair.

❿ JOHN WALKER'S BLUES from **JERUSALEM**
Who else would or could write a song from the point of view of an incarcerated American Taliban fighter, other than the Woody Guthrie of his times?

Nigel Williamson

Easy Rider

If the morning bus ride to work takes place in your imagination on a throbbing Harley on a dead-straight stretch of two-lane blacktop, then this is the soundtrack you've been searching for. Whip out those mirror shades, give the finger to the man and let's burn rubber.

❶ MOTORBIKIN' DEE DEE RAMONE from
GREATEST & LATEST
The original lacks the guts of Dee Dee's version, to which Chris Spedding (who wrote the song and took it to the charts back in 1977) chips in guitar skills and studio expertise.

❷ BORN TO BE WILD THE CULT from **ELECTRIC**
Ian Astbury gets back to his hard-rockin' roots in this superior reworking of the old Steppenwolf number. Rick Rubin's masterful production adds a hard and sharp 80s edge.

❸ WHITE LINE FEVER MERLE HAGGARD from
OKIE FROM MUSKOGEE
Your bike might be fast, but Merle reminds you that no matter what you do, "the years keep flying by like the highline poles" and that all those miles will just put wrinkles on your forehead.

❹ THE ROAD'S MY MIDDLE NAME
BONNIE RAITT from **NICK OF TIME**
She's wild and free, and she lives for the thrill of a motorcycle ride. Sadly, she doesn't exist – except in songs like this gem from Bonnie.

❺ MOTORBIKE BEAT THE REVILLOS from
TOTALLY ALIVE IN LONDON
A cylinder-cracking piece of rock'n'roll, complete with engine effect and the echoing vocals of Ms Fay Fife.

❻ ROLL ON DOWN THE HIGHWAY
BACHMAN-TURNER OVERDRIVE from **THE COLLECTION**
The big, bearded fellers from Canada tell it like it is in this slice of motorcycle outlaw life. Will make you yearn for the smell of petrol.

❼ TWO-LANE BLACKTOP ROB ZOMBIE from
PAST, PRESENT AND FUTURE

Hard-grinding road song that revs and throttles like an overloaded Bonneville pushing over a bad stretch of hill.

❽ TAKE THE HIGHWAY THE MARSHALL TUCKER BAND from ANTHOLOGY: THE FIRST 30 YEARS

A country-coloured tale of farewell in which the pull of the endless trail wins out over the desire to remain with the one you love.

Al Spicer

Eels

Eels – really just Mark Everett, or "E" – have been turning out weird, well-crafted, Aaron Copland-esque pop for over a decade.

❶ OVERTURE from OH, WHAT A
BEAUTIFUL MORNING

From the live album, this Eels primer blends bits of all the band's hits into a theatrical, over-the-top overture.

❷ NOVOCAINE FOR THE SOUL from
BEAUTIFUL FREAK

Eels' big break in the mid-90s, much weirder than most radio hits, and still sounding fresh a decade later.

❸ LAST STOP: THIS TOWN from
ELECTRO-SHOCK BLUES

Bizarre baroque pop song, one of E's best, with an infectious rhythm track, shout-along chorus and guitar freakout bridge.

❹ CLIMBING TO THE MOON from
ELECTRO-SHOCK BLUES

Heartbreaking centrepiece of E's best record, perhaps written from the perspective of his late, mentally ill sister.

❺ GRACE KELLY BLUES from DAISIES OF
THE GALAXY

The forlorn, pedal steel-adorned first track from

E's "happy" album, with joyful lyrics like "I think, you know, I'll be okay".

❻ MR E'S BEAUTIFUL BLUES from DAISIES OF
THE GALAXY

One of E's catchiest pop gems, and typical of his foul-mouthed enthusiasm for life: "Goddamn right it's a beautiful day".

❼ SOULJACKER, PART 1 from SOULJACKER

The standout from Everett's "hard" album, a grungey, tribal, fuzzed-out rave-up about a serial killer called "Souljacker".

❽ RAILROAD MAN from BLINKING LIGHTS AND
OTHER REVELATIONS

E heads out on the rails in this foot-tappin', countryfied ramblin' song from his return-to-form album.

**❾ THINGS THE GRANDCHILDREN SHOULD
KNOW** from BLINKING LIGHTS AND OTHER REVELATIONS

E's last will and testament, where the enigmatic songwriter declares: "If I had to do it all over again, it's something I'd like to do".

❿ P.S. YOU ROCK MY WORLD from
ELECTRO-SHOCK BLUES

Electro-Shock Blues, which grew out of the death of E's mother and sister, ends with this tragic yet oddly life-affirming masterpiece.

Hunter Slaton

English eccentrics

Be they quirky, irritating or just plain mad, the eccentrics of gentle English pop are numerous enough to fill a laughing academy all their own.

❶ TRAMS OF OLD LONDON ROBYN HITCHCOCK
from I OFTEN DREAM OF TRAINS

A lovely evocation of some of the city's most charming street names and districts, marred only by the unforgivable couplet "Oh, it seems like ancient myth/They once ran to Hammersmith".

❷ GOOD BOY KEVIN COYNE from **MARJORY RAZORBLADE**
Viciously patronizing compliments from some unspecified authority blended with hostility from ill-defined peers and accompanied by the most angry acoustic guitar you've ever heard.

❸ SUNSHINE SUPERMAN DONOVAN from **SUNSHINE SUPERMAN**
Once he stumbled out of Dylan's shadow, Donovan created some great psychedelia, such as this splendid little number, which struts like a hippy grooving up Portobello Road.

❹ KING'S LEAD HAT BRIAN ENO from **BEFORE AND AFTER SCIENCE**
Gleefully intense, happily pointless and guaranteed to pack experimental disco dancefloors, this is Eno at his pre-ambient best, all feathers, flounces and random synth settings.

❺ AT LAST I AM FREE ROBERT WYATT from **HIS GREATEST MISSES**
Wyatt couldn't have picked a more poignant tune to cover, and couldn't have treated it with greater respect.

❻ EFFERVESCING ELEPHANT SYD BARRETT from **BARRETT/THE MADCAP LAUGHS**
Before the Pink Floyd founder plunged into seclusion, he recorded a brace of solo albums that show him still welling over with creativity and stoned stories for kids, like this charming tale of life in the jungle.

❼ CRACKS ARE SHOWING VIV STANSHALL from **TEDDY BOYS DON'T KNIT**
After the Bonzo Dog Band, Viv made it to the studio on several occasions, letting a hint of his madness and misery slip through into tracks such as this.

❽ SAFESURFER JULIAN COPE from **PEGGY SUICIDE**
Close lyrical analysis reveals this song to have some connection with love in a time of plague,

prophylaxis and seduction. But forget the details – check out that guitar solo!

❾ WUTHERING HEIGHTS KATE BUSH from **THE WHOLE STORY**
Kate's master musicianship is often neglected in the rush to describe her eccentricities, but this catchy, complex track – with precise, coloratura vocals – still has the power to stun.

❿ CHILD OF MY KINGDOM ARTHUR BROWN from **THE CRAZY WORLD OF ARTHUR BROWN**
A stoned soul picnic. Arthur contributes mystic folderol and viola; his merry men bring along music-hall stylings and some ripe, cheesy jazz.

Al Spicer

21st-century English folk

Most of the great "source" artists of English traditional music are long gone, the giants of the 60s folk revival are now whiskery oldsters, and Irish and Scottish music has held the limelight in the UK for several decades. But in the 21st century there has been a rebirth of passion for English traditional folk song and dance music, with a new generation of artists injecting new life into old forms.

❶ PRETTY PLOUGHBOY ELIZA CARTHY from **ANGLICANA**
Singer, fiddler, bandleader, writer – this scarily talented scion of the Waterson/Carthy dynasty takes no prisoners.

❷ MONKEY COKEY JOHN SPIERS & JON BODEN from **TUNES**
As a melodeon, fiddle and vocal duo or fronting their eleven-piece big-band Bellowhead, "Squeezy & Stompy" have even inspired crowd surfing at recent festivals.

❸ LORD BATEMAN CHRIS WOOD from
THE LARK DESCENDING
An entrancing singer and fiddler, and a peerless arranger and writer, Chris Wood shines on
this traditional number.

**❹ THE WEDDING/BECAUSE HE WAS
A BONNY LAD KATHRYN TICKELL** from
DEBATABLE LANDS
Tickell's take on this slice of the Northumbrian
tradition shows the trailblazing piper (who was
a role model for the new wave of performers in
the 80s) at her best.

❺ GYPSIES JIM MORAY from **SWEET ENGLAND**
Controversial, original and questing, Jim Moray
was the man who dared take a laptop to folk
gigs. Here he adds crisp electric guitar to a
well-worn number.

❻ THE LYKE WAKE DIRGE ALASDAIR ROBERTS
from **NO EARTHLY MAN**
Roberts came from an indie-rock background
to become one of the most intriguing writers
of songs in the traditional style – and then a
performer of the old ones, such as this great
lyric-ballad.

❼ DOWNHILL DREAM HEKETY from **FURZE CAT**
A great piece of "e-ceilidh", the new wave of
country dancing that's proving to be one of the
fastest-growing strands of English folk.

**❽ POLLY OLIVER EMILY PORTMAN & LAUREN
MCCORMICK** from **SONG LINKS 2**
A fine showcase for two stunning young sing-
ers – both of them graduates of Newcastle
University's recently inaugurated folk-music
course.

❾ THE CREEL THE DEMON BARBER ROADSHOW
from **WAXED**
All English folk life is here – a core folk/rock
band fronted by Damien Barber and Bryony
Griffith, plus fast moving rappers, and morris
and mini-skirted clog dancers. Spectacular!

**❿ BARHAM DOWN/ THE YELLOW JOAK THE
GLOWORMS** from **BEAM**
Impressive hornpipes from the English country

dance trio headed up by dynamo fiddler and
folk advocate Laurel Swift.

Ian Anderson

Brian Eno

**Eno doesn't have a TV so he has more time
than other people. Or that's his story. But
to leaf through his credits, since forming
and leaving Roxy Music 30 years ago, is
quite awesome. He invented Ambient
as a genre decades before its time; has
produced outstanding work from Bowie,
U2, John Cale and Talking Heads; and his
own songs are quiet treasures. He declined
to contribute a playlist to this book by the
way: he doesn't approve of "list culture".**

❶ BABY'S ON FIRE from **HERE COME THE
WARM JETS**
It's 1973 and Eno is not long out of Roxy, citing
musical differences. But this great funk number
would have been a huge Roxy hit. Instead, it
got treated to a fabulous Fripp guitar solo.

❷ ON SOME FARAWAY BEACH from **HERE COME
THE WARM JETS**
Simplicity itself: two notes that gradually build
to a swirl of orchestral voices and guitar before
almost as an afterthought a song drifts in.

❸ I'LL COME RUNNING (TO TIE YOUR SHOE)
from **ANOTHER GREEN WORLD**
You don't think of Eno as a lyricist, but this is a
witty, affecting song. What a great title – and
the treated guitar is splendid, too.

❹ ANOTHER GREEN WORLD from **ANOTHER
GREEN WORLD**
A slice of artful wistfulness that most Brits can
actually hum (due to years of use as the theme
tune for BBC arts doc *Arena*).

❺ SLOW WATER from **MUSIC FOR FILMS**
Music For Films is a wonderful album including
some pieces that sound like they *should* be

used in movies, and others that really are, such as this delicate wonder, which graced Derek Jarman's *Jubilee*.

❻ WARSZAWA DAVID BOWIE from **LOW**
Summoned to Berlin by Bowie, Eno propelled him in a new direction that spawned his last great song, Heroes, and this wordless wonder.

❼ HERE HE COMES from **BEFORE AND AFTER SCIENCE**
Catchy as they come: a great tune, set to a glimmer of guitars. Eno picked it to kick off his own Desert Island selection of his work.

❽ 1/1 from **MUSIC FOR AIRPORTS**
More ambient than a cloud of helium, this is a sumptuous cut from Eno's most influential instrumental set.

❾ DEEP BLUE DAY from **APOLLO**
Originally written to accompany footage of the Apollo space missions, these tones were more recently heard on the soundtrack of *Trainspotting*.

❿ AND THEN SO CLEAR from **ANOTHER DAY ON EARTH**
Just when you thought Eno had forsaken songs, back he comes with an album full of them, including this marvel of Vocodered voice.

Mark Ellingham

Duke Ellington

When it comes to jazz nobility, no one holds a higher position than the Duke, one of the greatest composers – and certainly the greatest bandleader – in twentieth-century music. His recorded legacy was immense, so the following selection only highlights the tip of an enormous iceberg.

❶ BLACK AND TAN FANTASY from **MASTERPIECES**
A 1927 minor blues designed to show off the extraordinary plunger mute work of co-writer Bubber Miley.

❷ SINGLE PETAL OF A ROSE from **THE QUEEN'S SUITE**
From a 1959 suite privately recorded, pressed on a single disc and delivered to Queen Elizabeth at Buckingham Palace, this lovely arpeggiated piano piece shows Ellington at his most sumptuous.

❸ THE MOOCHE from **MASTERPIECES**
A prowling, haunting 1928 theme for wailing clarinets, named after the shuffling dance craze of the late 20s but performed by Duke's orchestra into the 60s.

❹ ROCKIN' IN RHYTHM from **MASTERPIECES**
Tightly arranged for the saxophone section, this intricate 1931 melody pointed the way for the big-band swing era and became one of Ellington's most enduring instrumentals.

❺ REMINISCING IN TEMPO from **MASTERPIECES**
After flirting with longer forms (notably the Creole Rhapsody) Ellington expressed his grief following his mother's death in 1935 with this dense and beautiful 13-minute composition.

❻ CARAVAN from **MASTERPIECES**
An early attempt to import musical textures from foreign lands, this 1937 piece of Eastern exotica featured the Latin-tinged trombone of co-composer Juan Tizol.

❼ KO-KO from **MASTERPIECES**
Dark and mysterious, this 1940 composition is a series of increasingly intense blues choruses, with star soloists Tizol and Jimmy Blanton (bass) contributing to the sultry heat.

❽ CONCERTO FOR COOTIE from **MASTERPIECES**
A subtly arranged 1940 showcase for trumpeter Cootie Williams, who delivers three distinct themes on mute, growl plunger and open horn.

❾ MADNESS IN GREAT ONES from **SUCH SWEET THUNDER**
From Duke's 1957 Shakespearean Suite, an imaginative portrait of Hamlet's unbalanced state with high-note specialist "Cat" Anderson providing suitably frantic musical hysteria.

⑩ ISFAHAN from **FAR EAST SUITE**
Co-composed with Billy Strayhorn in 1965, this lusciously harmonized piece was a perfect showcase for Johnny Hodges' liquid alto sax.

Chris Ingham

Eminem

More than just another white guy selling black music to middle-class kids so they can scare their parents, Eminem has brought a healthy dose of humour and self-doubt into a scene crippled by machismo and bragging.

① MY NAME IS from **THE SLIM SHADY LP**
Eminem exploded onto the scene with this, one of the great "this is me, who tha fuck are you?" songs. Stylistically, Snoop Dogg is never far away.

② '97 BONNIE & CLYDE from **THE SLIM SHADY LP**
Chilling little fairytale of spousal murder couched in terms of a daddy taking his li'l daughter to the beach with mom's corpse in the trunk.

③ JUST DON'T GIVE A FUCK from **THE SLIM SHADY LP**
You're a teenager, you're alienated, you just got ordered to clean your room. You need this song, whose beats are heavy enough to cover up your stomping compliance.

④ STAN from **THE MARSHALL MATHERS LP**
OK, it unleashed a tide of Dido on a world that deserved better, but as a response/coda to '97 Bonnie And Clyde, it can't be beat.

⑤ THE WAY I AM from **THE MARSHALL MATHERS LP**
Our man Marshall muses on the price of fame.

⑥ THE REAL SLIM SHADY from **THE MARSHALL MATHERS LP**
Kinda ironic, coming from a guy who dresses like a clone from the zone, but this ditty of imitation is one of his funniest tunes.

⑦ WHITE AMERICA from **THE EMINEM SHOW**
Eminem roars his defiance (again) with some masterful use of the English language.

⑧ CLEANIN OUT MY CLOSET from **THE EMINEM SHOW**
Hmm, interesting use of the word closet. Just what, apart from airing dirty washing, might be hidden in there?

⑨ WITHOUT ME from **THE EMINEM SHOW**
A consummate piece of white hip-hop. Committed, erudite even, our hero explains his stand and why he's still essential to the rap scene.

⑩ LOSE YOURSELF from **8 MILE SOUNDTRACK**
From Eminem's movie debut, this ode to stage-fright, overcoming it and the sheer rush that follows encapsulates the feeling that turns every performer into an addict.

Al Spicer

E.S.T.

Since their first release in 1993, the Esbjörn Svensson Trio has been tirelessly re-inventing the traditional jazz trio format of piano, bass and drums. There's no other pianist like Svensson, and his is a jazz trio that rocks!

① WHEN GOD CREATED THE COFFEE BREAK from **STRANGE PLACE FOR SNOW**
Esbjorn and bassist Dan Berglund put together one of the most savage bass patterns in modern jazz. Not to be played while driving.

② GOOD MORNING SUSIE SOHO from **GOOD MORNING SUSIE SOHO**
The title-track from E.S.T.'s third album, this has become the band's signature piece.

③ BEMSHA SWING from **ESBJÖRN SVENSSON TRIO PLAYS MONK**
A top cut from the only E.S.T. album where the material is not original. Monk would be proud.

❹ SERENADE FOR THE RENEGADE from STRANGE PLACE FOR SNOW

Subtle electronics and piano "treatments" (such as the placing of a steel pipe on the instrument's strings) give way to a wonderfully haunting, lilting melody.

❺ MINGLE IN THE MINCING-MACHINE from SEVEN DAYS OF FALLING

Dan Berglund's fuzzed-out double-bass solo is like nothing else in jazz-trio history.

❻ SEVEN DAYS OF FALLING from SEVEN DAYS OF FALLING

What EST does best. Sit back, close your eyes and be transported.

❼ LOVE IS REAL VIKTORIA TOLSTOY from SHINING ON YOU BY

This cover of EST's Believe, Beleft, Below is 100% true to the original, but Tolstoy has a far better voice than Svensson. One of the most beautiful jazz ballad recordings ever made.

Geoff Colquitt

Euro-reggae

Reggae is alive and well in Europe, with committed scenes in both France and Germany, where local producers and musicians are creating strange hybrids.

❶ SEE MI YAH WILLI WILLIAMS from RHYTHM & SOUND

Old hero Willi Williams meets two cutting-edge Berlin-based techno producers. The result is Germany's deepest and most spiritual reggae sound.

❷ NE DANS LES RUES DE PARIS PIERPOLJAK from JE FAIS C'QUE J'VEUX

Opening with melancholic accordion, this sounds real Frenchie, but there's Bob Marley lurking around the corner.

❸ DEM GONE GENTLEMAN from JOURNEY TO JAH

Would you believe this is by a German reggae artist? Tilmann Otto sings in perfect Jamaican patois using studios and riddims from the loudest island in the world.

❹ LA FILLE DU SELECTOR MASSILIA SOUND SYSTEM from 3968 CR 13

A soundsystem from Marseille that blends local roots music and dancehall. Here they sing in troubadour style about a girl who is cursed by a selector.

❺ DICKES B SEEED from NEW DUBBY CONQUERORS

From a big-band who perform with three singers and a mighty horn section comes maybe the best hymn to Berlin ever written.

❻ TOMBER LA CHEMISE ZEBDA from TOMBER LA CHEMISE MAXI

Multi-culti outfit from Toulouse with a dancefloor stomper that went to #1 in France.

❼ MEI GUADA FREIND HANS SÖLLNER from OI WEI I

He's been listening to the two Bobs – Marley and Dylan – and you can hear echoes of Chimes Of Freedom in this moving ballad about a departed friend.

❽ STOP DA WAR SERGENT GARCIA from BEST OF SERGENT GARCIA

Overtly political "salsamuffin" in dancehall style with Latin horns and vocal stints by famous French rapper Bionik and Hector Caramelo.

Jean Trouillet

Eurovision

Inexplicably taken seriously by audiences across continental Europe, despite the screaming histrionics, lyrical inanities and vaguely scary dance routines, the Eurovision Song Contest is viewed in the UK as a piece of camp heaven. Here's a selection of cheese that the French Agricultural Commission would be proud of.

Ian Anderson's
European roots

IAN ANDERSON has edited *fRoots* – the pioneering folk/world music magazine formerly known as *Folk Roots* – for the past twenty odd years. He has championed the idea of listening to the music of other countries and cultures – and in particular the many roots-based styles found across Europe. But he puts it all much better:

"You may think, when you turn on your radio in any European capital – London no exception – that globalized American pop has obliterated most traces of regional individuality. But down at the roots you can increasingly find joyful new noises as local cultures fight back in a myriad of inventive ways. The new music starts here."

❶ LA FIESTA AMPARANOIA from **SOMOS VIENTO**
Leading Spain's mestizo scene, Amparo Sanchez's party band mix roots from Mexico to the Balkans with songs and a voice to die for.

❷ LO GABIAN MOUSSU T E LEI JOVENTS from **MADEMOISELLE MARSEILLE**
This spin-off group from ragamuffins Massillia Sound System creatively fire up the cultural blender that is Marseille.

❸ I KRIES KOLENDE MOJMIR NOVAKOVIC from **IVO I MARA**
Croatian folklore looking outwards: big vocals, bagpipes, lijericas and beatboxes.

❹ AIRE DE RIEN JAUNE TOUJOURS from **BARRICADE**
Like their Belgian compatriots Think Of One, Jaune Toujours have a high-energy mix of roots musics from across Europe with brass, rock and politics.

❺ O TURCO NISTANIMERA from **CHORÉ**
From the deep south of Italy where there's still a Greek-speaking minority, and North Africa is closer than most of Europe.

❻ LO PRUMIER DE MAI LA TALVERA from **POBLE MON POBLE**
Occitan folk music from southern France, collected at source and given a 21st-century spin.

❼ RAMBLING SAILOR BELLOWHEAD from **E.P.ONYMOUS**
England erupts in a blaze of brass, strings and squeezebox: Benjamin Britten meets Kool & The Gang.

❽ CLOSE MY EYES KRISTI STASSINOPOULOU from **THE SECRET OF THE ROCKS**
Out of the Athens rock underground, adapting electronica and world music to Greek island traditions and inspirations.

❾ MAKEDÓN BESH O DROM from **CYI!**
Futuristic hi-energy Hungarian wedding band: Balkan Gypsy meets jazz and a scratching DJ.

❿ GRIMBORG GJALLARHORN from **GRIMBORG**
Nordic folk musicians do cool and moodily atmospheric as second nature: this Swedish quartet do it with a special energy.

❶ NEL BLU DI PINTO DI BLU ("VOLARE")
DOMENICO MODUGNO from **THE STORY OF EUROVISION**

A 1958 corker straight outta *La Dolce Vita* and responsible in part for the world's romantic adoration of la bellissima Italia.

❷ POUPÉE DE CIRE POUPÉE DE SON FRANCE GALL from **THE STORY OF EUROVISION**

Strangely, this engaging 1965 ditty failed to do the same for the Luxembourg tourist industry.

❸ CONGRATULATIONS CLIFF RICHARD from EUROVISION VOL 2

Shredding the little credibility he'd carried into the era of free love, Cliff was first inflicted on the wider European audience with this 1968 entry – a piece of irrepressible singalong dross.

❹ WATERLOO ABBA from EUROVISION VOL 2

ABBA turn the bloody carnage of 1815 into a jaunty metaphor for total submission in love.

❺ SAVE YOUR KISSES FOR ME BROTHERHOOD OF MAN from EUROVISION 1956–1999

Known to a generation of school kids as "Kippers For Tea", this 1976 entry launched BoM into a career in cruise-ship entertainment and northern British cabaret clubs. Justice is done.

❻ NE PARTEZ PAS SANS MOI CÉLINE DION from Eurovision Vol 2

Born in Quebec, previously unrecognized as an outpost of the Swiss empire, Dion was nonetheless chosen to warble this uninspired material to the top of the Eurovision chart.

❼ DIVA DANA INTERNATIONAL from EUROVISION VOL 2

This victorious 1998 entry from Israel (part of the Eurovision TV distribution network) captures the ideals of the contest better than any.

❽ MY NUMBER ONE HELENA PAPARIZOU from MY NUMBER ONE

In 21st-century entries such as this (Greece, 2005) the "la la la" is replaced by a synthesized "boom boom boom". But, as ever, the music is corny, the outfits outrageous and the presenters hilariously sincere. Long live Eurovision!

Al Spicer

Eurythmics

The finest of the his'n'hers synth'n'diva duos. Both Dave and Annie have enjoyed successful solo careers, but nothing to match up to the best of their joint heyday.

❶ TAKE ME TO YOUR HEART from IN THE GARDEN

Though airbrushed out of history, Eurythmics's Conny Plank-produced debut album contains a couple of excellent songs. On this one Ann Lennox (as she was then) sings unshowily and directly.

❷ NEVER GOING TO CRY AGAIN from IN THE GARDEN

Tim Wheater's flute nails down the obsessive chorus here, and there's a fleeting appearance from Can's Holgar Czukay on French Horn.

❸ SWEET DREAMS ARE MADE OF THIS from SWEET DREAMS

Lennox in all her gender-bending dominatrix glory. It's hard to believe this triumphant symphonic torrent was made on an eight-track.

❹ HERE COMES THE RAIN AGAIN from TOUCH

The apogee of the electronic singles, with Lennox floating melismatically against swooning strings and trickling keyboards.

❺ AQUA from TOUCH

Above a loping tribal chant, Stewart's keyboards screech and stutter as Lennox numbly begs to be drowned. It's clear why this was never a single.

❻ WOULD I LIE TO YOU from BE YOURSELF TONIGHT

Suddenly they started rocking out: a mean female chorus responds to Lennox's calls while Stewart exploits his electric guitar.

❼ BALL AND CHAIN FROM BE YOURSELF TONIGHT

An insistent circular rhythm, played slightly too fast for its own good, subverts this bright and shiny 80s production.

❽ THERE MUST BE AN ANGEL from
BE YOURSELF TONIGHT
The harmonica just pours out of Stevie Wonder
while Lennox flutters up and down the octaves.

❾ MISSIONARY MAN from **REVENGE**
An in-your-face classic. Get this version (rather
than the truncated single on the *Greatest Hits*
album) for its moody intro.

❿ KING AND QUEEN OF AMERICA from **WE TOO
ARE ONE**
By the time of their last "proper" album, Dave
and Annie were pretty much a spent force. But
this brassy lament looks the listener in the eye
and dares you to pity them.

David Honigmann

Bill Evans

**The most influential jazz pianist of his
generation, Evans was universally admired
for the lyricism of his playing, his harmonic
inventiveness and sheer musicality. His
cocaine-induced death robbed the jazz
world of one of its finest.**

❶ SO WHAT MILES DAVIS from **KIND OF BLUE**
Though supporting Davis, Evans is a corner-
stone in this, one of jazz's greatest tracks.
Subtlety, sophistication – Evans in his early
prime.

❷ I LOVES YOU PORGY from **AT THE MONTREUX
JAZZ FESTIVAL**
A tender yet passionate solo rendering of this
wistful Gershwin song. Don't be put off by
the tinkling wineglasses: the live atmosphere
seems to create real urgency in Evans' playing.

❸ WALTZ FOR DEBBIE from **NEW JAZZ
CONCEPTIONS**
One of Evans' few compositions, written for
his three-year-old niece. A beautiful song

without words (until Tony Bennett got his voice
round it).

❹ MY FOOLISH HEART from **THE TONY BENNETT/
BILL EVANS ALBUM**
Evans brings out the best of Bennett in this
intimate and inspired collaboration. With
just piano accompaniment, Bennett's voice is
exposed but richly expressive.

❺ OUR LOVE IS HERE TO STAY from **AT SHELLY'S
MANNE-HOLE**
A jaunty, melodic right hand soars above dar-
ingly chromatic harmonic sequences. Fabulous
trio playing with Chuck Israels (drums) and
Larry Bunker (bass).

❻ PEACE PIECE from **EVERYBODY DIGS BILL EVANS**
Six and a half minutes of haunting and utterly
absorbing impressionistic improvisation. Satie,
Debussy, Evans…

❼ BLUE IN GREEN from **PORTRAIT IN JAZZ**
A pensive Evans composition (which Miles
Davis tried to claim as his own) played with
Scott LeFaro (bass) and Paul Motian (drums)
– arguably the greatest jazz trio of all time.

❽ ALICE IN WONDERLAND from **SUNDAY AT THE
VILLAGE VANGUARD**
A joyous example of how 3/4 time lent itself to
Evans' floating right hand and complex harmo-
nies. Weeks later, bassist LeFaro was dead.

❾ THE WASHINGTON TWIST from **EMPATHY**
Evans is in perfect syncopation with Shelly
Manne's exciting drums in this edgy 12-bar
blues. Parts of your anatomy will move uncon-
trollably.

❿ JUST YOU, JUST ME from **CONVERSATIONS
WITH MYSELF**
A unique insight into Evans' musical psyche.
His brilliant, never-to-be-repeated idea
was to make an album of three overdubbed
piano tracks – all his own. Almost too much
to take in.

Alastair Rolfe

misogynistic, but it shows the band doing what they did best – heads-down rock'n'roll.

❼ CINDY INCIDENTALLY from OOH LA LA
Top Rod lyric – and he's nice to the lady this time.

❽ POOL HALL RICHARD from OOH LA LA
Ode to a wayward lad. What was Rod thinking?

❾ OOH LA LA from OOH LA LA
Rod didn't want to sing this as he didn't think it was good enough, so Ronnie Wood took over. (He likes it now.)

❿ YOU CAN MAKE ME DANCE, SING OR ANYTHING (EVEN TAKE THE DOG FOR A WALK) from GOOD BOYS WHEN THEY'RE ASLEEP
The band's swansong – and a fantastic single, too.

Dave Atkinson

The Faces

The original good-time, straight-forward rock'n'roll party band of the early 70s, The Faces even had a bar on stage with them. Hugely influential and a great springboard for Rod Stewart's solo career.

❶ THREE BUTTON HAND ME DOWN from FIRST STEP (AKA "SMALL FACES")
Organ, slide guitar, four-to-the-floor rhythms and a terrific tune (pinched from Can't Get Next To You). The shape of things to come.

❷ MAYBE I'M AMAZED from LONG PLAYER
A magnificent version of a great Paul McCartney tune.

❸ RICHMOND from LONG PLAYER
Folky song from Ronnie Lane, sounding very similar to Slim Chance, his next group.

❹ YOU'RE MY GIRL (I DON'T WANT TO DISCUSS IT) from FIVE GUYS WALK INTO A BAR
From a BBC session, the only Faces version of this brilliant tune previously recorded by Amen Corner.

❺ HAD ME A REAL GOOD TIME from LONG PLAYER
Back to their raving best – a full on, loud and groovy, live favourite.

❻ STAY WITH ME from A NOD IS AS GOOD AS A WINK … TO A BLIND HORSE
Lyrically this could be regarded as a little

Fado

The new millennium has seen a major revival of this bittersweet and quintessentially Portuguese music, spearheaded by a new generation of artists. While adding their own new twists, they are of course indebted to their forebears. Here are some choice cuts from both.

❶ FADO INÚTIL AMÁLIA RODRIGUES from FADO, THE SOUL OF PORTUGAL
The undisputed queen of fado is at the peak of her extraordinary powers in this 1951 recording. Talk about transcending the genre…

❷ ADEUS MOURARIA CARLOS RAMOS from BIOGRAFIAS DO FADO: CARLOS RAMOS
This 1957 recording is a fond farewell to the streets of Mouraria – the *bairro* (neighbourhood) of Lisbon most commonly namechecked in fado lyrics.

❸ BAIRROS DE LISBOA ALFREDO MARCENEIRO WITH FERNANDA MARIA from BIOGRAFIAS DO FADO: CARLOS RAMOS

A good example of the now rare *desgarrada* form of improvised duet, with one of the godfathers of 20th-century fado and a less familiar but rather feisty partner.

❹ FADO ZÉ ANTÓNIO MARIA TERESA DE NORONHA from FADO PORTUGUÊS VOL 1

Restrained passion was the trademark of this fine singer, who enjoyed a brief international career in the 60s.

❺ TROVA DO VENTO QUE PASSA ANTÓNIO BERNADINO from THE ROUGH GUIDE TO FADO

The best-known singer from Coimbra (the second city of fado, after Lisbon) performing a song which became an anthem of hope in the dark days of Portugal's dictatorship.

❻ MEMÓRIAS DE UM CHAPÉU CAMANÉ from ESTA COISA DA ALMA

Despite not having really capitalized outside Portugal on the recent fado revival, Camané is still the leading male voice of the "new school" at home. This is a singer who really uses his nose.

❼ TRAGO ALENTEJO NA VOZ ANTÓNIO ZAMBUJO from O MESMO FADO

A popular tune celebrating this promising young singer's home in the Alentejo region. His voice brims with emotion and is very highly rated in Lisbon, his adopted home.

❽ SOU DO FADO, SOU FADISTA ANA MOURA from GUARDA-ME A NA MÃO

A great version of a song by writer/producer Jorge Fernando. Moura's is a natural fado voice that we should be hearing a lot more from.

❾ O QUE FOR HÁ-DE SER KATIA GUERREIRO from NAS MÃOS DO FADO

A magnificent reworking of Dulce Pontes' song Ciranda. This may not strictly be fado, but Guerreiro is a fado fundamentalist and really gives it the treatment.

Mariza's
Voices

"I could have made a list of great fado singers", says Portuguese fadista **MARIZA**, who has become one of the biggest names in world music in recent years. "But I love great voices whether they're singing jazz, classical or pop and that's mostly what I went for in this list."

❶ ERA NÃO ERA DO TAMANHO DE UM PARDAL GAITEIROS DE LISBOA from MACAREU

❷ UPA NEGUINHO ELIS REGINA from ELIS REGINA LIVE IN MONTREUX

❸ WHAT'S GOING ON MARVIN GAYE from WHAT'S GOING ON

❹ BLUE MOON BILLIE HOLIDAY from BILLIE'S BLUES

❺ DO NOTHIN' TILL YOU HEAR FROM ME NINA SIMONE from SINGS ELLINGTON

❻ O SUAVE FACIULLA MARIA CALLAS from ROMANTIC CALLAS

❼ CANÇÃO VERDES ANOS CARLOS PAREDES from O MELHOR DE CARLOS PAREDES

❽ DONGO WALDEMAR BASTOS from RENASCENCE

❾ DINDI FRANK SINATRA & ANTONIO CARLOS JOBIM from FRANCIS ALBERT SINATRA & ANTONIO CARLOS JOBIM

❿ NEW YORK STATE OF MIND TONY BENNETT from PLAYIN' WITH MY FRIENDS

⑩ HÁ UMA MÚSICA DO POVO MARIZA from
TRANSPARENTE

Backed by Jaques Morelenbaum's subtle
orchestral arrangements, the leading contemporary female fadista kicks off her third album
with new-found maturity and restraint.

Jon Lusk

Brenda Fassie

**South Africa – no Africa's – top diva,
Brenda was blessed with a voice that
could stop anyone in their tracks. Until her
untimely death in 2004 she blasted out
some of the continent's finest pop tunes.**

① VUL'NDLELA from MEMEZA

Brenda's biggest-ever hit – a rousing wedding
song set to a stomping *mbaqanga* beat – this
later became an ANC campaign anthem.

② WEEKEND SPECIAL from GREATEST HITS

Her first hit, from 1983, features Brenda in the
role of weekend lover of a married man. It
became an instant and deserving disco classic.

③ GOOD BLACK WOMAN from TOO LATE
FOR MAMA

Recorded in the nightmarish late 80s, this is full
of strength and pain.

④ TOO LATE FOR MAMA from TOO LATE FOR MAMA

Silly lyrics but who cares? A bubblegum classic.

⑤ NTSWARE-NDIBAMBE from MALI

One of her last recordings, with Brenda almost
growling at times, the voice laced with compelling menace.

⑥ NGOHLALA NGI NJE from MINA NAWE

Builds beautifully from quavering solo to rousing anthem in inimitable Brenda fashion.

⑦ BAXAKEKILE OXAM' from MYEKELENI

A great mix of jazz and Xhosa traditional
rhythms, with Brenda's voice soaring and swirling above them.

⑧ SUM' BULALA from MEMEZA

A gentle, beautiful ballad, with Brenda's voice
the epitome of understated power.

Gregory Salter

Fairport Convention

**The original electric folk band are still
going, and that longevity means their
origins as Britain's answer to Jefferson
Airplane often gets overlooked. Not here.**

① A SAILOR'S LIFE from UNHALFBRICKING

The song that invented electric folk is spiky
and spooky like The Velvet Underground playing trad. Sandy Denny's singing is luminous.

② WHO KNOWS WHERE THE TIME GOES from
UNHALFBRICKING

Given extra poignancy by Sandy Denny's early
death, this ballad succeeds in slowing down
the time whose speed it mourns.

③ SLOTH from FULL HOUSE

Guitarist Richard Thompson and fiddler Dave
Swarbrick do battle on this anti-war dirge.

④ TAM LIN from LIEGE AND LIEF

Electric folk at its best: a tricky tempo and a
slashing riff giving meat to an off-with-the-
fairies tale of, well, fairies and fair maidens.

⑤ FOTHERINGAY from WHAT WE DID ON
OUR HOLIDAYS

Denny's evocation of Mary Queen of Scots'
sequestering floats on a wash of acoustic
guitars and voices.

⑥ I'LL KEEP IT WITH MINE from WHAT WE DID
ON OUR HOLIDAYS

Pre-trad Fairport were top Dylan interpreters.
Here's a stunning version of an obscure gem.

⑦ MATTY GROVES from LIEGE AND LIEF

A romp of adultery, tell-tale servants and

Marianne Faithfull's
Icons

An icon in her own right, and a role model to generations of female singers, from Chrissie Hynde to PJ Harvey, MARIANNE FAITHFULL picks tracks from ten of the most iconic artists of the 20th century.

❶ ONE MORE CUP OF COFFEE BOB DYLAN from DESIRE

❷ PAIN IN MY HEART OTIS REDDING from DESIRE

❸ REDEMPTION SONG BOB MARLEY from UPRISING

❹ CHAIN OF FOOLS ARETHA FRANKLIN from LADY SOUL

❺ FINE & MELLOW BILLIE HOLIDAY from THE SOUND OF JAZZ

❻ LUST FOR LIFE IGGY POP from LUST FOR LIFE

❼ MOTHER JOHN LENNON from PLASTIC ONO BAND

❽ FIRST WE TAKE MANHATTAN LEONARD COHEN from I'M YOUR MAN

❾ THAT'S ALL RIGHT ELVIS PRESLEY from THE SUN SESSIONS

❿ DELIA'S GONE JOHNNY CASH from AMERICAN RECORDINGS

---

murder which the Fairports attack full throttle, finishing up in a rollickingly inappropriate reel.

❽ THE LOBSTER from FAIRPORT CONVENTION
Neglected pre-Denny Fairport: a precursor of their VU folk sound. Oddball, creepy but captivating.

❾ ROSIE from ROSIE
Utterly uncharacteristic – almost poppy – mature Fairport. Charming.

❿ MEET ON THE LEDGE from WHAT WE DID ON OUR HOLIDAYS
The enduring Fairport theme song, a roustabout hymn to friendship past and present.
Toby Manning

Marianne Faithfull

From the innocent convent girl of As Tears Go By to the raging harpie of Why D'Ya

Do It, Marianne Faithfull's career has zig-zagged unconventionally from triumph to disaster – and then back again.

❶ AS TEARS GO BY from MARIANNE FAITHFULL
The first song Mick Jagger and Keith Richards ever wrote.

❷ IS THIS WHAT I GET FROM LOVING YOU? from THE VERY BEST OF MARIANNE FAITHFULL
A Goffin-King number that deserved to chart much higher in 1967 than the modest #43 it achieved.

❸ SISTER MORPHINE from THE VERY BEST OF MARIANNE FAITHFULL
It took Mick Jagger twenty years to admit that Marianne had helped write the words and to add her name to the credits on The Stones' version.

❹ THE BALLAD OF LUCY JORDAN from BROKEN ENGLISH
A magnificently warm rendition of the Shel Silverstein song from the 1979 album that redefined her career.

⑤ WHY D'YA DO IT? from **BROKEN ENGLISH**
Based on a poem by Heathcote Williams, this is a raging, X-rated rant, the like of which we'd never heard from a woman in rock before.

⑥ BALLAD OF THE SOLDIER'S WIFE from **LOST IN THE STARS: THE MUSIC OF KURT WEILL**
As this track shows, away from her pop career, Marianne has become a compelling interpreters of the Brecht/Weill songbook.

⑦ THE MYSTERY OF LOVE from **BEFORE THE POISON**
The best of the five tracks written and produced by PJ Harvey for MF's 2004 album.

Nigel Williamson

The Fall

The Fall's cranky, shambling, Mancunian incomprehensibility generates instant love or loathing. Here are some reminders for those who have forgotten – and tasters for those who have yet to catch the bug.

❶ VARIOUS TIMES from **EARLY SINGLES**
Creepy keyboards, spooky guitar and our man Mark E. Smith rambling on about witch trials, Nazi camp guards and weak beer.

❷ NO XMAS FOR JOHN QUAYS from **TOTALE'S TURNS**
Barely keeping the lid on, this is a band playing their hearts out.

❸ SPECTRE VS RECTOR from **DRAGNET**
The best of The Fall's early epics, and a tale scarier than *The Exorcist*.

❹ NEW FACE IN HELL from **GROTESQUE**
Government-induced paranoia, a guitar riff strong enough to build bridges from, and a whole bunch of throwaway one-liners.

❺ HIP PRIEST from **HEX ENDUCTION HOUR**
Making the most of that double drummer line-up.

❻ HIT THE NORTH from **THE FRENZ EXPERIMENT**
Celebrating the glorious countryside of Greater Manchester and urban Lancashire, the Fall do their bit for regional tourism.

❼ KURIOUS ORANJ from **I AM KURIOUS, ORANJ**
A strange tie-in to a ballet suite performed by Michael Clark's dance troupe, and a searing indictment of the Oranges.

❽ BIRMINGHAM SCHOOL OF BUSINESS SCHOOL from **CODE: SELFISH**
Dreamy, laid-back MES sounds like a Mancunian Sly Stone as he drools a lyric of the purest contempt and the band circle endlessly through one of their best riffs.

❾ HEY! STUDENT from **MIDDLE CLASS REVOLT**
This used to be called Hey! Fascist, but after swapping it to a rant against the complacency of the educated elite, it works just as well.

❿ STRYCHNINE from **THE COMPLETE PEEL SESSIONS 1978–2004**
Recorded in 1993 after a good few years in the business, Mark and the band proudly demonstrate no musical progress whatsoever.

Al Spicer

Fatboy Slim

Norman Cook's most successful alter-ego first appeared in 1996 with the *Better Living Through Chemistry* album, a slab of keyboard and computer trickery and dubious legality welded together by a man possessed of the spirit of funk and the Big Beat. Since then he's gone on to become a superstar artist, producer and DJ who these days clears the rights to samples before using them on his records.

❶ GOING OUT OF MY HEAD from **BETTER LIVING THROUGH CHEMISTRY**
Starting from Yvonne Elliman's cover of the Who's I Can't Explain and layering on the

effects like a chef sprinkling sugar, Norman whips up a cotton-candy tribute to getting out of your head.

❷ EVERYBODY NEEDS A 303 from **BETTER LIVING THROUGH CHEMISTRY**
Norm's ode to man's best friend – the Roland TB303 bassline generator.

❸ THE ROCKAFELLER SKANK from **YOU'VE COME A LONG WAY, BABY**
Norman's greatest hit so far – as catchy as the black plague. (But why didn't he just call it Right About Now, The Funk Soul Brother?)

❹ PRAISE YOU from **YOU'VE COME A LONG WAY, BABY**
Takes you to a beautiful place where scratch-happy MCs, gospel divas and twangy axe-players shake their asses in unison.

❺ STAR 69 from **HALFWAY BETWEEN THE GUTTER AND THE STARS**
Hip-hop in a Brighton stylie: enormous waves

of electronic beats, merciless basslines and naughty lyrics ideal for shouting out en masse.

❻ WEAPON OF CHOICE from **HALFWAY BETWEEN THE GUTTER AND THE STARS**
If Bootsy Collins joins your team then anything you do will be 100% funky. Convince Christopher Walken to donate some menace to the video and the result is a trip to Planet Silly, where the fun never stops.

Al Spicer

Finger-pickin' guitar

In most hands the folk guitar provides little more than a simple strummed accompaniment. But during the 60s folk and acoustic blues revival, a number of virtuoso performers (most of them Brits

---

Bert Jansch's
Influential 10

The doyen of English acoustic folk guitarists, BERT JANSCH is revered as an influence by the likes of Jimmy Page and Neil Young. His own musical tastes run to jazz, blues, rock and soul, all of which are reflected in his rather eclectic playlist.

❶ BLUES RUN THE GAME' JACKSON C. FRANK from **BLUES RUN THE GAME**

❷ BLACKWATERSIDE ANNE BRIGGS from **A COLLECTION**

❸ KEY TO THE HIGHWAY BIG BILL BROONZY from **TROUBLE IN MIND**

❹ PROUD MAISRIE DAVEY GRAHAM AND SHIRLEY COLLINS from **FOLK ROOTS, NEW ROUTES**

❺ OH LORD, DON'T LET THEM DROP THAT ATOMIC BOMB ON ME CHARLES MINGUS from **OH YEAH**

❻ (I'M YOUR) HOOCHIE-COOCHIE MAN' MUDDY WATERS from **THE BEST OF MUDDY WATERS 1947–55**

❼ BYKER HILL MARTIN CARTHY WITH DAVE SWARBRICK from **BYKER HILL**

❽ THE FROG GALLIARD JOHN DOWLAND from **JULIAN BREAM VOL 7: FANTASIES, AYRES & DANCES**

❾ CHARLOTTE HOPE SANDOVAL AND THE WARM INVENTIONS from **BAVARIAN FRUIT BREAD**

❿ GREEN ONIONS BOOKER T & THE MGS from **THE VERY BEST OF BOOKER T & THE MGS**

but some Americans too) took plucking and picking to a completely new level – with dazzling results.

❶ BLACKWATERSIDE BERT JANSCH from **JACK ORION**
A tune so good that Jimmy Page borrowed and recorded it with Led Zeppelin as Black Mountain Side – and cheekily claimed the writing credit for his own.

❷ SWEET POTATO JOHN RENBOURN from **SIR JOHN ALOT OF MERRIE ENGLAND**
Renbourn's guitar duets with Jansch were heard to brilliant effect in Pentangle and he was equally adept playing folk-blues or in the ornate style he called "mock Tudor".

❸ ANGIE DAVY GRAHAM from **GUITAR PLAYER PLUS**
Graham was just 21 when he recorded this stunning instrumental, later covered by both Jansch and Paul Simon.

❹ SCARBOROUGH FAIR MARTIN CARTHY from **MARTIN CARTHY**
Controversially nicked by Paul Simon, who failed to credit Carthy's arrangement, resulting in the two men not speaking for thirty years.

❺ BLUES RUN THE GAME JACKSON C FRANK from **BLUES RUN THE GAME**
An American who came to London in the mid-60s to become Sandy Denny's boyfriend and bequeath this much-covered tune.

❻ RANDOM JIG RICHARD THOMPSON from **STRICT TEMPO!**
Thompson's songwriting and electric guitar work often overshadowed the fact that he was a genius acoustic picker, as he proved on his 1981 album of jigs, reels, hornpipes and polkas.

❼ DAZZLING STRANGER WIZZ JONES from **THE LEGENDARY ME**
"Wizz was *the* guy to listen to in the early days", John Renbourn says. "But he didn't actually have any gigs 'cos he had such long hair and bare feet that he wasn't allowed into most of the folk clubs".

❽ THE DRIVING OF THE YEAR NAIL LEO KOTTKE from **SIX AND TWELVE STRING GUITAR**
The American-born Kottke drew on the blues as well as the folk tradition but this instrumental displays his dazzling dexterity to awesome effect.

❾ ON THE SUNNY SIDE OF THE OCEAN JOHN FAHEY from **THE TRANSFIGURATION OF BLIND JOE DEATH**
Fahey was a cult figure with a style as idiosyncratic as it was complex. This track is beautiful and impressionistic yet slightly bluesy and dissonant. It displays the man's technical genius and his weird and wonderful musical vision.

❿ MAPLE LEAF RAG STEFAN GROSSMAN from **YAZOO BASIN BOOGIE**
Another American folk-blues legend with an astonishing pickin' technique, Grossman is heard to brilliant effect on his guitar transcription of the Scott Joplin classic.

Nigel Williamson

Ella Fitzgerald

The First Lady of jazz song, and a genius of scat, Ella possessed one of the most dazzling voices of the 20th century – pure, polished and powerful, with a massive three-octave range. She put it to use during a prolific four-decade recording career, of which the following only scrapes the surfaces.

❶ IT'S ONLY A PAPER MOON from **ELLA AND HER FELLAS**
Ella's easy-swinging 1945 version of this Harold Arlen and Yip Harburg standard. The Delta Rhythm Boys provide creamy harmony.

❷ HOW HIGH THE MOON from **BEBOP SPOKEN HERE**
Ella announced her musical allegiance with the modern jazz movement on this brilliant 1947 scat reading of one of bop's great anthems.

❸ MY ONE AND ONLY LOVE from ELLA AND ELLIS

This soaring tune is just one highlight from the immaculate 1950 album recorded with pianist Ellis Larkins.

❹ EV'RY TIME WE SAY GOODBYE from THE COLE PORTER SONGBOOK

From her first songbook album, this famous, touching 1956 recording ensured the hitherto underexposed Cole Porter tune a place in the pantheon of all-time standards.

❺ A SHIP WITHOUT A SAIL from THE RODGERS AND HART SONGBOOK

One of the more obscure Rodgers and Hart songs from Ella's second songbook and a plaintive gem from the 1930 show *Heads Up*.

❻ DAYDREAM from THE DUKE ELLINGTON SONGBOOK

Part of the magnificent album recorded with Duke's orchestra in 1956, this is a truly shimmering version of the Strayhorn/Ellington ballad.

❼ STOMPIN' AT THE SAVOY from ELLA AND LOUIS AGAIN

The Ella and Louis albums made with the Oscar Peterson Trio in 1956–57 were full of magic. From the rematch, spurred on by producer Norman Granz, this hits an extraordinary level of excitement and spontaneity.

❽ THERE'S A LULL IN MY LIFE from LIKE SOMEONE IN LOVE

Arranged by Frank De Vol in 1957, this gorgeous Harry Revel song suited Ella's sweetly sad ballad style perfectly and makes for one of her most divine performances.

❾ BLUE SKIES from THE IRVING BERLIN SONGBOOK

The remarkable scat feature from the otherwise restrained and respectful *Berlin Songbook*, recorded with Paul Weston in 1958.

❿ JUST YOU, JUST ME from ELLA SWINGS LIGHTLY

Ella is typically virtuosic over Marty Paich's *Birth Of The Cool*-style arrangement.

Chris Ingham

Flamenco

One of the great musical forms of Europe, flamenco has a history and repertoire that few traditional or folk cultures can match. Today it thrives both in its "pure" form and in countless new flavours borrowing influences from all over the world.

❶ ENTRE SABANAS DE HOLANDA LA NIÑA DE LOS PEINES from LA NIÑA DE LOS PEINES VOZ DE ESTAÑO FUNDIDO

A key voice of the 20th century sings a glorious folk piece.

❷ LA VOZ DEL TIEMPO TOMATITO & EL CAMARÓN DE LA ISLA from TOMATITO

Underpinned by an upbeat chorus and the guitar of Tomatito, this track confirms the late El Camarón to be "the voice of the time".

❸ MOGUER ESTRELLA MORENTE from MY SONGS AND A POEM

A poem by Juan Ramón Jiménez (exiled during the Franco regime) set to music by this young star's illustrious father, Enrique Morente.

❹ LA VIDA SALE JOSE MERCÉ from AIRE

The rough-edged chorus, blasts of trumpet, vamping piano, percussion and above all the rusty, yearning voice of Mercé make this an unbelievably sexy number.

❺ JARABI KETAMA WITH TOUMANI DIABATÉ from KETAMA

A fine example of the passion and energy of 80s New Flamenco, this is a beautiful encounter between the Ketama ensemble, Malian kora player Toumani Diabaté and bassist Danny Thompson.

❻ DAME TU BOCA JAVIER RUIBAL from SAHARA

Pure musical seduction from this flamenco-influenced singer-songwriter.

❼ EL YEDDI HAG ENNAS RADIO TARIFA from FIEBRE

An unbeatable live version of this compelling song, with a wild sax solo to boot.

⑧ CORAZÓN LOCO BEBO Y CIGALA from LÁGRIMAS NEGRAS
A sublime flamenco telling of a classic Latin tale – a man torn between wife and lover.

⑨ TIEMPO DE SOLEA OJOS DE BRUJO from BARI
A superb *solea* from this cutting-edge Barcelona collective.

⑩ COGE LA ONDA EL LEBRIJANO CON LA ORQUESTA ARÁBIGO ANDALUZA from CASABLANCA
Consummate Arabic-Spanish fusion partnering the earthy voice of Juan Peña with Hassan Jebelhbibi and Arabic chorus.

Jan Fairley

Fleetwood Mac

Around the eternal nucleus of Mick Fleetwood (drums) and John McVie (bass), Fleetwood Mac have battled through triumph, disaster and countless personnel changes since 1967 and, amazingly, they're still around to tell the tale. Their story has been described as the ultimate rock soap opera, but even the most imaginative scriptwriter would struggle to dream up such a litany of success, failure, love, hate, alcoholism, disappearance, sex and drugs. And that was just 1971.

❶ ALBATROSS from ENGLISH ROSE
Atypically gentle, this windswept instrumental was a #1 hit in Britain.

❷ BLACK MAGIC WOMAN from ENGLISH ROSE
Better known in the classic version by Santana, Fleetwood Mac's original has a stronger undercurrent of mystery and dread.

❸ OH WELL from THEN PLAY ON
One of the most astonishing cuts of the late 60s: a blistering rock track segues into a dramatic instrumental with classical overtones.

❹ GREEN MANALISHI (WITH THE TWO-PRONGED CROWN) from 25 YEARS: THE CHAIN
Later covered by Judas Priest, this aggressively menacing song was one of the last that vocalist/guitarist Peter Green wrote for the band.

❺ HYPNOTIZED from MYSTERY TO ME
One of the highlights of the Bob Welch era: a breezy tune with just the right hint of mystery, and a precursor to the combination of moods that would make the band wildly successful in the late 70s.

❻ RHIANNON from FLEETWOOD MAC
The first of the great Stevie Nicks songs – and the one that came to define her public persona.

❼ GO YOUR OWN WAY from RUMOURS
Lindsay Buckingham's chiming rhythm and scorching lead guitars frame the song that summed up the band's internal personal tangle.

❽ YOU MAKE LOVING FUN from RUMOURS
The fourth and final single from *Rumours* was one of the best songs on the radio in 1977.

❾ SISTERS OF THE MOON from TUSK
A moody work reflecting Stevie Nicks's fascination with nocturnal imagery and mysterious female characters.

❿ BROWN EYES from TUSK
A slightly unusual Christine McVie track displaying some of the dark undercurrents found in Nicks' best work. It's said to include uncredited guitar work from Peter Green.

Butch Lazorchak

Flying Nun

Famously feted by the late John Peel as a model independent record label, Flying Nun took punk's DIY ethic (also a defining feature of New Zealand culture) and nurtured the "pop primitive" sound that defined Kiwi music from the early 80s.

❶ NOTHING'S GOING TO HAPPEN TALL DWARFS from **HELLO CRUEL WORLD**
Quite untrue; this lo-fi but poetic and adventurous debut single by the maverick duo augured well for the future. Plenty did happen.

❷ POINT THAT THING SOMEWERE ELSE THE CLEAN from **ANTHOLOGY**
The ghost of the Velvet Underground hovers heavy over this driving early tune. David Kilgour's distinctive narcoleptic vocal mumbles through mix. God knows what it's about.

❸ PINK FROST THE CHILLS from **HEAVENLY POP HITS: THE BEST OF THE CHILLS**
An early 7" by this Dunedin band, which has a wonderfully dark but luminous quality to it. Somehow The Chills' albums never quite sustained the giddy rush of such pop thrills.

❹ DEATH AND THE MAIDEN THE VERLAINES from **YOU'RE JUST TOO OBSCURE FOR ME**
This stop-start strummer transcends its literary pretensions. Another band that inspired the "Dunedin Sound" tag, which a lot of Flying Nun material was saddled with.

❺ RANDOLPH'S GOING HOME SHANE CARTER & PETER JEFFRIES from **THE FLYING NUN RETROSPECTIVE COMPILATION: GETTING OLDER 1981–91**
A suspenseful, melancholic one-off single that's become a collector's item in its original 7" format. Shane Carter went on to form Straightjacket Fits and Dimmer.

❻ THE MAN WITH NO DESIRE EXPENDABLES from **TUATARA**
Jay Clarkson's haunting jazz-tinged voice hints at possibilities that were never quite realized in a career that showed lots of early promise.

❼ DADDY'S HIGHWAY THE BATS from **DADDY'S HIGHWAY**
Skirling guitars suggest the influence of Scotland, where this band were well received. Prolific songwriter Robert Scott's inability to sing in tune only adds to their charm.

❽ NOT GIVEN LIGHTLY CHRIS KNOX from **MEAT**
Honest-to-goodness lurve song (very unusual!)

by the godfather of Kiwi punk (The Enemy, Toy Love, Tall Dwarfs), which remains by far his biggest hit.

❾ NUDE STAR GARAGELAND from **LAST EXIT TO GARAGELAND**
Musings on the fame that pretty well eluded them outside New Zealand. For a time they were the label's big hope of the 90s, but they broke up after three albums.

❿ PIRATE LOVE THE D4 from **6TWENTY**
The best song on their 2001 debut is actually a cover of a Johnny Thunders song – fitting in a way, since this Auckland foursome's pop punk isn't exactly typical Nun fare.

Jon Lusk

Folk-rock 1: English & Irish

English folk-rock peaked early: Fairport Convention's 1970 release *Liege and Lief* fused trad ballads and rock rhythms so perfectly that the form had really nowhere left to go. Its Irish cousin proved to have longer legs, largely thanks to the disorderly beahviour of the Pogues, until singer Shane McGowan became so legless he could barely get on a stage.

❶ A SAILOR'S LIFE FAIRPORT CONVENTION from **UNHALFBRICKING**
Liege and Lief was their landmark , but it was this track a year earlier which created the template for that album and first unleashed the remarkable interplay between Richard Thompson's guitar and Dave Swarbrick's violin.

❷ THOMAS THE RHYMER STEELEYE SPAN from **NOW WE ARE SIX**
Produced by Jethro Tull's Ian Anderson and featuring, of all people, David Bowie on saxophone.

❸ WHISKEY IN THE JAR THIN LIZZY from
VAGABONDS OF THE WESTERN WORLD
Basically a hard-rock act, Phil Lynott's band
nevertheless achieved folk-rock immortality
with this brilliantly reworked Irish trad ballad.

❹ MORRIS CALL ALBION BAND from MORRIS ON
The opening track from the classic 1972 album
by Ashley Hutchings' all-star folk-rock supergroup – if that's not an oxymoron.

❺ THE HANGED MAN MR FOX from GYPSY
Volatile, classic early-70s English folk-rock from
the soon-to-be-divorced Bob and Carole Pegg.

❻ ENGLISH MEDLEY ROBIN AND BARRY
DRANSFIELD from ROUT OF THE BLUES
The Yorkshire brothers actually turned down
an invitation to join Steeleye. This track from
their seminal 1970 debut shows why.

❼ TRIBUTE TO PAEDAR O'DONNELL
MOVING HEARTS from THE STORM
Synthesizers and bodhrans from the band
that legends Christy Moore and Donal Lunny
formed after leaving Planxty.

❽ HAL-AN-TOW OYSTERBAND from STEP OUTSIDE
These days they call it "English roots" rather
than folk-rock, but this explosive version of the
trad standard from Osterband's landmark 1986
album helped to keep the flame alive.

❾ DIRTY OLD TOWN THE POGUES from
RUM, SODOMY AND THE LASH
The Clash meet The Dubliners in a combus-
tible cocktail of amphetamine sulphate and
Guinness.

Nigel Williamson

Folk-rock 2: 60s America

Combining the best of both worlds,
American folk-rock started when The Byrds
put Bob Dylan to a Beatles beat, setting

the scene for some of the most enduring
musical statements of the 60s.

❶ MR TAMBOURINE MAN THE BYRDS from
MR TAMBOURINE MAN
The Transatlantic #1 hit that started it all in
1965, combining Bob Dylan's poetry, Roger
McGuinn's jingle-jangle electric 12-string and
the Byrds' skyscraping harmonies.

❷ TURN! TURN! TURN THE BYRDS from
TURN! TURN! TURN!
What The Byrds did for Dylan they also did
for Pete Seeger, turning a folk dirge into an
anthem of peace and tolerance.

❸ LIKE A ROLLING STONE BOB DYLAN from
HIGHWAY 61 REVISITED
Cathedral-filling organ, hard blues-rock guitar
and sneering, spiteful vocal coalesce on the hit
that delivered Dylan to a rock audience.

❹ FOR WHAT IT'S WORTH BUFFALO
SPRINGFIELD from BUFFALO SPRINGFIELD
An on-the-ground report of unrest on Sunset
Strip, with an indelible chorus and Neil Young's
ringing guitar notes acting as the hooks.

❺ THE SOUND OF SILENCE SIMON & GARFUNKEL
from SOUNDS OF SILENCE
It might be an allusion to modern alienation,
but it was so beatifically harmonized that it
had no trouble making the duo into superstars.

❻ CALIFORNIA DREAMIN' THE MAMAS & THE
PAPAS from IF YOU CAN BELIEVE YOUR EYES AND EARS
Deftly woven male–female harmonies and an
absurdly catchy melody transform California
into Utopia.

❼ GET TOGETHER THE YOUNGBLOODS from
THE YOUNGBLOODS
A Utopian vision for not just California but all of
humankind, steered clear of sappiness by Jesse
Colin Young's gentle yet soulful vocals.

❽ DO YOU BELIEVE IN MAGIC THE LOVIN'
SPOONFUL from DO YOU BELIEVE IN MAGIC
The Beatles-meets-Motown melody and an
uplifting chorus cement this declaration of

the healing powers of rock'n'roll. Folk-rock at its sunniest.

⑨ BOTH SIDES NOW JUDY COLLINS from WILDFLOWERS

Joni Mitchell's classic taking-stock folk song, turned into a glittering folk-rock hit with a multi-hued orchestral arrangement and Collins's pristine singing.

⑩ TODAY JEFFERSON AIRPLANE from SURREALISTIC PILLOW

A heartbreakingly pretty, largely acoustic ballad of cup-runneth-over hippy love that could have been a big hit, saved from schmaltziness by thundering Spectorian percussion.

Richie Unterberger

Foo Fighters

Foo Fighters have made life after Nirvana worth persevering with. And main man Dave Grohl has proved to be something of an ace songwriter to boot.

① ALL MY LIFE from ONE BY ONE

This track hinges on a cool stuttering riff which swings psychotically between loud and soft and lets Grohl indulge in some of his finest screaming to date.

② AURORA from THERE IS NOTHING LEFT TO LOSE

There's no hiding the sense of aching loss and bittersweet memories in this teasingly enigmatic, delicate yet powerful number.

③ BIG ME from FOO FIGHTERS

Short but very sweet, this gentle strumalong is a welcome antidote to Grohl's imposing guitar violence.

④ LEARN TO FLY from THERE IS NOTHING LEFT TO LOSE

Textbook songwriting, with shimmering guitars, soaring vocals, and a killer chorus. Grohl makes it all sound outrageously simple.

⑤ MONKEY WRENCH from THE COLOUR AND THE SHAPE

An intensely melodic punk tune with one hell of a memorable hook.

⑥ TIMES LIKE THESE from ONE BY ONE

Even if there were no vocals on this you'd be humming it for days after hearing it just once.

Essi Berelian

George Formby

Still no sign of him on iTunes, but the Brylcreemed, ukelele-bashing, Wigan-born singer/actor was once Britain's highest-paid entertainer. You'll find the following tracks on any number of greatest hits compilations, all of which will take you to a lost world of seaside fancies and triple entendres.

① THE EMPEROR OF LANCASHIRE

George the Cotton King returns home to throw a big tripe party for everyone. Oddly moving, and a great little dance tune.

② WHY DON'T WOMEN LIKE ME?

The Smiths used to play this one. Chorus: "If women like them like men like those, why don't women like me?"

③ YOU DON'T NEED A LICENCE FOR THAT

Such is the bureaucracy of post-War Britain that the only thing George doesn't need a licence for is "two bobs' worth of dark" (a snog in the cinema).

④ CHINESE LAUNDRY BLUES

Mr Wu, knickers and other classic Formbyisms.

⑤ WITH MY LITTLE STICK OF BLACKPOOL ROCK

"It may be sticky but I never complain/It's nice to have a nibble at it now and again."

❻ OUR FANNY'S GONE ALL YANKEE

The perils of GI infiltration into north-west England. Woodbines replaced by Camels, and "ee bah gum" replaced by "okay big boy".

Simon Garfield

Aretha Franklin

Under Jerry Wexler's supervision at Atlantic, the arrangements, choice of material and musicians all came together to create the perfect setting for Aretha's voice, which soared as it had never done before (and never has since). With the exception of Never Grow Old, all of the following can be found on *Respect – The Very Best Of Aretha Franklin*.

❶ I NEVER LOVED A MAN (THE WAY I LOVE YOU) from I NEVER LOVED A MAN THE WAY I LOVE YOU

One of just two tracks Aretha laid down at Muscle Shoals for her Atlantic debut – and what a debut! Outside gospel, had anyone heard a woman express emotion like this on record before?

❷ DO RIGHT WOMAN – DO RIGHT MAN from I NEVER LOVED A MAN THE WAY I LOVE YOU

The other Muscle Shoals track. Written by top country-soul songwriters Dan Penn and Chips Moman, this – incredibly – was the B-side of I Never Loved A Man. A restrained but heartfelt plea for equality and respect, which takes us up to…

❸ RESPECT from I NEVER LOVED A MAN THE WAY I LOVE YOU

More an answer record than a cover of Otis Redding's original, this remains as anthemic as the day it was recorded. Sock it to me!

❹ DR FEELGOOD (LOVE IS A SERIOUS BUSINESS) from I NEVER LOVED A MAN THE WAY I LOVE YOU

Originally the B-side of Respect, making Aretha's second Atlantic single another strong contender for the best 45 ever. The passion in her voice is almost frightening.

❺ (YOU MAKE ME FEEL LIKE) A NATURAL WOMAN from LADY SOUL

Aretha turns this Goffin-King-Wexler composition into a hymn to the redemptive power of human love.

❻ I SAY A LITTLE PRAYER from ARETHA NOW

Written by Bacharach and David for Dionne Warwick, but the sheer expressiveness and dynamic range of Aretha's voice make this the definitive version.

❼ THINK from ARETHA NOW

Another clarion call for respect (and freedom), immortalized on film in *The Blues Brothers*.

❽ LET IT BE from THIS GIRL'S IN LOVE WITH YOU

Paul McCartney is said to have written this with Aretha in mind, and you can see why: once again, she takes the song on to a higher plane.

❾ BRIDGE OVER TROUBLED WATER from GREATEST HITS

Paul Simon took his inspiration from a gospel song, and Aretha takes it back where it belongs. A transformation.

❿ NEVER GROW OLD from AMAZING GRACE

And she never will, on these recordings at least. Aretha, the preacher's daughter, back home in church – amazing grace indeed.

Neil Foxlee

Franz Ferdinand

This Scottish four-piece brought art-rock back to the mainstream with their eponymous 2004 debut album, from which all the following tracks are drawn.

❶ TAKE ME OUT

The song that established Franz Ferdinand in the public eye, thanks to one of the catchiest riffs of the new century.

❷ DARTS OF PLEASURE
FF's first single, though lauded in the music press for its clever use of syncopation and dynamics, wasn't the hit it deserved to be.

❸ MICHAEL
Frontman Alex Kapranos expresses homoerotic desires in the band's most risqué single to date.

❹ JACQUELINE
The philosophy of the modern British worker – "it's always better on holiday" – ironically expressed over clangy guitar and bass riffs.

❺ THE DARK OF THE MATINEE
Kapranos yearns for solitude and meaning in his life while being interviewed on BBC2 by Terry Wogan.

Ben Garfield

Free

Featuring Paul Rodgers' warm vocals and Paul Kossoff's ace guitar talents, these legendary bluesy youngsters possessed soul and maturity way beyond their years.

❶ ALL RIGHT NOW from FIRE AND WATER
A hooky stop-start riff, Rodger's sexy yelp and some seriously funky bass and percussion make this a feel-good classic.

❷ FIRE AND WATER from FIRE AND WATER
Paul Rodgers is hurtin' bad, mama, and he's just gotta get it off his (very hairy) chest. Kossoff makes his guitar cry like a true pro.

❸ HEAVY LOAD from FIRE AND WATER
How can a piano sound so world-weary? A beautifully wrought slice of misery with guitars relegated to the searing climax.

❹ LYING IN THE SUNSHINE from FREE
Summer heat turned into a liquid guitar refrain and complemented by Rodgers' languid vocals – he almost sounds like he's melting.

❺ MOUTHFUL OF GRASS from FREE
The sense of peace and space conjured up by this blissful instrumental is almost celestial. Less is definitely more.

❻ OH I WEPT from FIRE AND WATER
A gentle and lilting effort – Rodgers' voice almost cracks from the emotional struggle. Another economical but profound classic.

❼ SOLDIER BOY from FREE AT LAST
Martial drum rolls lead you into battle. Dark and troubled in tone, the song features some simple yet powerful guitar work.

❽ THE HUNTER from TONS OF SOBS
Just listen to Kossoff's guitar wail on this ferocious makeover of an R&B classic. Amazing to think the band were just teenagers at this time.

❾ THE STEALER from HIGHWAY
Andy Fraser's slippery, almost squelchy bass gives this track – which edges more towards rock – a fine and funky groove.

❿ WISHING WELL from HEARTBREAKER
A lot heavier and darker than their early stuff, with a stonking riff that makes this an early heavy-rock masterpiece.

Essi Berelian

Chansons Françaises

Okay, our French friends do not do le rock, but when it comes to songs – well, they are the masters. We could, maybe should, have done a whole list for many of the figures below, especially Charles Trenet (he of "Boum!"), who graced half the classic French movi es of the post-war years. Oh well, next edition…

❶ LA MER CHARLES TRENET from LA MER
Bobby Darin reworked this as Beyond The Sea

but Trenet's haunting original is the one to play as you cruise the Croisette in your 2CV.

❷ LA VIE EN ROSE EDITH PIAF from **SONGS OF A SPARROW**
The Little Sparrow's best-known song may be Je Ne Regrette Rien but this swirling accordeon-backed ballad is her finest work as both performer and lyricist.

❸ ET MAINTENANT GILBERT BECAUD from **L'ESSENTIEL**
Becaud was the epitome of a singing French heart-throb – his Et Maintenant became Shirley Bassey's What Now, My Love. Becaud gives his original the famous sex-charged 100,000 volts.

❹ SOUS LE CIEL DE PARIS JULIET GRECO from **THE BEST**
You can almost smell the Gauloises and taste the Ricard in this classic rendering of a song that conjures up 60s Paris, when Greco was the über hippy chick of the Left Bank.

❺ LA CHANSON DE JACKY JACQUES BREL from **INFINIMENT**
Belgian-born Brel inspired a generation of songwriters, from David Bowie to Marc Almond and Scott Walker, who had a hit with this track in English. Insist on the original.

❻ COMME D'HABITUDE CLAUDE FRANÇOIS from **COMME D'HABITUDE**
Paul Anka took this gentle reflection on unrequited love and turned it into Sinatra's balls-out My Way. Again, enjoy the more thoughtful and melancholic original.

❼ LE GORILLE GEORGE BRASSENS from **LE GORILLE**
Brassens remains an iconic French figure who composed thoughtful, witty songs. This one's about a well-endowed gorilla who escapes captivity and sodomises a judge.

❽ JE T'AIME... MOI NON PLUS SERGE GAINSBOURG & JANE BIRKIN from **JANE BIRKIN & SERGE GAINSBOURG**
English actress Birkin took over the singing role originally intended for Brigitte Bardot in this orgasmic romp censured by the Vatican.

❾ VOUS QUI PASSEZ SANS ME VOIR JEAN SABLON from **C'EST SI BON**
Sablon's song was a big hit in France in 1937, when he rivalled Maurice Chevalier on the world stage. To be taken with a glass of cognac in the wee small hours.

❿ J'ATTENDRAI TINO ROSSI from **J'ATTENDRAI**
Corsican-born Rossi was a great pre-War pin-up who produced a string of hits, and none better than this lush, atmospheric ballad.

Frank Barrett

Dodgy French lyrics

Somehow, putting a few French mots in an otherwise anglais song pretty much guarantees serieux kitsch. Blondie manage to get away with it; way down at the other end of the scale, there's Bill Wyman.

❶ DENIS BLONDIE from **PLASTIC LETTERS**
The lyrics are equally indecipherable in either French or English. But in general, Denis-dippy-doo, it's safe to assume that Blondie is in love with you-ah-oo. (In fact, she loves you so much she wants "a giant, everlasting fuck", to translate the last line of the French verse accurately).

❷ LE FREAK CHIC from **C'EST CHIC**
"Young and old are doing it, I'm told." Aaaaaah freak off.

❸ HIT ME WITH YOUR RHYTHM STICK IAN DURY AND THE BLOCKHEADS from **SEX & DRUGS & ROCK & ROLL**
"Das ist gut, c'est fantastique" – not just French, but German too! Hit me! Hit me! Hit me!

❹ I'M NOT SCARED EIGHTH WONDER from **FEARLESS**
The Pet Shop Boys' Neil Tennant asks us to "debarasse-moi de ces chiens/Avant qu'ils mordent". Yes, please get these dogs away from him before they bite.

5 JE NE SAIS PAS POURQUOI KYLIE from KYLIE
Sadly, we don't know why either. Maybe Kylie should have thought about it first?

6 JOE LE TAXI VANESSA PARADIS from M&J
OK, so she's French, but the lyrics are so bizarrely awful that her only excuse should have been being English. (And er, the title has the word "Joe" in it.)

7 LADY MARMALADE LABELLE from NIGHTBIRDS
Voulez-vous coucher avec moi? If you put it like that, then yes. A cover of a 1974 song about New Orleans prostitutes by The Eleventh Hour. Much covered since – by All Saints, and the lethal combination of Christina Aguilera, Lil' Kim, Mya & Pink (who you'd think were more likely to insist).

8 MICHELLE THE BEATLES from RUBBER SOUL
"… ma belle/These are words which go together well". Or perhaps not.

9 PSYCHO KILLER TALKING HEADS from TALKING HEADS '77
"Qu'est-ce que c'est/Fa fa fa fa fa fa fa fa fa fa/Far better". As David Byrne admits, "you're talkin' a lot, but you're not sayin' anything".

10 SI SI JE SUIS UN ROCK STAR BILL WYMAN from BILL WYMAN
Bill habite à south of France. Voulez-vous partir wiv' 'im? Unforgettable. (Unfortunately.) Actually, the English lyrics are better still: "We can take a hovercraft/Across the water/They'll think I'm your dad/And you're my daughter." Umm…

James McConnachie

French roots

The French roots music scene is big and vital and the country has numerous and strong regional strands. But the most fun to be had is in the South, so that is the emphasis here.

1 JOHNNY BRATSCH from RIEN DANS LES POCHES
Bratsch are the foremost band in France, having played together for 30 years now. Here these mad instrumentalists join forces with Hungarian Gypsy musicians Ando Drom on a song made famous by Edith Piaf.

2 A L'ARENE DES AUDACIEUX LO JO from AU CABARET SAUVAGE
Lo Jo is a wildly eclectic musical collective from Angers. With an imaginative array of instruments, and fronted by two North African sisters, they kick like hell on this.

3 PAS DE CI FABULOUS TROUBADORS from ERA PAS DE FAIRE
A professor of linguistics and a B-boy fuse the Troubadours, Brazilian nordestina and reggae. Inspired lyrics (in French and Occitan) are the icing on the cake.

4 PAGHJELLA DONNISULANA from PER AGATA
Donnisulana were revolutionaries in Corsican traditional music. Until they came on the scene women were allowed only to sing to their babies and mourn the dead.

5 LOS GOJATS COMPAGNIE LUBAT DÉ GASCONHA from SCATRAP JAZZCOGNE
Four free-jazz musicians relocate to the small southern town of Uzeste to create a mindblowing mix of jazz, rap, reggae and roots.

6 VOLI PAS MAI MOLZER LAS VACAS LA TALVERA from PAMPALIGOSSA
An outstanding combination of Southern France traditionals and dub-infused reggae.

7 ONDA LES NOUVELLES POLYPHONIES CORSES from LES NOUVELLES POLYPHONIES CORSES WITH HECTOR ZAZOU
An almost ambient rendering of traditional polyphonic singing with electronics, Ryuichy Sakamoto's piano and the clarinet of Ivo Papasov from Bulgaria.

8 MIRLIN TURKI ERIC MARCHAND ET LE TARAF DE CARABENSEBES from +DOR
Breton Eric Marchand combines with a gypsy band from Romania on this outing, which gives a new jazzy jazz feel to both musics.

❾ FACE A LA MER LES NEGRESSES VERTES from
10 REMIXES 87–93
The Negresses did a fantastic infusion of rock
with roots. Here Massive Attack reconstructed
their song about a cemetery by the beach.

❿ CAMINA DUPAIN from **CAMINA**
A Provençal song from this Marseilles band, set
to plaintiff trumpet, hurdy gurdy and vocals.
Ancient roots but 100% contemporary.

Jean Trouillet

Funk

**Ten tracks that will put the bump in your
trunk, the glide in your stride and the dip
in your hip.**

❶ GET OUT OF MY LIFE WOMAN LEE DORSEY
from **RIDE YOUR PONY**
The greatest drum beat of all-time?

❷ FUNKY BROADWAY DYKE & THE BLAZERS from
FUNKY BROADWAY
More "unnh" than anyone this side of James
Brown.

❸ WICKI WACKY FATBACK BAND from
KEEP ON STEPPIN'
Proof that funk doesn't have to bash you over
the head – it can slowly insinuate itself into
your hips.

❹ IT'S YOUR THING ISLEY BROTHERS from **DOIN'
THEIR THING**
A sexist load of bollocks, but my gosh, does
it groove.

❺ HOOK 'N' SLING EDDIE BO from **THE BEST OF**
One of the most rhythmically outrageous
records ever.

❻ EXPRESS YOURSELF CHARLES WRIGHT &
THE WATTS 103RD STREET RHYTHM BAND from
EXPRESS YOURSELF
Percolating bassline and goofy nonsense
psychedelia – what more do you need?

❼ DAP WALK ERNIE & THE TOP NOTES from
NEW ORLEANS FUNK
A dirtier, stankier version of Archie Bell & The
Drells with an octopus for a drummer.

❽ JUST KISSED MY BABY THE METERS from
REJUVENATION
New Orleans' finest at their most "nastay" and
most accessible.

❾ ROCK CREEK PARK THE BLACKBYRDS from
CITY LIFE
Perhaps the ultimate mellow summer jam.

❿ MORE BOUNCE TO THE OUNCE ZAPP
from **ZAPP**
Handclaps, synth bassline and stoopid Vocoder
make for one of the "slamminest" records ever.

Peter Shapiro

Peter Gabriel

After six albums with Genesis, Peter Gabriel walked, reinventing himself as a sound collagist – more landscape gardener, you might say, than rock god.

❶ SOLSBURY HILL from PETER GABRIEL 1
A deceptively simple acoustic guitar riff runs throughout this celebration of artistic freedom and the pleasures of rural Somerset.

❷ HERE COMES THE FLOOD ROBERT FRIPP from EXPOSURE
On *Peter Gabriel 1* this song was operatic. Here, on a Robert Fripp solo album, it emerges sparsely from dripping electronica and is all the more effective for it.

❸ GAMES WITHOUT FRONTIERS (MASSIVE/ DB REMIX) from STEAM
A West Country trip-hop remix freshens up this warhorse and restores its playfulness.

❹ ACROSS THE RIVER from THE BEST OF MUSIC AND RHYTHM
Gabriel wails and drums crash in an early example of his interest in world music. It first appeared on this album to pay off the debts incurred by the first WOMAD festival.

❺ WALLFLOWER from PETER GABRIEL 4
Unlike his song Biko (which he gave initially to Robert Wyatt), this human rights anthem has an anonymous hero facing interrogation from "clean white coats", Fairlight synthesizer samples rising from the shadows.

❻ MERCY STREET from SO
A rippling melody, one notch above ambient, drives this song about the poet Anne Sexton.

❼ SLEDGEHAMMER from SO
A song that inspires genuine affection even from non-fans – and one of the few occasions where Gabriel's love of steam-driven Motown-tinged funk pays off.

❽ BLOOD OF EDEN from US
A second cousin to Gabriel's duet with Kate Bush, Don't Give Up, this sees him teaming up with Sinead O'Connor, as brilliant and berserk as ever. The mix is loose and supple, with a keening duduk refrain.

❾ WHILE THE EARTH SLEEPS from THE STRANGE DAYS SOUNDTRACK
A collaboration with Belgian sonic colonialists Deep Forest sets Gabriel against Congolese pygmies for a mesmeric dance workout.

❿ DOWNSIDE UP from OVO
The Gabriel-soundtracked theatrical circus show was the one redeeming feature of the Millennium Dome: his music celebrated multi-cultural Britain and stood up in its own right.

David Honigmann

Galaxyquest

Space, the final musical frontier. Meet the songwriters who have boldly gone where no songwriters have gone before, exploring the universe's vast potential for cosmic metaphor.

❶ LIFE ON MARS? DAVID BOWIE from HUNKY DORY
Describing a young girl's escapism through cinema, this is prime Bowie, building from simple piano to a towering orchestral finale.

❷ SATURN STEVIE WONDER from SONGS IN THE KEY OF LIFE
Paradise is nowhere to be found on Earth, according to a world-weary Stevie. Above

futuristic synth effects, he says he's "going back to Saturn where the people smile".

❸ PLANET CLAIRE B52S from THE B52S
A perfect introduction to this band of cosmic crazies, Planet Claire is a wonderfully nonsensical cut of kitsch post-punk pop. Peter Gunn-esque strains and Fred Schneider's raving about aliens make for a surefire party starter.

❹ PLANET EARTH DURAN DURAN from DURAN DURAN
The Brummie pin-ups' blistering debut single. In between the catchy "bop-b'dop"s, Simon Le Bon alludes to impending global disaster.

❺ APOLLO 9 ADAM ANT from VIVE LE ROCK
Prince Charming waxes philosophical about a female who's escaped his attentions by hopping onto a passing star. Such misfortune doesn't seem to deter his high-spirited whoopsin' and jammerin', though.

❻ SATURN 5 INSPIRAL CARPETS from DEVIL HOPPING
A nostalgic jaunt through the heyday of space exploration, courtesy of Oldham's bowl-cut-wearing baggies. Clint Boon's childhood fascination with the 60s moon landings is complemented by the band's cheerful energy and telltale organ tinkling.

❼ FLY ME TO THE MOON FRANK SINATRA from SINATRA AT THE SANDS
Ol' Blue Eyes gave us the definitive version of this popular song which namechecks a few other celestial bodies for good measure. This 1966 live recording showcases Sinatra and Count Basie at their best.

❽ ROCKET MAN ELTON JOHN from HONKY CHATEAU 1972
Bernie Taupin's lyrics explore the isolation of an astronaut (a topical theme for the period), while Elt provides his inimitable flourish.

❾ GIRL FROM MARS ASH from 1977
Wistful memories of the eponymous sweetheart are moulded into an energetic speed ballad by the then-teenage Tim Wheeler and co.

❿ SATURN RETURN REM from REVEAL
Rich, electronic background music is kept in check, ceding centre-stage to Michael Stipe's reflective, confessional tone. A simple, but effective example of understated elegance.

Ed Wright

Garage rock

Decades before garage rock was synonymous with fake brother-and-sister bands or poseur boarding school alumni, the term meant nondescript American teens and college kids desperately trying to imitate the Stones. It was everything rock'n'roll is supposed to be.

❶ LOUIE LOUIE THE KINGSMEN from THE KINGSMEN IN PERSON
The Rosetta Stone of rock'n'roll.

❷ WOOLY BULLY SAM THE SHAM & THE PHARAOHS from WOOLY BULLY
Strip-joint R&B taken out into the stratosphere by a guy wearing a turban. There's a long-running debate on what the words are, or mean. "Got a cold haddock" is a possible opener.

❸ PSYCHO THE SONICS from HERE ARE THE SONICS
Drunken frat boys try to sing soul with gloriously sloppy results.

❹ DIRTY WATER THE STANDELLS from DIRTY WATER
As close as the Yanks got to the snarl and strut of The Rolling Stones.

❺ YOU'RE GONNA MISS ME THE 13TH FLOOR ELEVATORS from THE PSYCHEDELIC SOUNDS OF THE 13TH FLOOR ELEVATORS
Surf guitar + crazy electric jug + the punkiest vocals before Iggy Pop came along = perhaps the most intense garage record.

❻ 96 TEARS ? & THE MYSTERIANS from 96 TEARS
The record that definitively proved how much power one single note can have.

7 HEY JOE THE LEAVES from **HEY JOE**
Byrds jingle-jangle meets lysergic feedback freakout.

8 LAST TIME AROUND THE DEL-VETTS from **OH YEAH! THE BEST OF DUNWICH RECORDS VOL 1**
Total Yardbirds rip-off but when the results are this fuzzy and wild, who cares?

9 PSYCHOTIC REACTION COUNT FIVE from **PSYCHOTIC REACTION**
Even groovier than the group's stage apparel, which was no mean feat, as the Five all wore Dracula capes.

10 ACTION WOMAN THE LITTER from **DISTORTIONS**
The venom of The Stones gets teleported "out there" by one of the great guitar wig-outs of the 60s.

Peter Shapiro

Jan Garbarek

The cathedral-toned Norwegian saxophonist Jan Garbarek defined the "ECM sound" – sepulchral Northern European jazz. He moves seamlessly through Norwegian folk, Indian idioms, medieval polyphony, even electronica.

1 BEAST OF KOMMODO from **AFRIC PEPPERBIRD**
Terje Rypdal on electric guitar, Arild Andersen on bass and Jon Christensen on percussion provide an exotic rhythmic ground over which Garbarek howls and growls on tenor and flute: a far cry from his later reverent stillness.

2 VIDDENE from **DIS**
Ralph Towner's backdrop of twelve-string guitar and wind-harp throbs and breathes as Garbarek declaims on soprano. A couple of minutes in, the mood turns almost Spanish.

3 LILLEKORT from **EVENTYR**
Nana Vasconcelos's talking drums ripple underneath a duet between Garbarek and John Abercrombie's mandolin.

4 SAGA from **RAGAS AND SAGAS**
Pakistani musicians joined Garbarek for four ragas and one saga. On the former, Garbarek keeps a respectful distance; the saga is a fuller collaboration, Garbarek's sax bouncing off Ustad Fateh Ali Khan's singing.

5 BROTHER WIND SONG from **TWELVE MOONS**
After a couple of minutes of fragmented chaos, a determined melody starts, which swells into a march. Towards the end, Rainer Bruninghaus takes a perfect, trickling piano solo.

6 PARCE MIHI DOMINE from **OFFICIUM**
The Hilliard Ensemble and Garbarek play a mass for the dead. Garbarek's chorister-like soprano responds and rises up in praise.

7 O LORD IN THEE IS ALL MY TRUST from **MNEMOSYNE**
A return to the monastery: in this case, it is Thomas Tallis's anthem over which Garbarek swoops, rising nearer God with each verse.

8 IN PRAISE OF DREAMS from **IN PRAISE OF DREAMS**
Garbarek and viola player Kim Kashkashian slip in and out of time with each other to increasingly fractured and unsettling effect.

David Honigmann

Judy Garland

Child star, adult diva, showbiz legend and the Mistress of POW!

1 YOU MADE ME LOVE YOU from **BROADWAY MELODY OF 1938**
15 years old and sounding 30, in the movie Judy delivers this emotional version of the 1913 warhorse while gazing at a photograph of movie star Clark Gable.

2 OVER THE RAINBOW from **THE WIZARD OF OZ**
Rescued from being cut during previews, the definitive version of the yearning Arlen/Harburg song appeared in the 1939 classic. It made Judy a star.

❸ THE TROLLEY SONG from **MEET ME IN ST LOUIS**
Best of a string of great Blaine/Martin songs
(Have Yourself A Merry Little Christmas, The
Boy Next Door) in the movie. Garland's rhyth-
mic fizz and energy are irresistible.

❹ A COUPLE OF SWELLS from **EASTER PARADE**
A genuinely funny duet number with Fred
Astaire from the 1948 movie *Easter Parade*, for
which Judy and Fred portray tramps.

❺ FOR ME AND MY GAL from **LIVE AT THE PALACE**
Judy was reinvented by husband Sid Luft as a
concert performer after MGM sacked her and
this version of an old Garland movie song is
from her 1951–52 residency in New York. Her
charisma shines through the lo-fi recording.

❻ THE MAN THAT GOT AWAY from
A STAR IS BORN
From the 1954 movie that (briefly) re-launched
her film career after an unstable period, a
devastating, single-take tour de force of the
Arlen/Gershwin song.

❼ ZING WENT THE STRINGS OF MY HEART
from **JUDY IN LOVE**
A Garland favourite first heard in the 1938
movie *Listen, Darling*, Nelson Riddle recasts
it as a hard swinger on her 1958 album for
Capitol, and Judy comes out guns blazing.

❽ WHEN YOU'RE SMILING from **JUDY AT
CARNEGIE HALL**
It was in concert that mature Judy made sense;
from her legendary 1961 live album, her opening number sets the tone; sentimental, funny,
powerful and utterly unforgettable.

❾ MEDLEY from **JUDY, FRANK AND DEAN**
After some amiable fun with guests Sinatra
and Martin, Judy steals her own 1962 TV
special with a final mesmerizing selection of
vaudeville and movie oldies.

❿ BY MYSELF from **I COULD GO ON SINGING**
From her final movie in 1963 in which Judy
virtually played herself, a heartstopping version of the Deitz/Schwartz ballad.

Chris Ingham

Marvin Gaye

From his early solo hits and duets with
Tami Terrell and others, to his later, more
political and more confessional work,
Marvin Gaye was perhaps the most diverse
and original soul artist of all time.

❶ WHAT'S GOING ON? from **WHAT'S GOING ON?**
Motown soul music gets political. This initiated
Gaye's ground-breaking song-cycle of religion,
poverty and the modern world.

❷ LET'S GET IT ON from **LET'S GET IT ON**
The steamy opener on Gaye's remarkable
and equally unprecedented album of sex and
relationships grooves.

❸ MERCY MERCY ME from **WHAT'S GOING ON?**
Not only was this song's subject-matter – the
environment – unusual for its time, especially
for a soul artist, but the stark arrangement,
gently repetitive rhythm, gutsy sax and stagey
ending make it a piece of pure innovation.

❹ JUST TO KEEP YOU SATISFIED from
LET'S GET IT ON
Gaye's voice is never better than on this soaring, painfully explicit valediction to his wife
and failed marriage. Perhaps the most poignant piece of music he ever produced.

**❺ WHEN DID YOU STOP LOVING ME; WHEN
DID I STOP LOVING YOU?** from **HERE MY DEAR**
Gaye's attack on his ex-wife Anna Gordy, from
the album whose royalties he was ordered
to pay to her as alimony, is a rambling affair,
but this track is as passionate as anything he
recorded.

❻ SEXUAL HEALING from **MIDNIGHT LOVE**
The comeback song, with Gaye returning to
form – and sobriety – in Belgium and writing
this solid sexy groove in twenty minutes.

❼ TOO BUSY THINKING ABOUT MY BABY
from **MPG**
Not the obvious solo Marvin track from this

era, but displaying all the right Motown credentials – great song, great arrangement, and inch-perfect delivery.

❽ HOW SWEET IT IS (TO BE LOVED BY YOU) from HOW SWEET IT IS (TO BE LOVED BY YOU)
Marvin at the zenith of his solo pop career – his biggest seller before Grapevine.

❾ YOU'RE ALL I NEED TO GET BY MARVIN GAYE & TAMMI TERRELL from THE COMPLETE DUETS
This symbiotic duet represents the pinnacle of Marvin's time with probably his greatest partner, Tammi Terrell, before she died tragically young. They were perhaps the ultimate singing duo.

❿ MAIN THEME FROM TROUBLE MAN from TROUBLE MAN
Marvin wrote every note of this Blaxploitation soundtrack, and it is an overlooked gem: cool, spare, not unlike What's Going On in mood. And one of Gaye's own favourites.

Martin Dunford

Genesis

With their widdly diddly keyboards and crazy concept albums, the original Genesis were synonymous with prog rock, until Phil Collins led them into the world of 80s pop. Here's a selection from both camps.

GABRIEL DAYS

❶ THE FOUNTAIN OF SALMACIS from NURSERY CRYME
Greek gods and nymphs meet in this odd little Prog drama. Sun-dappled waters and isolated glades never sounded more enchanting.

❷ SUPPER'S READY from FOXTROT
At nearly 23 minutes this is an early defining epic. Surreal, blackly humorous and cryptic, you'll hear something new every time.

❸ I KNOW WHAT I LIKE (IN YOUR WARDROBE) from SELLING ENGLAND BY THE POUND
The band's first proper hit. Typically wacky lyrics about sentient lawnmowers (or something) from Gabriel and some great whirring effects.

❹ THE LAMB LIES DOWN ON BROADWAY from THE LAMB LIES DOWN ON BROADWAY
Concept albums ahoy! A majestic opening to a classic album, Gabriel's loopy lyrics joyously defy logic.

❺ IN THE CAGE from THE LAMB LIES DOWN ON BROADWAY
Beware weird time signatures. Gabriel seems to manifest multiple personalities and Banks' twiddly synths run rings around your brain.

❻ THE CARPET CRAWLERS from THE LAMB LIES DOWN ON BROADWAY
This could have been a pop song if it wasn't just so damn weird. The melody and lush layered vocals almost hypnotize through their beautiful simplicity.

PHIL TAKES THE MIKE

❼ ROBBERY, ASSAULT AND BATTERY from A TRICK OF THE TAIL
A jolly and ironic little tale of crime and punishment.

❽ ALL IN A MOUSE'S NIGHT from WIND AND WUTHERING
Gorgeously arranged, this proggy Tom and Jerry cartoon set to swirling synths must rank among the more eccentrically humorous post-Gabriel efforts.

❾ FOLLOW YOU, FOLLOW ME from ...AND THEN THERE WERE THREE...
Light and commercial without being too sugary. Tony Banks' light keyboards give the song a pop feel while harking back to their prog past.

❿ MAMA from GENESIS
Sweat drips down the walls and a dim light flickers in the corner – Collins sounds improbably sinister in this steamy, slowbuilding epic.

Essi Berelian

Dizzy Gillespie

The beret-sporting, goateed figurehead of the modern jazz revolution, a stunning trumpeter and as dizzy as a fox.

❶ WOODY 'N' YOU from THE DIZZY GILLESPIE STORY
It was Coleman Hawkins's date in 1944 but this carefully cascading chord sequence (apparently arrived at during the session itself and hurriedly recorded) is the unmistakable work of the far-thinking young trumpeter.

❷ BE BOP from THE DIZZY GILLESPIE STORY
Tenor saxophonist Don Byas does well with this uptempo 1945 exercise in minor-chord improvisation but Dizzy's blistering, bubbling solo is a virtuosic revelation.

❸ GROOVIN' HIGH from THE DIZZY GILLESPIE STORY
Fashioned ingeniously from the extended chords of old chestnut Whispering, it's an intricately arranged 1945 chart that sets up perfectly Diz's midway grandstanding four-bar break before an lovely half-time coda.

❹ SALT PEANUTS from THE DIZZY GILLESPIE STORY
The offbeat humour of the minimalist theme and daft vocal barely distract from the dazzling instrumental skill of Parker and Gillespie on this sizzling 1945 I Got Rhythm variation.

❺ THINGS TO COME from THE DIZZY GILLESPIE STORY
A jaw-dropping Gill Fuller/Gillespie theme extending the minor theme of "Bebop" to ludicrously intricate levels in 1946 and proving that a big band could handle the new music.

❻ A NIGHT IN TUNISIA from THE DIZZY GILLESPIE STORY
He'd recorded his exotic classic with Bird at a 1945 studio session but this extended 1947 Carnegie Hall rendition – again with Parker – has five full minutes of mature bop genius.

❼ MANTECA from THE DIZZY GILLESPIE STORY
A mighty 1947 example of Dizzy's blending of latin rhythms, big band textures and bebop language to create an exciting hybrid genre, later dubbed "Cubop".

❽ OOL-YA-KOO from THE DIZZY GILLESPIE STORY
One of Dizzy's occasional scat novelties (see also Oo-Bop-Sh'Bam and Oo-Pop-A-Da), as usual the tonsil twisting on this 1947 bop blues contains a wealth of musical detail.

❾ CON ALMA from AFRO
Based on chords inspired by Bach, this bewitching piece dates back from his first big band but was revisited by Dizzy throughout his career including this effectively latinized 1954 version.

❿ THE ETERNAL TRIANGLE from SONNY SIDE UP
Dizzy acts as wise old ringmaster in the 1957 cutting contest between Sonny Stitt and Sonny Rollins and gets in some sparkling stuff of his own on this fiendish Stitt theme taken at breakneck speed.

Chris Ingham

Classic girl groups

The finest professional pop songwriters of the early to mid 60s, layered production packed with imagination, the catchiest tunes on the hit parade, and young women who believed what they sang – that was the classic girl group sound.

❶ BE MY BABY THE RONETTES from THE BEST OF
Drums boom like the hearts of the most infatuated young lovers on Phil Spector's grandest production. Ronnie Spector delivers a bewitching invitation that's impossible to refuse.

❷ LEADER OF THE PACK THE SHANGRI-LAS from THE BEST OF
Rock's most excessive and most effective minimelodrama, garnished by violent motorcycle

crash effects and a hammering, tragedy-foretelling piano.

❸ HE'S SO FINE THE CHIFFONS from THE BEST OF
It's a simple upward-climbing riff, but it's among pop's most magical hooks. The plain-spoken devotion of the lyric is amplified by the Chiffons' lilting "doo-lang doo-lang"s.

❹ HE'S A REBEL THE CRYSTALS from THE BEST OF
Adolescent rebellion often lurked behind the good-hearted curtain of the girl group sound, as in this proud idolization of a misfit hero.

❺ SALLY GO ROUND THE ROSES THE JAYNETTS
from THE BEST OF THE GIRL GROUPS, VOL 1
One of the most memorable one-hit wonder smashes of all time, its elliptical piano riff and enigmatic lyric saturated with foggy mystery.

❻ WILL YOU STILL LOVE ME TOMORROW
THE SHIRELLES from 25 ALL-TIME GREATEST HITS
"Yes!" is the no-brainer answer to this winsome plea dusted with dancing strings and an immensely likable Gerry Goffin/Carole King-penned melody.

❼ TELL HIM THE EXCITERS from THE BEST OF THE GIRL GROUPS VOL 2
Staccato strings that jab like a doctor's needle, the stern, proud admonitions of the verse giving way to a chorus of bullfight-cheering strength.

❽ ONE FINE DAY THE CHIFFONS from THE BEST OF
Insanely raucous piano catapults this into overdrive and keeps it there, buoyed by another outstanding Goffin-King tune and waves of "shoo-be-do-be-do-be-do-be-bo-bop-bop"s.

❾ MY ONE AND ONLY, JIMMY BOY
THE GIRLFRIENDS from EARLY GIRLS VOL 3
Perhaps the finest imitation Phil Spector production of all, its combination of defiantly grinning vocal and pummelling rhythm is the equal of any Crystals hit.

❿ REMEMBER (WALKIN' IN THE SAND)
THE SHANGRI-LAS from THE BEST OF
Shaky rehearsal hall-quality piano, a Moonlight

Sonata-like melody, mournful vocals, and chattering seagull effects add up to a downbeat girl group classic.

Richie Unterberger

Girls Just Wanna Have Fun

Yes, the 80s had big hair, gummy bracelets from wrist to elbow, underwear worn as outerwear and fingerless lace gloves (thank you, Ms Ciccone), but what saved the decade from casualty were the bouncy guitar licks, quirky vocals and hopelessly catchy lyrics of its sassy girl pop.

❶ MICKEY TONI BASIL from WORD OF MOUTH
New Wave novelty Toni Basil pom-pommed her way into 80s consciousness with a flirty ditty to match her gum-smacking, cheerleading video persona, early MTV making her famous for fifteen minutes.

❷ MORNING TRAIN (NINE TO FIVE)
SHEENA EASTON from THE SINGLES COLLECTIONS
Scots lass Easton injects synthesizer sass into the morning commute: sprightly, rousing and entertainingly vacuous. It clearly captivated Prince, who promptly signed her up.

❸ VACATION THE GO GOS from VACATION
Significant? No. Deep? Hardly. Fun and frothy? Absolutely.

❹ QUEEN OF HEARTS JUICE NEWTON from JUICE
The queen of crossover unleashed this slick country-pop hit, rooted in down-home twang with a healthy dollop of dancey New Wave.

❺ GIRLS JUST WANNA HAVE FUN CYNDI
LAUPER from SHE'S SO UNUSUAL
This pop paean sparkled with hiccupy, perky hooks and a galvanizing "Go, girl!" theme, rendered in a giddy, baby-doll voice. Sensitive yet subversive, the song (and Lauper, in all her

rainbow-hued hair) will be forever radiantly tied to the decade.

❻ FLASHDANCE… WHAT A FEELING
IRENE CARA from **WHAT A FEELING**
Legwarmers notwithstanding, Cara's throaty, soaring anthem managed to rise above the cheesy overproduction, inspiring a generation with its earnest message – "Take your passion, and make it happen".

❼ LIKE A VIRGIN **MADONNA** from **LIKE A VIRGIN**
Writhing in a wedding dress on a Venetian gondola, the diva of the decade mined a heady, taboo-busting mix of religion and sex, and the public reacted like they were being "touched for the very first time".

❽ CRUEL SUMMER **BANANARAMA** from **BANANARAMA**
An evocative smash with sweet smears of bubblegum and plaintive New Wave peeking through the girl trio's messy hair.

❾ WALKING ON SUNSHINE **KATRINA AND THE WAVES** from **WALKING ON SUNSHINE**
Feel-good 60s beat dressed up as a glittery, 80s dance mix with a sunny refrain that begs to be belted out at the top of one's lungs.

❿ MANIC MONDAY **THE BANGLES** from **DIFFERENT LIGHT**
A glossy, jaunty, Prince-penned chart-topper, its hummable harmonies were spiked with pop-punk attitude and it was an effervescent antidote to the morning blues.

AnneLise Sorensen

Glam rock

For a brief but rather wonderful spell in the early to mid 70s, pop music in the UK resolutely refused to take itself seriously. Grown men – and sometimes even a few women – put stars on their foreheads, glitter under their eyes and platform soles on their big shiny boots.

❶ ALL THE YOUNG DUDES **MOTT THE HOOPLE** from **ALL THE YOUNG DUDES**
A little Bowie magic went a long way for this otherwise rather dull band. He sang backing vocals, did handclaps, and wrote and produced what would turn out to be their best song by a long shot.

❷ VIRGINIA PLAIN **ROXY MUSIC** from **THE BEST OF ROXY MUSIC**
Though Roxy soon became something both more suave and more strange, glam rock seemed like a fitting pigeonhole for early work such as their dazzling first single. It's hard to imagine them minding much, given their collective dress sense.

❸ GUDBUY T'JANE from **GET YER BOOTS ON: THE BEST OF SLADE**
Is it the red-hot riff, Noddy Holder's lusty, bellowed vocal, the insistent maracas or the stoopid spelling of the title that made this the best single of the 70s? Discuss…

❹ ZIGGY STARDUST **DAVID BOWIE** from **THE RISE AND FALL OF ZIGGY STARDUST…**
A theatrical masterpiece. The hilarious lyrics squirm with febrile rock'n'roll imagery and epic myth-making, such as: "He took it all too far/But boy could he play guitar!"

❺ SOLID GOLD EASY ACTION **T REX** from **20TH CENTURY BOY: THE ULTIMATE COLLECTION**
In 1973, I asked my dad to buy me this single. "You'll be sick of it in a week!" he declared, before relenting. He still likes it. Marc Bolan at his most gloriously juvenile.

❻ HELLO! HELLO! I'M BACK AGAIN **GARY GLITTER** from **32 GLAM HITS**
Five words you're unlikely to ever hear again from the exiled-in-disgrace Leader Of The Gang.

❼ SEE MY BABY **JIVE WIZZARD** from **SINGLES As & Bs**
The most hummable hit from this rather OTT band fronted by the charismatic ex-ELO member Roy Wood, whose excessive make-up emphasized a pair of wildly staring eyes.

❽ 48 CRASH SUZI QUATRO from **GREATEST HITS**

This leather clad, bass-toting singer was a role model for a whole generation of female rockers and more besides. Suzi always gave a good chorus, as this rousing rocker shows.

❾ BALLROOM BLITZ SWEET from **THE BEST OF SWEET**

Fantastic energy and an unforgettable vocal by the late Brian Connolly. Backed by the brilliant songwriting duo Chinn and Chapman, Sweet had a string of hits at the height of glam.

❿ PERSONALITY CRISIS THE NEW YORK DOLLS from **THE NEW YORK DOLLS**

The leading stateside exponents of glam rock were a bunch of hard-rockin' cross-dressing New York substance abusers, whose raucous output anticipated punk.

Jon Lusk

Dexter Gordon

With his cavernous tone and impeccable phrasing, Gordon's name and sound are synonymous with the smoky clubs of jazz cliché. However, despite his preference for popular tunes, he was one of jazz's great interpreters, with an unparalleled ability to communicate through simplicity.

❶ DON'T EXPLAIN from **A SWINGIN' AFFAIR**

Dexter Gordon doing what he does better than anyone else: telling a love story in the early hours.

❷ ERNIE'S TUNE from **DEXTER CALLING**

Another towering ballad from the master, his sax sound more human than ever.

❸ I GUESS I'LL HANG MY TEARS OUT TO DRY from **GO**

The title's clumsy but the playing is gorgeous.

❹ LOVE FOR SALE from **GO**

A jumpy rendition of the Cole Porter classic. Gordon's line is clipped and accurate.

❺ SCRAPPLE FROM THE APPLE from **OUR MAN IN PARIS**

Gordon harks back to his hard-bop roots with this fluid version of Charlie Parker's tune.

❻ A NIGHT IN TUNISIA from **OUR MAN IN PARIS**

Dizzy gets the Dexter treatment: an energetic and muscular version of the trumpeter's best-known composition.

❼ DOXY from **BOTH SIDES OF MIDNIGHT**

Gordon is at his bluesy, breezy best in this imperious take on a Sonny Rollins number.

❽ FRIED BANANAS from **MORE POWER!**

A swinging example of the perfection of the saxophonist's tone and phrasing

Nat Defriend

American gospel

Religion aside, gospel is the bedrock of just about all Anglo-American popular music. Sinners, free thinkers and fence-sitters one and all will appreciate this lot.

❶ HONEY IN THE ROCK BLIND MAMIE FOREHAND from **AMERICAN PRIMITIVE VOL 1**

The ideal accompaniment to a dark night of the soul.

❷ MOTHER'S CHILDREN HAVE A HARD TIME BLIND WILLIE JOHNSON from **THE COMPLETE BLIND WILLIE JOHNSON**

Blind Willie's grammar may be flawed (it should read "motherless"), but it's hard to imagine a more perfect record.

❸ I'LL BE RESTED (WHEN THE ROLL IS CALLED) BLIND ROOSEVELT GRAVES & BROTHER from **AMERICAN PRIMITIVE VOL 1**

Guitarist John Fahey called this the hottest religious record ever made – it's hard to disagree.

④ GOSPEL TRAIN GOLDEN GATE JUBILEE QUARTET from **THE GOLDEN GATE QUARTET VOL 1**
This swings like nobody's business.

⑤ MOVE ON UP A LITTLE HIGHER MAHALIA JACKSON from **HOW I GOT OVER: THE APOLLO SESSIONS**
There surely has never been a performance captured on record as physically powerful.

⑥ MILKY WHITE WAY THE TRUMPETEERS from **MILKY WHITE WAY**
One of the best selling gospel records ever, and for good reason.

⑦ BY AND BY THE SOUL STIRRERS from **SHINE ON ME**
Long before Sam Cooke joined the group, they were the best of the male gospel groups. This shows why.

⑧ MARY DON'T YOU WEEP THE SWAN SILVERTONES from **THE SWAN SILVERTONES**
Hard gospel at its most acrobatic and intense.

⑨ OLD LANDMARK ARETHA FRANKLIN from **AMAZING GRACE**
Gospel, or any other music, doesn't get any more fiery than this.

⑩ MARION WILLIAMS GO DOWN MOSES from **THE GREAT GOSPEL WOMEN VOL 2**
Archaic sounding, and sometimes stilted, this performance nevertheless shows why many critics call Williams the greatest singer ever.

Peter Shapiro

South African gospel

It doesn't come much more stirring than South African gospel, and these tracks range from solo divas to massed choirs.

❶ NGIYEKELENI REBECCA MALOPE from **NGIYEKELENI**
Perhaps the greatest track from the pint-sized but full-voiced queen of SA gospel.

❷ NOH! NOH! SEBEHLALA BEJABULA JABU HLONGWANE from **JOYOUS CELEBRATION 3**
Massive choral sound, assuring listeners that we will always be happy in heaven. If it sounds anything like this up there, it must be true.

❸ AVULEKILE AMASANGO ISHMAEL from **GOSPEL GROOVES**
"The gates of heaven are opening" sings Ishmael in this heartstring-tugging classic.

❹ IMVUSELELO YASE NATALI IZIGI from **IZIGI**
Superbly rousing choral number. The lyric's claim "I can feel the stamping" says it all.

❺ VUYO MOKOENA PURE MAGIC NJALO from **NJALO**
Smooth singing Vuyo is the Barry White of SA gospel and this is his finest song.

❻ DIPHALA DI RAPEDISA MOPORESIDENTE THABO MBEKI SOLLY MOHOLO from **MOTLHANG KE KOLOBETSWA "DIE POPPE SAL DANS"**
The best of the Zionist gospel singers, Moholo wishes the President well in this stirring epic.

❼ VUMA BRENDA FASSIE from **MINA NAWE**
"Allow Him in", advises Brenda, "and you'll be saved." Agree or not, this is a beautifully moving gospel song.

❽ MBULALI WAMI MARIA LE MARIA from **MARIA LE MARIA**
A moving ode to a murderer from his victim, singing "we'll meet in heaven…"

❾ JERUSALEMA MANDOZA from **GOSPEL GROOVES**
Mandoza's best known for his stomp rock kwaito, but he's a fine gospel artist, too, as this rasping hymn to Jerusalem amply proves.

❿ EKUSEN' EMATHUNENI LADYSMITH BLACK MAMBAZO from **LIPH' IQINISO**
The still sadness of the morning after the crucifixion is the subject of this Joseph Shabalala poem, immaculately arranged, and beautifully delivered by the celebrated LBM.

Gregory Salter

g

Goth

Acres and acres of black and a fear of bright lights. Be afraid. Be very afraid.

❶ DESIRE GENE LOVES JEZEBEL from **DISCOVER**
Driven and achingly melodic, its ethereal guitar lines ricochet all over the shop.

❷ I WALK THE LINE ALIEN SEX FIEND from **ALL OUR YESTERDAYS**
Surf rock in midnight black: Nik Fiend walks the line between good and evil in this twangy, grim and grandiose goth gem.

❸ LOVE ME TO DEATH THE MISSION from **GOD'S OWN MEDICINE**
Jangly, romantically doomed guitar heaven. Poor Wayne Hussey sounds like he's got it bad.

❹ LUCRETIA (MY REFLECTION) THE SISTERS OF MERCY from **FLOODLAND**
A strident, pumping bass and drum machine (named Doktor Avalanche) hammer this beautifully bleak track right into the dancefloor.

❺ PREACHER MAN FIELDS OF THE NEPHILIM from **DAWNRAZOR**
A subtle Ennio Morricone homage launches this dusty, spaghetti-western-inspired drama. McCoy's supernaturally deep voice sounds as parched as the Mexican desert.

❻ SEBASTIANE SEX GANG CHILDREN from **FALL: THE COMPLETE SINGLES**
This is way out there. A heaving bassline, screeching violins and Andi Sexgang's barking mad vocals topping the melodramatic madness.

❼ SPELLBOUND SIOUXSIE AND THE BANSHEES from **JUJU**
As hypnotically enchanting as the title suggests, this is also starkly violent, the spiralling melody meshing tightly with Siouxsie's possessed vocals.

❽ SPIRIT WALKER THE CULT from **DREAMTIME**
The seeds of stadium rock are present but the chiming guitars and Ian Astbury's wolf child howl ensure the track remains shrouded in the cloak of Goth.

❾ THE PASSION OF LOVERS BAUHAUS from **MASK**
A tense and turbulent masterpiece with a twisting rhythm hooked on a hyperactive bassline. Peter Murphy's vocals sound gloriously aloof throughout.

❿ WALK INTO THE SUN THE MARCH VIOLETS from **THE BOTANIC VERSES**
Goths and sunlight? Surely some mistake? This is a bouncy, manic little tune complete with a bright and sprightly little sax solo in the middle.

Essi Berelian

Grateful Dead

From spaced-out acid rock to mellow Americana, Grateful Dead covered the whole musical waterfront until the untimely death of their avatar Jerry Garcia in 1995.

❶ DARK STAR from **LIVE DEAD**
All these years on, this twenty-minute intergalactic jam recorded live in 1969 still represents the high tide of West Coast acid rock.

❷ TURN ON YOUR LOVELIGHT from **LIVE DEAD**
A showcase for the talents of Pigpen, the blues-and-whisky drenched singer who was the first of three keyboardists to die on the band over the years.

❸ UNCLE JOHN'S BAND from **WORKINGMAN'S DEAD**
The joyous opening track from the album on which they swapped extended acid jams for tightly constructed country-rock songs.

149

David Gray's
Lost Songs

DAVID GRAY has sold more albums in the 21st century than any British artist except Dido. Needless to say, his playlist is heavily dominated by singer-songwriters – with one or two surprises.

① **IT'S ALRIGHT MA (I'M ONLY BLEEDING)** BOB DYLAN from BRINGING IT ALL BACK HOME

② **PARASITE** NICK DRAKE from PINK MOON

③ **MANSION ON THE HILL** BRUCE SPRINGSTEEN from NEBRASKA

④ **BALLERINA** VAN MORRISON from ASTRAL WEEKS

⑤ **MERCY MERCY ME** MARVIN GAYE from WHAT'S GOING ON

⑥ **REFUGE OF THE ROADS** JONI MITCHELL from HEJIRA

⑦ **DREAM GERRARD** TRAFFIC from WHEN THE EAGLE FLIES

⑧ **DESIRE** TALK TALK from THE VERY BEST OF

⑨ **JUST LIKE TOM THUMB'S BLUES** NINA SIMONE from TO LOVE SOMEBODY

⑩ **QUIET NIGHT OF QUIET STARS** FRANK SINATRA & ANTONIO CARLOS JOBIM from FRANCIS ALBERT SINATRA & ANTONIO CARLOS JOBIM

---

④ **TRUCKIN'** from AMERICAN BEAUTY
Autobiographical anthem of the band's busts and a stirring manifesto of defiance.

⑤ **RIPPLE** from AMERICAN BEAUTY
Exquisite tune from Garcia with Zen-like lyrics by Robert Hunter

⑥ **SUGAR MAGNOLIA** from AMERICAN BEAUTY
Another classic from their most flawless album, this time written and sung by Bobby Weir

⑦ **PLAYING IN THE BAND** from GRATEFUL DEAD
Brilliant exposition of the communal Deadhead philosophy from the 1971 live album affectionately known to fans as "Skullfuck", a title not surprisingly vetoed by Warner Brothers.

⑧ **JACK STRAW** from EUROPE 1972
By the early 70s the Dead were so prolific that many of their best songs never found their way onto a studio album. This cowboy-song gem only ever appeared on a triple live set in 1972.

⑨ **UNBROKEN CHAIN** from FROM THE MARS HOTEL
Classically-trained bassist Phil Lesh wrote only

a handful of songs for the band over the years. This complex, jazzy 1974 offering was his finest moment and later gave its name to his charitable foundation.

⑩ **TOUCH OF GREY** from IN THE DARK
After seven years away from the studio, they returned in triumph in 1987 with an album that included Touch of Grey, their only American top ten single.

Nigel Williamson

Al Green

No one sings soul quite like Al Green; even though he has been minister at his own Memphis church for the last 25 years, you only have to see him in concert to realize that the tortured sensuality that infused his 70s classics still resounds from every note he sings.

❶ TIRED OF BEING ALONE from **AL GREEN GETS NEXT TO YOU**
Green's first hit, in 1971, saw him very definitely on the lookout for love.

❷ LET'S STAY TOGETHER from
LET'S STAY TOGETHER
Al himself didn't like his biggest hit when he first recorded it in 1971; record buyers made him an international star regardless.

❸ LOVE AND HAPPINESS from
I'M STILL IN LOVE WITH YOU
A strangely compelling 1972 saga of love and jealousy, almost like eavesdropping on someone else's confidences.

❹ I'M GLAD YOU'RE MINE from
I'M STILL IN LOVE WITH YOU
From its supremely funky drum break onwards – courtesy of Al Jackson – a truly irresistible love song.

❺ SIMPLY BEAUTIFUL from
I'M STILL IN LOVE WITH YOU
Another perfect love song, imbued with overwhelming tenderness.

❻ FUNNY HOW TIME SLIPS AWAY from **CALL ME**
The rueful longing in Green's voice makes this Willie Nelson song his own. One of his many attempts to out-do Elvis.

❼ JESUS IS WAITING from **CALL ME**
A sublime, almost private meditation from 1973, in which Green duets beautifully with his own multi-tracked self.

❽ TAKE ME TO THE RIVER from
AL GREEN EXPLORES YOUR MIND
By 1974, as Green moved further towards the church, the gospel elements in his secular work were becoming ever more pronounced.

❾ PEOPLE GET READY from
GREATEST GOSPEL HITS
A spell-binding rendition of Curtis Mayfield's gospel anthem.

Al Green
Plays

One of the greatest soul singers of our age, AL GREEN's playlist recognizes the influences of such classic voices as Sam Cooke and Otis Redding on his own style but also reveals tastes that range from jazz to hip-hop.

❶ JUST FOR THE LOVE JOHN COLTRANE from **LEGENDS OF JAZZ**

❷ MOON DREAMS MILES DAVIS from **BIRTH OF THE COOL**

❸ YOU SEND ME SAM COOKE from **GREATEST HITS**

❹ THE WIND CRIES MARY JIMI HENDRIX from **ARE YOU EXPERIENCED**

❺ TRY A LITTLE TENDERNESS OTIS REDDING from **COMPLETE AND UNBELIEVABLE: THE OTIS REDDING DICTIONARY OF SOUL**

❻ HIGHER GROUND STEVIE WONDER from **INNER VISIONS**

❼ WHERE DO WE GO FROM HERE CHICAGO from **CHICAGO II**

❽ SIMPLY BEAUTIFUL QUEEN LATIFAH from **THE DANA OWENS ALBUM**

❾ IF I AIN'T GOT YOU ALICIA KEYS from **THE DIARY OF ALICIA KEYS**

❿ THE FACT IS (I NEED YOU) JILL SCOTT from **BEAUTIFULLY HUMAN: WORDS AND SOUNDS, VOL 2**

⑩ STRAIGHTEN OUT YOUR LIFE from **GREATEST GOSPEL HITS**

This impassioned 1983 summons to the righteous life marked Green's finest moment in gospel.

Greg Ward

Green Day

World-beating punk-pop and then some. Since breaking through with the hit album *Dookie*, singer/guitarist Billie Joe and co have developed well beyond mere three-chord thrashes.

❶ AT THE LIBRARY from **39/SMOOTH**

It ain't slickly produced but it is charming in a simple but affecting boy-lusts-after-girl-who-doesn't-know-he-exists kind of way.

❷ BLOOD, SEX AND BOOZE from **WARNING**

A jolly little S&M ditty which bounces along like a Rottweiler on a spacehopper.

❸ DON'T LEAVE ME from **39/SMOOTH**

Our hero's got the girl, but not for much longer by the sounds of it. A concise and speedy number with acres of great pop harmonies.

❹ GOOD RIDDANCE (TIME OF YOUR LIFE) from **NIMROD**

Drenched in nostalgia, this acoustic number is simple but effective – only a few well-placed strings underline the melancholy tone.

❺ HITCHIN' A RIDE from **NIMROD**

Size ten boots and knuckledusters await the unwary in this cautionary tale, which gives you a good going over right from the opening bars.

❻ JESUS OF SUBURBIA from **AMERICAN IDIOT**

A punk rock concept suite? Surely some mistake? Nope, here's a nine-minutes-plus epic flowing from one rambunctious section to the next.

❼ MISERY from **WARNING**

Fancy a change of pace? Try this bizarre polka punk'n'folk effort complete with accordion, violins and mandolin.

❽ WAKE ME UP WHEN SEPTEMBER ENDS from **AMERICAN IDIOT**

Gently strummed acoustic guitars and delicate chimes build to a crashing chorus.

Essi Berelian

Grunge

The early 90s sound of Seattle that burst forth onto an unsuspecting audience, fusing the core elements of rock'n'roll, metal and punk in a reaction to the growth of the over-commercialized music mainstream. Thus was born a new post-punk genre, striking raw, imperfect chords, first with disaffected teenagers, then dollar-tinged ones with ad execs.

❶ ABOUT A GIRL NIRVANA from **BLEACH**

Grunge's most celebrated purveyors break away from their typical screeching guitars and percussive thuds. An undulating melody and laid-back strumming allow Kurt Cobain's voice alone to provide the emotional intensity.

❷ TOUCH ME I'M SICK MUDHONEY from **SUPERFUZZ BIGMUFF**

The Grunge pioneers combine distorted guitars, pulverizing drums and blood-curdling vocals to create down'n'dirty rock music. Poetic it's not, but for breakneck, bluesy, bar-room brawl beats, it can't be topped.

❸ JESUS CHRIST POSE SOUNDGARDEN from **BADMOTORFINGER**

Straddling heavy metal and punk, Soundgarden's hard rock beats fell snugly into the grunge pot by their third album's release. This six-minute opus is an energetic barrage of riffs, feedback and lung-bursting singing.

❹ JEREMY PEARL JAM from TEN

An MTV favourite, this hit from the band's debut album showcases their signature classic rock melodies and Eddie Vedder's stentorian vocals, combined with disturbing, provocative subject matter.

❺ WOULD? ALICE IN CHAINS from DIRT

Formed in 1987, AiN went on to incorporate the bleak, introspective and self-destructive sensibilities of their grungier Seattle peers. Here, Layne Staley and Jerry Cantrell nail druggy musings onto the latter's beguiling guitar playing on a standout track from the band's breakthrough LP.

Ed Wright

Guitar breaks

"Heads down meet you at the end" guitar riffs have their own list elsewhere in this book. But then there's the guitar break where the singer has to content himself with shaking a tambourine while the man with the axe seriously gets to show off.

❶ RED HOUSE JIMI HENDRIX from ARE YOU EXPERIENCED?

On which he teases and twists a standard twelve-bar blues into places it had never been before…

❷ SHOULDN'T HAVE TOOK MORE THAN YOU GAVE ERIC CLAPTON from DAVE MASON'S ALONE TOGETHER

The best example of wah-wah guitar God – or anyone else – ever recorded.

❸ ALIVE MIKE McCREADY from PEARL JAM'S TEN

And he then modestly admitted he'd copped the lick from Kiss's Ace Frehley…

❹ SILVER AND GOLD BARRY MELTON from COUNTRY JOE AND THE FISH'S CJ FISH

If an alien landed and demanded to know what West Coast guitar was all about, this is what you'd play them.

❺ REELIN' IN THE YEARS ELLIOT RANDALL from STEELY DAN'S CAN'T BUY A THRILL

Elliott who? But it only takes one classic solo to achieve rock'n'roll immortality…

❻ STAIRWAY TO HEAVEN JIMMY PAGE from LED ZEPPELIN IV

Yes, the song's pretty daft. But when Robert Plant has finished warbling, Page cuts loose on one of his most lyrical solos – which thousands have tried to copy since.

❼ SAMBA PA TI CARLOS SANTANA from ABRAXAS

Proving that guitar virtuosity doesn't have to be about how fast you could play.

❽ HURRICANE NEIL YOUNG from STARS AND BARS

Neil's solos were always built around the minimal number of notes, but therein lies his effectiveness.

❾ DARK STAR JERRY GARCIA from THE GRATEFUL DEAD'S LIVE DEAD

Intergalactic guitar explorations from the man they called "Captain Trips"…

❿ LOAN ME A DIME DUANE ALLMAN from BOZ SCAGGS

Like Clapton, some of brother Duane's best playing was kept for other people's records.

Nigel Williamson

Guns N' Roses

The most dangerous rock band in the world? Probably not. Though when they actually bothered to release albums they were among the very best.

❶ CIVIL WAR from USE YOUR ILLUSION II

A snippet from the movie Cool Hand Luke launches into a stunningly heartfelt lyric about the nature of conflict. Who'd have thought the Gunners had it in them?

❷ ESTRANGED from USE YOUR ILLUSION II

One of the finest tunes the Gunners ever

recorded. Expertly arranged, the aching guitar refrain frames Axl's emotionally tormented vocals perfectly.

❸ MR BROWNSTONE from APPETITE FOR DESTRUCTION

You want drug songs? This paean to getting wrecked is an addictively succinct effort riding high on a superbly sleazy riff. A real jewel from the gutter.

❹ PARADISE CITY from APPETITE FOR DESTRUCTION

The masterful riff owes a major debt to Aerosmith while the anthemic chorus gets entire stadiums singing along.

❺ PERFECT CRIME from USE YOUR ILLUSION I

A fast and frenetic rocker, when GN'R are in the groove they're unstoppable. Slash's solo is a ripper and Axl unleashes venomous expletives like a true pro.

❻ RECKLESS LIFE from GN'R LIES

Originally from the band's debut EP, this live track positively reeks of the band's nothing-to-lose attitude. It's fast, tacky and stinks of cheap booze and drugs.

❼ SWEET CHILD O' MINE from APPETITE FOR DESTRUCTION

Could this be Slash's best solo ever? A major hit, this gorgeously arranged love song reveals Axl's sensitive side without a hint of schmaltz.

❽ WELCOME TO THE JUNGLE from APPETITE FOR DESTRUCTION

This is one hell of a way to kick off your debut album: violent, nasty and completely brilliant.

Essi Berelian

Woody Guthrie

With Woody it is as much the idea and the romantic notion of a better, less mean world as it is the music. The music though is the clear forerunner to Dylan and then

The Clash. So this is a selection of songs with typical hard hitting content.

❶ I AIN'T GOT NO HOME from DUSTBOWL BALLADS

Quintessential Guthrie, the song of a man for whom a singing, preaching life was the only one he could live.

❷ BIGGEST THING THAT MAN HAS EVER DONE from COLUMBIA RIVER COLLECTION

Fighting Fascists was Woody's mission, and this one is a rallying call for freedom.

❸ THIS LAND IS YOUR LAND from ASCH RECORDINGS VOLUME 1

The People's National Anthem. Forget GW Bush hijacking it, this song was written for everybody: "This Land belongs to you and me."

❹ JESUS CHRIST from ASCH RECORDINGS VOL 1

The truest vision of Radical Christian Socialism: Woody saw Jesus as a martyr put to death by the Boss Classes.

❺ DANVILLE GIRL from ASCH RECORDINGS VOL 2

A love song about a girl spotted on a station platform, who "wore her hat on the back of her head, like high born people all do". Perfect.

❻ JOHN HENRY WOODY GUTHRIE AND CISCO HOUSTON from WOODY GUTHRIE AND CISCO HOUSTON

Great example of the beautiful close harmonies the duo perfected, and another great working man's song.

❼ HARD TRAVELIN' from ASCH RECORDINGS VOL 3

Again, telling it like it is, the life of a hard working man, "busted, disgusted, not to be trusted".

❽ PRETTY BOY FLOYD from ASCH RECORDINGS VOL 4

The Dustbowl folk romanticized robbers and rebels, and this one is about Pretty Boy Floyd who would leave $50 bills with people who helped him hide from the Cops.

❾ TOM JOAD from DUSTBOWL BALLADS

Steinbeck's character from *Grapes of Wrath* is a template for all Woody's characters, a man for whom the struggle is everything, and camaraderie comes first.

🔟 CAR SONG from **ASCH RECORDINGS 1**
And just to prove Woody could delight three-year-olds, too, a song based around "Brrm Brrm". Delightful.

Richard Baker

Gypsy music

The Romany – commonly known as Gypsies – trace their nomadic origins to India and feature strongly in the music-making of many nations.

❶ DZELEM, DZELEM **ESMA REDZEPOVA** from **GYPSY QUEENS**
The Romany anthem as sung by Macedonia's Gypsy Queen.

❷ EDERLEZI AVELA **KOCANI ORKESTAR** from **L'ORIENT EST ROUGE**
Tough, dense brass music from eastern Macedonia that celebrates Ederlezi (the Romany holy day).

❸ BALADA CONDUCATOROLUI **TARAF DE HAIDOUKS** from **MUSIQUE DES TZIGANES DE ROUMANIE**
Violin and cymbalom weave a weird, dissonant ballad that celebrates the fall of Romanian dictator Nicolae Ceausescu.

❹ SOY GITANO **CAMARON DE LA ISLA** from **SOY GITANO**
The greatest flamenco singer of the past fifty years toasts his roots. Paco De Lucia adds fluid flamenco guitar.

❺ BAMBOLEO **GIPSY KINGS** from **GIPSY KINGS**
Hoarse vocals, rumba rhythms, flamenco melodies… it can only be the Gipsy Kings.

❻ PELNO ME SAM **SABAN BAJRAMOVIC** from **A GYPSY LEGEND**
The golden voiced Serbian wildman sings the Gypsy blues.

❼ CINE ARE FATA MARE **DONA DUMITRU SIMINICA** from **CINE ARE FATA MARE**
Eerie, haunted music that suggests a darker Transylvania than even Bram Stoker ever dared imagine.

❽ BASAL FERUS **FERUS MUSTAFOV** from **KING FERUS**
Bright Balkan dance tune named in honour of the little Macedonian sax and clarinet giant who plays it.

❾ IAG BARI **FANFARE CIOCARLIA** from **IAG BARI**
The fastest, funkiest brass band on the planet bust a collective gut and truly go for it.

🔟 OTPISANI **BOBAN MARKOVIC ORKESTAR** from **LIVE IN BELGRADE**
Horns blazing and sweat pouring, Boban leads a full-on Balkan brass experience.

Garth Cartwright

H

Herbie Hancock

Herbie Hancock: a bit of a legend. His 60s Blue Note work is impeccable, he was a bedrock of Miles Davis's quintet, and he invented jazz-funk fusion in the 70s. Great sideman, too.

❶ WATERMELON MAN from **TAKIN' OFF**
Hancock's first hit, originally in a version by Mongo Santamaria. On Hancock's own take, Freddie Hubbard and Dexter Gordon punch out the huge Latin brass riffs.

❷ MAIDEN VOYAGE from **MAIDEN VOYAGE**
George Coleman's tenor sax drifts over Hancock's rhythmic piano.

❸ DOLPHIN DANCE from **MAIDEN VOYAGE**
One of Hancock's loveliest compositions: hear also the version by the Jazz Jamaica All-Stars.

❹ CANTALOUPE ISLAND from **EMPYREAN ISLES**
US3 hip-hopped this into Cantaloop Island but they couldn't improve on the musical chassis of the original, with Freddie Hubbard's trumpet over Hancock's repeated piano arc.

❺ RIOT from **SPEAK LIKE A CHILD**
Starts slow for a riot but descends into flurrying whirlpools of piano.

❻ CHAMELEON from **HEADHUNTERS**
Jazz-funk starts here, with a quintessentially squelchy synth pattern woven contrapuntally with percussion and sax lines.

❼ WATERMELON MAN from **HEADHUNTERS**
A revisit for Watermelon Man in Headhunters style: the pygmy noises are made by percussionist Bill Summers blowing into a beer bottle.

❽ PALM GREASE from **THRUST**
A ride into deep space, with synthesizers like a murmured dispute between two alien species.

❾ JIMBASING HERBIE HANCOCK AND FODAY MUSA SUSO from **JAZZ AFRICA**
Hancock collaborating with the Gambian kora player and his dynamic band.

❿ ROCKIT from **FUTURE SHOCK**
An early and influential hip-hop track, extravagantly scratched, showed Hancock was still ahead of the curve.

David Honigmann

Happy Mondays

Proof that, given enough drugs, a bunch of unskilled scallywags from the bleak wreckage of England's industrial north could cook up some decent funk.

❶ STEP ON from **PILLS 'N' THRILLS AND BELLYACHES**
Owing more than a little to the John Kongos classic He's Gonna Step On You Again, the Mondays' masterpiece shambles along like it's been sniffing glue all afternoon. Couldn't stomp if they tried to.

❷ WROTE FOR LUCK (WFL) from **LIVE**
Forget about having your melons twisted, this one'll mess your head right up. The band's all time best closing number recorded on a night of pharmaceutical euphoria.

❸ KINKY AFRO from **PILLS 'N' THRILLS AND BELLYACHES**
Laid back easy funk confessions from a man old enough to know better.

❹ HALLELUJAH (CLUB MIX) from **GREATEST HITS**
Monkish chanting, soul girl screams and a

big baggy stomping beat that'll pull even the desperately mashed-up out of their seats.

⑤ RAVE ON from **THE HALLELUJAH SINGLE**
Finest acid squelches, stolen basslines, purloined lyrics and a dangerously medicated sounding Shaun take the listener way back to nights spent in muddy fields on dodgy pills.

⑥ LOOSE FIT (PERFECTO MIX) from **GREATEST HITS**
The coolest groove ever to leave Lancashire for a cheeky week in Ibiza

⑦ BOB'S YER UNCLE from **PILLS 'N' THRILLS AND BELLYACHES**
Shaun Ryder never sounded sleazier, the band groove on like they're playing on stage in a Latin bordello. Harks back to Why Did You Do It by Stretch, and no bad thing either.

⑧ COUNTRY SONG from **BUMMED**
The Mondays were so urban they had tarmac up their spines so why this attempt at country and north-western? I blame the drugs…

Al Spicer

Hardcore USA

Punk rock may have been invented in New York, but it was in California and Washington DC – as hardcore – that it received its most extreme expression in the god-fearing United States.

① I LOVE LIVIN' IN THE CITY FEAR from **THE RECORD**
Not quite light speed yet, but as raw as you can bear.

② WE MUST BLEED THE GERMS from **GI**
One of the first American punk records to ratchet up the speed to masturbatory bleat.

③ PAY TO CUM BAD BRAINS from **BAD BRAINS**
Zero to Mach 1 in one minute and thirty seconds.

④ HOLIDAY IN CAMBODIA DEAD KENNEDYS from **FRESH FRUIT FOR ROTTING VEGETABLES**
A brutal parody of the condescension and contradictions of white liberalism.

⑤ IN MY EYES MINOR THREAT from **MINOR THREAT**
Where American punk broke from Britain and turned intense and earnest.

⑥ RISE ABOVE BLACK FLAG from **DAMAGED**
The high point of Henry Rollins' career.

⑦ JOHN WAYNE WAS A NAZI THE STAINS (AKA MDC) from **MILLIONS OF DEAD COPS**
Classic right-wing baiting.

⑧ I'M NOT A LOSER DESCENDENTS from **MILO GOES TO COLLEGE**
Everyone from Green Day to Good Charlotte owes their careers to this record.

⑨ MY OLD MAN'S A FATSO ANGRY SAMOANS from **BACK FROM SAMOA**
Self-conscious and satirical, and nails one of hardcore's central conundrums: "My old man's a fatso, but you know he owns this house."

⑩ BASKET CASE GREEN DAY from **DOOKIE**
Nostalgic Descendents tune with more hooks.

Peter Shapiro

Roy Harper

England's premier –only? – fried prog-folk poet, a hero of Floyd, Zeppelin and Kate Bush, and still going strong in his 60s.

① ONE OF THESE DAYS IN ENGLAND from **BULLINAMINGVASE**
The nearest Harper ever came to a hit, this very English epic is, typically, both angry and pastorally pretty. The McCartneys sing back-up.

② WHEN AN OLD CRICKETER LEAVES THE CREASE from **HQ**
Harper's favourite, and another of his greatest paeans to Englishness. Delicate, nostalgic and

born aloft by the Grimethorpe Colliery brass band.

❸ ME AND MY WOMAN from STORMCOCK

Harper's sentiments – culminating aptly in some comments on cuckoos – are matched excess for excess by David Bedford's extravagant orchestration. Prog folk at its finest.

❹ ANOTHER DAY from FLAT BAROQUE AND BERSERK

A touching song of never-consummated romance. The modal melody, quavery vocal and first use of strings audibly inspired Jethro Tull, plus an 80s cover by This Mortal Coil.

❺ I HATE THE WHITE MAN from FLAT, BAROQUE AND BERSERK

Skip the waffling hippie intro if you must, and you'll witness the best of Harper's acoustic phase: ostensibly Dylan-esque, its angry, poetic intensity is wholly Harper.

❻ HORS D'OEUVRES from STORMCOCK

The overture to Harper's best album, all tart lyrics, meandering melody and one-man falsetto chorale.

❼ SAME OLD ROCK from STORMCOCK

Epic anti-religious rant given additional gravitas by the sterling presence of pal Jimmy Page on lead guitar.

❽ THE LORD'S PRAYER from LIFEMASK

Daunting but rewarding, a brush with death brought on this sidelong suite, shifting from poem to acid incantation. Again featuring Page on guitar.

❾ HALLUCINATING LIGHT from HQ

From Harper's most rock-oriented album comes this beautiful electric ballad, with Harper's vocal in particularly aching form.

❿ YOU from THE UNKNOWN SOLDIER

The last gasp of the classic era, this angular, rocky number finds Harper doing battle with the wailing of Kate Bush and David Gilmour's guitar.

Toby Manning

Emmylou Harris

An early protégé of Gram Parsons, the great Emmylou Harris should be queen of the country establishment. Yet she has somehow managed to maintain "outsider" status, continuing to take risks throughout a long and stellar career.

❶ LOVE HURTS WITH GRAM PARSONS from DUETS

Recorded with the late lamented country rock pioneer a year before Emmylou's debut, when she was still carving out her reputation as a harmony vocalist with a rare empathy.

❷ TILL I GAIN CONTROL AGAIN from ELITE HOTEL

From the second of two albums she released in 1975, this Rodney Crowell song seems made for Emmylou's soulful wail.

❸ PONCHO & LEFTY from LUXURY LINER

A wonderful rendering of Townes Van Zandt's signature tune. Emmylou really inhabits the sad poetic storyline, helped by great backing vocals from Rodney Crowell and Albert Lee.

❹ MY FATHER'S HOUSE from THIRTEEN

An austere reading of this powerfully cinematic Bruce Springsteen song, from what Emmylou erroneously considers to be her 13th solo album; she disowned her true debut.

❺ IF YOU WERE A BLUEBIRD from BLUEBIRD

A suspenseful shimmer of mandolin introduces this gorgeous Butch Hancock ballad, hinged on a series of country-spun conditionals.

❻ ROLLIN' AND RAMBLIN' (THE DEATH OF HANK WILLIAMS) from BRAND NEW DANCE

A heartfelt tribute to the honky-tonk hero, powered by rootsy fiddle and accordion.

❼ CRESCENT CITY from COWGIRL'S PRAYER

Vibrant Cajun-flavoured cover of a Lucinda Williams number from this excellent 1994 album, the quality of which hinted at what was on the horizon.

Emmylou Harris's
Roots 9

The queen of alt-country, EMMYLOU HARRIS has duetted with everyone from Gram Parsons and Bob Dylan to Neil Young and Ryan Adams. As you might have expected, her playlist has a strong American roots flavour, but with an interesting detour to Eastern Europe.

❶ DREAMING MY DREAMS WITH YOU WAYLON JENNINGS from THIS TIME, THE RAMBLIN' MAN

❷ UNCLOUDY DAY STAPLE SINGERS from UNCLOUD DAY

❸ UP ON CRIPPLE CREEK THE BAND from THE BAND

❹ TALK TO ME OF MENDOCINO KATE AND ANNA McGARRIGLE from KATE & ANNA McGARRIGLE

❺ THE EMPEROR OF WYOMING NEIL YOUNG from NEIL YOUNG

❻ MANSION ON THE HILL BRUCE SPRINGSTEEN from NEBRASKA

❼ THE MAKER DANIEL LANOIS from ACADIE

❽ POLEGNALA E TODORA (THEODORA IS DOZING) ENSEMBLE OF THE BULGARIAN REPUBLIC CONDUCTED BY PHILIP KOUTEV from MUSIC OF BULGARIA

❾ NOT DARK YET BOB DYLAN from TIME OUT OF MIND

❽ WHERE WILL I BE from WRECKING BALL
The dazzling opener from Emmylou's 1995 reinvention album, which made a daring break with previous work in the choice of rock material and Daniel Lanois' grainy production.

❾ BANG THE DRUM SLOWLY from RED DIRT GIRL
Co-written with Guy Clark, this ghostly, bittersweet recollection of her father is deeply autobiographical.

❿ LITTLE BIRD from STUMBLE INTO GRACE
Canadian sisters Kate and Anna McGarrigle have long been influential on Emmylou, and this pretty and delicate co-write has their magic stamped all over it.

Jon Lusk

George Harrison
Some highlights of the solo output of the dark horse of The Beatles.

❶ I'D HAVE YOU ANYTIME from ALL THINGS MUST PASS
The opening track of George's post-Beatles 1970 masterpiece, a marvellous, surprising collision of Harrison's luscious major seventh chords and Bob Dylan's lusty chorus.

❷ MY SWEET LORD from ALL THINGS MUST PASS
The second track, uncomfortably similar to the Chiffons' He's So Fine (an "unconscious plagiarism" for which George coughed up £600,000 in 1976), is nevertheless a remarkably rousing, inspirational record.

❸ GIVE ME LOVE (GIVE ME PEACE ON EARTH) from LIVING IN THE MATERIAL WORLD
The single from his 1973 album and the hopeful highlight of it.

❹ YOU from EXTRA TEXTURE
His albums had become semi-inspired ragbags by the mid-70s but this 1975 Springsteen-esque single had some fire in it, courtesy of Jim Horn's saxophone.

⑤ BLOW AWAY from **GEORGE HARRISON**
From 1979, one of Hari's most delightful choruses, an infectious featherweight celebration of the optimism that love can inspire.

⑥ ALL THOSE YEARS AGO from **SOMEWHERE IN ENGLAND**
A 1981 tribute to the recently assassinated Lennon featuring contributions from Paul and Ringo, boogiesome and big of heart.

⑦ THAT'S THE WAY IT GOES from **GONE TROPPO**
A marvellously judged blend of fatalistic humility and spiritual wisdom in an unfussy strum-a-long setting, typical early 80s Harrison.

⑧ WHEN WE WAS FAB from **CLOUD NINE**
An ingenious and affectionate Jeff Lynne-produced Beatles pastiche from George's excellent 1987 "comeback" album.

⑨ NEVER GET OVER YOU from **BRAINWASHED**
Brainwashed, released a year after his death in 2001, was an alluring mix of lyrical density and musical modesty. This romantic ballad is one of the highlights.

Chris Ingham

PJ Harvey

Practically a grand dame of indie-rock these days, PJ Harvey's career performs a regular swerve from cult to mainstream and back again. Here's a chronological tour.

❶ DRESS from **DRY**
The debut single: typically uncompromising, railing against conventional femininity, over choppy cello and her own scratchy violin.

❷ O MY LOVER from **DRY**
Dripping with accusatory irony, this harmonium laced ballad boasts one of the best and most dismissively despairing – grunts in rock.

❸ RID OF ME from **4 TRACK DEMOS**
Even more intense than the album version, this solo version absolutely howls outraged

rejection, voices and guitars hacking like blunt, bloodied machetes.

❹ MISSED from **RID OF ME**
The two Marys at Jesus's grave isn't an ordinary rock topic, but so extraordinary is this tortured, thudding ballad it's practically a religious experience.

❺ TECLO from **TO BRING YOU MY LOVE**
Tracks like this lush spaghetti-western ballad with literal bells on took PJ Harvey right away from her hardcore harridan image. The hot pink jumpsuits helped, too.

❻ SEND HIS LOVE TO ME from **TO BRING YOU MY LOVE**
The aggression of this acoustic midpacer summarizes Harvey's agony/ecstasy contradictions.

❼ THE DANCER from **TO BRING YOU MY LOVE**
Another tune that combines the spiritual and the carnal: aptly organ-heavy and featuring a supremely orgasmic vocal.

❽ IS THAT ALL THERE IS? from **DANCE HALL AT LOUSE POINT (WITH JOHN PARISH)**
This wry version of an old Peggy Lee tune is rare evidence of Harvey's sense of humour. Black humour, naturally.

❾ LOVE TOO SOON from **PASCAL COMELADE'S L'ARGOT DU BRUIT**
This little-known collaboration with a kind of French Tom Waits highlights the showtune diva Harvey only hints in her own work.

❿ WE FLOAT from **STORIES FROM THE CITY, STORIES FROM THE SEA**
Swooningly seductive addition to Harvey's subgenre of water songs puts a confident full-stop to her biggest-selling album so far.

Toby Manning

The hat acts

The rise of the music video and CMT – the country equivalent of MTV – helped to

create a new kind of male country star. Well scrubbed and usually clean shaven, they looked like football players, except that they dressed in cowboy boots and outsize hats. Musically they tended to be neo-traditionalists but with a strong pop sensibility, prime for chart action. Star player was Garth Brooks who by the early 90s was challenging Michael Jackson as the biggest star in America.

❶ AIN'T GOING DOWN ('TIL THE SUN COMES UP) GARTH BROOKS from IN PIECES

He had a degree in marketing from a business university and became Nashville's biggest commodity in Nashville in the 90s.

❷ BOOT SCOOTIN' BOOGIE BROOKS & DUNN from BRAND NEW MAN

Two hats for the price of one from Kix and Ronnie who invented a particularly dopey line dance with this song and now rival Simon & Garfunkel and Hall & Oates as the best-selling duo in musical history.

❸ NEVER KNEW LONELY VINCE GILL from WHEN I CALL YOUR NAME

Former bluegrass musician turned country crooner who has also become familiar as the super-smooth presenter of Nashville's annual Country Music Awards.

❹ ALL MY EXS LIVE IN TEXAS GEORGE STRAIT from OCEAN FRONT PROPERTY

The original 80s cowboy-in-a-hat, Strait was a major influence on the likes of Garth Brooks and Alan Jackson.

❺ ACHY BREAKY HEART BILLY RAY CYRUS from SOME GAVE ALL

Love him or hate him, you couldn't ignore this line dancing favourite – or the extraordinary mullet he revealed when he took off his hat.

❻ DON'T GET ANY COUNTRIER THAN THIS TIM MCGRAW from NOT A MOMENT TOO SOON

"I'm a redneck and I admit it," this platinum-selling son of a baseball hero asserted.

❼ A THOUSAND MILES FROM NOWHERE DWIGHT YOAKAM from THIS TIME

The closest any of the hat acts has ever got to rock'n'roll credibility and the only one to get on MTV, he once even covered a Clash song.

❽ TOO GONE TOO LONG RANDY TRAVIS from ALWAYS AND FOREVER

For a while he seemed to be the heir to George Jones's honky-tonk crown, although his star has waned in recent years.

❾ WHERE WERE YOU (WHEN THE WORLD STOPPED TURNING) ALAN JACKSON from DRIVE

Country music demanded an immediate reaction to 9/11 and Jackson obliged with this simple but effective commentary…

❿ COURTESY OF THE RED, WHITE AND BLUE TOBY KEITH from UNLEASHED

…but Oklahoma's Toby Keith offered a far uglier response on this song that threatened to "put a boot in your ass" if you mess with the US of A.

Nigel Williamson

Hawaiian music

For a spell in the 20s and 30s Hawaii provided the world's favourite pop sounds. It has to be said much of the early stuff now sound like novelty songs, but the best maintain real charm. Meantime, in contemporary Hawaii, there's a vibrant roots-based scene, spearheaded by guitarist Gabby Pahinui: more serious fare, but with the trademark steel-guitar lilt still as evocative of paradise as ever. The ten tracks here are a trawl through both ancient and modern.

❶ OUA OUA KANUI & LULA from HAWAII'S POPULAR SONGS

Strange but true: this irresistible 1929 slice

of ukulele–backed doggerel was a #1 hit in Austria in 2001.

❷ LEPE ULAULA SAM ALAMA & HIS HAWAIIANS from HAWAII'S POPULAR SONGS
A lovely early classic, this time from 1936.

❸ HI'ILAWE GABBY PAHINUI from LEGENDS OF FALSETTO
The first major recording by the father of contemporary Hawaiian music, from 1947.

❹ ALIKA GENOA KEAWE from ROUGH GUIDE TO HAWAII
Infectiously enjoyable 1974 performance by one of Hawaii's greatest falsetto singers.

❺ KA ULUWEHI O KE KAI HAPA from HAPA
This Maui band revitalized the Hawaiian scene with their debut 1992 album.

❻ HAWAII '78 ISRAEL KAMAKAWIWO'OLE from FACING FUTURE
The sadly-missed Iz, who died in 1997, included this Hawaiian sovereignty anthem on his seminal 1993 album, *Facing Future*.

❼ KAWAIPUNAHELE KEALI'I REICHEL from KAWAIPUNAHELE
Since this first 1994 hit, Maui-based hula teacher Reichel has released a succession of beautiful albums.

❽ ALOHA KA MANINI ISRAEL KAMAKAWIWO'OLE from E ALA E
Iz really deserves his own playlist; this is a sublime rendition of a Hawaiian standard.

❾ HANAIALI'I NUI LA EA AMY HANAI'ALI'I GILLIOM from HAWAIIAN TRADITION
The leading modern exponent of the falsetto tradition, on fine form in 1997.

❿ KU'U LEI CYRIL PAHINUI AND BOB BROZMAN from FOUR HANDS SWEET & HOT
Gabby's son Cyril, and roving musician Bob Brozman, released this gorgeous slack-key guitar duet in 1999.

Greg Ward

Isaac Hayes

Starting out as a house writer for Stax Records in Memphis, Isaac Hayes went on to invent symphonic soul and become a multi-platinum-selling artist – as well as a film and TV star. Now he's the voice of Chef in South Park and the world's funkiest scientologist.

❶ BY THE TIME I GET TO PHOENIX from HOT BUTTERED SOUL
Isaac takes the Jimmy Webb tune on an 18-minute journey. Little happens musically but the Voice grabs you and refuses to let go.

❷ THEME FROM SHAFT from SHAFT
"Who's the black private dick that drives all the chicks crazy?" asks Isaac not so much about the film's stud cop but about, uh-hum, himself.

❸ WALK ON BY from HOT BUTTERED SOUL
The Dionne Warwick song gets stretched. "Walk on!" scream the gospel chorus. Fuzz guitar bleeds. Ike sighs. Listen and melt.

❹ NEVER CAN SAY GOODBYE from BLACK MOSES
Another classic extended work-out.

❺ IKE'S MOOD from INSTRUMENTALS
Hugely atmospheric mood music. Much sampled by trip and hip-hoppers.

❻ IKE'S RAP 1 from TO BE CONTINUED
Ike's talking over minimal piano-drum backing, telling his woman that Uncle Sam's called him up but stay true cos he'll be back. A soul sermon of sorts.

❼ SOULSVILLE from SHAFT
"Some are trying to ditch reality with a $50 high/Only to find out you can never touch the sky." Ike was deep, no doubt.

❽ JOY from JOY
Isaac in rare, up-tempo form and laying the seduction on thick: "Sweetness is the name for you, sugar."

⑨ IKE'S RAP 4/A BRAND NEW ME from
BLACK MOSES
Gorgeous descending bassline that Tricky built
a career on anchors this twenty-minute epic.

⑩ NO NAME BAR from **SHAFT**
An instrumental that conjures up a-bad-place-
to-be. Huge horn riffs, thick organ, dizzy flute,
brassy sax: this is the sound of the 70s.

Garth Cartwright

Jimi Hendrix

**Modern guitar heroics start here. Six-
string abuse doesn't come wilder or more
passionate than Jimi in full flight.**

① ALL ALONG THE WATCHTOWER from
ELECTRIC LADYLAND
Jimi takes Bob Dylan's tune and creates what
many feel is the timeless and magical definitive
version. Simply awesome.

② BURNING OF THE MIDNIGHT LAMP from
ELECTRIC LADYLAND
Almost a Wall Of Sound-style production with
celestial backing vox, harpsichord and some
terrific guitar building to a huge layered climax.

③ DOLLY DAGGER from **FIRST RAYS OF THE NEW
RISING SUN**
She drinks her blood from a jagged edge,
don'tcha know? A terrifically funky number
with a cracking closing solo.

④ LITTLE WING from **AXIS: BOLD AS LOVE**
A deceptively simple and lyrically gorgeous little song. The closing solo relies more on soulful
flow than flashy histrionics.

⑤ MACHINE GUN from **LIVE AT THE FILLMORE EAST**
War? What is it good for? Drums rattle and Jimi
puts his guitar almost literally through the
emotional grinder on this awesome political
thriller.

⑥ PURPLE HAZE from **ARE YOU EXPERIENCED**
'Scuse me while I kiss the freakin' sky, baby!

From the famously choppy intro to the psych
overload climax, a stone-cold classic.

⑦ SPANISH CASTLE MAGIC from **THE JIMI
HENDRIX EXPERIENCE**
Fancy a trip on a dragonfly? A nice long version
here, so hold tight for a great rolling riff and
some fantastic soloing.

⑧ STAR SPANGLED BANNER from **LIVE AT
WOODSTOCK**
The guitar god lays waste in an historic performance. A shrieking, howling, life-affirming
noise.

⑨ THIRD STONE FROM THE SUN from **ARE YOU
EXPERIENCED**
A simply wild interstellar trip with a beautifully
flowing bassline and Hendrix in weird free-
form poetry mode.

⑩ VOODOO CHILD (SLIGHT RETURN) from
ELECTRIC LADYLAND
Another famous intro, those wacka-wacka licks
erupt into an incendiary frenzy and Jimi starts
felling mountains with the edge of his hand.

Essi Berelian

Herb superb

**Some people might say that ganja and
reggae music are somehow inseparable,
but, to be honest officer, I couldn't possibly
comment. Less open to interpretation,
though, is the fact that there are an
inordinate number of reggae songs written
in veneration of the so-called herb superb.
This is a selection from a list so long it
would take up your entire MP3 player. Now
there's a thought – never mind U2, what
about a special edition iPod that's useless
before midday and plays the same dodgy
old tune over and over again at three
o'clock in the morning?**

❶ **LEGALIZE IT** PETER TOSH from **LEGALIZE IT**
The daddy of all weed songs, that has Tosh as Marketing Director as, over the choppiest of beats, he stacks up the reasons for a change in the law.

❷ **SENSEMILLA** BLACK UHURU from **20 GREATEST HITS**
Percolating, popping, disco-esque rhythm from Sly & Robbie, while the militant vocals make the case against the forces of Babylon and their hardline approach to the weed.

❸ **UNDER MI SLENG TENG** WAYNE SMITH from **SLENG TENG EXTRAVAGANZA**
Accepted as the first reggae record not to have a bassline, this nagging buzzsaw of a tune as Smith exposes the joys of being off his face.

❹ **HERBMAN HUSTLING** SUGAR MINOTT from **HERBMAN HUSTLING**
An escalating selection of drumbeats are all Minott needs to bolster up his salesman's tale in a superb example of how, on planet reggae, digital didn't have to mean dismal.

❺ **GANJA SMUGGLING** EEK-A-MOUSE from **WA-DO-DEM**
The Mouse "skeddebeng"s and "diddidung"s his way through a concise explanation of the economics of the collie trade and how Kingston life can revolve around it.

❻ **I LOVE MARIJUANA** LINVAL THOMPSON from **I LOVE MARIJUANA**
No nonsense roots music, with a hymn to the herb as unequivocal as the title. It "keeps the natty dreadlocks singing", apparently.

❼ **KAYA (LEE PERRY PRODUCTION)** THE WAILERS from **THE ESSENTIAL BOB MARLEY**
Lee Perry's inherent understanding of how a circular reggae beat can be taken to a place beyond merely insistent creates a flawless framework for The Wailers' slow, drawn out harmonizing and Bob's very stoned lead.

❽ **NATURAL COLLIE** FREDDIE MCGREGOR from **THE ANTHOLOGY**
A pleading, soulful love song offering up collie weed as an escape route from the tribulations of Jamaican poverty.

❾ **CHALICE IN THE PLACE** U-ROY from **DREAD IN A BABYLON**
Over the classic rocksteady of Queen Majesty, U-Roy toasts a truly absurd tale of licking the chalice in Buckingham Palace that blurs into a dancehall love song. Fabulous stuff.

❿ **PASS THE KOUTCHIE** THE MIGHTY DIAMONDS from **CHANGES**
Laidback in the extreme, multi-layered for a comforting cushion of a rhythm, soothingly harmonized, this record drifts about like a big cloud of particularly pungent smoke. Musical Youth later took a smoke-free version to the top of the UK charts.

Lloyd Bradley

Highlife

An early African music phenomenon, highlife had long golden years from the 50s to the 70s. Ghana was the epicentre of this easygoing good time music, though Nigeria and several nearby countries produced their own variants.

❶ **ALL FOR YOU** E.T. MENSAH from **ALL FOR YOU**
An early 50s highlight from the undisputed king of highlife, whose career spanned an incredible six decades.

❷ **THE QUEEN'S VISIT** KING BRUCE from **GOLDEN HIGHLIFE CLASSICS**
This genteel number anticipates Queen Elizabeth 11's 1959 visit to Ghana. After all that, HRH did a no-show! Contains the immortal line: "This is the day five million Ghanaians will go gay." How times have changed.

❸ **BONE BIARA SO WO AKATUA** NANA AMPADU & THE AFRICAN BROTHERS from **THE ROUGH GUIDE TO HIGHLIFE**
Poor recording quality can't stifle this phenomenal groove. With their "Afrohili" brand of

guitar-band highlife, Nana Ampadu and his band were at the top of their game through much of the 60s and 70s.

❹ KYENKYEN BI ADI M'AW U.K. FRIMPONG AND HIS CUBANO FIESTAS from AFRO-ROCK VOL 1
This evergreen minor key highlife from 1976 has been sampled by several contemporary "hiplife" artists.

❺ MATUTU MIRIKA ERIC AGYEMAN from HIGHLIFE SAFARI
Infectiously danceable party fave by this modernizer of Kumasi's "sikyi" style. The simple, insistent horn motif would be a ring tone if they'd had mobile phones in Ghana in 1978.

❻ THE LORD'S PRAYER SUPER SWEET TALKS from THE LORD'S PRAYER
They say the devil has all the best tunes, but this proves that's a lie. A.B. Crentsil's late-70s masterpiece is enough to make godless souls shout "Amen!"

❼ OYOLIMA CHIEF STEPHEN OSITA OSADEBE from THE ROUGH GUIDE TO NIGERIA AND GHANA
A slinky, laid back number with muted trumpet, understated guitar, atmospheric percussion and the honeyed vocals of Nigeria's master of Igbo highlife.

❽ NULAKE KPLE FUWO BLIND DZIMSON AND HIS MORKPOLAWO GROUP from THE GUITAR AND GUN
Hawaiian guitar adds sweetness and an exotic touch to this wonderful chugging tune recorded in 1983 at John Collins' legendary Bokoor Studios in Accra.

❾ FRIENDS TODAY, ENEMIES TOMORROW
THE BEACH SCORPIONS from ELECTRIC HIGHLIFE
An epic 1989 song in Pidgin English, which floats in the air for nearly ten minutes.

❿ MAFE WO ALEX KONADU from THE HIGHLIFE ALLSTARS/SANKOFA
Known as "One Man Thousand" for his forceful stage presence, Kumasi-based Konadu was a major figure in 70s highlife. He made this gloriously retro recording in 2001.

Jon Lusk

Lauryn Hill/ The Fugees

By age 23, Hill had had two smash hit albums with The Fugees and a solo effort that recalled the ambition of 70s Stevie Wonder. Then, bar an acoustic MTV album, she disappeared. Here's why we miss her.

FUGEES

❶ RUMBLE IN THE JUNGLE from WHEN WE WERE KINGS OST
Her intricate, complex, conscious rhymes wipe the floor with such legends as Q-Tip and Busta Rhymes, as well as prefiguring the conscious soul hip-hop she would make her own with *Miseducation*.

❷ FU-GEE-LA from THE SCORE
The album version, with higher-mixed keyboards, and the Haitians' breakthrough hit. Wyclef and Pras live up to Hill's standard.

❸ KILLING ME SOFTLY from THE SCORE
Too close to the original perhaps, but Hill doesn't so much recall Roberta Flack as out-sing her, note for note in her unique baritone.

❹ READY OR NOT from THE SCORE
Hill covers this Delfonics song supremely, asserting the hook with absolute authority before showing off her considerable rap skills. Did she really need The Fugees?

LAURYN HILL

❺ EX FACTOR from THE MISEDUCATION OF LAURYN HILL
This (apparent) account of her tortuous relationship with fellow Fugee Wyclef Jean has an embarrassment of choruses, while its massed harmonies lift it to heartbroken euphoria.

❻ DOO WOP (THAT THING) from THE MISEDUCATION OF LAURYN HILL
Doo-wop, sprightly, poppy – Hill at her most

charming. And there's wit in the sexual sententiousness.

7 I GOTTA FIND PEACE OF MIND from MTV UNPLUGGED

From the otherwise patchy Unplugged, this showcases Hill's deft acoustic guitar technique and way with words, before the devastating moment when she begins to cry mid-song.

8 TO ZION from THE MISEDUCATION OF LAURYN HILL

Fuwho? Self-deifying though it is ("and then an angel came to me," etc), there's still something very moving about Hill's epiphanal paean to her baby son.

9 THE MISEDUCATION OF LAURYN HILL from THE MISEDUCATION OF LAURYN HILL

Perfect summation of that extraordinary debut, Hill sounding like Roberta Flack and Stevie Wonder's love child, the piano evoking 70s conscious soul, the vinyl crackles a lifetime love of hip-hop.

10 TELL HIM from THE MISEDUCATION OF LAURYN HILL

Tucked away as a bonus track at the end of the UK version of the album, this is actually a highlight: a delightfully simple acoustic hip-hop ballad, with one of Hill's most heartfelt vocals.

Toby Manning

Hip-hop classics

Hip-hop has a real history: 25 years of stylistic and technological developments, as well as countless changes in direction and perception. But for this list of classics, completely unscientifically, I've narrowed the territory down to genre-defining tunes from those half a dozen years (late 80s/early 90s) in between old-skool and gangsta, when it was still naive enough to be musically open-minded, was just beginning to visualize its own long-term

future, and had yet to define itself by MTV-oriented guidelines.

1 SOLILOQUY OF CHAOS GANG STARR from DAILY OPERATION

A restless, computerized string section loop moves this spooky rhythm around what sounds like a glockenspiel and a nagging drumbeat, while Guru's rapping is of a gig that turned into a riot.

2 IT'S TRICKY RUN-DMC from GREATEST HITS

Proving they didn't need to share a stage with Aerosmith to craft raucous heavy metal embracing hip-hop, the twosome swap rhymes with considerable aplomb and a good humour seldom associated with Run-DMC.

3 I CAN'T LIVE WITHOUT MY RADIO LL COOL J from RADIO

If one single track summed up what hip-hop was originally about, this is it. A big, belligerent teenager playing his ghetto blaster too loud. No wonder it took so long to go mainstream.

4 PUSH IT SALT'N'PEPA from HOT, COOL & VICIOUS

B-girls with more front than Selfridges, this noisy, crisply cut up stomper proves it's entirely possible to take rap pop without giving an inch of attitude.

5 PAID IN FULL (ORIGINAL MIX) ERIC B & RAKIM from PAID IN FULL

This is what lay underneath a seemingly endless number of remixes, and being only semi-vocal it showcases Eric B's phenomenal turntable skills as well as the rapper's verbal dexterity.

6 LADIES FIRST QUEEN LATIFAH from ALL HAIL THE QUEEN

Built on an almost breezy horn sample this feminist diatribe is powered by so charming a tune that it comes across as engaging and never hectoring.

7 DOOWUTCHALIKE DIGITAL UNDERGROUND from PLAYWUTCHALIKE

Anything other than a diatribe of any description, this record is a rap frat house party anthem if anybody remakes Animal House in a hip-hop stylee, this will be its Louie Louie.

⑧ WELCOME TO THE TERRORDOME PUBLIC ENEMY from FEAR OF A BLACK PLANET
Public Enemy at their most overwhelming: the samples are sliced up and stacked four or five deep as the best's carried by a buzz saw, seemingly random phrases are thrown in, Chuck isn't going to let anybody off lightly and Flav works hard to counterpoint this finely focused fury.

⑨ BASSLINE MANTRONIX from MANTRONIX
Always at the cutting edge of sound science and sampling experimentation this is the point at which electro osmosed into straight ahead hip-hop, setting up some wonderfully involved beat arrangements.

⑩ PEOPLE EVERYDAY ARRESTED DEVELOPMENT from GREATEST HITS
Gentler, thoughtful, tuneful rap, built around Sly Stone's Everyday People, from the group that put "hippie" into hip-hop.

Lloyd Bradley

Global hip-hop

Hip-hop has conquered the world and in Africa it is now the dominant music. Away from the US, however, attitudes come very different, and (like reggae before it) hip-hop is more often a vehicle for sharp political and social comment than for chat about guns and 'hos.

❶ 537 C.U.B.A ORISHAS from A LO CUBANO
European-based Cuban rappers who cheekily sampled Buena Vista's Social Club's Chan Chan on this track from their debut album.

❷ BOOMERANG DAARA J from BOOMERANG
Wolof rhymes, West African melodies and hip-hop beats as they celebrate the music's homecoming – "born in Africa, brought up in America, rap has come full circle".

❸ ANGELA SAIAN SUPA CREW from KLR
Global hip-hop in the truest sense as rap, R&B, raga and zouk all collide on a track that gave this Parisian street crew the biggest-selling French-language single of 2000.

❹ BOUGE DE LA MC SOLAAR from QUI SEME LE VENT RECOLTE LE TEMPO
The 1990 debut single from the biggest hip-hop star in France, the world's biggest hip-hop market outside America. It translates as "move out of the way".

❺ MEEN ERHABE DAM from ARABRAP (COMPILATION)
Palestinian rappers telling it like it is in the Occupied Territories. The title means "who is a terrorist" and the rap includes such lines as "I'm not against peace – peace against me."

❻ DIVIDE AND CONQUER SUBLIMINAL from THE LIGHT AND THE SHADOW
But rap can give out many messages, as right-wing Israeli rapper and self-confessed Zionist Subliminal proves here as he sneers at the Middle Eastern peace accords and those who support the creation of a Palestinian state.

❼ BLAW POSITIVE BLACK SOUL from NEW YORK/PARIS/DAKAR
The longest-established first Senegalese hip-hop group and the best known – at least until Daara J came along.

❽ RETURN OF THE TRES DELINQUENT HABITS from MERRY GO ROUND
Tequila-injected hip-hop with a mariachi twist.

❾ BEYROUTH ECOEUREE CLOTAIRE K from LEBANESE
Arabic instruments and programmed beats on a track about the war that tore the heart out of Beirut.

❿ AHA MAASAI HIP-HOP X PLASTAZ from TANZANIA
With a lyric apparently about tracking gazelles, wildebeest and buffalo. Eat your heart out, Snoop Doggy Dog.

Nigel Williamson

Robyn Hitchcock

The surreal lyrics about fish, fowl and flesh often obscure his deft guitar-work and melodic gifts, but he's as much the progeny of The Beatles and Bob Dylan as Syd Barrett. Or indeed The Band, on whom he contributed a playlist to this book.

❶ AIRSCAPE from **ELEMENT OF LIGHT**
Over a ringing Byrds-like riff, a ruminative elegy of man's place in the universe … or something like that.

❷ BRENDA'S IRON SLEDGE from **BLACK SNAKE, DIAMOND RÔLE**
Robyn at his manic and just-this-side-of-silly best; the jet-propelled riff practically begs you to hop aboard for the ride.

❸ THE FLAVOUR OF NIGHT from **I OFTEN DREAM OF TRAINS**
A haunting, moody and intimate piano song; how many guys can make the line "you with your ice cream hands" sound this romantic?

❹ FILTHY BIRD from **MOSS ELIXIR**
The deconstructed bridge evokes Sgt Pepper-era Beatles, but it's the sliding guitar chords that hypnotize from the onset.

❺ EGYPTIAN CREAM from **FEGMANIA!**
Bizarre sexual identity issues surround this keen pop melody, powered by the lush, upbeat instrumentation of his new old backing band.

❻ SLEEPING WITH YOUR DEVIL MASK from **GLOBE OF FROGS**
Robyn's fixation with birds, ghosts, fish and guys with funny names like Gareth reaches a fitting conclusion next time round, he'll be a trout.

❼ LINCTUS HOUSE from **EYE**
Lovely, dexterous acoustic guitar work supports alternately amusing and heartrending lines on a faded relationship.

❽ YIP SONG from **RESPECT**
It's a fine line between absurd and touching; the latter somehow wins out while you marvel at how many times he can repeat the word "yip" during a eulogy to his father and without taking a breath.

❾ UNDERWATER MOONLIGHT from **UNDERWATER MOONLIGHT (SOFT BOYS)**
Some unbelievably catchy hooks and harmonies make you question why this immaculate slice of psychedelia wasn't a hit. Perhaps because it was about two statues heading off for an evening dip…

❿ NO, I DON'T REMEMBER GUILDFORD from **JEWELS FOR SOPHIA**
A folksy, fizzy exercise in amnesia, sung as if floating on a pool on a lazy afternoon. The yowling harmonica is purest Dylan.
Andrew Rosenberg

Billie Holiday

Billie Holiday invested jazz song with the emotional immediacy of the blues. Her voice, with its subtle tremolo and hint of rasp, was as irresistible as her effortlessly liquid, behind-the-beat phrasing. Billie's life was full of tragedy and there's a fragility even to her swinging cuts from the 1930s; in the later years, almost everything she sang was imbued with a profound melancholia – a sense of total acquiescence to some eternal sadness.

❶ THE MAN I LOVE from **LADY DAY**
Billie's never found the knight in shining amour of Gerhwin's song. The closest she came was saxophonist Lester Young, whose weighty, velvety solo grounds this performance.

❷ BODY & SOUL from **LADY DAY**
As this classic take shows, with Billie there's always a fine line between sorrow and seduction.

❷ ON THE SUNNY SIDE OF THE STREET from THE COMMODORE MASTER TAKES
Proof that Billie wasn't all pain and tears, this take of the Louis Armstrong favourite is brimming over with infectious joy.

❸ IN MY SOLITUDE from LADY DAY
"In my sar-li-tude…". There's an almost crystal-line delicacy to Billie's account of this Ellington number.

❹ GOD BLESS THE CHILD from LADY DAY
There are eighteen recordings of this Billie signature tune, co-written with Arthur Herzog. This 1941 take shows Billie's voice at its technical peak.

❻ STRANGE FRUIT from LADY IN AUTUMN
Written for Holiday, Lewis Allan's anti-lynching song was hugely potent for American audiences of the 1940s, as the hushed atmosphere of this intense live version demonstrates.

❼ I LOVE YOU PORGY from THE LEGEND OF BILLIE HOLIDAY
Billie brings an unmatched tenderness to this highlight from Gershwin's "folk opera". When the rhythm section quietly drops in for the second verse, the tears start rolling.

❽ LOVE FOR SALE from LOVE FOR SALE
Billie's forlorn account of this Cole Porter tune is powerful enough on its own terms. Once you learn that she was a prostitute in her teenage years, her delivery cuts like a blade.

❾ YESTERDAYS from LADY IN AUTUM
No one was better suited than Billie to this wistful Jerome Kern number, and in this 1953 version her poised vocal is closely miked, with Oscar Peterson's spacey Hammond providing extra bite.

❿ FINE & MELLOW from THE LEGENDARY SOUND OF JAZZ TELECAST
Recorded for TV, this extended version of Billie's self-penned blues saw her reunited with old sideman and dear friend Lester Young – just two years before both would be dead.

Duncan Clark

Holland–Dozier–Holland

Quite simply, Eddie Holland, Lamont Dozier and Brian Holland were the greatest song-writing and production team in the history of popular music. Here's why.

❶ CAN I GET A WITNESS MARVIN GAYE from ANTHOLOGY
H-D-H inject Motown's finest singer with rocking and rolling holy roller fervour.

❷ LEAVING HERE EDDIE HOLLAND from HEAVEN MUST HAVE SENT YOU: THE H-D-H STORY
A rollicking number that has since become something of a standard for groups like Motor City punkers The Rationals and Motörhead.

❸ WHERE DID OUR LOVE GO THE SUPREMES from THE ULTIMATE COLLECTION
The H-D-H formula in a nutshell: simple, sing-song melody surrounded by pure dynamism.

❹ LOVE IS LIKE AN ITCHING IN MY HEART THE SUPREMES from THE ULTIMATE COLLECTION
Some of the most electric music in Motown's supercharged catalogue.

❺ NOWHERE TO RUN MARTHA & THE VANDELLAS from LIVE WIRE!
The Vandellas shadow Martha Reeves' vocals like they're stalking her, while Funk Brothers' James Jamerson's bassline and that insistent tambourine propel the music to almost unbearable levels of intensity.

❻ REACH OUT I'LL BE THERE THE FOUR TOPS from ANTHOLOGY
Forget Phil Spector – this is the real "wall of sound".

❼ TAKE ME IN YOUR ARMS (ROCK ME A LITTLE WHILE) KIM WESTON from HEAVEN MUST HAVE SENT YOU…
A pulsating plea for love and affection that's been covered numerous times by rockers.

h

8 HEAVEN MUST HAVE SENT YOU THE ELGINS from **HEAVEN MUST HAVE SENT YOU...**
Perhaps the sexiest and most beautiful ballad in the H-D-H songbook.

9 GIVE ME JUST A LITTLE MORE TIME CHAIRMEN OF THE BOARD from **HEAVEN MUST HAVE SENT YOU...**
One of the records that created the blueprint for the pop-easy listening-soul crossover.

10 GOING BACK TO MY ROOTS LAMONT DOZIER from **HEAVEN MUST HAVE SENT YOU...**
A stirring, truly moving record about alienation – and proof that you can go back home again.
Peter Shapiro

John Lee Hooker

Miles Davis called John Lee Hooker "the funkiest man alive" – and who's to argue? The man created a mesmeric stomping boogie sound, and the staggering scale of his output across six decades puts him in pole position for the most individually compelling bluesman of them all.

1 BOOGIE CHILLEN from **THE LEGENDARY MODERN RECORDINGS**
Hooker unleashed his trademark boogie in his very first recording, from Detroit in 1948.

2 CRAWLIN' KING SNAKE from **THE VERY BEST OF**
The first version of a theme to which Hooker was to return again and again, as delivered in 1949.

3 HUCKLE UP BABY from **THE VERY BEST OF**
A stunning free-form re-interpretation of Paul Williams' signature tune, from 1950.

4 I'M IN THE MOOD from **THE VERY BEST OF**
Though supposedly inspired by Glenn Miller's In The Mood, this early Hooker gem is much more boogie than brass.

5 DIMPLES from **THE VERY BEST OF**
This 1956 hit was the most musically straight-forward of all Hooker's songs, which is probably why it inspired so many white rock bands.

6 BOOM BOOM from **THE VERY BEST OF**
This odd but successful blues-pop hybrid, cut with the Motown house band in 1962, gave Hooker a rare hit single.

7 YOU KNOW, I KNOW from **THE VERY BEST OF**
A hypnotically compelling Chess single from 1966.

8 BURNING HELL from **THE VERY BEST OF**
This tour de force was recorded with Canned Heat in 1970.

9 THIS IS HIP from **MR LUCKY**
A rumbustious romp from 1991.

10 STRIPPED ME NAKED from **MR LUCKY**
Octogenarian rap from 1991; Hooker rants about the judge who handled his divorce, atop a jazz-tinged accompaniment from Carlos Santana.
Greg Ward

House

"…House is an uncontrollable desire to jack your body and as I told you before this is our house and our house music…"

1 ACID TRAX PHUTURE from **TRAX RECORDS: ACID CLASSICS**
Original 303 acid house from Chicago.

2 JACK YOUR BODY STEVE HURLEY from **BEST OF HOUSE [UK]**
For a demonstration of the art of "jacking" just watch a room full of people moving to this.

3 FRENCH KISS LIL LOUIS from **FRENCH KISSES-COMPLETE MIX COLLECTION E.P.**
The woman in the breakdown definitely likes this slightly embarrassing house classic.

Nick Hornby's
10 great songs you might not know

Author **NICK HORNBY** proved himself a master of lists with his debut, *Fever Pitch*, and took the form to a new art in *High Fidelity*, and his collection of music writing, *31 Songs*. He says, about this list, "Of course, I have no idea what you know and don't know. But I have managed to introduce these songs even to people who listen to a lot of music; maybe you have somehow managed to have missed them."

❶ **WATCH YOUR STEP** BOBBY PARKER from **BENT OUT OF SHAPE**
❷ **START ALL OVER AGAIN** TYRONE DAVIS from **ATLANTIC RHYTHM & BLUES: VOL 7**
Two 60s R&B songs, one slightly menacing, the other exuberant, both of them absolutely irresistible.

❸ **FORMULA, COLA, DOLLAR DRAFT** MARAH From **LET'S CUT THE CRAP…**
The first three stages of man, neatly encapsulated in four minutes and what seems like a million urgent words, with a beautiful and unusual banjo outro. It rocks, twangs and uplifts.

❹ **I CAN'T BE ME** EDDIE HINTON from **HARD LUCK GUY**
The singer Jerry Wexler described Hinton as a white Otis Redding, and as a writer whose songs were covered by Aretha Franklin and Percy Sledge. "I Can't Be Me" was recorded just before he died in 1995, and he'd just about perfected blue-eyed soul by then.

❺ **A LONG WAY BACK AGAIN** PETER WOLF from **FOOL'S PARADE**
More white R&B – the former singer with J Geils is growing older with dignity and, on

this evidence, just the right amount of regret and melancholy.

❻ **GOIN' BACK TO CALI** LL COOL J from **ALL WORLD-GREATEST HITS**
❼ **BRIDGING THE GAP** NAS from **STREET'S DISCIPLE**
Hip-hop for people who don't think they'll like hip-hop. Blues riffs, trumpets, and the same kind of excitement you'd find in any great rock'n'roll.

❽ **PIECE OF CLAY** MARVIN GAYE from **THE MASTER**
❾ **STRANGER IN MY OWN TOWN** ELVIS PRESLEY from **THE MEMPHIS RECORD**
You may think you know all you need to know about these two. But Gaye's Piece of Clay is a haunting, mournful ballad released after his death (and, given the circumstances of his death, the first line is pretty chilling); Stranger In My Own Town is from the fantastic Memphis sessions, when Elvis briefly twitched back into glorious life after his long, slow 60s death, like one of the characters in *Awakenings*. Colonel Parker soon put a stop to his fun.

❿ **I WANT TO KNOW WHAT LOVE IS** NEW JERSEY MASS CHOIR from **BEGINNER'S GUIDE TO GOSPEL**
⓫ **WALK OF LIFE** CHARLES MANN from **THE ESSENTIAL COLLECTION**
Yes, the Foreigner song and, yes, the Dire Straits song. One is done gospel, the other Cajun, and both make you doubt every aesthetic judgement about songs you've ever made.

⓬ **ME JUST PURELY** BRENDAN BENSON from **ONE MISSISSIPPI**
A heartbreaking, simple ballad, possibly about giving up drugs. I don't know. I never know what songs are about.

❹ FOLLOW ME ALY-US from SINGLE
If you don't get this uplifting end-of-the-night anthem, then you don't get house music.

❺ YOU CAN'T HIDE FROM YOUR BUD
DJ SNEAK from SINGLE
Impeccably filtered disco house: a one-bar loop that twists and winds like a funky snake.

❻ COLOSSUS THOMAS BANGALTER from TRAX ON DA ROCKS, VOL 2
Most famous for his poppier Daft Punk tunes, Bangalter can also put together unstoppable underground house tracks like this.

❼ DOUBLE DOUBLE DUTCH DOPE SMUGGLAZ from DOUBLE DOUBLE DUTCH
Put this house version of Malcolm McLaren's "Double Dutch" on at a party and watch it erupt into carnival bacchanal.

❽ EMOTIONS ELECTRIC A GUY CALLED GERALD from THE CHILLOUT SESSION IBIZA SUNSETS
Warm, breathy synths, spacious production, and a wailing diva vocal made this a rush-inducing staple of "Summer of Love" raves.

❾ GOOD LOVE (REESE DEEPER MIX) INNER CITY from SINGLE
A relatively recent release from Kevin Saunderson's seminal house outfit, which aptly updates the Good Time vocal sound.

❿ STRINGS OF LIFE RHYTHIM IS RHYTHIM from SINGLE
Derrick May presents a sparse, mechanical version of house that still retains the crucial funk.

Dan May

Howlin' Wolf

Howlin' Wolf always seemed more of an elemental force than a flesh-and-blood human being. Crammed into his mighty frame were all the essential ingredients of the blues, the rage and passion of the Mississippi Delta, and the electric thunder and urgency of Chicago.

❶ HOW MANY MORE YEARS from MOANIN' IN THE MOONLIGHT
The Wolf's earliest great howl, recorded at Memphis Sun Studios in 1951 by Sam Phillips who always considered Wolf a greater discovery even than Elvis.

❷ EVIL from MOANIN' IN THE MOONLIGHT
Bellowing with pain, bristling with menace, Wolf is at his scariest in this 1954 recording.

❸ FORTY FOUR from MOANIN' IN THE MOONLIGHT
You wouldn't want to cross the Wolf in this mood, prowling with his loaded pistol.

❹ SMOKESTACK LIGHTNIN' from MOANIN' IN THE MOONLIGHT
Probably the Wolf's finest hour, from 1956; he's howling partly with longing and partly in emulation of the train on which he's leaving.

❺ I ASKED FOR WATER (SHE GAVE ME GASOLINE) from MOANIN' IN THE MOONLIGHT
Early mentor Tommy Johnson taught Wolf this one back in Mississippi; he electrified it in Chicago in 1956.

❻ WANG DANG DOODLE from MOANIN' IN THE MOONLIGHT
Wolf is said to have loathed Willie Dixon, who he famously called "that fat fuck"; Dixon's songs nonetheless suited him down to the ground.

❼ BACK DOOR MAN from MOANIN' IN THE MOONLIGHT
Another Dixon tour de force, also from 1960. "The men don't know, but the little girls understand."

❽ SPOONFUL from MOANIN' IN THE MOONLIGHT
And Dixon too was responsible for converting this song by Wolf's boyhood mentor Charlie Patton into an electric blues hit in 1960.

⑨ THE RED ROOSTER from **MOANIN' IN THE MOONLIGHT**

The Rolling Stones championed Howlin' Wolf during their earliest American tours, and had a hit single covering this 1961 song.

⑩ DON'T LAUGH AT ME from **MOANIN' IN THE MOONLIGHT**

An intriguing self-penned masterpiece from 1965, in which Wolf lays his vulnerabilities bare.

Greg Ward

The Human League

From a minimal electronic outfit with bad haircuts to dancy 80s chart regulars: let's hear it for Phil Oakey and the glamorous Susanne Sulley and Joanne Catherall.

❶ ALMOST MEDIEVAL from **REPRODUCTION**

Harsh and almost discordant, the squishy synths and pounding rhythms turn this into a paranoid yet utterly compelling nightmare.

❷ ARE YOU EVER COMING BACK? from **CRASH**

Another relationship on the rocks makes for an underrated, smooth and catchy mid 80s electro-pop gem. Should have been a hit.

❸ BEING BOILED from **TRAVELOGUE**

Not the minimal original but a turbocharged reworking with a throbbing rhythm and decorated with weird distorted handclaps.

❹ BLIND YOUTH from **REPRODUCTION**

There is room for optimism in the big bad city after all. The futuristic vibe is brisk, positive and most importantly highly danceable.

❺ DON'T YOU WANT ME from **DARE**

With that classic boy–girl vocal split, no 80s disco is complete without at least one spin of this. Guaranteed to get people singing.

❻ (KEEP FEELING) FASCINATION from **THE VERY BEST OF**

A super rubbery bassline to this one with Phil sounding particularly suave so why didn't this great song end up on 1984's *Hysteria*?

❼ THE LEBABNON from **HYSTERIA**

Just get a load of those corking Big Country-meets-U2-style guitars. Stadium rock meets the spirit of the dancefloor.

❽ LOVE ACTION (I BELIEVE IN LOVE) from **DARE**

This is Phil talking, kids! The chant-along mid section is (unintentionally) cheesily brilliant and the tink-a-tink rhythm track is terrific, too.

❾ THE SOUND OF THE CROWD from **DARE**

A mesmerizing beauty this. You've just got to love the pumping bassline, and the escalating gunshot-style drums are ace, too.

❿ SOUNDTRACK TO A GENERATION from **ROMANTIC?**

Oh wow! Holy cow! The girls' exclamations are so bright and upbeat you just have to laugh. A great hear-it-once-sing-it-forever chorus, too.

Essi Berelian

Iceland: rock's coolest outpost

It's not just Björk. Despite a tiny population, Iceland and in particular its capital Reykjavik boasts a thriving rock scene noted for its left-field approach. Blur's Damon Albarn is a regular visitor and part owns a bar called the Kaffibarrin in the city.

❶ BIRTHDAY SUGARCUBES from LIFE'S TOO GOOD
The first the world heard of the extraordinary voice of Björk Gudmundsdottir on her band's debut single back in 1988.

❷ ARMY OF ME BJÖRK from POST
It's imposible to represent her solo career with a single track, but this menacing, sinister-sounding iceberg of a song made waves when it was used in the film *Tank Girl*.

❸ AGAETIS BYRJUN SIGUR ROS from AGAETIS BYRJUN
The Icelandic My Bloody Valentine with added glacial soundscapes … the aural equivalent of an Icelandic postcard.

❹ THE SPELL LEAVES from ANGELA TEST
While this lot, with a lead vocalist who was once an opera singer, have been called the Icelandic Coldplay.

❺ CALM WATER EINAR ORN from GHOSTIGITAL
Once in The Sugarcubes with Björk, Orn was signed up by Damon Albarn to make a weird and wonderful solo album for his Honest Jon's label. It included this piece of dark oddness.

❻ MODERN HAIRCUTS MINUS from JESUS CHRIST BOBBY
Iceland's noisiest and nastiest heavy metal champions. This song also features Einar Orn.

❼ THE LAND BETWEEN SOLAR SYSTEMS MÚM from FINALLY WE ARE NO ONE
An epic, gurgling lullaby sung by twin sisters – two Björks for the price of one.

❽ WEDNESDAY'S CHILD EMILIANA TORRINI from LOVE IN THE TIME OF SCIENCE
It was her voice you heard singing the haunting Gollum's Song over the closing credits of *Lord Of The Rings: The Two Towers*, but this equally eerie track comes from her 2000 debut solo album.

❾ AM I LIVIN'? TRUBROT from LIFUN
Contrary to popular opinion, Icelandic rock did not begin with The Sugarcubes. Trubrot were the country's leading hippie band of the early 70s, whose finest hour came on the prog concept album *Lifun*, which chronicled "the trip we all take from birth to death", no less.

❿ HIROSHIMA UTANGARDSMENN from GEISLAVIRKIR
Briefly Iceland's biggest band around the time of the punk explosion, they once supported their idols The Clash in Reykjavik. This was their biggest hit. Sample lyric: "You will all, you will all, you will all… DIE!"

Nigel Williamson

Idlewild

This Edinburgh quartet have come a long way in a decade, developing from their early latterday punk frenzy into a mature and thought-provoking band. Vocalist Roddy Woomble leads the ship with cool assurance.

❶ THESE WOODEN IDEAS from **100 BROKEN WINDOWS**
The sudden jangled intro is overtaken by a hypnotic keyboard motif that underpins the excitement of the guitar-driven chorus. For post-modernists everywhere.

❷ TELL ME TEN WORDS from **THE REMOTE PART**
The surprising banjo-picked intro soon gives way to the more accustomed crash of crisp guitar and symbols and more great melodies.

❸ LET ME SLEEP (NEXT TO THE MIRROR) from **100 BROKEN WINDOWS**
The piercing guitar intro preludes a magnificent verse-hook-chorus that is bound to tickle the hairs on the back of your neck.

❹ PAINT NOTHING from **HOPE IS IMPORTANT**
This early number points the way towards later glories.

❺ QUIET CROWN from **100 BROKEN WINDOWS**
The gentle, almost folky intro is laden with harmonies and harmonics that pave the way for another killer chorus.

Nick Edwards

Industrial

With a brutal aesthetic that drew its inspiration from blighted, noise-polluted cityscapes, industrial music came of age in the 80s and early 90s, though Purists reserve the "industrial" tag for the mid-70s output of the Industrial Records label. Intoxicating sampling coupled with savage shouting and provocative imagery created a distinctive scene.

❶ UNITED THROBBING GRISTLE from **GREATEST HITS: ENTERTAINMENT THROUGH PAIN**
Sparse electronica with the bleakest of vocals from the pioneering London experimentalists who consciously chose to play unattractive music.

❷ 13 LOECHER (LEBEN IST ILLEGAL)
Einsturzende Neubauten from **KALTE STERNE**
Groundbreaking musical subversion from "Collapsing New Buildings", the ultimate demolition mob when it comes to razing such niceties as harmony and melody, and constructing new foundations from the raw soundscapes of electric drills and girders.

❸ ASSIMILATE SKINNY PUPPY from **BITES**
Most accessible entry point for the Vancouver band who specialize in otherworldy growls and agonized cries. Closing with a chant of "death, death, death", it creeps through your mind like the wounding excesses of an earthbound hellzone.

❹ HEADHUNTER FRONT 242 from **FRONT**
Relentlessly pounding stomper that shunned the dissonance of earlier industrial and gave rise to the term "electro body music" to encapsulate this new dancefriendly direction. Quite possibly the best industrial track of the 80s.

❺ THIEVES MINISTRY from **THE MIND IS A TERRIBLE THING TO TASTE**
Al Jourgensen leads his seminal Chicago outfit at a churning grind, crashing into a terrifyingly thrashy chorus as he seethes with venom and contempt for a society bleeding with thieves, liars and hypocrites.

❻ BEERS, STEERS AND QUEERS REVOLTING COCKS from **BEERS, STEERS AND QUEERS**
Affectionately called Revco, this Ministry offshoot supplied, according to Jourgensen, "disco for psychopaths". This cut is a godless hoedown, complete with crazed "yee-haws".

❼ HEAD LIKE A HOLE NINE INCH NAILS from **PRETTY HATE MACHINE**
A pulsating industrial dance anthem, written and played entirely by Trent Reznor, an individual so steeped in the macabre that he once lived at 10050 Cielo Drive, the house where Charles Manson murdered Sharon Tate.

❽ I GIVE TO YOU NITZER EBB from **EBBHEAD**
Orchestral beats and tortured lyrics collide in this outpouring from Essex electronic trio Bon Harris, David Gooday and Douglas McCarthy.

Mark Ellen picks
The Incredible String Band

MARK ELLEN edits *Word* magazine, the lastest in a string of music magazines he has created, including *Smash Hits*, *Q* and *Mojo*. Ellen has a longstanding passion for ISB. He explains: "The Incredible String Band were a pair of wildly adventurous psychedelic folk gypsies who, at their peak in the late 60s, were a major influence on John Lennon, George Harrison and Led Zeppelin (among others). A lot of their material is impossibly dated now but these songs still sound immortal."

❶ THREE IS A GREEN CROWN from **THE HANGMAN'S BEAUTIFUL DAUGHTER**
Indian raga masterpiece knocked out after genius multi-instrumentalist Robin Williamson had "followed the Tarot to Fez" and returned with an oud, assorted flutes, ethnic drums and a bowed gimbri.

❷ NO SLEEP BLUES from **5000 SPIRITS OR THE LAYERS OF THE ONION**
Naïve psychedelic whimsy in a daft folk shuffle.

❸ KOEEOADDI THERE from **THE HANGMAN'S BEAUTIFUL DAUGHTER**
A miniature song-cycle on the theme of creation, awash with cosmic riddles and including a section seen from the eyes of a small child. Nothing like this has ever been attempted before or since.

❹ WITCHES HAT from **THE HANGMAN'S BEAUTIFUL DAUGHTER**
Bizarre slice of atmosphere that sounds like it fell through a wormhole in time from the 16th century.

❺ COLD FEBRUARY from **HARD ROPE AND SILKEN TWINE**
The title of their pinnacle album, *The Hangman's Beautiful Daughter*, was an image of British recovery after WWII (both Williamson and Mike Heron were born in wartime). This late-period live recording was a reflection on the war that preceded it.

❻ OCTOBER SONG from **THE INCREDIBLE STRING BAND**
Homage to the English and Gaelic folk tradition that Dylan mined just as successfully in the early 60s.

❼ WALTZ OF THE NEW MOON from **THE HANGMAN'S BEAUTIFUL DAUGHTER**
Robert Plant once told me that Led Zeppelin had bought a copy of *The Hangman's Beautiful Daughter* "and simply followed the instructions". This, he thought, was the most thrilling and mysterious opening line to a song he'd ever heard in his life – "I hear that The Emperor Of China used to wear iron shoes with ease."

❽ SWIFT AS THE WIND from **THE HANGMAN'S BEAUTIFUL DAUGHTER**
Heron's dark, faintly Victorian account of a terrified child waking from a nightmare. Wood blocks clack disturbingly in the background. Absolute genius.

❾ DEAR OLD BATTLEFIELD from **LIQUID ACROBAT AS REGARDS THE AIR**
Lost gem buried in the mire of their ill-advised "folk-rock" interlude.

❿ FIRST GIRL I LOVED from **THE 5000 SPIRITS OR THE LAYERS OF THE ONION**
Williamson's touching recollection of a love affair when he was 17. Everyone hearing this smiles knowingly to suggest that they, too, once had a similarly deep relationship.

Produced by Alan Wilder, it's like early Depeche Mode, only harder.

⑨ SKINFLOWERS YOUNG GODS from **TV SKY**
This track from Scandinavian noisenik Franz Treichler builds to a quirky, Swiss-inflected bellow, while synth-phasers and electro guitar riffs burst through the thunderous, dominating drum machine.

⑩ SAVED DOUBTING THOMAS from **THE INFIDEL**
Cevin Key and Duane Goettel of Skinny Puppy showcase their masterful programming techniques with this dark slice of instrumental electronica. An intricate industrial masterpiece.

Ed Wright

Irish roots

Accordionist Brendan Begley called it "the only acceptable form of madness". Maybe so. Ireland's traditional music has survived the exigencies of poverty, famine and emigration as a fully living form. And it seems to resist commercial pressures, too, despite the global success of its top artists.

❶ THE LARK MOVING HEARTS from **THE STORM**
A staggering thirteen-minute musical exploration encapsulating all the Hearts' passion.

❷ RAGGLE TAGGLE GYPSY/TABHAIR DOM DO LÁMH PLANXTY from **PLANXTY**
The classic song and rousing pipes-led tune combination which still creates a storm thirty years on.

❸ CO. DOWN DANÚ from **THE ROAD LESS TRAVELLED**
Tommy Sands' modern-day emigration song, vibrantly delivered by Muireann Nic Amlaoidh.

❹ THE HOLLAND HANDKERCHIEF MARY MCPARTLAN from **THE HOLLAND HANDKERCHIEF**
Stunningly arranged and evocatively sung.

❺ TOMMY PEOPLES/THE WINDMILL/ FINTAN MCMANUS'S ALTAN from **ISLAND ANGEL**
Three sparkling reels from the awesome *Island Angel* album.

❻ THE LAMENT FOR STAKER WALLACE/THE GREEN GOWNED LASS MATT MOLLOY from **MATT MOLLOY**
An evocative air followed by a typically sprightly reel.

❼ NA CEANNABHÁIN BHÁNA/THE BLACK ROGUE/WILLIE CLANCY'S SECRET JIG CRAN from **LOVER'S GHOST**
A rollicking jig-song segues naturally into two rousing jigs.

❽ NA CONNERYS NIOCLÁS TÓIBÍN from **RINN NA NGAEL**
One of the "big" songs in the sean-nós tradition, sung impeccably.

❾ THE CHICKEN'S GONE TO SCOTLAND/ KITTY THE HARE/JIM ERWIN'S/THE DRUNKEN MAIDS OF ARDNAREE GERRY O'CONNOR from **JOURNEYMAN**
This is how fiddle music should sound – a gem of a highland and three fine reels.

❿ THE BUTLERS OF GLEN AVENUE/SLIABH RUSSELL/CATHAL MCCONNELL'S LÚNASA from **OTHERWORLD**
Fiddle, flutes, pipes and whistles combine to gorgeous effect.

Geoff Wallis

Iron Maiden

Having ridden in on the late 70s' so-called New Wave Of British Heavy Metal, Maiden are a rock phenomenon still able to sell-out stadiums worldwide with supreme ease.

❶ 12 MINUTES TO MIDNIGHT from **POWERSLAVE**
A countdown to the apocalypse, featuring great lyrics, a classy galloping bassline and some ace soloing.

❷ DIE WITH YOUR BOOTS ON
from **LIVE AFTER DEATH**
This is a real fist-pumping, crowd-pleasing do-or-die anthem with a cracking singalong chorus.

❸ DREAM OF MIRRORS from **BRAVE NEW WORLD**
A deeply troubled set of lyrics, exploring second sight and the power of dreams, married to a huge and memorable chorus.

❹ IRON MAIDEN from **IRON MAIDEN**
Almost punky in its speed, this gritty effort stuffs loads of ideas into just three and a half minutes of spitfire energy.

❺ PASCHENDALE from **DANCE OF DEATH**
The stench of violent death is almost palpable in this intelligent epic dramatizing one of the First World War's bloodiest battles. Complex, mature and emotional stuff.

❻ PHANTOM OF THE OPERA from **IRON MAIDEN**
A tune bursting with youthful zeal; the arrangement hints at the proggy influences Maiden would explore more fully later in their career.

❼ RUN TO THE HILLS from **NUMBER OF THE BEAST**
This cowboys'n'injuns corker features a thumping Steve Harris bassline and one of the most famous intros in metaldom.

❽ RUNNING FREE from **IRON MAIDEN**
Thundering war drums and Paul DiAnno's rough'n'ready vocals give this a neat street-level punch.

❾ THE NUMBER OF THE BEAST
from **NUMBER OF THE BEAST**
Hammer horror meets the best of British metal. A terrific creepy intro and one of Bruce Dickinson's best ear-shattering screams. Be afraid, be very afraid.

❿ THE TROOPER from **PIECE OF MIND**
The flash of steel, the crack of muskets, the clamour of war – a stunning Maiden battle tune complete with a classic duelling riff.

Essi Berelian

Isley Brothers

Beginning as a gospel group in 1955, the adaptable Isleys have moved on through doo-wop, R&B, Motown, psychedelic soul, disco and just about every other form of black American popular music and are still going strong half a century on…

❶ SHOUT from **SHOUT**
An early single from 1959 and five years later a big hit for the 15-year-old Lulu…

❷ TWIST AND SHOUT from **TWIST AND SHOUT**
Another song that led to a rather famous cover by a group from Liverpool …

❸ TESTIFY from **IT'S OUR THING**
Featuring the guitar of a then obscure member of their backing band named Hendrix.

❹ THIS OLD HEART OF MINE from **THIS OLD HEART OF MINE**
Their first single for Tamla Motown, penned by the ubiquitous Holland, Dozier and Holland team.

❺ I GUESS I'LL ALWAYS LOVE YOU from **THIS OLD HEART OF MINE**
The Motown hit factory does its stuff again.

❻ SUMMER BREEZE from **3+3**
Written by naff folk duo Seals and Crofts but transformed by the brothers' mighty soul voices…

❼ THAT LADY from **3+3**
Almost six minutes long, this 1973 single sold more than a million copies, after they split it into two on both sides of the disc.

❽ HARVEST FOR THE WORLD from **HARVEST FOR THE WORLD**
Heavily influenced by the sentiments of Marvin Gaye's Mercy Mercy Me (The Ecology), this protest song made the UK Top 10 in 1976.

Nigel Williamson

Michael Jackson

Although the family business was really only ever about Michael, it wasn't until he left the brothers behind that he, well, left the brothers behind and began to show what he was truly capable of.

❶ OFF THE WALL from **OFF THE WALL**
Mike's watershed song, in which you can hear him, gloriously, sounding like he's surprising himself as much as everybody else.

❷ ROCKIN' ROBIN from **GOT TO BE THERE**
Funky, frantic and loadsa fun, yet, in the best possible way, this is never more than half an inch away from being completely cheesy.

❸ THE WAY YOU MAKE ME FEEL from **BAD**
With the chugging background stripped down for so much of the song (well, stripped down as relative to other MJ records) this gives his voice's natural swing a chance to be heard.

❹ WHY YOU WANNA TRIP ON ME
from Dangerous
Teddy Riley-produced swingbeat that stirs in an electric guitar and creates a taut, tough tune that was always woefully underrated.

❺ AIN'T NO SUNSHINE
from **GOT TO BE THERE**
Big strings and a chugging rhythm provide a goose-down duvet of an arrangement for Michael to wrap himself up in and croon this evergreen tale of loss.

❻ PEOPLE MAKE THE WORLD GO ROUND
from **BEN**
A Bell/Creed composition, with a delightfully brassy, almost easy listening, Gene Page arrangement; it's Michael's contribution to the post-What's Going On ecology debate.

❼ I WANNA BE WHERE YOU ARE
from **GOT TO BE THERE**
Though an overly fussy orchestration takes up too much of the mix, Michael works incredibly hard and pulls off a fantastic performance.

❽ BILLIE JEAN from **THRILLER**
Divorce this track from the video and you've got possibly the best example of jumping, pumping pop/funk that it'll ever be your privilege to dance to.

❾ WE'RE ALMOST THERE from **FOREVER MICHAEL**
A cool hustle of a beat and an orchestration that manages not to overwhelm the funk.

❿ ROCK WITH YOU from **OFF THE WALL**
Probably the greatest Jackson solo track. Over a gently rocking beat, the arrangements are deceptively smooth but the singer's evident excitement injects a soulful exuberance.

Lloyd Bradley

The Jackson 5

The Jackson 5? Who are we kidding? From the moment that prepubescent performer launched into I Want You Back, it's only ever been Michael & Four Taller Blokes. That said, The Jackson 5 canon remains a fabulous record of Wacko's early years.

❶ THE LOVE YOU SAVE from **ABC**
Mike's clearly been on the orange squash, hence this song is much more exciting than anything else on which he was forced to share vocals with Jermaine.

❷ DANCING MACHINE from **GET IT TOGETHER**
The taut rhythm pumps it all up and, thanks to

clever holes in the instrumentation, Michael discovers the freedom to be found within a song: he even sounds like he's enjoying it.

❸ BLAME IT ON THE BOOGIE from **DESTINY**
The J5 get funky with a thumping disco beat, popping bass and harmonizing that has Mike sound like part of a quintet instead of a singer and his backing vocalists.

❹ LOOKING THROUGH THE WINDOWS from **LOOKING THROUGH THE WINDOWS**
Great big orchestrations that push the vocals to the point at which they turn around and triumphantly kick some over-arranged arse.

❺ NEVER CAN SAY GOODBYE from **MAYBE TOMORROW**
The brothers opt for a dead straight, finger-snappin', old-school-type backing while 13-year-old Michael soars to the rafters.

❻ I'LL BE THERE from **THIRD ALBUM**
Mike's heart-wrenching, unreserved and fragile enough to be rescued by Jermaine as his voice gets to the very edge of cracking.

❼ I BET YOU from **ABC**
Brooding low key funk with everybody except Marlon taking a turn on lead. George Clinton co-wrote this when he was a Motown staffer.

❽ SHOW YOU THE WAY TO GO from **THE JACKSONS**
Tight, sophisto-funk Gamble & Huff orchestrations give The J5 the space they need to stretch out in their first post-Motown hit.

❾ SANTA CLAUS IS COMING TO TOWN from **THE JACKSON FIVE CHRISTMAS ALBUM**
It's done with great gusto and is as corny as hell, but that's the whole point.

❿ I WANT YOU BACK from **DIANA ROSS PRESENTS THE JACKSON FIVE**
They never quite recaptured this rush as that cascading piano introduced the world's youngest superstar and the J5 spun off each other like apprentice Temptations.

Lloyd Bradley

Jailhouse Pod

As a rule, they do not allow iPods in county jails. If they did, these are the songs that would be on there.

❶ FOLSOM PRISON BLUES JOHNNY CASH from **JOHNNY CASH AT FOLSOM PRISON**
The quintessential prison song: you get murder, guns, trains and longing. It's all backed by the steady chug of an old guitar and the apocalyptical voice of the man in black.

❷ IN THE JAILHOUSE NOW JIMMIE RODGERS from **FIRST SESSIONS, 1927–1928**
A cheerful lament about the penalties for playing with cards, dice and loose women.

❸ STACKOLEE DOC WATSON from **TROUBLE IN MIND**
A fast blues tune recorded by everyone from Roy Bookbinder to Dave Von Ronk. Watson's version shows off his trademark, intricate guitar picking.

❹ JAILHOUSE ROCK ELVIS PRESLEY from **THE BLUE SUEDE SHOES COLLECTION**
An obvious choice. You can't help singing along even as you ponder what exactly he means when he sings "If you can't find a partner use a wooden chair."

❺ BLACKJACK COUNTY CHAINS DEL MCCOURY BAND from **COLD HARD FACTS**
A haunting cover of a Willie Nelson tune. Del's voice is extra high here, and extra lonesome.

❻ WISE COUNTY JAIL DOCK BOGGS from **HIS FOLKWAYS YEARS: 1963–1968**
A performer of some note in the 1920s, coal miner Dock Boggs put away his banjo until the 60s, when Mike Seeger called him out of hiding.

❼ WOMEN'S PRISON LORETTA LYNN from **VAN LEAR ROSE**
There's not much cheer in this track from Lynn's 2004 comeback album, but there is something uplifting in the grind of Jack White's electric guitar.

j

❽ STONE WALLS AND STEEL BARS
RALPH STANLEY & JUNIOR BROWN
from CLINCH MOUNTAIN COUNTRY
High lonesome meets low lonesome in a
traditional duet about cheating, killing, doing
time and the end of the line.

❾ MAMA TRIED
MERLE HAGGARD from MAMA TRIED
Another upbeat lament, this classic is one in a
slew of prison songs penned from the pages
of Haggard's life in juvenile detention halls and
San Quentin. Outlaw country at its finest.

❿ MOTORCYCLE MAMA
NEIL YOUNG from COMES A TIME
Because what's a prison set without some hope
of breaking free?

Madelyn Rosenberg

The Jam

**Three angry young men in sharp suits
who stormed out of the suburbs and over
the frenzy of punk to become one of the
biggest band in the UK.**

❶ IN THE CITY from AT THE BBC
This is suburban soul mod style, delivered in
the language of purest punk-rock. Even more
raw and urgent in this no-frills BBC production.

❷ MODERN WORLD
from THIS IS THE MODERN WORLD
Claimed by both the punks and resurgent mod
movement at the time of release, this is still the
greatest song The Who never wrote.

❸ DAVID WATTS from ALL MOD CONS
Cover version of The Kinks' number that
stomps all over the original – more bitter, more
twisted, more venom.

❹ A BOMB IN WARDOUR STREET
from ALL MOD CONS
A sketched slice of punk life as the London
scene disintegrated into warring factions.

❺ STRANGE TOWN from VERY BEST OF
One of the best "small town boy in the big bad
city" songs ever written. Weller's pithy sum-
maries of cockney-fashioned brush-offs sound
depressingly accurate.

❻ ETON RIFLES from SETTING SONS
With Weller settling comfortably into his role as
chronicler of the peculiarities of British society,
this is one of his lyrical high points and one of
the Jam's true greatest hits.

❼ GOING UNDERGROUND from VERY BEST OF
Precision guided lyrical attacks on the bunkers
of establishment orthodoxy delivered through
intercontinental ballistic soul music.

❽ START! from SOUND AFFECTS
Mindless, nameless, soulless sex might not be
that satisfying, but it's a start. Great to dance to,
just ignore the detumescent lyrics.

❾ THAT'S ENTERTAINMENT
from SOUND AFFECTS
As the Jam's main man started looking around
for something a little more challenging, his
growing disgust with the scene became
increasingly apparent, as this lyric indicates.

❿ BEAT SURRENDER from VERY BEST OF
This, one of the band's farewell songs, shows
them leaving the stage with the crowd still
begging for more.

Al Spicer

Jamaican vocal trios

**The sublime harmonies of Jamaica's all-
male vocal trios have been responsible
for creating many of ska, rocksteady and
reggae's most enduring classics.**

❶ SATTA MASSAGANA THE ABYSSINIANS
from SATTA MASSAGANA
The definitive rasta anthem, from 1975.

② **TWO SEVENS CLASH** CULTURE
from TWO SEVENS CLASH
Produced by Joe Gibbs, this 1976 piece of
prophesying rocketed Culture to worldwide
acclaim.

③ **TRAIN TO SKAVILLE** THE ETHIOPIANS
from EVERYTHING CRASH: THE BEST OF
Early ska classic from 1967.

④ **HELLO CAROL** THE GLADIATORS
from DREADLOCKS THE TIME IS NOW
During the 70s, before they lost their way
imitating The Wailers, The Gladiators produced
a string of classic hits like this Studio One gem.

⑤ **WHY WORRY?** ISRAEL VIBRATION
from THE SAME SONG
Utterly magnificent music from 1976.

⑥ **ARK OF THE COVENANT** THE CONGOS
from HEART OF THE CONGOS
Under Lee Perry's direction in 1977, The
Congos produced the greatest reggae vocal
album of all time.

⑦ **COOL RASTA** THE HEPTONES
from THE MEANING OF LIFE: BEST OF
A laidback jewel from 1976.

⑧ **I NEED A ROOF** THE MIGHTY DIAMONDS
from THE RIGHT TIME
Exquisite 1976 harmonies from the depend-
able Diamonds.

⑨ **WATCH THIS SOUND** THE UNIQUES
from TIGHTEN UP – VOLUME 1
A deliciously soulful reinterpretation of a
Buffalo Springfield original, from 1969.

⑩ **JAH JAH GIVE US LIFE** WAILING SOULS
from PUTUMAYO PRESENTS THE BEST OF REGGAE
The Wailing Souls delivered the best work of
their glittering career at Channel One in 1978.

Greg Ward

Keith Jarrett

**From the free and ecstatic to the honed
and romantic to the deeply introspective,
the expressive range of one of jazz's great
communicators is as wide as it is deep.**

① **GYPSY MOTH** from EL JUICIO (THE JUDGEMENT)
A contagious, rolling piece of gospel-flavoured
jamming from the American Quartet (featuring Dewey Redman, Charlie Haden and Paul
Motian) in 1971.

② **THERE IS A ROAD (GOD'S RIVER)**
from EXPECTATIONS
The climax of his ambitious 1972 double album
for Columbia, a joyous melange of pumping
piano, rock guitar and celestial strings.

③ **THE WINDUP** from BELONGING
Stupidly tricksy and utterly compelling, the
European Quartet (featuring Jan Garbarek,
Palle Danielsson and Jon Christensen) make
light work of Jarrett's asymmetrical theme in
1974 before the pianist takes flight.

④ **PART 1** from THE KÖLN CONCERT
Of the scores of Jarrett's solo improvisations
available, the extraordinary opening half-hour
of his famed and best-selling Köln concert from
1975 is as approachable and rewarding as any.

⑤ **MY SONG** from MY SONG
Simple harmonies, a lyrical, almost childish
tune and soaring quasi pop saxophone from
Garbarek; from 1978, Jarrett's other extreme.

⑥ **SPIRITS 20** from SPIRITS
Featuring his own overdubbed sax, flute,
percussion and recorder, this meditative, faintly
ethnic music from 1985 has few adherents
in the jazz world though some may detect a
mysterious healing quality.

⑦ **BOOK OF WAYS 18** from BOOK OF WAYS
Beautiful Bach-like ruminations on solo clavi-
chord from 1986.

Chris Ingham

Jazz ballads

Classics from the intimate side of the improvisational art … nice.

❶ BODY AND SOUL
COLEMAN HAWKINS from THE SWING ERA
Not written by a jazzer, but presented in 1939 with such imagination by tenor saxophone titan Hawkins, it was almost a gauntlet for the hundreds of versions which followed.

❷ PRELUDE TO A KISS
DUKE ELLINGTON from BRAGGIN' IN BRASS
Later turned into a song, this chromatic melody works best as an Ellington instrumental with fulsome harmony and the tune handled by the sensual alto sax of Johnny Hodges.

❸ ROUND ABOUT MIDNIGHT THELONIOUS MONK from THE COMPLETE THELONIOUS MONK ON BLUE NOTE
This Thelonious Monk ballad was turned into the song Round Midnight, which attracted countless vocal interpretations.

❹ IF YOU COULD SEE ME NOW
SARAH VAUGHAN from YOUNG SASSY
A bebop ballad composed by Tadd Dameron and based on the famous coda to Dizzy Gillespie's Groovin' High, it received its definitive reading from Sarah Vaughan in 1946.

❺ MISTY ERROLL GARNER from THE ORIGINAL MISTY
Composed in the head of the pianist on a plane on the way to a Chicago recording session, this inaugural 1954 recording of this most covered of romantic melodies was reportedly the first time he ever played it.

❻ CHELSEA BRIDGE
DUKE ELLINGTON from MASTERPIECES
Composed by Billy Strayhorn, this is an extraordinarily evocative piece of jazz impressionism.

❼ GOODBYE PORK PIE HAT
CHARLES MINGUS from MINGUS AH UM
A serpentine melody over an altered blues sequence forms this rich 1959 tribute by the mighty bassist/composer to the recently deceased and much-loved tenor saxophonist Lester Young.

❽ BLUE IN GREEN MILES DAVIS from KIND OF BLUE
Based on the chords of pianist Bill Evans, this wounded, sensuous theme from 1959 hypnotizes like an Escher staircase.

❾ CHILD IS BORN HANK JONES from LIVE AT MAYBECK RECITAL HALL
Master pianist Hank Jones examines his brother Thad's classic jazz waltz in 1991 and produces elegance and invention.

❿ DOLPHIN DANCE HERBIE HANCOCK from MAIDEN VOYAGE
From Hancock's 1965 cerebral classic of modal jazz, a piece that perfectly exemplifies a modern ballad; rich, intense and moving.

Chris Ingham

Blue Note jazz

The label that, to many, is synonymous with jazz, its iconic artwork and staggering music defined a zeitgeist.

❶ HAT AND BEARD ERIC DOLPHY from OUT TO LUNCH
Angular modernism at its most alarming.

❷ FRANKENSTEIN JACKIE MCCLEAN from ONE STEP BEYOND
A hunchbacked waltz, its revenant choruses lumber woozily with all their limbs in the wrong places.

❸ TWO PIECES OF ONE: RED
TONY WILLIAMS from SPRING
Icy and sparse, a chilly fanfare and forensic percussion heralds nothing less than Blue Note's very own Rite Of Spring.

❹ GHETTO LIGHTS
BOBBY HUTCHERSON from DIALOGUE
Freddie Hubbard's sly muted trumpet and

Hutch's conspiratorial vibraphone conjure a snide, abstracted blues.

❺ DEDICATION ANDREW HILL
from POINT OF DEPARTURE
Eric Dolphy's mournful lowing and dizzying cascades sometimes temper, sometimes augment, the lyricism of Hill's almost quasi-New Orleans lament.

❻ SPECTRUM ANDREW HILL
from POINT OF DEPARTURE
Quizzical, avian, fast-paced debate radically recontextualizes itself half-way through, pulling itself together to stick out its collective tongue at us.

❼ THE EGG HERBIE HANCOCK from EMPYREAN ISLES
Herbie boldy strides "out there" with an insistent riff, while Freddie Hubbard essays a cod-Spanish theme.

❽ EVOLUTION
GRACHAN MONCUR III from EVOLUTION
Startlingly discordant, precise and doggedly held chords from the horns render this arguably the starkest and most jarring recording among the Blue Note reels.

❾ CONQUISTADOR
CECIL TAYLOR from CONQUISTADOR
Cecil Taylor's scarily dynamic piano playing sounds like mice in a milk-bottle factory, while the horns of Jimmy Lyons and Bill Dixon – once they've recovered their breath – wake up to his weltanschauung sharpish.

Matt Milton

Jazz fusion

Jazz fusion developed as a result of the blending together of jazz and rock styles, but fusion also draws from the harmonic and rhythmic aspects of soul music. No slow dancing allowed!

❶ BIRDS OF FIRE MAHAVISHNU ORCHESTRA from BIRDS OF FIRE
John McLaughlin, Billy Cobham and Jerry Goodman created the defining fusion album and song with *Birds of Fire*. It remains the benchmark by which fusion is measured.

❷ STRATUS BILLY COBHAM from SPECTRUM
Shortly after Cobham left Mahavishnu Orchestra, he recorded this blistering solo album. Stratus is a fusion tour de force.

❸ SCHIROKKO PASSPORT
from DOLDINGER JUBILEE CONCERT
Klaus Doldinger's Passport recorded amazing fusion albums from 1970 through the end of the decade.

❹ EXPRESSO GONG from GAZEUSE
What do you do when you no longer want to be a drugged-out space-rock hippie band? Become a fusion band, of course!

❺ I BRAKE 4 MONSTER BOOTY JOHN SCOFIELD
from UBERJAM
After dabbling for years in a more rock influenced arena Uberjam marked the return to fusion for guitarist Scofield.

❻ BIRDLAND WEATHER REPORT
from HEAVY WEATHER
With the song Birdland, Weather Report generated the biggest fusion hit ever.

❼ HEY TEE BONE MVP (MARK VARNEY PROJECT)
from CENTRIFUGAL FUNK
This trio trade pyrotechnic solos that will make your jaw drop. Simply awesome.

❽ GOOD-BYE PORK PIE HAT
JEFF BECK from Wired
Jeff Beck is one of the most creative guitarists of the modern age and this arrangement of a Mingus classic is one of the best examples of fusion on record.

Geoff Colquitt

Jazz guitar geniuses

Ten great spankers of the plank.

❶ NUAGES DJANGO REINHART from **CLASSICS**
A clawed left hand didn't stop the Belgian gypsy acoustic guitarist being one of the most freewheeling, witty instrumentalists in jazz.

❷ AIR MAIL SPECIAL CHARLIE CHRISTIAN from **THE GENIUS OF THE ELECTRIC GUITAR**
In Christian's hands the single note melodic solo on the electric guitar became as valid a solo voice as any in jazz.

❸ LET'S COOK BARNEY KESSEL from **LET'S COOK**
Boppish and bluesy, Kessel was a studio musician for much of his career but remained a thrilling jazz player.

❹ TAKING A CHANCE ON LOVE TAL FARLOW from **THE SWINGING JAZZ GUITAR OF TAL FARLOW**
His smooth, almost uninflected fluency and bop melodicism mark Farlow as one of the great players. This is from his rich Verve period in the mid 50s.

❺ CHITLINS CON CARNE KENNY BURRELL from **MIDNIGHT BLUE**
Restrained, contained and deeply bluesy, Burrell grooves in a medium-hard bop style.

❻ WEST COAST BLUES WES MONTGOMERY from **INCREDIBLE JAZZ GUITAR**
This original jazz waltz from 1960 captures the essence of Wes's plectrum-free, self-taught style and prodigious melodic imagination.

❼ IF I SHOULD LOSE YOU GRANT GREEN from **BORN TO BE BLUE**
Green's achievements as Blue Note's house guitarist in the 60s should not be overshadowed by the dull funk he made in the 70s.

❽ STELLA BY STARLIGHT
JOE PASS from **VIRTUOSO**
In the 70s, when most jazz guitarists were exploring rockier climbs, Pass was an oasis of straight-ahead virtuosity.

❾ GIANT STEPS PAT METHENY from **TRIO 99/00**
Often heard in sunny fusion settings, latter day outings have emphasized Pat's lyrical, unprocessed invention, like this 1999 bossa nova reworking of Coltrane's classic.

❿ DARN THAT DREAM MARTIN TAYLOR from **SOLO**
Adept in all styles from contemporary to Django-style swing, Taylor excels as a solo performer.

Chris Ingham

Jazz rock

It was Miles Davis's influence which launched rock music's flirtation with jazz in the late 60s. Quite separate from jazz fusion (essentially jazz musicians moving into crossover territory), jazz rock approached the hybrid from the opposite direction.

❶ SMILING PHASES BLOOD, SWEAT AND TEARS from **BLOOD, SWEAT AND TEARS**
Astonishingly, they were the second highest-paid act at Woodstock after Jimi Hendrix.

❷ 25 OR 6 TO 4 CHICAGO from **CHICAGO II**
They later became associated with soft-rock ballads but this 1970 track combined Terry Kath's rock guitar and a full-on horn section in thrilling style.

❸ A LOVE SUPREME CARLOS SANTANA & JOHN McLAUGHLIN from **LOVE DEVOTION AND SURRENDER**
They shared an Indian guru – and a love of John Coltrane.

❹ BEWARE THE IDES OF MARCH COLOSSEUM from **THOSE ABOUT TO DIE**
Classic British progressive jazz-rock from 1969 with the late Dick Heckstall-Smith on sax.

⑤ MOON IN JUNE SOFT MACHINE from THIRD

A nineteen-minute suite featuring the vocals of Robert Wyatt.

⑥ O CAROLINE

MATCHING MOLE from MATCHING MOLE

After leaving Soft Machine, Wyatt formed the esoteric Matching Mole and had a minor hit with this affecting love song.

⑦ PEACHES EN REGALIA

FRANK ZAPPA from HOT RATS

Instrumental jazz-rock of astonishing invention from his 1969 solo album.

⑧ GOD MUST BE A BOOGIE MAN

JONI MITCHELL from MINGUS

From the album she dedicated to the great man and which employed the brilliant Jaco Pastorius on bass.

⑨ SHINE RY COODER from JAZZ

From his 1978 tribute to Dixieland, with arrangements by Joseph Byrd.

⑩ CAT FOOD

KING CRIMSON from IN THE WAKE OF POSEIDON

Featuring the virtuoso jazz piano of Keith Jarrett.

Nigel Williamson

Jefferson Airplane

Formed in San Francisco in 1965, the Jefferson Airplane helped to create acid rock from a melodic folk-rock sensibility, an artistic desire to explore and a solid grounding in the blues. Oh, and psychedelic drugs. Their best work comes from the period up to 1970.

❶ CHAUFFEUR BLUES

from BLUES FROM AN AIRPLANE

The basics: Memphis Minnie's 30s blues song,

belted out by original vocalist Signe Anderson, who left to have a baby.

❷ SOMEBODY TO LOVE from SURREALISTIC PILLOW

Its direct descendant, sung by new vocalist Grace Slick (late of The Great Society) and written by her (ex)husband Darby Slick.

❸ WHITE RABBIT from SURREALISTIC PILLOW

This classic of lysergic pop mixes *Alice In Wonderland* with a commanding bolero beat. It still sounds great today.

❹ COMING BACK TO ME

from SURREALISTIC PILLOW

It's often forgotten that Marty Balin founded the band. His gentle love song of reconciliation illustrates the group's more poetic side.

❺ EMBRYONIC JOURNEY

from SURREALISTIC PILLOW

A brief acoustic instrumental from the band's powerful guitarist Jorma Kaukonen and inventive bassist Jack Cassidy (who later returned to rootsier music in Hot Tuna).

❻ BALLAD OF YOU AND ME AND POONEIL

from AFTER BATHING AT BAXTERS

Rhythm guitarist Paul Kanter sings leads on one of the more accessible tracks from the album's disorienting psychedelic experiments and extended "suites".

❼ IF YOU FEEL (LIKE CHINA BREAKING) from CROWN OF CREATION

Driving wah-wah guitars power Balin's exhilarating "if it feels good, do it" rocker, leading the return to more conventional structures.

❽ LATHER from CROWN OF CREATION

Grace Slick is in gentle mood in this compassionate, haunting song about the loss of innocence.

❾ THE OTHER SIDE OF THIS LIFE from BLESS ITS POINTED LITTLE HEAD (LIVE)

The band take the freewheeling sentiment of Fred Neil's (the Neil in Pooneil) folk-blues song and turn it into a rocker.

⑩ GOOD SHEPHERD from **VOLUNTEERS**

The *Volunteers* album, which saw the band turning further towards revolutionary politics and science fiction, makes more sense as a whole but Kaukonen's enchanting reworking of this traditional song stands out.

Ian Cranna

The Jesus And Mary Chain

Hailing from East Kilbride, Scotland, the Mary Chain were a band (primarily brothers Jim and William Reid) that harnessed the kind of guitar feedback unheard since the days of The Velvets; for a while they were rulers of the UK indie scene.

❶ UPSIDE DOWN from **BARBED WIRE KISSES**

Their debut single – three minutes of saturated guitar scree, pounding drums and a perfect-pop melody. A nihilistic classic.

❷ IN A HOLE from **PSYCHOCANDY**

A standout cut from a standout first album. Again white noise dominates proceedings.

❸ SOME CANDY TALKING from **PSYCHO CANDY**

At the time of release this junky's lament was boycotted by UK DJs, but still made it into the Top 20. It's a blinding song which unashamedly displays the Reid brothers' love of Phil Spector-styled drums and production.

❹ HEAD from **BARBED WIRE KISSES**

A dark and claustrophobic assault on the ears, Head is one of several early B-sides that growls with defiant experimentation and edgy charm.

❺ DARKLANDS from **DARKLANDS**

The gentle melody and classic pop "do-do-dos" of this second-album cut surprised many after the thunder of *Psychocandy*.

❻ SIDEWALKING from **THE COMPLETE JOHN PEEL SESSIONS**

Peel was host to easily the best version of this grinding classic. The drum machine pounds away alongside a killer bassline while William proceeds to wring unearthly howls from his overdriven guitar.

❼ TEENAGE LUST from **HONEY'S DEAD**

One of the better cuts from the band's later albums. The bass and drums slide against each other like pole-dancing lizards, while wah-wahed guitars slice through your speakers.

❽ JUST LIKE HONEY from **PSYCHOCANDY**

With drums and guitars drenched in top-end and reverb, this album-opener stands as one of those great lost love songs; it was used to great effect in the film *Lost In Translation*.

Peter Buckley

Jethro Tull

Hoary old folk-blues warriors with a bit of one-legged flute virtuosity thrown in. Leader/linchpin Ian Anderson is not to be confused with the guitar-wielding editor of *Folk Roots* and contributor to this guide.

❶ FALLEN ON HARD TIMES from **BROADSWORD AND THE BEAST**

Broadsword And The Beast saw Jethro Tull turn away from folk-blues towards synthesizer-heavy metallic rock.

❷ THICK AS A BRICK from **BURSTING OUT LIVE**

The twelve minutes of this song start as a folky strum and builds to a rocking roar.

❸ SAID SHE WAS A DANCER from **CREST OF A KNAVE**

The guitar work on this has been fed through an industrial-strength Knopflerizer, but the tale of a cautious encounter with an Eastern European femme fatale is pure Anderson.

❹ HUNTING GIRL from **SONGS FROM THE WOOD**
Ah, the sexual allure of jodhpurs. Even a hunt saboteur would thrill to this.

❺ AQUALUNG from **AQUALUNG**
Wheezing tramp chic: a shambling blues riff that heralded popular culture's highest-profile asthma sufferer until Darth Vader.

❻ MINSTREL IN THE GALLERY
from **MINSTREL IN THE GALLERY**
Unashamed folk rock.

❼ FLUTE SOLO IMPROVISATION/GOD REST YE MERRY GENTLEMEN/BOUREE
from **BURSTING OUT LIVE**
The channelled spirit of Roland Rashaan Kirk, a Dickensian carol and JS Bach – just to give the band a break between songs.

❽ LIVING IN THE PAST from **LIVING IN THE PAST**
Uncharacteristic smoothness from this roughest and certainly hairiest of bands.

❾ ORION from **STORMWATCH**
Guitars crash like thunder and the drums sound like beaten anvils, while the verses provide a brief haven of hush.

❿ WONDERING ALOUD from **AQUALUNG**
A moment of calm amid the breathy locomotions of *Aqualung*.

David Honigman

Elton John

He may be a fat old has-been with dodgy hair, but the 70s were an extraordinarily creative time for Elton John, who – at least for a while – was a more serious and original singer, songwriter and musician than most people nowadays give him credit for.

❶ TINY DANCER from **MADMAN ACROSS THE WATER**
On the road in California, with Elt, Bernie and his girlfriend.

❷ LEVON from **MADMAN ACROSS THE WATER**
For all those people who hate their parents – and love huge, overblown string arrangements.

❸ TAKE ME TO THE PILOT from **17.11.70**
Elton rocks, particularly on this live version. But who knows what he's talking about?

❹ HONKY CAT from **HONKY CHATEAU**
Country-ish hocus with great brass and great singing.

❺ ROCKET MAN from **HONKY CHATEAU**
Elton's stab at the 70s space alienation genre.

❻ BENNY AND THE JETS from **GOODBYE YELLOW BRICK ROAD**
Falsetto heaven on this glam classic.

❼ BURN DOWN THE MISSION
from **TUMBLEWEED CONNECTION**
The slaves are revolting! The climax of Elt and Bernie's Wild West tumbleweed adventure.

❽ CAPTAIN FANTASTIC AND THE BROWN DIRT COWBOY from **CAPTAIN FANTASTIC AND THE BROWN DIRT COWBOY**
The story of how it all began.

❾ DON'T LET THE SUN GO DOWN ON ME
from **CARIBOU**
Lyrics soaked in melodrama, the Beach Boys on backing vocals – what more could anyone want from this live barnstormer.

❿ FUNERAL FOR A FRIEND/LOVE LIES BLEEDING from **GOODBYE YELLOW BRICK ROAD**
Pompous 70s prog-rock instrumental, laden with synthesizers, which segues beautifully into the glorious pop-rock of Love Lies Bleeding.

Martin Dunford

Robert Johnson

Even if modern scholars have proved he didn't literally write every word of his songs, Robert Johnson remains the "King of the Delta Blues". Immortalized thanks to two brief recording sessions, in 1936 and 1937, he lived the life and died the death (by poisoning) of the archetypal bluesman.

❶ CROSS ROAD BLUES
from THE COMPLETE RECORDINGS
The legend that Johnson sold his soul to the Devil at a lonesome Delta crossroads was fuelled by this saga of fear and despair.

❷ SWEET HOME CHICAGO
from THE COMPLETE RECORDINGS
Even if the words may say next to nothing, the boogie behind them went on to change the world.

❸ HELLHOUND ON MY TRAIL
from THE COMPLETE RECORDINGS
Beneath his delicate imagery, Johnson's sense of the hopelessness of trying to outrun his doom is overwhelming.

❹ COME ON IN MY KITCHEN
from THE COMPLETE RECORDINGS
A rare tender love song, quite beautiful in its simplicity.

❺ 32-20 BLUES from THE COMPLETE RECORDINGS
Johnson in a less metaphysical mood, threatening to shoot his baby with a Gatling gun.

❻ ME AND THE DEVIL BLUES
from THE COMPLETE RECORDINGS
Perhaps the most chilling of all Johnson's recordings, culminating in the threat that his "evil spirit" would continue to roam the highways after his death.

❼ LOVE IN VAIN
from THE COMPLETE RECORDINGS
A concise poetic narrative of loss and loneliness, as covered by The Rolling Stones.

❽ STOP BREAKIN' DOWN BLUES
from THE COMPLETE RECORDINGS
This song's deadpan arrogance made it too perfect for The Rolling Stones.

❾ WALKING BLUES
from THE COMPLETE RECORDINGS
Johnson borrowed the song from Son House, but made its desolation all his own.

❿ MILKCOW'S CALF BLUES
from THE COMPLETE RECORDINGS
This Kokomo Arnold original was covered by a remarkable triumvirate – Robert Johnson, Elvis Presley and Bob Dylan.

Greg Ward

Elvin Jones

Drummer Elvin Jones achieved prominence with perhaps the greatest jazz group of all time: the Coltrane Quartet of 1961–65. His deep-swinging polyrhythms set a standard for improvization and, with McCoy Tyner and Jimmy Garrison, moved rhythm section playing from the background to the foreground in a way that had never been done before.

❶ MY FAVORITE THINGS
JOHN COLTRANE from MY FAVOURITE THINGS
A beautiful, lilting and understated performance from Jones over 'Trane's 6/8 rendition of the Rogers and Hammerstein classic.

❷ DAHOMEY DANCE
JOHN COLTRANE from OLÉ
Elvin's impossibly deep swing is high in the mix and pings off the bass duo of Art Davis and Reggie Workman.

❸ SOFTLY AS IN A MORNING SUNRISE
JOHN COLTRANE from THE COMPLETE VILLAGE VANGUARD RECORDINGS
All crisp brushwork and delicate emphasis. Brain therapy from the rhythm master.

④ MR DAY JOHN COLTRANE
from **COLTRANE PLAYS THE BLUES**
Jones's increasing telepathy with his fellow band members is evident in this upbeat track from a great album.

⑤ OUT OF THIS WORLD JOHN COLTRANE from **THE CLASSIC QUARTET – THE COMPLETE IMPULSE RECORDINGS**
Popping candy for the ears.

⑥ JUJU WAYNE SHORTER from **JUJU**
Epic and apocalyptic drumming. The only logical explanation for the speed, accuracy and fury is that Jones has cloned himself.

⑦ A LOVE SUPREME, PART II – RESOLUTION JOHN COLTRANE from **A LOVE SUPREME**
The standard is set for group improvization in Coltrane's groundbreaking masterwork. Jones at his most inventive.

⑧ LOVE JOHN COLTRANE from **Meditations**
Set free from regular rhythmic structure, Elvin delivers mighty power in this swirling statement of a collective vision.

⑨ LIVING SPACE
JOHN COLTRANE from **LIVING SPACE**
Astonishing drumming. Jones in total, angular synchronicity with bassist Jimmy Garrison and pianist McCoy Tyner.

⑩ CONTEMPLATION
McCOY TYNER from **THE REAL McCOY**
A languid outing compared to the exertions of the last four tracks, this swings right through to your kidneys.

Nat Defriend

George Jones

"George Jones is not just one of country music's master vocalists. He's one of the greatest American song stylists of the 20th century. Care to argue?" asked Kurt Wolff in *The Rough Guide To Country Music*.

① BARTENDER'S BLUES
from **BARTENDER'S BLUES**
James Taylor wrote it. George turned it into his tour de force.

② THESE DAYS (I BARELY GET BY)
from **THE BEST OF**
Co-written by Tammy Wynette, who went and left him two days after he recorded the song.

③ A GOOD YEAR FOR THE ROSES from **BURN**
The Honky Tonk Broken marriage classic from 1970, later covered by Elvis Costello.

④ THE GRAND TOUR from **THE GRAND TOUR**
A number one hit in 1974 at the height of his productive partnership with producer Billy Sherrill.

⑤ STILL DOIN' TIME from **STILL THE SAME OLE ME**
A tale of drunken shame and, like so many of his songs, George had certainly been there…

⑥ HE STOPPED LOVING HER TODAY
from **I AM WHAT I AM**
"He kept some letters by his bed, dated 1962, he had underlined in red every single 'I love you.'" And the today, of course, was the day he died.

⑦ IF DRINKING DON'T KILL ME (HER MEMORY WILL) from **I AM WHAT I AM**
Mostly he sang other people's songs but this heartfelt lyric was all his own.

⑧ SHE THINKS I STILL CARE
from **THE GEORGE JONES COLLECTION**
At his most pained on this ballad from 1962.

⑨ WHITE LIGHTNING
from **WHITE LIGHTNING AND OTHER FAVOURITES**
His first #1 from 1959, written by J.P. Richardson, better known as the Big Bopper.

⑩ I'M RAGGED BUT I'M RIGHT
from **COUNTRY SONG HITS**
Under the influence of Hank Williams on one of his earliest recordings from 1956, based on a trad song originally recorded by Riley Pucket.

Nigel Williamson

Janis Joplin

She shrieked, she screeched, she moaned, she sang the psychedelic-soul-rock blues with the ear-shattering intensity of no other singer before or since.

❶ BALL AND CHAIN BIG BROTHER & THE HOLDING COMPANY from CHEAP THRILLS
An ominous epic of anguished romance, her croon-to-a-scream vocal ideally complemented by Big Brother's wobbly, crazed guitar wails and swoops.

❷ ME AND BOBBY MCGEE from PEARL
Could Janis handle country-folk-blues songs that required sensitivity, not just intensity? Yes she could; this American #1 hit proved it.

❸ PIECE OF MY HEART BIG BROTHER & THE HOLDING COMPANY from CHEAP THRILLS
Joplin made this R&B hit by Erma Franklin (sister of Aretha) her own, particularly on the scarifyingly supplicating chorus.

❹ DOWN ON ME BIG BROTHER & THE HOLDING COMPANY from BIG BROTHER & THE HOLDING COMPANY
Gospel transformed into psychedelic rock, with the combination of desperation and ecstasy heard in many of Joplin's best vocals.

❺ SUMMERTIME BIG BROTHER & THE HOLDING COMPANY from CHEAP THRILLS
The George Gershwin standard never sounded like this, either in Janis's rasp-croon of a vocal or the underrated Big Brother's snaky dirge of an arrangement.

❻ HALF MOON from PEARL
Another indication of Joplin's growing versatility in her final months, the funk-rock groove dissolving into delectably buttery phrasing in the jazzy chorus.

❼ COO COO BIG BROTHER & THE HOLDING COMPANY from BIG BROTHER & THE HOLDING COMPANY
A thunderous adaptation that stands an overdone folk standard on its head, powered by a maelstrom of raga-rock guitar.

❽ MOVE OVER from PEARL
Joplin's best original composition is an insistent stomper that sounds like a hit single that never was.

❾ TRY (JUST A LITTLE BIT HARDER) from I GOT DEM OL' KOZMIC BLUES AGAIN MAMA!
The best cut from her underachieving debut solo album, signifying her drift from psychedelia into sexy urgent soul.

❿ GET IT WHILE YOU CAN from PEARL
As the concluding song on her final album, an apt epitaph for a woman who wrenched everything she could from her voice.

Richie Unterberger

Joy Division

There's a dark side to every story of love, and Ian Curtis wrote the music. When he heard Captain and Tenille singing Love Will Keep Us Together, his response was to write Love Will Tear Us Apart.

❶ SHE'S LOST CONTROL from UNKNOWN PLEASURES
Closely observed, almost clinical description of a nervous breakdown in progress. Manic electro drums exquisitely capture the nature of obsession.

❷ ATMOSPHERE from STILL
The world's greatest break-up song; Ian and the band teeter on the very brink of melodrama.

❸ LEADERS OF MEN from SUBSTANCE 1977–1980
Desperate clashes of sheet-steel guitar fence with Ian's equally desperate vocals.

❹ NO LOVE LOST from SUBSTANCE 1977–1980
Piercing insight into the heart of the artist as fickle lover.

❺ HEART AND SOUL from CLOSER
The tragedy of love is that there's never a happy ending to it.

⑥ ATROCITY EXHIBITION from CLOSER

Compelling yet repellent, this display of deformity and perverted human imagination scarcely needs Ian Curtis to act as its carnival barker. Great drums, too.

⑦ DAY OF THE LORDS from UNKNOWN PLEASURES

Menacing basslines shiver up against guitars frozen beyond all pity and care. The lyrics are no barrel of laughs either.

⑧ INTERZONE from UNKNOWN PLEASURES

Based no doubt on some of Manchester's less attractive areas, this combines the fear of a Velvet Underground trip out to score with an urban zone far more menacing than anything dreamed of by William Burroughs

⑨ SISTER RAY from STILL

Who would have thought a band from Manchester could make such a totally New York song completely its own

⑩ LOVE WILL TEAR US APART
from UNKNOWN PLEASURES

Ian sounds wretched, like a priest burying his own mother, as he intones the saddest and most honest lyric to emerge from the whole northern English wave of post-punk depression.

Al Spicer

Jungle

Skirting around "coffee-table", "jazzy", and "intelligent" drum'n'bass, this list selects ten of the ruffest, most badboy jungle tunes ever released.

❶ THE HELICOPTER TUNE DEEP BLUE

An unbelievably funky beat and two chords; nothing else is required. This track still tears up pirate radio stations today, over ten years after its release.

❷ SUPER SHARP SHOOTER DJ ZINC

The singalong hip-hop vocal ("The S, the U,

the P...") made this a hit in student unions as well as with junglists, but a signature Ganja Kru bassline is the real pull.

❸ SHADOW BOXING NASTY HABITS

Proving you don't have to be happy to dance, this cut's doom-laden synth line and chopping beat impact like a karate chop.

❹ PHIZICAL RONI SIZE

From Roni's pre-superstar days, this winning combination of a chunky beat and subtly used sax sample is aimed squarely at the dancefloor.

❺ THE LIGHTER SOUNDS OF THE FUTURE

A true old-skool anthem.

❻ PROTON ED RUSH AND NICO

A monstrously dark hoover bassline and tearing Amen beat brought carnage to dancefloors in the mid 90s.

❼ THE RUCKUS TECHNICAL ITCH

Just as "dark jungle" was beginning to look tired, this 2002 track proved you can always go one step more evil.

❽ CONSCIENCE A HANG DEM DJ C/CAPLETON

Flying the flag for ragga jungle in 2005, Dj C's productions fuse ragga, jungle, gabba and whatever else he can think of.

❾ BAD ASS MICKEY FINN AND APHRODITE

From the Kings of the "wobbly bassline", this is a prime example of the Urban Takeover label's speaker-busting jump-up sound.

❿ ORIGINAL NUTTAH SHY FX AND UK APACHE

This infectious slice of ragga jungle made the British pop charts in 1994, but is no sell-out material. It made Shy FX's name.

Dan May

Just desserts

It's a common misconception that musicians are too busy thinking about sex to be interested in food. In fact, bluesmen

would do almost anything for a nice bit of jelly; while fruit of all kinds, especially when baked in a pie, remains beloved by rock'n'rollers young and old.

① BANANA IN YOUR FRUIT BASKET
BO CARTER from **BANANA IN YOUR FRUIT BASKET**

② GOOD JELLY BIG BILL BROONZY
from **KEY TO THE HIGHWAY**

③ IT MUST BE JELLY ('CAUSE JAM DON'T SHAKE LIKE THAT) GLENN MILLER
from **THE GOLDEN YEARS**

④ I LIKE MY BABY'S PUDDING
WYNONIE HARRIS from **RISQUÉ BLUES VOL.1**

⑤ WATERMELON MAN HERBIE HANCOCK
from **WATERMELON MAN**

⑥ SUGAR DUMPLING SAM COOKE
from **THE MAN AND HIS MUSIC**

⑦ HONEY PIE THE BEATLES from **THE WHITE ALBUM**

⑧ COUNTRY PIE BOB DYLAN
from **NASHVILLE SKYLINE**

⑨ BROWN SUGAR THE ROLLING STONES
from **STICKY FINGERS**

⑩ ICE CREAM MAN JONATHAN RICHMAN AND THE MODERN LOVERS from **THE MODERN LOVERS LIVE**

Greg Ward

K

Paul Kelly

Arguably Australia's greatest singer-songwriter Paul Kelly's extensive catalogue ranges across places and icons like a guidebook, although often zeroing in on Melbourne.

❶ TO HER DOOR from **UNDER THE SUN**
A classic "trying to sort things out, will she gives me another chance?" song.

❷ ON A WHITE TRAIN from **GOSSIP**
We've all got friends who are trouble and this suicidal mate is clearly a big problem.

❸ FROM ST KILDA TO KINGS CROSS from **POST**
Not only does it link Melbourne and Sydney's sin (and backpacker) centres, it's also the most perfect Sydney put down song.

❹ FORTY MILES TO SATURDAY NIGHT
from **UNDER THE SUN**
It's the quintessential outback night out, get in that ute and head to the pub, it's only forty miles away.

❺ SYDNEY from **A 727 FROM COMEDY**
We spend so much time listening to music in planes it's a wonder there aren't more songs about flying places.

❻ DUMB THINGS from **UNDER THE SUN**
In a punchy cry from the heart, Kelly regrets just about everything.

❼ FROM LITTLE THINGS BIG THINGS GROW
from **COMEDY**
Occasionally Paul Kelly ranges outside intensely personal song-stories to tell bigger tales, like this moving story of the fight for Aboriginal land rights.

Tony Wheeler

Kids' songs not sung by purple dinosaurs

Here's a list tested extensively on pre-school kids. Sure, there may be tots who can't get enough of The Itsy Bitsy Spider. But this is for ones who prefer The Who's Boris and other rock'n'roll nonsense.

❶ SURFIN' BIRD
THE RAMONES from **ROCKET TO RUSSIA**
A rocking cover with vocal effects that sound as if Joey is hiccuping into a toilet bowl.

❷ HELLO GOODBYE
THE BEATLES from **MAGICAL MYSTERY TOUR**
A layered but gentle introduction to the concept of opposites by a group that lays out the fundamental building blocks of rock'n'roll.

❸ HOUND DOG ELVIS PRESLEY
from **ELVIS' GOLDEN RECORDS**
Another song chock full of fundamental building blocks. Plus, kids like songs about dogs.

❹ VEGETABLES THE BEACH BOYS
from **SMILEY SMILE/WILD HONEY**
Even kids who forgo the green stuff will like this upbeat ode, where the harmonies are blended more smoothly than mashed peas.

❺ MAGIC BUS THE WHO from **MAGIC BUS**
The percussion – often Keith Moon knocking on a wooden block – gets the bus moving and the Pete Townshend/Roger Daltrey exchange:

"I want it, I want it, I want it!"/"You can't have it" hits children where they live.

❻ GOO GOO MUCK THE CRAMPS from **PSYCHEDELIC JUNGLE**
A punkabilly monster song in the spirit of those old K-Tel offerings but with rocking guitar and bass and a creature whose jungle trill evokes old Tarzan movies.

❼ MOLE IN THE GROUND BASCAM LAMAR LUNSFORD from **BALLADS, BANJO TUNES AND SACRED SONGS OF WESTERN NORTH CAROLINA**
This old-time tune with a seemingly simple banjo drone is often treated as a children's song, though the verses vary according to year recorded and who's doing the singing.

❽ OLD McDONALD HAD A FARM
RUFUS THOMAS from **FUNKY CHICKEN**
There's no telling what kind of impact Old McDonald could have if pre schoolers sang it Thomas' way.

❾ LOOKIN' OUT MY BACK DOOR CREEDENCE CLEARWATER REVIVAL from **COSMO'S FACTORY**
This tune about elephants and flying spoons has the added advantage of introducing kids to the CCR guitar innovation of "the choogle".

❿ MR. SPACEMAN THE BYRDS from **FIFTH DIMENSION**
Jangly electric guitars and a small silly factor open up the possibility of a rock'n'roll universe.

Madelyn Rosenberg

Cool kids music

Okay, okay, by 10 or so, kids have their own taste in music, hopefully entirely at odds with your own. But at 6, 7, 8, they're still very much up for direction, especially if you can provide fun tunes and memorable lyrics. Reggae and ska often go down well, as do classic Beatles, Monkees, T Rex and Bowie.

❶ ABOMINABLE SNOWMAN IN THE SUPERMARKET JONATHAN RICHMAN from **23 GREAT RECORDINGS**
Jonathan Richman can do "dark" with the best of them, but dozens of his early songs are for or about childhood.

❷ BAGGY TROUSERS
MADNESS from **DIVINE MADNESS**
The daft ska of Madness strikes a chord with most kids, and even more so if you get a DVD with all their very funny pop videos.

❸ KEEP'N IT REAL
SHAGGY from **HOLES (SOUNDTRACK)**
Holes is a cool kids' movie with a top soundtrack, which includes this warm rap-reggae from Shaggy.

❹ JOE LE TAXI SHARLENE BOODRAM from **THE ROUGH GUIDE TO CALYPSO AND SOCA**
This has all the ingredients: great tune, fun rap, novelty intro (taxi screeching to a halt) and soca soul-reggae riddim.

❺ YELLOW SUBMARINE
THE BEATLES from **REVOLVER**
Blinding tunes, memorable lyrics: The Beatles hit a chord with kids, from She Loves You to Here Comes the Sun. And does anyone not commit Yellow Submarine to memory?

❻ I'M A BELIEVER
THE MONKEES from **THE DEFINITIVE MONKEES**
Hey hey, how can anyone resist? And this is a perfect way in, familiar from the Smash Mouth version in *Shrek*.

❼ CHANGES DAVID BOWIE from **HUNKY DORY**
You wouldn't wish Tin Machine on kids, but 70s Bowie songs – from Hunky Dory and Ziggy Stardust – have a singalong magic.

❽ A LITTLE LESS CONVERSATION (JXL REMIX) ELVIS PRESLEY from **30 #1 HITS**
It's remarkable how kids respond to Elvis – the songs and the image – and this fabulous remix is the very best introduction.

❾ GET IT ON T REX from **ELECTRIC WARRIOR**
The US passed on Marc Bolan but in Europe he filled the gap for kids left by The Beatles and The Monkees. Start with this spark of genius.

❿ MAKE 'EM LAUGH DONALD O'CONNOR from **SINGIN' IN THE RAIN SOUNDTRACK**
Is Julie Andrews getting embarassing? There's no need to give up on musicals – and this is the funniest number from the greatest of them all.

Mark Ellingham

Kids' TV

Some of the best, most memorable themes belong to kids' shows – but how to track them down? Check out albums by the composers themselves or try some of the *Cult Fiction* compilations from Virgin for instant gratification.

❶ THE BANANA SPLITS THE BANANA SPLITS
The nutty "Tra-la-la-la" song! The kind of insanely sunny theme that would have you bouncing madly around the playground during break. Essential.

❷ DR WHO Delia Derbyshire
By far the best Who effort is Delia Derbyshire's arrangement of Ron Grainer's immortal classic, promising plenty of hide-behind-the-sofa Tom Baker action.

❸ GRANGE HILL Alan Hawkshaw
As soon as this timeless effort kicks off you can just picture the comic-style opening, that fork and the sausage!

❹ HONG KONG PHOOEY Scatman Crothers
Hanna Barbera's nutty answer to Bruce Lee featured the amazing Scatman Crothers' voice and loads of thwacky-wacky sound effects.

❺ JOE 90 Barry Gray
A real gem from Barry Gray, this far-out psych-edelic tune sounds more like a strobe-lit 60s wig-out than a kids TV theme. Groooovy baby!

❻ MAGPIE Spencer Davis Group
ITV's hipper rival to Blue Peter had one hell of a rocking theme from the Spencer Davis Group – check out the lashings of wicked Hammond organ!

❼ ROOBARB & CUSTARD Johnny Hawksworth
A green dog, a pink cat plus lots of wobbly animation equals a classic.

❽ THUNDERBIRDS Barry Gray
Thunderbirds are GO! Those marching martial drums and blaring trumpet fanfares mean business in this full-on orchestral arrangement from Barry Gray.

❾ TOMORROW PEOPLE Dudley Simpson
Next to Dr Who's, the SF theme most likely to scare the life out of you was this.

❿ WHITE HORSES Jackie Lee
Jackie Lee had a hit with the theme to *Rupert The Bear* in 1971 but her wistful vocals sound effortless on this Top 10 hit from 1968.

Essi Berelian

BB King

He celebrated his 80th birthday in 2005 and he's been the king of the blues guitar for more than half a century. Everyone from the Stones to U2 has played with him.

❶ EVERY DAY I HAVE THE BLUES from **THE COMPILATION KING OF THE BLUES**
Released as a single in 1955, the song that became his signature tune.

❷ SHE'S DYNAMITE from **THE COMPILATION KING OF THE BLUES**
Recorded in Memphis in 1951 by Sam Phillips – who three years later would discover Elvis.

❸ THREE O'CLOCK BLUES from **THE COMPILATION KING OF THE BLUES**
His first rhythm and blues #1 recorded at the black YMCA in Memphis.

❹ ROCK ME BABY
from **THE COMPILATION KING OF THE BLUES**
A storming version of a Lowell Fuslom song
that hit #1 in the American R&B chart in 1952.

❺ SWEET LITTLE ANGEL from **LIVE AT THE REGAL**
A classic blues song from one of the all-time
classic live albums recorded in the mid 60s.

❻ THE THRILL IS GONE
from **THE COMPILATION KING OF THE BLUES**
"I'd been carrying around that song for six
or seven years but it would never come out
how I wanted it," BB recalls. Then producer Bill
Szymczyk suggested putting strings on it.

❼ LUCILLE from **LUCILLE**
A tribute to the love of his life – Lucille, the
name he gave his gold-plated, pearl-inlaid
Gibson 335 guitar.

❽ WHEN LOVE COMES TO TOWN
from **RATTLE AND HUM**
Bono wrote him a song, they recorded it
together, stuck it on a U2 album and he suddenly found a whole new audience.

❾ PAYIN' THE COST TO BE THE BOSS
from **DEUCES WILD**
Backed by a combo called The Rolling Stones
on his 1997 all-star duets album.

❿ KEY TO THE HIGHWAY
from **RIDING WITH THE KING**
The Big Bill Broonzy tune done acoustically
from his 2001 Grammy-winning album with
Eric Clapton.

Nigel Williamson

The Kinks

**Ray Davies blended pop with nostalgia
and a music hall sensibility, and created
something peculiarly English and more
than a little eccentric. He's a national
treasure, and should be protected by law.**

❶ YOU REALLY GOT ME from **THE KINKS**
The ultimate riff-driven statement of instant
lust/obsession. It's not only dumb-but-great in
its own right, but without it we wouldn't have
had The Who or The Troggs.

❷ WATERLOO SUNSET from **SOMETHING ELSE**
Soundtrack for a Swinging London movie: Terry
(Stamp) kisses Julie (Christie) on the bridge,
and the concrete wilderness of the South Bank
turns into Paradise.

❸ DAYS from **THE VILLAGE GREEN PRESERVATION
SOCIETY (BONUS TRACK)**
Simple but elegant. As a song of celebration
and gratitude.

❹ LOLA from **KINKS PART 1: LOLA VERSUS
POWERMAN AND THE MONEYGOROUND**
The song that put transvestism on the map,
years before Bowie. Never has pop sexuality
been quite so laissez faire.

❺ DAVID WATTS from **SOMETHING ELSE**
Fifth-form angst, as Ray idolizes the "pure and
noble" paragon who captains both the school
and the team.

❻ SUNNY AFTERNOON from **FACE TO FACE**
Vicious tax demand? Girlfriend left you and
taken the car? Ah, well – at least the weather's
nice. Mustn't grumble?

**❼ THE VILLAGE GREEN PRESERVATION
SOCIETY**
from **THE VILLAGE GREEN PRESERVATION SOCIETY**
Like Ian Dury, Ray Davies had a talent for
compiling lists of things he liked – in this case
enshrining all the endangered ingredients of a
vanishing England.

❽ DEAD END STREET
from **FACE TO FACE (BONUS TRACK)**
Poverty, hopelessness, appalling living condi-
tions – and all with no hope of getting out. This
one's practically a call to armed revolution.

❾ AUTUMN ALMANAC
from **SOMETHING ELSE (BONUS TRACK)**
Fantastic singalong ode to the joys of autumn

– everything from rustling leaves to football and roast beef.

⑩ COME DANCING from **COME DANCING WITH THE KINKS (COMPILATION)**
Rueful regrets about bad town planning, and the lost arts of 50s romance: ie the doorstep snog and the knee-trembler.

Pete Hogan

Knocked down, but I get up again

Life will occasionally deliver a roundhouse punch to the jaw that sets you spinning on your heels. Here's some music to listen to while the cartoon stars and chirping birdies whirl about your head.

① COMPLETE CONTROL THE CLASH from **FROM HERE TO ETERNITY LIVE**
Betrayed by evil faceless suits at the record company who put out the wrong album track as the band's second single, The Clash turned their song writing skills to this tale of defiance.

② REBEL MUSIC (3 O'CLOCK ROADBLOCK) BOB MARLEY AND THE WAILERS from **NATTY DREAD**
Misbehaving maybe but doing no harm, when you put into a patrol in the middle of the night then throw out your little 'erb stalk.

③ I WILL SURVIVE GLORIA GAYNOR from **THE BEST OF**
Ripped apart by a million drunks, heartbroken and with mascara running figuratively if not literally down their cheeks, this is perhaps the ultimate "end of the affair" song.

④ TAKE THIS JOB AND SHOVE IT DEAD KENNEDYS from **BEDTIME FOR DEMOCRACY**
A more vicious, venomous and downright personal version than Johnny Paycheck's original.

⑤ MAGGIE'S FARM RAGE AGAINST THE MACHINE from **RENEGADES**
Bob Dylan wrote this, RATM added the spine, muscle, grit, sweat and anger.

⑥ WORKING CLASS HERO MARIANNE FAITHFUL from **BROKEN ENGLISH**
Ms Faithfull croaks a spine-chilling indictment of traditional life choices that neither she nor the writer (Lennon) ever had to face.

⑦ SIXTEEN TONS THE REDSKINS from **NEITHER WASHINGTON NOR MOSCOW**
Cold, miserable yet defiant through the darkest days of the 80s, the Redskins could always be relied on to give the man the finger.

⑧ WORKIN' FOR THE MAN ROY ORBISON from **ALL TIME GREATEST HITS**
Great lyric about putting up with a remarkable amount of bullshit from the boss while sneakily romancing his daughter.

⑨ CAREER OPPORTUNITIES THE CLASH from **THE CLASH**
Brilliant dose of teenage frustration by a band on the verge of immense success

⑩ PISS FACTORY PATTI SMITH from **LAND 1975–2002**
Superb, uplifting tale of factory life beaten out by solo voice and percussive pianomatics. Patti tells it straight about fighting the machine.

Al Spicer

Kool & The Gang

The skill and subtlety of Kool & The Gang's early instrumentations plus their almost transcendental understanding of how a groove works is what has given their pop productions such lasting depth. It's no wonder James Brown was moved to describe them as "the second baddest out there".

❶ WILD AND PEACEFUL from **WILD AND PEACEFUL**

Nine minutes of deeply funky, jungle-influenced jazz, washing over you in waves.

❷ STREET CORNER SYMPHONY from **LIGHT OF WORLDS**

The bassline's grumbling is, presumably, a reaction to its having to hold up the heaviest horn section that doesn't involve Fred Wesley.

❸ FUNKY STUFF/MORE FUNKY STUFF from **WILD AND PEACEFUL**

The tune that introduced the whistle as regulation club-going paraphernalia, and so dedicated to the groove it proves every instrument can be turned into a rhythmic device.

❹ GET DOWN ON IT from **SOMETHING SPECIAL**

Only a band with their intrinsic understanding of how much work you need to do inside a single riff to stop it getting boring could have taken this one this far.

❺ LADIES NIGHT from **LADIES NIGHT**

A hen night classic – with nothing as distracting as lyricism or instrumental twiddliness to get in the way.

❻ OPEN SESAME PTS 1&2 from **OPEN SESAME**

A pounding up-tempo rhythm is such a solid anchor, even with a bonkers, Ali Baba-ish theme.

❼ NT from **LIVE AT PJS**

Rubberized bass keeps everything on the bounce; percussion spirals around the mix; and the guitars fall in on themselves.

❽ LET THE MUSIC TAKE YOUR MIND from **KOOL AND THE GANG**

As teenagers showing off in 1969, they shout, crack jokes, play solos, musically joust but never stray too far from the beat as they build up a track of awesome funk power.

❾ RATED X from **GOOD TIMES**

A string section, a clavinet and an ARP synthesizer put such a perfect cushion between the rhythm section and the brass.

❿ SUMMER MADNESS from **LIGHT OF WORLDS**

At their most introspective, losing the horns to make a spiritual statement that maintains an astonishing tension.

Lloyd Bradley

Kraftwerk

The showroom dummies from Düsseldorf invented the pop world of pristine shimmering surfaces that we now inhabit. These are the ten cuts that made this brave new world possible.

❶ RUCKZUCK from **KRAFTWERK 1**

It begins with synth washes before becoming a jam session that has more to do with 60s avant-garde New York than the future.

❷ KLING KLANG from **KRAFTWERK 2**

One of their earliest synthscapes, and, despite its name, it's glistening and rather gorgeous.

❸ AUTOBAHN from **AUTOBAHN**

A pastoral ode to the freeway – one of their greatest and cheekiest records.

❹ RADIOACTIVITY from **RADIOACTIVITY**

Techno, synth-pop, techno-pop and all other electronic genres start here.

❺ TRANS-EUROPE EXPRESS from **TRANS-EUROPE EXPRESS**

The synth washes from "Ruckzuck" return on one of the most influential records of the last thirty years.

❻ METAL ON METAL from **TRANS-EUROPE EXPRESS**

The rhythmic motif of Trans-Europe Express transposed to tin cans.

❼ NEON LIGHTS from **MAN-MACHINE**

Yet another of this band's pastorales dedicated to urbanization.

❽ POCKET CALCULATOR from **COMPUTER WORLD**

By this point (1981) most of the world had

caught up with them, but no one else was able to craft such great pop from grating sounds.

⑨ NUMBERS from **COMPUTER WORLD**
Another outlandish exploration of the rhythmic possibilities of the synthesizer.

⑩ TOUR DE FRANCE
from **TOUR DE FRANCE SOUNDTRACKS**
The technology of cycling may be comparatively ancient, but it inspired what may be this band's best record.

Peter Shapiro

Krautrock

A couple of generations worth of enforced alienation from African-American music caused young Germans in the early 70s to rethink the role of rhythm in popular music. These are ten of the most startling records that resulted from the experimentation.

❶ THE WITCH THE RATTLES
from **RATTLES' GREATEST HITS**
Germans try to play a Bo Diddley riff and end up inventing psychedelic glam rock.

❷ ARCHANGEL THUNDERBIRD
AMON DÜÜL II from **YETI**
Gothic, spacy dronerock recast as Teutonic heavy metal.

❸ HALLELUWAH CAN from **TAGO MAGO**
Guitarist Michael Karoli and keyboardist Irmin Schmidt throw shapes everywhere and sculpt with their battery of effects pedals.

❹ WHY DON'T YOU EAT CARROTS?
FAUST from **FAUST**
Surreal rock concrète in which Faust lay waste to everything that came before them.

❺ HALLOGALLO NEU! from **NEU!**
The definitive motorik rhythm loop.

❻ LIGHT: LOOK AT YOUR DARKNESS ASH RA TEMPEL from **SCHWINGUNGEN**
A bluesy doom march into the gloomy bowels of psychdom.

❼ LAILA, PART 2 AGITATION FREE from **SECOND**
Krautrock at its jazziest and most Grateful Dead-like.

❽ HOLLYWOOD CLUSTER from **ZUCKERZEIT**
Decades ahead of its time, people are still trying to catch up to this record's synth tones and programming sophistication.

❾ CHA CHA 2000 LA DUSSELDORF from **VIVA**
Twenty minutes of pure kosmische slop.

❿ E2-E4 MANUEL GÖTTSCHING from **E2-E4**
On paper, a single-track, instrumental concept album about chess is the worst idea ever; in practice, it's a shimmering masterpiece.

Peter Shapiro

Kronos Quartet

Without the Kronos Quartet, the state of contemporary composition would be dramatically poorer. Since violinist David Harrington founded the string quartet in 1973, the ensemble has commissioned some six hundred new works and ranged across musical boundaries to take in tango flavours, East European Gypsy music and Bollywood glitz as well as promoting the work of avant garde composers such as Philip Glass and Steve Reich.

❶ BLACK ANGELS from **BLACK ANGELS**
Groundbreaking electric string quartet composed by George Crumb as an ode to the Vietnam War.

❷ GORECKI'S QUARTET NO. 1: ALREADY IT IS DUSK from **HENRYK GORECKI**
Alternatively sombre and furious, a fervent

David Harrington's
Discoveries

As leader of the Kronos Quartet, DAVID HARRINGTON has been in the vanguard of commissioning the best of modern composition, and has pioneered the field of world music/classical crossover. Every day of his working life, he puts aside two hours to listen to new music.

❶ FUNERAL CHANT from **ANTHOLOGY OF THE MUSIC OF THE AKA PYGMIES**
This track features the voices of an entire village lamenting a death. The collective grief heard here is transformed by the community into an awesome beauty.

❷ ARTISTS IN A TIME OF WAR HOWARD ZINN from **ALTERNATIVE RADIO, HOSTED BY DAVID BARSAMIAN**
As a source of real in-depth thought about world events, *Alternative Radio* is unsurpassed. Howard Zinn's voice and observations give hope for the future.

❸ BACH'S GOLDBERG VARIATIONS
played by **GLENN GOULD**
A testament to the power of the imagination, the Variations continue to astonish. In this performance, Gould charted new areas of commitment and virtuosity, setting a standard which is totally off the scale.

❹ LINDA MUSIC BANDA LINDA from **CENTRAL AFRICAN REPUBLIC: BANDA POLYPHONY**
A recording that features amazing choirs of horns. Each player is responsible for a note and a rhythm. I am always inspired by the raw beauty and interconnectedness this music and these performers have.

❺ STAR-SPANGLED BANNER
JIMI HENDRIX from **WOODSTOCK**
Hendrix's performance transformed our national anthem into a meaningful response to world events – using only sound.

❻ PARI INTERVALLO RITVA KOISTINEN from **NEW FINNISH KANTELE**
Ritva Koistinen's performance of Arvo Paert's *Pari Intervallo* sets a new standard of beauty, clarity and holiness. It has its own aura.

❼ DVORAK'S HUMORESQUE
from **FRITZ KREISLER PLAYS ENCORES**
The first note Kreisler plays is the most gentle, beautiful note I've ever heard on a violin: an endless source of inspiration. With his sound, he seems to embody the essence of the violin.

❽ SCHUBERT'S QUINTET IN C MAJOR played by **PABLO CASALS ET AL**
The depth and generosity of Schubert's imagination is unparalleled and in this one piece we have available to us a pinnacle of human expression. The performance is a landmark of interpretation, as though each note comes directly from the source of inspiration.

❾ RAGA TODI/RUPAK TAL from **RAVI SHANKAR LIVE AT MONTEREY 1967**
Ravi Shankar and tabla player Alla Rahka gave a new generation of listeners another way to hear music. This recording captures the exciting moment when these peerless virtuosos are swept up in the thrill of sharing their tradition with a culture far from home.

❿ ST. LOUIS BLUES
from **BESSIE SMITH: THE COLLECTION**
Bessie Smith's voice is perfectly counterbalanced by the harmonium and trumpet of Louis Armstrong, and she reveals areas of feeling instrumentalists can only hint at.

prayer for deliverance from the great Polish composer.

❸ TURCEASCA (TURKISH SONG) from CARAVAN
A collaboration with Romania's Taraf de Haidouks as conservatoire training collides with wild, untamed Gypsy passion.

❹ ESCALAY FOR TAR & STRING QUARTET: WATERWHEEL from PIECES OF AFRICA
Composed by the Sudanese oud master Hamza El Din for the Quartet's ground-breaking African album.

❺ MORTON FELDMAN'S PIANO AND STRING QUARTET from PIANO QUARTET
Written by the composer for the Kronos in 1987 shortly before his death.

❻ G-SONG, FOR STRING QUARTET & SYNTHESIZER from 25 YEARS: RETROSPECTIVE
The first of several pieces written for the Kronos by composer Terry Riley, based on a sixteen-bar theme of G minor scales played asymmetrically over a jazz chord progression.

❼ MISSA SYLLABICA
from 25 YEARS: RETROSPECTIVE
Written by Arvo Pärt for the quartet, who have been consistent champions of the Estonian-born composer.

❽ MEHBOOBA MEHBOOBA from YOU'VE STOLEN MY HEART: SONGS from R.D. BURMAN'S BOLLYWOOD
Indian singer Asha Bhosle joins the Quartet on a song written by her late husband, the film composer R.D. Burman.

❾ FIVE TANGO SENSATIONS FOR BANDONEÓN & STRING QUARTET
from FIVE TANGO SENSATIONS
The quartet go tango with Astor Piazzolla on a composition he wrote to play with them.

❿ DIFFERENT TRAINS FOR DOUBLE STRING QUARTET & TAPE
from DIFFERENT TRAINS/ELECTRIC COUNTERPOINT
Steve Reich's haunting response to the Holocaust.

Nigel Williamson

Fela Kuti

Fela Anikulapo Kuti was a musician, a politician, a utopian and, above all, a provocateur. In a Nigeria where the authorities responded to provocation with fury, his was a game played for blood. From the 70s until his death in 1997, he melded elements of Nigerian highlife and American funk into irresistibly jazzy dance music.

❶ LADY from SHAKARA
One of Fela's best-known songs, later covered by Hugh Masekela at a stripped-down five minutes. Ingenious attempts have been made to reclaim this denunciation of uppity women as a feminist anthem, but they are a stretch: Fela's sexual politics were never his strong point.

❷ WATER NO GET ENEMY from EXPENSIVE SHIT
An uncharacteristically lyrical piano line dominates this extended workout.

❸ ZOMBIE from ZOMBIE
A provocation of the army, which had disastrous results: Fela's compound, the self-proclaimed Kalakuta Republic, was raided by soldiers. One of them threw Fela's mother out of a window, causing injuries from which she later died.

❹ NO AGREEMENT from NO AGREEMENT
A rolling, boisterous repeated bass riff, with swirling organ and hammering brass solos.

❺ UNKNOWN SOLDIER from UNKNOWN SOLDIER
An inquiry into the Kalakuta raid blamed an "unknown soldier" – one of the thousand present – for the death of Fela's mother. He was vilified here.

❻ COFFIN FOR HEAD OF STATE
from COFFIN FOR HEAD OF STATE
The mass funeral of Fela's mother, herself a leading campaigner for independence and for women's rights, is remembered in this song.

❼ I.T.T. (INTERNATIONAL THIEF THIEF)
from **I.T.T.**
The target here is the multinationals profiting from Africa, and in particular the conglomerate ITT.

❽ ARMY ARRANGEMENT
from **ARMY ARRANGEMENT**
Still baiting the army: Fela hadn't learned.

❾ TEACHER DON'T TEACH ME NONSENSE from **TEACHER DON'T TEACH ME NONSENSE**
The former colonial nations are cast as teachers telling lies to the African countries and their citizens.

❿ BEASTS OF NO NATION
from **BEASTS OF NO NATION**
The eponymous beasts are Botha, Reagan and Thatcher, slated for their supposed support for Apartheid.

David Honigmann

Kwaito killers

South Africa's kwaito (hip-hop) tunes aren't generally built to endure, but rather to fizz and spark until the next hit comes along. Still, here's a selection that have managed to implant themselves as long-lasting dancefloor classics

❶ NDIHAMBA NAWE MAFIKIZOLO
from **SIBONGILE**
Wonderfully catchy anthem that was a huge hit on release and still always gets the kwaito line dancers going.

❷ NKALAKATHA MANDOZA from **NKALAKATHA**
Classic and enjoyable stomp rock/kwaito tune.

❸ DLALA MAPANTSULA TKZEE
from **HALLOWEEN**
Laid back vibes from kwaito maestros TKZee, so sure of themselves they don't mind what you think. As they put it "dance if you want to dance, whatever…".

❹ THATH'ISIGUBHU BONGO MAFFIN
from **CONCERTO**
Another line dancing classic, as Bongo Maffin implore us to "take the drum".

❺ LIFE 'ISKOROKORO BROTHERS OF PEACE
from **THE D PROJECT**
Contemporary house/kwaito tune with a great dubwise middle section.

❻ UBABA UYAJOLA CHICCO
from **STREET BASH 2**
"Mum's at home while Dad's partying next door", warns Chicco in this retro kwaito masterpiece.

❼ KHAULEZA ARTHUR from **YIYO**
Arthur crowned himself the king of kwaito – an exaggeration perhaps, but this hit alone made him a strong contender.

❽ DOWN SOUTH REVOLUTION, FEATURING JIMMY DLUDLU from **ANOTHER LEVEL**
Jazz, house and kwaito all rolled into one from this talented Durban outfit.

❾ MAFIKIZOLO MAFIKIZOLO from **SIBONGILE**
Superb and ever-green mid-tempo kwaito cut from one of SA's top pop acts.

❿ THE WAY KUNGAKHONA BONGO MAFFIN
from **BONGOLUTION**
Sunny and upbeat, with great vocals from the lovely Thandiswa, who has since gone solo.

Gregory Salter

Kylie

Australia's pop princess has defied all expectations with the longevity of her career and the durability of her hits.

❶ JE NE SAIS PAS PORQUOIS
from **KYLIE MINOGUE**
It's those hard J's that make this so irresistible.

❷ HAND ON YOUR HEART from **ENJOY YOURSELF**
The first really great Kylie song, with a melody that would stand up in any arrangement, though-long term fans are still waiting for the unplugged version.

❸ BETTER THE DEVIL YOU KNOW from **RHYTHM OF LOVE**
Whether she was talking about Stock, Aitken or Waterman remains unclear, but sticking with the infamous production/songwriting team for her first four albums did her no harm.

❹ STEP BACK IN TIME from **RHYTHM OF LOVE**
The hilarious video pointed the way forward for Kylie. The desert photo shoots for the album introduced a note of possibly unintended humour.

❺ CONFIDE IN ME from **KYLIE MINOGUE**
One of Kylie's least typical hits, and the best of the Deconstruction wilderness years. Again, lifted by a great video.

❻ WHERE THE WILD ROSES GROW DUET WITH NICK CAVE from **MURDER BALLADS.**
Kylie honestly sounds a bit out of her depth here, though it's kind of appropriate given what happens to her character in the song. The most enduring legacy of her ill-advised "indie" period.

❼ SPINNING AROUND from **LIGHT YEARS**
"I'm spinning around/Get out of my way." This girl is serious about dancing. And it shows.

❽ ON A NIGHT LIKE THIS from **LIGHT YEARS**
An admittedly slight addition to the Kylie canon was transformed when she performed it at the Sydney Olympics opening ceremony, assuring that post-millennial comeback.

❾ BURY ME DEEP IN LOVE DUET WITH JIMMY LITTLE from **CORROBORATION**
This little known gem from a 2001 compilation of leftfield Aussie acts pairs Kylie with Aboriginal cabaret crooner Jimmy Little on a great Triffids song.

❿ CAN'T GET YOU OUT OF MY HEAD from **FEVER**
Millions of others couldn't either – Kylie's biggest hit ever even struck gold in the US, which generally hasn't quite "got" Kylie.

Jon Lusk

LA, I'm your's

LA is romanticized the world over, and for good reason. This collection of stars, dreams, drunks and – of course – sunshine is to get you in an LA state of mind.

1 I WILL TALK AND HOLLYWOOD WILL LISTEN ROBBIE WILLIAMS from SWING WHEN YOU'RE WINNING

2 I LOVE L.A. RANDY NEWMAN from DOWN AND OUT IN BEVERLY HILLS

3 LOS ANGELES, I'M YOURS THE DECEMBERISTS from HER MAJESTY

4 LA ELLIOTT SMITH from FIGURE 8

5 L.A. WOMAN THE DOORS from L.A. WOMAN

6 ODE TO L.A. THE RAVEONETTES from PRETTY IN BLACK

7 FREE FALLIN' TOM PETTY & THE HEARTBREAKERS from FULL MOON FEVER

8 A HOUSE IS NOT A MOTEL LOVE from FOREVER CHANGES

9 UNDER THE BRIDGE RED HOT CHILI PEPPERS from BLOOD SUGAR SEX MAGIK

10 GOODNIGHT, HOLLYWOOD BLVD. RYAN ADAMS from GOLD

Hunter Slaton

Lambchop

"Music by which to drift down river, cowboy hat on head, open beer in hand." Actually we didn't write that. We found it, unattributed, on the Internet, but thought it summed up the charm of Kurt Wagner's alt-Nashville collective so perfectly that we couldn't improve upon it. Here are ten to float downstream to…

1 UP WITH PEOPLE from NIXON
Alt-country meets Curtis Mayfield on a track that was also dramatically remixed by Zero 7.

2 YOUR FUCKING SUNNY DAY from THRILLER
Exquisite country-soul again, this time with a Muscle Shoals influence.

3 I SUCKED MY BOSS'S DICK from THE EP HANK
OK, it's not Kurt's greatest song. But it's got to be his greatest song title.

4 THE SATURDAY OPTION from WHAT ANOTHER MAN SPILLS
A tender but oddly lurid account of bed-time ritual, like Desmond Morris set to music.

5 I'VE BEEN LONELY FOR SO LONG from WHAT ANOTHER MAN SPILLS
Kurt's usual baritone drawl turns falsetto on a wonderful cover of Frederick Knight's old hit.

6 THE NEW COBWEB SUMMER from IS A WOMAN
Whispered, gossamer beauty from the 'Chop's most deliciously understated album.

7 THE BUTCHER BOY from NIXON
An old murder ballad from Harry Smith's *Anthology of American Folk Music*, but given a new tune by Wagner.

8 IS A WOMAN from IS A WOMAN
Elegiac, unhurried and intimate – but with a surprising reggae-tinge.

⑨ NOTHING ADVENTUROUS PLEASE
from **AWCMON/YOU CMON**
Just to prove that they can rock out when they want to.

⑩ NOTHING BUT A BLUR FROM A BULLET TRAIN from **AWCMON/YOU CMON**
Gorgeous strings and intimate piano on a masterful minor key sound poem, with a typically impressionistic Wagnerian lyric that as far as we can tell has nothing to do with Britpop.

Nigel Williamson

Daniel Lanois

The Canadian artist/producer brings a characteristic shimmer to his own and other's work. Speciality: rescuing stuck careers, often in collaboration with Eno.

❶ ICE from **ACADIE**
Acadie is Lanois's finest outing under his own name, a blend of ambient electronica and Francophone folk.

❷ THE MAKER from **ACADIE**
A slow march with reverberating bass and drums, a trick Lanois would repeat with many of his production clients.

❸ FALLEN ANGEL ROBBIE ROBERTSON from **ROBBIE ROBERTSON**
A farewell to Robertson's Band-mate Richard Manuel. Come down Gabriel, blow your horn, implores Robertson and lo, Peter Gabriel agonizes on backing vocals.

❹ YELLOW MOON THE NEVILLE BROTHERS from **YELLOW MOON**
Aaron Neville's falsetto is one of Lanois's favourite voices, here used in service of the premier New Orleans funk band.

❺ MAN IN THE LONG BLACK COAT BOB DYLAN from **OH MERCY**
A spooky nod to the Band's Long Black Veil.

❻ BLOOD OF EDEN PETER GABRIEL from **US**
The original version of this, from the film *Until The End Of The World*, is unaccountably stiff: this album version sounds like a lot more fun.

❼ A SORT OF HOMECOMING U2
from **THE UNFORGETTABLE FIRE**
With chiming guitar and a yearning chorus, this set the tone for U2's move from indie energy to stadium mastery.

❽ WHERE WILL I BE EMMYLOU HARRIS
from **WRECKING BALL**
An ethereal melody that sounds like an old Appalachian hymn, and a sharp snare drum kick off Emmylou Harris's best album.

Essi Berelian

Latin soul

The blend of Cuban rhythms and jazz was some 20 years old by the time a new generation of Puerto Rican immigrants came of age in the 60s. Instead of looking to the jazz of their parents' age, they affirmed their Americanness by blending the sounds of their homeland with the rhythmically more aggressive soul music.

❶ EL SEÑOR EMBAJADOR RICARDO RAY
from **SE SOLTO**
Perhaps the very first boogaloo by the man who would become el rey del shingaling.

❷ BANG BANG JOE CUBA
from **WANTED DEAD OR ALIVE**
Only a complete killjoy can remain unmoved by this boogaloo classic.

❸ I LIKE IT LIKE THAT PETE RODRIGUEZ
from **I LIKE IT LIKE THAT (A MI ME GUSTA ASI)**
Boogaloo at its partying best.

❹ ACID RAY BARRETTO from **ACID**
In which psychedelia and effects entered the vernacular of Latin music.

5 HEAT! PUCHO & THE LATIN SOUL BROTHERS from HEAT!
One of the most seamless blends of Latin and soul-jazz rhythms.

6 YROCO JIMMY SABATER from EL HIJO DE TERESA
A bewitching combination of hard funk rhythms, horns, guitars, percussion and chants.

7 HARLEM RIVER DRIVE (THEME SONG) EDDIE PALMIERI & HARLEM RIVER DRIVE from HARLEM RIVER DRIVE
Salsa, soul, jazz – Palmierei fuses it all on this magnificent record.

8 LATIN STRUT JOE BATAAN from SALSOUL
Monstrous Latin-funk jam that helped clear the way for disco.

9 BABALONIA RICARDO MARRERO from NU YORICA!
Released on Don King's (yes, that Don King) label, this is an almighty Latin funk jam.

10 DO IT ANY WAY YOU WANNA LOUIE RAMIREZ from A DIFFERENT SHADE OF BLACK
Seriously funky, Latin-tinged cover of Peoples' Choice's disco classic.

Peter Shapiro

Leadbelly

The son of sharecropping parents, Huddie Ledbetter was not just another Delta blues singer. He was a repository of American popular music whose repertoire of five hundred plus songs included blues, spirituals, folk ballads, prison songs, field hollers, Cajun dance tunes and even cowboy songs. He died virtually penniless in 1949 but his recordings are widely available and his songbook has been plundered by rock artists ever since. Here are ten that he wrote or recorded – and some of the artists who covered them.

1 BOURGEOIS BLUES Ry Cooder: Billy Childish; Arlo Guthrie; Taj Mahal

2 GALLIS POLE Led Zeppelin; Odetta

3 IN NEW ORLEANS (HOUSE OF THE RISING SUN) Bob Dylan; The Animals; Nina Simone; Dolly Parton

4 GOONIGHT IRENE Frank Sinatra; Ry Cooder; Little Richard; Johnny Cash; Jim Reeves; Jimi Hendrix; Jerry Lee Lewis; Van Morrison; The Weavers

5 ROCK ISLAND LINE Lonnie Donegan; Johnny Cash

6 COTTONFIELDS The Beach Boys; Elton John; Credence Clearwater Revival; the Pogues

7 BLACK BETTY Ram Jam; U2

8 IN THE PINES Nirvana (as Where Did You Sleep Last Night); Smog

9 MIDNIGHT SPECIAL Credence Clearwater Revival; Van Morrison; Jimmy Smith

10 PICK A BALE OF COTTON Abba; Johnny Cash

Nigel Williamson

Led Zeppelin

The daddies of heavy metal to some, Robert Pant (vocals), Jimmy Page (guitar), John Paul Jones (bass/keyboards) and John Bonham (drums) created some of the most diverse and magnificent rock music ever.

1 ACHILLES' LAST STAND from PRESENCE
Over ten minutes of manically driven rock built around a thumping rhythm track; the interplay between Bonham and Jones is breathtaking.

2 DAZED AND CONFUSED from LED ZEPPELIN I
Plant is on top my-woman-done-me-wrong form with this loping, smouldering blues monster.

3 IMMIGRANT SONG from LED ZEPPELIN III
That supernatural Plantian wail says it all. And

it's about Vikings. Really, what more do you need to know? Just succumb to the hammer of the gods.

❹ IN MY TIME OF DYING from **PHYSICAL GRAFFITI**
A lengthy and turbulent blues-rock work-out. Plant pleads for heavenly salvation and the rest of the band lay waste with a collective sonic sledgehammer.

❺ MISTY MOUNTAIN HOP from **LED ZEPPELIN IV**
Plant wants to get down with the love generation but The Man just wants to give them all grief. Bonham's drumming really makes this track what it is.

❻ NO QUARTER from **HOUSES OF THE HOLY**
Plant sounds like he's singing underwater on this mystical and atmospheric little epic. Jones' keyboard work is nothing short of awesome.

❼ STAIRWAY TO HEAVEN from **LED ZEPPELIN IV**
Are those recorders at the start?! One of the most famous rock songs ever, featuring some of the best lyrics ever, and one of the best solos ever. Period.

❽ THE RAIN SONG from **HOUSES OF THE HOLY**
The typical Zeppelin bombast is jettisoned in favour of a gorgeously simple guitar melody and some touchingly intimate vocals. An understated, underrated gem.

❾ TRAMPLED UNDER FOOT
from **PHYSICAL GRAFFITI**
Naughty little Robert wants to check your oil pressure with his greasy dipstick, baby. Sex and cars, sex in cars – a timeless rock'n'roll combination.

❿ WHOLE LOTTA LOVE (LIVE)
from **HOW THE WEST WAS WON**
The version on Led Zep II is a classic, but this concert take exceeds the twenty-minute mark and throws in a bunch of blues standards for good measure.

Essi Berelian

Led Zeppelin solo

Robert Plant has spent much of his solo career denying the Zeppelin legacy and flirting with a variety of musical forms – anything but hard rock, in fact. Jimmy Page, on the other hand, remained an axe hero but failed to match the output of his former band. Until Page & Plant, that is.

❶ SHINE IT ALL AROUND
from **MIGHTY RE-ARRANGER**
Plant gets just the right mix of Middle Eastern rhythms and dinosaur riffs on this; the various trance remixes are also worth checking out.

❷ SATISFACTION GUARANTEED from **THE FIRM**
The combination of Page and ex-Free/Bad Co. singer Paul Rodgers in *The Firm* should have been a winner, but this gorgeous ballad proved to be one of the few high points.

❸ ROCKIN AT MIDNITE The Honeydrippers
from **THE HONEYDRIPPERS VOL 1**
And rock he (Plant) does, with guests Page, Beck et al on his superb 50s Big Band project.

❹ EO/EO STEPHEN STILLS from **RIGHT BESIDE YOU**
Jimmy plays a blinder on this salsafied funk offering from Stephen Stills.

❺ WHO'S TO BLAME
from **DEATHWISH 2 SOUNDTRACK**
Neighbour Michael Winner got Page to write him a soundtrack, and this track was the best part of it.

❻ LIFE BEGINS AGAIN WITH AFRO CELT
SOUNDSYSTEM from **66 TO TIMBUKTU**
Tribal drumming, flutes and Plant's inimitable wailing. It could have been a mess, but instead is inspired.

❼ COLOURS OF A SHADE from **FATE OF NATIONS**
Plant in full rustic lyricism mode. File under folk-rock.

Robert Plant's
Solid gold

With Led Zeppelin he was the golden god. But at heart, ROBERT PLANT remains above all a music fan, as he proves on this diverse selection of his faves, old and new.

1 HOME IN YOUR HEART SOLOMON BURKE from HOME IN YOUR HEART

2 DOUBLE TROUBLE OTIS RUSH from GOOD'UNS: THE CLASSIC COBRA RECORDINGS

3 OH DEATH RALPH STANLEY from MAN OF CONSTANT SORROW

4 SHE'S EVERYTHING RAL DONNER from YOU DON'T KNOW WHAT YOU'VE GOT

5 FARMER IN THE CITY SCOTT WALKER from FIVE EASY PIECES

6 MACH SCHAU AND THEY WILL KNOW US BY THE TRAIL OF DEAD from SECRET OF ELENA'S TOMB

7 SHINE IT ON VERNON GARRETT from KENT'S CELLAR OF SOUL

8 TOO CLOSE THE STAPLE SINGERS from GLORY! IT'S THE STAPLE SINGERS

9 MATCH BOX BLUES BLIND LEMON JEFFERSON from CLASSIC BLUES

10 THE SAME OLD ROCK ROY HARPER from STORMCOCK

8 DARKNESS DARKNESS from DREAMLAND
A haunting Jesse Colin Young number from Plant's collection of (mostly) 60s covers.

9 DON'T LEAVE ME THIS WAY from COVERDALE/PAGE
A rare return to the blues from this brief, and testosterone-heavy, collaboration.

10 ANNIVERSARY from MANIC NIRVANA
Sounds more like the anniversary of a tragedy. Gut-wrenching guitar solo, too.

Chris Coe

John Lennon

Poet, peace campaigner, visionary and inspiration to millions, Lennon's reputation currently lurks in the dark, hidden by the many hypocrisies of his life as a rich recluse. These titles from his solo career should help his rehabilitation

1 INSTANT KARMA from THE JOHN LENNON COLLECTION
One of the ex-Beatle's earliest solo outings, this shows him to be just as accomplished a master of pop as his erstwhile song-writing partner.

2 AISUMASEN (I'M SORRY) from MIND GAMES
The best "Sorry, darling" song he ever wrote.

3 WHATEVER GETS YOU THRU THE NIGHT from WALLS AND BRIDGES
Upbeat ode to the delights of a chemical smile. This funky tune bounces along in a sunshine of its own making.

4 NUMBER 9 DREAM from WALLS AND BRIDGES
Lennon explored the hidden crannies of falling and being in love with unique dedication, and continually found new ways to celebrate his emotional attachments and dependencies.

5 MIND GAMES from MIND GAMES
Lennon's worship of Yoko formed the backbone of his solo career. This perceptive and gentle meditation on the peculiar telepathy of

sweethearts is applicable to all who are truly in love.

⑥ COLD TURKEY from **LIVE PEACE IN TORONTO**
Credited to the Plastic Ono Band as Lennon tried to be just one of the guys in the group.

⑦ WORKING CLASS HERO from **JOHN LENNON/ PLASTIC ONO BAND**
Bitter tears on the lyric sheet, blood on the guitar strings. Despite John's upwardly aspirant upbringing, he manages to bring a blood curdling authenticity to this dark moment.

⑧ GIMME SOME TRUTH from **IMAGINE**
With hardened attacks of barbed lyricism such as this to contend with, it's a wonder Nixon endured so long.

⑨ I DON'T WANNA BE A SOLDIER from **IMAGINE**
This is one of his most powerful outings, and forms a major part of his legacy as a lasting campaign song for right-thinking peaceniks.

⑩ JUST LIKE STARTING OVER from **DOUBLE FANTASY**
Proof that an honest, sincere love song is never embarrassing.

Al Spicer

The Libertines/ Babyshambles

The Libertines are on hold and Carl Barat is at the time of writing unsure of his next musical step, while Pete Doherty's pharmaceutical/romantic decline is being steepened by intense media interest and Babyshambles' continuing desire to be paid in hard cash. So catch 'em quick.

① CAN'T STAND ME NOW from **THE LIBERTINES**
Remember the sadness of your first unrequited love, the shock of a best friend's betrayal? Three minutes of whining self-pity never sounded so good.

② WHAT BECAME OF THE LIKELY LADS from **THE LIBERTINES**
If you can ignore that it's one of those "love you man!" songs born of hard drugs and alcohol, this is the best brotherhood song of the decade.

③ DEATH ON THE STAIRS from **UP THE BRACKET**
One for all bands that have been knocked back by arrogant pieces of corporate ordure working in A&R.

④ UP THE BRACKET from **UP THE BRACKET**
Ammunition for those in search of the next band to take over from The Clash. Fast, tighter than a snake's new skin and just as stylish.

⑤ HORRORSHOW from **UP THE BRACKET**
The best song about using heroin since, well, Heroin by the Velvet Underground, with much more to offer than a tired "just say no" and suitably scruffy guitar work.

⑥ I GET ALONG from **UP THE BRACKET**
Carl croons his way through this, slithering over the words like a debauched lizard on warm glass, paying no mind to the road wreck guitar thrash that's piling up behind him.

⑦ DON'T LOOK BACK INTO THE SUN from **THE LIBERTINES**
Catchy, one might even say class A and addictive, this is the biggest hit the Libertines had.

⑧ SKINT AND MINTED from **DON'T LOOK BACK EP**
Scrappy production and a less than totally focused performance give this demo a vintage psychedelic garage rock sound.

⑨ FOR LOVERS WOLFMAN AND PETE DOHERTY from **FOR LOVERS**
Apparently scribbled down after a night of riotous crack smoking this song is so tender and sweet that the royalties ought to provide a solid pension.

⑩ KILLAMANGIRO BABYSHAMBLES from **KILLAMANGIRO**
This swaggers and sneers head and shoulders above the competition.

Al Spicer

Lighters in the air

The lights go down low and those first sweet'n'slow chords are met by a sea of cigarette lighters held aloft in salute. It's time for the big rawk ballad.

❶ EVERY ROSE HAS ITS THORN POISON
from **OPEN UP AND SAY AHH!**
If it's good enough to get Bill & Ted into heaven it's good enough for this list. Hair metallers take on the mantle of cowboy troubadours.

❷ HOME SWEET HOME MÖTLEY CRÜE
from **THEATRE OF PAIN**
Even sleazy glam rockers get tired of life on the road. Great keyboards plus a massive swaying chorus and widdling guitar solo.

❸ I WANT TO KNOW WHAT LOVE IS
FOREIGNER from **AGENT PROVOCATEUR**
Better fill up that Zippo. Lou Gramm needs a lesson in lurve, baby, and he's got a great big choir to back him up on this super-soft rocker.

❹ IS THIS LOVE WHITESNAKE from **1987**
Here we have a pristine vocal and a chorus guaranteed to make the laydeez go weak at the knees.

❺ MORE THAN WORDS EXTREME
from **PORNOGRAFFITTI**
So what if your mum knows all the words? You just can't beat clean vocal harmonies with a lilting acoustic accompaniment.

❻ NEVER SAY GOODBYE BON JOVI
from **SLIPPERY WHEN WET**
Jon gets all misty-eyed and nostalgic. Richie Sambora's insistent and heartstring-tugging guitar refrain is the magic ingredient here.

❼ NOTHING ELSE MATTERS METALLICA
from **METALLICA**
Even real men need to get sensitive once in a while.

❽ NOVEMBER RAIN GUNS N' ROSES
from **USE YOUR ILLUSION I**
The Gunners outdo themselves and everyone else. At nearly nine minutes in length this has piano violins, and enough guitar solos for at least three songs.

❾ STILL LOVING YOU THE SCORPIONS
from **LOVE AT FIRST STING**
A textbook example of the classic rock ballad: a slow build-up to a rousing and blisteringly melodic guitar solo climax.

❿ WHEN LOVE AND HATE COLLIDE
DEF LEPPARD from **VAULT**
Past masters of the smouldering slowie, the Leps pull out all the stops here. Just listen to those sugary strings and ultra-lush vocals.

Essi Berelian

London is the place for me

Tourist brochures and picture postcards present a rose-tinted view of life in the big smoke, but songwriters invariably lay bare the bones of the city they call home. These insider snapshots, in all their skewed and subjective glory, give you a lifetime's worth of London highs and lows, and all in just a few short minutes.

❶ THE GUNS OF BRIXTON THE CLASH
from **LONDON CALLING**
From a seminal album that embraced rock, punk, ska and reggae, The Clash hammered their right-on politics onto skanking beats for this raw, Jamaican-filtered scowl at authority.

❷ TWENTY-FOUR MINUTES FROM TULSE HILL CARTER USM from **101 DAMNATIONS**
From Carter's debut album, Jim Bob and Fruitbat aim their south-of-the-river bombast to public transport – a whistle-stop tour of the highs and lows of their local train service.

Tony Wheeler's
Lonely Planet

TONY WHEELER set up Lonely Planet with his wife Maureen in the early 70s, fresh off the Southeast Asia hippy trail. They named the company after a (mis-heard) line from a Joe Cocker song. In a shock transfer to Rough Guides' music division, Tony has also contributed playlists on Paul Kelly, Counting Crows, Route 66, and others to this book. He says: "Lots of businesses seem to have a soundtrack: this is Lonely Planet's, including the song which gave us our name."

❶ WAKE UP SUNSHINE CHICAGO from **CHICAGO**
In 1971 when Maureen and I lived together in London this was the standard Sunday morning wake-up song; years later we used it on our kids.

❷ ABRAXAS SANTANA from **ABRAXAS**
When we followed the hippy trail through Afghanistan in 1972, Sigis was the place to eat on Chicken Street in Kabul and Santana's Abraxas was the background music of choice.

❸ EAGLE ROCK DADDY COOL from **EAGLE ROCK**
At the end of our 1972 Asia overland trip we landed from a yacht on a west Australian beach and hitchhiked across to Sydney with Ross Wilson and Daddy Cool's favourite Aussie anthem playing on every truck radio and every pub jukebox.

❹ SPACE CAPTAIN JOE COCKER & LEON RUSSELL from **MAD DOGS & ENGLISHMEN**
In that classic rock-band-on-the-road film

from the 60s Joe Cocker belts out the line that gave Lonely Planet its name. Except I misheard it.

❺ GOODBYE TIGER RICHARD CLAPTON from **GOODBYE TIGER**
Australia's pub-rock troubadour of the late 70s came up with some classic Aussie stand-ards including this look back to those "dolce vita times".

❻ DR WU STEELY DAN from **KATY LIED**
During a year in San Francisco in the mid 80s Steely Dan was the music of choice, particularly on K-FOG, our favourite radio station.

❼ CONEY ISLAND VAN MORRISON from **AVALON SUNSET**
Maureen's a Belfast girl and on a return trip in the early 90s there was no better guide to Northern Ireland than Van the Man talking his way across the north.

❽ AICHA KHALED from **AICHA**
In 1996 we lived in Paris for a year and Khaled, the "King of Rai", crooning to Aicha to "ecoutez moi" was clearly the king of the Paris airwaves.

❾ PIU BELLA COSA EROS RAMOZZOTTI from **PIU BELLA COSA**
After years of Asian and developing world travel we got back in to Europe in the 90s and one trip was backgrounded by this soaring number.

❿ LOVE IS EVERYTHING KD LAING from **HYMNS OF THE 49TH PARALLEL**
If there's a song on high rotation for us in 2005 it's KD Laing positively breaking hearts with this Jane Silbery tearjerker.

❸ DON'T GO BACK TO DALSTON RAZORLIGHT
from **UP ALL NIGHT**

If the rumours about its inspiration are true, Londoner Johnny Borrell was just urging a rock-star friend to clean up his life.

❹ WATERLOO SUNSET THE KINKS
from **SOMETHING ELSE BY THE KINKS**

Like a diary extract, Ray Davies's musings seem almost too personal for public consumption as they describe life viewed from afar, beyond his bedroom window.

❺ PRIMROSE HILL LOUDON WAINWRIGHT III
from **LITTLE SHIP**

Ever the witty social observer, compassionate folkster Wainwright imagines life as a Tennants-swigging tramp in posh north London.

❻ WEREWOLVES OF LONDON WARREN ZEVON
from **EXCITABLE BOY**

Zevon's mischievous wordplay elevated his status among American singer-songwriters. If the opening verse doesn't draw you in, the lupine howling will.

❼ A RAINY NIGHT IN SOHO THE POGUES
from **THE ULTIMATE COLLECTION**

The Irish folk-rockers' main man Shane MacGowan penned a clutch of London songs, but this dreamy ballad is the best of them.

❽ DOWN IN THE TUBE STATION AT MIDNIGHT THE JAM from **ALL MOD CONS**

The urgent music is set against tube trains in motion, with the song's tempo changing accordingly, ratcheting the tension further.

❾ MILE END PULP from **TRAINSPOTTING**

A vital contribution to the sound of *Trainspotting*, this fusion of jangly, upbeat rhythms and tales of bedsit squalor is the ideal song to accompany student life.

❿ PLAISTOW PATRICIA IAN DURY
from **NEW BOOTS AND PANTIES**

Dury recounts a sad but spirited account of the eponymous junkie and her riotous behaviour. Outrageous, knees-up rocking at its best.

Ed Wright

Love

Achingly pretty folk-rock-psychedelia with a bitter lemon twist, usually though not always from the pen of leader Arthur Lee.

❶ ALONE AGAIN OR from **FOREVER CHANGES**

Second banana Bryan Maclean's shining moment in Love was also their best track, mixing flamenco, mariachi horns, soaring strings and quavering doubt.

❷ SHE COMES IN COLORS from **DA CAPO**

Jubilant jazzy folk-rock, its title often rumoured to have been lifted by The Rolling Stones for She's A Rainbow.

❸ 7 AND 7 IS from **DA CAPO**

60s garage rock at its punkiest, powered by nonstop drum rolls, jaws-of-doom guitar chords, and a simulated nuclear explosion.

❹ MY LITTLE RED BOOK from **LOVE**

Another glorious venting of Love's tougher side – who could believe it was a cover of a Bacharach/David song?

❺ ANDMOREAGAIN from **FOREVER CHANGES**

Exhibit A in the unsurpassed blend of acoustic guitars, violins and inscrutable lyrics that typified the classic *Forever Changes* album.

❻ THE GOOD HUMOR MAN HE SEES EVERYTHING LIKE THIS from **FOREVER CHANGES**

Another string-heavy *Forever Changes* ballad that lulls you into bliss.

❼ MAYBE THE PEOPLE WOULD BE THE TIMES OR BETWEEN CLARK AND HILLDALE from **FOREVER CHANGES**

A kaleidoscopic hot smoggy look down Sunset Boulevard in 1967, set to a psychedelic bossa nova beat.

❽ STEPHANIE KNOWS WHO from **DA CAPO**

Wild free jazz meets garage rock, barked out with the ludicrous bravado of a man who knows where he's going even if we don't.

⑨ MUSHROOM CLOUDS from **LOVE**

Devastatingly sad acoustic lament of nuclear holocaust that never makes Love collections.

⑩ LIVE AND LET LIVE from **LOVE**

An amazingly intelligent, probing rock song, considering it begins with the narrator watching snot caking on his pants.

Richie Unterberger

Love & marriage

There are love songs and cheating songs aplenty. Rarer are the tracks that deal with the state in between. Maybe it's just not rock'n'roll to be married.

❶ SAGINAW, MICHIGAN **LEFTY FRIZELL**
from **THE BEST OF LEFTY FRIZELL**

A disapproving father gets his comeuppance from his street-smart, love-struck son-in-law, sung with a wink by one of country's best crooners.

❷ WOULDN'T IT BE NICE **BEACH BOYS**
from **PET SOUNDS**

With their high, pitch-perfect harmonies, The Beach Boys wax wistful on the album's catchy, layered opening track.

❸ LOVE AND MARRIAGE **FRANK SINATRA**
from **THE VERY BEST OF**

Sinatra's songs are such a part of pop culture now that it's hard to think of them just as the well-orchestrated musical pieces they are, replete with big band and that suave, velvet voice.

❹ SOMETHING TO BRAG ABOUT **GEORGE JONES & TAMMY WYNETTE** from **SOMETHING TO BRAG ABOUT**

You don't need much if you've got love. This is Tammy and George in their happier days,

before the loving stopped. Jones' voice is young and pliable, his range open and wide; Wynette is a milkshake of sass and grace.

❺ I KNEW THE BRIDE (WHEN SHE USED TO ROCK 'N' ROLL) **NICK LOWE**
from **BASHER: THE BEST OF**

A great marriage song for realists and rockers, I Knew The Bride begins with a churchy intro and then amps it up.

❻ YOU NEVER CAN TELL **CHUCK BERRY**
from **CHUCK BERRY: SAINT LOUIS TO LIVERPOOL**

Rollicking piano accents this song, used in a dance scene in the 1994 film *Pulp Fiction*.

❼ TAKE ME BACK TO TULSA **BOB WILLS**
from **TAKE ME BACK TO TULSA**

The fiddle has a voice of its own in this upbeat tune about running from the altar. Western swing, sweet and neat.

❽ LET'S GET MARRIED **AL GREEN**
from **IMMORTAL SOUL OF AL GREEN**

Punctuated by organ blasts, Green's singing is soulful and smooth. And when he's done belting it out, the reverend can always perform the nuptials.

❾ BIG BAD BILL (IS SWEET WILLIAM NOW)
LEON REDBONE from **CHAMPAGNE CHARLIE**

Recorded in the late 70s but evoking a long ago night club – the kind with "stardust" in the title – Redbone's baritone wraps you up warmer than your grandmother's mink.

❿ TWO SLEEPY PEOPLE **FATS WALLER**
from **THE VERY BEST OF**

With a playful, raspy voice that sounds at times like a muted trumpet, Waller sets an intimate mood as he tickles the ivories and sings about being too in love to fall asleep.

Madelyn Rosenberg

❼ MINUIT from **IN SEARCH OF THE LOST RIDDIM**

A gorgeously flowing electro-acoustic treat.

❽ TROUBLE SLEEP from **RED HOT & RIOT**

An example of Baaba's AIDS campaigning, recorded for a Fela Kuti tribute album with Antibalas, Taj Mahal and the late Kauding Cissoko on kora.

❾ ALLAH ADDU JAM
from **MISSING YOU (MI YEEWNII)**

Mesmerizing electric hoddu, an extraordinary vocal and some hardcore percussion animate the closing track on this marvellously atmospheric return-to-roots album.

Jon Lusk

Baaba Maal

Possessed of the most startling voice, and always dressed to kill, Baaba Maal has thanks to his songwriting talent and strong social conscience long been an unofficial ambassador for Senegal, and in particular the Pulaar culture it shares with neighbouring Mauritania.

❶ MUUDO HORMO from **DJAM LEELII**

A pulsing, starkly atmospheric piece from the "nearly lost" album Baaba made with friend and long-term collaborator Mansour Seck.

❷ WANGO ARTI from **THE BEST OF THE EARLY YEARS**

Seriously cutting cross rhythms and a restless groove on this poppy electric mbalax outing. The title means "Tribal Dance Comeback".

❸ BOUYEL from **BAAYO**

Finger snapping simplicity and a joyous vibe. This is one of several great songs on Baaba's seriously beautiful 1991 acoustic roots album.

❹ DANIIBE from **LAM TORO**

Despite the language barrier, Baaba's compelling skills as a storyteller are very much in evidence here.

❺ TABAKALY from **N'DER FOUTA TOORO VOL 1**

A long meditative song with just the tiny banjo-like hoddu for accompaniment.

❻ AFRICAN WOMAN from **FIRIN' IN FOUTA**

Latin music is big in Senegal, as this celebration of African womanhood attests.

Kirsty MacColl

One of Britain's best-loved female songsmiths who collaborated with an extraordinary range of artists before she was killed in a boating accident in 2000. This pick celebrates that variety.

❶ A NEW ENGLAND from **GALORE**

Kirsty's take on Billy Bragg's classic gives a poignancy to this tale of a twentysomething's love trysts.

❷ WALKING DOWN MADISON
from **ELECTRIC LANDLADY**

Gloriously bassy and energetic, this collaboration with former Smiths' frontman Johnny Marr even includes a rap.

❸ FREE WORLD from **KITE**

A bustling, purposeful song that bristles with MacColl's genius. Makes you smile.

❹ DAYS from **KITE**

Covering Ray Davies's saga of life's ups and downs, KIrsty reveals her rich vocal range.

❺ THEY DON'T KNOW ABOUT US from **GALORE**

A typically upbeat account of the strifes of love from the early years.

❻ MY AFFAIR from **ELECTRIC LANDLADY**
Samba beat, soaring strings, parping brass and Kirsty's mellifluous tones. A divine mix.

❼ THERE'S A GUY WORKS DOWN THE CHIP SHOP SWEARS HE'S ELVIS from **WHAT DO PRETTY GIRLS DO?**
Do lyrics get any madder than this? Brings country music twang to the chippy.

❽ FAIRYTALE OF NEW YORK from **GALORE**
Kirsty's lasting legacy will be this Irish-spiced duet with the Pogues' frontman Shane McGowan. Forever Christmas, with rich MacGowan grit and MacColl spring.

Tim Pollard

Madagascar

Not just a location for Hollywood cartoons and habitat for cute furry primates, the huge Indian Ocean island of Madagascar oozes diverse musical cultures and classy performers like few other places on earth.

❶ TSY ZANAKRA MPANARIVO JAOJOBY from **MALAGASY**
The omnipresent electric band music of the northern regions is the driving, skittering 6/8 salegy. Its undisputed kings are Jaojoby and his band – one of the world's greatest dance machines.

❷ KOBA TARIKA from **SOUL MAKASSAR**
Nominated by *Time* magazine as one of the ten best bands in the world, Tarika's high energy acoustic pop utilizes most of the island's traditional instruments and inspired harmonies.

❸ ZAZA SOMONDRARA D'GARY from **AKATO MESO**
Fearsomely talented acoustic guitarist who's up there with anybody that nearby Africa – a continent of guitar heroes – can throw at you.

❹ RAMANJAREO (NY ANY AMINAY) RAKOTOZAFY from **VALIHA MALAZA**
Late, legendary and influential virtuoso player

of the marovany, Madagascar's double-sided box zither. Rakotozafy has been called the Robert Johnson of Madagascar.

❺ MIERITRERETA RASOA KININIKE from **MOLIA RIHA CHERIE**
In the deep southwest, the local music is a pumped up groove called tsapiky, full of startling guitars and full-scream, uninhibited arse-rotating singers like the fabulous Rasoa.

❻ FOKAFOKA NY ANTSALY from **FOLKLORE DE MADAGASCAR**
In the 1950s, this trio led by valiha (bamboo tube zither) master Sylvestre Randafison were the first group to tour extensively abroad.

❼ EKA LAHY REGIS GIZAVO from **SAMY OLOMBELO**
Regis Gizavo plays a massive button accordeon like it's the simplest instrument on earth. Highly in demand as a session player in France, he is also a sensational live soloist.

❽ TADIDIKO RY ZALAHY MAHALEO from **TADIDIKO**
An iconic band in the local student upheavals of the 70s, thirty years on the Beatles of Madagascar are now doctors and parliamentary deputies, but they can still fill stadiums with their anthemic songs.

❾ ERA VAKOKA from **INTRODUCING VAKOKA**
Not an artist, but a project in which many of the island's current roots musicians workshopped together to produce an inspiringly unified album of the same name.

❿ ZAMAGILA SOLOMIRAL from **GASIKARA**
This band of brothers call their music vakojazzana – a fusion of vakodrazana traditional music and jazz.

Ian Anderson

Madness

Rarely out of the UK singles charts or off *Top Of The Pops* during the 80s, the Nutty Boys were the epitome of ska-tastic pop brilliance.

❶ BAGGY TROUSERS from **ABSOLUTELY**
Superb lyrics, lashings of bonkers sax and ter-rific plinky-plonk piano – to use the technical expression – equals a total pop classic.

❷ CARDIAC ARREST from **SEVEN**
Having the old ticker pack up never sounded quite so enjoyable. The jaunty tune belies the everyday sadness of the lyrics.

❸ DAY ON THE TOWN from **SEVEN**
Eating chips and fare dodging with the lads. This features a neat reggae swagger, some cool percussion and an ironic lyrical twist.

❹ HOUSE OF FUN from **COMPLETE MADNESS**
A fantastic coming-of-age comedy, but a warning lurks beneath the laughs. The swirling fairground-style keyboards are superb.

❺ IN THE MIDDLE OF THE NIGHT
from **ONE STEP BEYOND**
A naughty little tune about a saucy night-time knicker thief. Wonder if he's mates with Pink Floyd's Arnold Lane?

❻ MY GIRL from **ONE STEP BEYOND**
Hell hath no fury and all that. Written very much in the style of Ian Dury, Suggs plays the poor everyman suffering woman trouble.

❼ NEW DELHI from **THE RISE AND FALL**
An unusual tune conjuring up the oppressive heat of India through weird travelogue-style lyrics…or is it all just a feverish delusion?

❽ NIGHT BOAT TO CAIRO from **ONE STEP BEYOND**
A long instrumental intro and plenty of par-ping sax. Exactly the kind of insistent Madness tune that demands serious dancefloor action.

❾ OUR HOUSE from **THE RISE AND FALL**
Shamelessly nostalgic and evocative, this is a fantastic slice-of-life tune, with a great vid too.

❿ YESTERDAY'S MEN from **MAD NOT MAD**
Madness did melancholy exceedingly well, and the low-key sax and resigned vocals make them sound suitably world weary.

Essi Berelian

Madonna

The ever-provocative entertainer was never much of an album producer; most of her best songs were singles. But what singles they were – if they don't make you shut up and dance, little will.

❶ BURNING UP from **MADONNA**
The most worthy relic from her early, bubble-gum dance period, with a funky, percolating bassline and a convincingly uncoy lyric.

❷ OPEN YOUR HEART from **TRUE BLUE**
An utterly perfect pop confection, built on a joyous, horn-inflected chorus.

❸ LIKE A PRAYER from **LIKE A PRAYER**
The gospel-choir backing vocals, the spiritual lyrics, the controversial video – Madonna reaches her dance-pop apotheosis.

❹ LIVE TO TELL from **TRUE BLUE**
Her dramatic chops were put to better use on this powerful ballad than any piece of celluloid she's ever made; a huge leap in vocal maturity.

❺ RAY OF LIGHT from **RAY OF LIGHT**
On this spirited, swirling track. Madonna successfully catches up to electronica with the help of William Orbit; she hits high notes too.

❻ MATERIAL GIRL from **LIKE A VIRGIN**
Maybe not her defining musical moment, but ingratiating good fun nonetheless – and who can forget the Marilyn-inspired video?

❼ INTO THE GROOVE from **THE IMMACULATE COLLECTION**
Quintessential Madonna – a great beat with a lyric basically about enjoying a great beat. It's best to seek out the CD single, which has the uncut version in its full glory.

❽ DON'T TELL ME from **MUSIC**
An unlikely marriage of sounds and style: bor-rowed lyrics from her brother-in-law Joe Henry (off a vaguely Tom Waits-like song), built over a stuttering, electro-countrified riff.

9 SECRET from **BEDTIME STORIES**

As stealthy as its title, this seductively mellow groove wants to worm its way off your headset and into your bedroom.

10 MUSIC from **MUSIC**

The kind of celebratory, anthemic sing-along that she just keeps one-upping herself at; Madonna has rarely sounded so sure of her place in the pantheon.

Andrew Rosenberg

Now that's what I call Mali

Mali has an ancient musical culture, which owes much to its extraordinary Mande Empire, founded 800 years ago. Passed down by generations of griots (members of the traditional musicians' caste), it hosts Africa's "classical music" – intricate songs accompanied on the sitar-like kora – and some red-hot rock'n'roll.

1 MANDJOU AMBASSADEURS INTERNATIONAL SALIF KEITA from **THE MANSA OF MALI**

An epic, meandering praise song – the most iconic of Salif Keita's early career. This original 1978 recording was made along with the rest of the album in two hours of stolen studio time. Crime really does pay.

2 MALIYO SUPER RAIL BAND DU BAMAKO from **NEW DIMENSIONS IN RAIL CULTURE**

A wonderfully dreamy, meditative cut from their stunning 1982 album, featuring vocals by Lafia Diabaté and the inimitable guitar of Djelimady Tounkara.

3 SENE ADAMA DIABATE from **JAKO BAYE**

From an overlooked 1995 CD, this gorgeous, bouncy track features gutsy griot vocals, sublime n'goni playing by husband Makan Tounkara, and spectacular tempo changes.

4 MOUSSOLOU OUMOU SANGARE from **MOUSSOLOU**

Hair raising stuff from the groundbreaking 1990 debut by the "Songbird of Wassoulou". The hypnotic, loping rhythm and her soaring voice make for a high goose-pimple rating.

5 BENIDIAGNAMOGO BOUBACAR TRAORÉ from **SAHARA: BLUES OF THE DESERT**

Bewitching acoustic guitar and a searing vocal on an intensely melancholic song by one of the country's most celebrated and long serving artists.

6 HAWA DOLO ALI FARKA TOURÉ from **THE SOURCE**

Mali's leading sorcerer of the guitar at his most gentle, playing an acoustic instrument, accompanied only by sympathetic percussion and backing vocals.

7 SUPER 11 TAKAMBA SUPER ONZE from **FESTIVAL IN THE DESERT 2003**

Don't even try counting the cross rhythms on this passionate and mesmerizing slice of desert blues! Recorded live, not very far from Timbuktu.

8 LA RÉALITÉ AMADOU & MARIAM from **DIMANCHE A BAMAKO**

The blues-rocking duo from Bamako get a fairydust turbo-charge courtesy of Manu Chao on this driving number from their hugely successful crossover collaboration.

9 NANGA MADY KÉLÉTIGUI DIABATÉ from **SANDIYA**

Having contributed so much to albums made by other musicians, Mali's most in-demand player of the balafon (wooden xylophone) calls in a favour or two on his own – in this case a sparkling performance by guest kora virtuoso Toumani Diabaté.

10 NAWEYE TORO ALI FARKA TOURÉ AND TOUMANI DIABATÉ from **IN THE HEART OF THE MOON**

Two geniuses for the price of one on this sublime pulsing duet between kora and guitar. Music to drift down a river to.

Jon Lusk

Manchester: a lot to answer for

There's a well-balanced feel to Manchester bands; buffetted by the weather and by competition from Britain's other great metropolises, they tend to come with a chip on each shoulder. It gives them a fine swaggering attitude – all sneer and "prove it then!".

❶ PSYKICK DANCEHALL THE FALL from **DRAGNET**
One of the highlights of Salford Council's bus tour celebrating the Fall is visiting the actual Psykick Dancehall of the title. A busy, clanging, glamorous mass of music.

❷ HAND IN GLOVE THE SMITHS from **HATFUL OF HOLLOW**
With lyrics that include "the sun shines out of our behinds", this Morrissey number could have been born only in Manc.

❸ FRIENDS OF MINE BUZZCOCKS from **SPIRAL SCRATCH**
Howard Devoto and Pete Shelley emerged from the city's community of art students, documenting some of the peculiarly Manc tastes for excess in this amphetamine grinder.

❹ ROCK 'N' ROLL STAR OASIS from **DEFINITELY MAYBE**
Rather than pass the traditional torch from one generation to the next, in Manchester the sun sets in one bottom to dawn anew, shining from yet another backside, the next day.

❺ INTERZONE JOY DIVISION from **UNKNOWN PLEASURES**
An eerie tale lined with hidden menace as our protagonist scoots round the city's meaner streets, on foot and vulnerable.

❻ BYE BYE BADMAN THE STONE ROSES from **THE STONE ROSES**
Hidden within one of the Roses' finest songs is a lyric of stone-throwing, street-fighting rebel-

lion. Every city boasts its crew of such kids, and this is the anthem for the Manc chapter.

❼ GOD'S COP HAPPY MONDAYS from **PILLS 'N' THRILLS AND BELLYACHES**
Chief Constable Anderton had it coming. He claimed biblical authority for assertions like "gays are swilling around in a cesspool of their own making". They don't make chiefs like that any more, nor these sublime ecstatic grooves.

❽ GETTING AWAY WITH IT JAMES from **THE COLLECTION**
Scamming the system, working for cash in hand, and spending the dough on messing up your brain are traits perfectly celebrated in Manc music.

❾ BEAST INSIDE INSPIRAL CARPETS from **THE BEAST INSIDE**
Dark, cold and miserable as a Tuesday night in November, the Carpets waltz gloomily through an elegant little ditty of betrayal and love.

❿ SHADOWS OF SALFORD DOVES from **SOME CITIES**
To the accompaniment of a rickety pub piano, and an almost angelic chorus of backing vocals, Jimi Goodwin provides the perfect tune for sunset over the post-industrial wasteland.

Al Spicer

Manic Street Preachers

Welsh agit rockers, provocative punk terrorists, poly-decibel polemicists, call 'em what you will – so long as you realize they're "4 Real" (as legendary missing guitarist Richey Edwards once carved on his arm with a razor).

❶ A DESIGN FOR LIFE from **EVERYTHING MUST GO**
Personal in content but grand and vast in execution, this is widescreen rock at its best, and the lone drums ending is genius.

② FASTER from **THE HOLY BIBLE**

This song simply rages, vocalist James Dean Bradfield sounding weirdly Dalek-like on the opening lines.

③ FOUND THAT SOUL from **KNOW YOUR ENEMY**

On this raw and emotionally driven rocker, a piano is hammered to matchwood beneath the main riff – and the guitar solo is a ripper.

④ FROM DESPAIR TO WHERE from **GOLD AGAINST THE SOUL**

The band go for a big rawk production. Polished, melodic guitars plus a sophisticated string section make for a nice, slick sound.

⑤ IF YOU TOLERATE THIS YOUR CHILDREN WILL BE NEXT from **THIS IS MY TRUTH TELL ME YOURS**

Slow but majestic. Throw in lyrics you can actually sing and some seriously swooping strings, and you have a big hit single.

⑥ INTRAVENOUS AGNOSTIC from **KNOW YOUR ENEMY**

The verses sound almost polite before turbulent layers of squalling, thrashing guitars punch you in the gut. A gloriously messy track.

⑦ THE MASSES AGAINST THE CLASSES from **FOREVER DELAYED**

Starts off like something by The Monkees before blazing into life with distorted vocals and unleashing a thousand guitars.

⑧ PCP from **THE HOLY BIBLE**

A cool post-punk influence pervades this relentless political onslaught. Frantic from first to last.

⑨ REPEAT (UK) from **GENERATION TERRORISTS**

A real chant-along sloganeering rocker, absolutely guaranteed to offend readers of the *Daily Mail*, and a cool guitar solo to boot.

⑩ YOU LOVE US from **GENERATION TERRORISTS**

The politics of the rock'n'roll spectacle laid bare. A great riff and even greater solos, topped off with a major shift up the gears.

Essi Berelian

Aimee Mann

The underdog heroin of literate pop songwriters has crafted a signature brand of mid-tempo rock, following label troubles and the early, flukey success of *Voices Carry*.

① SHOULD'VE KNOWN from **WHATEVER**

Pure power pop, with lyrics ("I don't know what else to say, but I think you get it") and guitars that sting like a slap in the face.

② DEATHLY from **MAGNOLIA SOUNDTRACK**

Perhaps her most powerfully rendered and emotionally wrought lyric, this was the epic around which the movie *Magnolia* was built.

③ PAVLOV'S BELL from **LOST IN SPACE**

Vintage Aimee: a character-driven anti-love song, slowly but steadily rocking, and once in your head impossible to get out.

④ SAVE ME from **MAGNOLIA SOUNDTRACK**

So dreamy you may feel no urgency at all to save her from the "ranks of the freaks, who suspect they could never love anyone."

⑤ RED VINES from **BACHELOR NO. 2**

From the unassuming intro to the tinkling piano outro, Mann produces something nearly cinematic; every effect works to perfection.

⑥ THAT'S JUST WHAT YOU ARE from **I'M WITH STUPID**

A bouncing, sing-songy kiss-off, with not an extraneous word or note. Nice background harmonies from the Squeeze guys too.

⑦ LITTLE BOMBS from **THE FORGOTTEN ARM**

The rhythmic strumming gently ticks along, channeling Paul Simon by way of Son Volt; on top of that, little bombs explode in the form of fraught, resigned observations.

⑧ IT'S NOT SAFE from **I'M WITH STUPID**

With raucous guitar bursts and rousing harmonies, Aimee gives a vigorous word of warning to those who might cross her path.

Andrew Rosenberg

Marilyn Manson

You want coruscating industrial metal, guaranteed to offend even the most liberal sensibilities? All hail the self-proclaimed God of Fuck!

❶ THE BEAUTIFUL PEOPLE
from **ANTICHRIST SUPERSTAR**
The stop-start riff and tribal drumming alone are fabulous. Throw-in some cool expletive-driven lyrics and you have a top track.

❷ COMA WHITE from **MECHANICAL ANIMALS**
A coolly observed snapshot of potential suicide. Detached yet perversely beautiful verses drip with hopelessness and despair.

❸ DISPOSABLE TEENS from **HOLYWOOD**
A fist-bangingly heavy glam stomp with an irritatingly catchy chorus. Off-the-peg nihilism never sounded quite so attractive.

❹ THE FIGHT SONG from **HOLYWOOD**
Vicious voice-and-percussion verses boil over into a glamorously violent and electrifyingly provocative chorus. A celebration of defiance.

❺ I DON'T LIKE THE DRUGS (BUT THE DRUGS LIKE ME) from **MECHANICAL ANIMALS**
Like being invited to an infernal discothèque. Manson does strutting industrial cyber funk complete with great soulful female backing vocals.

❻ LUNCHBOX from **THE LAST TOUR ON EARTH**
An object lesson in how to work a crowd: great riff, wild synths and Manson teetering on the edge of homicide.

❼ MOBSCENE (SIC)
from **THE GOLDEN AGE OF GROTESQUE**
One of those great big angry anthems Manson specializes in that makes you want to break things. The cheerleaders are terrific too.

❽ THE REFLECTING GOD from **ANTICHRIST SUPERSTAR**
There's nothing quite like a slow building

torrent of industrial-strength bile. A great minimal bassline leads to aural apocalypse.

❾ TAINTED LOVE from **LEST WE FORGET: THE BEST OF**
A song ideally suited to Manson's edgy delivery. The backing vocals are spooky and the distorted guitars build menacingly to the climax.

❿ THIS IS THE NEW SHIT
from **THE GOLDEN AGE OF GROTESQUE**
Like being trapped in the heart of a very dark machine. Excellent electronic percussion melds perfectly with Manson's stuttering verses.

Essi Berelian

Thomas Mapfumo

Zimbabwe's Thomas Mapfumo is the king of chimurenga: a blend of traditional mbira music and Western instrumentation so rootsy and hypnotic that it might have just welled up from the ground. A furious critic of the despotic regime of President Mugabe – as he was of 70s' white-minority rule – Mapfumo has been the torch-bearer of political resistance for thirty years.

❶ MURAMBADORO from **CHAMUNORWA**
God only knows what they were thinking when they remixed this for CD. The original vinyl version is mbira-laden genius, guaranteed to convert anyone to the chimurenga cause!

❷ MHONDORO from **GWINDINGWI RINE SHUMBA**
One of the songs that had the world music fraternity jumping through hoops in the 1980s, Mhondoro is Mapfumo and the Black Unlimited stripped to the bone.

❸ HOKOYO! from **HOKOYO!**
"Watch out!" Mapfumo's warning earned him three months in prison in 1979. Rocks with the joy of impending Zimbabwean independence.

❹ NYAMUTAMBA NEMOMBE from **SINGLES 77–86**

Pure, quintessential chimurenga. Somewhere it had to exist!

❺ KUPERA KWEVANHU from **CORRUPTION**

You don't have to understand the lyrics to understand the sorrow of war and famine in Mozambique.

❻ JUANITA from **MR. MUSIC**

Heavy on the horns, completely repetitive; your toes will not stop tapping from beginning to end.

❼ MUGARA NDEGA
from **CHIMURENGA FOR JUSTICE**

This collaboration between the Black Unlimited and Misty in Roots must be one of the most mesmerizing slabs of reggae ever produced.

❽ NGOMA YARIRA from **TAKE ONE**

Phenomenal proto-chimurenga from the Hallelujah Chicken Run Band, featuring Mapfumo and legendary guitarist Joshua Dube.

Tom Bullough

Bob Marley & The Wailers

With Bob virtually beatified, it's worth remembering that Peter Tosh and Bunny Livingstone made the original Wailers a great harmony group. The strength of much of their Island material, on the other hand, was down to the Jamaican practice of successfully "versioning" their best songs from nearly a decade's worth of back catalogue.

❶ ONE LOVE from **EXODUS**

First ska, then reggae. With lyrics partly borrowed from the Curtis Mayfield/Impressions classic, this inclusive, "let's get together and feel all right" song was an ideal choice for the BBC Song of the Millennium.

❷ I'M STILL WAITING from **SONGS OF FREEDOM**

Doowop delight – achingly beautiful harmonies from the Wailers, in their finest Impressions style.

❸ PUT IT ON from **BURNIN'**

Originally a defiant rude boy tune, the Island version is pure pleasure – "feel all right now".

❹ DREAMLAND from **BLACKHEART MAN**

Based on "My Dream Island" by the El Dorados, this is a gorgeous song with lovely lyrics, beautifully sung by Bunny.

❺ STIR IT UP from **CATCH A FIRE**

Johnny Nash made this Marley composition a UK hit in 1972, but Bob's slower five-and-a-half-minute version makes time stand still.

❻ PASS IT ON from **BURNIN'**

A sublime Marley song, with lead vocals by Bunny Wailer, from the group's best (studio) album.

❼ TRENCHTOWN ROCK from **LIVE!**

A Jamaican #1, this song was an inspired choice to open the legendary London Lyceum concerts, celebrating both their ghetto origins and the power of music itself.

❽ LIVELY UP YOURSELF from **NATTY DREAD AND LIVE!**

Previous incarnations are paradoxically languorous, but the live version is absolutely electrifying – just listen to the audience!

❾ NO WOMAN NO CRY
from **LIVE!**

Although Rita Marley's revelations about her husband's macho misbehaviour make the title seem bitterly ironic, they can't detract from the magic of the music.

❿ REDEMPTION SONG from **UPRISING**

Marley's musical epitaph. To be compared with Hendrix's acoustic "Hear My Train A Coming".

Neil Foxlee

The Martians are coming!

Mysterious emanations from the Red Planet have exerted a strange influence on the minds of certain songwriters, leading them into flights of fancy and up the paths of whimsy.

❶ HERE COME THE MARTIAN MARTIANS
JONATHAN RICHMAN from ROADRUNNER
According to JoJo, when they come, we shouldn't be surprised to see them riding on their Martian bikes.

❷ MARTIAN GIRL THE AQUABATS from FURY OF THE AQUABATS
Cheerful, ska-coloured knees-up with the usual everyday tale of interplanetary attraction gone awry.

❸ LIFE ON MARS FLAMING LIPS from THIS HERE GIRAFFE CD SINGLE 1 (WARNER; 1996)
So wistful and distorted you'd swear Wayne Coyne was pining for his dusty ole home back on the red planet, the Lips' cover of this Bowie classic is more lonesome and much further out there than the original.

❹ I TURNED INTO A MARTIAN THE MISFITS from WALK AMONG US
Coming in at under two minutes, this song gets straight to the point and kicks off with all the reverb, distortion and slam-dance energy that The Misfits have come to represent.

❺ MARTIAN MOMMA KING KURT from ALCOHOLIC RAT
Meaty, blaring horns, a cool guitar riff and lyrics of purest nonsense combine to make this a must for any interplanetary dance party.

❻ MARTIAN HOP ROCKY SHARPE & THE REPLAYS from ROCK-IT-TO MARS
The original, by The Ran-Dells, was the first track to use "additive synthesis" from a wave generator. This updated version is hooked with high-pitched "space" voices, bouncy guitars and tasty laser gun effects.

❼ MARTIAN SCREAMING BLUE MESSIAHS from TOTALLY RELIGIOUS
Set the interstellar overdrive to automatic and groove to the red shift as the SBMs take you into warp speed.

❽ MARTIAN SAINTS MARY LOU LORD from MARTIAN SAINTS EP
Spooky Theremin sounds, yes. Usual nonsense lyrics? No way. Ms Lord was scooped up from the Boston subways to blossom into one of the most interesting songwriters to have emerged on the east coast in years.

❾ BACK FROM MARS AQUA from AQUARIUS
Ultra-cheery pop nonsense on a track that has no more connection to Mars than to any other chocolate bar – but we all need a little Euro-beat in our lives.

❿ BALLROOMS OF MARS T REX from THE SLIDER
Marc Bolan was at the peak of stardom when *The Slider* was first released; its stately, swanking blues-based progression has lyrics from Planet Rubbish but a guitar solo that'll put you into orbit.

Al Spicer

John Martyn

John Martyn's best work fits into the decade-long gap between the Scottish folkie's discovery of jazz and his discovery of synthesizers. Perfect music for a long hot summer .

❶ SOLID AIR from SOLID AIR
A glorious tribute to troubled pal Nick Drake: lazy jazz acoustic, shimmering organ, Danny Thompson's rumbling bass and Martyn's drunkenly slurred growl.

❷ SMALL HOURS from ONE WORLD
Recorded across a lake at 3am, Small Hours

absolutely oozes ambience, Martyn's echo-drenched guitar going places no-one previously imagined.

❸ I DON'T WANT TO KNOW from SOLID AIR

Martyn at his most poppy, all righteous testifying, hazy electric pianos and a wall of soulful harmonies. You do want to know.

❹ MAY YOU NEVER from SOLID AIR

As touching a tribute as Solid Air, this breezy acoustic confection seems to belong to some folk memory of perfection (Clapton cover notwithstanding).

❺ SO MUCH IN LOVE WITH YOU from INSIDE OUT

Rarely has passion sounded so strangulated: *Inside Out* was the extreme of Martyn's Echoplex phase: treated, twisted guitar topped by equally gnarled vocals.

❻ BLESS THE WEATHER from BLESS THE WEATHER

This irresistible early appearance of Martyn's snapping acoustic style is just one highlight from a gorgeous album: summery, wistful, woozy.

❼ STORMBRINGER from STORMBRINGER

From the best of his two collaborative albums with wife Beverley: a twinkling, folk-rock wall of sound.

❽ LOOK IN from INSIDE OUT

Martyn's rocky side emerges: a killer, distorted four-note riff, explosive drums and one of his roaring best vocals.

❾ JUST NOW from BLESS THE WEATHER

Some of Martyn's most plangently pure singing: an airy piano ballad that's almost unbearably touching.

❿ SPENCER THE ROVER from ONE WORLD

A late return to the trad style of his youth, now Martyn's voice adds whole worlds of weariness and regret to this tale of a heart-broken wanderer.

Toby Manning

Massive Attack & Bristol-hop

The trip-hop squad and the music they made sauntered out of Bristol puffing on a big spliff, hitched up to London and spent a summer in the spotlight before seeing the light and going back home.

❶ UNFINISHED SYMPATHY MASSIVE ATTACK from BLUE LINES

Stately, elegantly paced, delicate and supreme, this is the track that announced Massive Attack to a stunned listening public.

❷ TEARDROP MASSIVE ATTACK from MEZZANINE

Sharp resonant imagery that sits, composed and calm, like a master calligrapher's representation of the perfect haiku.

❸ INERTIA CREEPS MASSIVE ATTACK from MEZZANINE

The darkest track on an album steeped in the oppressive reek of too much time in the studio and too many unresolved tour-bus arguments.

❹ PROTECTION MASSIVE ATTACK from PROTECTION

Tracey Thorn's ethereal vocals provide an armour-glass shield of defiance in her duty of care to the one she loves.

❺ RADIATION RULING THE NATION (PROTECTION DUB) MASSIVE ATTACK VS. MAD PROFESSOR from NO PROTECTION

The ultimate urban producer from the mean streets of Southeast London takes on the dark lords of Bristol under manners.

❻ SPYING GLASS MASSIVE ATTACK from PROTECTION

By updating Horace Andy's original track of paranoia with a sturdy 90s' digital backing, Massive Attack regenerated his career and landed themselves another supremely talented vocalist.

❼ I SPY (SPYING GLASS DUB) MASSIVE ATTACK VS. MAD PROFESSOR from NO PROTECTION
Even better suited than Protection to the medicine developed by the Mad Professor, this track is an almighty dub mix strong enough to bend your speaker mounts. Turn it up!

❽ BLACK STEEL TRICKY from MAXINQUAYE
When the most frightening character in Bristol walks into the studio to rasp his way through an updated Public Enemy track, you stand back and let the gentleman do his thing.

❾ HELL IS ROUND THE CORNER TRICKY from MAXINQUAYE
This is darker and far colder than outer space, and comes with an eerie beat sampled perhaps from a wounded human crawling towards the phone.

❿ WANDERING STAR PORTISHEAD from DUMMY
Portishead came and went on a burst of acclaim that would have swamped many a more experienced collective. This was their finest piece, recorded before the attention melted them down.

Al Spicer

Curtis Mayfield

Singer-songwriter-producer-guitarist-entrepreneur-social commentator: Curtis was a Chicago genius and soul music's artistic conscience.

❶ GYPSY WOMAN from DEFINITE IMPRESSIONS
The haunting ballad that established The Impressions. A song of timeless beauty.

❷ PEOPLE GET READY from DEFINITE IMPRESSIONS
Biblical Civil Rights song featuring the finest guitar break in recorded history. The Mount Everest of soul songs.

❸ I'M SO PROUD FROM DEFINITE IMPRESSIONS
Curtis is proud of his girl, proud to be loved by her, proud to be with her. Listening to him, I'm proud to be human.

❹ CHOICE OF COLORS from THE YOUNG MOD'S FORGOTTEN STORY
"If you had a choice of colors, what would you choose?" Curtis asked America in 1969. Tough question. Uneasy answers were sure to follow.

❺ IF THERE'S A HELL BELOW WE'RE ALL GONNA GO from CURTIS
Curtis solo espouses hard funk fuelled with dread.

❻ FREDDIE'S DEAD from SUPERFLY
Bad movie gets great soundtrack. Curtis, the soul Buddha, sings a lament for fallen drug dealer Freddie, bringing the pain and compassion right back home.

❼ PUSHERMAN from SUPERFLY
Rappers sample this as a celebration of dealers. Curtis sang it with harsh irony: "got some dope/want some speed?".

❽ SO IN LOVE from THERE'S NO PLACE LIKE AMERICA TODAY
Lovely laidback groove as Curtis celebrates how fine love is. Gorgeous.

❾ DIRTY LAUNDRY from HONESTY
Overlooked when released, this comment on political and social corruption saw Curtis in exceptional form.

❿ NEW WORLD ORDER from NEW WORLD ORDER
A last whisper of song from the paralyzed artist finds Mayfield still searching for human reconciliation.

Garth Cartwright

Mazzy Star

Since forming in LA in 1990, guitarist Dave Roback and vocalist Hope Sandoval have ploughed their very own furrow of melancholic, trance-inducing Indie country

rock. Music that is very much at the bleaker end of the psychedelic spectrum.

❶ HARRIET BROWN OPAL from EARLY RECORDINGS
Bohemian story-song from Roback's previous, Syd Barrett-inspired band.

❷ HAPPY NIGHTMARE BABY OPAL from HAPPY NIGHTMARE BABY)
Raw Sex covers Siouxsie Sioux.

❸ RIDE IT ON from SHE HANGS BRIGHTLY
Spare and echoing. As if Nashville's moved to Transylvania.

❹ BEFORE I SLEEP from SHE HANGS BRIGHTLY
Like a lullaby from the end of the world.

❺ FADE INTO YOU from SO TONIGHT THAT I MIGHT SLEEP
Almost lush-sounding piano-led piece.

❻ FIVE STRING SERENADE from SO TONIGHT THAT I MIGHT SLEEP
Sandoval's barely-there drawl gets back-up from five guitar strings and a tambourine.

❼ ALL MY SISTERS from AMONG MY SWAN
Slick psychedelic production. Like falling into a whirlpool.

❽ DROP HOPE SANDOVAL AND THE WARM INTENTIONS from BAVARIAN FRUIT BREAD
Acoustic cover of the Jesus and Mary Chain B-side.

Rachel Coldicutt

Paul McCartney

Okay, Lennon brought out the best in McCartney and when they split there was no concealing the pain. But it wasn't just silly love songs. There's at least a playlist of solo Paul that's Beatles class.

❶ MAYBE I'M AMAZED from MCCARTNEY
A classic from the get-go, this graced Macca's much-derided first solo outing. Affecting lyrics – "Maybe I'm a lonely man who's in the middle of something that he doesn't really understand" – and an all-time great vocal.

❷ UNCLE ALBERT-ADMIRAL HALSEY from RAM
A lovely slice of whimsy from the consistently inventive *Ram* album: it would have been hailed as a masterpiece by, say, 10CC.

❸ MY LOVE from RED ROSE SPEEDWAY
Even if the album wasn't so great, this is a big, big McCartney song: "My love does it good" indeed. Macca does the ballad to perfection.

❹ BAND ON THE RUN from BAND ON THE RUN
This zany story of a jailbreak was proof at last that Paul was motoring on, charm intact.

❺ JET from BAND ON THE RUN
And this showed that he hadn't forgotten how to rock. Jet comes from the same mould as Back in the USSR, and packs similar punch.

❻ LIVE AND LET DIE from THE MOVIE
The best Bond theme song since *Goldfinger*. "When you've got a job to do, you gotta do it well; You gotta give the other fella hell!!"

❼ VENUS AND MARS/ROCKSHOW from VENUS AND MARS
Beautifully modulated, shifting from dreamy introspection to uproarious rock'n'roll.

❽ SILLY LOVE SONGS from WINGS AT THE SPEED OF SOUND
"What's wrong with that? I'd like to know" Nothing at all, mate. Keep 'em coming.

❾ SAY, SAY, SAY from ALL THE BEST
One of two great collaborations with Jacko in 1983. Supremely danceable and retro.

❿ PIPES OF PEACE from ALL THE BEST
As the nuclear arms race intensified, Thatcher promised Reagan that she'd follow him to the end of the world. This was Paul's response.

Sebastian Secker Walker

Danny McNamara's
Influences

"These were the first ten tracks to influence me, listed in chronological order of me discovering them," says DANNY McNAMARA, lead singer with Embrace, whose debut album *The Good Will Out* gave them a UK #1 in 1998 and who returned to the top of the album charts with 2004's *Out Of Nothing*. "The next ten would include The Pixies, Primal Scream , Happy Mondays, Boo Radleys, Pavement, Velvet Underground, Beach Boys, Sly & The Family Stone, P.J.Harvey and Elvis Costello," he adds. "But these got there first…"

❶ LOVE ME TENDER ELVIS PRESLEY from JAILHOUSE ROCK/LOVE ME TENDER

❷ KINGS OF THE WILD FRONTIER ADAM AND THE ANTS from KINGS OF THE WILD FRONTIER

❸ TAINTED LOVE SOFT CELL from NON-STOP EROTIC CABARET

❹ BAD U2 from THE UNFORGETTABLE FIRE

❺ DO IT CLEAN ECHO AND THE BUNNYMEN from CROCODILES

❻ HOW SOON IS NOW THE SMITHS from HATFUL OF HOLLOW

❼ LOVE WILL TEAR US APART JOY DIVISION from SUBSTANCE

❽ SO CENTRAL RAIN REM from RECKONING

❾ PERFECT TIME RIDE from WAVES

❿ I AM THE RESURRECTION THE STONE ROSES from THE STONE ROSES

Kate & Anna McGarrigle

While the French-Canadian sisters may now be in danger of becoming better known as mother and aunt, respectively, of Rufus and Martha Wainwright, their folky songwriting has won them admirers from Emmylou Harris to Linda Ronstadt.

❶ HEART LIKE A WHEEL from KATE AND ANNA MCGARRIGLE
A series of similes about the nature of love, famously covered by Linda Ronstadt.

❷ SWIMMING SONG from KATE AND ANNA MCGARRIGLE
Written by Kate's ex-husband Loudon Wainwright III (with more subtlety than usual), this could be a metaphor for sexual awakening – or it could just be about swimming.

❸ COMPLAINTE POUR STE CATHERINE from FRENCH RECORD
French folk-reggae? Oui, s'il vous plait.

❹ MOVE OVER MOON from LOVE OVER AND OVER
Vocoder can't quite hide the honky-tonk roots here.

❺ LOVE OVER AND OVER from LOVE OVER AND OVER
Mark Knopfler strolls in for a guitar solo, adding a little FM sheen to a more polished but still quirky album.

❻ HEARTBEATS ACCELERATING from HEARTBEATS ACCELERATING
As close to electronica as the McGarrigles ever

got, but still recognizably call-and-response between the sisters.

❼ GOIN' BACK TO HARLAN from MATAPEDIA
Emmylou Harris released this one first, but it is classic McGarrigle work: rustic, allusive, and pretty without being soft.

❽ PETITE ANNONCE AMOUREUSE
from LA VACHE QUI PLEURE
Encore du French folk reggae, and their best song for years.

David Honigmann

Blind Willie McTell

As Bob Dylan put it, "Nobody sings the blues like Blind Willie McTell"; in a career that spanned from the 1920s to the 1950s, the itinerant Georgian bluesman produced a legacy of astonishing individuality and force.

❶ WRITIN' PAPER BLUES from COMPLETE RECORDED WORKS VOL 1
The very first song McTell ever recorded, in 1927, and already his gifts were fully in place.

❷ MAMA, TAIN'T LONG FO' DAY from COMPLETE RECORDED WORKS VOL 1
There's an almost feminine delicacy to the young McTell's voice on this 1927 masterpiece.

❸ STATESBORO BLUES from COMPLETE RECORDED WORKS VOL 1
A definitive blues classic, from 1928; McTell's deft finger-picking beautifully complements the poignant words.

❹ RAZOR BALL from COMPLETE RECORDED WORKS VOL 1
McTell's most infectious dance number, from 1930.

❺ SOUTHERN CAN IS MINE
from COMPLETE RECORDED WORKS VOL 1
Another piece of entertaining if misogynist hokum, this time from 1931.

❻ BROKE DOWN ENGINE BLUES
from COMPLETE RECORDED WORKS VOL 1
McTell returned repeatedly to this song throughout his recording career, but it was never more powerful than in this 1931version.

❼ SCAREY DAY BLUES
from COMPLETE RECORDED WORKS VOL 1
McTell's perfect blending of voice and guitar makes this 1931 recording irresistible.

❽ LITTLE DELIA from ATLANTA TWELVE STRING
By the time McTell cut a superb batch of songs for the Atlantic label in Atlanta in 1949, his voice was much rougher and gruffer; small wonder Johnny Cash later covered this one.

❾ DYING CRAPSHOOTER BLUES
from ATLANTA TWELVE STRING
A bravura triumph, this 1949 saga of a dying gambler who asks his friends to "dig my grave with the ace of spades" wouldn't sound out of place on one of Dylan's finest albums.

❿ MOTHERLESS CHILDREN HAVE A HARD TIME from ATLANTA TWELVE STRING
A lovely demonstration of McTell's instrumental virtuosity, again from 1949.

Greg Ward

Natalie Merchant & 10,000 Maniacs

Quintessential college-rock band, yoking good-time party-boy musicians to a solemn singer-songwriter. When the contradictions became too hard to handle, Merchant took off for a solo career.

❶ HEY JACK KEROUAC from **IN MY TRIBE**
Only Natalie Merchant could have taken this enduring symbol of masculine freedom and worry-warted about the peripatetic pisspot's relationship with his mother.

❶ DON'T TALK from **IN MY TRIBE**
Merchant pushes through thickets of guitar to reach a haunting minor-key melody.

❷ LIKE THE WEATHER from **IN MY TRIBE**
A song about greyness that somehow avoids being grey itself.

❸ EAT FOR TWO from **BLIND MAN'S ZOO**
A tale of teenage pregnancy, the narrator's folly growing inside her.

❹ THESE ARE DAYS from **OUR TIME IN EDEN**
A slow march for the end of the band.

❺ TROUBLE ME from **MTV UNPLUGGED**
A song of solidarity, second cousin to REM's Everybody Hurts.

❻ BECAUSE THE NIGHT from **MTV UNPLUGGED**
A perfect version of Patti Smith and Bruce Springsteen's anthem, here with the guitar solos taken by the violin.

❼ CARNIVAL from **TIGERLILY**
Now solo, Merchant agonizes about street-level inequality over an intoxicating patter of Brazilian percussion.

❽ THIS HOUSE IS ON FIRE from **MOTHERLAND**
The strongest of Merchant's solo albums opens with this: Merchant's thick voice, oud and Middle Eastern strings set to a reggae swagger.

❾ WHICH SIDE ARE YOU ON?
from **THE HOUSE CARPENTER'S DAUGHTER**
An oddity, this album: a ragbag of cover versions and old folk songs, including this union ballad from Kentucky miner's wife Florence Reece.

David Honigmann

Mercury Rev

Flaming Lips' only rivals as the most original American band of the last fifteen years. Here are ten tracks that combine whacked-out psychedelic droning, spooked orchestrations and an instinctive empathy with what Greil Marcus once called "the old, weird America…"

❶ VERY SLEEPY RIVERS from **YERSELF IS STEAM**
Thirteen dizzying minutes of hypnotic, twinkling post-pop genius.

❷ RACING THE TIDE
from **SEE YOU ON THE OTHER SIDE**
Delirious psychedelic joy from their first album, after oddball vocalist David Baker had been kicked out of the band.

❸ SUDDEN RAY OF HOPE
from **SEE YOU ON THE OTHER SIDE**
Sure they'd clearly been listening to *Pet Sounds* – but Brian Wilson himself could hardly have synthesized what they heard better.

❹ THE DARK IS RISING from **ALL IS DREAM**
Cinematic splashes of orchestral colour and Jonathan Donahue's most fragile falsetto.

❺ METH OF A ROCKETTE'S KICK from **BOCES**
Ten epic minutes of piercing feedback, doo-wop harmonies, guitars, flutes, harps, and brass – and a choir for good measure.

❻ TIDES OF THE MOON from **ALL IS DREAM**
Unearthly theramins and ethereal glocken-spiels on a typically brooding Rev piece.

❼ CAR WASH HAIR from **YERSELF IS STEAM**
This sublime Velvet Underground-influenced single was added as a bonus track to the reis-sue of their 1991 debut album.

❽ DELTA SUN BOTTLENECK STOMP
from **DESERTER'S SONGS**
Tumultuous slide guitar on one of the band's most audacious sonic experiments.

⑨ HOLES from **DESERTER'S SONGS**
Bowed saws, majestic violins, fluttering flutes
and a positively eerie vocal on the sensational
opening track of their most acclaimed album.

⑩ OPUS 40 from **DESERTER'S SONGS**
Majestic pocket pop symphony with The
Band's Levon Helm on drums.

Nigel Williamson

Metal Classics

**You want screaming axes, and amps on
eleven? Give your eardrums a serious
pounding with these classic metal cuts.**

① A LIGHT IN THE BLACK RAINBOW from **RISING**
Everything about this is great: Ritchie
Blackmore's bonkers guitar, Cozy Powell's
deadly drumming, and Dio's chest-beating
vocals.

② AM I EVIL? DIAMOND HEAD
from **LIVING ON BORROWED TIME**
Want to know where Metallica got their ideas?
Look no further. This song boasts one of the
best and heaviest riffs in metaldom.

③ ANOTHER PIECE OF MEAT THE SCORPIONS
from **LOVEDRIVE**
With Michael Schenker on lead guitar, The
Scorpions were truly a force to be reckoned
with. This represents them at their aggressive
best.

④ COLD SWEAT THIN LIZZY
from **THUNDER AND LIGHTNING**
One of the heaviest things Phil Lynott wrote
– it'll rock you right out of your leather strides.
John Sykes' mental soloing is a joy.

⑤ ELECTRIC EYE JUDAS PRIEST
from **SCREAMING FOR VENGEANCE**
On this fabulous tune about cyber-surveillance
gone mad, singer Rob Halford sounds suitably
chilling and dispassionate as the malevolent
spy in the sky.

⑥ FOREARM SMASH BUDGIE from **POWER SUPPLY**
A song that does exactly what its title suggests:
it brings you down and then jumps up and
down on your spine. But in a good way.

⑦ HOT FOR TEACHER VAN HALEN from **1984**
Thundering tribal drums and a wicked fret-
burning run even before the main riff! Singer
David Lee Roth never wanted to end up in
detention so bad.

⑧ SLAVE TO THE GRIND SKID ROW
from **SLAVE TO THE GRIND**
This is so heavy it could easily be mistaken for
Metallica. There's nothing fancy going on here,
just an honest-to-goodness pummelling and
killer chorus.

⑨ STILL OF THE NIGHT WHITESNAKE from **1987**
A shameless Led Zep rip-off this may well be,
but there's no disguising the sheer metallic
splendour of the stuttering stop-start riff and
David Coverdale's howling vocals.

⑩ STRONG ARM OF THE LAW SAXON
from **STRONG ARM OF THE LAW**
A metal band getting hassled by The Man?
Whatever next? A relentless bassline, crunchy
riff and tasty solo make this a tried-and-tested
live fave.

Essi Berelian

Metallica

**From cult thrash fiends to one of the
biggest bands in the world, Metallica are
stadium-bothering behemoths of metal.**

① AIN'T MY BITCH from **LOAD**
The success of this bellicose little ditty hinges
purely upon James Hetfield repeatedly snarling "Biiii-tchaaaaaa!", as though he is sneezing
violently, throughout the whole thing.

② BATTERY from **MASTER OF PUPPETS**
A celebration of Metallica doing what they do
best. Don't be fooled by the gentle classical
intro.

❸ CREEPING DEATH from **RIDE THE LIGHTNING**
Who'd have thought the Bible could provide such convincing metal fare? The Old Testament recycled into a bludgeoning blood-soaked extravaganza.

❹ DISPOSABLE HEROES from **MASTER OF PUPPETS**
War, what is it good for? Eight-minutes-plus of pure, unrestrained energy, about soldiers bred as cannon fodder.

❺ ENTER SANDMAN from **METALLICA**
The night brings with it wonders and terrors beyond imagining. This features one mother of a riff and a genius pause in the action just before the end.

❻ FUEL from **RELOAD**
Not the first metal tune about the need for speed, but a compact and turbo-charged beauty all the same.

❼ ONE from **...AND JUSTICE FOR ALL**
Based on a Dalton Trumbo anti-war story, the horror of the central character's life takes us from melodic climes to a rampant, violent climax.

❽ RIDE THE LIGHTNING from **RIDE THE LIGHTNING**
You could build a fortress with a riff this big and heavy – a fortress of twisted metal.

❾ WELCOME HOME (SANITARIUM) from **MASTER OF PUPPETS**
One of those tunes that sounds as though it's going to be your friend – until it tries to rip your ears off, and climaxes like a runaway juggernaut.

❿ WHIPLASH from **KILL 'EM ALL**
A full-on, red-blooded thrasher and then some, on which James Hetfield shrieks like he's trapped his left nut in the top string. Ouch.

Essi Berelian

Michelle Shocked

Michelle Shocked came to prominence when a bootleg tape of a solo acoustic appearance at a folk festival became a surprise hit. For a few years the punk-styled folk-blues-swing-whatever singer could do no wrong; for longer, afterwards, she could seemingly do no right. But her fans remained loyal, and 2005 saw the simultaneous release of three new albums.

❶ ANCHORAGE from **SHORT SHARP SHOCKED**
Shocked's calling card for years, this is the one that casual fans shout out for. The true story of an old friendship reawakened.

❷ MEMORIES OF EAST TEXAS from **SHORT SHARP SHOCKED**
Texan pastoral, as Shocked reminisces about learning to drive on dirt back roads.

❸ SLEEP KEEPS ME AWAKE from **CAPTAIN SWING**
When everyone wanted a sequel to *Short Sharp Shocked*, its author took a sudden detour into Western Swing, complete with brass section. This is bluesier than the rest, but retains the same sly charm.

❹ MONA LISA from **CAPTAIN SWING**
The most seductive song on *Captain Swing*, a melancholy violin lament set to a walking bassline and garlicky puns about robbing the Louvre blind.

❺ PRODIGAL DAUGHTER from **ARKANSAS TRAVELER**
Arkansas Traveller mingled uneasy meditations on race with the kind of down-home, old-time music, way before *O Brother* made it fashionable. Prodigal Daughter, a feminist retake on Cotton-Eyed Joe, stings while it swings.

❻ STILLBORN from **KIND-HEARTED WOMAN**
Kind-Hearted Woman starts with this stark song

about a midwife walking home in the early morning after attending a stillbirth, and gets more depressing from there.

❼ CAN'T TAKE MY JOY from **GOOD NEWS**
A capella Pentecostalism in full exuberant flow: this is the music that saw Shocked through dark times.

❽ GOOD NEWS from **DEEP NATURAL**
A burst of religious fervour (marital heartache saw Shocked turn to God) combining ecstatic joy with fuzzbox guitar.

❾ EARLY MORNING SATURDAY from **DON'T ASK DON'T TELL**
Don't Ask Don't Tell kisses off Shocked's ex-husband in direct and brutal style, but this, its opener, has a lazy yawning stretch.

❿ MATCH BURNS TWICE from **MEXICAN STANDOFF**
Mexican Standoff digs around in the Mexican roots of both Shocked's Texan birthplace and her adopted home in Los Angeles. Match Burns Twice lopes like mariachi reggae.

David Honigmann

Midnight

Many a fine song has probably been written around the witching hour, and some have even taken it as their subject.

❶ MOANIN' AT MIDNIGHT HOWLIN' WOLF from **THE BEST OF HOWLIN' WOLF**
What else would a wolf do at this time of day? An early hit by the massively influential bluesman.

❷ IN THE MIDNIGHT HOUR WILSON PICKETT from **WILSON PICKETT'S GREATEST HITS**
The best known song by this Alabama-born singer is a stompin' soul classic. Pickett was aided in no small way by having Booker T and the MGs as his backing band.

❸ MIDNIGHT SPECIAL CREEDENCE CLEARWATER REVIVAL from **WILLIE AND THE POOR BOYS**
Swinging prison song revived from the Great American Songbook by these good ole boys from California.

❹ I'M A MIDNIGHT MOVER BOBBY WOMACK from **MIDNIGHT MOVER. THE BOBBY WOMACK STORY**
The soul sensation wasn't backwards in coming forward, judging by the way he struts his stuff here.

❺ MIDNIGHT RAMBLER THE ROLLING STONES from **LET IT BLEED**
Not everybody out and about after dark has good intentions. Mick Jagger sounds suitably demonic on their bluesy 1969 masterpiece.

❻ LADY MIDNIGHT LEONARD COHEN from **SONGS FROM A ROOM**
An early composition by the Canadian balladeer. There are plenty of other far more original subjects among his lyrics, however.

❼ MIDNIGHT LADY MARVIN GAYE from **MIDNIGHT LOVE**
The upbeat track that opens the tragic singer's final album isn't really typical of what made him so special, but prefigures a lot of what happened in dance music after his death.

❽ HORA ZERO ASTOR PIAZZOLLA from **LUNA**
This spooky instrumental vividly evokes the midnight wanders around Buenos Aires that Argentina's tango maestro and his musicians used to take between late-night sets.

❾ MIDNIGHT FEAST LAL WATERSON & OLIVER KNIGHT from **ONCE IN A BLUE MOON**
A mercurial songwriting talent, perhaps overshadowed by more famous members of her family.

❿ ROUND MIDNIGHT FRED HERSCH from **THELONIOUS**
The opening number on the 1997 album subtitled *Fred Hersch Plays Monk* is a spectral treasure – one celebrated pianist putting his own stamp on another's work.

Jon Lusk

Charles Mingus

Once upon a time, Charles Mingus was the bad boy of jazz, his music sneered at by the purists. Today, it sounds less like a tearing up of the rulebook than an intelligent and heartfelt synthesis of all that was great about the bebop, Big Band swing, honking R&B and gospel soul of his era.

❶ PITHECANTHROPUS ERECTUS from PITHECANTHROPUS ERECTUS
A menacing bassline and unreasonable horns render this the aural equivalent of a prelude to a mugging.

❷ SOLO DANCER from THE BLACK SAINT AND SINGER LADY
Archetypal big-band Mingus, his trademark glissandos in the horns smeared all over the two-chord see-saw of the main theme.

❸ VASSARLEAN from MYSTERIOUS BLUES
Recorded by Mingus elsewhere as Weird Nightmare, this version has all the eldritch benefits of Eric Dolphy's porcine sax snuffling.

❸ HOG CALLIN' BLUES from MINGUS OH YEAH!
A burst of scatted vocalese from Charles cues in some minatory hi-hat and low-end piano; then the insistent riff begins to build up, barked out by threatening horns.

❹ NEW NOW KNOW HOW from MINGUS DYNASTY
Many Mingus tunes have the ghosts of other corners of both his own and the classic jazz songbooks. Here it's Stars Fell On Alabama, given a zippy Thelonious Monk-like treatment.

❺ FREEDOM (PART ONE) from THE COMPLETE TOWN HALL CONCERT
A rap from Mingus, sloppy handclaps, and a world-weary chorus from his band builds up into a hollerin' and testifyin' frenzy.

❻ GUNSLINGING BIRD from MINGUS DYNASTY
Hopping peculiarly, a xylophone punctuates another Monkish melody rapped out by impa-tient horns, with all the cadres of Mingus' band seemingly one step ahead of each other.

❼ GOODBYE PORK PIE HAT from MINGUS AH UM
A lyrical tribute to the late Lester Young, its spare, breathy sax melody treads carefully, with respect but never reverence.

❽ FABLES OF FAUBUS from MINGUS AH UM
Smoky but sharp, cool but alert, it's Mingus playing things relatively straight – a little like a Henry Mancini soundtrack given a more adventurous, discordant edge.

❾ THE SHOES OF THE FISHERMAN'S WIFE ARE SOME JIVE ASS SLIPPERS from LET MY CHILDREN HEAR MUSIC
Sustained chords swell upward, like a discordant hymn, into a scrupulous and complex piece of Ellingtonia, with duelling, vamping brass counterpoint that suggests cubist facets of the old standard Brazil.

Matt Milton

Ministry

Masterminded by evil genius Al Jourgensen, Ministry are highly influential pioneers of scorching industrial metal, designed to test your pain threshold to its limit. Break out the ear protectors...

❶ ANIMOSITY from ANIMOSITISOMINA
It could be a guitar solo in the middle, then again it could be an angle grinder on an iron girder. A bile-fuelled bullet to the brain.

❷ BAD BLOOD from DARK SIDE OF THE SPOON
A mediocre album, perhaps, but this is a wild-eyed bruiser. It sounds like someone's thwacking sheet steel just before the guitar solo takes your head off.

❸ BREATHE from THE MIND IS A TERRIBLE THING TO TASTE
You want an environmentalist diatribe to end them all? Choking and claustrophobic, the

more the screams order you to breathe the harder it becomes.

❹ JESUS BUILT MY HOTROD from **PSALM 69**
Industrial thrash as the good Lord intended. Butthole Surfers' Gibby Haynes delivers the infamously gibberish vocals to a juiced-up, ass-kicking rhythm track.

❺ THE LAND OF RAPE AND HONEY
from **THE LAND OF RAPE AND HONEY**
An object lesson in the sonic architecture of electro-metal. Layer upon layer of samples and instrumentation create a monumental Wall Of Noise.

❻ NO "W" from **HOUSES OF THE MOLÉ**
Ministry get even more intense and bitter. The ammunition combines industro-metal with screaming hardcore punk, and George Dubya is in the firing line.

❼ N.W.O. from **PSALM 69**
That's President Bush Snr. sampled talking about a New World Order amid the tortured screams and mercilessly pummelling beats. Truly deadly.

❽ WRONG from **HOUSES OF THE MOLÉ**
Dubya gets it in the neck again. Venomous lyrics, spat with heartfelt conviction, compete with a boiling torrent of industrial punk noise.

Essi Berelian

Mirror mirror

When artists peer into the looking glass, just what *do* they see? Here are nine songs that provide some surprising answers.

❶ MIRROR MIRROR DOLLAR from **PRODUCED BY TREVOR HORN**
Therese Bazaar and David Van Day jog on the spot, clutching each other tight – it's them against the world! That is until they split, when it seemed like it was every David for himself.

❷ HALL OF MIRRORS KRAFTWERK from **TRANS-EUROPE EXPRESS**
The eerie electronic nightmare tale of an artist who becomes beguiled by his own reflection.

❷ HALL OF MIRRORS SIOUXSIE AND THE BANSHEES from **THROUGH THE LOOKING GLASS**
On this more sensual rendering of the Kraftwerk classic, Siouxsie's mesmeric voice wafts round a compelling harp-plucking beat.

❹ I COULD GIVE YOU (A MIRROR) EURYTHMICS from **SWEET DREAMS**
Annie and Dave rock out in this car-crash ride version of a song that was also heard on the B-side of the Sweet Dreams single.

❺ MIRROR MAN HUMAN LEAGUE from
Quite a rarified outing from the League here, with the ladies cooing their simple oooohs and aaaahs around Phil, to a quasi-Motown chug.

❻ I'LL BE YOUR MIRROR VELVET UNDERGROUND from **VELVET UNDERGROUND & NICO**
The Velvets covered all the bases from gorgeously dank to powerfully healing. Here's a prime example of the latter, with Nico's brittle quavering voice attempting to offer support to a friend in deep existential need.

❼ MIRRORS SALLY OLDFIELD from **MIRRORS**
Dreamy Hawaiian harmonies lilting through Sally's classic. Here, she's a mirror of the sun, finding it impossible to do anything else but reflect the love that surrounds her.

❽ MAN IN THE MIRROR MICHAEL JACKSON from **BAD**
Well into his stride, almost a decade after *Off The Wall*, Michael ponders the changes we must make in ourselves if we are to hope to change the world around us.

❾ MIRROR BEAUTIFUL SOUTH from **BLUE IS THE COLOUR**
The Beautiful South doing what they do best: effortless soulful strumming that welcomes you onto its gingham picnic blanket and invites you into its comforting country hamper.

Link Hall

Mississippi Delta blues

The origins of Mississippi's Delta blues, which flowered early in the twentieth century, remain mysterious; certainly the African heritage is strong, but musicologists also trace the influence of vaudeville, and even of Hawaiian guitarists. What's certain however is the early Mississippi bluesmen – and not only Robert Johnson (see his individual playlist) – laid the basic template for rock'n'roll.

❶ **WALKING BLUES** SON HOUSE from PREACHIN' THE BLUES

❷ **CYPRESS GROVE BLUES** SKIP JAMES from THE COMPLETE EARLY RECORDINGS OF SKIP JAMES

❸ **NOBODY'S DIRTY BUSINESS** MISSISSIPPI JOHN HURT from AVALON BLUES: THE COMPLETE 1928 OKEH RECORDINGS

❹ **THAT'S NO WAY TO GET ALONG** ROBERT WILKINS from THE ORIGINAL ROLLING STONE

❺ **LEAD PENCIL BLUES** JOHNNIE TEMPLE from THE ROOTS OF ROBERT JOHNSON

❻ **FIXIN' TO DIE BLUES** BUKKA WHITE from THE COMPLETE BUKKA WHITE

❼ **ROLL AND TUMBLE BLUES** HAMBONE WILLIE NEWBERN from THE ROOTS OF ROBERT JOHNSON

❽ **WHEN THE SUN GOES DOWN** LEROY CARR from THE ROOTS OF ROBERT JOHNSON

❾ **PONY BLUES** CHARLEY PATTON from FOUNDER OF THE DELTA BLUES

❿ **BIG ROAD BLUES** TOMMY JOHNSON from TOMMY JOHNSON & ASSOCIATES

Greg Ward

Joni Mitchell

First and foremost a Canadian, whose career in the US has always subtly reflected her roots. Joni Mitchell is a total artist – a painter with words, music and even the images that often grace her album covers. While she was a child of the 60s, the 70s were her decade, as this selection suggests:

❶ **BOTH SIDES NOW** from CLOUDS
A much covered early hit from Joni's second album, which came out in 1969. Only on her third did she really hit her stride.

❷ **BIG YELLOW TAXI** from LADIES OF THE CANYON
Joni's feeling for rhythm, the environment and pop music are all expertly rolled into this snappy little song.

❸ **WOODSTOCK** from LADIES OF THE CANYON
The flower-child naïvety here still sounds charming, while the odd vocal gymnastics at the end hint at a passion for jazz which would later develop.

❹ **CALIFORNIA** from BLUE
A strong sense of place is probably the best reason for calling Joni Mitchell's music "folk", and nowhere is that better demonstrated than here.

❺ **YOU TURN ME ON I'M A RADIO** from FOR THE ROSES
The only hit on this largely forgotten 1972 album, which bridged the stylistic gap between two far more famous efforts.

❻ **FREE MAN IN PARIS** from COURT AND SPARK
Just one of half a dozen possible representative cuts from an album that masterfully fused jazz, rock and folk.

❼ **DON'T INTERRUPT THE SORROW** from THE HISSING OF SUMMER LAWNS
Joni really got rhythm on her 1975 album, utilizing the services (long before world music

was thought of) of the Drummers of Burundi. This sophisticated, urbane track is a real highlight.

❽ AMELIA from **HEJIRA**
A cinematic treat with a travelling-through-the-desert vibe. Sounds like it should have been on the soundtrack to Antonioni's *Zabriskie Point*.

❾ PAPRIKA PLAINS from **DON JUAN'S RECKLESS DAUGHTER**
This epic track filled a whole side of vinyl on its original release in 1977, and inspired bass player Charlie Mingus to approach the artist with a proposal.

❿ THE WOLF THAT LIVES IN LINDSEY
from **MINGUS**
Joni's 1979 album was both a tribute to and a collaboration with jazz great Mingus. Even some timber wolves got involved on this abstract off-the-wall gem.

Jon Lusk

Moby

It hasn't always been advert soundtracks from the man with the teashop in Manhattan. In fact, he's done just about everything. Here's the cream.

❶ GO from **MOBY**
The *Twin Peaks*-sampled favourite never tires with every listen. Simplicity at its most brilliant.

❷ WHISPERING WIND from **PLAY/THE B SIDES**
The haunting Vocoder vocal and simple piano riff proves Moby can turn any bpm into a great track.

❸ MOVE (YOU MAKE ME FEEL SO GOOD)
from **MOVE EP**
A rave gem with classic piano and anthemic singing. Hands in the air.

❹ PORCELAIN from **PLAY**
Hey, woman. Delicate name, delicate track. *Play*'s finest.

Moby
Stretches Out

From techno to blues via heavy metal and acid house, MOBY's music touches many bases over his 15 year solo career. No surprise, then, that his eclectic playlist stretches from Johnny Cash to Donna Summer.

❶ I ONLY HAVE EYES FOR YOU THE FLAMINGOS from **THE BEST OF THE FLAMINGOS**

❷ UTOPIA GOLDFRAPP from **FELT MOUNTAIN**

❸ I FEEL LOVE DONNA SUMMER from **THE BEST OF**

❹ NORTHERN SKY NICK DRAKE from **BRYTER LAYTER**

❺ STRINGS OF LIFE DERRICK MAY from **INNOVATOR**

❻ HELPLESS CROSBY, STILL, NASH & YOUNG from **DÉJÀ VU**

❼ OVER THE WALL ECHO AND THE BUNNYMEN from **HEAVEN UP HERE**

❽ THE MERCY SEAT NICK CAVE from **TENDER PREY**

❾ HURT JOHNNY CASH from **AMERICAN IV: THE MAN COMES AROUND**

❿ MEMORIES CAN'T WAIT TALKING HEADS from **FEAR OF MUSIC**

⑤ FIRST COOL HIVE from **EVERYTHING IS WRONG**
Surrounded by hyper beats on the album, this sticks out for all the right reasons.

⑥ SICK IN THE SYSTEM
from **NATURAL BLUES SINGLE**
Strings, piano and beats with an uplifting chord progression – wasted as a B-side.

⑦ FEELING SO REAL from **EVERYTHING IS WRONG**
Another rave classic amid the more recent smoother sounds that Moby has made his current trademark. Incredible energy.

⑧ EXTREME WAYS from **18**
Taking the *Play* sound into the twenty-first century with relative ease. The stand-out track from *18*.

⑨ WHY DOES MY HEART FEEL SO BAD?
from **PLAY**
Only two tracks from *Play*? Yes, but this sorrowful ditty shines through.

⑩ NEXT IS THE E from **RARE: THE COLLECTED B-SIDES (1989-1993)**
Mental beats and the token drug reference made this track a stand-out during the rave era. Still sounding fresh today.

Marten Sealby

Mogwai

Though sometimes labelled "post-rock" or "second-generation shoegazers", Mogwai are a band with a sound all of their own. Here's a handful of their finest glacial slabs.

① HELICON 2 from **TEN RAPID**
A slow and graceful instrumental that perfectly represents the band's ability to capture a fine melody.

② ANGELS VERSUS ALIENS from **TEN RAPID**
Guitars layer and deepen like falling snow, culminating in an explosion of overdrive and stampeding xylophone.

③ SECRET PINT from **ROCK ACTION**
The piano line and vocals are beautiful and sad, while the clattering rattle of cymbals sets the tempo.

④ HUNTED BY A FREAK from **HAPPY SONGS FOR HAPPY PEOPLE**
A Vocoder-blessed gem of shimmering guitarchords and strings. Also search out the Peel session version on *Government Commissions*.

⑤ LIKE HEROD from **GOVERNMENT COMMISSIONS**
An eighteen-minute holocaust that first lulls you into a near-slumber and then hurls you into the path of a distortion tornado.

⑥ MOGWAI FEAR SATAN (MY BLOODY VALENTINE REMIX) from **MOGWAI FEAR SATAN REMIXES EP**
Kevin Shields works his magic on a Mogwai original – beats melt into a goo of saturated sounds that'll leave you gasping for air.

Peter Buckley

Thelonious Monk

The most original and iconoclastic of all jazz composers, Monk's music is immediately recognizable. His splintery piano playing is equally individual – simultaneously homely and alien, it's a beautiful law unto itself.

① THELONIOUS
from **GENIUS OF MODERN MUSIC VOL 1**
Thumped-out, morse-code piano wakes up an ornery drumkit before everything starts swinging beneath a circular thirteen-chord fanfare.

② MONK'S MOOD from **THELONIOUS HIMSELF**
Monk alone at the piano is made all the more affecting for John Coltrane and Wilbur Ware unassumingly (and unexpectedly) joining in towards the very end.

❸ HORNIN' IN
from **GENIUS OF MODERN MUSIC VOL 2**
Trilling and acerbic, this tune is Monk at his nastiest and is as insinuating as a splinter.

❹ FOUR IN ONE
from **GENIUS OF MODERN MUSIC VOL 2**
A generous tangle of a tune, its tricky knots are both challengingly captious and warmly inviting.

❺ PANNONICA from **BRILLIANT CORNERS**
Monk plays piano with one hand, celeste with the other, adding a delicate clarity to this sidelong lullaby.

❻ BEMSHA SWING FROM BRILLIANT CORNERS
Max Roach doubles on timpani on a tune which, aided by Sonny Rollins' thick-set but measured tone, manages to sound both muscular and wistful.

❼ OFF MINOR (TAKE FIVE)
from **MONK'S MUSIC**
The dynamic duo of Lester Young and John Coltrane add some stab to Monk's punchy dischords, throwing his minors even further off.

❽ SWEET AND LOVELY
from **MULLIGAN MEETS MONK**
Gerry Mulligan's sax tone is as fuzzy as mouldy chocolate, laying back while Monk vamps some of his splayed hammy clusters on a gorgeously discordant ballad.

❾ BOO BOO'S BIRTHDAY (TAKE 2)
from **UNDERGROUND**
Dedicated to his daughter, this 1968 tune is quintessential Monk, questing and explorative but fundamentally tumbling around a single nagging note.

❿ INTROSPECTION from **SOLO MONK**
A gymnastic farrago of sudden twists, turns and reversals; the tune's key changes as abruptly and multifariously as if the tape had been spliced.

Matt Milton

The Monkees

Even if the prefabricated four – Micky Dolenz, Davy Jones, Peter Tork and Mike Nesmith – never had any pretensions to greatness, they were masters of apparently disposable, yet surprisingly durable, pop.

❶ DAYDREAM BELIEVER
from **GREATEST HITS**
Wondrously wistful, ultra-contagious, and sweetly sung by Davy Jones, this feelgood smash was the best thing to come out of that bizarre late-60s flowering known as bubblegum pop.

❷ I'M A BELIEVER from **GREATEST HITS**
Covered for the movie *Shrek*, used in an episode of *South Park*, this Neil Diamond composition is a once-heard, frequently-hummed timeless shout of joy about the moment when love begins to click.

❸ RIO
from **FROM A RADIO ENGINE TO THE PHOTON WING**
Hypnotically indecisive, charmingly melodic solo effort from Mike Nesmith, in which his predicament – should he go to Rio or not? – doesn't seem to matter that much.

❹ ALTERNATE TITLE (RANDY SCOUSE GIT)
from **GREATEST HITS**
One of the most inventive pop hits of the 1960s, this is an authentic, angry, freewheeling marvel from the pen of Micky Dolenz.

❺ (I'M NOT YOUR) STEPPING STONE
from **GREATEST HITS**
The band's struggles with their own label inspired this bitter diatribe. The furious lyrics, aimed at a feckless lover, could just as easily apply to the Machiavellian figures who run the music industry,

❻ WHAT AM I DOIN' HANGING 'ROUND?
from **THE BEST OF THE MONKEES**
A simple slice of corny country pop by Michael Martin Murphey. The Monkees cover, complete

with banjo from Doug Dillard, prefigures Nesmith's later move into cult country rock.

❼ PLEASANT VALLEY SUNDAY
from **GREATEST HITS**
Noted, at the time, for its mild social protest, this song is far broader, striking a chord with anyone who's ever endured a pointless Sunday.

❽ LAST TRAIN TO CLARKSVILLE
from **GREATEST HITS**
Pop is full of train songs and this one has worn well; possibly because neither The Monkees nor Boyce and Hart who wrote it, felt obliged to include "choo choo" and "train" in the lyric.

❾ VALLERI from **GREATEST HITS**
Short, unpretentious, lyrics about the girl next door, wailing trumpets, Davy Jones on vocal and none of the other Monkees on it at all.

❿ PORPOISE SONG from **GREATEST HITS**
With sweeping organ, swaying vocals from Dolenz, and cries of encouragement in the chorus from Jones, this theme to the band's movie *Head* is a real fan's favourite.

Paul Simpson

Monty Python

They're winning awards again with the Broadway musical, Spamalot. But the Pythons, ably abetted by Neil Innes, always did a nice song. Like the sketches, many sound distinctly dated or dodgy, but the best remain brilliant.

❶ ALWAYS LOOK ON THE BRIGHT SIDE OF LIFE from **MONTY PYTHON SINGS...**
Who could resist a toe-tapping crucifixion feel-good number? With a whistling chorus? It just ain't possible. What you got to lose? Cheer up you old bugger, give us a grin.

❷ LUMBERJACK SONG
from **MONTY PYTHON SINGS...**
Michael Palin never wanted to be a weather forecaster. He wanted to be a lumberjack, and to sing, sing, sing this classic transvestite woodcutters' anthem. He's okay.

❸ ERIC THE HALF A BEE
from **MONTY PYTHON SINGS...**
ABCDEFG, Eric the half a bee. Perhaps one of Python's finest philosophical numbers, writ in song.

❹ HEIDEGGER from **MONTY PYTHON SINGS...**
Were the world's greatest philosophers all piss-heads? It would appear so. Wonderful rhymes and startling logic ("René Descartes was a drunken fart, I drink therefore I am") to a didgeridoo backing.

❺ GALAXY SONG from **MONTY PYTHON SINGS...**
Python's last film, *The Meaning of Life*, may have been a stinker, but it spawned this lovely Eric Idle number about the universe: "...and pray there's intelligent life somewhere out in space 'cos there's bugger all down here on earth."

❻ EVERY SPERM IS SACRED
from **MONTY PYTHON SINGS...**
This absurdly ambitious number (also from *The Meaning of Life*) has a cast of hundreds, getting across the immutable Catholic belief: "If a sperm is wasted, God gets quite irate."

Mark Ellingham

Alanis Morissette

Her remarkable 1995 album *Jagged Little Pill* may not have been Morissette's debut, but it was the one that put her on the map. Inevitably she's struggled to match its teenage themes of sexual jealousy and confused anger ever since, and half of this list comes from that one album. But we've rounded up a few gems from her later work, too.

❶ YOU OUGHTA KNOW from JAGGED LITTLE PILL
On which Alanis rivals Marianne Faithfull for the bitterness with which she berates an ex-lover.

❷ ALL I REALLY WANT from JAGGED LITTLE PILL
Brilliant pop production by Glen Ballard.

❸ IRONIC from JAGGED LITTLE PILL
Alanis doesn't quite appear to understand the strict dictionary definition of the word, but a great song, nonetheless.

❹ YOU LEARN from JAGGED LITTLE PILL
Lessons in life from a precocious nineteen-year-old.

❺ HAND IN POCKET from JAGGED LITTLE PILL
Ballsy but accessible, perfect radio-friendly pop-rock.

❻ THANK U from SUPPOSED FORMER INFATUATION JUNKIE
This was the best song from an otherwise disappointing album. "Thank you India, thank you terror, thank you disillusionment" she sings. What could she be on about?

❼ THAT I WOULD BE GOOD from SUPPOSED FORMER INFATUATION JUNKIE
A chill-out track in which she intriguingly wonders how she would react if she lost all the fame and wealth that *JLP* had brought.

❽ 21 THINGS I WANT IN A LOVER from UNDER RUG SWEPT
Tick 'em off and count 'em to see how well you measure up.

❾ KING OF PAIN from ALANIS UNPLUGGED
A surprising cover of the Police song from her 1999 MTV outing.

❿ DOTH I PROTEST TOO MUCH from SO-CALLED CHAOS
The mature Alanis circa 2004 asking a question she would never have contemplated at the time of You Oughta Know.

Nigel Williamson

Ennio Morricone

Not only did Morricone recast Western movie music as we know it, he effectively invented a whole new genre with his innovative blend of eerie desert sounds, weird abstract vocals and superb orchestration.

❶ THE ECSTASY OF GOLD from THE GOOD, THE BAD AND THE UGLY
A simply gorgeous piece. Understated piano, tolling chimes and oboe motif lead to a slowly building abstract vocal and orchestral arrangement.

❷ THE GOOD, THE BAD AND THE UGLY from THE GOOD, THE BAD AND THE UGLY
No introduction necessary for this total and utter classic. One of the most famous movie themes (spaghetti western or otherwise) ever written.

❸ GUITAR NOCTURNE from DEATH RIDES A HORSE
As the desert sun sets… A mellow and minimal arrangement of hazy voices and percussion floats around a beautiful acoustic guitar solo.

❹ INVENZIONE PER JOHN from A FISTFUL OF DYNAMITE
Building upon the vocal and melodic motifs of the main theme, this stunning nine-minute piece moves effortlessly through a variety of emotional moods.

❺ LA RESA DEI CONTI from FOR A FEW DOLLARS MORE
The fragile chimes of a pocket watch erupt into terrifyingly strident church organ chords – a moment of stark epiphany.

❻ MAN WITH A HARMONICA from ONCE UPON A TIME IN THE WEST
Regularly sampled and borrowed, the epic strains of an eerily distant harmonica introduce an arrangement heavily pregnant with brooding violence.

7 L'ULTIMA TROMBA from **A FIST GOES WEST**

A distant cousin to Man With A Harmonica, on which the haunting tones are leavened by lyrical trumpet and oboe solos, soft voices and soothingly strummed guitars.

8 PER QUALCHE DOLLARO IN PIÙ from **FOR A FEW DOLLARS MORE**

A Jew's harp twangs away in the baking midday heat, and a distant whistled melody ushers in some superb guitar and chanting vocals.

9 SE SEI QUALCUNO E' COLPA MIA from **MY NAME IS NOBODY T**

Introduced by a ticking clock, the sense of suspense is epic. Brilliantly distorted electric guitars add to the crucial nail-biting tension.

10 THEME FROM A FISTFUL OF DOLLARS from **A FISTFUL OF DOLLARS**

Stately and sombre in pace; while the vocals play their part, it all hinges around a single mournful trumpet. The sense of emotion is palpable.

Essi Berelian

Morrissey

Bequiffed legend; monarch of miserabilism; aloof eccentric; father of Britpop. Whatever your take on Morrissey, he remains one of Britain's most seminal artists of the past twenty-five years.

1 EVERY DAY IS LIKE SUNDAY from **VIVA HATE**

An epic song from Mozzer's first solo album, perfectly capturing the drudgery of modern life. Makes Britain's "silent and grey" seaside towns achingly beautiful.

2 HAIRDRESSER ON FIRE from **BONA DRAG**

Proof that Morrissey is strangely addictive: tunes like this touch parts that others just can't reach.

3 WE HATE IT WHEN OUR FRIENDS BECOME SUCCESSFUL from **YOUR ARSENAL**

The arch put-down is a dish best served dripping with Morrissey wit and razor-sharp lyrics. An elegant riposte to his critics.

4 SING YOUR LIFE from **KILL UNCLE**

Proof that Moz can do uplifting as well as downbeat.

5 IRISH BLOOD, ENGLISH HEART from **YOU ARE THE QUARRY**

Wily musings on the artist's own identity crisis, writ to the catchiest of pop tunes.

6 MARGARET ON THE GUILLOTINE from **VIVA HATE**

"People like you make me feel so tired. When will you die?" A poetic outburst aimed at Britain's former prime minister, Margaret Thatcher.

7 SUEDEHEAD from **VIVA HATE**

Morrissey's best solo pop song shares much of its genetic make-up with the finest of The Smiths' back catalogue.

8 MUTE WITNESS from **KILL UNCLE**

Perhaps one of 1991's oddest songs, stuttering from slow piano ballad to pumping guitar rock. Marvellously strange.

9 I DON'T MIND IF YOU FORGET ME from **VIVA HATE**

Soaring indie guitar track fizzing with energy and lovers' angst. An outsider's anthem.

10 TOMORROW from **YOUR ARSENAL**

Morrissey at his awkward best: impassioned singing about pain and lovelorn loneliness. Trademark yodelling and edgy guitars.

Tim Pollard

Van Morrison

A professional musician since he was fifteen, the Belfast bard, uncommon one, and veteran rock-blues-jazz-folk-soul

fusionist, has developed into one of the great masters of modern music.

❶ AND THE HEALING HAS BEGUN from **INTO THE MUSIC**
Momentum-building celebration of love and life with a new age tinge. Violin and vocals chase each other across the groove.

❷ BROWN EYED GIRL from **BLOWIN' YOUR MIND!/THE BEST OF VAN MORRISON**
Van's only jukebox perennial and karaoke fixture: "…Do you remember when, we used to sing?"

❸ BESIDE YOU from **ASTRAL WEEKS**
"High" point (in all sorts of ways) of Van's most original, most must-have album. Ecstatic, poetic with risk-takingly committed vocals.

❹ I FORGOT THAT LOVE EXISTED from **POETIC CHAMPIONS COMPOSE**
From the darker side of the oeuvre – "heart-ache after heartache" – one of several smooth and moody tracks from *Champions*.

❺ MOONDANCE from **MOONDANCE**
A "marvellous night" indeed. Van at his smoothest and lounge-iest.

❻ STREETS OF ARKLOW from **VEEDON FLEECE**
A fine example of Morrison's Celtic strain, with flute, pastoral lyrics and wandering vocals.

❼ A TOWN CALLED PARADISE from **NO GURU, NO METHOD, NO TEACHER**
Smooth, saxy redemption song from a beauti-fully produced fine late album.

❽ SUMMERTIME IN ENGLAND from **THE COMMON ONE**
Far out – not just for the lyrics about Wordsworth and Coleridge "smokin' dope in Kendal"– mystic marathon from an underrated album.

❾ WILD NIGHT from **TUPELO HONEY**
Hit the town and dance. Brisk, breezy rocky Van-lite.

❿ YOU DON'T PULL NO PUNCHES, BUT YOU DON'T PUSH THE RIVER from **VEEDON FLEECE**
Go with the flow. Not as trance-inducing as the comparable Listen to the Lion, but delightfully off-the-wall lyrics and superb musicianship weave a magic spell.

Andrew Lockett

Motown

The Detroit-based company was the first successful label to be owned and run by African-Americans. The Motown style reached perfection in the 60s and 70s. The following are ten finely-tuned vehicles from Berry Gordy's Hit Factory.

❶ MONEY (THAT'S WHAT I WANT) BARRETT STRONG from **THE BEST OF BARRETT STRONG**
It was bigger for The Beatles, but this gritty piece of soul put Motown on the map.

❷ (LOVE IS LIKE A) HEATWAVE MARTHA AND THE VANDELLAS from **HEATWAVE**
Holland-Dozier-Holland sizzler that shows off the classic Hitsville backing-vocal sound.

❸ GET READY THE TEMPTATIONS from **GETTING READY**
Solid, driving soul from the Motown backbone.

❹ NEEDLE IN A HAYSTACK THE VELVELETTES from **BEST OF THE VELVELETTES**
Catchy three-girl harmony, backed up with a rhythmic playground feel.

❺ BABY LOVE THE SUPREMES from **WHERE DID OUR LOVE GO**
Shimmering pop—soul crossover from Berry's brightest stars.

❻ HEARD IT THROUGH THE GRAPEVINE GLADYS KNIGHT AND THE PIPS from **EVERYBODY NEEDS LOVE**
Lowdown and languorous. A stunning version of the Marvin Gaye hit.

❼ THIS OLD HEART OF MINE (IS WEAK FOR YOU) THE ISLEY BROTHERS from **THIS OLD HEART OF MINE**
Weeping string and double drums underpin this #1 ballad.

❽ TEARS OF A CLOWN SMOKEY ROBINSON & THE MIRACLES from **MAKE IT HAPPEN**
Inspired by the opera *I Pagliacci*, Smokey takes the circus sound 4 to the floor.

❾ GOTTA GIVE IT UP (PART 1) MARVIN GAYE from **LIVE AT THE LONDON PALLADIUM**
Skin-tight 70s party groover.

❿ LIVIN' FOR THE CITY STEVIE WONDER from **INNERVISIONS**
Motown gets funky on the wrong side of the tracks.

Rachel Coldicutt

Motörhead

With the legendary Lemmy at the helm, the battle-scarred warhorse that is Motörhead remains the true embodiment of body-slamming rock'n'roll.

❶ ACE OF SPADES from **ACE OF SPADES**
Brain-rattling drums, *that* riff and Lemmy's rapid-fire bass nailing it all home with snake-eye precision. One of the most famous tunes in metaldom.

❷ BOMBER from **NO SLEEP 'TIL HAMMERSMITH**
Rawer and dirtier than the studio version, this is delivered with the kind of ferocity that would kill any normal band.

❸ BURNER from **BASTARDS**
A psychotic cousin to the Ace Of Spades, with a spiky off-kilter chorus that could have your eye out.

❹ DANCING ON YOUR GRAVE from **ANOTHER PERFECT DAY**
The 'Head went vaguely tuneful for a while

thanks to guitarist Brian Robertson – but this under-rated effort slays all the same.

❺ LOCOMOTIVE from **NO REMORSE**
This must contain some of the fastest drumming ever to grace a 'Head tune, and that's really saying something. Casey Jones it ain't.

❻ MOTÖRHEAD from **NO SLEEP 'TIL HAMMERSMITH**
Yet another gonzoid belter with Lemmy proving his speedfreak credentials. This live version makes the original sound like a nursery rhyme.

❼ ORGASMATRON from **ORGASMATRON**
Lemmy does cynical evil brilliantly and nowhere more so than on this grinding, black-hearted epic.

❽ OVERKILL from **NO SLEEP 'TIL HAMMERSMITH**
This rocket-fuelled live version is faster and more chaotic than in the studio and still boasts two ace false endings.

❾ R.A.M.O.N.E.S from **1916**
Kindred rock'n'roll spirits with Da Brudders from Noo Yoik, this spot-on tribute number is a blur of bad attitude.

❿ SMILING LIKE A KILLER from **INFERNO**
Chucklesome and chilling Lemmy is a master of blackly funny lyrics – even your pets aren't safe from the warty one's homicidal instincts.

Essi Berelian

Mott The Hoople & Ian Hunter

Most famous for that excellent smash hit (see #1 below), these glammy hard rockers enjoyed reasonable success in the 1970s before splintering. Ace songwriter Ian Hunter is still packing 'em in though.

❶ ALL THE WAY FROM MEMPHIS from **MOTT (MOTT)**
Some fantastic ivory-bashing from Hunter, plus

snazzy saxophone and guitar interplay give this a cool vintage rock'n'roll flavour.

❷ ALL THE YOUNG DUDES from **ALL THE YOUNG DUDES**

It looked like the end of the line for the lads before David Bowie revived them with this classic anthem. Listen carefully and you might catch him on backing vox.

❸ CRASH STREET KIDDS from **THE HOOPLE**

Look out, they're dressed to kill! And just when you think it's finished early, those guitars suddenly jump all over you.

❹ THE GOLDEN AGE OF ROCK'N'ROLL from **THE HOOPLE**

There's tons going on here. Ian Hunter gives the vocals some serious welly amid the piano, parping saxophones and glamorous backing vocals.

❺ SATURDAY GIGS from **GREATEST HITS**

The band's last hit single, and the biographical lyrics are tearjerkingly nostalgic – worth it just to hear them name-check Croydon!

❻ ALL AMERICAN ALIEN BOY from **ALL AMERICAN ALIEN BOY**

Very cool and funky autobiographical tune with some great female backing vox. Ends with an awesome rapidfire list of Native American chiefs' names.

❼ CLEVELAND ROCKS from **YOU'RE NEVER ALONE WITH A SCHIZOPHRENIC**

A staple tune in the Hunter live set to this day, this is nothing less than a storming melodic rocker with an irresistible hook.

❽ ONCE BITTEN TWICE SHY from **IAN HUNTER**

Surely one of Hunter's best lyrics, with some great bar-room piano. Sounds like low-key genius until those Mick Ronson guitars kick in.

❾ SHIPS from **YOU'RE NEVER ALONE WITH A SCHIZOPHRENIC**

Bizarrely, Barry Manilow covered this and had a huge US hit. A gentle ballad that is genuinely touching without wallowing in schmaltz.

❿ WHO DO YOU LOVE from **IAN HUNTER**

Another real cracker, with a terrific bouncy bass, and Mick Ronson conjuring up some fiery fretboard magic. Love the cool finger-clicking intro too.

Essi Berelian

Mozambique

The world comes together in the music of Mozambique. Down on the shores of the Indian Ocean, influences from Indonesia, Brazil, the Congo, New York, India and the Middle East (to name just a few) meet a wealth of traditional styles and instruments and are born again.

❶ ELISA GOMARA SAIA ORCHESTRA **MARRABENTA STAR DE MOÇAMBIQUE** from **INDEPENDANCE**

The original marrabenta outfit, complete with Wazimbo on vocals and a full horn section. Here with steam coming out of their ears.

❷ RAMBANANE TIMBILA MUZIMBA from **CONTA PROPRIA**

Timbila Muzimba turn sax, drums, bass and a defiantly jazz outlook onto traditional timbila music.

❸ MARIA TERESA DILON DJINDJI from **DILON**

A recent recording of a 50s' classic about a man caught between two women, by the man they call the King of Marrabenta.

❹ NUNO MAALANI EYUPHURO from **MAMA MOSAMBIKI**

The great Zena Bakar leads this group from Nampula, in the Islamic north of the country. Her voice flies in this song about motherhood.

❺ MBHOLE MBHOLE NA YONE DJAAKA from **MBHOLE MBHOLE NA YONA**

Rootsy brilliance from Beira's finest. A bit like Zimbabwean chimurenga, but built around the patterns of Mozambican timbila (traditional Chopi xylophones).

❻ M'TSITSO VENANCIO MBANDE
from **TIMBILA TA VENANCIO**
The king of timbila, Mbande performs a
call and response with his thirty-two piece
orchestra.

❼ WUKATI LAKUKAWA HINENGUE FELICIANO
GOMES from **FORGOTTEN GUITARS FROM MOZAMBIQUE**
Proper marrabenta of the 50s, featuring acous-
tic guitars, drums and a traditional form of rap.

❽ A FÚRIA DAS ÁGUAS FACE OCULTA
from **ATENÇÃO: DESMINAGEM!**
Studio Kandonga (Underground) is the mainstay of Mozambique's hip-hop scene. Chilled
beats and floating voices, but the fury's never
far beneath the surface.

❾ TOMA QUE TI DOU ZAIDA E CARLOS CHONGO
from **HOMENAGEM À ZAIDA**
Irresistible Mozambican pop, with the late,
much-lamented Zaida Chongo on lead vocals
and Carlos Chongo playing that dreamy lead
guitar. Best served with lots of sunshine!

Tom Bullough

Oliver Mtukudzi

**No-one in African music makes you want to
dance, weep and laugh at the same time
quite like the great "Tuku". The biggest
star in Zimbabwe for years, he has now
taken over on the international stage as
well, playing his soulful, socially conscious
songs. He's released 48 albums to date, but
here are some good places to start.**

❶ NDIMA NDAPEDZA from **TUKU MUSIC**
This is the album that broke him internationally, and if any one track swung it…

❷ RAKI from **BVUMA/TOLERANCE**
More about weeping than dancing. That great,
deep voice over layers of delicate guitar and
wailing backing singers.

❸ CHIDO CHENYU from **THE OTHER SIDE**
A 1970s classic, this is stomping dance music
about "those who sleep in the forest": that is,
the guerrillas in the war of independence.

❹ PINDIRAI from **NHAVA**
Among the first recordings made at his new
studio in Norton, Zimbabwe, this 2005 number
is the sound of Tuku at home.

❺ ZIWERE from **ZIWERE MUCOPENHAGEN**
This live standard, originally released on 1978's
Ndipeiwo Zano, is one of Oliver's most playful,
joyful songs.

❻ NERIA from **NERIA**
The lovely, gentle theme song from Tuku's
award-winning soundtrack to Zimbabwe's
second feature film, in which he also starred.

❼ NDAKUVARA from **VHUNZE MOTO**
His voice cracks with passion. The bass rocks
and thunders. The dancefloor fills up (if it isn't
full already).

❽ UCHAROYA CHETE from **KUVHAIRA**
With a rare marimba (traditional xylophone)
playing in the band, Ucharoya Chete points
straight to Tuku's roots.

Tom Bullough

Mudhoney

**Nirvana had the hits, but Mudhoney kept it
real. This is grunge as it was first conceived,
an unholy sub-Stoogian racket filtered
through the prism of punk.**

❶ A THOUSAND FORMS OF MIND
from **TOMORROW HIT TODAY**
The loping riff could almost have been written
by Black Sabbath's Tony Iommi circa 1971. The
organ flourishes add a cool vintage vibe.

❷ HATE THE POLICE from **HERE COMES SICKNESS,
THE BEST OF THE BBC RECORDINGS**
Mudhoney's infamous Dicks cover captured at

245

the Reading festival is far more dangerous and frenetic than its studio version.

❸ IN 'N' OUT OF GRACE from **SUPERFUZZ BIGMUFF**
A completely unhinged riff and a fabulously discordant guitar solo compete to give you the migraine of your life. Welcome to grunge, baby.

❹ INTO THE DRINK from **EVERY GOOD BOY DESERVES FUDGE**
There's a 60s pop song lurking somewhere beneath the garage grease and grime. It must be the acoustic guitar way down in the mix.

❺ JUDGEMENT, RAGE, RETRIBUTION AND THYME from **MY BROTHER THE COW**
You've got to love the excellent Simon and Garfunkel title pisstake, while that scything, sliding guitar could easily have your ears off.

❻ LET IT SLIDE
from **EVERY GOOD BOY DESERVES FUDGE**
Is that a guitar solo ending the song or is it a drunken fingers-jammed-through-the-strings job? Sounds great either way.

❼ SUCK YOU DRY from **PIECE OF CAKE**
The band reckon this turned out just as they intended it. The spirit of 60s garage rock condensed to a mere two-and-a-half minutes.

❽ THIS GIFT from **MUDHONEY**
A sinister but tuneful little ditty featuring an understated reverbed guitar motif burbling away underneath the verses.

❾ TOUCH ME I'M SICK from **MARCH TO FUZZ**
The drums sound like they're being thrown downstairs, and the guitars grind under industrial levels of distortion.

❿ YOU GOT IT from **MUDHONEY**
This sounds almost controlled and tuneful by Mudhoney standards, which is to say, it's merely chaotic rather than utter bedlam.

Essi Berelian

Murakami's music

The Japanese novelist Haruki Murakami ran a jazz club in Tokyo, with his wife Yoko, for seven years and is said to have a collection of six thousand records and CDs. Music permeates his novels and stories, even shapes them to a degree, and many of his characters discuss music with passion and knowledge.

❶ THE GIRL FROM IPANEMA STAN GETZ AND ASTRUD GILBERTO from **GETZ–GILBERTO**
Murakami wrote a whole story about this song, musing – riffing, you might call it – over how the girl looks at the sea in 1963, and, unchanging, two decades later.

❷ NORWEGIAN WOOD THE BEATLES from **RUBBER SOUL**
Norwegian Wood was a huge bestseller in Japan, where it was titled *Forest In Norway*, which is how the Beatles song was originally (mis)translated. The novel's three million sales led to a light orchestral version of the song going to #1 in Japan.

❸ DEAR HEART HENRY MANCINI from **DEAR HEART & OTHER SONGS**
The main character in *Norwegian Wood*, Watanabe, gives a copy of this to Naoko, and it is the first song that Reiko plays to him before the two make love near the book's end.

❹ DANCE, DANCE, DANCE THE DELLS from **OH WHAT A NIGHT: THE VERY BEST OF THE DELLS**
The Dells' song –"I gotta dance dance dance now the beat's really hot right on the spot" – later covered by The Beach Boys – gave Murakami the title of his next novel.

❺ STAR CROSSED LOVERS DUKE ELLINGTON
Hajime, the jazz bar owner in *South of the Border, West of the Sun*, has his club pianist play

Charlie Gillett rates
Muscle Shoals

DJ and writer **CHARLIE GILLETT** is best known for his ever-intriguing World Music shows on BBC Radio London and World Service World. But he remains a big soul and R&B fan, having begun his career with the now-classic book on American music, *The Sound of the City*. The studios of Muscle Shoals, Alabama – Fame, Muscle Shoals, Quinvy – have produced many of the greatest R'n'B songs of all time. Here are ten classic singles.

❶ **I'LL TAKE YOU THERE** THE STAPLE SINGERS from **MUSCLE SHOALS**

❷ **I'VE NEVER LOVED A MAN** ARETHA FRANKLIN from **FAME**

❸ **WHEN A MAN LOVES A WOMAN** PERCY SLEDGE from **QUINVY**

❹ **STEALING IN THE NAME OF THE LORD** PAUL KELLY from **MUSCLE SHOALS**

❺ **IT'S BETTER TO HAVE AND DON'T NEED** DON COVAY from **MUSCLE SHOALS**

❻ **I'D RATHER GO BLIND** ETTA JAMES from **FAME**

❼ **YOU LEFT THE WATER RUNNING** MAURICE & MAC from **FAME**

❽ **HOLD WHAT YOU GOT** JOE TEX from **FAME**

❾ **YOU BETTER MOVE ON** ARTHUR ALEXANDER from **FAME**

❿ **UP TIGHT, GOOD MAN** LAURA LEE from **FAME**

---

this over and over again (Casablanca fashion) until suddenly it no longer moves him.

❻ **THE THIEVING MAGPIE** ROSSINI from **ROSSINI OVERTURES CONDUCTED BY CLAUDIO ABBADO**
The "monotonous melody" of Rossini's overture preoccupies Toru Okada, protagonist of *The Wind-Up Bird Chronicle*.

❼ **TARA'S THEME** THE PERCY FAITH ORCHESTRA from **THE COLLECTION**
Again in *The Wind-Up Bird Chronicle*, Okada hears this at the dry cleaners. The tune brings him good memories of taking his girlfriend to see the movie, *A Summer Place*.

❽ **D MAJOR (HEAVENLY) SONATA** FRANZ SCHUBERT
Oshima, the guiding character in *Kafka On The Beach*, listens to Schubert's D Major Piano Sonata when he's driving, so as to "feel the

limitations of what humans are capable of" in its imperfect performance.

❾ **THE ARCHDUKE TRIO** BEETHOVEN performed by **THE MILLION DOLLAR TRIO**
Hoshino, the truck driver, falls for the Archduke Trio, and tells Oshima of this recording. Oshima rates it, though he himself prefers the version by the Czech group, the Suk Trio.

❿ **FIVE SPOT AFTER DARK** CURTIS FULLER from **BLUESETTE**
Asked "What musical pieces would you include on a Murakami playlist?", the novelist replied: "Whenever I write a novel, music just sort of naturally slips in… When I was writing my newest novel, *After Dark*, the melody of Curtis Fuller's Five Spot After Dark kept running through my head".

Mark Ellingham

My Bloody Valentine

The undisputed kings of UK indie noise, MBV were a band who released few albums, but when they did appear the results were stupendous and consistently groundbreaking. The group has now all but dissolved, with frontman Kevin Shields only occasionally resurfacing for remix and production work and, most recently, to contribute to the blinding *Lost In Translation* soundtrack.

❶ SOFT AS SNOW (BUT WARM INSIDE) from **ISN'T ANYTHING**
A machine gun of drums paves the way for luscious whale-song guitars and a silky Shields vocal.

❷ SEVERAL GIRLS GALORE from **ISN'T ANYTHING**
So good. The guitars phase and chug over Shield's vocal foil Belinda Butcher.

❸ YOU MADE ME REALISE from **ISN'T ANYTHING**
A single that saw thousands of mop-headed indie kids shaking their thing on student union dancefloors up and down the nation during the late 80s (even if they never quite knew what to do during the extending guitar storm toward the end of the cut).

❹ SAFE IN YOUR SLEEP from **ECSTACY AND WINE**
An early jangler that's very much of its time, though all the elements of the band's future glories are already in place.

❺ SLOW from **YOU MADE ME REALISE**
Basslines don't come much dirtier and sexier than this. A great B-side, and with lyrics that'll either make you blush or head straight to the bedroom.

❻ CIGARETTE IN YOUR BED
from **YOU MADE ME REALISE**
A beautiful song that introduced many to MBV

when it appeared on the Creation Records *Doing It for The Kids* LP – a classic indie playlist in itself.

❼ SOON from **LOVELESS**
This single (the A-side of the *Glider* EP) broke the band's mould and presented a radical collision of guitar loop chaos and a killer dance break.

❽ TO HERE KNOWS WHEN from **LOVELESS**
This whole album is a sumptuous fest of guitar texture and angelic vocals, and should really be taken as a whole … regularly. But if we have to single out one cut, this one's a corker.

❾ COME IN ALONE from **LOVELESS**
The guitars are dense and uplifting, creating a wall of sound that would send Phil Spector running for cover.

❿ GLIDER from **GLIDER EP**
This instrumental B-side doesn't make for relaxing listening – the guitar loops grind and whine like dental drills looking for soft root pulp. Hypnotic and extreme.

Peter Buckley

My Boy Lollipop UK Reggae Hits

Britain's love affair with Jamaican music began well before Bob Marley. Despite the anti-reggae bias of the BBC at the time, all the records listed here made the UK Top Fifty. Others sold just as many, but not in the white-oriented shops that were used for compiling chart returns. All those below are available on *Young, Gifted And Black*.

❶ MY BOY LOLLIPOP **MILLIE**
Based on a 50s R&B song by Barbie Gray, Millie Small's worldwide hit was actually recorded in London, with a pop-ska arrangement by top Jamaican guitarist Ernest Ranglin.

❸ AL CAPONE PRINCE BUSTER

The gangster gimmick and sound effects gave the record novelty appeal, but it's the brilliant brass work – notably by tenor-sax player Val Bennett – that makes this an enduring classic.

❹ TRAIN TO SKAVILLE THE ETHIOPIANS

Despite the title, the suitably chugging rhythm is rock steady rather than ska. Apparently the horn riff derives from Johnny Cash's Ring Of Fire, of all things.

❺ ISRAELITES DESMOND DEKKER

This topped the charts in half a dozen countries, including South Africa, and reached #9 in the US – not bad for a song that compared the plight of Jamaicans "slaving for bread" to that of the Israelites in Egypt/Babylon!

❻ RETURN OF DJANGO THE UPSETTERS

Nominally inspired by a spaghetti western, this perennial party favourite turned out to be an instrumental version of a cover of Chris Kenner's R&B tune Sick And Tired. The sax solo is by the great Val Bennett.

❼ YOUNG, GIFTED AND BLACK BOB AND MARCIA

Sweetened with strings for its UK release, this pop-reggae version of the Nina Simone song remains a joyous affirmation of black potential.

❽ DOUBLE BARREL DAVE AND ANSELL COLLINS

Dave was Dave Barker, a fine falsetto singer who also specialized in vocal interjections, the keyboardist was Ansell Collins, and a young Sly Dunbar was on drums.

❾ EVERYTHING I OWN KEN BOOTHE

Boothe transforms David Gates' sensitive song about the death of his father into a timeless and super-soulful lovers' tune.

Neil Foxlee

N

Youssou N'Dour

The most famous Senegalese person ever, Youssou is also arguably the most successful African artist of the last quarter-century. He's had his ups and downs, but here are a few of the former.

❶ JALO from **ETOILE DE DAKAR VOLUME 1 – ABSA GUEYE**
Slow, slinky, understated gem recorded live in 1979 in a Dakar nightclub. As with much of Youssou's early work, the accompanying players and vocalists (especially the gruff voiced El Hadji Faye) are key to its appeal.

❸ THIAPA THIOLY from **ETOILE DE DAKAR VOLUME 2 – THIAPA THIOLY**
A restless twelve-minute epic, complete with wildly clattering tama (small talking drum), spidery guitar, Cuban timbales and chopping mbalax rhythms. Spicy stuff!

❹ IMMIGRÉS/BITIM REW from **IMMIGRÉS**
The breakthrough hit, which gained an international release in 1984. This is Youssou at his white-hot artistic peak, on a creative roller coaster ride. A real tour de force.

❺ RUBBERBAND MAN from **NELSON MANDELA**
Youssou puts a different spin on The Spinners' hit. A memorable and truly peculiar piece from a largely forgotten album.

❻ SEVEN SECONDS from **THE GUIDE (WOMMAT)**
Easily Youssou's biggest hit, this 1994 duet with Neneh Cherry addressed the insidious nature of racism and struck a chord worldwide.

❼ GUISS GUISS from **NE LA THIASS**
Proving he's not just a great lead singer, Youssou does ghostly chorus vocals on this hypnotic collaboration with dreadlocked protégé Cheikh Lô.

❽ BIRIMA from **JOKO**
The best track on a much-derided album. Does not feature any guest appearance by Sting, Peter Gabriel, or Wyclef Jean. Fortunately.

❾ MBËGGÉÉL NOONU LA ('BECAUSE LOVE'S LIKE THAT) from **NOTHING'S IN VAIN**
Back to mbalax basics, on this surging upbeat number from the album that signalled a return to form after a rather dull period from the mid-90s onwards.

❿ TIJANIYYA from **EGYPT**
A great cut from Youssou's most recently released album, celebrating his devotion to the Mouride faith. Actually recorded in 1999, but delayed by the anti-Islamic fall-out from 9/11.

Jon Lusk

Willie Nelson

These days Willie Nelson is an elder statesman, but he was the original country music rebel, growing his hair and turning against the slick Nashville establishment that made his name. The last decade has seen him on better form than ever – releasing great albums, working with big names from all genres, and with his trademark throaty quaver and studiedly artless guitar-picking never better.

❶ CRAZY from **CRAZY: THE DEMO SESSIONS**
Patsy Cline made this great, great song famous, but this 1960s demo version is still the best.

❷ BLUE EYES CRYIN' IN THE RAIN from **RED-HEADED STRANGER**
Willie's first country number #1, from the pared-back *Red-Headed Stranger* album.

❸ GETTING OVER YOU from **ACROSS THE BORDER**
Willie may be a duet tart, but this recording, with Bonnie Raitt, is one of his best, and a highlight of the 1992 album that initiated the last great blooming of his genius.

❹ ME AND PAUL
from **THE ESSENTIAL WILLIE NELSON**
This picaresque ballad details the adventures of Willie and his sidekick Paul English on the road in the late 1950s.

❺ NIGHTLIFE from **THE ESSENTIAL WILLIE NELSON**
Written on his way to a gig in Pasedena – "It ain't no good life, but it's my life".

❻ FUNNY HOW TIME SLIPS AWAY from **THE ESSENTIAL WILLIE NELSON**
Again, a bigger hit for someone else, but Willie's voice and the deliberately low-key arrangement of this version is the benchmark.

❼ YESTERDAY'S WINE from **THE ESSENTIAL WILLIE NELSON**
Crooning classic from the RCA years.

❽ BLOODY MARY MORNING from **THE ESSENTIAL WILLIE NELSON**
Still pop, still country, but closer to the narrative songs and spartan arrangements of later Willie.

❾ NEVER CARED FOR YOU from **TEATRO**
Willie's 60s classic updated with a Latin tilt – a perfect example of just how dynamic his output has been in recent years, both with regard to his own songs and others.

❿ SOMEBODY PICK UP MY PIECES from **TEATRO**
A late, great Willie song that draws a great performance from Emmylou Harris; and the band is totally on the button. A fine example of Willie's uneducated, snap-gut guitar style.

Martin Dunford

The Neville Bros & The Meters

The preternaturally funky Neville Brothers have been at the forefront of New Orleans music for more than fifty years, as solo artists and in bands like The Meters, as well as in the Neville Brothers group itself – still going strong with the addition of various offspring and other relations.

❶ MARDI GRAS MAMBO **THE HAWKETTS** from **TREACHEROUS**
Eldest brother Art Neville's debut offering, from 1954, remains a carnival classic.

❷ TELL IT LIKE IT IS **AARON NEVILLE** from **TREACHEROUS**
Brother Aaron's astonishingly pure voice propelled this enduring soul classic to the top of the US charts in 1967.

❸ CISSY STRUT **THE METERS** from **FUNKIFY YOUR LIFE**
Art's "other" band, The Meters, were at their funkifying best on this 1969 instrumental.

❹ MEET DE BOYS ON THE BATTLEFRONT **THE WILD TCHOUPITOULAS** from **THE WILD TCHOUPITOULAS**
Joining up with their uncle's Mardi Gras Indian tribe marked a return to their New Orleans roots for the Nevilles in 1976.

❺ BROTHER JOHN / IKO IKO **THE NEVILLE BROTHERS** from **FIYO ON THE BAYOU**
Throughout the 1980s, the Nevilles profitably mined a deep vein of New Orleans funk/R&B.

❻ PLEDGING MY LOVE **AARON NEVILLE** from **ORCHID IN THE STORM**
Aaron's transcendent tones were perfect for a 1986 EP of doo-wop covers.

❼ MICKEY MOUSE MARCH **AARON NEVILLE** from **STAY AWAKE**
Just to prove Aaron could move you to tears singing the phone book, he delivered this

show-stopping rendition on a 1988 album of Disney covers.

❽ DON'T KNOW MUCH AARON NEVILLE AND LINDA RONSTADT from **CRY LIKE A RAINSTORM**
The soaring duet that made Aaron an unlikely pop star once again in 1989.

❾ YELLOW MOON THE NEVILLE BROTHERS from **YELLOW MOON**
Also in 1989, the Nevilles made a superb comeback album with hip producer Daniel Lanois, of which this was the title track.

❿ AMAZING GRACE AARON NEVILLE from **GOSPEL ROOTS**
Aaron continues to bring the house down each year in the gospel tent at New Orleans' Jazzfest; this 2003 recording shows he's still at his peak.

Greg Ward

New Order

New Order were seen as the pretty pop butterfly that emerged from the dour chrysalis of Joy Division after Ian Curtis's suicide. Despite a back catalogue impressively peppered with limited releases, alternative mixes, and ultra rare imports from around the globe, they remain best loved as a singles band, knocking out hits for a chemically enhanced generation of new pop kids.

❶ TRUE FAITH from **SUBSTANCE 1987**
Available in a good half-dozen remixed flavours – all delicious, but with The Pet Shop Boys' at the top of the pile – this is the most divine evocation of the ecstasy experience.

❷ BIZARRE LOVE TRIANGLE from **BROTHERHOOD**
The soundtrack to some elegant nightclub where disco and electronica hook up for a few friendly drinks with rock'n'roll. Bernard's vocals take continual dives at the right note, occasionally scoring bang on target.

❸ THIEVES LIKE US from **THE BEST OF**
Masterful swirling keyboards and a slow funk groove make this track an unwitting tribute to The Human League's own brand of electro-lounge music.

❹ RUINED IN A DAY from **REPUBLIC**
Massive acoustic guitar chords establish a lush minor-key carpet where the finest of beats and keyboard swirls are displayed, and Bernard waxes melancholy.

❺ BLUE MONDAY from **POWER, CORRUPTION AND LIES**
Factory agreed to release this track in such a bewildering combination of remixes, deluxe sleeves and different formats that it lost money on every copy sold. Great tune though, no matter which version you load onto your player.

❻ PERFECT KISS from **LOW-LIFE**
Funky, in the way the chalk-white Mancunians have made their own, with superb right-on-the-money beats and bass working in harmony. A perfect piece of dance music.

❼ REGRET from **REPUBLIC**
There's joy, celebration and a bunch of pop hooks in this track that will always brighten the mood into a warm summery feeling.

❽ VANISHING POINT from **TECHNIQUE**
Not as obvious a tribute to the speed-thriller of the same title as Primal Scream's, but a good, heavy, asphalt-pounding driver of a tune.

❾ CONFUSION from **SUBSTANCE 1987**
The mix used in the *Blade* soundtrack comes ready mixed for an in-car rave, with beats to focus the mind on the white lines dividing the lanes of traffic. Wiser to stick with the plain-vanilla version that went into *Trainspotting*.

❿ EVERYTHING'S GONE GREEN from **SUBSTANCE 1987**
Written soon after Ian's departure from both Joy Division and this mortal coil, Everything's Gone Green sounds like a younger, less electronic version of Blue Monday.

Al Spicer

New Orleans R&B

When it comes to music, New Orleans has always been a law unto itself. During the 1960s in particular, the birthplace of jazz was home to some of the funkiest musicians on the planet, and the Crescent City produced a stream of insanely catchy R&B hits.

❶ BIG CHIEF – PART 2 PROFESSOR LONGHAIR from 'FESS: THE PROFESSOR LONGHAIR ANTHOLOGY

❷ MOTHER IN LAW ERNIE K-DOE from HIGHLIGHTS FROM CRESCENT CITY SOUL

❸ RULER OF MY HEART IRMA THOMAS from SATURDAY NIGHT FISH FRY – NEW ORLEANS FUNK & SOUL

❹ I LIKE IT LIKE THAT CHRIS KENNER from HIGHLIGHTS FROM CRESCENT CITY SOUL

❺ OOH-POO-PAH-DOO JESSIE HILL from HIGHLIGHTS FROM CRESCENT CITY SOUL

❻ IKO IKO THE DIXIE CUPS from HIGHLIGHTS FROM CRESCENT CITY SOUL

❼ EVERYTHING I DO GONH BE FUNKY LEE DORSEY From SATURDAY NIGHT FISH FRY – NEW ORLEANS FUNK & SOUL

❽ WHO SHOT THE LA LA? OLIVER MORGAN from GREATEST HITS

❾ SEA OF LOVE PHIL PHILLIPS from NEW ORLEANS PARTY CLASSICS

❿ BAREFOOTIN' ROBERT PARKER from HIGHLIGHTS FROM CRESCENT CITY SOUL

Greg Ward

New York rockers

The Big Apple has long been fuelled by the dialectic between glitter and grime and nowhere more so than in its rock. These are the ten records that best walk that perilous tightrope.

❶ HELIUM HEAD SIR LORD BALTIMORE from SIR LORD BALTIMORE (MERCURY, 1970)
The term "heavy metal" was coined to describe the sound of this Big Apple train wreck.

❷ WALK ON THE WILD SIDE LOU REED from TRANSFORMER
The definitive New York rock'n'roll record.

❸ PERSONALITY CRISIS NEW YORK DOLLS from NEW YORK DOLLS
They may have squawked in doltish New Yawkese, but they were palookas with wit, hooligans with a sense of irony, dandies with chutzpah.

❹ NEXT BIG THING THE DICTATORS from THE DICTATORS GO GIRL CRAZY!
What the Dolls would have sounded like if they wore wrestling gear instead of makeup.

❺ BLITZKRIEG BOP THE RAMONES from THE RAMONES
Let Malcolm McLaren and Johnny Rotten have their delusions – this is the first punk rock record.

❻ DON'T FEAR THE REAPER BLUE ÖYSTER CULT from AGENTS OF FORTUNE
Proof you don't have to wear corpse paint or have infernal croaking vocals to be truly scary.

❼ LOVE COMES IN SPURTS RICHARD HELL & THE VOIDOIDS from BLANK GENERATION
Legendary guitarist Robert Quine at his best.

⑧ NEW YORK GROOVE ACE FREHLEY
from **ACE FREHLEY**
Indomitable glitter disco stomp.

⑨ HOT WIRE MY HEART SONIC YOUTH from
SISTER
Blistering downtown guitar rave-up, even if the song was originally from San Francisco.

⑩ YÜ GUNG PUSSY GALORE from **SUGARSHIT SHARP**
New York scuzz punk dares to make a rap-prochement with hip-hop.

Peter Shapiro

Randy Newman

If you only know Randy Newman from quirky but fundamentally warm movie soundtracks such as *Toy Story*, the acerbic cynicism and sheer emotional nakedness of his classic albums might just blow you away.

① MAMA TOLD ME NOT TO COME from **12 SONGS**
Newman casts himself as the quintessential outsider; it's as though the Mr Jones who didn't know what was happening in Dylan's Ballad of a Thin Man gets to sing his own song.

② REDNECKS from **GOOD OLD BOYS**
Singing as a redneck and flaunting the "n" word in every chorus, Newman lambasts Southern racism and lazy Northern liberalism in equal measure.

③ LOUISIANA 1927 from **GOOD OLD BOYS**
A glorious, wistful account of the Mississippi flood of 1927.

④ BIRMINGHAM from **GOOD OLD BOYS**
A beautifully realized character sketch of blue-collar life in Alabama, with the delicious line "my daddy was a barber, a most unsightly man."

⑤ SAIL AWAY from **SAIL AWAY**
The stunning title song from Newman's finest album; a ballad extolling the joys of slavery, sung in Africa by a recruiter for the slave trade. As Newman put it "How else could I do it – slavery is bad?"

⑥ YOU CAN LEAVE YOUR HAT ON
from **SAIL AWAY**
Adopted as the bump-and-grind anthem of strippers everywhere, but never more sleazy than in its original form.

⑦ GOOD MORNING
from **GOOD OLD BOYS (REISSUE)**
Newman sings both voices in a duet between two estranged parents on their child's birthday; the father's malignant litany of "fuck offs" might explain why it was left off the original release.

⑧ GOD'S SONG (THAT'S WHY I LOVE MANKIND) from **SAIL AWAY**
In which God, backed by some elegiac piano, explains why he just can't help loving us: "I take from you your children, and you say 'how blessed are we'".

⑨ POLITICAL SCIENCE from **SAIL AWAY**
Newman at his most sardonic; granted that the rest of the world hates Americans, then "Let's drop the big one and see what happens".

⑩ MY LIFE IS GOOD from **TROUBLE IN PARADISE**
The definitive skewering of Tinseltown aggression, pretension and paranoia in the coke-fuelled LA of the early 1980s.

Greg Ward

Nirvana

Kurt Cobain's grunge pioneers still cast the longest shadow over today's indie outfits. Partly the music, partly the myth.

① RAPE ME from **IN UTERO**
Controversial, aggressive and innocent. Atop a typically simple and effective four-chord riff, loveable Cobain cries out to be abused.

② **SLIVER** from **INCESTICIDE**

A futile attempt by Cobain to leave his grand-parents' house is split between a whiny guitar as he pleads to go home and Chris Novoselic's upbeat bass riff as his grandparents attempt to cope with him.

③ **ABOUT A GIRL** from **BLEACH**

Bleach's only indication of Nirvana's progressively more poppy sound: the girl is probably Cobain's former lover Tracy, who complained that he never wrote about her.

④ **HEART-SHAPED BOX** from **IN UTERO**

A gentle arpeggiated riff sets the tone as Cobain writes about a child with cancer.

⑤ **FLOYD THE BARBER** from **BLEACH**

Typical of Nirvana's early metal sound, a trip to the hairdresser goes horribly wrong.

⑥ **WHERE DID YOU SLEEP LAST NIGHT?** from **MTV UNPLUGGED**

Cobain makes this Leadbelly cover his own, growling over clean acoustics.

⑦ **COME AS YOU ARE** from **NEVERMIND**

The bellowing guitar riff shrouds the song's mad undercurrent as Cobain tempts an old friend to pay one last visit.

⑧ **LITHIUM** from **NEVERMIND**

Novoselic's finest bassline echoes all the way through what has to be Nirvana's most optimistic song.

⑨ **THE MAN WHO SOLD THE WORLD** from **MTV UNPLUGGED**

Bowie's epic, strung out on acoustic and gawd knows what else.

⑩ **SMELLS LIKE TEEN SPIRIT** from **NEVERMIND**

The unmistakeable riff that brought Nirvana to the mainstream. If this is all you know, you'll love the songs above.

Ben Garfield

Stina Nordenstam

Swedish-born Stina Nordenstam has one of the most distinctive voices you'll hear: breathy, indefinably delicate, and at times so impenetrable you wonder if she really is singing in English. But the texture of her sound is sensational, and her writing is as atmospheric as anything in rock music.

① **I SEE YOU AGAIN**
from **AND SHE CLOSED HER EYES**

This gorgeous soundscape should hook you on Stina for life, with its opening of seductive obscurity, and a trumpet break to die for.

② **LITTLE STAR** from **AND SHE CLOSED HER EYES**

Little Star featured, memorably, in Baz Luhrmann's *Romeo + Juliet*. It begins with just guitar and voice, and builds to a huge sound, with Latin chant, before vanishing into thin air.

③ **SAILING** from **PEOPLE ARE STRANGE**

Yes – the Rod Stewart song. But you'd never believe it could be this great, reduced to a handful of piano chords, rain, and voice.

④ **PURPLE RAIN** from **PEOPLE ARE STRANGE**

Another wonderfully idiosyncratic reading on this album of covers. The Prince song is slowed down, stripped down, to strange beauty.

⑤ **CLOTHE YOURSELF FOR THE WIND** from **THIS IS STINA NORDENSTAM**

1 minute 35 seconds. And yet it feels like a whole movie. One of the great tracks on Stina's finest album to date.

⑥ **EVERYONE ELSE IN THE WORLD**
from **THIS IS STINA NORDENSTAM**

The saddest, most harmonious chorus – "Everyone else in the world would love me by now, would love me from day one, but not you". And the song needs hardly another word.

⓻ FROM CAYMAN ISLANDS WITH LOVE from **THE WORLD IS SAVED**

Much of Stina's recent work is pared down, with the voice carrying songs: this by contrast is almost orchestral, yet miraculously restrained.

⓼ THE END OF A LOVE AFFAIR from **THE WORLD IS SAVED**

"A scene from a movie," Stina sings, and doesn't it just feel that way: a song with this poise and power cries out for use in an indie film.

Mark Ellingham

Northern Soul

That strange phenomenon in which young men from the industrial wastelands of the north of England worshipped American soul records – the rarer and more obscure the better – with a zeal and piety that would shame anyone but the most devout religious followers. These ten records will make believers out of anyone.

❶ DO I LOVE YOU (INDEED I DO) FRANK WILSON from **NORTHERN SOUL CONNOISSEURS**

The most expensive record in the world, but also one of the best.

❷ PLEASE LET ME IN JJ BARNES from **THE GROOVESVEILLE MASTERS**

As impassioned as, and grittier than, anything released by Ric-Tic's more famous crosstown Detroit rivals.

❸ STORM WARNING THE VOLCANOS from **NORTHERN SOUL: ON THE PHILADELPHIA BEAT**

Woefully underrated early Philly soul, rescued by British soul fans.

❹ HIT & RUN ROSE BATISTE from **THE GOLDEN AGE OF NORTHERN SOUL**

Certainly more soulful and sassy than The Supremes.

❺ EXUS TREK LUTHER INGRAM ORCHESTRA from **HIPSHAKER**

Big, bold colours and dramatic arrangement make for a three-minute instrumental epic.

❻ (COME ON BE MY) SWEET DARLIN' JIMMY (SOUL) CLARKE from **THE GOLDEN AGE OF NORTHERN SOUL**

As uplifting and joyful as any record in the Northern soul canon.

❼ TAINTED LOVE GLORIA JONES from **THE WIGAN CASINO STORY: FINAL CHAPTER**

One of the better examples of dancing as exorcism.

❽ SLICED TOMATOES JUST BROTHERS from **THE GOLDEN TORCH STORY**

Sounds like it was recorded for a 60s' surf flick, but so groovy that it was sampled heavily by Fatboy Slim.

❾ KEEP ON KEEPING ON N.F. PORTER from **THE GOLDEN TORCH STORY**

The driving but ghostly arrangement keeps this track shrouded in mystery.

❿ IT REALLY HURTS ME GIRL THE CARSTAIRS from **DAZZLE: DISCO DELIGHTS FROM NEW YORK CITY**

The record that tore the Northern Soul scene asunder, but at least it's worth fighting over.

Peter Shapiro

Laura Nyro

Prophetically named after a song, Laura Nyro had talent to burn, and then some. Her late 60s and early 70s work is peerless and hugely influential. What a loss to music when her life was cut short in 1997.

❶ WEDDING BELL BLUES from **MORE THAN A NEW DISCOVERY (A.K.A. THE FIRST SONGS)**

Like several of Laura's best songs, this is probably most familiar from one of many anaemic covers, none of which can touch the original.

❷ AND WHEN I DIE from **MORE THAN A NEW DISCOVERY (A.K.A. THE FIRST SONGS)**

Laura wrote this memorable gospel-flavoured piece at the age of seventeen. Its maturity is a staggering testament to her imagination and "a certain folk wisdom that teenagers have", as she put it.

❸ STONED SOUL PICNIC from **ELI AND THE THIRTEENTH CONFESSION**

Captures the magical bohemian spirit of the 60s' counterculture like nothing else. Another song many tried to cover. Roy Ayers and The 5th Dimension, eat your heart out!

❹ TIMER from **ELI AND THE THIRTEENTH CONFESSION**

Breathtaking tempo changes, a crazily brilliant, free-ranging song structure and an extraordinary exuberance. This is Laura's Bohemian Rhapsody.

❺ NEW YORK TENDABERRY from **NEW YORK TENDABERRY**

Just Laura, accompanying herself on piano. The stark and soulful title cut from her third album, an oddly austere soundtrack to what she calls her "wild years".

❻ SAVE THE COUNTRY from **NEW YORK TENDABERRY**

Peace and love, Nyro style. This became an anthem for a generation. It's still painfully relevant.

❼ WHEN I WAS A FREEPORT AND YOU WERE THE MAIN DRAG from **CHRISTMAS AND THE BEADS OF SWEAT**

This album gave notice that the fiery creativity of Laura's muse was on the wane. But it still has a handful of songs to die for, like this one.

❽ MET HIM ON A SUNDAY/THE BELLS from **GONNA TAKE A MIRACLE**

In 1971, Laura teamed up with Labelle to revisit some of her favourite soul songs. That choice proved an inspired move, as this fantastic double-barrelled intro shows.

❾ YOU REALLY GOT A HOLD ON ME from **GONNA TAKE A MIRACLE**

Smokey Robinson must have been proud of such a radical reworking. Unlike lesser artists who piggybacked on the genius of her work, Laura added something unique to her covers.

❿ OH YEAH MAYBE BABY (THE HEEBIE JEEBIES) from **WALK THE DOG AND LIGHT THE LIGHT**

Laura's last studio album has some pretty resonant echoes of former glories, and this is the clearest of them all.

Jon Lusk

Oasis

At their peak, Oasis were the finest rock band in the UK, and they remain so steeped in their own myth that even at their worst they still seem to believe it. Recent recordings hint at a return to form, but in truth, it's only their earliest material that continues to sheeeee-iiiiiine.

❶ ROCK 'N' ROLL STAR from **DEFINITELY MAYBE**
A song so full of itself, reeking of testosterone, cheap aftershave and bottled lager, that it might offer you outside for a fight somewhere between the second and third verses.

❷ LIVE FOREVER from **DEFINITELY MAYBE**
The Gallagher brothers, when they meshed together in their earliest days of success, had the world by the balls, knew it, and could write songs about it too.

❸ SUPERSONIC from **DEFINITELY MAYBE**
The protagonist of this little gem believes himself king of the world for the short time that his wrapper of happiness lasts him.

❹ WONDERWALL from **(WHAT'S THE STORY) MORNING GLORY**
The hypnotically obscure and enigmatic lyrics place the loved one in the role of saviour surrounded by an impermeable barrier of shyness and tongue-tied adoration.

❺ DON'T LOOK BACK IN ANGER from **(WHAT'S THE STORY) MORNING GLORY**
Never more Lennon-esque than in the rambling first verses, Noel suddenly gives the game away in the chorus, turning it into a majestic love song.

❻ CHAMPAGNE SUPERNOVA from **(WHAT'S THE STORY) MORNING GLORY**
Sure, it's replete with the atmosphere of "you'll all be sorry when I'm dead, won't you", but even if it positively reeks of spoilt teenagers storming off to bed, there's a more mature, bitter taste under the surface

❼ I AM THE WALRUS (LIVE) from **THE MASTERPLAN**
The set closer that rewarded only the most appreciative of crowds. Anthemic, monumental, bloody loud and, of course, a tune The Beatles themselves never played to a live audience.

❽ MORNING GLORY from **(WHAT'S THE STORY) MORNING GLORY**
Despite its anthemic, 80s rock guitar run, this is a bleak slice of misery and jaundiced self-loathing.

❾ SHE'S ELECTRIC from **(WHAT'S THE STORY) MORNING GLORY**
Cheerful, harmless, pop rock of the instantly memorable yet totally meaningless jauntiness school.

❿ CAST NO SHADOW from **(WHAT'S THE STORY) MORNING GLORY**
The strongest, most musicianly track that the band's original line up ever recorded, and an excellent, well-crafted lyric of maturity and poignancy

Al Spicer

Sinéad O'Connor

Born to be a star? Sinead O'Connor has always had a difficult relationship with her fame. She may not want what she hasn't

Sinéad O'Connor's
Roots Reggae

It was Bob Marley's *War* that longtime reggae fan SINÉAD O'CONNOR was singing on American TV in 1992 when she notoriously tore up that picture of the Pope, an incident that came close to ending her career in the US. Yet she still loves the song enough to include a version of it on her latest album *Throw Down Your Arms*, recorded in Jamaica with reggae veterans Sly & Robbie. Unsurprisingly, it heads her list of her ten favourite roots reggae tracks...

❶ WAR BOB MARLEY AND THE WAILERS from RASTAMAN VIBRATION

❷ DOWNPRESSOR MAN PETER TOSH from EQUAL RIGHTS

❸ MARCUS GARVEY BURNING SPEAR from MARCUS GARVEY

❹ VAMPIRE LEE PERRY from ARKOLOGY

❺ Y MAS GAN THE ABYSSINIANS from SATTA MASAGANA

❻ PROPHET HAS ARISE ISRAEL VIBRATION from THE SAME SONG

❼ UNTOLD STORIES BUJU BANTON from TIL SHILOH

❽ CURLY LOCKS JUNIOR BYLES from BEST OF JUNIOR BYLES AND THE UPSETTERS

❾ THROW DOWN YOUR ARMS BURNING SPEAR from DRY AND HEAVY

❿ DOOR PEEP BURNING SPEAR from BURNING SPEAR

got, but what she has got is a voice with few equals.

❶ MANDINKA from THE LION AND THE COBRA
The first real hit – a driving rocker that owes little in the way of musical influence to its West African namesake.

❷ NOTHING COMPARES TO YOU from I DO NOT WANT WHAT I HAVEN'T GOT
Certainly, Prince's version doesn't compare to Sinéad's. This is the song that really propelled her into the mega-league – and not just because of that tear-jerking video.

❸ THE LAST DAY OF OUR ACQUAINTANCE from I DO NOT WANT WHAT I HAVEN'T GOT
Sinéad's songwriting and storytelling genius really came into their own on her second album, from which this is a key cut.

❹ BEWITCHED, BOTHERED AND BEWILDERED from AM I NOT YOUR GIRL?
Phil Ramone's extravagant orchestral arrangements never upstage Sinéad's delicate vocal delivery.

❺ IN THIS HEART from UNIVERSAL MOTHER
Staggeringly beautiful a cappella track featuring the backing vocals of the little known but wonderful Irish trio Voice Squad. But what a patchy album, otherwise!

❼ THIS IS TO MOTHER YOU from THE GOSPEL OAK
A typical cris de coeur on the theme of motherhood, with the line "what your own mother didn't do" hanging heavy in the air. The *Gospel Oak* EP should really have been an album

❽ THIS IS A REBEL SONG from I DO NOT WANT WHAT I HAVEN'T GOT
Perhaps the most perfect marriage of the political and the personal she's ever recorded.

Andrew Loog Oldham's
Bogota picks

When he parted company with the Rolling Stones in 1967, ANDREW LOOG OLDHAM was still only 23. He'd discovered them, managed and moulded them, and produced all their early hits, and in addition had set up the Immediate label where he had hits with such acts as The Small Faces and Chris Farlowe. In recent years, he has written two acclaimed volumes of autobiography and remains a sharp observer of the music scene. He sent us this list from Bogota, Columbia, where he now lives.

❶ RUBY BABY DION from BRONX BLUES: THE COLUMBIA RECORDINGS (1962-1965).

❷ SUMMERTIME BLUES EDDIE COCHRAN from MEMORIAL ALBUM

❸ BABY, I DON'T CARE ELVIS PRESLEY from ESSENTIAL ELVIS: THE FIRST MOVIES

❹ SUR LA ROUTE 66 EDDY MITCHELL from FRENCHY

❺ LA GOTA FRIA CARLOS VIVES from CLASICOS DE LA PROVINCIA

❻ LET'S SPEND THE NIGHT TOGETHER THE ROLLING STONES from BIG HITS (HIGH TIDE AND GREEN GRASS)

❼ HELLO GOODBYE THE BEATLES from MAGICAL MYSTERY TOUR

❽ BEYOND THE SEA BOBBY DARIN from THAT'S ALL

❾ CHRISTMAS (BABY PLEASE COME HOME) DARLENE LOVE from A CHRISTMAS GIFT FOR YOU FROM PHIL SPECTOR

❿ I HEARD IT THROUGH THE GRAPEVINE MARVIN GAYE from IN THE GROOVE

Like her best writing, this sounds like it could almost be a traditional song.

❾ RELEASE from COLLABORATIONS
This joint effort with Afro Celt Sound System is one of her better collaborations. If you really must jump up and down in a field, you could do a lot worse than this.

❿ NO MAN'S WOMAN from FAITH AND COURAGE
An uplifting pop rocker and a strong statement of independence – the soundtrack to Sinéad's controversial "coming out" in the media.

Jon Lusk

Will Oldham

Oldham's world view is peculiar, and his songs are strange and beautiful in equal measure. For well over a decade he has pedalled his alt. country creations under numerous monikers, most famously Bonnie 'Prince' Billy and the various incarnations of the "Palace" franchise. Oldham is a true American songwriter to be cherished.

❶ RIDING PALACE BROTHERS
from THERE IS NO-ONE WHAT WILL TAKE CARE OF YOU
Oldham's plaintive voice lazily sings a tale of incest and damnation over distant drums and a gently twanging guitar.

❷ HORSES PALACE MUSIC
from **LOST BLUES AND OTHER SONGS**

The vocal strains and cracks over mellow country atmospherics before the electrics kick in with an hilariously noodling solo.

❸ I SEE A DARKNESS BONNIE 'PRINCE' BILLY from **I SEE A DARKNESS**

He sure does. This woefully sung ballad pulls piano and bass together into a masterful, surprisingly uplifting composition.

❹ DEATH TO EVERYONE BONNIE 'PRINCE' BILLY from **I SEE A DARKNESS**

Console yourself, as Will does, in the fact that we're all gonna be worm food sooner or later.

❺ I AM A CINEMATOGRAPHER BONNIE 'PRINCE' BILLY from **SINGS GREATEST PALACE MUSIC**

A jaunty, full-country-band version of an old Palace number, from a great album of full-country-band versions of old Palace numbers.

❻ BEAST FOR THEE BONNIE 'PRINCE' BILLY & MATT SWEENEY from **SUPERWOLF**

This gorgeous track stands as Oldham's most memorable of recent times; the delicate guitar work skates along beneath a subtle lyric.

❼ YOU HAVE CUM IN YOUR HAIR AND YOUR DICK IS HANGING OUT PALACE from **ARISE THEREFORE**

With a title like that how could this song not be worth hearing?

❽ O LORD ARE YOU IN NEED? PALACE BROTHERS from **THERE IS NO-ONE WHAT WILL TAKE CARE OF YOU**

A simply strummed guitar and pendulum drum track waltz into the sunset as Oldham's lyric drifts downriver.

❾ COME IN PALACE BROTHERS from **LOST BLUES AND OTHER SONGS**

From a strangely disjointed beckoning at the song's opening, the instrumentation rises to accompany another quiet classic.

Peter Buckley

Olympian vocals

For some singers and their voices, bigger is invariably better. Hitting those high notes and trying to nail every other on the way and back has become their life's work, it seems. For that perseverance and their impressive vocal chords, we salute them. The Olympic medallists in warbling are:

GOLD

❶ EMOTIONS MARIAH CAREY from **EMOTIONS)**

Mariah's five-octave range is used to great effect here (were it seven octaves – as some enthusiasts believe – she'd have as many notes as a grand piano). Just don't put the kettle on while this is playing.

❷ MY HEART WILL GO ON CELINE DION from **LET'S TALK ABOUT LOVE**

The *Titanic* theme tune was a heartfelt weepie and the French-Canadian songbird delivered the lip-quivering goods, emoting to a staggering fifty million record buyers with every fibre of her being.

❸ I WILL ALWAYS LOVE YOU WHITNEY HOUSTON from **THE BODYGUARD**

After landing a starring role in *The Bodyguard*, Whitney's memorable theme tune revisited Dolly Parton's classic in spectacular fashion. She and her reverberations ended up stealing not only Kevin Costner's heart, but the whole show.

SILVER

❹ WUTHERING HEIGHTS KATE BUSH from **THE KICK INSIDE**

Kate Bush's update of Emily Brontë's novel won over a legion of adolescent fans. Even now, the damsel-in-distress's melodramatic vocals make men of a certain age tremble in admiration.

❺ BELIEVE CHER from **BELIEVE (WARNER, 1998)**

Cher's dazzling reinvention as a modern disco diva employed a welter of writers and technical jiggery-pokery. The "wibbly" bits of the chorus were distorted via a Vocoder, creating clubby electro-pop perfection.

BRONZE

⑥ HUMAN BEHAVIOUR BJÖRK from DEBUT
On Human Behaviour, Björk's staccato enunciation and alternately quiet and loud singing found the wide audience she deserved. She has since cornered the market in quirky power-yodelling.

⑦ LORELEI COCTEAU TWINS from TREASURE
Liz Fraser's ethereal warbling became a hallmark of The Cocteau Twins' unique oeuvre. On Lorelei, swirling guitars enhance her vocals to create an otherworldly sound.

Ed Wright

On the road

A classic road song doesn't just roll down some anonymous road, it should name the road, the route and point out the roadside attractions. We can make exceptions.

① ROUTE 66 BOBBY TROUP from KICKS ON 66
The Stones made it their own but whoever sings it – see our separate Route 66 list – this is the classic road song. Route 66 remains the place to get your kicks, anywhere from Chicago to LA, more than 2000 miles all the way.

② RUNNING ON EMPTY JACKSON BROWNE from RUNNING ON EMPTY
In 1965 Jackson Browne was seventeen and running up 101, the inland road between Los Angeles and San Francisco. He rolled down 295 out of Portland, Maine, on the same album.

③ DEEP WATER RICHARD CLAPTON from GOODBYE TIGER
There were plenty of road stories during Richard Clapton's late-70s moment in the sun, but sitting out on the Palm Beach Road (it runs north from Sydney), drunk and with a car that won't go, was a peak.

③ LAKE CHARLES LUCINDA WILLIAMS from CAR WHEELS ON A GRAVEL ROAD
Travelling down the Louisiana Highway, across Lake Ponchartrain, and in a yellow El Camino listening to Howlin' Wolf to boot, Williams turns a road trip into a tragedy.

④ THE LAST CHANCE TEXACO RICKIE LEE JONES from RICKIE LEE JONES
Tiptoeing along I-9, Rickie Lee Jones turns that last Texaco gas station into a metaphor for all our last chances.

⑤ VENTURA HIGHWAY AMERICA from HOMECOMING
It was in the sunshine and the days were longer; the real highway is the coast stretch of 101 out of Los Angeles, before it turns inland.

⑥ GRACELAND PAUL SIMON from GRACELAND
The actual road is never specified, but we know it follows the river, and since it's in the cradle of the civil war it's clearly in the Deep South, even before we're told it runs to Graceland.

⑦ ROLL ME AWAY BOB SEGER from THE DISTANCE
He's heading west, he's on a big motorcycle and when he picks up the girl who rides with him awhile he's twelve hours out of Mackinaw City in Michigan – what more do we need to know?

⑧ 24 HOURS FROM TULSA GENE PITNEY from THE VERY BEST OF GENE PITNEY
Apart from being a day's drive from Tulsa, Oklahoma, it's unclear where Gene met that temptress but this is a road song warning about motels, cafes and jukeboxes.

⑨ AUTOBAHN KRAFTWERK from AUTOBAHN
The German techno pioneers never name which autobahn they're on but no matter, "wir fahr'n fahr'n fahr'n auf der autobahn."

⑩ A13 TRUNK ROAD TO THE SEA BILLY BRAGG from THE ESSENTIAL BILLY BRAGG
OK, it's a piss take on Route 66, but why not take that road that "starts down in Wapping"?

Tony Wheeler

The Orb

The Orb provided the interface at which prog rock met ambient music: the chill out zone, where whacked-out ravers – still grinning but too messed up to dance attractively – sat their twitching spines down for some recuperation time.

❶ POMME FRITZ (MEAT 'N' VEG) from **U. F. OFF**
At its best, The Orb's music will calm you down, take your mind off your problems and give you a gurgling keyboard sound to play with and put that smile back on your face.

❷ BLUE ROOM from **U. F. OFF**
Too beat-drenched to hold its own in the chill-out room, this is the track that grabs you by the lapel and leads you back to the dancefloor for one more cheeky half and a bit of a dance.

❸ HUGE EVER GROWING PULSATING BRAIN ... from **ADVENTURES BEYOND THE ULTRAWORLD**
Masterful, like Pink Floyd for a new generation taking different drugs. Classy, involved and deeply interesting music that makes you want to sit down, skin up and really think about things.

❹ LITTLE FLUFFY CLOUDS from **ADVENTURES BEYOND THE ULTRAWORLD**
Sampling Rickie Lee Jones reminiscing about her early life somewhere on a distant planet. This is always a trip, and a real floor filler.

❺ OOBE from **UFORB**
This is The Orb at the meatier end of the spectrum. A harmless, unpretentious, four-to-the-floor dance hall stomper.

❻ PERPETUAL DAWN from **ADVENTURES BEYOND THE ULTRAWORLD**
Just plain silly. Vulgar mouth noises made by a man with the voice of a 1950s radio presenter, back-to-basics beats and totally irresistible.

❼ SPANISH CASTLES IN SPACE from **ADVENTURES BEYOND THE ULTRAWORLD**
Alex Patterson and the studio working together as one to show just how psychedelic a track can be.

❽ TOWERS OF DUB from **UFORB**
Youth (ex-Killing Joke) made his contribution to the album most felt on this track, reflecting both his massive bass and taste for dub.

❾ TOXYGENE from **ORBLIVION**
Late period Orb single, which came as a double CD set of endless remixes. For once, however, they're all worth more than a single spin.

❿ U. F. ORB from **UFORB (ISLAND; 1996)**
Immense low-frequency throbbing from Youth and a swirl of highly tweaked computer generated keyboard effects from Alex.

Al Spicer

Roy Orbison

The high priest of romantic paranoia and rock's first monarch of miserablism, whose soaring songs were as dark as his shades. He has even been compared to John Dowland by no less a luminary than Harrison Birtwistle.

❶ IN DREAMS from **ALL TIME GREATEST HITS**
If Roy Orbison hadn't existed, David Lynch would have had to invent him. This song, which haunts Lynch's *Blue Velvet*, is one of rock and roll's great dream songs.

❷ SHE'S A MYSTERY TO ME from **MYSTERY GIRL**
Written by Bono, this is the greatest work of the Big O's 80s comeback and one of his greatest vocal performances, ending with a flourish that recalls his soaring climax to Crying.

❸ BLUE BAYOU from **ALL TIME GREATEST HITS**
Another classic dream song, the product of Orbison's productive partnership with Joe Melson. Almost as familiar through the cover

versions – by Linda Ronstadt and Mireille Mathieu – as the original.

❹ OH, PRETTY WOMAN
from ALL TIME GREATEST HITS

A strutting, rocking, rollicking tale of a man who turns a pretty woman's head on the street. Since 1964, men on streets all over the world have replayed this scenario.

❺ RUNNING SCARED
from ALL TIME GREATEST HITS

A paranoid bolero, with a Mexican ambience, and a twist ending – to his own obvious disbelief, Roy gets the girl. Marvellous.

❻ IT'S OVER from ALL TIME GREATEST HITS

You get the full Orbison *sturm und drang* here: lonely sunsets, falling stars, weeping rainbows and betrayal. Impassioned and overblown, this is a truly chilling ballad, as the wronged lover faces a life sentence of lovelessness.

❼ BLUE ANGEL from ALL TIME GREATEST HITS

Though this was initially dismissed as too much of a clone of Only The Lonely, the passages where Roy wordlessly sympathizes with his blue angel's heartbreak are simply out of this world.

❽ CRYING from ALL TIME GREATEST HITS

An iconic song of heartache, this is based on a real encounter between Orbison and an old flame.

❾ YOU GOT IT from MYSTERY GIRL

A late, insistent, celebration of love, almost a companion piece to Oh, Pretty Woman, which shows that, even in the late 80s, the Big O still had, as Barry Gibb said, "the voice of God".

❿ DANNY BOY from MEMPHIS

Almost everybody has recorded this tear-jerking Irish folk standard, but Orbison's cover is exceptionally powerful.

Paul Simpson

Outkast

Big Boi and Dre, two Georgia rapper-producers, blended musical idioms like no one since Prince and gave the Dirty South a soul New Orleans' thugs lacked.

❶ HEY YA from THE LOVE BELOW/SPEAKERBOX

"Shake it like a Polaroid picture" commands Dre. The world obliged. The best party tune of the twenty-first century? Easy.

❷ PLAYERS BALL from SOUTHERNPLAYALISTICA DILLACMUZIK

A celebration of a pimps' and hustlers' convention. Ghetto fabulous? This is it.

❸ ROSA PARKS from AQUEMINI

Civil Rights icons are rarely celebrated in hip-hop. Perhaps understandably: Rosa Parks sued them for using her name!

❹ MS JACKSON from STANKONIA

Over an organ drone and staccato drum pattern, Dre and BB celebrate their babies while asking for peace from the mamas.

❺ SO FRESH, SO CLEAN from STANKONIA

"We are the coolest motherfuckers on the planet/the sky is fallin', aint no need to panic" raps Big Boi in this slow jam hymn to their fine selves

❻ SOUTHERNPLAYALISTICADILLACMUZIK
from SOUTHERNPLAYALISTICADILLACMUZIK

This early track saw Outkast mouthing gangsta clichés, yet the groove, languid as an Atlanta summer afternoon, means ya gotta love it.

❼ ELEVATORS (ME & YOU) from ATLIENS

A 1996 reflection on early days. They're raking green, yeah, but there's a long way to go says Dre. Some understatement.

❽ SPOTTIEOTTIEDOPALISICIOUS from AQUEMINI

Rough gigs, falling in love, raising a daughter and failing a Post Office drug test are among the concerns tackled here.

❾ THE WHOLE WORLD from BIG BOI & DRE
PRESENT… OUTKAST
Outkast celebrate their own success. The
closest they've come to a conventional hip-
hop tune.

❿ CRUMBLIN' ERB from SOUTHERNPLAYALISTIC
ADILLACMUZIK
A hymn to getting high. Message: smoking
herb is better than doing drive-bys.

Garth Cartwright

Outlaw Country

"Outlaw Country" took its name from
Waylon Jennings' 1972 album *Ladies Love
Outlaws* and soon came to apply to a host
of artists who refused to play the Nashville
game. Partly it was about image, but the
movement's main objective was creative
control for the artists and songwriters who
came to be associated with it. Here are ten
who refused to toe the line…

❶ BLUE EYES CRYIN' IN THE RAIN WILLIE
NELSON from RED HEADED STRANGER
So stripped-down and low key that at first
Columbia refused to release the album, this
song eventually gave Willie his first #1.

❷ ARE YOU SURE HANK DONE IT THIS WAY?
WAYLON JENNINGS from DREAMING MY DREAMS
The song that summed up the frustration with
how Nashville had lost touch with its roots.

❸ PANCHO AND LEFTY TOWNES VAN ZANDT from
THE LATE, GREAT TOWNES VAN ZANDT
More than any of the outlaws, Townes lived the
life he made in song and Willie Nelson, Merle
Haggard and Emmylou Harris all covered this
classic.

❹ SOLD AMERICAN TOMPALL GLASER
from CHARLIE
A fantastic version of Kinky Friedman's
bottomed-out cowboy lament from the least

celebrated of the quartet who recorded the
classic *Wanted! The Outlaws* album.

❺ YOU MEAN TO SAY JESSI COLTER
from WANTED! THE OUTLAWS
Waylon's wife and one of the few female
"outlaws", she achieved immortality by appear-
ing on *Wanted! The Outlaws* alongside with
Waylon, Willie and Tompall.

❻ ME AND BOBBY MGEE KRIS KRISTOFFERSON
from ME AND BOBBY MCGEE
Covered by everyone from Janis Joplin to The
Grateful Dead, the song that was the bridge
between Hank Williams and Bob Dylan.

❼ LONGHAIRED REDNECK DAVID ALLAN COE
from LONGHAIRED REDNECK
An outlaw anthem if ever there was one, from
the man whose other songs included Willie,
Waylon And Me and Take This Job And Shove
It.

❽ HONKY TONK HEROES BILLIE JOE SHAVER from
HONKY TONK HEROES
Waylon recorded an entire album of his songs,
of which this was the title track. But in addition
to being a great songwriter, Shaver was a fine
performer in his own right.

❾ DESPERADOS WAITING FOR A TRAIN GUY
CLARK from OLD NO 1
A Texas compadre of Townes Van Zandt, this is
the best-known of his eloquent country-folk
narratives.

**❿ UP AGAINST THE WALL, REDNECK
MOTHER** JERRY JEFF WALKER from VIVA TERLINGUA
Although Jerry Jeff wrote Mr Bojangles, this
classic Texas bar-room sing-along was penned
for him by Ray Wylie Hubbard.

Nigel Williamson

Oz Rock

Australia has long harboured a high-
energy rock scene to rival any in the world.
Here are eight of the most visceral rockers

from down under, along with two wild cards to prove that they're not all he-man surfer dudes.

❶ YOU'RE DRIVING ME INSANE THE MISSING LINKS from **THE MISSING LINKS**
Totally unhinged maximum R&B.

❷ FRIDAY ON MY MIND THE EASYBEATS from **FRIDAY ON MY MIND**
Even better than Loverboy's Working For The Weekend.

❸ (I'M) STRANDED THE SAINTS from **I'M STRANDED**
Snarl, groove, venom, hooks, momentum – is this the best rock record ever?

❹ NEW RACE RADIO BIRDMAN from **RADIOS APPEAR**
The faint right-wing gang overtones are a bit scary, but my god does this move.

❺ WILD WEEKEND PSYCHO SURGEONS from **DO THE POP!**
Don't let the hint of melody at the beginning fool you, this is pure Neanderthal stomp.

❻ DO THAT DANCE PRIMITIVE CALCULATORS from **PRIMITIVE CALCULATORS**
Spiky, agitated post-punk with electronics that owe a large debt to Cabaret Voltaire.

❼ 24 HOURS (SOS) THE CELIBATE RIFLES from **SIDEROXYLON**
An awesome combination of jingle-jangle and high voltage rifferama.

❽ BE MY GURU HOODOO GURUS from **STONE AGE ROMEOS**
Big, dumb and stoopid – perfect trashy surfer rock.

❾ CATTLE AND CANE THE GO-BETWEENS from **BEFORE HOLLYWOOD**
Gorgeous melancholia from Oz's greatest troubadours.

❿ BYE BYE GIRL HARD-ONS from **DO THE POP!**
Two minutes of thrashy perfection.

Peter Shapiro

Pacifica

… or Polynesian music, if you like. And that includes New Zealand, even though it's hardly tropical, because so many artists have made their homes there. See also the Hawaii playlist.

❶ FRENCH LETTER HERBS
from **LISTEN: THE VERY BEST OF**
1983's defining moment for this multicultural Pacific Island/Maori group, telling French nuclear testers to get out of the Pacific in no uncertain terms.

❷ ALOHA MEANS I LOVE YOU TAU MOE FAMILY WITH BOB BROZMAN from **THE TAU MOE FAMILY WITH BOB BROZMAN**
The globe-trotting family band with hyperactive hippy Brozman in tow. A truly charming collaboration.

❸ HAWAI'I '78 INTRODUCTION ISRAEL KAMAKAWIWO 'OLE from **FACING FUTURE**
Bittersweet recollections of family life from "Iz", the unlikely giant of Hawaiian music, who died in 1997 at the age of 38.

❹ HOW BIZARRE OMC from **HOW BIZARRE**
A worldwide hit by the Otara Millionaires Club, aka Pauly Fuemana. You couldn't avoid this song in 1996, but where is he now?

❺ THE DAVID TUA THEME BROTHER D
from **URBAN PACIFIKA: PIONEERS OF A PACIFIKAN FRONTIER**
Crunching hip-hop tribute to Samoa's diminu-

tive boxing star: "He packs a punch … He made the big nations aware of little islands."

❻ MIHI TUATAHI WAI from **WAI 100%**
Innovative Maori music for the new millennium, by singer Mina Ripia and programmer/producer Maaka McGregor.

❼ MISTY FREQUENCIES CHE FU from **NAVIGATOR**
A smoother-than-satin vocal treat by the leading light of Pacific/Kiwi soul, hip-hop and R&B…Che Fu is a hard man to pigeonhole!

❽ FOR THE PEOPLE NESIAN MYSTIK
from **POLYSATURATED**
Joyful, upbeat Pacific R&B by a boy band with a difference.

❾ LAKILUA TE VAKA from **TUTUKI**
Chunky, rootsy log-drums from Pan-Polynesian group who are worldwide festival favourites.

❿ HOPE FAT FREDDY'S DROP
from **BASED ON A TRUE STORY**
Deeply soulful, urban Pacific reggae grooves, featuring the amazing velvet vocals of Dallas Tamaira, aka Joe Dukie. This seven-piece are currently the hottest thing in New Zealand.

Jon Lusk

Paisley underground

This loose amalgamation of early-80s Californian bands were seen as a "movement" thanks to their allegiance to late-60s artists like Pink Floyd, Jimi Hendrix and Neil Young – plus their sartorial tendencies. They reinvigorated underground rock just as commercial music reached its new-wave nadir.

❶ DAYS OF WINE AND ROSES DREAM SYNDICATE from **DAYS OF WINE AND ROSES**
This potent blast starts at a frenetic clip with

Dennis Duck's pounding drums, and ends as lead guitarist Karl Precoda rings every last jolt of electricity out of the air.

❷ THIS CAN'T BE TODAY RAIN PARADE
from **EMERGENCY THIRD RAIL POWER TRIP**

A rare up-tempo song from Rain Parade, who epitomized the gentler end of the scene, with a keyboard-driven sound that was a dead ringer for early-70s Pink Floyd.

❸ HE'S GOT A SECRET THE BANGLES
from **ALL OVER THE PLACE**

This compelling song from the debut album by The Bangles is built around pile-driving power chords from guitarist Vicki Peterson.

❹ NARCOLEPSY GREEN ON RED
from **GRAVITY TALKS**

Riding the mid-60s garage sound hard, this nugget incorporates swelling organ and chiming rhythm guitar in its hypnotic pallet.

❺ HOLOCAUST RAINY DAY from **RAINY DAY**

Big Star tune, drawn from loose-knit supergroup Rainy Day's 1984 covers album, and sung by Kendra Smith of The Dream Syndicate.

❻ FELL FROM THE SUN SMITH, ROBACK AND MITCHELL from **FELL FROM THE SUN**

After leaving The Dream Syndicate, Kendra Smith teamed up with David Roback of The Rain Parade and drummer Keith Mitchell. When Smith left, they morphed into Mazzy Star.

❼ ROCKET MACHINE OPAL
from **HAPPY NIGHTMARE BABY**

This grinding, chugging T-Rex pastiche opened Opal's debut album.

❽ JET FIGHTER THE THREE O'CLOCK
from **SIXTEEN TAMBOURINES**

Bassist/vocalist Michael Quercio's helium-pitched vocals carry this soaring song from the L.A. band most wed to mid-60's soft-rock.

❾ TOO CLOSE TO THE LIGHT THE LONG RYDERS
from **NATIVE SONS**

A sweetly melodic song from hard-core Byrds fanatics The Long Ryders.

❿ SOME VELVET MORNING THIN WHITE ROPE
from **WHEN WORLDS COLLIDE**

An intense version of Lee Hazlewood's totally strange 1968 composition.

Butch Lazorchak

Charlie Parker

Every jazz musician who came after Charlie Parker (1920–55) was influenced by him – even in the (rather unlikely) event they didn't know him. Dating from the era of 78 rpm singles and largely pre hi-fi, his music enormously repays listening through the crackles. All the following are drawn from Proper's 4CD boxed set, *Boss Bird*.

❶ KO-KO

An astonishing virtuoso display from the first real be-bop recording session, in 1945. Parker soars over the complex chords with a freedom and audacity then quite new to jazz.

❷ NIGHT IN TUNISIA

Based on a bass riff, built around two exotic chords and ending on a fade, Gillespie's 1946 composition was a first in many ways. Parker's vertiginous four-bar solo-break still thrills, and every solo which follows is a classic.

❸ KLACTOVEESEDSTENE

The first of two takes of this tune, from 1947. Parker reaches new levels of abstraction, building a solo out of a jigsaw of motifs while drummer Max Roach pushes him on.

❹ EMBRACEABLE YOU

Again producing his masterpiece on the first of two 1947 takes, Parker recomposes Gershwin's tune completely, working from a limpid five-note phrase into a breathtaking solo.

❺ BIRD OF PARADISE

Recorded on the same day as Embraceable You, and featuring a solo so inspired and logical that it has often been transcribed and played as a melody in its own right.

6 PARKER'S MOOD

Parker was always a great blues player, and this 1948 track is one of his best – a slow Kansas City blues framed by a haunting minor-key cry on the alto.

7 JUST FRIENDS

1949's "with strings" sessions still divide fans – but once you get used to the sweet-and-sour sound, you can hear one of Bird's great solos.

8 BLUE'N'BOOGIE

The live 1951 reunion of Bird, Dizzy and pianist Bud Powell is less well known than the Massey Hall concert of a couple of years later, though it produced better music.

9 FINE AND DANDY

Most live Parker "airshots" offer poor recording quality; this remarkably clear 1953 one shows the altoist fronting an excellent big band.

10 NOW'S THE TIME

Revisiting one of his 1945 blues riffs in 1953, Parker sounds like his old self. From now on, until his death less than two years later, it was all downhill.

Alex Webb

Gram Parsons

In a tragically short but intense career, stretching from The International Submarine Band, via The Byrds, The Flying Burrito Brothers and even The Rolling Stones to his own beautiful, ethereal solo records, and ended by his untimely death in 1973, Gram Parsons can take credit as the leading progenitor of country rock.

1 SHE from GP

Parsons' voice is at his most poignant in this gently insistent examination of his quasi-Christian beliefs.

2 HOT BURRITO #1
from THE GILDED PALACE OF SIN

A choked and vulnerable ballad that shows off Gram's voice to great effect.

3 A SONG FOR YOU from GP

The sparse arrangement of this gospel-ish song perfectly offsets Gram's throaty quaver.

4 RETURN OF THE GRIEVOUS ANGEL
from GRIEVOUS ANGEL

An acid-driven road movie of a song, full of sadness for brief encounters and long lost soulmates.

5 $1000 WEDDING from GRIEVOUS ANGEL

Gram's voice soars sublimely with Emmylou Harris's on this bitter lament.

6 IN MY HOUR OF DARKNESS
from GRIEVOUS ANGEL

A medium-tempo country lament for the deaths of three close friends. Great playing, and gorgeous singing from Emmylou.

7 HICKORY WIND
from SWEETHEART OF THE RODEO

Parsons' ode to his southern roots, and a general commentary on good old American lonesomeness.

8 LOVE HURTS from GRIEVOUS ANGEL

Not a Parsons song, but a great one, showcasing Gram and Emmylou Harris at their very best.

9 DARK END OF THE STREET
from THE GILDED PALACE OF SIN

The Flying Burritos Brothers' yearning interpretation of a southern soul classic – perhaps the ultimate evocation of Parsons' "Cosmic American Music".

10 DO YOU KNOW HOW IT FEELS TO BE LONESOME? from THE GILDED PALACE OF SIN

Originally cut for *Safe At Home*, Gram's first venture with The International Submarine Band, and reprised in this slicker version with the Flying Burritos.

Martin Dunford

Dolly Parton

Larger than life but the real deal, country music has never seen anything quite like Dolly Parton. Singer, songwriter, country traditionalist and pop crossover superstar, she was never a dumb blonde.

❶ COAT OF MANY COLORS
from **COAT OF MANY COLORS**
Moving autobiographical account of Dolly's dirt-poor upbringing in the Smokey Mountains.

❷ JUST BECAUSE I'M A WOMAN
from **JUST BECAUSE I'M A WOMAN**
Despite her male-pleasing image ("It costs a lot of money to make me look this cheap", she once cracked), there was always a strong streak of feminism to her songs…

❸ DADDY WAS AN OLD TIME PREACHER MAN from **ONCE MORE**
Among the finest of the many duets Dolly recorded with Porter Wagoner.

❹ JOLENE from **JOLENE**
Her first big hit after splitting from Porter had to be something special. And it was.

❺ I WILL ALWAYS LOVE YOU from **JOLENE**
Forget Whitney Houston. Dolly wrote this as a tribute to Wagoner, who took her desertion from his show as a personal betrayal.

❻ MY TENNESSEE MOUNTAIN HOME from **MY TENNESSEE MOUNTAIN HOME**
Dolly was never better than when singing about her Appalachian roots…

❼ HERE YOU COME AGAIN from **HERE YOU COME AGAIN**
The one that crossed her over from country into the pop charts.

❽ 9 TO 5 from **9 TO 5 AND ODD JOBS**
The infectious title song written for the 1980 film of the same name.

❾ MULE SKINNER BLUES from **THE ESSENTIAL DOLLY PARTON**
Dolly's first solo hit in 1970 was this vivacious interpretation of Jimmie Rodgers' classic song.

❿ THOSE MEMORIES OF YOU from **TRIO**
Magnificent, mournful bluegrass from a 1987 album with Emmylou Harris and Linda Ronstadt.

Nigel Williamson

Pavement

College rockers supreme, Stephen Malkmus and Scott "Spiral Stairs" Kannenberg became reluctant leaders of the alt:rock school of indie music in the 90s. Their band Pavement created quirky beauty and elegance from the ugliest and most mismatched of musical components. Funny, deadpan and unique.

❶ FROM NOW ON
from **WESTING (BY MUSKET AND SEXTANT)**
Pavement's earliest declaration of how they planned to take on the world and win.

❷ ANGEL CARVER BLUES/MELLOW JAZZ DOCENT from **WESTING (BY MUSKET AND SEXTANT)**
Epic, twisted mountain pathway of a tune that leads you blindly on until boom, revelation comes as you reach the summit.

❸ SUMMER BABE from **SLANTED AND ENCHANTED**
An early crowd pleaser, encouraging fans to join in and help out with the harmonizing.

❹ CUT YOUR HAIR
from **CROOKED RAIN, CROOKED RAIN**
Comparatively straightforward rocker with the anthemic "No Big Hair" hook.

❺ HIT THE PLANE DOWN
from **CROOKED RAIN, CROOKED RAIN**
Scott goes all Mark E. Smith, one last, magnificent time.

Stephen Malkmus
Esoterica

The main man with Pavement, one of America's most influential alternative rock acts of the 90s, STEPHEN MALKMUS created a suitably esoteric and alternative playlist for us, right down to opting for just the nine numbers. Less is the new more.

❶ DRIFTING LEIGH STEPHENS
from **RED WEATHER**

❷ SWEETIES THE HANDSOME BEASTS
from **THE BEASTIALITY**

❸ SPARE CHAYNGE JEFFERSON AIRPLANE
from **AFTER BATHING AT BAXTERS**

❹ KEEP ON TRYING ENGLISH GYPSY
from **ENGLISH GYPSY**

❺ BUY CHISWICK RECORDS RADIO STARS
from **SONGS FOR SWINGING LOVERS**

❻ THE ROYAL PLAN ABNER JAY
from **SWANNEE WATER AND COCAINE BLUES**

❼ PREPARE TO LIVE SECTION 25
from **FROM THE HIP**

❽ BEAT THE REAPER LAURIE STYVERS
from **SPILT MILK**

❾ OUR SONG STRAY from **STRAY**

❻ RANGE LIFE from **CROOKED RAIN, CROOKED RAIN**
Laid-back musings on the life of an averagely successful college band – the tours, the gigs, the petty rivalries – to a gentle acoustic setting.

❼ RATTLED BY THE RUSH from **WOWEE ZOWEE**
A four-minute exploration of the inside of Stephen's brain, beautifully illustrated with odd-job guitars and deadpan delivery.

❽ STEREO from **BRIGHTEN THE CORNERS**
The first single from this set, an art-rock jam guaranteed never to bother the charts.

❾ THE HEXX from **TERROR TWILIGHT**
While Pavement never quite evolved away from their roots as garage band and studio kids, by now they could turn small ideas into major workouts like this ominous heavy rocker.

❿ FLUX=RAD from **WOWEE ZOWEE**
Pavement's take on music to cruise by – groovy singalong lyrics and, hey, it's a toe-tapper!

Al Spicer

Peel faves

Long-standing champion of the weird and wonderful in modern music, DJ John Peel made the occasional bad choice, but when he threw his weight behind an act, you could guarantee it was something special. Though Peelie's gone, his work will live on, as long as there are "Peel Sessions" tapes to be unearthed and reissued.

❶ INDUSTRIAL ESTATE THE FALL
from **COMPLETE PEEL SESSIONS**
John claimed The Fall set a yardstick by which all other acts had to be judged, they played so many Peel sessions that the collection clocks in at six tightly packed CDs. This track captures their spiky, brilliant, enigmatic appeal.

❷ TEENAGE KICKS THE UNDERTONES
from **THE BEST OF**
The best single ever, according to the great man, recorded on zero budget by what was

then the only punk band in Ireland.

❸ IRK THE PURISTS HALF MAN HALF BISCUIT
from **TROUBLE OVER BRIDGEWATER**
Permanently funny, shambling and amateurish, no matter how dour the delivery, HMHB were the consummate Peel band. This is by several lengths their best track.

❹ DOWN DOWN STATUS QUO from **XS ALL AREAS**
Controversial, quirky and possibly the only Quo track in this entire volume, Down Down was John's "if all else fails" dancefloor filler. From student discos to the Reading Festival, Peel exhorted the crowds to get down, deeper and down. Apparently it never failed.

❺ SURE 'NUFF & YES I DO CAPTAIN BEEFHEART
& THE MAGIC BAND from **SAFE AS MILK**
John loved the Captain and would regularly play his 1968 live rerecording of this track, despite its appalling quality.

❻ 19 HEADACHES AUTECHRE
from **THE PEEL SESSIONS VOL.2**
Clearing the mental palate like sandpaper on a furred tongue, Autechre's aural assaults were a frequent delight on John's shows. This suitably titled track pokes into all the electro-noise closets and rattles the contents of our pleasure.

❼ YOU DON'T SEND ME BELLE AND SEBASTIAN
from **DEAR CATASTROPHE WAITRESS**
Nothing if not eclectic in his musical tastes, our hero had his moments of gentle whimsy, as shown by this late slice of B&S.

❽ PAWN SHOPPE HEART THE VON BONDIES from
LET PAWN SHOPPE HEART
Detroit noise-mongers like the Von Bondies, with their bad attitude and dirty habits, were meat and drink to John. Blast your brains with this slice of raw power.

❾ MR BLUE SKY THE DELGADOS
from **ALL YOU NEED IS HATE**
The none-more-indie Glasgow miserablists performed this ELO cover on the show, but this version has more gloss and finesse.

❿ Y CONTROL THE YEAH YEAH YEAHS
from **FEVER TO TELL** V
To the end of his life, John Peel championed the over-driven, raw end of the rock'n'roll circus. Finishing this list with The Yeah Yeah Yeah's loudest, most distorted and glorious track to date seems only right.

Al Spicer

Art Pepper

Altoist par excellence Art Pepper made the transition from California cool cat to harrowing balladeer via a lifetime of heroin addiction.

❶ SUZY THE POODLE from **SURF RIDE**
Bop, west coast-style; Pepper comes on like a slick, sun-tanned Charlie Parker on his intricate 1952 variation on the chord sequence of Indiana.

❷ BEGIN THE BEGUINE from **ART OF PEPPER**
From a splendid series of Blue Note albums made after returning from prison on narcotics charges, this charged, hypnotic 1957 performance proved he'd lost none of his sparkle.

❸ IMAGINATION
from **MEETS THE RHYTHM SECTION**
Unprepared, undernourished and without a decent instrument, Pepper wings it in 1957 with Miles's rhythm section, and triumphs with playing of spirit and surprise.

❹ SHAW 'NUFF from **MODERN JAZZ CLASSICS**
The 1959 album featured beautifully hip, rich arrangements for an eleven-piece band; at the centre an insouciantly brilliant Pepper dances through Gillespie's fiendish bop flagwaver.

❺ TEARS INSIDE from **SMACK UP**
A rigorous reading of the Ornette Coleman tune from a 1960 session featuring some particularly limber work from pianist Pete Jolly.

⑥ GONE WITH THE WIND from **INTENSITY**

This 1960 collection of ballads and standards was the last in a tremendous series of albums for Contemporary. The smooth, west coast approach was already transforming into something more rugged and ragged.

⑦ THE SUMMER KNOWS from **THE TRIP**

By 1975, the long, hard haul back into shape plus the influence of Coltrane had made its impact on Pepper, but his ballads – like this bruised, sobbing reading of the Michel Legrand tune – were a compelling experience.

⑧ BLUE BOSSA from **SAN FRANCISCO SAMBA**

Pepper's late-period passion and intensity was particularly potent on Latin grooves as on this Kenny Dorham classic, recorded live in 1977.

⑨ WHEN THE SUN COMES OUT from **WINTER MOON**

Not until 1980 did Pepper get to rhapsodize over a string orchestra. It was worth the wait, with Bill Holman providing the arrangements and Pepper playing like a man set free.

⑩ DON'T LET THE SUN CATCH YOU CRYING from **GOIN' HOME**

Months from death in 1982, and alone with pianist George Cables, Pepper was in unflinching mood on this Joe Greene heartbreaker.

Chris Ingham

Lee Perry productions

As a producer, in his 70s heyday, at the mixing desk in the legendary Black Ark Studio which he ultimately burned down, reggae giant Lee "Scratch" Perry was responsible for an astonishing range of seminal recordings. All were infused with his bizarre imagination and seemingly intuitive technical wizardry.

① BEAT DOWN BABYLON JUNIOR BYLES from **TROJAN JAMAICAN HITS**

Perry's early collaborations with Byles, like this one from 1972, have seldom been surpassed.

② BETTER DAYS CARLTON & THE SHOES from **JUNGLE LION**

An uplifting rasta-inspired chant from 1972.

③ WORDS OF MY MOUTH THE GATHERERS from **JUNGLE LION**

Eerie, inspirational sounds from 1973, with the vocals pushed back behind some trademark dub ex-Perry-mentation.

④ POLICE AND THIEVES JUNIOR MURVIN from **POLICE AND THIEVES**

The big summer hit of 1976, as later reinterpreted by The Clash.

⑤ WAR IN A BABYLON MAX ROMEO from **WAR IN A BABYLON**

Another 1976 hit, based on the much-recycled Sipple Out Deh rhythm.

⑥ PROPHET LIVE PRINCE JAZZBO from **ITAL CORNER**

Freeform toasting from the underrated Jazzbo in 1976.

⑦ RASTA TRAIN RAPHAEL GREEN AND DR ALIMANTADO from **ARKOLOGY**

One of the very best of the Upsetter's 12-inch vocal-plus-DJ singles, from 1977.

⑧ ARK OF THE COVENANT THE CONGOS from **THE HEART OF THE CONGOS**

This 1977 album has to be Perry's finest hour; magnificent falsetto harmonizing, atop astonishing rhythms.

⑨ TO BE A LOVER (HAVE SOME MERCY) GEORGE FAITH from **ARKOLOGY**

The title track of a totally successful 1977 album that synthesized heavy dub with Philly soul.

⑩ TALK ABOUT IT THE MIGHTY DIAMONDS from **TROJAN ROOTS**

More delightful harmonies from1977; the dub

version, featuring Perry's caterwauling kids, is less appealing.

Greg Ward

The Pet Shop Boys

The Pet Shop Boys are a byword for pop of outstanding beauty – elegant crooning over cutting-edge electronica that veers from ethereal wispiness to amyl-fuelled techno.

❶ WEST END GIRLS (DANCE MIX) from **PLEASE [ENHANCED]**
The first the world heard of Neil Tennant and Chris Lowe; so good they had to release it twice before the public could believe its ears. Pop perfection, with that trademark slightly bitter taste already in place.

❷ ALWAYS ON MY MIND / IN MY HOUSE from **INTROSPECTIVE [ENHANCED]**
Neil sacrilegiously applies his Noël Coward routine to an Elvis song, then Chris kicks off a blasphemous house-inspired keyboard'n'computer workout. Guaranteed to have the King revolving in his grave (or wherever he is).

❸ BEING BORING (EXTENDED MIX) from **BEHAVIOUR [ENHANCED]**
The boys have a unique ability to whip up frothy concoctions that are somehow robust enough to support the crushing lyrics of regret, farewell and shame that are draped over them.

❹ CAN YOU FORGIVE HER? from **VERY [ENHANCED]**
Lyrics this arch deserve to be viewed in a grand public square, surrounded by fountains. The jaunty melody sugars an extremely bitter pill of confused sexuality and denial.

❺ SO HARD (EXTENDED DANCE MIX) from **BEHAVIOUR [ENHANCED]**
Ever fallen in love with someone you shouldn't have fallen in love with? Of course you have. And did they cheat on you? Of course they did. And did you love them all the same? This one's for you, sucker.

❻ RENT from **ACTUALLY [ENHANCED]**
Majestic, awesome, heartbreaking and enigmatic lyrics, telling either of true love or of the oldest financial transaction in the world. When the protagonist declares "I love you. You pay my rent", is that missing "and" or "because"?

❼ DJ CULTURE from **BEHAVIOUR [ENHANCED]**
Knowing words of vacuous 80s disco/nightclub lifestyle, set to one of Chris' most deliberately soulless arrangements.

❽ OPPORTUNITIES [LET'S MAKE LOTS OF MONEY] (12" MIX) from **PLEASE [ENHANCED]**
Many pop bands write a declaration of their intent to rule the world; few match this for brazenness, elegance or wit.

❾ HEART (DISCO MIX) from **ACTUALLY [ENHANCED]**
A shirts-off, poppers-huffing muscle-mary of a tune, all red-faced, steroid-toned and ever-so-slightly menacing.

❿ I WOULDN'T NORMALLY DO THIS KIND OF THING (BEATMASTERS EXTENDED NUDE MIX) from **DISCO 2**
Neil's tongue is so far in his cheek as he delivers a lyric so blatantly untrue that, like the song's character, you might also want to burst out laughing and dance naked in the rain.

Al Spicer

P-funk

It's safe to say that nobody has traversed the mind-booty divide more audaciously than George Clinton, with his Parliafunkadelicment Thang. Here are ten records that prove that funk "can not only move, but remove, ya dig?"

❶ (I WANNA) TESTIFY THE PARLIAMENTS
from **I WANNA TESTIFY**
One of the very first records to blend guitar psychedelia with vocal-group harmonizing.

❷ MAGGOT BRAIN FUNKADELIC
from **MAGGOT BRAIN**
Ten minutes of devastatingly emotive post-Hendrix guitar; the result of Clinton directing Eddie Hazel to play like his "mother had just died".

❸ UP FOR THE DOWN STROKE PARLIAMENT
from **UP FOR THE DOWN STROKE**
Preposterously funky monolithic groove.

❹ COSMIC SLOP FUNKADELIC from **COSMIC SLOP**
A remarkable tale of a mother turning tricks to feed her kids.

❺ CHOCOLATE CITY PARLIAMENT
from **CHOCOLATE CITY**
White stereotypes of insatiable black hyper-sexuality, turned into a black power fantasy to keep George Wallace and Enoch Powell awake at night.

❻ GIVE UP THE FUNK (TEAR THE ROOF OFF THE SUCKER) PARLIAMENT
from **MOTHERSHIP CONNECTION**
One of Clinton's most outlandish sci-fi funk fantasies.

❼ VANISH IN OUR SLEEP BOOTSY'S RUBBER BAND from **STRETCHIN' OUT IN BOOTSY'S RUBBER BAND**
A scary/funny, acid-soaked conflation of Eros and Thanatos.

❽ FLASH LIGHT PARLIAMENT from **FUNKENTELECHY VS. THE PLACEBO SYNDROME**
The collective's greatest groove was one of the first records truly to appreciate the synth's abilities as a rhythm machine.

❾ ONE NATION UNDER A GROOVE
FUNKADELIC from **ONE NATION UNDER A GROOVE**
Clinton's most unabashedly anthemic record.

❿ ATOMIC DOG GEORGE CLINTON
from **COMPUTER GAMES**
The synth stomp that launched a thousand G-Funk rap records.

Peter Shapiro

The Philly sound

Under the guiding hands of producers like Kenny Gamble, Leon Huff and Thom Bell, Philadelphia soul – with its warmth, pinpoint instrumental definition and gently uplifting momentum – marked a new direction for African-American music in the late 60s and early 70s.

❶ YES, I'M READY BARBARA MASON
from **Yes, I'm Ready**
With its gushing string cascades, this 1965 torrent of virginal teen longing counts served as a prototype for the emerging genre.

❷ THE DELFONICS LA-LA MEANS I LOVE YOU
from **LA LA MEANS I LOVE YOU**
The most unctuous record ever made?

❸ ONLY THE STRONG SURVIVE JERRY BUTLER
from **THE ICEMAN COMETH**
With its creamy guitar licks and resonant vibraphone, the production on this 1969 classic is like slipping on a smoking jacket and relaxing in front of the fire with a snifter of brandy.

❹ DROWNING IN THE SEA OF LOVE JOE SIMON
from **DROWNING IN THE SEA OF LOVE**
The contrast of Simon's foghorn vocals and the roiling waves of strings, horns and guitar is one of Philly's greatest glories.

❺ BACK STABBERS THE O'JAYS
from **BACK STABBERS**
Perhaps the best introduction in the history of popular music – and things only get better.

⑥ HAROLD MELVIN & THE BLUE NOTES
THE LOVE I LOST from BLACK & BLUE
Drummer Earl Young basically invents disco with his snare pattern and hi-hat work on this 1973 gem.

⑦ I'LL ALWAYS LOVE MY MAMA
THE INTRUDERS from SAVE THE CHILDREN
An almost African-sounding guitar line makes this sheer delight, even if lead singer Little Sonny Brown wanders off pitch like a drunk trying to walk a straight line.

⑧ LOVE IS THE MESSAGE MFSB
from LOVE IS THE MESSAGE
The fast section is the national anthem of disco.

⑨ DO IT ANY WAY YOU WANNA
PEOPLE'S CHOICE from BOOGIE DOWN USA
Philly at its funkiest.

⑩ LIFE ON MARS DEXTER WANSEL
from LIFE ON MARS
The cosmic synths of keyboardist Wansel takes Philly into outer space .

Peter Shapiro

Wilson Pickett

Handsome, arrogant, sensual and owner of one of the most raw and powerful voices in 60s soul, Wilson Pickett was nicknamed "The Wicked Pickett". Cutting hit after hit in Memphis and Muscle Shoals, he ranks as one of the great soul men.

❶ IN THE MIDNIGHT HOUR from IN THE MIDNIGHT HOUR
Wilson blew the charts apart in 1965 with this storming party anthem.

❷ NINETY-NINE AND ONE-HALF (WON'T DO) FROM THE EXCITING WILSON PICKETT
Backed by Booker T & The MGs, the leather-lunged Pickett's declaration of perfection

suggested how Southern soul was facing up to Motown's pop onslaught. Hardcore!

❸ LAND OF 1000 DANCES
from THE EXCITING WILSON PICKETT
Not the first version of a tune since covered by a thousand bands – but the chart-topper everyone remembers.

❹ 634-5789 from THE EXCITING WILSON PICKETT
"If you need a little lovin'/call on me" boasts the Wicked Pickett over a funky groove and snarling horns.

❺ MUSTANG SALLY from THE WICKED PICKETT
Hard rhythms, snorting horns and fat'n'greasy organ – what a groove! – allow Wilson to lay back and tell Sally to leave her Mustang alone.

❻ FUNKY BROADWAY from THE SOUND OF WILSON PICKETT
Sizzling proto-funk, as Pickett struts down Broadway like he owns the goddam street.

❼ HEY JUDE from HEY JUDE
Atlantic Records made their soul singers tackle Beatles tunes to win over the white audience, usually to dire effect. Here Wilson, with Duane Allman in tow, fries Lennon-McCartney in boiling soul juice.

❽ I'M IN LOVE from MIDNIGHT MOVER
Wilson takes his buddy Bobby Womack's tune and sings it slow and soulful. If he wasn't such a badass stud you'd almost believe him.

❾ GET ME BACK ON TIME, ENGINE NUMBER 9 from WILSON PICKETT IN PHILADELPHIA
Mutant funk that still sounds spacey today.

❿ DON'T KNOCK MY LOVE
from DON'T KNOCK MY LOVE
Pickett's last big hit: driving bass, surging horns and a vocal that pleads and threatens.

Garth Cartwright

Pink Floyd

From psychedelic dandies to space rock adventurers to stadium-sized chroniclers of the human condition… let's stop before we get to the 90s reformation.

❶ SEE EMILY PLAY from **RELICS**
The peak of the Syd Barrett era, a perfect summations of Summer 67 psychedelia: yearning, childlike, chockfull of ideas.

❷ ECHOES from **MEDDLE**
This 25-minute oceanic "tone poem" features some of the most gorgeous melodies and harmonies in the Floyd canon.

❸ TIME from **DARK SIDE OF THE MOON**
The explosion of clocks was a handy demo for 70s hi-fis, but the song is a demonstration of melodic songcraft that's entirely timeless. Nice tuned tom-toms too.

❹ US AND THEM from **DARK SIDE OF THE MOON**
Rippling with organ, sax and harmonies; rarely has anger – against war, poverty and racism – been couched in such laidback music.

❺ BRAIN DAMAGE/ECLIPSE
from **DARK SIDE OF THE MOON**
An epic conclusion to an epic album: one minute deep in the madness of Syd Barrett, the next a shopping list of, well, life itself.

❻ WISH YOU WERE HERE
from **WISH YOU WERE HERE**
An irresistible acoustic riff, while Gilmour's impassioned vocal on this country pastoral transforms a cliché into a cry for help.

❼ SHINE ON YOU CRAZY DIAMOND PARTS 1–5 from **WISH YOU WERE HERE**
Barrett's madness inspires both Waters' fractured lyric and some brilliant space-blues guitar from Gilmour.

❽ NOBODY HOME from **THE WALL**
A simple piano ballad, boasting one of Water's most touching – and funny – lyrics.

❾ COMFORTABLY NUMB from **THE WALL**
Immune to camp cover versions, this epic account of crack up and retreat into fabled childhood boasts not one but two of the greatest guitar solos ever.

❿ ANOTHER BRICK IN THE WALL (PART TWO) from **THE WALL**
A Christmas #1. The disco beat and children's choir weren't typical; the contrasting scathing lyric/liquid guitar solo combo were though.

Toby Manning

The Pixies

Frank Black and Kim Deal's soaring guitar riffs and surreal lyrics fizz with energy. Forget the small name: The Pixies are a giant of a band.

❶ DEBASER from **DOOLITTLE**
Classic Pixies, from the first hopping bassline to the strained, sing-scream of an impassioned Black. Who knows what the hell a debaser is anyway? Who cares?

❷ ALLISON from **BOSSANOVA**
Synthy effects, strumming rhythms, a tale about Allison. All in one minute and twenty seconds. A real rollercoaster.

❸ MONKEY'S GONE TO HEAVEN from **DOOLITTLE**
One of their biggest hits, this is a dark environmental plea, brought to life by The Pixies' sharply rendered melodies and thumping bassline.

❹ CACTUS from **SURFER ROSA**
A dark, almost bloodthirsty love song. Black sounds desperate while scratchy guitars and pounding drums conjure a dry desert heat.

❺ PLANET OF SOUND from **TROMPE LE MONDE**
Dark, edgy and raw, this fine cut builds to an eponymous wall of noise.

⑥ GOUGE AWAY from **DOOLITTLE**
Gruesomely raw lyrics gouge away at your brain. This is Black at his punchiest.

⑦ TAME from **DOOLITTLE**
Whispering, naughty, screaming, clashing guitars. No other band sounds like this.

⑧ GIGANTIC from **SURFER ROSA**
The title says it all: one of the band's biggest hits, sung by Kim Deal. Wonderful layers of sound build up to give that Pixies DNA.

⑨ HEY from **PIXIES AT THE BBC**
The Pixies do soft, kicking off with a gloriously moody Black and bass guitar. It all gets loud again at the end of this BBC session, though. They wouldn't have it any other way.

⑩ WHERE IS MY MIND from **SURFER ROSA**
Rightfully one of The Pixies' best loved tracks. By turns hauntingly beautiful and surprising even when you hear it for the hundredth time. Medicine for the soul.

Tim Pollard

Pizza pie

Those sentimental guys with the easy manner and the smooth voices; ladies and gentlemen, the crooners.

① DEEP NIGHT RUDY VALLÉE from **VINTAGE VALLÉE**
With a straightforward style, a megaphone and a "Heigh Ho, everybody", Vallée invented pre-microphone crooning, and also co-composed this 1929 hit.

② THREE LITTLE WORDS BING CROSBY
from **1926–1932**
The new-fangled microphone, invented just months before Crosby's recording debut, did much to transmit his warmth and intimacy into the hearts of millions. This relaxed take on Kalmer/Ruby's early-30s hit is classic early Bing.

③ PRISONER OF LOVE RUSS COLUMBO
from **PRISONER OF LOVE**
A rival for Crosby's crooning crown, with his louche style Columbo, as heard on his self-penned early-30s hit, was almost as influential as Bing on those who followed.

④ THE VERY THOUGHT OF YOU AL BOWLLY
from **THE AL BOWLLY STORY**
Britain's most popular singer during the 30s, Bowlly was lighter and stiffer than Crosby, but in his own way as pleasing on the ear.

⑤ EMBRACEABLE YOU FRANK SINATRA
from **THE BEST OF THE COLUMBIA YEARS**
Though Frank loved Bing, he went out of his way to develop a distinctively legato style, as on this archetypally sensual 1946 hit.

⑥ STRANGER IN PARADISE TONY BENNETT
from **TONY'S GREATEST HITS**
A little hotter and more spontaneous than the average crooner, Bennett nevertheless has his roots in the idiom, as his massive 1954 hit with the *Kismet* song displays.

⑦ THAT'S AMORE DEAN MARTIN
from **BEST OF**
Filtering Crosby's approach through Italy and lacing it with booze, Martin brought a whole new detachment to novelty balladeering, as on his mid-50s hit.

⑧ PAPA LOVES MAMBO PERRY COMO
from **PERRY COMO**
The man who in Bing Crosby's words "invented relaxed" scored many solo hits in the 40s, but this kind of silly-but-sweet novelty was his style in the 50s.

⑨ STARDUST NAT "KING" COLE
from **20 GREATEST HITS**
A jazz pianist who made his fortune wrapping his silky tonsils around ballads. Some were corny, some, like his immaculate 1957 reading of Stardust – composer Hoagy Carmichael's all-time favourite version – were classics.

⑩ YOUNGER THAN SPRINGTIME VIC DAMONE
from **ON THE STREET WHERE YOU LIVE**

A singer cited by his biggest influence Sinatra as having "the best set of pipes in the business", Damone has produced decades of mellow, musical vocals on high-quality material, including this *South Pacific* ballad from 1964.

Chris Ingham

Iggy Pop & The Stooges

Detroit's heaviest industry since they closed down the car plants, The Stooges swooped out from under the wing of The MC5 to unleash some of the mightiest riffs in dumb-ass rock'n'roll. When the drug-induced haze cleared, Iggy Pop was a solo artist, godfather of punk, ready to stomp the world in his dinosaur boots.

① I WANNA BE YOUR DOG from **THE STOOGES**

The Stooges' masterwork, boasting the Midwest's biggest, bestest riff ever. Iggy slips into his submissive role while the boys work up a four-chord hymn to degradation and bad behaviour of the most enjoyable kind.

② NO FUN from **THE STOOGES**

A cooler response to teenage boredom than that offered by the Sex Pistols' cranked-up cover, implying that what ever the boys do, they'll get into trouble doing it.

③ SEARCH AND DESTROY from **RAW POWER**

The rock'n'roll equivalent to the evil helicopter-driven assault in *Apocalypse Now*. Skinny little Iggy describes himself as "a street-walking cheetah with a heart fulla napalm", and gets away with it.

④ GIMME DANGER from **RAW POWER**

Iggy gets all Midwestern vampire, doom-mongering in his echoing baritone before the aforesaid cheetah persona claws its way out of

the sack and he bites the throat out of the tune while the band pummels its body into pulp.

⑤ FALL IN LOVE WITH ME from **HIPPODROME PARIS 77**

Put Iggy in front of a crowd, set the tape rolling and watch the magic unfold. Recorded while the man was still in recovery from a terrible pill habit, this shows him pulling out a big showbiz production from a distinctly shaky start.

⑥ FUNTIME from **THE IDIOT**

A sordid little slice of emotionless, twitchy desire, based on the cocaine and drag-queen debauches of Iggy and Bowie in Berlin and shining a tight beam of peculiarly coloured light on desires best left in the dark.

⑦ NIGHTCLUBBING from **THE IDIOT**

Follows on perfectly from *Funtime* by leading you, drunk and befuddled, on a head-spinning tour of the seedy side of urban entertainment. Sleazy horn music for all you sleazy whores.

⑧ PASSENGER from **LUST FOR LIFE**

A killer riff and a perfect lyric of life as a rock star, insulated by cocaine and armour-glass both from reality and those forced to inhabit it.

⑨ JOHANNA from **KILL CITY**

A classic Iggy melodrama, a love song of passion and commitment wrenched from a man who could barely feel his face.

⑩ REAL WILD CHILD from **BLAH-BLAH-BLAH**

Recorded at an age when most rock stars of his generation are looking forward to a free bus pass and reduced-rate haircuts on a Wednesday, Iggy hunts down a wild, untamed, rockabilly tune and wrestles it to the ground.

Al Spicer

Elvis Presley

Rock's one essential star without whom so much else – such as The Beatles, Bob Dylan, and Cliff Richard – might never have come to pass. Uh-huh-huh…

p

❶ LAWDY MISS CLAWDY from **ELVIS PRESLEY**

Elvis sounds confusingly chirpy as he bemoans the faithlessness of his partner in his scintillating cover of Lloyd Price's classic, egged on by Shorty Long's pounding piano.

❷ MYSTERY TRAIN from **ELVIS AT SUN**

A confident, almost insolent, appropriation of Junior Parker's mournful tale of a love leaving town on a train sixteen coaches long. Scotty Moore and Bill Black supply the locomotion to back Elvis's cheeky vocal.

❸ LONG BLACK LIMOUSINE
from **FROM ELVIS IN MEMPHIS**

Soulful backing singers, Chips Moman's finest production values, and Elvis' most impassioned indignant vocal make this country song sound like a protest number.

❹ HIS LATEST FLAME from **No1s**

Apparently effortless, yet brilliantly studied and executed, this classic slice of love-gone-wrong popshuffles along to a beautiful Bo Diddley beat, driven by Floyd Cramer's fine piano and a wonderfully judged vocal.

❺ TOMORROW IS A LONG TIME
from **TOMORROW IS A LONG TIME**

Gentle, hypnotic and unaffected, Bob Dylan's favourite cover version of one of his songs is utterly unlike anything else Elvis ever recorded.

❻ GOOD ROCKING TONIGHT from **ELVIS AT SUN**

As writer Nick Tosches said, not a song so much as an invitation to a holocaust. A rawer, heavier, urgent precursor to *Jailhouse Rock*.

❼ I'M LEAVIN' from **BURNING LOVE**

The King's most chilling ballad – experimenting with his voice, he sounds almost suicidal as he contemplates life without his love.

❽ IN THE GHETTO from **FROM ELVIS IN MEMPHIS**

A white multi-millionaire singing about a black ghetto? Come off it! But Elvis carries it off, sounding majestic, compassionate and sincere, pointedly – and subtly – underlining the double meaning in the line "Well the world turns".

❾ HEARTBREAK HOTEL from **No1s**

If Edgar Allan Poe had cut a pop record, it would have sounded like this.

❿ ONE NIGHT from **No1s**

While they cleaned up the lyrics of Smiley Lewis's lament, they couldn't hide the intensity and the passion in Elvis's vocal as he stutters and spits out the words.

Paul Simpson

The Pretenders

Chrissie Hynde's Pretenders survived death and disaster to created some of the finest love songs in pop history, delivered by one of its finest voices: equal parts honey and heartache.

❶ TALK OF THE TOWN from **PRETENDERS II**

An epic ballad of yearning and unrequited love – not to mention oh-no-everybody-knows paranoia. Worth the price of admission for the jangly guitar intro alone.

❷ BRASS IN POCKET from **PRETENDERS**

Even though Chrissie's telling you exactly how she's going to make you notice her, she's still going to succeed in seducing you – and there's nothing you can do about it.

❸ 2000 MILES from **LEARNING TO CRAWL**

Possibly the best Xmas record of all time. If you've ever been separated from your loved one at that time of year, this'll send shivers up your spine.

❹ DON'T GET ME WRONG from **GET CLOSE**

By this point, Chrissie had distilled the self-deprecating love song to a fine art – and this is very fine indeed. If the middle-eight doesn't get you, then you've never really been in love.

❺ BACK ON THE CHAIN GANG
from **LEARNING TO CRAWL**

After half her band had killed themselves with overdoses, Chrissie came up with this: a statement of pride in her own survival, and a recognition of the necessity of starting to live again.

❻ HYMN TO HER from **GET CLOSE**
A pagan celebration of womanhood as the Triple Goddess of maiden, mother and crone.

❼ KID from **PRETENDERS**
Is it about the problems of single motherhood, or the problems of having a much younger lover? Either way, it works, and it's wonderful.

❽ POPSTAR from **VIVA EL AMOR!**
In which Chrissie amusingly trashes the (younger) competition and current pop/media trends. They don't make 'em like they used to? Damn straight.

❾ STOP YOUR SOBBING from **PRETENDERS**
How to take a minor Kinks song that nearly everyone had forgotten and turn it into one of the 70s' most impressive pop debuts. Having Nick Lowe as producer certainly didn't hurt.

❿ I'LL STAND BY YOU
from **LAST OF THE INDEPENDENTS**
Love, loyalty and commitment: an epic teen love ballad for grown-ups.

Pete Hogan

Primal Scream

The band that broke the rock'n'roll mould of the 90s by throwing dance, techno and house into the mix.

❶ MOVING ON UP from **SCREAMADELICA**
Producer and DJ Andrew Wetherall doused Gillespie's rock'n'roll jangly guitars with dance and techno and the ambitious, innovative Moving On Up exploded onto the dancefloor.

❷ LOADED from **SCREAMADELICA 1991**
Slugging a powerful bass groove at I'm Losing More Than I'll Ever Have, and removing most of its original instruments, Weatherall scorched decks for miles around.

❸ ROCKS from **GIVE OUT BUT DON'T GIVE UP**
Primal Scream returned to their 70s' hard-rock roots with this catchy, stay-up-all-night party anthem.

❹ TRAINSPOTTING from **VANISHING POINT**
Scream's reaction to poor reviews for *Give Out But Don't Give Up* was to come back with the dark theme to 1996's *Trainspotting*, richly laced with exotic trance.

❺ KOWALSKI from **VANISHING POINT**
A unique mix of Gillespie's creepy vocals and a menacing beat that propelled the Scream to their highest UK chart place – #3.

❻ IF THEY MOVE, KILL 'EM
from **VANISHING POINT**
This instrumental mix of acid house, rock and a banging hip-hop beat along with a crushing brass section transports you to the hazy drug-fuelled ride of a 70s road trip.

❼ KILL ALL HIPPIES from **XTRMNTR**
Scream go all political on their last Creation album.

❽ SWASTIKA EYES from **XTRMNTR**
A raucous lyrical loop, pounding along at high speed.

❾ SHOOT/SPEED/KILL LIGHT from **XTRMNTR**
If this dark euphoric melody makes you think of Joy Division, that's because of Bernard Sumner's unmistakable guitar riff.

❿ SOME VELVET MORNING from **EVIL HEAT**
Lee Hazlewood and Nancy Sinatra made it a cult and now Gillespie has his muse Kate Moss to whisper and warble along with him in much the same way.

Lisa-Jane Ellis

Prince

High on God and sex, the Minneapolis imp reinvented soul, funk, rock and pop throughout the 80s.

1 I WANNA BE YOUR LOVER from **PRINCE**
Prince's first hit, a tasty funk number where he croons "I wanna be your lover/ the only one who makes you come … running."

2 DIRTY MIND from **DIRTY MIND**
Minimalist punk-funk, on which Prince sets out his manifesto for dominating women and the world.

3 WHEN YOU WERE MINE from **DIRTY MIND**
On this rockin' tune, Prince pleads to a girl who's dumped him that, hey, he now loves her more than when she was his.

4 1999 from **1999**
"Life is a just a party and parties weren't meant to last" intones Prince, mantra-like, over a huge, funked-up rip of The Band's *Chest Fever* riff.

5 LITTLE RED CORVETTE from **1999**
In which Prince wonders if he's man enough for his latest conquest, the used condoms in her pocket unsettling him. "A body like that's on the verge of being obscene," he observes; then leaps in.

6 WHEN DOVES CRY from **PURPLE RAIN**
Epic, spacey funk-rock that sounds like nothing recorded before or since. Prince contrasts his relationship with that of his parents – them ole dysfunctional blues never sounded better!

7 KISS from **PARADE**
Stunning hard funk with one of Prince's funniest lyrics: "Act your age not your shoe size," he commands his latest paramour.

8 SIGN O' THE TIMES from **SIGN O' THE TIMES**
Urban horror show detailed over dubby keyboard, tough drum machine and nasty guitar licks. No one in popular music was making music that came anywhere near this in 1987.

9 IF I WAS YOUR GIRLFRIEND
from **SIGN O' THE TIMES**
Prince talks dirty, sings tender and uses a speeded-up voice to make one of his strangest and most entertaining of songs.

10 ALPHABET STREET from **LOVESEXY**
A car-wreck of funk, in which sounds and voices come from everywhere. Altogether now: "Cat, we need you to rap!"

Garth Cartwright

The Prodigy

Liam Howlett and co. have produced some of the finest (and most controversial) dance tracks of the past fifteen years, and continue to evolve with each album. Here are ten of the highlights so far…

1 BREAK AND ENTER
from **MUSIC FOR THE JILTED GENERATION**
Breaking glass, cinematic strings, rumbling bass and a Baby D sample combine with melodic keyboard riffs and acid-tinged knob-twiddling to create an atmospheric opening track for The Prodigy's second album.

2 EVERYBODY'S IN THE PLACE
from **THE PRODIGY EXPERIENCE**
Still exhilarating, despite the abundant old-school ravey daftness.

3 FIRESTARTER from **THE FAT OF THE LAND**
Another distinct musical departure, from their third album. Keith Flint's more-rotten-than-Rotten vocals espouse the joys of being a wrong-un. A *Daily Mail* favourite.

4 MEDUSA'S PATH
from **ALWAYS OUTNUMBERED, NEVER OUTGUNNED**
An incredibly rich and multi-layered soundscape of syncopated rhythms, epic strings, distorted keyboard riffs and dubby basslines. Perhaps the best movie theme that never was.

5 POISON from **MUSIC FOR THE JILTED GENERATION**
Hip-hop drums, demented yelping and screeching vocals with a hint of didgeridoo, served up on a platter of teeth-rattling bass.

6 OUT OF SPACE from **THE PRODIGY EXPERIENCE**
Manic mix of classic Prodigy rave beats and

skanking reggae, topped off with helium-tinged vocals.

⑦ DIESEL POWER from **THE FAT OF THE LAND**
Hardcore hip-hop featuring long-standing Howlett favourite Kool Keith of the Ultramagnetic MCs on vocals.

⑧ CHARLY from **THE PRODIGY EXPERIENCE**
Often imitated, never bettered, The Prodigy's breakthrough tune represents the pinnacle of the crossover rave tunes bothering the charts in the early 90s.

⑨ SPITFIRE
from **ALWAYS OUTNUMBERED, NEVER OUTGUNNED**
Juliette Lewis takes over from Keith Flint on angry lyric-spouting duties and manages to surpass even him for rawness.

⑩ NO GOOD (START THE DANCE)
from **MUSIC FOR THE JILTED GENERATION**
The classic Prodigy template of strings, speeded up vocal and rave-inspired keyboard riffs, given a darker edge thanks to its clanking, industrial drums. The benchmark for British dance music in the mid-90s.

Brendan Waller

Prog rock

Always critically reviled, despite selling bucketloads in the 70s, prog rock has been revaluated post-Radiohead and now stands as restlessly experimental music that, at its best, remained intensely melodic. The Moody Blues deliberately excluded.

① CINEMA SHOW GENESIS
from **SELLING ENGLAND BY THE POUND**
Inspired by T.S. Eliot's *Wasteland*, the poetic acoustic section gives way to cinematic instrumental. Tony Banks on keyboards and Phil Collins on drums vie to see who can avoid playing the same thing twice.

② HEART OF THE SUNRISE YES from **FRAGILE**
Who knows what Jon Anderson is warbling on about on this bonkers epic? But with its spooky atmospherics, attention-deficit tempo shifts and glorious melody, who needs to?

③ EPITAPH KING CRIMSON
from **IN THE COURT OF THE CRIMSON KING**
The future Mr Wilcox's outfit pretty much invented prog with their debut, a feast of song-suites, like this eccentric power ballad, bristling with pipers, witches and mellotrons.

④ ECHOES PINK FLOYD from **MEDDLE**
An "epic tone poem", apparently. Which is to say 25 blissful minutes of oceanic effects, bird cries and – naturally – lots of guitar solos.

⑤ DARKNESS VAN DER GRAAF GENERATOR
from **THE LEAST WE CAN DO IS WAVE TO EACH OTHER**
One of Peter Hammill's most perfect distillations of mood (crepuscular, creepy) and melody (cyclical, ever-building).

⑥ MOCKING BIRD BARCLAY JAMES HARVEST
from **BARCLAY JAMES HARVEST**
Posh prog's unsung poor cousins, BJH did a lovely line in prog pastoral. This delicately anthemic orchestral ballad is among their best.

⑦ LOCOMOTIVE BREATH JETHRO TULL from
AQUALUNG
The piano intro manages to combine Beethoven and blues, before revving up to the riff-tastic folk-prog from which the band made an entire career.

⑧ THE MOON IN JUNE SOFT MACHINE from **THIRD**
Robert Wyatt's sidelong, near-solo evocation of exile from home and love, simultaneously aching and chatty, epic and cosy and absolutely stickled with hooks.

⑨ THE GOLDEN VOID HAWKWIND
from **WARRIORS AT THE EDGE OF TIME**
Prog's darker, scarier, more primitive wing show they could do grandiose if they chose – and create Hoover noises hitherto unheard to boot.

⑩ FANFARE FOR THE COMMON MAN
EMERSON LAKE AND PALMER from **WORKS VOLUME 1**
Ironically, the prog supergroup hit biggest in the summer of punk, the video finding them in furs in chilly Canada, blasting out this hard-rock attack on Copeland's classic.

Toby Manning

Protest songs

Every protest movement produces its own songs but from We Shall Overcome on, the best have tended to have a universality that transcends the specific circumstances of their writing. No Dylan because he's got his own separate list, but here are ten that tried to change the world…

❶ STRANGE FRUIT BILLIE HOLIDAY
from **THE BEST OF BILLIE HOLIDAY**
Abe Meeropol's song about lynching, so pow-erful some couldn't even sing it without their voices breaking.

❷ TRAMP THE DIRT DOWN ELVIS COSTELLO
from **SPIKE**
"When England was the whore of the world, Margaret was her madam." Not a big fan of Mrs Thatcher, then…

❸ OHIO CROSBY, STILLS, NASH AND YOUNG
from **SO FAR**
When four protesting students were shot dead at Kent State University, Ohio, in 1970, this Neil Young was written, recorded and in stores as a single within days.

❹ WAR EDWIN STARR from **WAR AND PEACE**
"War…huh. What is it good for? Absolutely nothing." Not exactly subtle, this rare protest from the avowedly apolitical Motown stable.

❺ FOR WHAT IT'S WORTH BUFFALO SPRINGFIELD from **BUFFALO SPRINGFIELD**
Written by Steven Stills after a 1966 riot on Sunset Strip, like all good protest songs this went on to become an all-purpose clarion call.

❻ GIVE PEACE A CHANCE PLASTIC ONO BAND
from **LENNON**
Had you told John and Yoko the song was simplistic, they'd have responded that the choice between war and peace was, indeed, very simple.

❼ B.O.B. OUTKAST from **STANKONIA**
B.O.B. stood for Bombs Over Baghdad, and was symptomatic of the way in which the second Gulf War repoliticized American music.

❽ WHAT'S GOING ON? MARVIN GAYE
from **WHAT'S GOING ON?**
The smoothest protest song of them all.

❾ POLITICAL SCIENCE RANDY NEWMAN
from **SAIL AWAY**
A devastating critique of American foreign policy, all the more potent for its rapier-like wit.

❿ BOB MARLEY AND THE WAILERS
GET UP STAND UP from **BURNIN'**
A universal anthem for the dispossessed and downtrodden the world over.

Nigel Williamson

Psychedelic guitar

Tune in the air guitar. Turn on the music. Drop out somewhere the other side of sanity.

❶ VOODOO CHILE JIMI HENDRIX
from **ELECTRIC LADYLAND**
The original, the best; in fact, the sound of Jimi chopping down a mountain. With the edge – or is that "ledge"? – of his hand.

❷ I'M ALIVE PEARL JAM from **TEN**
Grunge rockers find redemption in mindwarp guitar.

❸ IN EVERY DREAM HOME A HEARTACHE
ROXY MUSIC from FOR YOUR PLEASURE
Ferry languidly relates a tale of fetishistic obsession; then Phil Manzanera kicks in and attacks his guitar in a fashion that borders on the psychotic.

❹ HEY JOE SPIRIT from SPIRIT OF 76
Submit to Randy California's sublime riffing swathed in echo. On headphones if possible.

❺ DOWN BY THE RIVER ROY BUCHANAN
from SWEET DREAMS
He may have looked like a geography teacher, but he played this Neil Young song from some very dark corner of his soul.

❻ LIKE A HURRICANE NEIL YOUNG from DECADE
… and Neil himself gets lost in a fog of loneliness…

❼ MAGGOTBRAIN FUNKADELIC
from MAGGOTBRAIN
Those funk boys certainly knew how to get down, and also how to seriously come down. And some.

❽ SAFESURFER JULIAN COPE from PEGGY SUICIDE
Floored genius from the megalithic sage. Bonkers, of course.

❾ COMFORTABLY NUMB PINK FLOYD from PULSE
Dave Gilmour sets the controls for the heart of the storm.

❿ BIRD SONG THE GRATEFUL DEAD
from WITHOUT A NET
This tribute to Janis Joplin is a vehicle for Jerry Garcia to go to the places that only he could reach. And that's not a flute – just Jerry's guitar.

Chris Coe

Pub rock

Punk was not the only reaction against the bloated rock music of the 70s. The bands who emerged on London's pub rock circuit registered their dissatisfaction by playing rootsy R&B and country-tinged music in small rooms above insalubrious boozers. A few, like Ian Dury and Joe Strummer, made the transition from pub rock to punk, and Dire Straits somersaulted from a Deptford tavern to Wembley stadium. But many more were lost by the wayside when punk threw the baby out with the bathwater.

❶ (WHAT'S SO FUNNY 'BOUT) PEACE LOVE AND UNDERSTANDING? BRINSLEY SCHWARZ from THE NEW FAVOURITES
The Brinsleys practically invented pub-rock and gave us the sainted Nick Lowe, who never guessed in 1974 that this song would one day make his fortune via its inclusion in *The Bodyguard*.

❷ HOWLIN' WIND GRAHAM PARKER & THE RUMOUR from HOWLIN' WIND
Perhaps the most unlucky of all the pub-rockers whose careers were curtailed by punk. Tracks like this suggest Parker could have been a rival to Van Morrison.

❸ ROXETTE DR FEELGOOD from DOWN BY THE JETTY
Canvey Island's finest played estuary rock'n'roll with menace, even if their amphetamine-fuelled compulsion was perhaps never captured as well on record as live.

❹ CINCINATTI FATBACK ROOGALATOR from RIDE WITH YOUR ROOGALATOR
Led by American guitarist Danny Adler, Roogalator played this sort of James Brown riff better than any white boys had a right to.

❺ KEYS TO YOUR HEART 101ERS from ELGIN AVENUE BREAKDOWN
The Clash were not so much new wave radicals as old school traditionalists, and Joe Strummer's roots lay in pub rockers the 101'ers, whose high-octane originals included this early antecedent of White Riot.

⑥ UPMINSTER KID KILBURN AND THE HIGH ROADS from HANDSOME
The late, great Ian Dury first essayed his vignettes of Essex lowlife in the Kilburns, and long before Billericay Dickie and Plaistow Patricia there was the Upminster Kid.

⑦ CHOO CHOO CH'BOOGIE CHILLI WILLI AND THE RED HOT PEPPERS from BONGOES OVER BALHAM
Seminal country-rockers Chilli Willi even had a song called Goodbye Nashville, Hello Camden Town, but they usually opened their sets with a riotous version of this Louis Jordan number.

⑧ LITTLE DOES SHE KNOW KURSAAL FLYERS from BEST OF THE KURSAAL FLYERS
Named after their home town Southend's most famous landmark, the Flyers signed to Jonathan King's label and made the Top 20 with this 1975 Mike Batt-produced single.

⑨ DO ANYTHING YOU WANT TO DO EDDIE AND THE HOT RODS from THE BEST OF ... THE END OF THE BEGINNING
The Hot Rods' R&B-fuelled energy almost shaded into punk on this strident 1977 hit.

⑩ HOW LONG ACE from FIVE-A-SIDE
Most thought Paul Carrack's song was a simple tale of romantic infidelity. In fact, it was about a rival band attempting to steal their guitarist.

Nigel Williamson

Public Enemy

When they first hit the scene, PE seemed like the most revolutionary thing to hit popular culture since the electric guitar. Time hasn't blunted their best records, which still sound – as they put it – Louder Than A Bomb.

① YO! BUM RUSH THE SHOW
from YO! BUM RUSH THE SHOW
It may actually be about sticking it to the bouncers, but it sounds like a universal call for the disenfranchized to seize the means of pro-duction. Maybe that's all down to what sounds like a piano being dropped from a great height on the chorus.

② PUBLIC ENEMY NO.1
from YO! BUM RUSH THE SHOW
Still one of the best examples of hip-hop's "less is more" credo, using little more than a flatlining moog and dusty old drums to challenge the world's woofers, tweeters and sucker MCs.

③ BRING THE NOISE
from IT TAKES A NATION OF MILLIONS TO HOLD US BACK
The omnivorousness of the sampler ("Beat is for Sonny Bono/Beat is for Yoko Ono") and the perilous contingency of the black male ("How low can you go? Death row") are just two of this track's furious asseverations.

④ COLD LAMPIN' WITH FLAVOR from IT TAKES A NATION OF MILLIONS TO HOLD US BACK
"Ya eatin' death ... ya pick ya teeth with tombstone chips" accuses Flavor Flav gleefully, some bumptious funk transfiguring him into hip-hop's one and only voodoo avatar.

⑤ DON'T BELIEVE THE HYPE from IT TAKES A NATION OF MILLIONS TO HOLD US BACK
"Teach the bourgeois/And rock the boulevard" – PE party like it's Paris 68, barking out another boast-cum-manifesto over hyper-inflated sax squeals and paramilitary funk guitar.

⑥ FIGHT THE POWER
from FEAR OF A BLACK PLANET
"Most of my heroes don't appear on no stamps" asserts Chuck, smashing a few icons to the accompaniment of pneumatic funk and the insistent tocsin of a digital alarm clock.

⑦ BROTHERS GONNA WORK IT OUT
from FEAR OF A BLACK PLANET
The familial tropes of rock guitar and funk yelp are isolated, atomized, ruthlessly estranged and brutally disorientated by producers The Bomb Squad, until they become inimical spanners for petrified works.

⑧ POLYWANNACRACKA
from **FEAR OF A BLACK PLANET**

Sardonic whistling, snide scratching and a laidback creep of a pace help narrate a parable about interracial relationships.

⑨ BY THE TIME I GET TO ARIZONA
from **APOCALYPSE 91: THE ENEMY STRIKES BLACK**

A massive sludge of frazzled acid guitar that Funkadelic would have been proud of; and a testifyin' gospel choir make this a moving tribute to the individual's power of protest.

⑩ SHUT 'EM DOWN (PETE ROCK REMIX)
from **SHUT 'EM DOWN**

The album version (from *Apocalypse 91*) is stirring stuff, but this remix single really made the most of an uplifting anthem, one that inspires rather than hectors.

Matt Milton

Public Image Ltd

Originally genuine art rock pioneers and purveyors of the deepest dub and darkest cynicism, PIL grew first into John Lydon's own personal soapbox, then after collaborations with Afrika Bambaata and bids for chart success, into just another rock band.

① ANNALISA from **PUBLIC IMAGE FIRST ISSUE**
Annalisa dates back to when John Lydon was still beating Johnny Rotten out of his soul; its percussive nature shows how hard that was.

② PUBLIC IMAGE from **PUBLIC IMAGE LIMITED**
Perched miraculously on a fence where it could be seen by the old punk rockers and by the new audience facing the bleak moorland of the 80s, this swaggers with pride, berates the audience, and bigs up the band all at once.

③ SWAN LAKE / DEATH DISCO from **METAL BOX**
Keith Levene had no time for idols, and showed little respect when he stole the melody from Tchaikovsky's ballet score. Set to a groovy disco beat, it was written by John for his mum who had cancer. She thought it was very funny.

④ MEMORIES from **METAL BOX (SECOND EDITION)**
Heaven forbid anyone should say so to his face, but Lydon's lyric stands on its own as poetry. Keith and Wobble weave a hybrid of dance tune and devotional work , while his echoing mystic wail suddenly bursts into a confidential closeness, stripped of all studio effects.

⑤ CAREERING from **METAL BOX (SECOND EDITION)**
Not so much "dated" as "identifiably of its time" due to the synth drum assault and the whirring of dangerously overloaded electronics.

⑥ FLOWERS OF ROMANCE
from **FLOWERS OF ROMANCE**

This track kicks off like something by The Creatures, its lyrics pointing to a pastoral afternoon of birdwatching out at Box Hill – an extra-urban adventure Johnny Rotten would have found unimaginably boring.

⑦ THIS IS NOT A LOVE SONG (12" REMIX)
from **PLASTIC BOX**

PiL's dance remixes always had a hint of self-parody in them and this one hints heavily at Trevor Horn's work with Frankie Goes To Hollywood.

⑧ RISE from **ALBUM**
Lydon gets back to his roots on this late classic, with a refrain based on an old Irish farewell.

⑨ WARRIOR (12" EXTENDED VERSION) from **PLASTIC BOX**
Lydon warbles and blusters his rebellious way while the production team rifles the sound effects box; then the rhythm track kicks in and we're off on the nearest PiL ever got to trance.

⑩ THE SUIT from **METAL BOX (SECOND EDITION)**
A simple boom-chik on drums and a single bass riff repeated to the extent it burrows into your mind for the rest of the day.

Al Spicer

Pulp

The Sheffield misfits who triumphed over adversity to make it – all too briefly – as the most eloquent observers of social awkwardness.

❶ **COMMON PEOPLE** from **A DIFFERENT CLASS**
Truly an anthem of the 90s, combining all the things the band did best – lust, envy, bitterness, good jokes and melody.

❷ **SORTED FOR E'S AND WHIZZ**
from **A DIFFERENT CLASS**
The last word on the Summer of Love: one moment you're flying, the next your brain's destroyed.

❸ **MIS-SHAPES** from **A DIFFERENT CLASS**
Jarvis Cocker writes his biography, and suggests that people in weird clothes can indeed rule the world.

❹ **DO YOU REMEMBER THE FIRST TIME?**
from **HIS 'N' HERS**
Oh, teenage crushes and fumblings, remembered from a position of maturity.

❺ **BAR ITALIA** from **A DIFFERENT CLASS**
The perfect come-down tune, a tender Soho waltz as the day dawns and the sugar in the coffee replaces the chemicals in your veins.

❻ **THE FEAR** from **THIS IS HARDCORE**
Creepy panic-room stuff, plus an oblique reference to Paul Daniels.

❼ **BABIES** from **HIS 'N' HERS**
The joy of older sisters, as observed from inside a wardrobe. No one says "all right" quite like JC.

❽ **I SPY** from **A DIFFERENT CLASS**
More dark voyeurism, a stalking quest for revenge among the haves and have-nots.

❾ **DISHES** from **THIS IS HARDCORE**
A house-husband's lament, another brutally touching tune about simple lives.

Simon Garfield

Punk originals

Young, Loud and Snotty to the core, punk's trailblazers lived as fast as they played, dressed to kill and thrill only themselves.

❶ **SATELLITE** THE SEX PISTOLS from **KISS THIS**
Big kids from the big city sneering at the better-heeled suburban teens who'd go on to make them rich and famous. With a guitar line that has all the aggression of stuffing shells into a shotgun, and Rotten doing his worst, this is pure punk venom.

❷ **I DON'T WANNA WALK AROUND WITH YOU** THE RAMONES from **THE RAMONES**
Written and learned in desperation one afternoon when all the cover versions they tried proved too damn difficult to play, this has all the essence of the Ramones' appeal – a simple idea, stated simply, with a simple riff to follow.

❸ **NEW ROSE** THE DAMNED
from **DAMNED DAMNED DAMNED**
The First Ever Punk Rock Single and still one to set the goose-flesh tingling. Every pop kid knows the thrill of a meaningless love story shouted out loud with high speed guitar accompaniment and a drum beat to set the heartbeat racing.

❹ **WHITE RIOT** THE CLASH from **THE CLASH**
In retrospect, more than a little dumb and earnest but it kicks open the doors with wailing police sirens, knocks out the windows with a roaring football chant chorus and sets up tactical positions from which to lay down swathes of punk rock electric guitaaaaaaaaaaaaarrrrrrr!

❺ **RISE ABOVE** BLACK FLAG from **DAMAGED**
One of the hardest mosh pit anthems of all time, originally by The Misfits but here pimped up like a stolen ride on steroids. The tune now probably accompanies more gently jogging gymnasium freaks than tattooed skate punks out to scare the straight world but comes with all the power of a steam train running downhill outta control.

6 CALIFORNIA ÜBER ALLES DEAD KENNEDYS
from **FRESH FRUIT FOR ROTTING VEGETABLES**

Jello Biafra and the boys posit an eerie future where a celebrity takes control of the most powerful state in the union (so terribly prophetic, and to think we used to laugh at the DK's paranoia) predating The Cramps voodoo rockabilly acquisition of doolally reverb and beautifully encapsulating the band's unique blend of outrage and fear.

7 ALL THIS AND MORE DEAD BOYS from **YOUNG, LOUD AND SNOTTY**

One of punk's greatest love songs – smutty, sleazy and rotten to the bone. Stiv never sounded more debauched, while the boys egg him on to ever more depraved acts.

8 SUSPECT DEVICE STIFF LITTLE FINGERS
from **INFLAMMABLE MATERIAL**

Urgent, shocked lyrics of urban terrorism and a guitar line that sounds like all the emergency services arriving at once make SLF's greatest hit as relevant today as it was three decades ago.

9 (I'M) STRANDED THE SAINTS
from **I'M STRANDED**

Riding in on a Pacific wave like the biker-surf dudes from hell, The Saints perfected the turbine-whine guitar roar, cranked up the volume then bellowed the lyrics into the maelstrom.

10 BLANK GENERATION RICHARD HELL & VOIDOIDS from **BLANK GENERATION**

The New York punk anthem – nihilist and jerking around like a spikey-head at CBGBs, overwrought by speed and Breaker Malt Liquor.

Al Spicer

Punk's new kids

Punk headed underground in the 80s and stayed there, with all the best and most inventive acts doing the right thing and making the most of the small-scale joys that accompany limited success. Writing million-sellers and accumulating trust funds, groupie scabs and drug habits just isn't punk rock. Still, the kids seem to lap it up.

1 OLYMPIA WA RANCID
from **AND OUT COME THE WOLVES**

Rancid may well sell zillions of CDs and it's been some time since any of the band saw the inside of a trailer park, but this memoir of a less glamorous past life rings true as pure gold.

2 GONE AWAY THE OFFSPRING
from **IXNAY ON THE HOMBRE**

Too intellectual, too rich to be punk? Very possibly, but they do make a most convincing attempt at an authentic angry punk sound.

3 AMERICAN IDIOT GREEN DAY
from **AMERICAN IDIOT**

Now into their second decade of teenage rebellion, Green Day decided at the outset to sound like the Clash's kid brothers, and have no reason to change things now.

4 EASY TARGET BLINK-182 from **BLINK-182**

Great stuff about a female serial killer, turning the highways of southern California into her own twisted charnel house.

5 A.K.A. I-D-I-O-T THE HIVES from **BARELY LEGAL**

High-quality pop punk from the best dressed band in town – any town. Not quite as authentically "street" as the average leather-clad mohican, but a lot more fun to be with.

6 TAKE IT OFF THE DONNAS from **SPEND THE NIGHT**

Yeah! Hot girl lust from The Donnas, a band that knows the future is female, plays guitar, and has issues with traditional notions of masculinity. Loud, raw, dirty music. It doesn't get any better than this.

7 STILL WAITING SUM-41
from **DOES THIS LOOK INFECTED?**

Some reviewers detected the slow advance of a social conscience in Sum-41's follow-up to All Killer No Filler, but it doesn't take much effort to ignore it.

Al Spicer

p

Put that red dress on

Or take it off. Why are there so many songs where the singer instructs his girlfriend what she should be wearing?

❶ WRECKING BALL NEIL YOUNG from FREEDOM
Somehow, something pretty and white doesn't ring true with the aging grungemeister – but that's what he wants her to wear.

❷ ALISON ELVIS COSTELLO from MY AIM IS TRUE
The problem with Alison's party dress, from the Costello viewpoint, is that somebody else got to take it off.

❸ HI-HEEL SNEAKERS TOMMY TUCKER from HI-HEEL SNEAKERS
Assorted versions of this rock classic offer instructions not only to put on those footwear classics but also a red dress, a wig hat and possibly some boxing gloves, just in case.

❹ THE HEALING HAS BEGUN VAN MORRISON from INTO THE MUSIC
Van shows he can worry about fashion with the best of them; here it's instructions to put on a particular summer dress (the pretty one) and add an Easter bonnet as the finishing touch.

❺ ONE OF US CANNOT BE WRONG LEONARD COHEN from SONGS OF LEONARD COHEN
Predictably Leonard Cohen does a different take on the what-to-wear question. He doesn't want her to put on or take off that see-through dress, just to confess that he tortured it.

❻ ROSIE FAIRPORT CONVENTION from ROSIE
All Rosie has to take off is her coat (and settle down and listen to the band) but it remains one of Fairport's, and particularly Dave Swarbrick's, classics.

❼ CACTUS THE PIXIES from SURFER ROSA
This is undressing by remote control, with instructions to "take off the dress and send it to me", preferably soaking wet after wandering around in the desert heat.

❽ YOU CAN LEAVE YOUR HAT ON RANDY NEWMAN from SAIL AWAY
The coat, the shoes, the dress all have to come off and there are even instructions on how to do it – real slow – but the hat? That can stay on.

❾ ROXANNE THE POLICE from OUTLANDOS D'AMOUR
Well this is more democratic; Sting's instructions are that you don't have to wear that dress, or put on the red light for that matter.

❿ PASTIES & A G-STRING TOM WAITS from SMALL CHANGE
The gravel-voiced-one is totally straightforward in this ode to a beer-soaked strip joint: take off all your clothes.

Tony Wheeler

Qawwali

The word means "utterance", the style is perhaps the world's most swinging religious music. Live performances regularly last over three hours, with listeners falling into trance as they understand the deeper meaning of the words.

❶ MUNADJAAT NUSRAT FATEH ALI KHAN from EN CONCERT À PARIS VOL 2
Long a star in India and Pakistan, Nusrat launches his worldwide career performing this beautiful poem by the great Sufi Rumi at the studios of Radio France, in November 1985.

❷ HAAZYR HEIN HAAZYR HEIN SABRI BROTHERS from QAWWALI MASTERWORKS
The mighty two, Ghulam Farid (bass) and Maqbool Ahmed Sabri (tenor), caught in full flight on a wicked rhythm.

❸ THE FACE OF LOVE NUSRAT FATEH ALI KHAN & EDDIE VEDDER from DEAD MAN WALKING –THE SCORE
One of Nusrat's most striking collaborations, based on the ghazal Tery Bina, and featuring Ry Cooder on bottleneck guitar.

❹ ALLAH HU NUSRAT FATEH ALI KHAN from THE ECSTATIC QAWWALI II (JVC)
While it's not quite appropriate to speak of Qawwali "hits", Allah Hu was always much requested when Nusrat performed.

❺ YA SAHIB-UL-JAMAL
SABRI BROTHERS from YA HABIB
"O Beloved of God, so luminescent is your beauty that even the moon, the sun and the stars are shy in your presence." A moving tribute to the prophet Mohammed (PBUH).

❻ MUSTT MUSTT – DUCK POND DUB MIX
NUSRAT FATEH ALI KHAN REMIXED BY MASSIVE ATTACK from "MUST MUST"
Classic proof that qawwali works on the dancefloor too. The dramatic beats on the tabla work well with Massive Attack's tight reggae rhythm.

❼ GEET BAHAUDDIN QUTBUDDIN QAWWAL & PARTY from FLIGHT OF THE SOUL
A good example how qawwali is traditionally performed at the shrines of Sufi saints.

❽ ALLAH HI JANE KAUN BASHAR HAI AZIZ MIAN from ALLAH HI JANE
Aziz Mian stretches his incredible voice to the limit; some liken his music to punk, but, rest assured, it's still traditional qawwali.

❾ LAGI WALIAA NU NEEND NIA ONDHI ABIDA PARVEEN from HOMMAGE À NUSRAT FATEH ALI KHAN
A moving tribute to Nusrat, from *the* female voice of a genre largely dominated by males.

❿ NIGHT SONG NUSRAT FATEH ALI KHAN W. MICHAEL BROOK from NIGHT SONG
Nusrat sings a kind of *alaap* that sounds like a lament, against a very dark synth drone.

Jean Trouillet

¿Que? Rock hits not in English

English is the universal language of rock'n'roll; wherever you come from, record companies the world over will tell you that's the tongue you have to sing in if you want international success. Here are ten that slipped under the wire…

1 LA BAMBA RITCHIE VALENS
from **HIS GREATEST HITS**
A pop hit several times over since this 1958 version, the song actually comes from 19th-century Veracruz, Mexico. In truth, the lyric is nonsense in any language.

2 MI TIERRA GLORIA ESTEFAN from **MI TIERRA**
Few artists have combined English and Spanish releases more successfully; the *Mi Tierra* album even made the British top ten in 1993.

3 NON, JE NE REGRETTE RIEN EDITH PIAF
from **L'IMMORTELLE**
And then Sony crassly went and reissued it on an album they called *I Regret Nothing*…

4 JE T'AIME…MOI NON PLUS JANE BIRKIN & SERGE GAINSBOURG from **JANE BIRKIN & SERGE GAINSBOURG**
French was indeed the loving tongue, as this piece of aural eroticism went to #1 all over Europe in 1969.

5 MACARENA LOS DEL RIO
from **MACARENA NON STOP**
Los Del Rio had recorded more than thirty albums of traditional Spanish music when this became a freak international hit in 1996.

6 OYE COMO VA SANTANA from **ABRAXAS**
Written by Tito Puente, but brilliantly covered by Carlos and his band in 1970.

7 GUANTANAMERA THE SANDPIPERS
from **GUANTANAMERA**
The much-covered Cuban classic gave this trio of Californian singers a Top 10 hit in Britain and America in 1966.

8 PATA PATA MIRIAM MAKEBA from **PATA PATA**
According to Makeba, the lyric, sung in Xhosa, is "meaningless". That didn't prevent it being an international hit in 1967.

9 DIDI KHALED from **KHALED**
The first song in Arabic to chart in France in 1991, it was also a hit in Israel, Egypt and Saudi Arabia – and even, in Hindi, in India.

10 HAVA NAGILA SPOTNIKS from **HAVA NAGILA**
All right, this one's a cheat. This Swedish band took the Jewish folk song into the British Top 20 in 1963, but they left out the words and turned it into an instrumental.

Nigel Williamson

Queen

Queen – Freddie Mercury, Roger Taylor, John Deacon and Brian May – made the rocking world go round for much of the 70s. Their flamboyant epicentre, Mercury, had a rare genius for vaudeville, lyrics, music and crowd psychology.

1 MARCH OF THE BLACK QUEEN from **QUEEN II**
In tempo, harmony and key changes, this fans' favourite – more of a poem than a song – is as ambitious as Bohemian Rhapsody.

2 MELANCHOLY BLUES
from **NEWS OF THE WORLD**
2am, drink in hand, alone and slumped over in some lousy piano bar, say no more.

3 SOMEBODY TO LOVE FROM
from **A DAY AT THE RACES**
Full-throttle Freddie. The "Find Me Somebody to Love" chant, alternately bombastic and desperate, provided the blueprint for many brilliant ballads to come.

4 LOVE OF MY LIFE from **A NIGHT AT THE OPERA**
A heart-rending tale of unrequited love with Freddie's poignantly simple piano accompaniment. Get the hankies.

5 GOOD OLD FASHIONED LOVER BOY
from **A DAY AT THE RACES**
The band's last true vaudeville number fulfils Freddie's declared ambition that Queen songs should be works of brilliant escapism.

6 SPREAD YOUR WINGS
from **NEWS OF THE WORLD**
Perhaps the second finest contribution by John

Deacon, the band's most overlooked member, to their work.

❼ KILLER QUEEN from **SHEER HEART ATTACK**
One of the cleverest pop songs Freddie ever wrote, with nicely syncopated piano, and entertaining show-off lyrics.

❽ DROWSE from **A DAY AT THE RACES**
You're feeling sleepy, very sleepy. Talk about winding down, this Roger Taylor number, a secret favourite among Queen aficionados, will have you melting into the floor .

❾ BOHEMIAN RHAPSODY
from **A NIGHT AT THE OPERA**
This redefined the pop single, popularized the pop video, featured the longest lead melody of any single in its day, and left millions of schoolkids wondering who Scaramouche was and what he had to do with the fandango. Almost too familiar, but still plenty listenable.

❿ I WANT TO BREAK FREE from **THE WORKS**
Does he, doesn't he? Make your own mind up whether Freddie really wants to be out on his own or not. John Deacon's finest four minutes.

Lesley Simpson

Questions, questions...

Like all great artists, musicians down the centuries have always been renowned for asking the truly important questions in life.

❶ DO YOU LOVE ME? THE CONTOURS
from **GREATEST HITS**
Perhaps the crucial question in all pop music; their follow-up "Can You Jerk Like Me?" seemed somehow less important.

❷ WHO DO YOU LOVE? BO DIDDLEY
from **BO DIDDLEY**
Bo dares to push the questioning a little further.

❸ WHAT IS LIFE? GEORGE HARRISON
from **ALL THINGS MUST PASS**
Trust George to tackle the really big issues.

❹ WHY DON'T WE DO IT IN THE ROAD? THE BEATLES from **THE WHITE ALBUM**
And trust Paul to bring things back down to the gutter.

❺ CAN YOU PLEASE CRAWL OUT YOUR WINDOW? BOB DYLAN from **BIOGRAPH**
And trust Dylan to turn surreal on us.

❻ ARE YOU EXPERIENCED? THE JIMI HENDRIX EXPERIENCE from **ARE YOU EXPERIENCED?**
Jimi gets straight to the point. By the next year, the drugs had taken their toll, and he was demanding "Have You Ever Been (To Electric Ladyland)?"

❼ WHAT'S THE UGLIEST PART OF YOUR BODY? THE MOTHERS OF INVENTION from **WE'RE ONLY IN IT FOR THE MONEY**
Couldn't we just gloss over that one, Frank?

❽ DO YOU KNOW WHO I AM? ELVIS PRESLEY
from **FROM NASHVILLE TO MEMPHIS**
By the end of the 60s, Elvis had never been bigger…

❾ WHO AM I? ELVIS PRESLEY from **FROM NASHVILLE TO MEMPHIS**
Even if his memory was not what it had been.

❿ DO YOU WANT TO TOUCH ME?
GARY GLITTER from **GLITTERING GREATS**
If ever a question begged the answer "no", this was the one.

Greg Ward

Radiohead

Radiohead is one of those rare bands who can lift listeners to the heights yet also scare the pants off them, all while staying true to their utterly unique vision.

❶ CREEP from **PABLO HONEY**
The anthem of self-loathing that launched a towering career, once abandoned by the band, but now at least sometimes embraced again on stage.

❷ THE BENDS from **THE BENDS**
Classic loud-soft-louder Radiohead. Feel the catharsis when Thom pleads "I wanna live, breathe. I wanna be part of the human race!"

❸ POLYETHYLENE (PARTS 1 & 2) from **AIRBAG/HOW AM I DRIVING?**
A proto-*OK Computer* song (about plastic), the first part mumble-sung over picked acoustic, the second wailed over *Bends* bombast.

❹ PARANOID ANDROID from **OK COMPUTER**
Pure Radiohead DNA, in all its millennial glory and technofear. Thom and the band sound positively, perfectly, blissfully unhinged.

❺ EVERYTHING IN ITS RIGHT PLACE from **KID A**
After *OK Computer*, big things were expected from Radiohead – and they delivered on *Kid A*'s surreal, synth-heavy, alienating opener.

❻ IDIOTEQUE from **KID A**
Between *OK* and *Kid A*, the band reportedly listened to a lot of Warp Records stuff; this frenetic, freaked-out "dance" song is proof.

❼ PYRAMID SONG from **AMNESIAC**
Over a looping, stumbling piano line, Thom conjures "black-eyed angels" in a dream of life – or something like it – after death.

❽ LIFE IN A GLASS HOUSE from **AMNESIAC**
Bizarre New Orleans funeral dirge with sultry horns shot through with Thom's paranoia that "someone's listening in".

❾ A WOLF AT THE DOOR from **HAIL TO THE THIEF**
Classic closer, summing up in breathless, schizophrenic fashion – "dance you fucker don't you dare" – Thom's ongoing lyrical concerns.

❿ TRUE LOVE WAITS from **I MIGHT BE WRONG**
For all Radiohead's fear and paranoia, they believe in humanity's essential, if embattled, dignity. This delicate fan favourite is proof.

Hunter Slaton

Ragga

In the simplest terms, ragga is reggae made with electronic instruments. The form has dominated Jamaican music since it emerged in 1985.

❶ UNDER ME SLENG TENG WAYNE SMITH from **SLENG TENG**
The computerized portamento bassline that is the genesis of ragga.

❷ RING THE ALARM TENOR SAW from **STALAG 17, 18 AND 19**
While not strictly ragga – it uses 1973's "Stalag 17" riddim – the uncompromising attitude is pure ragga.

❸ TEMPO ANTHONY RED ROSE from **FIREHOUSE REVOLUTION**
Menacing, creeping ragga with ice water in its veins.

4 GREETINGS HALF PINT from 20 SUPER HITS
The record that gave the new genre its name
– "raggamuffin" shortened to two syllables.

5 BORDER CLASH NINJAMAN
from REGGAE ANTHOLOGY
The Don Gorgon of the dancehall shows off
one of ragga's unique vocal deliveries.

6 BANDOLERO PINCHERS from BANDOLERO
Utterly bewitching Wild-West bravado.

7 MURDER SHE WROTE CHAKA DEMUS & PLIERS
from ALL SHE WROTE
Sly Dunbar's "bhangra" riddim propelled this
irresistible record to trans-Atlantic pop success.

8 OH CAROLINA SHAGGY from PURE PLEASURE
The perfect postmodern Jamaican record,
reaching back to the burro drums of the first
Rastafarian rituals and to Cold War spy flicks.

9 LIMB BY LIMB CUTTY RANKS
from DANCEHALL 101 VOL 1
Breathtaking rockstone boasting – will take out
any soundbwoy.

10 WHO AM I BEENIE MAN
from MANY MOODS OF MOSES
The record that alerted hip-hoppers to the
sounds coming out of the dancehall.

Peter Shapiro

Raï music

Raï developed as the music of Algeria's
underclass, with values diametrically
opposed to the cultural mainstream,
speaking boldly of drinking, sex and
teenage kicks. Twenty years on, its biggest
stars, notably Khaled, have moved up to
world concert halls and festivals. They may
no longer be dangerous, but their music
retains its power and romance.

1 MAGHBOUN CHEB KHALED
from POP-RAI AND RACHID STYLE
Before global fame beckoned, young Khaled
sang his heart out for producer Rachid Baba
– with a bottle of wine in his hand.

2 DIDI KHALED from KHALED
Produced by Don Was, the bombastic bass-
driven Didi, and the Khaled album, blew rai
wide-open for thousands of non-Maghrebis,
charting from Europe to India.

3 SIDI MANSOUR CHEIKHA REMITTI
from SIDI MANSOUR
The ultimate rock-raï mix? In her 70s, Remitti
collaborates with Robert Fripp on one of the
most adventurous of crossovers.

4 ROCK EL CASBAH RACHID TAHA from TÉKITOI
Taha takes The Clash to Oran, cranks up the
percussion and strings, and brings in a football
terrace chorus. The perfect reinvention.

5 BAÏDA FAUDEL from BAÏDA
Brought up in the grim Parisian suburb of
Maintes-la-Jolie, Faudel is the new voice of Rai,
with sights set firmly on seducing "le grand
publique" in the manner of his childhood hero,
Khaled. He's got the voice to do it.

6 YA RAYAH KHALED, TAHA, FAUDEL
from 1, 2, 3 SOLEILS
The three modern champions of Algerian
music together, bringing the music full circle.

Chris Nickson

Raindrops keep falling

There's a song for every happy occasion,
but sometimes, when it rains on your
parade, you need a song for that, too.

1 I CAN'T STAND THE RAIN ANNE PEEBLES
from HOW STRONG IS A WOMAN
Also memorably covered by Eruption and Tina

Turner, this Memphis diva's original version is arguably the finest.

② SINGING IN THE RAIN GENE KELLY
from **SINGING IN THE RAIN**
And dancing too, come to think of it.

③ I DON'T CARE IF THE SUN DON'T SHINE
ELVIS PRESLEY from **SUNRISE**
Young Elvis had better things to do than worry about the weather.

④ RAINDROPS KEEP FALLING ON MY HEAD
B.J. THOMAS from **BACK-FORWARD**
Hal David's sad but optimistic lyric must have struck a chord with this performer, who had a long struggle with drug and alcohol dependency. His is the best-known cover of this song.

⑤ IT'S RAINING MEN THE WEATHER GIRLS from **SUPER HITS**
No need for an umbrella; they wanna get "absolutely soaking wet"! And who can blame them? A well-deserved camp classic from Izora Rhodes and Martha, err … Wash.

⑥ AIN'T NO SUNSHINE BILL WITHERS
from **GREATEST HITS**
A particularly lugubrious, not to say drenching, classic.

⑦ IT'S RAINING IRMA THOMAS
from **HIT SOUNDS OF NEW ORLEANS**
Complete with highly authentic "drip, drop" effects, this anthem to misery could bring anyone down.

⑧ RAINING IN MY HEART BUDDY HOLLY
from **GREATEST HITS**
Buddy can't have seen too much of the stuff in Lubbock, Texas. As he says, the sky was blue…

⑨ RAINY NIGHT IN GEORGIA RAY CHARLES
from **GENIUS & SOUL, THE 50TH ANNIVERSARY COLLECTION VOL 4**
Mr Soul knew all about hard times; he pours his heart into this one, as many others have since.

⑩ IT'S A RAINY DAY, SUNSHINE GIRL FAUST
from **SO FAR**
Gloriously, minimalist Krautrock; Faust are rendered so dumbstruck by the unanticipated clemency that they merely chant the title for seven thumping minutes.

Greg Ward & Jon Lusk

The Ramones

Life-affirming, good natured, high-speed pulse racing jollity from the kings of New York punk. This is the band that invented it, so sit back and rock rock rock all the way to Rockaway Beach.

① BEAT ON THE BRAT from **THE RAMONES**
Inspired by an exasperated mom's novel approach to discipline, as observed from Dee Dee's front steps in Queens. Everything there is to know about punk rock in one quick hit, for today's hurried, time-short listener.

② SHEENA IS A PUNK ROCKER from **ROCKET TO RUSSIA**
A perfect, buzzsaw-guitar-powered drive through four chords of urban landscape. New York City really has it all!

③ PINHEAD from **LEAVE HOME**
This touching tale of a pinhead's transformation by the healing power of love, inspired by Tod Browning's 1932 cult movie *Freaks*, gave the world the expression "Gabba Gabba Hey!".

④ BLITZKRIEG BOP from **THE RAMONES**
Possibly the dance we'd all be doing if the Third Reich had won WWII, though the lyrics are too meaningless to tell, this is the über-dumb punk rock theme performed by the undisputed masters of the scene.

⑤ ROCKAWAY BEACH from **ROCKET TO RUSSIA**
Surf music for the scummy expanses of urban grit spread out along the East Coast, this track celebrates sunburn in a heady atmosphere of petrol fumes and decaying marine life.

❻ I WANNA BE YOUR BOYFRIEND
from **THE RAMONES**
A slow, romantic ballad in the Shangri-Las' vein – they may have been lobotomized, but they still had big, dumb, fragile hearts.

❼ WE'RE A HAPPY FAMILY
from **ROCKET TO RUSSIA**
Hilarious, frenzied cartoon portrait of life back home at the Ramone family apartment; dysfunctional living at its modern best, ten floors up in the worst housing project in New York.

❽ I WANNA BE SEDATED from **ROAD TO RUIN**
Most bands that tour as much as The Ramones did sooner or later record a song about getting back home to the one you love. Of course, if you're Dee Dee, then the one you love comes powdered in bundles, and will sit you flat down on the base of your spine, drooling.

❾ TEENAGE LOBOTOMY from **ROCKET TO RUSSIA**
There was a dark, personal side to the band's fixation with mental illness, but it never crept into the music, which totally celebrated the brighter side of brain surgery and the fun to be had gobbling down the thorazines.

❿ JUDY IS A PUNK from **THE RAMONES**
Sheena's best pal and the perfect girlfriend for any right-thinking scion of the clan Ramone. Second verse, same as the first.

Al Spicer

Red Hot Chili Peppers

The band that made it and lost it in the 90s are now one of the world's greatest rock bands.

❶ BY THE WAY from **BY THE WAY**
A brooding opening bassline followed by a crisp opening verse which then explodes and pulls you into a chorus that leaves a lasting impression.

❷ UNDER THE BRIDGE
from **BLOODSUGARSEXMAGIK**
The classic track that made them famous and catapulted them to superstardom still stands the test of time.

❸ AEROPLANE from **ONE HOT MINUTE**
A great uplifting, track from a time when the band was dogged by tragedy.

❹ KNOCK ME DOWN from **MOTHER'S MILK**
A memorial track to Hillel Slovak who overdosed on heroin the year before. The upbeat pop melodies testify to Slovak's influence.

❺ OTHERSIDE from **CALIFORNICATION**
Another soft ballad, delivered in a way that makes you want to turn the volume up and belt it out.

❻ UNIVERSALLY SPEAKING from **BY THE WAY**
This track transports you back to the 60s, if not in style then in the feel of the lyrics.

❼ DOSED from **BY THE WAY**
A beautiful track where Kiedis truly lets go, unleashing his voice on a quasi-ballad built on guitar lines that almost become an addiction.

❽ CALIFORNICATION from **CALIFORNICATION**
One of the strongest tracks of the Peppers' career. The catchy bridge into the strong chorus leaves the listener wanting more.

❾ CAN'T STOP from **BY THE WAY**
A great return to funk rap, right down to the last note. Great drums, great riffs, great stuff.

❿ PARALLEL UNIVERSE from **CALIFORNICATION**
Upbeat and uptempo number, building into a wailing crescendo of rock.

Mike Symons

Otis Redding

The greatest male soul singer of all time? And then some. Otis Redding was only 26 when he died tragically in a plane crash in

1967, and so never had to go disco or sing duets with Phil Collins. Here are ten of his mightiest and most pitiful.

❶ MR PITIFUL from SINGS SOUL BALLADS
Despite its title, the song that gave him his nickname is actually one of his more upbeat numbers.

❷ I'VE BEEN LOVING YOU TOO LONG
from OTIS BLUE
The self-penned breakthrough that gave Otis his first Top 40 single.

❸ RESPECT from OTIS BLUE
Aretha's version is better known but Otis wrote it, and his version, sung from a man's perspective, makes a fascinating contrast.

❹ I CAN'T TURN YOU LOOSE
from THE COMPLETE STAX SINGLES
Otis at his earthiest on a song that was covered by The Rolling Stones.

❺ (I CAN'T GET NO) SATISFACTION
from OTIS BLUE
At the time, Mick and Keith reckoned being covered by Otis was one of the greatest thrills of their young lives.

❻ A CHANGE IS GONNA COME from OTIS BLUE
We can argue all night whether Sam Cooke or Otis recorded the definitive version. Fact is, both are genius.

❼ FA-FA-FA-FA-FA (SAD SONG)
from THE OTIS REDDING DICTIONARY OF SOUL
Backed – as on most of his Stax sides – by the peerless Booker T and the MGs.

❽ TRY A LITTLE TENDERNESS
from THE OTIS REDDING DICTIONARY OF SOUL
From the slow goose-bump-inducing beginnings to the storming, stomping finale, the all-time perfect soul song.

❾ TRAMP from KING AND QUEEN
A wonderfully witty duet with Carla Thomas about his backwoods upbringing in rural Georgia.

❿ (SITTIN' ON) THE DOCK OF THE BAY
from DOCK OF THE BAY
Rendered more potent by being released post-humously. If you're ever in San Francisco, you can visit the dock of the bay where he wrote it, just over the Golden Gate Bridge, in Sausalito.

Nigel Williamson

Lou Reed

The Dark Prince of the Velvet Underground continued to impress with his solo work – though often erratic, it proved he was capable of writing about much more than just low life, S&M and hard drugs.

❶ WALK ON THE WILD SIDE from TRANSFORMER
Reed soliloquizes about the bad habits of Andy Warhol superstars Holly (Woodlawn), Candy (Darling), "Little" Joe (Dallesandro) and the Sugar Plum Fairy (Joseph Campbell) – and turns it all into an irresistible pop song.

❷ PERFECT DAY from TRANSFORMER
The title says it all – a gentle description of true love and a perfect date, revived twenty years later for an all-star charity version.

❸ SATELLITE OF LOVE from TRANSFORMER
The lilting tune – and David Bowie's sublime production – make it easy to forget that this is actually a song about serial infidelity and the pain it can cause.

❹ DIRTY BLVD from NEW YORK
Celebrating the mean streets of New York City, and the lives of the downtrodden and neglected who reside there; even if no one else cares about them, Reed does.

❺ A DREAM from SONGS FOR DRELLA: A FICTION
Sung by John Cale but written by Reed, this is masterful: a reverie in the mind of the dying Andy Warhol. It's Reed's most moving tribute to his mentor.

Werner Pieper's
Reefer songs

WERNER PIEPER writes, publishes and compiles CDs under the name Grüne Kraft (Green Power) in Heidelberg, Germany. He was described by Timothy Leary as a "cyber-shamanic-psychedelic-performing-publisher and founding father of the European Green movement". His series of Flashback CDs include a marvellous volume of reefer songs. As he asserts, "Smoking dope and singing about it didn't start (or end) with the hippies."

❶ **MUGGLES** LOUIS ARMSTRONG
from **DOPE & GLORY**
One of the most famous pre-hippy dopers stretching his notes. What a wonderful music-world he opened up.

❷ **THE U.S.S. TITANIC** JAMIE BROCKETT
from **REMEMBER THE WIND AND THE RAIN**
Well, finally we know why the drama happened: the captain took a toke. The finest fourteen minutes of this mid-60s Boston singer-songwriter.

❸ **KNOCKIN' MYSELF OUT** BIG BILL BROONZY & JEAN BRADY from **HIGH & LOW**
One of the most recorded reefer-songs of all time, as if folks were smoking skunk sixty years ago.

❹ **THE HASHISHIN** RY COODER & BUFFY ST. MARIE from **PERFORMANCE SOUNDTRACK**
A Jack Nitzsche song from the movie *Performance*, with Buffy on mouth-bow and help from Jack Nitzsche.

❺ **MARIHUANA** THE FUGS from **THE FUGS**
A medival Gregorian chant, celebrating the herb in dozens of languages. A global statement.

❻ **AFRICAN REGGAE** NINA HAGEN BAND from **UNBEHAGEN**
This hymn to African dope is partly rapped in German, sung in English, with some yodelling thrown in – an oddly powerful mix.

❼ **GRUENZEUGKRISTALLE** ISCHEN IMPOSSIBLE from **DANCEHALLFIEBER 3**
An unbelievably fine debut recording by four girls from Cologne. A teenage opera in under five minutes.

❽ **PANAMA RED** PETER ROWAN from **PETER ROWAN**
Recorded solo by Peter, with Old And In The Way, by the New Riders and others. As long as the stuff is illegal, we should have more songs about dealers. (OK, let's not forget Traffic's Dealer, Dealer.)

❾ **VIPERS DRAG** FATS WALLER from **DOPE & GLORY**
"Dreamed about a reefer five feet long … the sky is high & so am I" … Louis and Fats stand for all those 30s and 40s musicians like Sidney Bechet, Mezz Mezzrow and Cab Reefer Man Calloway who recorded more dope songs than the hippies ever managed in the 60s.

❻ CAROLINE SAYS II from **BERLIN**

A disturbing portrait of domestic abuse and a disintegrating relationship – and quite probably a tribute to Reed's former lover Nico (as is the whole *Berlin* album).

❼ GROWING UP IN PUBLIC from **GROWING UP IN PUBLIC**

Proof positive that Reed can be downright funny, while also taking a scathing swipe at his own shortcomings. Shortly after this, he gave up both drugs and alcohol.

❽ THE BELLS from **THE BELLS**

Lengthy (nine minutes), jazzy and strange. Supposedly influenced by both Ornette Coleman and Edgar Allan Poe (*there's* arty), this improvised piece about a rooftop suicide is utterly compelling.

❾ I LOVE YOU, SUZANNE from **NEW SENSATIONS**

For all his literary merit, Reed can still also write great throwaway pop songs with dumb guitar riffs and dumber lyrics.

❿ MAGIC AND LOSS from **MAGIC AND LOSS**

In the last decade or so, Reed has frequently tackled a subject that other rock songwriters avoid like the plague: death. A tribute to dying friends that's as mature as rock will ever get.

Peter Really

Reggae: only the best

The ultimate reggae playlist is something of a tall order: ten tunes from the thousands made in a dozen styles over nearly fifty years on three different continents. But this is it, the unequivocal Ten Best Reggae Records Ever Made. Or at least this is what they are this afternoon.

❶ JOHNNY TOO BAD THE SLICKERS
from **THE HARDER THEY COME**

A cautionary tale of a rude boy's potentially sticky end, told with an appropriately swaggering early-reggae style.

❷ KING TUBBY MEETS ROCKERS UP TOWN
AUGUSTUS PABLO from **KING TUBBY MEETS ROCKERS UP TOWN**

Probably the most famous dub track ever committed to vinyl, and deservedly so, as inherent swing and discreetly persuasive echo sets up a matchless perpetual motion.

❸ MONEY IN MY POCKET (2ND VERSION)
DENNIS BROWN from **THE BEST OF**

This cut has a more rounded out bass, a harder working Hammond and springing percussion, brilliantly framing DB's subtle phrasings inside an apparently simple rhythm.

❹ ROCK (ALBUM MIX) MATUMBI
from **THE BEST OF**

Deep, grumbling, awesomely musically literate roots reggae that bases itself in Biblical prophecy and still involves a few minutes of jazzy flute and sax break that sounds suspiciously like Courtney Pine.

❺ SWING & DINE THE MELODIANS
from **RIVERS OF BABYLON**

At that beautiful junction where rock steady meets reggae, you'll find The Melodians' gentle harmonizing.

❻ THE BORDER GREGORY ISAACS from **LIVE**

Testament to the steamrolling power of the best reggae stage shows: The Cool Ruler at his uptempo, Jah Jah-praising best; the taut Roots Radics driving him to new heights; and an ecstatic crowd singing the choruses for him.

❼ BY HIS DEEDS VC from **BY HIS DEEDS**

Peter Tosh-level anger as, over the simplest beat box backing, VC rips into those who are doing the country and its people wrong. He recorded this tune with his redundancy pay when he was laid off; catching the mood of Jamaica, it was the biggest record of 2001.

Dennis Bovell's
Sound system

DENNIS BOVELL: founder and leader of Matumbi, musical director and bandleader for Linton Kwesi Johnson, leader of Dennis Bovell's Dub Band, and producer of acts as diverse as Orange Juice, The Slits and Bananarama. He says:

"If I still ran my Jah Sufferer sound system, and we were playing before the band (Matumbi) did their set, this is ten tunes I'd play and the order in which I'd play them."

❶ RASTAMAN VIBRATION BOB MARLEY
from RASTAMAN VIBRATION

❷ GET TO LOVING DENNIS BROWN
from GET TO LOVING

❸ SLAVERY DAYS BURNING SPEAR
from MARCUS GARVEY

❹ GROOVING IN LOVE INNER CIRCLE
from THE CAPITOL YEARS 1976–1977

❺ ONE WHEELIE WHEEL EARLY B
from ONE WHEELIE WHEEL

❻ Y MAS GAN THE ABYSSINIANS
from SATTA MASSAGANA

❼ MAN IN ME MATUMBI from MUSIC IN THE AIR

❽ ONCE AGO GREGORY ISAACS
from THE BEST OF GREGORY ISAACS VOL 2

❾ 54-46 WAS MY NUMBER TOOTS AND THE MAYTALS from ANTHOLOGY (1964–2000)

❿ THE HARDER THEY COME JIMMY CLIFF
from THE HARDER THEY COME

❽ IT'S ME AGAIN JAH LUCIANO
from WHERE THERE IS LIFE
Although the sounds are as sparse and seemingly hard-edged as anything else in the dancehall, Luci's stylish gospel-ish tones give this nu roots classic a genuine ital glow.

❾ THE LIQUIDATOR HARRY J ALL STARS
from TROJAN'S GREATEST HITS
A snapping, bubbling, popping, bouncing, Hammond-happy poptastic smash in 1969.

❿ LOVE A DUB RANKING DREAD from LOVE A DUB
Springy, eternally cheerful slice of dancehall nonsense, with the deejay sticking that long-standing reggae tradition and celebrating the music, himself and the dance in which the two have come together.

Lloyd Bradley

Roots reggae

More than simply loading up the chalice and praising Jah Rastafari, roots reggae had an earthy, almost organic feel to it that the best tunes expressed from beneath the palpable. It meant a vibe that was as close to Rasta's back to nature philosophies as was possible in a 70s Jamaican recording studio, and why there is a disproportionate number of Lee Perry productions on this particular playlist.

❶ AFRICA ASWAD from CRUCIAL TRACKS
Instrumentally complex, solidly rocking, cleverly harmonized and sound in its sentiments: who says British roots struggled to keep up?

❷ SATTA MASSA GANA THE ABYSSINIANS
from **SATTA MASSA GANA**
The ultimate in roots reggae, combining classic Jamaican three-piece harmony with a biblical epic of a song, atop big brass, a chugging rhythm and a bassline of awesome authority.

❸ CROAKING LIZARD PRINCE JAZZBO
from **SUPER APE**
A version of War In A Babylon in which Jazzbo's seemingly nonsensical righteousness is as artfully delivered as the cleanly cut-up chaos of Perry's production, taking the tune to an even higher level of reggae genius.

❹ THE GHOST BURNING SPEAR
from **GARVEY'S GHOST**
Lightly dubbed, hi-stepping instrumental cut of Marcus Garvey, all the more dread for allowing the horns and percussion to take centre stage, showing off the intrinsic atmospherics.

❺ COUNTRY LIVING THE MIGHTY DIAMONDS
from **COUNTRY LIVING**
So bright and breezy and altogether wholesome, this could almost qualify as easy listening, but it's exactly such peace'n'harmony that gives the song true roots consequence.

❻ SMALL AXE (LEE PERRY PRODUCTION)
THE WAILERS from **COMPLETE WAILERS 1967–72**
Jaunty Hammond-up "traditional" reggae backing leaves plenty of space for early-Perryisms, but, most importantly, there's room to frame the trio's totally sweet but entirely militant vocalizing.

❼ MOVE OUTTA BABYLON JOHNNY CLARKE
from **DREADER DREAD 1976–78**
Gently bubbling generic reggae beat supports Clarke's plaintive vocals; his touch is so delicate he could be crooning lovers' rock.

❽ CURLY LOCKS JUNIOR BYLES from CURLY LOCKS
The original roots/lovers' rock crossover sets Byles' voice off against a seemingly endless mount of subtly melodic touches going on waaaay back in the mix.

❾ EAST OF THE RIVER NILE AUGUSTUS PABLO
from **EAST OF THE RIVER NILE**
Slowing the rockers' pace down slightly, Pablo's melodica duels with a guitar to create a shifting-sand lullaby of a tune, that uses minimum dub techniques to maximum effect.

❿ RICO CHILDREN OF SANCHEZ
from **ROOTS TO THE BONE**
The wooziest, in-sight-of-Addis-Ababa jazz-influenced roots, with layering so clever it creates the illusion of dub. A masterpiece from the man who studied trombone under Don Drummond

Lloyd Bradley

R.E.M.

The original 80s college radio jangle-pop band that just won't quit. Michael Stipe's lyrics remain an oblique, enigmatic highlight.

❶ RADIO FREE EUROPE from MURMUR
Irresistibly jangly and definitively obscure, with a skewed call-to-arms chorus: "Calling all out in transit!" (We think.)

❷ SO. CENTRAL RAIN (I'M SORRY)
from **RECKONING**
Looks forward to Michael Stipe's later-period apology-songs to an unnamed third person – possibly a lover?

❸ FALL ON ME from LIFE'S RICH PAGEANT
Bassist Mike Mills sings beautiful harmonies with Stipe and takes a solo turn, too, revealing him to be R.E.M.'s secret vocal weapon.

❹ IT'S THE END OF THE WORLD AS WE KNOW IT (AND I FEEL FINE) from DOCUMENT
A tongue-twister party anthem if there ever was one, this has become R.E.M.'s concert-closing warhorse.

❺ COUNTRY FEEDBACK from OUT OF TIME
This brooding, impressionistic tone poem

Peter Buck's
Pick of the year

Even after a quarter of a century playing guitar with R.E.M., PETER BUCK remains one of the most astute and enthusiastic fans of new music. His list consists entirely of his favourite tracks from the best releases of 2005.

❶ NEW JESUS THE TURN-ONS from EAST

❷ THERE GOES THE SUN PERNICE BROTHERS from DISCOVER A LOVELIER YOU

❸ MEADOW ESPERS from ESPERS

❹ FACTORY MARTHA WAINWRIGHT from MARTHA WAINWRIGHT

❺ MY SOUL MY SOUL RICHARD THOMPSON from FRONT PARLOUR BALLADS

❻ ROCK BOTTOM RISER SMOG from A RIVER AIN'T TOO MUCH TO LOVE

❼ PENCIL ROT STEPHEN MALKMUS from FACE THE TRUTH

❽ PUT YOU TO SLEEP JEFF KLEIN from THE HUSTLER

❾ JACKSONVILLE SUFJAN STEVENS from ILLINOIS

❿ DARLINGHURST NIGHTS THE GO-BETWEENS from OCEANS APART

essays deep sadness with "a paperweight, a junk garage, winter rain, a honey pot".

❻ NIGHTSWIMMING from AUTOMATIC FOR THE PEOPLE

Piano-driven and heartbreaking, this nostalgic ode to the lost innocence of youth is maybe the best song from R.E.M.'s greatest album.

❼ E-BOW THE LETTER from NEW ADVENTURES IN HI-FI

In the vein of Country Feedback, E-Bow looks hard at fame and decides, appropriately for R.E.M., that "adrenaline tastes like fear".

❽ DAYSLEEPER from UP

Delicate and fuzzy-headed, Stipe here takes on the persona of one who works anonymous nights "colored headache grey".

❾ SATURN RETURN from REVEAL

With a drifting, cosmic piano line, Saturn Return shifts in the middle from canned to live drums, giving the listener a feeling of lift-off.

❿ FINAL STRAW from AROUND THE SUN

Though spare and acoustic, Final Straw is R.E.M.'s most politically pointed song ever, as Stipe implores George W. Bush to "tell me why".

Hunter Slaton

Rembetika

Songs of sorrow, betrayal and hashish made famous by the so-called *manges*, rebellious characters who adorned themselves with fancy wardrobes, hated the police and loved the holy smoke and beautiful ladies.

❶ TA HANOUMAKIA RÍTA ABADZÍ from GREEK-ORIENTAL REBETICA – THE GOLDEN YEARS: 1911–1937

This is great Smyrnaiko, Rembetiko in Asia Minor style, celebrating the "Hashish Harem", the girls taking care of the *nargile* (or hookah).

❷ MANA MOU ELLAS STAVROS XARCHAKOS/
NIKOS GATSOS from **AMAN-AMIN**
Taken from Kostas Ferris's stellar movie
Rembetiko, this sings the desperation of exile.

❸ EGO MANGAS PHENOMOUNA MICHALIS
JENITSARIS & PROSECHÓS from **SALTADOROS**
This song was a scandal, because it was written
by a youngster: "I was born to be a *mangas*,
I liked it, I learned to play bouzouki instead
of going to school." The last surviving hero of
Rembetiko, Jenitsaris died in May 2005.

**❹ TO VAPORI APO TIN PERSIA – THE BOAT
FROM PERSIA** VASILIS TSITSANIS from **FÜNF
GRIECHEN IN DER HÖLLE**
In this *zeybekiko*, Tsitsanis, a bouzouki player
from Piraeus, mourns the loss of eleven tons of
finest hashish.

❺ I FONI TU ARGILE STELLAKIS PERPINIADIS from
REMBETIKA – SONGS OF THE GREEK UNDERGROUND
1925–1947
"The voice of the *nargile*", recorded in 1935
using a real hookah, evokes the sorrow and
relief of an imprisoned *mangas*.

❻ EMAI ORFANOS APO PAIDHI NIKI TRAMBA,
ROSS DALY & LABYRINTH from **CAFE AMAN**
Star vocalist of the Rembetiko revival Niki
Tramba describes with personal metaphors the
fate of the Greeks uprooted from Asia Minor.

**❼ BAYAT/TRADITIONAL ARRANGEMENT
– IRINIKA** BRATSCH from **NOMADES EN VOL
– PORTRAIT**
French lovers of the genre who even enchant
Greek aficionados with their skilful play.

❽ YEDIKULE KUDSI ERGUNER ENSEMBLE from
ENSEMBLE REMBETIKO FROM ISTANBUL
What a great idea: Greek and Turkish musicians
have come together in this band to pay respect
to the roots of the genre, which lay in Asia
Minor from where the Greek population had
to flee in 1922.

❾ O PINOKLIS CAFÉ AMAN AMERICA ORCHESTRA
from **GREEK-AMERICAN SONGS REVISED AND REVISITED**
Another great idea: a Greek producer digs into

material recorded during the 20s and 30s in
the US, with a special focus on the then-used
language of Gringlish.

❿ ZEYBEKIKO DIONYSSIS SAVOPOULOS
from **THE DIASPORA OF REMBETIKO**
Famous rock singer who has expressed
through his music the struggles and dreams of
the generation of 1968, singing with two parallel mirrored voices as if one were broken.

Jean Trouillet

Jonathan Richman

**Having started out as not only the Velvet
Underground's most obsessive fan, but
also, with Modern Lovers, their greatest
emulator, Jonathan Richman soon
turned both more whimsical and more
emotionally revealing. He continues to
release excellent albums, and puts on a
great live show.**

❶ MONOLOGUE ABOUT BERMUDA from **HAVING
A PARTY WITH JONATHAN RICHMAN**
The perfect encapsulation of the live Richman
experience, this 1991 concert recording entertainingly describes the musical and personal
growth of the Modern Lovers.

❷ VELVET UNDERGROUND from **I, JONATHAN**
In which the mature Jonathan reflects on his
youthful obsession, and tackles the issue of
"How in the world were they making that
sound?" with a brief rendition of Sister Ray.

❸ I WAS DANCING IN THE LESBIAN BAR
from **I, JONATHAN**
A hymn to the sheer joy of being – and dancing – in the right place at the right time, given
a lovely twist by the technique of repeating
crucial lines at high speed.

④ ROADRUNNER (ONCE) from **ROCK'N'ROLL WITH THE MODERN LOVERS (REISSUE)**

Subtler than the punk thrash on the first Modern Lovers album, this glorious celebration of driving "with the radio on" gave Jonathan an unexpected chart hit in the UK.

⑤ PABLO PICASSO from **THE MODERN LOVERS**

A bona fide punk classic – "Girls would turn the colour of an avocado, when he would drive down the street in his El Dorado – Pablo Picasso never got called an asshole." Producer John Cale even recorded his own cover version.

⑥ I'M STRAIGHT from **THE MODERN LOVERS**

Few indeed were the rock musicians in 1972 who could so unabashedly beg the girl of their dreams to leave "Hippy Johnny" because he's always stoned, and let the "straight" Jonathan take his place.

⑦ GIRL FRIEND from **THE MODERN LOVERS**

Tiring of his lonely walks through the Museum of Fine Arts in Boston, young Jonathan yearns instead for a G-I-R-L-F-R-E-N.

⑧ THE NEIGHBORS from **JONATHAN GOES COUNTRY**

One of the great songs about serious adult relationships, even if Jonathan himself sounds remarkably truculent.

⑨ YOU'RE CRAZY FOR TAKING THE BUS from **JONATHAN GOES COUNTRY**

Greyhound never sounded so appealing as in this highlight from Jonathan's successful 1990 foray into the world of rhinestones and cowboy boots.

⑩ HEY THERE LITTLE INSECT from **JONATHAN RICHMAN AND THE MODERN LOVERS**

Jonathan's at his most child-like and innocent, but you can't help suspecting that if the little insect does come down to fool around, it may come to a sticky end.

Greg Ward

Riffs

The Stranglers said it best when they invited a "stranger from another planet" to just strap on his guitar and "play some rock'n'roll" (Get A Grip On Yourself). This list celebrates the riff – the simple yet magic combination of chords and rhythm that brings the guts, sweat and blood to rock music. Solos are for wimps!

① BAD TO THE BONE GEORGE THOROGOOD AND THE DESTROYERS from **30 YEARS OF ROCK**

With this as your soundtrack, you could kick open the saloon door, stride up to the bar and order a sarsaparilla like Bob Hope in *Paleface*, and no man would dare bat an eyelid.

② WILD THING THE TROGGS from **THE GREATEST HITS**

The most powerful application of three chords known to man. Play air guitar to this by all means, just don't try to do a sexy dance.

③ MY GENERATION THE WHO from **MY GENERATION**

"Hope I die before I get old," they sang. Is it bad taste to say "Two down, and two to go"? ["Yes" – Taste editor]

④ REBEL REBEL DAVID BOWIE from **DIAMOND DOGS**

Mick Ronson was the best rock'n'roll guitar-slinger that the old dame ever worked with, and this is the best riff he ever produced.

⑤ SMELLS LIKE TEEN SPIRIT NIRVANA from **NEVERMIND**

The tune that took over from Deep Purple's Smoke On The Water as the one most despised by guitar-shop employees.

⑥ JUMPING JACK FLASH THE ROLLING STONES from **40 LICKS**

Rule #1: Don't try to copy Keef's guitar licks. They don't call him "The Human Riff" for nothing, and his skills will leave yours crying in the dust. Rule #2: If you must, then you'll need to re-tune your guitar. Look it up on the Internet.

⑦ SHOULD I STAY OR SHOULD I GO? THE CLASH from **THE ESSENTIAL**

Mick and Joe made this one with spare parts from 60s pop hits, vintage R&B and a degree of cheek unmatched in the annals of pop.

⑧ SCHOOL'S OUT ALICE COOPER from **THE DEFINITIVE**

Magnificently snotty stuff from a band who were a parent's worst nightmare back in the innocent days of the 70s.

⑨ OH PRETTY WOMAN ROY ORBISON from **ALL TIME GREATEST HITS**

It's not hard to copy Roy's deceptively easy walking bassline once or twice, but it takes skill and stamina to keep it up all the way through the song.

⑩ I WANNA BE YOUR DOG THE STOOGES from **THE STOOGES**

This riff descended into Ron Asheton through a haze of drugs and exploded in his guitar-playing fingers with a burst of white hot inspiration.

Al Spicer

Riot Grrrl

While the indie boys had Seattle grunge, the girls had Riot Grrrl – a venomous explosion of feminist fury, punky guitars, tangled hair, big boots and babydoll dresses. These sisters clawed their way into the media spotlight, but after being all the alternative rage for a brief interlude in the early 90s, the grrrowling faded. Sleater-Kinney and Le Tigre are among the few still carrying the torch.

❶ TEENAGE WHORE HOLE from **PRETTY ON THE INSIDE**

Never knowingly understated, former teen stripper Courtney Love lays bare her muddled psyche in this insolent adolescent tirade.

❷ REBEL GIRL BIKINI KILL from **PUSSY WHIPPED**

A primal howl of a record from America's undisputed queens of Riot Grrrl, with toxic screeching from Kathleen Hannah.

❸ PRETEND WE'RE DEAD L7 from **BRICKS ARE HEAVY**

The poppiest and most famous Grrrl song, this entered the UK Top 20 (helped along by Donita Sparks' on-stage antics).

❹ HER JAZZ HUGGY BEAR from **TAKING THE ROUGH WITH THE SMOOCH**

As spiky as it is earnest, this is punked-up revolutionary-preaching from Britain's foremost Riot Grrrl band.

❺ BRUISE VIOLET BABES IN TOYLAND from **FONTANELLE**

On their accomplished third album, chief Babe Kat Bjelland ear-bashes a former bandmate with her alternately sweet and snarly vocals.

❻ THE DAY I WENT AWAY SLEATER-KINNEY from **SLEATER-KINNEY**

Tight, harmonious garage-punk reigns on the Olympia, Washington trio's debut LP.

Ed Wright

Rivers

Rivers have few peers as a rich source of pop song imagery... though things may not always be what they seem...

❶ CRY ME A RIVER JULIE LONDON from **THE BEST OF JULIE**

See what I mean? Water under the bridge! One great version among many.

❷ BIG RIVER JOHNNY CASH from **THE MAN IN BLACK**

This one's really about a woman. Johnny doesn't say how big she was, but apparently she loved Big River more than him.

❸ GREEN RIVER CREEDENCE CLEARWATER REVIVAL from GREEN RIVER

These California city boys did nostalgia for imagined roots far better than many more authentic bands.

❹ BLACK RIVER FALLS CATHAL COUGHLAN from BLACK RIVER FALLS

Typically opaque but spookily compelling number from the underrated former lead singer of Microdisney. Check him out!

❺ RIVER BOY WILLIE NELSON from THE COMPLETE LIBERTY RECORDINGS 1962–1964

An evocative early song about fishin'and longin' from the "good for nothin' River Boy". Yep, this one's actually about a girl.

❻ RIVER MAN NICK DRAKE from WAY TO BLUE

A suitably flowing tune by the tragic singer/songwriter, who achieved posthumous cult fame. Like the possible reasons for his death, the song is wide open to interpretation.

❼ RIVER DEEP, MOUNTAIN HIGH IKE AND TINA TURNER from PROUD MARY: THE BEST OF IKE & TINA TURNER

Pees from a great height over other covers by Eric Burden, Deep Purple, Neil Diamond and … The Shadows.

❽ MANY RIVERS TO CROSS JIMMY CLIFF from THE MESSENGER

The definitive take on a much-covered classic, Cliff's homesick, lonely lament resonates with washed up losers everywhere. Always.

❾ RIVERS OF BABYLON BONEY M from THE GREATEST HITS

These West German Caribbeans did wonders for this Jamaican song. Boney M were the unstoppable darlings of the disco in the 70s.

❿ THE RIVER BRUCE SPRINGSTEEN from THE RIVER

The river in question is just a muddy backdrop to this sorry tale of teenage pregnancy, economic downturn and lurve gone cold.

Jon Lusk

Smokey Robinson

Motown's most consistent hit writer penned classics for The Temptations, Marvin Gaye and many others. But he saved his very finest songs for The Miracles.

❶ SHOP AROUND from HI, WE'RE THE MIRACLES

Leading The Miracles, Smokey's pumping 1960 tune about not going for the first girl who puts out provided Motown with its first national hit.

❷ YOU'VE REALLY GOT A HOLD ON ME from ANTHOLOGY

1962 and this silky love ballad tops the R&B charts and sits at #2 in the pop charts. The master at work.

❸ MICKEY'S MONKEY from ANTHOLOGY

Remember the scene in *Mean Streets* where De Niro dances around Harvey Kietel's Cadillac to MM? The Miracles could cut dance tunes to match the best of them.

❹ GOING TO A GO-GO from GOING TO A GO-GO

Smokey's celebration of dancing remains one of the most infectious party tunes ever. Drop the needle and hit the dancefloor.

❺ THE TRACKS OF MY TEARS from GOING TO A GO-GO

Marv Tarplin's guitar lines are as poetic as the lyrics Smokey sings. Pop music doesn't get any more divine.

❻ OOO BABY BABY from GOING TO A GO-GO

This is the Motown soul ballad at its zenith and Smokey at his most silky: just listen to those voices harmonize and wrap around his high tenor.

❼ I SECOND THAT EMOTION from ANTHOLOGY

"If you feel like loving me/if you got the notion/I second that emotion." No wonder Dylan called him America's greatest living poet.

❽ THE TEARS OF A CLOWN
from **THE TEARS OF A CLOWN**

Co-written with Stevie Wonder in 1966. Smokey sings sad while James Jamerson and the Funk Brothers keep the music pulsing.

❾ CRUISING from **WHERE THERE'S SMOKE…**

Smokey's so laidback here he's near horizontal. Gorgeous bedroom ballad that hit #4 in the pop and R&B charts in the US.

❿ BEING WITH YOU from **BEING WITH YOU**

A hymn to love from the Detroit love god. Perfect soundtrack for a relaxed evening with your other half.

Garth Cartwright

Rockabilly

50s America; Eisenhower is President, reds hide under beds, all is normal … until a greasy hillbilly called Elvis seduces the youth with his hopped-up mix of country and blues: rockabilly.

❶ THAT'S ALRIGHT MAMA ELVIS PRESLEY
from **THE SUN SESSIONS**

Elvis, Scotty and Bill start messing around with an Arthur Crudup blues. The world begins to shake, civilization collapses.

❷ DIXIE FRIED CARL PERKINS
from **ORIGINAL SUN GREATEST HITS**

Carl celebrates a gone cat who pulls razors "but he aint shavin'". Primal rockabilly from the genre's poet laureate.

❸ WHOLE LOTTA SHAKIN' GOIN' ON JERRY LEE LEWIS from **18 ORIGINAL SUN GREATEST HITS**

"Shake baby, shake" commands the Killer over frantic, manic piano. Who would dare disagree?

❹ BE BOP A LULA GENE VINCENT
from **CAPITOL COLLECTORS SERIES**

Gene purrs the vocal. Cliff Gallup pulls out a sexy, menacing solo. John Lennon heard this and knew destiny lay in such a sound.

❺ TWENTY FLIGHT ROCK EDDIE COCHRAN
from **LEGENDARY MASTERS**

Fast, funny and hip, Eddie was a boy genius with hot guitar. Paul McCartney sang this to Lennon on their first meeting.

❻ THAT'LL BE THE DAY BUDDY HOLLY
from **20 GOLDEN GREATS**

Holly's hiccuping vocal and ripping guitar solos sounded a call to teenage arms and the kids took this to #1 on the US charts in 1957.

❼ FUJIYAMA MAMA WANDA JACKSON
from **ROCKIN' WITH WANDA**

In the 50s Wanda was the toughest white chick singing and Fujiyama Mama continues to detonate. A girl so gonzo even Elvis was in awe.

❽ TRAIN KEPT A ROLLIN'
JOHNNY BURNETTE TRIO from **TRAIN KEPT A ROLLIN'**

Mad, distorted music that inspired many a 1960s guitar hero. Go, cat, go!

❾ SUSIE-Q DALE HAWKINS
from **ROCK'N'ROLL TORNADO**

Lusty rockabilly anthem from the Louisiana wildman. The guitar solo from a teenage James Burton chewed up the ears of all who heard it.

❿ RUNAWAY BOYS THE STRAY CATS
from **THE STRAY CATS**

80s revivalists debuted with this roaring ode to a place "that the cops don't know". What's the address?

Garth Cartwright

The Rolling Stones

Of course we're all delighted to find The Rolling Stones still chugging away into the 21st century, but there's no denying that the (very strong) case for seeing them as the greatest rock'n'roll band of all time rests entirely on their first ten years together, up to 1972.

Keith Richards
In the mood

Over more than forty years as a professional guitar slinger, Richards has remained remarkably true to the music that originally inspired him. All ten of his picks here were recorded before The Rolling Stones even formed.

❶ PREACHIN' BLUES (UP JUMPED THE DEVIL) ROBERT JOHNSON
from KING OF THE DELTA BLUES

❷ ROLLIN' STONE MUDDY WATERS
from FEEL LIKE GOIN' HOME

❸ THE MIDNIGHT SPECIAL LEADBELLY from THE DEFINITIVE LEADBELLY

❹ GOOD GOLLY MISS MOLLY LITTLE RICHARD
from HIS GREATEST RECORDINGS

❺ YOU WIN AGAIN HANK WILLIAMS
from THE COMPLETE COLLECTION

❻ MOANIN' AT MIDNIGHT HOWLIN' WOLF
from HOWLIN WOLF RIDES AGAIN

❼ EVERYDAY I HAVE THE BLUES BB KING
from THE VINTAGE YEARS

❽ I'M IN THE MOOD JOHN LEE HOOKER
from THE LEGENDARY MODERN RECORDINGS

❾ TALKIN' TO YOUR MAMA BLIND WILLIE MCTELL from THE DEFINITIVE BLIND WILLIE MCTELL

❿ MARDI GRAS IN NEW ORLEANS PROFESSOR LONGHAIR & HIS SHUFFLING HUNGARIANS from AN INTRODUCTION TO PROFESSOR LONGHAIR

❶ NOT FADE AWAY from THE ROLLING STONES
The sheer energy of this Buddy Holly song made it stand out among the many cover versions on the Stones' first album in 1964, before Jagger and Richards had got into their stride as songwriters.

❷ (I CAN'T GET NO) SATISFACTION from HOT ROCKS
Keef's archetypal riff gave the Stones their crucial breakthrough hit in the US in 1965.

❸ PAINT IT, BLACK from HOT ROCKS
The creative stimulus of their rivalry with The Beatles spurred the Stones to this 1966 gem.

❹ STREET FIGHTING MAN from BEGGARS BANQUET
In retrospect, LSE graduate Jagger as socialist revolutionary no longer rings quite true, but in the heady days of 1968 anything seemed possible.

❺ PRODIGAL SON from BEGGARS BANQUET
It was the Stones' love of the blues that got them started in the first place; their 1968 rendition of Rev Robert Wilkins' That's No Way To Get Along remains one of their finest hours.

❻ GIMME SHELTER from LET IT BLEED
The Stones most perfectly realized album found them flirting with darkness, murder, mayhem; on its most atmospheric track, Keef's riffing is positively demonic.

❼ YOU CAN'T ALWAYS GET WHAT YOU WANT from LET IT BLEED
Kicking off with a children's choir, this 1969 classic is a magnificent anthem to negativity.

❽ HONKY TONK WOMEN from HOT ROCKS
The Stones were at their peak in 1969; at the same time as turning out complex albums of genuine depth and subtlety, they were still releasing perfect singles like this.

⑨ BROWN SUGAR from **STICKY FINGERS**

The last of the truly great Rolling Stones singles; one-dimensional, sure, but majestic in its simplicity.

⑩ HAPPY from **EXILE ON MAIN STREET**

While it's hard to pick out stand-out tracks from the quintessential Stones album – it's such a glorious primordial soup of grunge – Happy represents Keith at his definitive best.

Greg Ward

Solo Stones

❶ WANDERING SPIRIT MICK JAGGER
from **WANDERING SPIRIT**

One of the few moments in Jagger's solo career with enough zip to compare to the Stones finer efforts. Rollicking R&B.

❷ ||| KEITH RICHARDS from **MAIN OFFENDER**

Keef's solo outings have been wildly disappointing and generally as underproduced as Jagger's have been overproduced; this slab of swaggering noise is the exception.

❸ TESTIFY RON WOOD from **SLIDE ON LIVE**

Ron's raspy vocals seem to get better with age, and he gets seriously funky with this slice of born-again, deep-fried soul.

❹ GOD GAVE ME EVERYTHING MICK JAGGER
from **GODDESS IN THE DOORWAY**

One day, Lenny Kravitz dropped by the studio and gave Mick his best song in years. That was nice of him, wasn't it?

❺ ANGEL IN MY HEART MICK JAGGER
from **WANDERING SPIRIT**

A rare moment of gentleness from the ever-snarling Mick, harpsichord fills evoking memories of Lady Jane.

❻ MEMO FROM TURNER MICK JAGGER
from **THE SOUNDTRACK OF PERFORMANCE**

A nasty tale of gangsters and leather boys recorded during the sessions for *Beggar's Banquet*.

❼ SWAY MICK TAYLOR
from **MICK TAYLOR AND CARLA OLSEN LIVE**

Taylor was always one of rock's most eloquent guitarists and he really lets rip on this old Stones number, ably assisted by country rock chanteuse Carla Olsen.

❽ TROUBLE NO MORE MICK JAGGER & KEITH RICHARDS from **BLUES BLUES BLUES (JIMMY ROGERS)**

Mick'n'Keef ably support ageing bluesman Jimmy Rogers, and Mick reminds us of his prowess with a blues harp.

❾ SEVEN DAYS RONNIE WOOD from **SLIDE ON LIVE**

Bob Dylan gave the song to Ronnie, who doesn't disgrace on this raucous live rendition.

❿ DEAD FLOWERS KEITH RICHARDS
from **STARS AND GUITARS (WILLIE NELSON)**

Keef joins old timer Willie Nelson and young blood Ryan Adams on this gloriously sloppy rendition of the Stones' finest country moment. Fun was clearly had by all.

Route 66

Jazz pianist Bobby Troup wrote the song (Get Your Kicks On) Route 66 while on the road, arriving in LA with a tune celebrating the highway that brought everyone from dustbowl migrants to Chicago mobsters to California. Troup's song quickly became a standard, fuelling much of the mythology behind Americana.

❶ NAT KING COLE

The first to record Route 66. His version, leading on piano, is jazzy, light, a hipster's delight.

❷ ANITA O'DAY

Anita's a jazz singer but a tough, sassy one and the kicks she suggests getting are those best not mentioned in polite company.

❸ CHARLES BROWN

The smoothest blues singer going also took the song for a spin.

Rough Trade Shop
Gems

Even after thirty years, the Rough Trade Shop on Talbot Road, Notting Hill Gate, is still the place to go to search out those little nuggets that sound great, and will also provide a pension plan in later years. Here, Nigel House presents a selection that have made the staff's ears prick up over the years.

❶ LITTLE JOHNNY JEWEL TELEVISION
New York was the breeding ground for a new style of music in the mid 70s that eventually inspired the overthrow of the prog rock tyrant on this side of the pond.

❷ SPIRAL SCRATCH EP THE BUZZCOCKS
Rough Trade opened in 76, just in time to help kick-start the punk rock explosion. This was arguably the first indie punk 7", and it still sounds great today.

❸ LOVE BUZZ NIRVANA
The first release from Sub Pop's ground-breaking 7" singles club, and what a cracker. Mine is number 602 and, no, I haven't registered it on the owner's website.

❹ TIGERMILK BELLE AND SEBASTIAN
We heard tell of a Prince's Trust-financed label from Scotland and managed to score about half of the 500 pressing. For ages it was one of the most sought-after records, but now is available to everyone.

❺ EP 1 BADLY DRAWN BOY
Fantastic little dinked 7" from up north

that was so sketchy, but had that elusive something that made everyone look up and take notice.

❻ SAFETY COLDPLAY
We only had a couple of boxes of these, and I didn't like it that much, but I knew enough to know that all the majors would lap it up.

❼ SAWMILL EPS MUSE
When a Smashy or Nicey style man rings up I usually try and wriggle out of whatever he is proposing. This time I didn't and may you all forgive me if I had anything to do with helping this pomp rock monstrosity on the world.

❽ DE STIJL WHITE STRIPES
When Robin from Heavenly tells me that there is a band worth checking out I always listen. This time he was right on the button – for months we were one of the few shops selling what I think are still one the best bands of all time.

❾ FIRST 7 BLOC PARTY
Real old school style pressings from this fantastically on the button label.

❿ ALL NIGHT DISCO PARTY THE BRAKES
Out as a single or on the album. A side project for British Sea Power's singer together with other assorted south coast luminaries this harks back to post punk and yet is still very now and very catchy.

❹ CHUCK BERRY

More than any other song, Route 66 probably showed Chuck how to write detailed, witty songs. He rocks up Troop's tune until it sounds like a Berry original.

❺ THE ROLLING STONES

A stomping take on their 1964 debut album suggested the Stones saw Route 66 as the highway that lead to all kinds of American kicks.

❻ THEM

A young Van Morrison ripped through Route 66 on Them's debut album. Has any singer ever sounded hungrier to get on that highway?

❼ ASLEEP AT THE WHEEL

On *Wheelin' And Dealin'* the Western swing band cut a roaring version accompanied by several veteran musicians from Bob Wills' Texas Playboys. Smokin'!

❽ MARCIA BALL

Ball's a classy blues pianist and singer who lives on the road. Listen to her name those towns and realize she knows them all too well.

Garth Cartwright

Roxy Music

The definitive art/rock group whose work contained everything from 50s rock to the Velvets to Can to the poetry of John Donne, the wit of Dorothy Parker and the romantic genius of Humphrey Bogart. The definitive line-up – Bryan Ferry, Brian Eno, Phil Manzanera, Andy Mackay and Paul Thompson – only lasted two albums. But the band were reinvented as masters of elevator smooch music, while Ferry established an alternate career as lounge lizard, pop vampire and tuxedoed crooner.

❶ MOTHER OF PEARL from STRANDED

Ferry's finest lyric, Roxy's most versatile song – at times, too noisy for its own good, at others, inducing a trancelike state – this is the number where Ferry really does sound as if he's about to sink his teeth into your neck.

❷ IN EVERY DREAM HOME A HEARTACHE
from FOR YOUR PLEASURE

Pre-dating – and anticipating – both Talking Heads' bleak vision Once In A Lifetime and the Police's silly Be My Girl, this is Roxy's most ambitious song.

❸ BEAUTY QUEEN from FOR YOUR PLEASURE

When Roxy started, no one knew quite how to take Ferry's vocals – was he serious or what? Here he deploys every trick, sounding at times grandiose, indecipherable, cynical and impassioned.

❹ IF THERE IS SOMETHING? from ROXY MUSIC

As strange a song as Roxy ever cut – with the possible exception of Bitters End, the closer on the same album.

❺ THE THRILL OF IT ALL from COUNTRY LIFE

There are those who say that Duran Duran made a whole career out of rewriting this haunting anthem.

❻ MORE THAN THIS from AVALON

Quiet, lavish, efficient, heartfelt, chilling – the ultimate late Roxy performance, such a great song even Bill Murray's karaoke performance couldn't destroy it in *Lost In Translation*.

❼ THESE FOOLISH THINGS
from THESE FOOLISH THINGS

The first – and greatest – evidence that Ferry wasn't joking about his ambition to become a white tuxedoed nightclub singer.

❽ OH YEAH from FLESH AND BLOOD

This is a subtly played, brilliantly sung, ode to lost love, in which the lyrics move with startling economy – an expression in her eyes is all it takes to surprise and enchant the narrator. A master class in radio-friendly romantic pop.

Phil Manzanera's
Latin list

"People tend to need a bit of help in the area of Latin music," says Roxy Music guitarist PHIL MANZANERA, who grew up in pre-Castro Cuba in the 50s. "So, given my background, here's my alternative Latin playlist." He even plays on a couple of 'em.

❶ YOLANDA PABLO MILANES from CLASICOS DE CUBA

❷ PLAYA GIRON SILVIO RODRIGUEZ from CUBA CLASSICS 1 – CANCIONES URGENTES

❸ GUITARRA Y VOZ JORJE DREXLER from ECO

❹ J19 NOVIEMBRE CARLOS VIVES from VARIOUS SONGS OF CARLOS VIVES

❺ AMANECIO OTRA VEZ ANA BELEN Y CHAVELA VARGAS

❻ LA VACUNA ORISHAS from EL KILO

❼ CUCURRUCUCU CAETANO VELOSO from THE BEST OF CAETANO VELOSO

❽ HASTA SIEMPRE 801 LATINO from 801 LATINO

❾ PARA TI NENGON CORONCHO from CORONCHO

❿ CHAN CHAN BUENA VISTA SOCIAL CLUB from BUENA VISTA SOCIAL CLUB

---

❾ BOTH ENDS BURNING from SIREN
The finest fruit of Roxy's brief disco phase, which also gave us the glory that is Love Is The Drug.

❿ DO THE STRAND from FOR YOUR PLEASURE
A tribute to a dance craze's ability to distract us from mash potato schmaltz, and to Roxy's ability to give a work of pure satire such genuine power. The tumbling piano interlude is one of the song's underrated highlights.

Paul Simpson

Run-DMC

The self-appointed "Kings from Queens" reinvented New York hip-hop with their minimalist sound and sportswear look.

❶ IT'S LIKE THAT from RUN-DMC
Existential statement about how things are in Reagan's America. Message: they aint gonna change so get used to it.

❷ SUCKER MCS from RUN-DMC
Back in 83 no one shouted louder or boasted harder than Run and DMC.

❸ HARD TIMES from RUN-DMC
Rhyming over a blunt drum machine, the duo unleashed the new sound of young black America.

❹ CAN YOU ROCK IT LIKE THIS from KINGS OF ROCK
Fame and all its illicit fruit celebrated over big beats and power chords.

❺ MY ADIDAS from RAISING HELL
Product placement? Yeah. But if only all ads cut so fresh and hard.

❻ WALK THIS WAY from RAISING HELL
Producer Rick Rubin reinvents rap and rehabilitates Aerosmith. Everyone involved makes millions.

❼ IS IT LIVE from RAISING HELL
Furious rhyming, wild percussion and raw scratching.

❽ IT'S TRICKY from **RAISING HELL**
"It's tricky to rock a rhyme/to rock a rhyme/
that's right on time."

❾ MARY MARY from **TOUGHER THAN LEATHER**
The Monkees' tune gets a hip-hop makeover.
Ridiculous? Sure. But fun.

Garth Cartwright

Todd Rundgren

Rundgren is a polymath genius, at his best when he's at his most succinct, most tuneful and most vulnerable in affairs of the heart. You want adult pop? This is how it's done

❶ OPEN MY EYES from **NAZZ**
Exhilarating 1968 Anglophile rocker from his days in The Nazz, a Philadelphia power quartet.

❷ I SAW THE LIGHT from **SOMETHING/ANYTHING?**
A neat Carole King pastiche and a great song about the belated recognition of love.

❸ HELLO IT'S ME from **SOMETHING/ANYTHING?**
A tender song about trying not to trample on hurt feelings in an affair that won't last.

❹ CAN WE STILL BE FRIENDS?
from **SOMETHING/ANYTHING?**
A strained relationship comes to a good end.

❺ IT WOULDN'T HAVE MADE ANY DIFFERENCE from **SOMETHING/ANYTHING?**
Amazing the bite a bit of bitterness can add.
Defiance in the face of getting dumped.

❻ LOVE IS THE ANSWER
from **OOPS! WRONG PLANET**
Unusually restrained – and touchingly soulful – universal truth from the misbegotten Utopia.

❼ A DREAM GOES ON FOREVER from **TODD**
The military hint and "life's greatest tragedy" puts a new, wider slant on loved and lost.

❽ BE NICE TO ME
from **THE BALLAD OF TODD RUNDGREN**
Seeking short-term escape from the long-term expectations of a relationship.

❾ MARLENE from **SOMETHING/ANYTHING?**
"I'm in trouble if your folks get mean…" A jaunty but (fairly) innocent infatuation with a 17-year-old.

❿ TINY DEMONS from **I SAW THE LIGHT (BEST OF)**
"They won't ever leave, but they won't show their faces to me…" Todd on insecurities. A 1981 gem (from the Healing sessions) but relegated to a B-side, for goodness sake.

Ian Cranna

Salsa

You can't pin salsa down to one style or dance or rhythm, so even these brilliant dance tracks can't do justice to a continent and some's worth of dazzling music. Wherever you stand in the Latin world, you'll hear a very different playlist.

❶ **LA NOCHE** JOE ARROYO from *32 CANONAZOS*
All the ingredients of Arroyo's *caribeño* sound: lilting Colombia-Caribbean salsa, shot with trumpets and topped by his unmistakeably, earthy, rhythmic voice.

❷ **DECISIONES** RUBEN BLADES from *BUSCANDO AMERICA*
The revolutionary singer-songwriter who turned salsa inside out with his social-realist lyrics never abandoned the dancers. This song broke every rule, weaving doowop and Cuban son with reggae and New York salsa.

❸ **DECARGA CACHAO** CACHAO from *CACHAO MASTER SESSIONS VOL 1*
The Latin world's greatest double-bass player leads a funky jam (*descarga*) with a glorious band of legendary soloists, produced by Hollywood's Andy Garcia.

❹ **CALLE LUNA, CALLE SOL** WILLIE COLON & HECTOR LAVOE from *LA EXPERIENCIA*
The sheer brilliance of these 20-something Nuyoricans, in 1973, is still astonishing. Role models for two generations of salsa musicians, Colon and Blades shine in this song of Old San Juan: Lavoe's fabulously emotive vocals, Colon's raw trombone, and the sparkiest percussionists in town.

❺ **DIOSA DEL RITMO** CELIA CRUZ & FANIA ALL STARS from *CELIA CRUZ WITH FANIA ALL STARS*
The irrepressible, eternal voice of La Reina, the Queen of Salsa, backed by the greatest American salsa band ever. This is packed with solos, and rocks to Cuban-American rhythms.

❻ **ESENCIA** DIEGO GALE from *ESENCIA LATINA*
Bright, brassy, youthful Colombian salsa, led by the reckless timbales player, Diego Gale.

❼ **CHOCO'S GUAJIRA** RUBEN GONZALEZ & IBRAHIM FERRER from *CHANCHULLO*
Elegant Cuban *guajira* from the Buena Vista dream team, recreating a classic with young conga wizard, Anga Diaz, and tres player, Papi Oviedo. Gonzalez's effortlessly rhythmic piano and Ferrer's yearning vocals are pure bliss.

❽ **CALCULADORA** OSCAR D'LEON from *ESENCIALES: THE ULTIMATE COLLECTION, VOL 1*
Luscious and swoony, this cover of a classic Cubancha cha-cha gets the Venezuelan, D'Leon treatment with swathes of violins and trombones, and his high, fragrant tenor.

❾ **EL CHIVO DE LA CAMPANA** ISMAEL RIVERA from *ISMAEL RIVERA: EL SONERO MAYOR*
Classic old-school Puerto Rican salsa, driven by Rafael Cortijo's congas, and a showcase for the voice of Rivera (the island's equivalent to Al Green or Sam Cooke).

Sue Steward

Samba

Samba from Rio's favelas is the soundtrack to the world's favourite carnival, and you never tire of it.

❶ **YAYA MASSEMBA** MARIA BETHÂNIA from *BRASILEIRINHO*
Bethania is a glorious Bahian singer with a rich, androgynous voice, here describing the

unspoiled tropical landscapes, painted by the guitars and percussion.

② REFAVELA GILBERTO GIL from **REFAVELA**
Gilberto Gil – singer, composer, now Minister of Culture – scored with this song in the 70s, and it's still greeted with cheers. Rippling guitar melodies open for Gil's gloriously honeyed voice in a deceptively harsh story of favela life.

③ SAO VICENTE MILTON NASCIMENTO from **CLUBE DA ESQUINA 2**
Brazil's greatest lyrical singer with his "Corner Club" group. Nascimento combines the legacy of choral singing with samba-esque guitars, and his unmistakeably African ancestry.

④ GODDESS OF EBANO VIRGINIA RODRIGUEZ from **NOS**
The exquisite operatic voice of this singer from Salvador, Bahia, pays homage to the Afro-Brazilian deities of candomble goddess Ebano as Celso Fonseca's guitar ripples, and a sublime chorus rises to join her.

⑤ VELHA INFANCIA TRIBALISTAS from **TRIBALISTAS**
This recent supergroup featuring singers Marisa Monte and Arnaldo Antunes, and percussionists Carlinhos Brown, raised Brazilian pop to new heights with gorgeously hypnotic harmonies and inventive arrangements. This song was an instant classic.

⑥ CANTO DO CIDADE DANIELA MERCURY from **SWING TROPICAL**
Bahia's best-loved young singer, Mercury has brought pop-sambas to the electronic beat generation. Canto Do Cidade is a heavy, rocking, street samba, which forces her voice to soar high above the crowds of revellers.

Sue Steward

San Francisco

"If you're going to San Francisco/Be sure to wear some flowers in your hair," waxed Scott McKenzie in 1967. These days wannabe hippies still hang out in the Haight but Silicon Valley exudes a much greater influence. Which may be why it's no longer a major music city.

① WHITE RABBIT JEFFERSON AIRPLANE from **SURREALISTIC PILLOW**
Acid-tinged soundtrack to the Summer of Love with Grace Slick convincingly suggesting wisdom may be found in Lewis Carroll.

② DANCE TO THE MUSIC SLY & THE FAMILY STONE from **GREATEST HITS**
Sly's male/female, black/white, psychedelic soul sound blew minds. Including Sly's once he'd shifted to LA.

③ I-FEEL-LIKE-I'M-FIXING-TO-DIE-RAG COUNTRY JOE & THE FISH from **WOODSTOCK**
Haight Ashbury's ambassador provides Woodstock's muddy masses with their anti-war anthem.

④ BLACK MAGIC WOMAN SANTANA from **SANTANA**
San Francisco has a large Mexican community although Carlos Santana is the only sonic evidence. Tasty Latin flavouring of the Fleetwood Mac tune.

⑤ A WOMAN LEFT LONELY JANIS JOPLIN from **PEARL**
JJ was a Texan blues-soul shouter who rose to fame fronting SF's psychedelic warriors Big Brother. But this slow-burning Dan Penn tune shows she really could sing.

⑥ RIPPLE GRATEFUL DEAD from **AMERICAN BEAUTY**
Zen country rock for the tie-died masses.

⑦ FORTUNATE SON CREDENCE CLEARWATER REVIVAL from **WILLIE AND THE POOR BOYS**
Roaring, rockin' prole anger directed at those who declare war then send po' boys off to fight.

⑧ LOAN ME A DIME BOZ SCAGGS from **BOZ SCAGGS**
Another transplanted white Texan who could sing the blues. Here Boz stretches out while Duane Allman sets fires with slide guitar.

❾ CALIFORNIA UBER ALLES DEAD KENNEDIES from **FRESH FRUIT FOR ROTTING VEGETABLES**

"You will jog for the master race": political satire of the highest order. Jello Biafra was the smartest, sharpest San Franciscan rocker.

❿ BASKET CASE GREEN DAY from **DOOKIE**

MTV-friendly punks won a huge adolescent audience with this celebration of being stoopid.

Garth Cartwright

Santana

Carlos Santana's fusion of Latin rhythms and blues-rock was way ahead of its time and his band's electrifying performance at Woodstock was one of the highlights of the festival. In the mid 70s he discovered jazz and Indian spiritualism, changed his name to Carlos Devadip and recorded John Coltrane tunes. By the end of the 90s he'd sunk into semi-obscurity but then surprised everyone by coming storming back with the best-selling album of his career, and winning eight Grammies.

❶ SOUL SACRIFICE from **WOODSTOCK**

This explosive piece also appeared on the band's first album but the "three days of love, peace and music" version is the one to go for.

❷ BLACK MAGIC WOMAN/GYPSY QUEEN from **ABRAXAS**

You wouldn't have thought anyone could improve on Fleetwood Mac's version of the Peter Green song… but you'd be wrong.

❸ SAMBA PA TI from **ABRAXAS**

A contender for the greatest instrumental track ever as Carlos rings every last drop of emotion out of his guitar.

❹ OYE COMO VA from **ABRAXAS**

A crash course in salsa for rock fans who'd

never heard of the song's author, Tito Puente.

❺ EVIL WAYS from **SANTANA**

The other standout track from the band's 1969 debut – and Santana's first big hit.

❻ SHE'S NOT THERE from **MOONFLOWER**

The old Zombies number gets the Black Magic Woman treatment

❼ EVERY STEP OF THE WAY from **CARAVANSERAI**

A bit unfair to single out one track from the band's fourth and most ambitious album, because its really one long suite that deserves to be listened to in its entirety. But if you're looking for a soundbite, try this.

❽ THE HEALER JOHN LEE HOOKER from **THE HEALER**

Santana's blistering guitar work on the title track of John Lee Hooker's 1989 comeback album had him sounding bluesier than in years.

❾ INCIDENT AT NESHABUR from **LOTUS**

Santana were a magnificent live ensemble in their early years and although this jazz-rock masterpiece first appeared on the immaculate *Abraxas*, the playing on this sixteen-minute version recorded live in 1973 is awesome.

❿ SMOOTH from **SUPERNATURAL**

On which the 50-something Carlos is rein-vented as a modern pop star with this monster hit featuring Matchbox 20 singer Rob Thomas.

Nigel Williamson

Scots rock

We're not talking Harry Lauder and Andy Stewart's White Heather Club here and sadly we also have to pass over the vibrant Scottish folk and roots scene. We're talking Scottish rock'n'roll. Here are ten who came over Hadrian's Wall to rock the world…

❶ SHOUT LULU

Scotland never had its own Beatles. But it did

have Marie MacDonald McLaughlin Lawrie, who recorded this rasping version of the Isley Brothers' song in 1964 when she was just 15.

② FALLING AND LAUGHING ORANGE JUICE from THE HEATHER'S ON FIRE

Strange to think that the Burroughs cut-up technique could play a part in this shimmering, delicate beauty. Arty but not fey or contrived – a thing of beauty and a joy for ever.

③ DOWN THE DIP AZTEC CAMERA from HIGH LAND, HARD RAIN

Written in a matter of minutes, this song of devotion is unusually direct for the unpredictable Roddy Frame, but it's the most memorable song on a memorable debut album.

④ NEXT! THE SENSATIONAL ALEX HARVEY BAND from NEXT

A Jacques Brel song about prostitutes and soldiers in wartime, given a powerful rendition by the godfather of Scottish punk.

⑤ MOLLY'S LIPS THE VASELINES from THE WAY OF THE VASELINES

Lanarkshire's finest with a song good enough to be covered by Nirvana.

⑥ SAY WHAT YOU WANT TEXAS from WHITE ON BLONDE

A 1997 Top 10 hit from band led by Sharleen Spiteri, Scotland's sexiest singer since Lulu.

⑦ SING TRAVIS from THE INVISIBLE BAND

For a brief while, their radio-friendly angst made them the biggest band in the UK – a unique achievement for a bunch of Scots.

⑧ PARTY FEARS TWO THE ASSOCIATES from SULK

Classic 80s post-punk pop from Billy MacKenzie, who tragically took his own life in 1997.

⑨ TAKE ME OUT FRANZ FERDINAND from FRANZ FERDINAND

The art school dance goes on for ever. Clever imagery and the spiky, angular rhythms of post-punk are reworked into something shiny and postmodern.

⑩ AN TOLL DUBH RUNRIG from RECOVERY

They even sang in Gaelic. McRespect.

Nigel Williamson/Ian Cranna

Screaming Trees & Mark Lanegan

For a decade the Screaming Trees, rated higher than Nirvana by the grunge faithful, were intrinsic to the Seattle scene. They always had more going for them than just grunge and singer Mark Lanegan has subsequently made a series of fine solo albums and collaborated with the mighty Queens of the Stoneage.

① IVY SCREAMING TREES from INVISIBLE LANTERN

Relentless and irresistible, this opener typifies the wall of sound and rough edges of the band's early efforts. The vocals froth over the wah-wah guitar.

② BLACK SUN MORNING SCREAMING TREES from BUZZ FACTORY

Vocals as harsh as Oregon logging saws as the Trees rage about ecological destruction. Van Conner's luscious bass runs maintain order.

③ BED OF ROSES SCREAMING TREES from UNCLE ANESTHESIA

The poppier side of the band is showcased, as Gary Lee serves up some disarmingly sweet riffs while Lanegan croons nonchalantly.

④ WINTER SONG SCREAMING TREES from SWEET OBLIVION

Honey-throated spirituality, honeycombed in jagged jangles and backwards guitars. Piercing hooks abound.

⑤ ALL I KNOW SCREAMING TREES from DUST

Hop, skip and boom – the Trees launch us into a helter skelter rush of whirling guitar and bouncy melodies.

6 **DYING DAYS** SCREAMING TREES from DUST

The acoustic intro is blown away by a blast of Zep-like proportions. Lanegan manfully bares his soul for the end times, while Gary Lee soars. Superb.

7 **EL SOL** MARK LANEGAN from WHISKEY FOR THE HOLY GHOST

Heartfelt and divine lament to the loss of sun and heaven. Lanegan's voice could make the angels weep as he wrenches out the simple refrain about waiting for some warmth a-coming down.

8 **STRANGE RELIGION** MARK LANEGAN from BUBBLEGUM

A folk/blues lullaby touching Lanegan's favourite topic of redemption meets road movie. Aided by Izzy Stradlin and a backing choir.

Nick Edwards

Seattle

The North Western city is famous for helming Bill Gates' Microsoft empire and the Starbucks chain but it's also long been home to a very raw rock scene.

1 **TALL COOL ONE** THE WAILERS from THE ORIGINAL GOLD CREST MASTERS

Primal garage band formed in 1958. All Seattle's guitar madness spills, more or less, from this gonzo combo.

2 **WALK DON'T RUN** THE VENTURES from WALK DON'T RUN: THE BEST OF THE VENTURES

The world's biggest guitar instrumental band formed just outside Seattle in 1959 and this is their twangy theme tune.

3 **PSYCHO** THE SONICS from PSYCHO-SONICS

Truly psychotic garage band legends. Cut in 1965 Psycho rocks harder than 99% of punk bands. Guaranteed.

4 **LOUIE LOUIE** THE KINGSMEN from THE BEST OF THE KINGSMEN

OK, they're from Portland, Oregon, but their cut on Louie is such a classic that every band in the North West learned it, so spiritually they're from Seattle.

5 **BARACUDA** HEART from LITTLE QUEEN

Sisters Ann and Nancy Wilson delivered this hard rocking ode to fast cars while leading the biggest band to come out of Seattle in the 70s.

6 **TOUCH ME, I'M SICK** MUDHONEY from SUPERFUZZ BIGMUFF

Grunge godfathers punk anthem. Mudhoney never got rich and never lost their soul, true Seattle heroes!

7 **BLACK HOLE SUN** SOUNDGARDEN from SUPERUNKNOWN

Doom … doom … on MTV and going platinum … doom. Soundgarden were real fun guys.

8 **SMELLS LIKE TEEN SPIRIT** NIRVANA from NEVERMIND

Has rock'n'roll ever sounded so good again? Crank it up and let it loose.

9 **RAIN WHEN I DIE** ALICE IN CHAINS from DIRT

Heavy smackheads unleash huge Sabbath riffs while vocalist Layne Staley wails about impending doom. Before the decade was out heroin fulfilled Layne's prophecy.

10 **HIT THE CITY** MARK LANEGAN BAND from BUBBLEGUM

Wonderful weary rumble of a rocker from former Screaming Trees vocalist. Give the guy a venti espresso, yeah?

Garth Cartwright

Sex Pistols

When you absolutely definitely want to knock out the upper register of your

hearing, there's no better way than with the noisiest, naughtiest boys ever to swagger out of West London and into the limelight.

❶ HOLIDAYS IN THE SUN from **NEVER MIND THE BOLLOCKS HERE'S THE SEX PISTOLS**
A paramilitary drum beat intro leads into a crashing guitar and a dive bomber riff – sounding just like Slade's angry little brothers, the Pistols released this track at the height of their pomp and never again reached this peak.

❷ SATELLITE from **SPUNK**
Raw and primitive. Jones and the band have all the equipment set on "SNARL" and Rotten is swigging open a bottle of poison in between lines of lyric, the better to spit it back in the face of the audience.

❸ NO FEELINGS from **NEVER MIND THE BOLLOCKS HERE'S THE SEX PISTOLS**
By the time they got round to recording the final album version, this song had slowed down a little for the lyrics to get through.

❹ SEVENTEEN (2ND VERSION) from **SPUNK**
Multi-tracked vocals mean Johnny sounds even more rotten, but this is one track that definitely shows the benefits of Malcolm's strong black coffees. Drums raining down like hailstones, sheets of cymbals, guitar trickery – the full English.

❺ NEW YORK (LOOKING FOR A KISS) from **SPUNK**
Chunkiest guitar line that Jonesy ever conjured and the perfect bass accompaniment – the kind you don't notice – from Matlock provide just the background needed for Rotten to lay into the New York Dolls, safe in the knowledge that David Jo and Johnny Thunders were still hanging out on the other side of the Atlantic.

❻ LIAR from **SPUNK**
The phased speakers on the guitar and crisp drumming are all very well but what makes this the definitive version of the Pistols' most vitriolic is, of course, Rotten's delivery.

❼ SUBMISSION (2ND VERSION) from **SPUNK**
Punk's only hymn to the delights of going down Mexico Way, and the only song ever to feature a solo blown on the whistle of an old-fashioned kettle.

❽ NO FUTURE (GOD SAVE THE QUEEN) from **SPUNK**
The occasional wrong note can be excused as a sign of the artists' desperate sincerity, the lyrics are best described as still to be finalized and it is quite obviously bolted together from two different takes, but this once-bootleg version sparks with more energy than that finally released on the album and as a single.

❾ PRETTY VACANT from **NEVER MIND THE BOLLOCKS**
Opening with the most crucial three-note alarm in the history of punk, Pretty Vacant hangs the guys out to dry – warts, haemoroids and all – as a dumb but lovely boy band.

❿ ANARCHY IN THE UK (1ST VERSION, AKA NOOKIE) from **SPUNK**
All guns firing at once, this is the definitive version of the song that made them famous. It bursts with red-faced rage, as Rotten roars like a very pissed-off caged beast, Jones hacks a Dolls-esque path through the chord chart, and Cook beats the fear of gods into his kit.

Al Spicer

Sheffield

They came out of Yorkshire armed with synthesizers and tape loops wanting to kill rock music. Instead, they managed to rejuvenate it. Here are nine songs that celebrate their noble experiment.

❶ NAG NAG NAG CABARET VOLTAIRE from **THE LIVING LEGENDS**
The guitar riff may have been straight out of the garage, but the dentist-drill synths and mosquito vocals bore a hole in your skull.

❷ BEING BOILED HUMAN LEAGUE from REPRODUCTION
Post-industrial doom-saying never sounded so good.

❸ LOVE ACTION (I BELIEVE IN LOVE) HUMAN LEAGUE from DARE!
A landmark of plasticity, garish artifice and shimmering surfaces, this made synth-pop's sangfroid the soundtrack to the look-but-don't-touch 80s.

❹ (WE DON'T NEED THIS) FASCIST GROOVE THING HEAVEN 17 from PENTHOUSE AND PAVEMENT
Ex-Human Leaguers Ian Craig Marsh and Martyn Ware proved that you didn't have to give up politics to be catchy.

❺ POISON ARROW ABC from THE LEXICON OF LOVE
Instead of embracing industrial decay, ABC tried to kill rock by drowning it in smarm and decadence.

❻ BREAKDOWN CLOCK DVA from ADVANTAGE
Terrifyingly bleak avant-funk noise collage.

❼ TRACK WITH NO NAME FORGEMASTERS from WARP 10
Minimalist, brutalist house music that kicked off Sheffield's finest label, Warp.

❽ TESTONE SWEET EXORCIST from WARP 10
Spartan electronic masterpiece from Cabaret Voltaire's Richard H Kirk that became one of the building blocks of British Hardcore.

❾ PHOTOGRAPH DEF LEPPARD from PYROMANIA
Proof that no matter how hard they tried, Sheffield's electronic naysayers just couldn't kill the beast.

Peter Shapiro

Wayne Shorter

One of the great exponents of the soprano and tenor saxophone, Shorter is also an outstanding composer, his output on the

Blue Note label and then as part of the legendary Miles Davis quintet of 1965–67 leaving a legacy of stunning compositions and even better performances. After co-founding the fusion group Weather Report, Shorter retired from live performance in 1985 until, in the last five years, he has returned to the stage with a new quartet and a series of fantastic concerts.

❶ FREE FOR ALL ART BLAKEY AND THE JAZZ MESSENGERS from FREE FOR ALL
An example from 1960 of Shorter's emerging and original style of composition as part of Blakey's school for future greats.

❷ FEE-FI-FO-FUM from SPEAK NO EVIL
A laid-back setting for Shorter and Freddie Hubbard to chat.

❸ DELUGE from JUJU
Spacious writing with Elvin Jones supplying joyous support. Shorter takes all the time he needs to say his piece.

❹ MAHJONG from JUJU
Another beautiful melody demonstrating Shorter's ability to use all his musicians to create a distinctive and coherent sound.

❺ IRIS MILES DAVIS from E.S.P
Shorter's first compositional effort for the Miles Davis quintet shows him at his most mournful and languid.

❻ FOOTPRINTS MILES DAVIS from MILES SMILES
The effortlessly fluid and loose sound which set this group apart demonstrated to perfection on this lovely track.

❼ ADAM'S APPLE from ADAM'S APPLE
Shorter gets funky with one of his more conventionally popular-sounding tracks. No one does it better though.

❽ SANCTUARY MILES DAVIS from BITCHES BREW
Shorter's contribution to the groundbreaking album retains the swelling, epic abstractness of

his earlier writing despite the different setting. Shorter plays soprano.

⑨ PALLADIUM WEATHER REPORT
from HEAVY WEATHER

An example of Shorter's composition for the influential fusion group. While the overall sound is unrecognizable from the acoustic material, the haunting timbre of Shorter's sax remains.

⑩ JUJU from FOOTPRINTS LIVE!

Shorter's present-day group gives a startling new flavour to this self-penned classic. Collective improvisation at its most impressive.

Nat Defriend

Jane Siberry

Siberry should be a star on a par with Kate Bush, possibly even fellow Canadian Joni Mitchell. Her caring insights into love and nature can be complex and deeply emotional, yet are strongly visual, engagingly conversational and leavened with gentle humour. Most of these songs are from the gorgeously melodic purple patch of her fourth and fifth albums (recorded with something like a conventional band) and can be found on the *Love Is Everything* anthology.

❶ MIMI ON THE BEACH from NO BORDERS HERE
An early landmark: an eight-minute mini-movie with two spoken monologues (Siberry exhorts a young surfing girl to achieve something with her life) yet almost a hit in Canada.

❷ RED HIGH HEELS from THE WALKING
A small church, snow on the fields and a girl going home, thinking of a past love. Sweet and spirited.

❸ THE WALKING AND CONSTANTLY from THE WALKING
"Your shoes, you left your hat/ It's on the bed

or else the chair I don't know, I don't know, I…" The pain and confusion of being unable to let go of a failed romance.

❹ THE LOBBY from THE WALKING
"So I go down to the lobby and everybody stares/ They say, take off that foolish hat, put down that chair…" Spellbinding, slow-motion song about failure to connect.

❺ BOUND BY THE BEAUTY
from BOUND BY THE BEAUTY

"The slowness of the falling leaves across this warm November door/And the geese the flying southness the arms out evermore…" A loving hymn to Mother Earth.

❻ EVERYTHING REMINDS ME OF MY DOG
from BOUND BY THE BEAUTY

A jaunty song of affection to the world that makes you laugh every time you hear it.

❼ LOVE IS EVERYTHING
from WHEN I WAS A BOY

A cry of pain and dismay turns into a determination to love bigger and better still. This Eno-produced flood of emotion is one of her most heartfelt.

❽ CALLING ALL ANGELS
from WHEN I WAS A BOY

"We're hoping, we're trying, we're hurting, we're loving, we're crying… because we're not sure how this goes" – a song of supplication, a duet with KD Lang, and her biggest hit.

Ian Cranna

Simon & Garfunkel

At their best, they recast the Everly Brothers' harmonies for a brighter, more optimistic generation. At their worst, they rehashed the Everly Brothers' incessant squabbling.

❶ THE SOUND OF SILENCE from **WEDNESDAY MORNING 3AM**
Later souped up with a drum track, but just right in this quiet acoustic form.

❷ I AM A ROCK from **WEDNESDAY MORNING 3AM**
As solipsistic as they come, but done with enough conviction to stick in the memory.

❸ HOMEWARD BOUND from **GREATEST HITS**
Allegedly written on Widnes railway station during Simon's sojourn as a struggling song-writer in England. Again, look for this version without a drum track.

❹ KATHY'S SONG from **SOUNDS OF SILENCE**
While in England, Simon learned at the feet of the English folk revivalists, notably Martin Carthy. His influence and that of Bert Jansch can be heard here.

❺ THE 59TH STREET BRIDGE SONG (FEELIN' GROOVY) from **PARSLEY, SAGE, ROSEMARY AND THYME**
Not sure whether to be grandiose or finger-clickin'; eventually, happily, plumps for the latter.

❻ AMERICA from **BOOKENDS**
A Greyhound bus journey becomes a quest for the soul of the nation itself. As they do.

❼ A HAZY SHADE OF WINTER from **BOOKENDS**
The Bangles made this into pure power pop: listening to the original, it's striking how little they had to do.

❽ MRS ROBINSON from **BOOKENDS**
Works as a song even for those who haven't graduated.

❾ CECILIA from **BRIDGE OVER TROUBLED WATER**
John Lennon thought this the most carnal song imaginable: what could be more deca-dent than making love in the afternoon?

❿ MY LITTLE TOWN from **OLD FRIENDS**
A few years after going their separate ways, Simon wrote this cynical, brass-driven song

for Art's sake. They sang it together and it appeared on both their solo albums of the time.

David Honigmann

Paul Simon

Paul Simon strained at the leash as the better half of a duo with Art Garfunkel: his interest in developing a broader palette could be heard in songs like El Condor Paso. Solo, he gave this compulsion full rein, covering New Orleans jazz, embryonic reggae, South African township music, Braziliana and points south. His lyrical preoccupations, however, remained firmly rooted in New York.

❶ FATHER AND DAUGHTER from **THE WILD THORNBERRYS SOUNDTRACK**
A chiming African guitar call opens this charm-ing meditation on a father's love for his daugh-ter – hidden away on a kids' soundtrack album, but as good as anything from his solo career.

❷ DARLING LORRAINE from **YOU'RE THE ONE**
The story of a marriage, it patters on happily until it runs into rocky ground in the penulti-mate verse, rocked by tiny brass stabs like slaps to the face; but it comes through smiling.

❸ THE OBVIOUS CHILD from **RHYTHM OF THE SAINTS**
A rainstorm of drumming from Olodum, a Brazilian carnival bloc, heralds this opening track from *Rhythm Of The Saints*, an attempt to do for South America what Graceland had done for South Africa. As a whole, the album is less successful, but this is musically forceful and lyrically elliptical in true Simon style.

❹ CAN'T RUN BUT from **RHYTHM OF THE SAINTS**
This, by contrast, ripples quietly, folding back on itself as it goes so that it seems to have no beginning and no logical end.

⑤ BOY IN THE BUBBLE from GRACELAND
Groaning opening accordion chords kick off this unmistakable Sotho stormer before massive drumbeats usher in a bassline like floorboards being ripped up with a crowbar. Across the world, the sound of 1986 was the sound of South Africa.

⑥ DIAMONDS ON THE SOLES OF HIS SHOES from GRACELAND
As light as Boy In The Bubble was heavy, this married the breathy choral singing of Ladysmith Black Mambazo to trilling guitar.

⑦ RENE AND GEORGETTE MAGRITTE WITH THEIR DOG AFTER THE WAR from HEARTS AND BONES
Belgian surrealism meets 50s doo-wop.

⑧ STILL CRAZY AFTER ALL THESE YEARS from STILL CRAZY AFTER ALL THESE YEARS
An exaggerated lazy calm, rising into a truncated saxophone solo, serves as defence against the tough talk from an old flame.

⑨ 50 WAYS TO LEAVE YOUR LOVER from STILL CRAZY AFTER ALL THESE YEARS
Only Simon could turn a light ditty to teach rhyming schemes to a child into a tale of romantic desolation.

⑩ LOVES ME LIKE A ROCK from THERE GOES RHYMIN' SIMON
Joyful gospel, backed by the Dixie Hummingbirds, harking back to the soundtrack of Simon's 50s childhood.

David Honigmann

Nina Simone

She set her heart on being a classical pianist and never wanted to be a singer at all. But, despite her reluctance, she could sing her laundry list and make it sound soulful and she became one of the great vocal stylists of the last fifty years. These ten span jazz, blues, pop, swing and soul.

① FEELING GOOD from I PUT A SPELL ON YOU
The High Priestess of Soul at her mid-60s peak.

② MY BABY JUST CARES FOR ME from LITTLE GIRL BLUE
From her very first album in 1959 – though it wasn't a hit until 1987.

③ MISSISSIPPI GODDAM from IN CONCERT
She sang a lot of covers but she was also a fine songwriter. This was one of her most potent civil rights anthems.

④ I PUT A SPELL ON YOU from I PUT A SPELL ON YOU
With one of the best scat passages you will ever hear – copied note for note by Van Morrison and Them.

⑤ STRANGE FRUIT from PASTEL BLUES
Simone found this song so harrowing that she broke down every time she sang it and eventually had to drop it from her repertoire.

⑥ I WANT A LITTLE SUGAR IN MY BOWL from SINGS THE BLUES
At her most delightfully risqué…

⑦ I WISH I KNEW HOW IT WOULD FEEL TO BE FREE from SILK & SOUL
Effortlessly swinging and now forever associated with Barry Norman's TV programme.

⑧ TO BE YOUNG GIFTED AND BLACK from BLACK GOLD
Another of her own compositions, dedicated to her late friend, the playwright Lorraine Hansberry and typical of her growing militancy in the late 60s.

⑨ SAVE ME from SILK & SOUL
Originally released as the B-side of Young Gifted and Black, this version of the Aretha Franklin classic was the funkiest thing she ever recorded.

⑩ FOUR WOMEN from WILD IS THE WIND
This hymn to black feminism is one of her most moving compositions.

Nigel Williamson

The Simpsons

One of the funniest, longest running shows on TV is also chock full of great music. You can track down the episodes – which will yield plenty of musical material unavailable elsewhere – or just grab *Songs In The Key Of Springfield* and *Go Simpsonic With The Simpsons*.

❶ FLAMING MOE'S from **FLAMING MOE'S**
A great TV theme gets the Simpsons' overhaul. Cheers' famous tune didn't have lyrics quite this close to the bone, however.

❷ HAPPY BIRTHDAY MR BURNS from **ROSEBUD**
Short and sweet, just like their own songs, the Ramones put the boot into both Mr Burns and one of the best known tunes in the world.

❸ IN A GADDA DA VIDA
from **BART SELLS HIS SOUL**
Bart decides to play a prank and the Iron Butterfly heavy rock classic gets the big church organ treatment. Sounds entirely appropriate.

❹ SCORPIO END CREDITS
from **YOU ONLY MOVE TWICE**
Spot the Bond theme. Imagine *Goldfinger* with ace lyrics about a homicidal megalomaniac providing his employees with great pensions and health plans.

❺ SEÑOR BURNS from **WHO SHOT MR BURNS?**
The legendary Tito Puente & His Latin Jazz Ensemble sizzle and swing with no small amount of style.

❻ THE GARBAGEMAN from **TRASH OF THE TITANS**
Candyman gets remodelled into a hilariously over-the-top tune about the joys of collecting trash.

❼ THE SIMPSON'S END CREDIT THEME
from **HOMERPALOOZA**
Insanely discordant and awash with ear-bleeding feedback, Sonic Youth thrash through the final credits.

❽ THE SIMPSON'S END CREDIT THEME
from **THE SIMPSONS CONNECTION**
There's nothing quite like a spot-on homage and the familiar theme is delivered in the style of Mike Post's classic *Hill Street Blues*.

❾ WE PUT THE SPRING IN SPRINGFIELD
from **BART AFTER DARK**
The entire Simpsons cast pitch in with this fabulous ragtime romp of a show tune recalling *The Best Little Whorehouse In Texas*.

❿ YOUR WIFE DON'T UNDERSTAND YOU
from **COLONEL HOMER**
A terrific Tammy Wynette tears-in-your-beer country homage. The lyrics mirror Homer's domestic woes and that pedal steel could make a grown man cry.

Essi Berelian

Frank Sinatra

The Voice of the Century with his greatest collaborator, the arranger Nelson Riddle.

❶ I'VE GOT THE WORLD ON A STRING from **THIS IS SINATRA!**
After the crooner of the 40s, the has-been of the early 50s, this 1954 variety of Sinatra, with a gleaming Riddle swing arrangement, was a strutting, swinging optimist.

❷ GET HAPPY from **SWING EASY**
Discreet modern tonalities and a roaring mid-point climax from Riddle with Frank in a freewheeling rhythmic mood, a highlight of his 1954 album.

❸ ILL WIND from **IN THE WEE SMALL HOURS**
At the other end of the emotional spectrum, both Riddle and Sinatra hit compelling depths in 1955 on Harold Arlen's Cotton Club ballad.

❹ I'VE GOT YOU UNDER MY SKIN from **SONGS FOR SWINGIN' LOVERS!**
The most overt example of Riddle's arranging following the intensity arc of sexual foreplay: Sinatra understands and after this flawless

1956 reimagining of Cole Porter's song, so do we all.

⑤ YOU MAKE ME FEEL SO YOUNG from SONGS FOR SWINGIN' LOVERS!

In which an unassuming 1947 romantic ditty is turned for all time by Riddle and Sinatra's Swingin' Lovers masterpiece into a swaggering, lusty celebration of senses awakened.

⑥ I GOT PLENTY O' NUTTIN' from A SWINGIN' AFFAIR!

An audacious 1956 reworking of the Gershwins' song from *Porgy And Bess* in which Riddle's brilliantly reharmonised bass trombone interlude shoots way off the hip-o-meter.

⑦ ONE FOR MY BABY from ONLY THE LONELY

The 1958 treatment of the ultimate saloon song blends Bill Miller's barroom pianistics with hazy strings and a deep Sinatra vocal to devastating effect.

⑧ NICE 'N' EASY from NICE 'N' EASY

Relaxed, swinging, with a hint of sleaze, this 1960 arrangement of a modern song is a rare example of a Sinatra/Riddle classic not built on a standard of the previous generation.

⑨ SUMMER WIND from STRANGERS IN THE NIGHT

Sinatra is winningly stately on Johnny Mercer's weather meditation Summer Wind and the intro riff alone – played on organ on a chord of mysterious properties – is worth the price of the otherwise rotten 1966 album.

⑩ SOMETHING from TRILOGY

Riddle's wondrous recasting of George Harrison's Abbey Road ballad in lush impressionist strings coaxes one of Sinatra's best late-period performances in 1979.

Chris Ingham

Ska

As Independence fever swept the island at the start of the 50s, ordinary, working-class Jamaicans rejected US R&B, or what was fed to them on the BBC-based national radio, in favour of the vociferous homegrown sound of ska. Thus, as an intrinsic expression of Jamaican-ness, it is always going to be hard to beat – certainly as far as these examples go.

① BOOGIE IN MY BONES LAUREL AITKEN from STORY SO FAR

A gloriously hard-partying example of ska's R&B-based forerunner, "JA boogie" and, rest assured, the Trades Description Laws clearly won't be troubling this particular title.

② TEAR UP THE SKATALITES (FEAT. ROLAND ALPHONSO) from STRETCHING OUT

This simplest of ska riffs is so uplifting you can hear Alphonso smiling through his saxophone as he blows some ridiculously cheerful solos.

③ SIMMER DOWN THE WAILERS from THE WAILING WAILERS

Teenage Wailers with the naked power to come out on top of an arrangement so raw it's probably been served its own ASBO.

④ CARRY GO BRING COME JUSTIN HINDS & THE DOMINOES from ANTHOLOGY 64–74

Big bass drum drives this song, meaning Hinds's perfectly weighted vocals can motor along with hardly any cause for as little fuss or strain.

⑤ EASTERN STANDARD TIME DON DRUMMOND from TROJAN INSTRUMENTALS

Contemplative, cool tempo instrumental ska from the master of the minor key, trombonist Don Drummond.

⑥ MADNESS PRINCE BUSTER from HUSH UP!!!

The Prince takes it easy with this hiccuping, rollicking riff, but it's the ultra-affability of his vocals that makes this such an infectious piece of music.

⑦ SKA-ING WEST SIR LORD COMIC & HIS COWBOYS from FROM THE DYNAMIC TREASURY VOL 2

Rudimentary Western-flavoured ska that jumps to the beat like a jack rabbit on the prairie, presided over by one of the first, and still the most laid back, toasters on record.

⑧ BROADWAY JUNGLE THE MAYTALS from **THE BEST OF**
Background shouting, jungle noises, chugging beat and a wailing trumpet, it's the perfect platform for Toots and the boys at their raucous, rasping best.

⑨ STORM WARNING LYNN TAITT & HIS COMETS from **TROJAN MOD REGGAE (BOX)**
A subtly melodic instrumental, that manages to sound optimistic in spite of the rumbling menace in the bassline. Duke Reid really should have produced more ska.

⑩ RAIN OR SHINE THE SKATALITES (FEAT. DON DRUMMOND) from **SKA AUTHENTIC VOL.2**
Three minutes of wild style eastern promise, as Drummond's mournful 'bone blows all the way to Addis Ababa, and the backing keeps up with a woozy, wavey brass-heavy extravaganza.

Lloyd Bradley

Slapp Happy/ Peter Blegvad

"Naive rock", Slapp Happy defined their style, as they embarked on a consciously low-key career in the mid-70s. They were madly out of time, coming at the height of prog rock, but their songs of "sinister whimsy", delivered by the marvellous Dagmar Krause, retain their magic. And in Peter Blegvad, they had a songwriter of most peculiar genius.

SLAPP HAPPY

① JUST A CONVERSATION from **SORT OF**
The quirkily joyous opener from their debut has Krause singing a chorus line over oddball lines of chat from Blegvad and Anthony Moore.

② CASABLANCA MOON from **ACNALBASAC NOOM**
"He used to wear fedoras but now he sports a fez, cabalistic inuendoes in everything he says," begins this very catchy, surreal narrative.

③ A LITTLE SOMETHING from **ACNALBASAC NOOM**
There's a perfection to this breathy love song, strummed on electro-acoustic, with a narrative "from the tip of Alaska to the edge of Spain…"

④ THE DRUM from **ACNALBASAC NOOM**
A quirky rocker, covered by Bongwater two decades on. The Slappy original was recorded by the trio in Germany with Faust.

⑤ SLOW MOON'S ROSE from **CASABLANCA MOON**
Virgin got Slapp Happy to re-record their UK debut album, and on this song, with its sweet, wistful sax break, they got it right.

PETER BLEGVAD

⑥ GOLD from **CHOICES UNDER PRESSURE**
This song is a huge country hit in waiting: a tale of the uselessness of gold, "the lowliest of metals, too soft for serious use, pretty of course…"

⑦ MEANTIME from **KING STRUT**
A train song with a difference: destination meantime, where you could wait for ever.

⑧ KING STRUT from **KING STRUT**
Blegvad's rocking narrative of a dreamer, featuring the terrific line "imagination like a muscle will increase with exercise".

⑨ DAUGHTER from **JUST WOKE UP**
An unusually straight but affecting song on parenthood: "that's my daughter in the water/ Everything she knows I taught her".

⑩ WASTE OF TIME from **CHOICES UNDER PRESSURE**
Perversely, Blegvad prefaced his retrospective album with this tale of "a devil in my cranium who wants to see me fail". Catchy, nonetheless.

Mark Ellingham

Peter Blegvad's
Rx (är'e˘ks')

n 1. A prescription for medicine or a medical appliance. 2. A remedy, cure, or solution for a disorder or problem.

❶ SANTA CLAUS SONNY BOY WILLIAMSON from **THE CHESS YEARS**

A shot of pure adrenaline in which Williamson tears his baby's crib apart (not his tot's cot, you dig) trying to find out "what did she bought me for Santy Claw". He leaps into each verse, piling the fantastic language up, the combo swinging harder and harder until finally he vents a happy "oh yeah!" and lets his harp wail.

❷ TIME FOR THE SUN TO RISE EARL KING from **SEXUAL TELEPATHY**

The haunting guitar has something of the sweetness of Hendrix's Little Wing, but with more primitive mystery and depth. The song evokes a mood of dreamy longing – "Sunrise, why must you come so soon/Sunrise, you don't suit me like the moon."

❸ WHO WILL SING FOR ME THE STANLEY BROTHERS from **16 GREATEST GOSPEL HITS**

Songs by the Stanley Brothers are sinister yet full of light. Heap good goose-bump medicine.

❹ MA'S DREAM BLUES MICHAEL HURLEY from **WATERTOWER**

One of the ruefullest songs ever, vulnerably voiced by the troubadour, cartoonist, former Holy Modal Rounder and occasional loup garrou known as Snock, Wood Bill and other handles to his devotees. Records can be got direct from the man himself at snocknews. com. In this song, Blind Willie McTell and Ma Rainey appear to the dreamer; Willie has regained his sight; Snock starts dancing but when he turns around he realizes…

❺ UP THE LAZY RIVER LOUIS ARMSTRONG

I lost my copy of this years ago. But as soon as I'm asked about all-time favourite tracks I hear it in my head. The scat solo in which Satchmo amazes himself: "Boy am I riffin tonight, I hope sumpin." The trumpet solo which comes up like glory, raising the dead. But memory swerves. Could it really be THAT stately and great? So I order a new copy, wait days, it arrives, I play it, and … that's me, prostrate, acknowledging the transcendent made manifest in my living room.

❻ I MUST HAVE THAT MAN BILLIE HOLIDAY from **LADY DAY, THE BEST OF**

My dad is a great jazz buff. I like to hear him tell how in the 60s Teddy Wilson came to our London flat after a gig and tickled the ivories on our out-of-tune upright. Wilson leads the classic line-up on this celebrated track. Lady Day at her youthful peak, transforming what would otherwise be a mere ditty into a masterpiece. Lester "Nijinsky of the saxophone" Young's solo is one of my favourite moments in music.

❼ MUSIC FOR GLASS HARMONICA (K617) W.A. MOZART from **MUSIC FOR GLASS HARMONICA**

Mozart's last piece of chamber music. The glass harmonica is a series of tuned glasses spinning on an axle and played with wet fingers. Devised by Benjamin Franklin, it makes an unearthly, ethereal sound. In the 18th century people were warned of its effect on sensitive temperaments. Mesmer used it as part of his "animal magnetism" treatments. Necromancers used it to summon the dead. Some of the instrument's most popular players went mad, and by the mid-19th century the instrument had been banned. In fact, it was probably poisoning from the lead in the glass which toppled their reason, so it's perfectly safe to listen to – though this piece does have addictive narcotic properties.

Slide guitar

Tune your guitar to some sort of chord, stick a glass or metal tube over a finger or hold some sort of metal bar in your hand, and slide it up and down the strings. It's a sound associated most strongly with the blues, is claimed by some to have started in Hawaii, but in truth crops up all over the world.

❶ WRITE ME A FEW LINES FRED MCDOWELL from MISSISSIPPI DELTA BLUES
"I don't play no rock'n'roll", claimed Fred, all the while pounding out driving, rattling, awesome country blues like this that made most rockers sound like pale ninnies.

❷ KEHARWA BRIJ BUSHAN KABRA DHUN from EXOTIC SOUNDS ON GUITAR
The father of Hindustani slide guitar, carried to the levels of musicianship required by Indian classical music.

❸ CAN'T BE SATISFIED MUDDY WATERS from THE ANTHOLOGY
He took the acoustic blues of Son House and Robert Johnson onto electric guitar and into the Chicago clubs. The world changed and his mojo henceforth worked.

❹ CAY TRUC XINH KIM SINH from THE ARTISTRY OF KIM SINH
The master of slithery Vietnamese guitar has adapted its sound to the lap Hawaiian version too.

❺ SONG OF THE RANGE JIM & BOB, THE GENIAL HAWAIIANS from HAWAIIAN STEEL GUITAR CLASSICS
They recorded very little in the early 30s, but their extraordinary version of Home On The Range is one of the all-time great slide guitar masterpieces.

❻ COLUMBUS STOCKADE BLUES DARBY & TARLTON from COMPLETE RECORDINGS
These days country music is awash with Dobros and pedal steel guitars, but that slidey sound was pioneered in the old timey music of the 20s.

❼ PALOLO SOL HOOPII from HAWAIIAN STEEL GUITAR CLASSIC
The hottest of the hot Hawaiians from the golden age in the 20s and 30s.

❽ ALALAKE SEKOU "DIAMOND FINGERS" DIABATE from THE SYLIPHONE YEARS
Slide reached Africa too: the aptly nicknamed Diabate showcased it in Guinea's mighty Bembeya Jazz, and it's used in Nigerian juju bands as well.

❾ KOLOPA BOB BROZMAN (WITH LEDWARD KAAPANA) from KIKA KILA MEETS KI HO'ALU
The world's greatest binge collaborationist has blended his virtuoso slide talents with those of players from Okinawa, India, Guinea, La Reunion, Hawaii and beyond.

❿ THE LOVER'S GHOST MARTIN SIMPSON from THE BRAMBLE BRIAR
One of England's finest acoustic guitarists adapts techniques learned from the blues to melodic English and Celtic folk tunes.

Ian Anderson

Sly Stone

The Beatles, The Rolling Stones, The Temptations and James Brown may have had more hits, but no one epitomized the late 60s/early 70s more than Sly & the Family Stone. While other bands paid lip service to such 60s ideals as racial integration, sexual equality and fighting the establishment, the erstwhile Sylvester Stewart and his clan of brothers, sisters and ofays put the rhetoric into practice with some of the most radical, perfectly crafted, galvanizing music ever.

❶ DANCE TO THE MUSIC from **DANCE TO THE MUSIC**

Blends James Brown and The Who so seamlessly that you can't figure out where the rock stops and the soul begins.

❷ M'LADY from **LIFE**

Churning funk almost identical to Dance to the Music, but the groove is so ferocious you won't care.

❸ I WANT TO TAKE YOU HIGHER from **STAND!**
Boom-lacka-lacka-lacka-boom.

❹ EVERYDAY PEOPLE from **STAND!**

Sly took pop's great subject, "everybody is a star", and made it a political statement of empowerment, belonging and belief.

❺ STAND from **STAND!**

In which Sly desperately tries to apply the solipsism of acid rock to the real world.

❻ THANK YOU (FALETTINME BE MICE ELF AGIN) from **GREATEST HITS**

Far removed from the anthemic heights of old, this is a snarling vamp that is the group's most uncompromisingly funky record.

❼ FAMILY AFFAIR from **THERE'S A RIOT GOIN' ON**

Perhaps Sly's best record about being trapped by fate.

❽ QUE SERA SERA (WHATEVER WILL BE, WILL BE) from **FRESH**

In which Sly turns the sickly sweet Doris Day chestnut into a gospel hymn.

❾ IF YOU WANT ME TO STAY from **FRESH**

As savage and brutal a kiss off as Bob Dylan's Positively Fourth Street.

❿ LOOSE BOOTY from **SMALL TALK**

A record that pops with weird energy, but what do Shadrach, Meshach and Abednego have to do with loose booty?

Peter Shapiro

The Small Faces & other mods

Though the mods were famous for masculine peacock finery of the most paisley-patterned rainbow-coloured kind, styles that look good even now were just the icing on the cake of the youth movement, which thrived on soul, bluebeat, ska, Tamla-Motown and the ear-cracking chimes rickenbacker guitars fed without mercy into overdriven amplifiers.

❶ ALL OR NOTHING THE SMALL FACES from **THE ULTIMATE COLLECTION**

Marriott had the voice, the attitude and credit in Carnaby Street strong enough to permit him this most macho of mod lyrics. Not a dance tune, but the perfect accompaniment to your tenth cup of cappuccino in the caff opposite the Flamingo Club.

❷ THE KIDS ARE ALL RIGHT THE WHO from **THE ULTIMATE COLLECTION**

They should have played more Tamla Motown covers and they never mastered Bluebeat, but The Who managed to define mod for a generation. In the lyrics hides a world of teenage confusion and turmoil, locked away behind a cool exterior of blocked (ho! ho!) emotions.

❸ THE 'IN' CROWD DOBIE GRAY from **THE ULTIMATE COLLECTION**

A song so cool that even Bryan Ferry couldn't totally mess it up. It delivers a concentrated distillation of the whole mod ethos painlessly and in less than three minutes.

❹ LET'S GO BABY (WHERE THE ACTION IS) ROBERT PARKER from **THE WARDELL QUEZERQUE SESSIONS**

Ultimate mod sentiments from a man who, oddly enough, wouldn't recognize a mod if one bit him on the leg. It is all about finding yourself the good times, where the beat goes

on and the people don't care about too much
but their clothes. A great dance tune, of course.

⑤ THESE HANDS (SMALL BUT MIGHTY)
BOBBY BLAND from **ANTHOLOGY**
Bland's unmistakeable voice yells his soul out
to the skies on wings of sweet, sweet brass
from the tightest horn section in the town of
Memphis.

⑥ DON'T BRING ME DOWN THE PRETTY THINGS
from **THE BBC SESSIONS**
Stereotypical cool classic British R&B from the
band that gave the Stones bad dreams and
cold sweats. This song of Saturday-night love
affairs was banned by the BBC for the suggestion contained in the lyric "…and when I
laid her on the ground, my head was spinning
round…", what can they have been thinking of?

⑦ HOLD ON I'M COMIN' THE CHORDS from **THIS IS**
WHAT THEY WANT
The mod revival that sprouted in the late 70s
produced some truly forgettable music. This
version of the Sam & Dave soul classic was the
exception. Mod was all about music like this;
fast, sweaty, wearing a huge beaming grin and
so cranked up that the boys can't blink.

⑧ WACK WACK THE YOUNG HOLT TRIO from
LOOKING GOOD (VARIOUS ARTISTS)
Time to break it down and bust yourself a
move or two to the piano stylings of a hot,
shuffling instrumental. Nothing's cooler than
singing along to the bassline like the guy
whose playing it, then freestyling across the
floor to the drum break.

⑨ I'M GONNA RUN AWAY FROM YOU
TAMIYA LYNN from **AT THE CLUB (VARIOUS ARTISTS)**
Lynn's coldly emotional vocal echoes like it was
recorded in the enormous freezer beneath a
meat warehouse, and the melody seems ready
to turn to ice with her. You treated her wrong,
you dog, and even though it breaks her heart,
she's gonna find someone better.

⑩ I GOT A WOMAN (PARTS 1 & 2) JIMMY
MACGRIFF from **GREATEST HITS**
A cool groove with the swinging Hammond
sounds of the man McGriff. Finish off your set

now, sprinkle that talcum on the floor and slide
your stride, but mind my mohair threads, OK?

Al Spicer

Smashing Pumpkins

**Seattle's post-grunge four-piece produced
three breathtaking records (and, it has to
be said, some dross) before imploding.**

① DISARM from **SIAMESE DREAM**
Church bells, strings and acoustic guitar back
Billy Corgan's bellow of rejection and isolation.

② ZERO from **MELON COLLIE AND THE INFINITE**
SADNESS
The definitive Pumpkins grungy rock song, a
rough ride through self-obsessed lyrics, heavy
bass and gnarly riffs.

③ 1979 from **MELON COLLIE AND THE INFINITE**
SADNESS.
The years without responsibility and consequence recalled over a slurry riff and drum
track.

④ TONIGHT TONIGHT from **MELON COLLIE AND**
THE INFINITE SADNESS.
A marching snare compliments a string quartet
as Corgan enthuses "the impossible is possible
tonight."

⑤ SIVA from **GISH**
From the Pumpkins' often forgotten first
album, Siva scruffs its way between soft
melodies and wailing solos.

⑥ TODAY from **SIAMESE DREAM**
The typical Pumpkins dynamic range, juxtapos-
ing a sweet riff against distorted guitar.

⑦ BULLET WITH BUTTERFLY WINGS from
MELON COLLIE AND THE INFINITE SADNESS
Squealing guitars and desperate lyrics: "Des-
pite all my rage I am still just a rat in a cage."

❽ AVA ADORE from ADORE

Like much of the band's later work, a more electronic and less gritty noise for Corgan to sing of selfish, uncompromising desires.

Ben Garfield

Elliott Smith

Having tragically died at the height of his powers, Smith left behind a clutch of albums that constitute a songbook of such quality that his name will not quickly be forgotten.

❶ NEEDLE IN THE HAY from ELLIOTT SMITH

Guitar and voice, simple and effective. The lo-fi production and Smith's near-whisper almost place him and his tape machine in the same room as you.

❷ ROMAN CANDLE from ROMAN CANDLE

A quiet song about anger like no other. An acoustic guitar boils while Smith softly spits venom.

❸ LAST CALL from ROMAN CANDLE

Perhaps this songwriter's finest moment and an unrivalled analysis of the troubled after-math of a relationship.

❹ INDEPENDENCE DAY from XO

An altogether sunnier number that bounces along in a Beatles-esque fashion.

❺ SOMEBODY THAT I USED TO KNOW
from FIGURE 8

Another uptempo amble through Smith's head. He can pretend all he wants that he doesn't care. It's clear that he does.

❻ COAST TO COAST
from FROM A BASEMENT ON THE HILL

This opening cut of Smith's posthumously released final collection is a full throttled stomper that's hard to shake out of your head.

Peter Buckley

Patti Smith

You can forget Tony Soprano and Bruce Springsteen. New Jersey's toughest export is Patti Smith – poet, artist, performer. Although she can occasionally be irritating and scattershot in her work, when she gets it right, there's nobody to match her for purity, intensity and the mystic quasi-religious mania of genius.

❶ REDONDO BEACH from HORSES

The band's incongruously chirpy white reggae at first hides the unfolding story of love gone wrong, arguments, tantrums and suicide down at the beach.

❷ ROCK 'N' ROLL NIGGER from EASTER

The Patti Smith group has no peers when it comes to tales of life in the music world. This track celebrates and glorifies the outsider status of true-blue dyed-in-the-wool rockers. Takes guts to drop the "N-bomb", too, if you're a white woman outta NJ.

❸ FREE MONEY from HORSES

This should be the National Lottery Show theme tune. It's a blue-collar, coupon-clipper's hymn, poignant in its desperate reliance on the gods of chance for a way out of their miserable lives, that builds to a fantastic, liberating peak of release.

❹ PEOPLE HAVE THE POWER
from DREAM OF LIFE

So when we've burned down all the lottery ticket outlets, let's move on to overthrow the system and fight the power. This shall be our rallying song. Patti leads the band and the audience into a singalong, out onto the streets and, waving flaming torches, up to City Hall.

❺ BREAK IT UP from HORSES

Hallucinatory lyrics from childhood fever dreams take the listener up a staircase built from Lenny Kaye's swooping guitar, in one of Patti's greatest moments. Inspiration struck her at Jim Morrison's grave, so the story goes.

Ed Smith's
Pavilion playlist

England cricketer ED SMITH compiled this list of the music he listens to before going out to bat. Smith is also a broadcaster and author of *On and Off the Field*. He writes of his list: "A pavilion, particularly the dressing room, witnesses just about every human emotion: joy, affection, despair, rage, hope, laughter, tears. Team sport leads us to experience the full range, alongside our peers, and music provides a great bond along that journey"

❶ BORN TO RUN BRUCE SPRINGSTEEN from **BORN TO RUN**
Adrenalin-driven but intelligent rock'n'roll. Makes you feel anything is possible.

❷ INTO THE MYSTIC VAN MORRISON from **MOONDANCE**
Cricket attracts Van Morrison fans. My old Kent team-mate Graham Cowdrey has seen him 187 times (seriously). Into The Mystic perfectly captures Morrison's plaintive mysticism. I don't know what it's about and that's just fine.

❸ THE RESCUE BLUES RYAN ADAMS from **GOLD**
"Everybody wants you to be special", runs the opening line, reminding us sports people that we all once harboured hopes of being the best. And for almost everyone, that hope is slowly dashed.

❹ TINY DANCER ELTON JOHN from **MADMAN ACROSS THE WATER**
There are few happier moments than a win followed by a team sing-song. This is the most sing-along-able I know.

❺ IT MAKES NO DIFFERENCE
THE BAND from **THE LAST WALTZ**
In making *The Last Waltz*, Martin Scorsese not only captured a great concert, but also the whole essence of life on the road. Sportsmen, just like musicians, understand the road only too well. While providing a constant stream of new adventures, it makes us vulnerable to nostalgia and introspection.

❻ EVERYBODY'S CHANGING
KEANE from **HOPES AND FEARS**
Tim Rice-Oxley, Keane's keyboardist, played with me in the same Tonbridge School First XI (bowling handy inswingers). He was the same brilliant musician and intelligent, modest man that he is now. Ten years on, Keane were an instant hit in the pavilion – catchy, evocative, moody – and this song is my favourite.

❼ SIMPLE TWIST OF FATE BOB DYLAN from **BLOOD ON THE TRACKS**
Luck, destiny, fate – sport's recurring themes.

❽ EAST MARAH from **20,000 STREETS UNDER THE SKY**
Sometimes you need straight-shooting, no bullshit rock'n'roll. The question is: does anyone make it these days? Marah do, and East is their best – like an early Springsteen song.

❾ FIRE AND RAIN JAMES TAYLOR from **YOU'VE GOT A FRIEND, THE BEST OF JAMES TAYLOR**
Bitter-sweet and melancholic but not depressing, Fire And Rain makes people stop talking and listen (for about a minute).

❿ MOST OF THE TIME BOB DYLAN from **OH MERCY**
Dylan sings this brilliantly: no irony, no bitterness, just straight heartache. Four decades of emotion expressed in five minutes.

6 AIN'T IT STRANGE from **RADIO ETHIOPIA**

While the band click out some precise, uneasy reggae, Patti jolts and stumbles through a trip of imagery all her own, with girls in white dresses, boys shooting white stuff and books of gold.

7 PISSING IN A RIVER from **RADIO ETHIOPIA**

Great song, with intense lyrics that under examination don't appear to mean much to anyone living outside of Patti's head.

8 BECAUSE THE NIGHT from **EASTER**

Smith's magnificent take on a lyric by Bruce Springsteen takes it to an entirely different place.

9 KIMBERLY from **HORSES**

Named after Patti's sister, the one who found it even harder to escape the many tentacles of love in the Smith household, this song hangs in the memory like a promise of rescue left by an escaped cellmate.

10 GLORIA from **HORSES**

The song that started it all for Patti begins with the best line she ever wrote – "Jesus died for somebody's sins, but not mine." Her version of Van Morrison's song blossoms into a bump and grind that climaxes in a breathless ascent of the highest bell tower in the universe.

Al Spicer

The Smiths

The ultimate student bedsit to Los Angeles poolside: the misery of Manchester still sounds sublime.

1 THERE IS A LIGHT THAT NEVER GOES OUT from **THE QUEEN IS DEAD**

The most romantic traffic pile-up in the world – car, ten-ton truck and double-decker bus – with a string section and Morrissey at his sweetest as it unfolds.

2 HOW SOON IS NOW from **HATFUL OF HOLLOW**

Johnny Marr cascades and stutters in a tribute to crippling social inadequacies.

3 THE QUEEN IS DEAD from **THE QUEEN IS DEAD**

"I know you, and you cannot sing," the monarch announces. To which Morrissey would now respond, "But you should hear Camilla play piano."

4 HEAVEN KNOWS I'M MISERABLE NOW from **HATFUL OF HOLLOW**

Desolation, blushing, genuinely funny lyrics and a falsetto. When people parody the Smiths, this is the song they use.

5 MEAT IS MURDER from **MEAT IS MURDER**

The most complete example of The Smiths as a band rather than simply a Moz/Marr duet. And the one that made young vegetarians of thousands.

6 THE HEADMASTER RITUAL from **MEAT IS MURDER**

Cold showers and pupil abuse in all guises – Morrissey sings as if he enjoyed school a great deal.

7 A RUSH AND A PUSH AND THE LAND IS OURS from **STRANGEWAYS HERE WE COME**

A revolutionary call to stand up for yourself in an uncaring world.

8 HAND IN GLOVE from **THE SMITHS**

A mouth-organ heralds a defiantly happy private love story. But not to worry: it's all dashed at the end.

9 I KNOW IT'S OVER from **RANK**

A heartbreaking confessional, it's also the band's most stirring live performance.

10 PANIC from **THE WORLD WON'T LISTEN**

"Hang the DJ" was the singalong, but "the music that they constantly play says nothing to me about my life" summed up precisely why The Smiths stood out.

Simon Garfield

Sonic Youth

Sonic Youth are more of a New York institution than a rock band. Their catalogue is vast and largely essential; as such, this list barely scrapes the surface.

❶ DEATH VALLEY 69 from **BAD MOON RISING**
Thurston and special guest Lydia Lunch scream their way through this blood-shedding aural road movie while hallmark super-fast open-tuned guitar scree falls all around them.

❷ TEENAGE RIOT from **DAYDREAM NATION**
It's impossible not to get swept away by this song; the opening bars gently tuck you in before a whirlwind of killer riffs rip the roof off your house.

❸ SUPERSTAR from **IF I WAS A CARPENTER**
The Youth have tackled many covers over the years, this take on the Carpenters' classic is brilliant, and surprisingly faithful.

❹ SCHIZOPHRENIA from **SISTER**
This radical rework of an old Skip Spence song opens an entire album that no home should be without. Guitars duck and dive and tempos shift with every single note and sound slotting into place like parts of a jigsaw.

❺ I DREAMED I DREAM from **SONIC YOUTH**
An early excursion of menacing power and precision. Could be the soundtrack to a creeping lava flow.

❻ EXPRESSWAY TO YR SKULL from **EVOL**
A slow burning excuse for some amplifier abuse hidden behind a great hook and tune.

❼ BULL IN THE HEATHER
from **EXPERIMENTAL JET SET, TRASH AND NO STAR**
From 1994, this single finds Kim Gordon at the mic for a stripped back stab of angular weirdness.

❽ COTTON CROWN from **SISTER**
Kim and Thurston duet over layers of crunching guitar.

❾ SKIP TRACER from **WASHING MACHINE**
When he's not been busy melting guitar scratch plates, Sonic Youth's Lee Ranaldo has taken the time to write and sing some of the band's most memorable lyrics. This one is a prime example.

❿ WALKING THE COW LUCKY SPERMS from **WALKING THE COW EP**
Track down this SY offshoot project (featuring Mike Watt) if you can. The track was originally by Daniel Johnston and this version of it is genius.

Peter Buckley

Soul ballads

The best of it all came from the same place, the heart, and ended up in roughly the same vicinity, the bedroom. But it was never merely a seduction tool – the soul ballad is the epitome of soul music itself, no matter what era it was recorded in.

❶ THE FIRST TIME EVER I SAW YOUR FACE ROBERTA FLACK
Straightforward and almost startling in its purity of voice and instrumentation. Ballads don't get more soulful than this.

❷ MY GIRL THE TEMPTATIONS
In spite of all the Motown sophistication in the backing, the Temps still manage to sound touchingly naïve, as if they can hardly believe their collective luck.

❸ MUNCHIES FOR YOUR LOVE BOOTSY'S RUBBER BAND
This bonkers, viscous, all-embracing love song practically oozes out of your speakers.

❹ ORDINARY PEOPLE JOHN LEGEND
By taking a satisfyingly lo-fi approach Legend ensures none of his inherent soulfulness gets lost in whatever's going on around him.

Jazzie B's
Soul set

A bit of a polymath, JAZZIE B. The founder of Soul II Soul – who have a good claim to putting British soul on the international map – he has also worked as a producer (James Brown is among his credits), a label boss, and sometime DJ with Kiss FM. "This", he says, "is a playlist of ten records that would be played in my set, and the order in which I'd play them."

❶ FLIP-JACK HUSTLERS OF CULTURE from FAT JAZZY GROOVES
A cult club track, I've been playing this for over five years now and it still commands dancefloor respect.

❷ ONE SWEET LOVE TO REMEMBER ROY AYERS from SOUTHPORT WEEKENDER VOLUME 3
One of those Classic Ayers tracks that is such a big boogie tune.

❸ YOU MAKE LOVE LIKE SPRING TIME TEENA MARIE from IRONS IN THE FIRE
The Lady of Soul. So full of passion, heart, emotion.

❹ AS GENE HARRIS from THE WONDER OF STEVIE
A Stevie Wonder tune, and this updated version really works for me.

❺ LET'S GET IT ON MARVIN GAYE from LET'S GET IT ON
A classic that has been given a new lease of life with an updated backing track, and the original vocals re spun on top.

❻ SUNNY JAMES BROWN from LIVE IN JAPAN
The great Mr Brown with a Japanese re-make that totally blows up the dancefloor.

❼ BATTLE WOOKIE from BATTLE SINGLE
His greatest commercial track.

❽ DUTCH PTA MIX BOOTLEG
A Missy Elliot re-make. This bootleg gets respect.

❾ AS IF YOU READ MY MIND STEVIE WONDER from HOTTER THAN JULY
The don ... 'nuff said!

❿ BACK TO LIFE (SPECIAL MIX) SOUL II SOUL from BACK TO LIFE SINGLE
How could my set be complete without this?

❺ GYPSY WOMAN CURTIS MAYFIELD
On this cool updating of an Impressions' classic Curtis and his guitar are backed by bass, drums, another guitar and a hyperactive bongo player. It's all over much too soon.

❻ I CAN'T STAND THE RAIN ANN PEEBLES
The other half of the Hi sound, with that Hammond organ, the Memphis horns and a Willie Mitchell production buoying up one of the 70s' finest female voices.

❼ JOY & PAIN MAZE
Always a Saturday night anthem, it has to be the live version for this chunky, funky, philosophical approach to lurrrve to make any sense.

❽ ALONE JODECI
Slowed-down swingbeat that allows the group's post-hip-hop attitude to square itself with their no nonsense notions of seduction to create a true love song for the 90s.

⑨ HOMELY GIRL THE CHI-LITES

This has a bizarre country feel to it, backed up by an almost military beat, yet the simple sentiments and smooth harmonizing pulls it all together into a pop soul masterpiece.

⑩ SHE'S SO GOOD TO ME LUTHER VANDROSS

Crisp, percussion-laden and tied up with just the right amount of strings, Luther's voice leads us around a celebration of his love.

Lloyd Bradley

70s Soul

This decade always had a great deal going for it. Following the social upheavals of the 60s, black music had an enormous confidence and sense of purpose and was yet to gobbled up by the mainstream record industry and spat out as disco. Musicians controlled the technology, and not the other way round. Thus 70s soul had a good few years to play by its own rules, pleasing nobody but itself.

① WHO IS HE WHAT IS HE TO YOU? CREATIVE SOURCE

Almost twelve minutes of shimmering percussion, wood-chopping wah-wahs, darting horns and towering vocals, building into a crescendo of paranoia that's borderline psycho.

② THE LOVE I LOST HAROLD MELVIN AND THE BLUE NOTES

Probably the ultimate Gamble & Huff tune: Teddy Pendergass on lead vocal; seemingly random four-part backing harmonies; broken-hearted subject matter; and a bassline that takes no prisoners.

③ LOVE'S THEME LOVE UNLIMITED ORCHESTRA

A forty-piece orchestra works hard to keep up with a rhythm section urged on by a relentless wah-wah guitar in a production as big as Barry White himself. More bling than this and we'd all go blind.

④ BE THANKFUL FOR WHAT YOU GOT WILLIAM DEVAUGHN

Cool, breezy and delicately put together, this easy-rocking hymn to the virtues of poverty is so infectious it makes not having a car sound like a good idea.

⑤ FAMILY AFFAIR SLY & THE FAMILY STONE

Larry Graham percolates his bass under the sparsest organ and guitar, whilst Sly oozes over everything with lyrics quite scary in their whacked-out, self-absorbed pointlessness.

⑥ GHETTO: MISFORTUNE'S WEALTH 24-CARAT BLACK

A classical-type orchestra and choir that moved protest soul into a new, symphonic world, this is an intimidating, bubbling funk slice of a revolutionary opera.

⑦ RIVERS OF MY FATHERS GIL SCOTT HERON/BRIAN JACKSON

Brian Jackson's centre-stage piano, the lowest profile bass and drums, and a world weary Gil all yearn for a better life. There was always much more to Heron than anger and irony.

⑧ THE GHETTO DONNY HATHAWAY

Built almost entirely on an electric piano that doesn't know how to stop and lyrics that limit themselves to "the" and "ghetto". These are eleven minutes of the soul of Donny Hathaway.

⑨ GYPSY MAN WAR

A groove so relentless it could crumble concrete is peppered with percussion and laced with electronica, but it's the harmonica that grabs the tune by its lapels and hurls it into a place beyond street funk.

⑩ WATCHA SEE IS WATCHA GET THE DRAMATICS

There's a riot going on in the background as the instrumentation works against itself. The delivery is mad as hell and the lyrics are a veiled rallying cry, yet it's one of the smoothest soul songs you'll ever hear.

Lloyd Bradley

Blue-eyed soul

In essence, this is soul music made by white singers with great voices, although the lines tend to blur into pop, blues and rock.

❶ REASON TO BELIEVE ROD STEWART from **EVERY PICTURE TELLS A STORY**
Surely the king of British blue-eyed soul, in splendid form with this majestic cover of the Tim Hardin classic.

❷ GROOVIN YOUNG RASCALS from **GROOVIN**
Magnificent mid-60s American group who managed to cross musical boundaries and successfully merge soul and pop. Those voices…

❸ BREAKFAST IN BED DUSTY SPRINGFIELD from **DUSTY IN MEMPHIS**
If Rod's the British King then Dusty is his Queen. This is from perhaps the greatest blue-eyed soul album of them all and written by the great Eddie Hinton.

❹ YOU'VE MADE ME SO VERY HAPPY BOBBIE GENTRY from **ODE TO BOBBIE GENTRY**
Bobbie Gentry crossed several different musical styles from country to pop to soul and always managed to make it sound great. This is a storming cover of the Blood, Sweat & Tears hit.

❺ EVERY KIND OF PEOPLE ROBERT PALMER from **DOUBLE FUN**
Underrated in his lifetime but held by many as a great lost talent. Robert Palmer liked to experiment with styles but rarely sounded better than when he was singing soul.

❻ SHE'S GONE HALL & OATES from **ABANDONED LUNCHEONETTE**
Massively influenced by soul, especially the sound of Philadelphia, Hall & Oates' early work is as good as blue eyed soul gets.

❼ HARDLUCK GUY EDDIE HINTON from **HARD LUCK GUY**
Eddie Hinton was a fantastic songwriter, arranger, musician and singer but never found much fame in his lifetime. Far more a background musician than a star, he died penniless in 1995.

❽ SOUL QUEEN OF NEW ORLEANS AVERAGE WHITE BAND from **SOUL SEARCHING**
Scottish soul music? Well yes indeed and damn fine it is as well. These boys could really, really play funk, soul, even disco and with more than a smattering of panache.

❾ 20 MILLION THINGS TO DO LOWELL GEORGE from **THANKS I'LL EAT IT HERE**
The late leader of the great Little Feat only managed to record one solo album. Buy it, you won't regret it. Beautiful voice, stirring tune and lyrics to break your heart.

❿ HOW LONG ACE from **FIVE A SIDE**
Led by Paul Carrack, owner of a great set of pipes, this was Ace's biggest hit and it has hardly aged at all.

Dave Atkinson

Sounds familiar

A selection of songs with stories to tell about the intricacies of copyright law.

❶ MY SWEET LORD GEORGE HARRISON from **ALL THINGS MUST PASS**
Harrison was successfully sued for subconsciously plagiarizing the Chiffons' "He's So Fine" when writing this tune.

❷ YOU SHOWED ME THE TURTLES from **THE TURTLES PRESENT THE BATTLE OF THE BANDS**
De La Soul sampled a significant portion of this tune in their song Transmitting Live From Mars and found themselves on the wrong end of one of the most significant early copyright cases regarding sampling.

❸ PRETTY WOMAN 2 LIVE CREW from **GREATEST HITS, VOL 2**
This parody version of the Roy Orbison classic was the subject of a lawsuit that went all the way to the US Supreme Court.

❹ OLD MAN DOWN THE ROAD JOHN FOGERTY
from **CENTERFIELD**
This contentious song formed the basis of a lawsuit filed by Fogerty's former label Fantasy Records in which they claimed that he was plagiarizing himself and, by extension, his former band Creedence Clearwater Revival, whose catalogue they owned.

❺ DAZED AND CONFUSED JAKE HOLMES
from **THE ABOVE GROUND SOUND OF JAKE HOLMES**
Jake Holmes' 1967 recording undoubtedly influenced Led Zeppelin's better-known version that appeared on their 1969 debut album, though for unknown reasons he received no songwriting credits.

❻ THE QUEEN AND I JUSTIFIED ANCIENTS OF MU MU from **1987 (WHAT THE FUCK IS GOING ON?)**
Abba discovered that the JAMS had borrowed liberally from their track Dancing Queen in the construction of this song, and subsequently sued, forcing the band to destroy the remaining copies of the records (a process the band documented on the cover of their *History of the Jams* album).

❼ U2 NEGATIVLAND from **U2**
Negativland appropriate and reassemble U2's I Still Haven't Found What I'm Looking For, leading to a lawsuit that almost bankrupts the band and their label.

❽ BITTERSWEET SYMPHONY THE VERVE from **URBAN HYMNS**
The British band was forced to forfeit its songwriting royalties from this massive hit due to an unauthorized sample of the Andrew Oldham Orchestra's 1966 instrumental version of the Rolling Stones' The Last Time."

❾ 99 PROBLEMS DANGERMOUSE from **THE GREY ALBUM**
This ingenious mash-up of The Beatles' *White Album* and Jay-Z's *The Black Album* garners cease-and-desist orders but stays alive via Internet downloads.

❿ 100 MILES AND RUNNIN' N.W.A.
from **100 MILES AND RUNNIN'**
N.W.A.'s three-note sample from Funkadelic's Get Off Your Ass and Jam provided the subject matter for a 2004 case that effectively raised the possibility that any unauthorized music sampling would be illegal under US law.

Butch Lazorchak

South African jazz

In the 50s, Sophiatown in Johannesburg and District Six in Cape Town played host to an African artistic renaissance in art and music and writing. The jazz scene combined American bop influences with the driving marabi rhythms to create a defiant music that was both fresh and doomed: most of its leading lights went into exile, and many met premature deaths.

❶ CHOBOLO SPOKES MASHIYANE from **KING KWELA**
Street-corner pennywhistle jive from the master.

❷ SWITCH CHRIS MCGREGOR AND THE CASTLE LAGER BIG BAND from **JAZZ – THE AFRICAN SOUND**
Chris McGregor would be a mainstay of South African expatriate jazz throughout the 70s with the Brotherhood of Breath. Here he leads a stellar big band on an insomniac recording session, with a tune by the altoist Kippie Moeketsi.

❸ NDENZENI NA? THE FATHER HUDDLESTONE BAND from **DRUM: SOUTH AFRICAN JAZZ AND JIVE**
Trevor Huddlestone was an unlikely jazz impresario as the headmaster of St Peter's, Sophiatown. This is an early outing for Hugh Masekela and Jonas Gwangwa.

❹ BLUES FOR HUGHIE THE JAZZ EPISTLES
from **VERSE 1**
Masekela, Gwangwa, Moekestsi in the front-

line, with Abdullah Ibrahim (then still Dollar Brand) on piano. South African jazz groups don't come much more stellar than that.

❺ SAD TIMES, BAD TIMES KING KONG CAST from THE KING KONG SOUNDTRACK
… unless it's here, in a musical based on the rise and fall of a celebrity black boxer. Starring Miriam Makeba and Nathan Mdledle of the Manhattan Brothers, and with musical support from Masekela and others, this Sophiatown take on *Guys And Dolls* led, indirectly, to most of its cast going into exile.

❻ MIRIAM AND SPOKES PATA PATA THE SKYLARKS from THE BEST OF MIRIAM MAKEBA AND THE SKYLARKS
Makeba and Spokes Mashiyane team up for a kwela jive, topped by some studio backchat in Zulu.

❼ MANNENBERG ABDULLAH IBRAHIM from VOICE OF AFRICA
Ibrahim's seven-note piano riff forms the base over which Basil Coetzee soloes endlessly on saxophone. Halfway between township and Harlem, this track sums up South African jazz.

❽ INGUGA HENRY ZUMA from JAZZ OFFERINGS FROM SOUTH AFRICA
South Africans will recognize this as the theme from the excellent polemical documentary series, *Beckett's Trek*. Everyone else can warm to its scratchy violin jive.

❾ UDF CHRIS MCGREGOR AND THE SOUTH AFRICAN EXILES from THUNDERBOLT
Dudu Pukwana joins McGregor and a scratch band of exile talent in 1986: a brief recapitulation of all that had been lost.

❿ IDUBE POPS MOHAMMED from ANCESTRAL HEALING
A modern mbaqanga stomper that builds from tiny pinpricks of thumb piano to a headlong torrent, in celebration of the 1994 elections.

David Honigmann

South African pop

South Africa has a hugely diverse pop music culture, dominated, currently, by gospel and kwaito –the home-grown hip-hop. Here are some (mostly) modern sounds.

❶ FASSIE VUL' NDLELA BRENDA FASSIE from MEMEZA
Brenda's biggest ever hit, with a great lyric about two gossips at a wedding, set to a classic rousing mbaqanga beat.

❷ THATH'ISIGUBHU BONGO MUFFIN from THE CONCERTO
Great feel-good kwaito number, perfect for line-dancing, township style.

❸ KHULA TSHITSHI LAMI BUSI MHLONGO from FREEDOM
Haunting Zulu ballad, beautifully arranged and produced, from a true maestro of urban roots.

❹ NDIHAMBA NAWE MAFIKIZOLO from SIBONGILE
Surely one of the all time great SA dance tunes, from one of the most potent groups on the kwaito scene today.

❺ NKALAKATHA MANDOZA from NKALAKATHA
Definitive stomp rock/kwaito combo that was a huge and deserved cross-over hit for Mandoza on release in 2000, and is still very popular.

❻ LELILUNGELO ELAKHO LADYSMITH BLACK MAMBAZO from THE VERY BEST OF
Exquisite vocals from Joseph Shabalala and crew, with a subtle and poetic lyric too.

❼ MBUBE SOLOMON LINDA'S ORIGINAL EVENING BIRDS from FROM MARABI TO DISCO
Recorded in 1939, and unquestionably one of the great South African tunes, frequently plagiarized but never bettered.

❽ IT IS WONDERFUL H2O from EXPRESSIONS: WORDS UNLIMITED
Lovely tune that re-works an old Ella Fitzgerald line, adding mellow, well-paced hip-hop lyrics.

❾ KUKE KWAGIJIM' IVENI MFAZ' OMNYAMA from NGISEBENZILE MAMA
A superb example of the Zulu maskanda style, ultra-masculine, yet graceful and melodic.

❿ SONDELA RINGO from SONDELANI
One of the finest SA love songs of recent years, beautifully rendered by the Xhosa heartthrob.

Greg Salter

Southern rock

Southern Rock relies on whiskey-fuelled guitar solos to propel the blues into an elongated boogie that still attracts fans from Atlanta to Aberdeen; despite multiple tragic band member deaths over the years, the genre is still dominated by the Allmans and Skynyrd.

❶ SWEET HOME ALABAMA LYNYRD SKYNYRD from SECOND HELPING.
With its irresistible chorus, defiant lyrics and nifty guitar/piano interplay, this was the high-point of Southern rock's foray into the charts

❷ JESSICA ALLMAN BROS from BROTHERS AND SISTERS
This slide-driven instrumental is the sound of summer, Georgia-style...and TV's *Top Gear*.

❸ FREEBIRD LYNYRD SKYNYRD from PRONOUNCED LEH-NERD SKIN-NERD
A plaintive ballad that develops into the most fiery guitar duel ever recorded.Truly awesome.

❹ GREEN GRASS HIGH TIDES THE OUTLAWS from THE OUTLAWS
The only song to come close to Freebird in fret-burning intensity; guitarist Hughie Thomassen later joined Skynyrd.

❺ MIDNIGHT RIDER ALLMAN BROS from IDLEWILD SOUTH
Much-covered ballad romanticizing Southern outlaws.

❻ THAT SMELL LYNYRD SKYNYRD from STREET SURVIVORS
Burns with indignation that friends could drink and drug themselves to death.

❼ THE DEVIL WENT DOWN TO GEORGIA CHARLIE DANIELS BAND from CHARLIE DANIELS BAND
A crossover hit that tells of a musical duel between the devil and some hapless hick. The fiddle playing is fiendish and, needless to say, the hick wins.

❽ THE WAY LYNYRD SKYNYRD from VICIOUS CYCLE
Never the rednecks of popular imagination, Skynyrd reference the Iraq debacle in this recent epic, as powerful as anything from their heyday.

Chris Coe

Space rock

Sonic properties receive the same emphasis as melody to create an otherworldly feel to the music. Space is the place where music and hallucination fused together.

❶ 2000 LIGHT YEARS FROM HOME THE ROLLING STONES from THEIR SATANIC MAJESTIES REQUEST
From the most unusual album in the Stones' catalogue comes the one song that all space rock music can trace its roots back to. Over thirty years later, this still ranks as one of the best Rolling Stones songs.

❷ LOST IN MY DREAM SPOOKY TOOTH from SPOOKY TWO
Back when Gary Wright was a real rock singer, Spooky Tooth wrote one of the spaciest songs ever. With dark, dreamy vocal imagery and fraz-zled guitars this is some spooky space indeed.

③ MYOPIC VOID CAPTAIN BEYOND
from **CAPTAIN BEYOND**

Captain Beyond came out of nowhere in 1972 and blasted the music scene with rock music that could only be described as "power space".

④ A SPRINKLING OF CLOUDS
GONG from **GONG YOU**

Just about any track from Gong's recordings are as spacey as you can get. Gong's history spans over thirty years and nearly as many albums.

⑤ SANDOZ IN THE RAIN AMON DUUL II from YETI

Sandoz In The Rain is the album's closer and is considered by many to be the birthplace of space rock.

⑥ SEA NATURE STEVE HILLAGE from GREEN

Sea Nature opens what many consider his best album and harkens to the desire for undersea life first explored by Jimi Hendrix on *Electric Ladyland*.

⑦ SET THE CONTROLS FOR THE HEART OF THE SUN PINK FLOYD from **A SAUCERFUL OF SECRETS**

Following the departure of bandmate Syd Barrett (who took a space trip and never returned), Pink Floyd gave everyone in the 60s a creative reason for hallucination. This is a space classic.

⑧ DAMNATION ALLEY HAWKWIND from QUARK, STRANGENESS & CHARM

A tad more polished than previous releases, the band was obviously trying to tighten their sound and become a little more accessible.

⑨ THE PSYCHEDELIC WARLORDS (DISAPPEAR IN SMOKE) HAWKWIND from **THE HALL OF THE MOUNTAIN GRILL**

With the demise of Gong in 1974, Hawkwind became the undisputed kings of space rock.

⑩ PSYCHEDELEKTRIKA TRIP SEQUENCE
NUKLI from **THE TIME FACTORY**

Caution! Put this into your playlist at your own risk. There's no map for the return trip from Nukli's sojourn into deep space!

Geoff Colquitt

Sparks

The most English act to have come out of America (hell, they even use irony!), the Mael brothers have influenced virtually every UK singer/synthesizer duo from Depeche Mode to Pet Shop Boys, and a few more besides; other fans included XTC, The Associates and early Simple Minds. Here's a joyful selection of their cleverest wit and snappiest melodies.

① TALENT IS AN ASSET from KIMONO MY HOUSE

"We're his parents/Everything's relative…" The young Albert Einstein is the focus of this precursor to XTC's Making Plans For Nigel with a dancing hook that sticks for days.

② AMATEUR HOUR from KIMONO MY HOUSE

Teenagers discover puberty in Sparks' second UK hit (with lyrics like "lawns grow thick in the hinterland" it's amazing it got any airplay): one of the best of their glam rock era.

③ THE NUMBER ONE SONG IN HEAVEN from **NO.1 IN HEAVEN**

"Gabriel plays it, God how he plays it…" Giorgio Moroder's driving electro-rhythms provided the perfect foil for the brothers' witty pop, with a neat twist of cynicism.

④ BEAT THE CLOCK from NO.1 IN HEAVEN

"Went to school when I was two/PhD that afternoon…" Not a new idea but wonderfully executed as Sparks are reborn with a production partnership that no one saw coming.

⑤ WHEN I'M WITH YOU from TERMINAL JIVE

"I never feel like garbage when I'm with you…" Sparks could hit tender areas under that deadpan humour; this moving, unexpectedly vulnerable love song is pure genius.

⑥ I WISH I LOOKED A LITTLE BETTER from IN OUTER SPACE

More self-mockery set to a piping Farfisa organ, driving beat and superb tune – a great lost hit from a great lost album.

7 ROCKIN' GIRLS from **IN OUTER SPACE**
"You're the only girl I ever met named Linda Lou/Maybe that's the reason I'm so in love with you…" Clever synth-pop reworking of rock'n'roll's tropes that works in its own right.

8 A FUN BUNCH OF GUYS from **IN OUTER SPACE**
"On our TVs in the sky/Your re-runs come in fine…" Slower deadpan humour as aliens introduce themselves ("here to get a tan and infiltrate") and sneak in a sly comment or two.

9 MUSIC THAT YOU CAN DANCE TO from **MUSIC THAT YOU CAN DANCE TO**
"… that and that alone is enough for me." Sparks' elegantly sardonic response to being rejected by London Records for not making simple enough dance music.

10 WHEN DO I GET TO SING MY WAY? from **GRATUITOUS SAX AND SENSELESS VIOLINS**
"When do I get to feel like Sinatra felt?" A neatly worked yet wistful look at the younger generation, who gained the success that eluded Sparks yet borrowed so heavily from them.

Ian Cranna

The Specials & Two-Tone

Although its revivalist ska and pop-art checkerboard logo were retro in style, Jerry Dammers' label embodied the sound and culture of Britain in the late 70s and early 80s.

1 GANGSTERS THE SPECIALS from **THE SPECIALS**
Prince Buster + punk energy = a revolution.

2 ON MY RADIO THE SELECTER from **GREATEST HITS**
A bouncy and irresistible pop classic.

3 A MESSAGE TO YOU RUDY THE SPECIALS from **THE SPECIALS**
It may have been a pretty straight cover of

Dandy Livingstone's twelve year-old song, but it captured the tenor of the times perfectly.

4 TEARS OF A CLOWN THE BEAT from **THIS ARE 2 TONE**
The group's only single for the label is one of the few Motown covers that actually work.

5 THE SPECIALS TOO MUCH TOO YOUNG from **THE SPECIALS**
This souped-up version of Lloyd Charmers' Birth Control was the label's first #1.

6 TOO EXPERIENCED THE BODYSNATCHERS from **THIS ARE 2 TONE**
Wavering, charming cover of Winston Francis' teen reggae classic.

7 MIRROR IN THE BATHROOM The Beat from **I JUST CAN'T STOP IT**
Savage, scornful, politically engaged – The Beat's finest record.

8 GHOST TOWN THE SPECIALS from **THE SINGLES COLLECTION**
One of the all-time great pop singles and the label's crowning achievement.

9 THE BOILER RHODA & THE SPECIAL AKA from **THIS ARE 2-TONE**
A chilling record about date rape that was unjustly ignored at the time.

10 NELSON MANDELA THE SPECIAL AKA from **THE SINGLES COLLECTION**
That rarest of political records – one that is as joyous as it is earnest.

Peter Shapiro

Phil Spector

The producer who originated the wall of sound, matching dense clusters of orchestration with rock-solid rhythms, fervently emotional singers, and a knack for amazingly catchy songs of love and heartbreak.

① BE MY BABY THE RONETTES from THE BEST OF THE RONETTES
Grabs you by the collar with that echoing opening drumbeat, after which Ronnie Spector's heart-tugging vocal won't let you go.

② HE'S A REBEL THE CRYSTALS from THE BEST OF THE CRYSTALS
A foot-stomping, almost martial beat anchors an anthem of devotion that's both proud and rebellious.

③ YOU'VE LOST THAT LOVIN' FEELIN' THE RIGHTEOUS BROTHERS from ANTHOLOGY 1962–1974
Operatic and booming orchestral pop, delivered as if it's announcing not just the end of a relationship, but the end of the world itself.

④ DA DOO RON RON THE CRYSTALS from THE BEST OF THE CRYSTALS
Where nonsense syllables say more about the thrill of an onrushing new romance than the most eloquent poetry. Great scampering piano, too.

⑤ RIVER DEEP, MOUNTAIN HIGH IKE & TINA TURNER from RIVER DEEP, MOUNTAIN HIGH
A maze-like mini-epic, jam-packed with ascending and descending riffs, rattling percussion, and ardent declarations of passion.

⑥ AWAITING ON YOU ALL GEORGE HARRISON from ALL THINGS MUST PASS
Harrison's pious religious sermonizing sounds like a call to party rather than prayer, owing to a mini-wall of thunderous percussion and chanting voices.

⑦ THEN HE KISSED ME THE CRYSTALS from THE BEST OF THE CRYSTALS
The insistent three-note riff that opens and motors this hit might be simple, but you'll never tire of it.

⑧ BABY I LOVE YOU THE RONETTES from THE BEST OF THE RONETTES
Another great, unstoppable hook in the wordless moaned chorus, Ronnie Spector's quivering voice melting the hardest hearts to jelly.

⑨ UPTOWN THE CRYSTALS from THE BEST OF THE CRYSTALS
Cinematic, Latin-tinged drama of American urban life, where the tenement changes from symbol of ghetto squalor to palace of sexual fulfillment.

⑩ WALKING IN THE RAIN THE RONETTES from THE BEST OF THE RONETTES
Complete with actual thunder effects, as dank and tempting as an actual wet walk huddled with your honey, with an especially anthemic chorus.

Richie Unterberger

Spirit

Spirit's brand of west coast psychedelia blended Randy California's guitar pyrotechnics with the jazz drumming genius of father-in-law Ed Cassidy, and it developed a cult following on both sides of the Atlantic.

① NATURES WAY from THE 12 DREAMS OF DR SARDONICUS
Randy's gentle ecology ballad that became an instant hippy anthem.

② LIKE A ROLLING STONE from SPIRIT OF 76
One of the great Dylan covers; the interplay between whispered vocals and delicate guitar refrains subverts the vitriol of the original.

③ MR SKIN from THE 12 DREAMS OF DR SARDONICUS
Founder member Jay Ferguson's brassy attack on pornographers.

④ RUN, RUN, RUN from JO JO GUNNE
OK, strictly speaking this isn't Spirit, but it would be a shame to ignore one of the all-time great rock singles, produced by Ferguson's solo project.

⑤ HAPPY from SPIRIT OF 76
The Stones re-invented with reverb and distortion.

6 HEY JOE from **SPIRIT OF 76**
Hendrix taught California guitar, and this trippy tribute to his mentor shimmers relentlessly under the weight of some mind bending guitar.

7 FARTHER ALONG from **FARTHER ALONG**
An instant classic from Spirit's period of re-invention in the late 70s.

8 THE OTHER SONG from **SON OF SPIRIT**
Cosmic blues interspersed with light jazz, and the kind of time changes that make Spirit so distinctive.

Dusty Springfield

The queen of British blue-eyed soul, embracing everything from lowdown R&B to show tunes with grace and grit.

1 I ONLY WANT TO BE WITH YOU from **THE VERY BEST OF DUSTY SPRINGFIELD**
Her first solo hit was not just dynamite soulful pop, but also among the most credible emulations of Phil Spector's wall of sound.

2 YOU DON'T HAVE TO SAY YOU LOVE ME from **THE VERY BEST OF DUSTY SPRINGFIELD**
Overblown it might be, but it's overblown to a purpose, and reined in by Dusty's ultra-commanding vocal.

3 WISHIN' AND HOPIN' from **THE VERY BEST OF DUSTY SPRINGFIELD**
The Merseybeats had a British hit with this Bacharach/David classic, but Springfield landed an American one with one of her most wistful performances.

4 I JUST DON'T KNOW WHAT TO DO WITH MYSELF from **THE VERY BEST OF DUSTY SPRINGFIELD**
More peerless Bacharach/David interpretation, Dusty unsurpassed in maintaining determined dignity as her love life falls to pieces.

5 SON OF A PREACHER MAN from **DUSTY IN MEMPHIS**
Justly acclaimed as one of the all-time 60s soul classics, from her much-vaunted recordings with genuine Memphis soul musicians.

Richie Unterberger

Bruce Springsteen

The new Boss is much the same as the old Boss: for more than thirty years, Bruce Springsteen has been delivering a spectacular rock'n'roll show that touches on masculinity, working-class solidarity and the quest for romance, in the widest sense, in an unromantic world.

1 THUNDER ROAD from **BORN TO RUN**
A carillon peal gives a carousel spin to this energetic opener to Springsteen's first really huge album.

2 MEETING ACROSS THE RIVER from **BORN TO RUN**
A short story of self-deception and doom, with a melancholy trumpet running through it like an undertow.

3 BADLANDS from **DARKNESS ON THE EDGE OF TOWN**
A thumping rocker: you'll be too busy chanting along even to wave a lighter in the air.

4 PROMISED LAND from **LIVE 1975/85**
In the studio (on *Darkness At The Edge Of Town*), this was fine, but a bit thin; the live version lifts it into another dimension.

5 THE RIVER from **THE RIVER**
The river starts as a symbol of liberation and end up as an emblem of despair: the narrator who starts of swimming comes to dream of drowning. A stark harmonica riff seals the leaden atmosphere.

6 I'M ON FIRE from **BORN IN THE USA**

Born In The USA was so triumphalist on the surface that Ronald Reagan referred to it approvingly, to the discomfort of the sterlingly Democratic Springsteen. This is a song so obsessive it borders on the creepy, with a metronomic drum tick pushing it along.

7 SEEDS from **LIVE 1975/85**

Only available in this live version, Seeds sets the travails of redundant oil workers to a spring-heeled bass lead.

8 BECAUSE THE NIGHT from **LIVE 1975/85**

A collaboration between Springsteen and Patti Smith: his version is smoother and easier than hers, and you can hear entire stadia singing along.

9 TUNNEL OF LOVE from **TUNNEL OF LOVE**

Springsteen bids farewell to his first marriage in this tale of a relationship that begins as a tunnel of love and ends as a haunted house.

10 THE GHOST OF TOM JOAD from **THE GHOST OF TOM JOAD**

Springsteen's quieter acoustic songs tend to favour lyrics over melody and are an acquired taste. But this one, about illegal immigrants into the border states, rises from a whisper into a barely sung chorus, precisely capturing its subjects' combination of invisibility and pride.

David Honigmann

The Stax sound

For a decade, from the early 60s to the early 70s, Stax Studios in Memphis was responsible for some of the greatest soul and blues music ever created, thanks in no small measure to a roster of musicians, songwriters and producers ranging from Booker T & The MGs to Isaac Hayes.

1 GREEN ONIONS BOOKER T & THE MGS from **GREATEST HITS**

The definitive funky soul instrumental.

2 SOUL FINGER THE BAR-KAYS from **GREATEST HITS**

A magnificent 1965 dance groove from the Bar-Kays, several of whom died in the plane crash that killed Otis Redding.

3 IN THE MIDNIGHT HOUR WILSON PICKETT from **GREATEST HITS**

An early classic of Southern soul, superbly delivered by the wicked Mr Pickett in 1965.

4 HOLD ON, I'M COMIN' SAM & DAVE from **THE BEST OF SAM & DAVE**

Yet another solid-gold slide of deep soul, co-written by Isaac Hayes in 1966.

5 KNOCK ON WOOD EDDIE FLOYD from **KNOCK ON WOOD**

Floyd's barnstorming 1967 hit was written with Steve Cropper in Memphis' Lorraine Motel, where Martin Luther King later died.

6 (SITTIN' ON) THE DOCK OF THE BAY OTIS REDDING from **THE OTIS REDDING ANTHOLOGY**

Otis Redding. Otis was the heart and soul of Stax; his biggest hit was recorded shortly before he died in 1967.

7 PRIVATE NUMBER WILLIAM BELL & JUDY CLAY from **THE BEST OF WILLIAM BELL**

Sublime soul duet from 1967.

8 THEME FROM SHAFT ISAAC HAYES from **SHAFT**

"Black Moses" established himself as the funkiest man on the planet with this 1971 movie soundtrack.

9 I WANNA GET FUNKY ALBERT KING from **I WANNA GET FUNKY**

The title track of a great 1972 album by the finest of Stax's small roster of blues artists.

10 RESPECT YOURSELF THE STAPLE SINGERS from **STAX-O'-SOUL**

Uplifting gospel/soul fusion from the veteran Staples in 1972.

Greg Ward

S

Steely Dan

There really are no half measures with Steely Dan. You either love the three ages of Dan or you hate them. From the first recordings 33 years ago through to the most recent, nothing revolutionary happens, it's just a clever pop groove.

❶ AJA from AJA
If you love drums enjoy, if you play them cry as Steve Gadd shows you how.

❷ THROUGH WITH BUZZ from PRETZEL LOGIC
It's short, it's sweet, its swirls. Quit drugs in 1 minute 32 seconds.

❸ DIRTY WORK from CAN'T BUY A THRILL
Early genius with Dave Palmer taking a rare non-Fagen lead vocal. All the elements are there that made everything that followed great.

❹ BAD SNEAKERS from KATY LIED
If the lyrical picture painting doesn't get you Michael Macdonald's backing vocals will sweep you away. His voice was amazing back then.

❺ COUSIN DUPREE from TWO AGAINST NATURE
The big return after twenty years and they were as clean and clever as ever. Fagen reminds us that our cousins can grow up to be sexy women.

❻ DEACON BLUES from AJA
The perfect late 70s song. There are no obvious clues to what its all about and it doesn't really matter. It just takes you somewhere else.

❼ ANY MAJOR DUDE from PRETZEL LOGIC
Listen to the words and it's very dark but the style and vibe is very light indeed. Lyrics that include phrases like "superfine" and " my funky one" just seem to work so well.

❽ MY RIVAL from GAUCHO
It rolls and grooves its way along with an extended fade-out that suggests an assured confidence. They had nothing left to prove.

❾ THE THINGS I MISS THE MOST from EVERYTHING MUST GO
Fagen is doing his best to cope with divorce but he is rather more obsessed with his material loss than any emotional one. It's nasty, funny and honest all at the same time.

❿ THE FEZ from ROYAL SCAM
The keyboard and guitar work is just superb. Who the hell cares what it's about – it just makes you smile. A song that could go on for forty minutes instead of four.

John Duhigg

Al Stewart

If he sounded less like Neil Tennant and had less of a weakness for Andrex-soft-rock he would be taken as seriously as he deserves. When they were both penniless Soho folk singers in the mid 60s, Paul Simon offered to sell Stewart his entire song catalogue. Stewart refused.

❶ ROADS TO MOSCOW from LIVE AT THE ROXY
An epic song by pop standards, but a lot shorter than *A Day In The Life Of Ivan Denisovitch*. The studio original starts with a botched cross-fade; this live version is flawless.

❷ ON THE BORDER from YEAR OF THE CAT
The title track of this album has become dulled by overfamiliarity, but this short, sharp, urgent tale of nocturnal gun-running still hums.

❸ OLD ADMIRALS from PAST, PRESENT & FUTURE
Probably the only song to have been inspired by First Sea Lord Jackie Fisher, a lament for old admirals who feel the wind but never put out to sea.

❹ NIGHT TRAIN TO MUNICH from BETWEEN THE WARS
The album tells the history of 30s Europe dancing into 1939 in a series of vignettes: this one comes on like a long-lost collaboration between Django Reinhart and Eric Ambler.

347

⑤ TRAINS from **FAMOUS LAST WORDS**
Steve Reich would explore the same imagery in Different Trains: a symbol of escape and freedom becomes the way to the Death Camps, the whole 20th century racing headlong down the tracks.

⑥ ANTARCTICA from **LAST DAYS OF THE CENTURY**
An icy flute motif frames an obsessive, busy song.

⑦ FIELDS OF FRANCE from **LAST DAYS OF THE CENTURY**
A delicate tale of World War I aviation, set to a fragile piano and flute duet.

⑧ POST WORLD-WAR TWO BLUES from **PAST PRESENT AND FUTURE**
British history from 1945 to 1973 condensed into a rollicking torrent.

⑨ SOHO (NEEDLESS TO SAY) from **RHYMES IN ROOMS**
If Subterranean Homesick Blues had been written in London, it would have sounded like this.

⑩ FLYING SORCERY from **YEAR OF THE CAT**
Vanished aviatrix as erotic touchstone.

David Honigmann

Stiff Records

"If it aint Stiff it aint worth a fuck" was the pioneering London independent label's motto. From 1975 to 77 it almost held true.

① WHAT'S SO FUNNY ('BOUT PEACE, LOVE AND UNDERSTANDING?) NICK LOWE from **PURE POP FOR NOW PEOPLE**
Cynical or serious? Nick never let on. Covered on *The Bodyguard* soundtrack, it made Lowe a millionaire. One imagines he laughed all the way to the bank!

② NEW ROSE THE DAMNED from **DAMNED DAMNED DAMNED**
The first 45 of the UK punk movement

unleashed the likes of Rat Scabies and Captain Sensible upon the world. Moronic but brilliant.

③ WATCHING THE DETECTIVES ELVIS COSTELLO from **THIS YEAR'S MODEL**
The girlfriend's hooked on TV cop shows; Costello's full of malice. His best ever song got to #15 in the UK charts in 1977.

④ SWEET GENE VINCENT IAN DURY AND THE BLOCKHEADS from **NEW BOOTS & PANTIES**
From a misfit to a misfit: Ian celebrates Gene in what could be cited as one of the few love songs of the punk era.

⑤ NEAT NEAT NEAT THE DAMNED from **DAMNED DAMNED DAMNED**
Even faster and funnier than New Rose. British rock'n'roll has rarely been so exhilarating.

⑥ ONE CHORD WONDERS THE ADVERTS from **CROSSING THE RED SEA**
The Adverts only had one chord but they made good use of it on this attempt at a punk anthem.

⑦ MY GIRL MADNESS from **ONE STEP BEYOND**
"My girl's mad at me," sang Suggs and the nation wanted to give him a cuppa and a cuddle.

⑧ HIT ME WITH YOUR RHYTHM STICK IAN DURY AND THE BLOCKHEADS from **DO IT YOURSELF**
Mix cockney innuendos, soft disco groove, screeching sax solo and proto-rap rhyming and what do you get? #1 UK for two weeks. Those were the days…

⑨ WHITE LINE FEVER MOTORHEAD from **THE BEST OF**
The metal lepers were given a break by Stiff in 1977 so they recorded a salute to amphetamine. Music to grind teeth to.

⑩ HOLE WIDE WORLD WRECKLESS ERIC from **WRECKLESS ERIC**
Eric thinks his dream girl just might live in Tahiti. He packs his lunch and heads off to find her.

Garth Cartwright

Sting/The Police

Not known for not taking himself seriously enough, the former teacher is also a sharp songwriter. The Police married tight white reggae to irresistible pop hooks; Sting's solo career spiced things up with jazz and world flavours.

❶ ROXANNE from THE SECRET POLICEMAN'S BALL
A solo version that brings out the song's cheeky pathos.

❷ MESSAGE IN A BOTTLE from REGGATTA DE BLANC
Ferociously energetic punk-reggae where hook and central image mesh like cork and bottleneck.

❸ WALKING ON THE MOON from REGGATTA DE BLANC
Slow and spacey in the right way, with Andy Summers' guitar defying gravity as Sting walks home dancing on air.

❹ DON'T STAND SO CLOSE TO ME from ZENYATTA MONDATTA
Now they were unstoppable enough to rhyme "shake and cough" with "Nabokov". For the time being, they got away with it. But the pretension police were noting it all down in Sting's criminal record.

❺ INVISIBLE SUN from GHOST IN THE MACHINE
The thumping bassline that runs through the verse drops away into a chasm for the chorus of this song about Northern Ireland, banned from radio broadcast on its first release.

❻ EVERY LITTLE THING SHE-DOES IS MAGIC from GHOST IN THE MACHINE
Two minutes of pure joy from an otherwise dark album.

❼ FORTRESS AROUND YOUR HEART from DREAM OF THE BLUE TURTLES
Schoolbook Sting, taking an outlandish metaphor and treating it seriously. Branford Marsalis is indispensable on saxophone.

❽ FRAGILIDAD from NADA COMO EL SOL
A quarter of *Nothing Like The Sun* was devoted

Michael Stipe's
Support network

REM always chose their support acts with great care and most of the artists on Michael Stipe's list have at one time or another supported the band on tour…

❶ IN THE SUN JOSEPH ARTHUR from COME TO WHERE I'M FROM

❷ WING PATTI SMITH from GONE AGAIN

❸ WE ARE NOWHERE AND IT IS NOW BRIGHT EYES from I'M WIDE AWAKE IT'S MORNING

❹ HIDDEN SONG ANGELA MCCLUSKEY from THE THINGS WE DO

❺ MERCEDES CHILDREN THE CHEEKS from WHAT YOU HEARD

❻ AUNT AVIS VIC CHESNUTT from DRUNK

❼ REVERSE NOW IT'S OVERHEARD from FALL BACK OPEN

❽ FAVOURITE WRITER MAGNAPOP from MAGNAPOP

❾ NIGHTS OF THE LIVING DEAD TILLY AND THE WALL from WILD LIKE CHILDREN

❿ H THE PRESIDENT FLASH TO BANG TIME from GLO

to songs about human rights abuses in South America. This version of Fragile does the logical thing and recasts the song in Spanish. It has deservedly become a standard.

⑨ I BURN FOR YOU from **BRING ON THE NIGHT**
Looser than the Police's version on the *Brimstone and Treacle* soundtrack, an impeccable slow blues.

⑩ DESERT ROSE from **BRAND NEW DAY**
Cheapened and sold out by its appearance in a car advert, but symbolic of Sting's continuing interest in world music, even if Cheb Mami's singing makes you wish that Sting would shut up for a moment.

David Honigmann

The Stone Roses

At the end of the 80s Ian Brown and cohorts were the messiahs of Manchester, delivering one of the greatest debut albums of all time. Contractual disputes and procrastination meant the long-awaited follow-up largely fell between the two stools of Led Zep and Happy Mondays so they broke up.

❶ I WANNA BE ADORED from **THE STONE ROSES**
The band announce their intent as rumbling bass emerges from some quiet noodlings before a tasty riff and a pop/psych tune take over.

❷ SHE BANGS THE DRUMS from **THE STONE ROSES**
A lovely bass run and shimmering guitars make this 60s-style paean to Lady Love flow like a paisley dress in the breeze.

❸ ELIZABETH MY DEAR from **THE STONE ROSES**
If the composer of Scarborough Fayre were around he would have sued for royalties on the intro. The ensuing pop masterpiece is closer to The Beatles by the end.

❹ SUGAR SPUN SISTER from **THE STONE ROSES**
The finest hook on the album precedes Brown's swing into "Sometimes I fantasise". There's even a touch of Latin semi-acoustic and a wailing electric solo.

❺ THIS IS THE ONE from **THE STONE ROSES**
Byrds jangles and a sudden three-chord stab surround Brown's plaintive vocals about what he's been waiting for all his life.

❻ I AM THE RESURRECTION from **THE STONE ROSES**
The tour de force album closer is almost a mini rock opera with offbeat drums, honeyed bass, killer riffs and pure psych vocals of punk vitriol. And they return for more just when you think they've done.

❼ TEN STOREY LOVE SONG from **SECOND COMING**
A quasi-eastern intro dissolves into the album's finest moment – pop magic with a haunting tune and the customary psychedelic sensibilities.

❽ HOW DO YOU SLEEP from **SECOND COMING**
Not a cover of the Lennon tirade against Macca but just as nasty, albeit wrapped in sugary tones and West Coast guitar fluidity.

Nick Edwards

The Stranglers

Previously known as the Guildford Stranglers, the "meninblack" had a head start on the competition when punk kicked off – they were already competent musicians, they had a mean way with a lyric and blended boyish smut with testosterone-induced rage in a manner most appealing.

❶ GET A GRIP (ON YOURSELF) from **IV RATTUS NORVEGICUS**
This jaundiced but jerkily energizing track contemplates the evils of life on the rock and roller

coaster: no money, no privacy, no appreciation, no personal hygiene, just the endless routine of turning up, tuning up, and playing the same set night after night after night.

❷ HANGIN' AROUND from IV RATTUS NORVEGICUS
There's a bad-taste pun lurking somewhere in the lyric about Christ "hanging around" on the cross but the song's main aim is to illustrate the boredom, listlessness and ennui of life on a 70s street corner.

❸ NO MORE HEROES from NO MORE HEROES
Two-fisted macho growling about one of punk's strongest articles of faith.

❹ SKIN DEEP from AURAL SCULPTURE
Hugh Cornwell croons a lyric of cynical disappointment, betrayal and friendship turned sour. He left the band shortly after.

❺ GOODBYE TOULOUSE from IV RATTUS NORVEGICUS
Harmonies in the backing vocals and a fiercely complicated rhythm meant this track stood out from the flood of punk rock that hit the streets in 1977.

❻ DUCHESS from THE RAVEN
Posh porno fantasy lyric of a naughty aristocrat with a taste for both quality and quantity in her desires. Frothy and lacking in social comment, but a damn fine tune and chortle-along refrain of "and the Rodneys are queueing up, God forbid".

❼ NICE 'N' SLEAZY from MENINBLACK
In a cellar club, people of indeterminate gender are removing their clothes while dancing. Somebody charges you a huge price for a watered-down drink and then you hear the music. As a hand slips into your jacket removing your wallet, you recognize it as this old time Stranglers' classic.

❽ GOLDEN BROWN from LA FOLIE
There's simply not enough harpsichord in rock music. Let's all listen to the delicately traced butterfly wing of a guitar solo and pretend it is nothing more than a gentle waltz-time song written to please a gently tanned lover.

❾ STRANGE LITTLE GIRL from LA FOLIE
A re-treading of the ground covered by the Beatles in She's Leaving Home but updated for a later and more dangerous period. Keyboards, strings and electric guitars all chip in to stop the heroine getting too bruised by the cold dark world she moved into.

❿ SOMETHING BETTER CHANGE from NO MORE HEROES
Now a dad-rock classic track that provokes inappropriate dancing with the first run through of its instantly recognizable opening riff, this is JJ Burnel's best known vocal and still one of the best of the punk rock originals.

Al Spicer

The Strokes

The band that transformed the musical landscape back in 2001, just when everyone thought rock was dead.

❶ HARD TO EXPLAIN from IS THIS IT
Music condensed to claustrophobic essentials: verse as catchy as chorus, chorus like a runaway train, inarticulacy as "fuck you" attitude.

❷ LAST NIGHT from IS THIS IT
The perfect meeting point between the Velvet Underground and Iggy Pop, but entirely Strokes in its compressed syncopation and shrugging melodicism.

❸ SOMEDAY from IS THIS IT
This melodic midpacer neatly combines melancholy and exuberance, the line "all my fears come back to me in threes" lunges straight for your pacemaker.

❹ REPTILIA from ROOM ON FIRE
Heed not those who slag the second album. A great catcalling vocal, and a scorching Nick Valensi guitar solo make this a Strokes classic.

⑤ 12:51 from **12:51** This Cars-influenced single is slow medicine, but over time its infectious synth-guitars, machine drums and mechanical claps become addictive.

⑥ THE MODERN AGE from **IS THIS IT**
Where it all started: those stuttering Lou Reed vocals and a heady sense that rock music was suddenly visceral and vital again.

⑦ TRYING YOUR LUCK from **IS THIS IT**
The nearest these cynics get to sounding romantic. Yearning, almost delicate in its intricacy with another fantastic Valensi solo.

⑧ BARELY LEGAL from **IS THIS IT**
A typically dismissively misanthropic Casablancas lyric wedded to totally exuberant music, clipped but excitable, concluding in a headrushing climactic lift.

⑨ WHAT EVER HAPPENED? from **ROOM ON FIRE**
Business-meaning opener to the second album: Casablancas at his most splenetically throaty and disaffected.

⑩ THE END HAS NO END from **ROOM ON FIRE**
More synth-like guitars criss crossing Casablancas' megaphone vocal, just as the delicate verse and crescendoing chorus criss-cross in turn.

Toby Manning

Studio One

Clement "Coxsone" Dodd's Studio One label launched the careers of many of Jamaica's greatest stars, including Bob Marley and Burning Spear. For many aficionados, the bass-heavy sound of Studio One's much-recycled rhythms is the definitive sound of classic reggae.

① WHAT KIND OF WORLD? THE CABLES from **WHAT KIND OF WORLD?**
The perfect Studio One formula; contempla-

tive harmonizing backed by a metronomic bass beat.

② BOBBY BABYLON FREDDIE MCGREGOR from **STUDIO ONE ROCKERS**
Despite his later success, McGregor never really topped his early Studio One hits, like this rasta anthem.

③ HOW CAN I GO ON? THE GAYLADS from **SOUL BEAT**
This young vocal trio cut a superb album for Studio One in the 60s.

④ FATTIE FATTIE THE HEPTONES from **THE HEPTONES 20 GOLDEN HITS**
Perhaps the Studio One group to beat them all, in fine voice.

⑤ MR BASSIE HORACE ANDY from **NICE UP THE DANCE – STUDIO ONE DISCOMIXES**
Still going as strong as ever in the 21st century, the high-voiced Horace produced a strong of Studio One classics.

⑥ SET ME FREE KEN BOOTHE from **STUDIO ONE SOUL**
A gloriously mellifluous extended version of The Supremes classic.

⑦ NICE UP THE DANCE MICHIGAN AND SMILEY from **NICE UP THE DANCE – STUDIO ONE DISCOMIXES**
Rollicking nonsense from the DJ duo at their youthful peak, once again backed by the Real Rock rhythm.

⑧ YAHO THE VICEROYS from **RESPECT TO STUDIO ONE**
Short and sweet, a lovely little piece of piratical nonsense.

Greg Ward

Summertime

Of the hundreds of versions in myriad styles of the song written in 1924 as part of Gershwin's "folk-opera" *Porgy And Bess*, here are ten crackers.

❶ SIDNEY BECHET from **JAZZ ANTHOLOGY 1939**
Bechet's soprano sax had an almost primeval howl, perfectly suited to the crying Gershwin melody.

❷ THE ZOMBIES from **THE ZOMBIES**
Revered British beat combo turned it into a hip jazz waltz on their 1964 debut album.

❸ THE THREE SOUNDS from **HERE WE COME**
Excellent relaxed swinging jazz trio from 1960 featuring the deeply groovy Gene Harris on piano.

❹ SANTO AND JOHNNY from **SANTO AND JOHNNY**
Best known for their 1959 instrumental hit Sleepwalk, the Farina brothers' version is hauntingly twangsome.

❺ ELLA FIZGERALD AND LOUIS ARMSTRONG from **PORGY AND BESS**
Two entirely different vocal approaches – the smooth and the rough – yet equally resonant and affecting.

❻ JONI MITCHELL from **GERSHWIN'S WORLD**
The first appearance of Joni as smoky jazz singer; the vocal is lived-in and luscious, and there's a gorgeous harmonica solo by Stevie Wonder.

❼ ALBERT AYLER from **MY NAME IS ALBERT AYLER**
A torrential highlight from the avant garde primitivist saxophonist's 1963 session.

❽ MILES DAVIS from **PORGY AND BESS**
Set among Gil Evans's cloudy Dorian horns, Miles's 1959 reading has an icy cool modality.

❾ LARRY ADLER from **GENIUS OF LARRY ADLER**
No one could tease out the beauty of his old friend George's melody like harmonica virtuoso Larry, or so Larry says anyway.

❿ PAUL MCCARTNEY from **CHOBA B CCCP**
Part of his Russia-only rock'n'roll release from 1988, a loose bluesy jamming attitude gives Macca a chance to tear into a risky vocal.

Chris Ingham

The Supremes & Diana Ross

Sweet sounds from the Queen Bees of Motor City.

❶ BUTTERED POPCORN THE SUPREMES from **MEET THE SUPREMES**
Florence Ballard delivers sexy, sassy, soul worthy of Etta James.

❷ WHEN THE LOVELIGHT STARTS SHINING THROUGH HIS EYES THE SUPREMES from **WHERE DID OUR LOVE GO**
Holland-Dozier-Holland get the girls on the dancefloor for their first proper pop song.

❸ WHERE DID OUR LOVE GO THE SUPREMES from **WHERE DID OUR LOVE GO**
Diana's barely-there vocal backed up with the Motown double-drum sound and a thousand "baby babys". Their first #1.

❹ LOVE IS LIKE AN ITCHING IN MY HEART THE SUPREMES from **SUPREMES A GO-GO**
Catchy as love hives.

❺ NO MATTER WHAT SIGN YOU ARE DIANA ROSS AND THE SUPREMES from **LET THE SUN SHINE IN**
The Supes get psyched. "I don't care about your rising sign", indeed.

❻ LOVE CHILD DIANA ROSS AND THE SUPREMES from **LOVE CHILD**
Funky-feeling delirious tenement-dwelling fantasy.

❼ STORMY THE SUPREMES from **NEVER-BEFORE-RELEASED MASTERS**
Sensitive rework of the easy-listening classic. Sweet enough to make a grown man cry.

❽ UP THE LADDER TO THE ROOF THE SUPREMES from **RIGHT ON**
New recruit Jean Terrell takes the helm for this Diana-a-like wah-wah fest.

9 SURRENDER DIANA ROSS from **SURRENDER**
Stripped down and serious. Ashford & Simpson deliver a soul classic for Diana's pre-disco album.

10 LOVE HANGOVER DIANA ROSS from **DIANA ROSS**
Breathless disco two-parter that sees Diana pull out the stops. She don't need no cure …

Rachel Coldicutt

Surf's up

The soundtrack to coastal Californian life in the early-to-mid 60s, whether it was instrumentals with oceanic guitar reverb or chipper odes to beach bumming by the Beach Boys and Jan & Dean.

1 SURF CITY JAN AND DEAN from **SURF CITY: THE BEST OF JAN & DEAN**
Two girls for every boy – the ultimate pre-women's lib male teenage fantasy. But what great falsetto harmonies from Beach Boy (and co-writer) Brian Wilson.

2 SURFIN' USA THE BEACH BOYS from **SURFIN' USA**
The tune was taken from Chuck Berry's Sweet Little Sixteen but the sun-baked harmonies and utopian ode to surf culture were all Beach Boys.

3 WIPE OUT THE SURFARIS from **SURFIN' HITS**
Infectious maniacal laughter, a drum roll solo copied by garage bands the world over, and an up-and-down guitar riff that won't quit.

4 PIPELINE THE CHANTAYS from **SURFIN' HITS**
Rubbery bass, pre-Doors mysterioso electric keyboards, and guttural guitar twang evoke both the majesty and fatal danger of the deep.

5 SURFIN' SAFARI THE BEACH BOYS from **SURFIN' SAFARI**
Their first big hit matches the guitar chug of Eddie Cochran with impeccably timed harmonized exhortations to get on the surfing bandwagon.

6 MISERLOU DICK DALE from **SURFIN' HITS**
Latin and middle eastern melodies collide, and wet staccato riffs mimic swelling waves, on the signature tune by the king of surf guitar.

7 SURFER GIRL THE BEACH BOYS from **SURFER GIRL**
Every surfing stud needs another half, lovingly idealized on this arching ballad, with another great falsetto vocal from Brian Wilson.

8 SURFIN' BIRD THE TRASHMEN from **SURFIN' HITS**
Two-chord jitter with delightfully moronic strangled vocals, taking an off-the-wall turn into the unaccompanied gargles of a drowning man halfway through.

9 CATCH A WAVE THE BEACH BOYS from **SURFER GIRL**
Riding the surf is made to sound like an almost holy experience, the vocal harmonies on the chorus rising like a tidal wave.

10 MAR GAYA THE FENDER IV from **GUITAR PLAYER PRESENTS LEGENDS OF GUITAR: SURF VOL 1**
Phenomenal machine-gun-fire surf guitar on this obscurity, which roars with the menace of an oncoming tsunami.

Richie Unterberger

Swingers

New Swing, or Jump Jive, was briefly huge in America in the late 90s and was further popularized by the cult movie *Swingers*. The new breed of big band swing has produced some of the finest music to dance to in years.

1 GO DADDY O BIG BAD VOODOO DADDY from **BIG BAD VOODOO DADDY**
This is seen by many as the essential track of the genre. Go Daddy O provides a high point in the cult film *Swingers*, delivered by one of the most exciting live bands of the time. It's a killer.

❷ RED LIGHT! INDIGO SWING from RED LIGHT!

Johnny Boyd has a beautiful, sweet, soulful voice and on Red Light he croons for all he's worth.

❸ ZIP GUN BOP (RELOADED) ROYAL CROWN REVIEW from THE CONTENDER

With a blistering mix of film noir, bebop and punk Zip Gun Bop fair races along. Anyone trying to dance to this one is likely to end up in traction. They call it Gangster Bop and I'm not arguing.

❹ JUMP JIVE & WAIL THE BRIAN SETZER ORCHESTRA from DIRTY BOOGIE

Ex-Stray Cats mainman Setzer updates Louie Prima's classic jump jive tune. It turned up in an advert, sold thousands of chino trousers and put Setzer's amazing live band at the forefront of the New Swing movement in America.

❺ BOOZIN' AND A CRUISIN' DEM BROOKLYN BUMS from THERE GOES THE NEIGHBOURHOOD

More Gangster Bop from another New York band. A live favourite which swings like the devil.

❻ SHE COULD BE A SPY SWINGERHEAD from SHE COULD BE A SPY

Band leader Michael Andrew is swing, from the collar of his leopard-print jacket to the very tips of his shoes. You can hear his love of Sinatra, Burt Bacharach and Bobby Darin in every second.

❼ EVERY SINGLE DAY JET SET SIX from LIVIN' IT UP

New York City's finest exponents of kitschy, lounge cool mix hipster swing and some good ol' 60s melodies with killer tunes and a great horn section.

❽ MR WHITE KEYS CHERRY POPPIN' DADDIES from ZOOT SUIT RIOT

Formed way back in 1989 by ex-punk rockers, The Daddies have a huge, ska-inspired sound and masses of attitude.

❾ RENAISSANCE IN HARLEM COMFY CHAIR from PARTY ON THE TITANIC

A band from San Francisco who play as either an acoustic three-piece or a hard rockin' four-piece. This one is from their debut album and shows just a hint of their full cabaret madness.

Gavin McNamara

Syliphone

The elephant's (syli was also an alias for president Sekou Touré) label was one of the most important and influential African labels of all times. What was published here was avidly listened to by fans and musicians alike throughout West Africa.

❶ INTRODUCTION/TENTEMBA BEMBEYA JAZZ NATIONAL from L'ANS DE SUCCÈS

The band starts a long intro and takes you on a maelstrom while the track progresses. Bembeya should be known as one of the best pop bands of all times!

❷ LA GUINEE MOUSSOLOU ORCHESTRE DE LA PAILLOTE from VOLUME 1

This is track one of the very first LP on Syliphone. Opened by a shady guitar this is a bolero which sings the praises of the Guinean women.

❸ N'NA KOUYATÉ SORY KANDIA from KOUYATÉ SORY KANDIA

Most of the recordings of this giant singer are with his "ensemble traditional", but this one blends perfectly electric guitar, saxophone and balaphon and the powerful mezzo soprano.

❹ KADIA BLUES ORCHESTRE DE LA PAILLOTE from 40ÈME ANNIVERSAIRE SYLIPHONE VOL 2

A spooky tune reminiscent of Louis Armstrong: a muffled trumpet, bluesy notes from a guitar, the snare played with brushes…

❺ PETIT SEKOU BEMBEYA JAZZ NATIONAL from DISCOTHÈQUE 76

A guitar scorcher from Sekou "Bembeya" Diabaté, aka Diamond Fingers. With an irresistible groove and calm, Diabaté shows off his talents.

⑥ SO I SI SA SUPER BOIRO BAND from **40ÈME ANNIVERSAIRE SYLIPHONE VOLUME 1**
Unbelievable keyboard playing with a pumping rhythm section that leads you straight to the dancefloor.

⑦ WHISKY SODA DEMBA CAMARA W. BEMBEYA JAZZ NATIONAL from **HOMMAGE À DEMBA CAMARA**
This is pure fun: one guy is singing the virtues of whisky soda and is getting tipsier throughout the song in an adaptation of a highlife rhythm.

⑧ MALOUYAME MIRIAM MAKEBA from **DISCOTHÈQUE 73**
Little is know about Miriam Makeba's stay in Guinea where she was looking for shelter with husband Stokely Carmichael. This one is also known as the widely popular "Bani", a traditional tune.

Jean Trouillet

David Sylvian

After leading the arty pioneers of the early 80s New Romantic explosion, the highly talented Sylvian headed off on an avant garde odyssey of his very own…

① FORBIDDEN COLOURS from **SECRETS OF THE BEEHIVE**
More graceful than the *Merry Christmas, Mr Lawrence* version, Ryuichi Sakamoto also tinkles the ivories on this simple and beautiful song.

② GHOSTS JAPAN from **TIN DRUM**
Who'd have thought something so oblique and odd could be a hit? Electronic bleeps and spectral chimes decorate a sparse vocal and haunting synth melody.

③ JEAN THE BIRDMAN DAVID SYLVIAN & ROBERT FRIPP from **THE FIRST DAY**
David Sylvian sounding almost playful? Who'd have thought it possible? An upbeat vocal bounces around a cool Robert Fripp guitar melody.

④ LATE NIGHT SHOPPING from **BLEMISH**
Icily detached yet bizarrely intimate, Sylvian's vocals are eerily perfect. The stark electronic handclap rhythm is particularly spooky.

⑤ MIDNIGHT SUN from **DEAD BEES ON A CAKE**
A weird amalgam of creaking delta blues and Sylvian sound art. Ryuichi Sakamoto provides the off-kilter brass arrangements.

⑥ MOTHER AND CHILD from **SECRETS OF THE BEEHIVE**
The acoustic bassline is simply divine and provides a perfect foil for Sylvian's dusty croon. The fractured jazz of the mid section is superb also.

⑦ NIGHTPORTER JAPAN from **GENTLEMEN TAKE POLAROIDS**
Sylvian sounds almost supernaturally miserable and lonely here. His fragile voice floats above a lost piano and ghostly cello.

⑧ QUIET LIFE JAPAN from **QUIET LIFE**
A more dancefloor-oriented effort with a crisp beat and some artfully drawn guitar lines weaving around the synth and bass interplay.

⑨ RIVER MAN from **GONE TO EARTH**
Robert Fripp provides strange and ethereal guitar textures while Sylvian sounds particularly contemplative. Great sax midway through, too.

⑩ TALKING DRUM JAPAN from **TIN DRUM**
Pop music as abstract art. Mick Karn's slippery fretless bass sounds as though it's turning to jelly in his hands.

Essi Berelian

T

June Tabor

The great tragedy queen of English folk, with a well-nigh infallible ear for a song. Most of her albums begin with A, like a taxi firm trying to be first in the Yellow Pages.

❶ A PLACE CALLED ENGLAND from A QUIET EYE
This Maggie Holland song argues for an English nationalism based on landscape and botany rather than ethnicity. Tabor's reading comes with a full jazz orchestra: the highpoint of a wonderful album.

❷ STRANGE AFFAIR from A CUT ABOVE
Tabor, here with Martin Simpson, folk guitarist extraordinaire, takes on a song from Richard and Linda Thompson. Electric from the very first line.

❸ I WONDER WHAT'S KEEPING MY TRUE LOVE TONIGHT from ALEYN
Also known as Green Grass It Grows Bonny, this song is common to both Scottish and Irish traditions: Tabor claims it for the English, too.

❹ NO MAN'S LAND/ FLOWERS OF THE FOREST from ASHES AND DIAMONDS
One of Eric Bogle's peerless Great War laments, twinned with the trad Flowers Of The Forest.

❺ SIR PATRICK SPENS from AN ECHO OF HOOVES
The album collected border ballads of horse thievery, kidnap and murder from the English-Scottish badlands. Sir Patrick Spens's doomed sailing expedition was top of these pops.

❻ DI NAKHT from ALEYN
On *Aleyn* Tabor cast her net wider than folk, including this Yiddish song of the 1920s that acquired a darker, sadder context over the coming decades.

❼ FALSE, FALSE from AGAINST THE STREAMS
Stark and accusing, with not a syllable wasted. Collected by Ewan McColl and Peggy Seeger from an Aberdeenshire traveller called Christina MacAllister, who sounds formidable.

❽ A PROPER SORT OF GARDENER from ALEYN
Another Maggie Holland horticultural song, about familial love.

❾ MISSISSIPPI SUMMER from FREEDOM AND RAIN (THE OYSTER BAND)
Taking a break from solo work to pose as rock chick singer with the ever reliable Oyster Band, Tabor and the Oysters brought life to this formerly arid delta blues.

❿ ROSE IN JUNE from ROSA MUNDI
Rosa Mundi was (of course) a concept album about rose growing. Tabor found a full song-book to explore, and the highlight was this, with words by Bob Copper, and a spring in its piano line that leaves the listener smiling.

David Honigmann

Talking Heads

David Byrne was half-geek, half-preacher; Chris Frantz and Tina Weymouth were an endlessly versatile rhythm section; Jerry Harrison had the funk. Together, they explored every style under the new wave sun, and still had time to make the only watchable concert film ever made.

❶ LOVE GOES TO BUILDING ON FIRE from SAND IN THE VASELINE: POPULAR FAVORITES
This early song has the nerdy plastic energy that drives all the band's early work.

❷ DON'T WORRY ABOUT THE GOVERNMENT
from **THE NAME OF THIS BAND IS TALKING HEADS**
From the early, scratchy punk-funk Heads, this is a celebration of strong central government that sounds like the military-industrial complex set to the music of the 50s.

❸ I ZIMBRA from **FEAR OF MUSIC**
Dadaist nonsense verse by Hugo Ball set to frenetic West African guitars.

❹ ONCE IN A LIFETIME from **REMAIN IN LIGHT**
The synthesizer riff gushes like a fountain as Byrne harnesses the demeanour of a charismatic preacher to a tale of alienation and anomie: "And you may ask yourself: How did I get here?" Eno chips in with the chorus.

❺ BURNING DOWN THE HOUSE
from **SPEAKING IN TONGUES**
This began life as a chanted Parliafunkadelicment chorus, but then evolved into one of the Heads' best-loved songs.

❻ THIS MUST BE THE PLACE (NAÏVE MELODY) from **STOP MAKING SENSE**
A tender song about domesticity: how un-rock can you get? In the film, Byrne can be seen at this point dancing with a standard lamp.

❼ STAY UP LATE from **LITTLE CREATURES**
A song that ackles and bounces like a demented toddler – which is pretty much what it is about.

❽ BLIND from **NAKED**
Central American menace pervades this jackhammer opener from the Heads' underrated sign-off album.

❾ MR JONES from **NAKED**
Any relation to Dylan's Mr Jones, who didn't know what was happening? Either way, he's back in town.

❿ (NOTHING BUT) FLOWERS from **NAKED**
Jocular guitar from Johnny Marr and backing vocals from Kirsty McColl sweeten this tale of a dystopian garden paradise.

David Honigmann

Tango

Though its musical treasures are many, Argentina has been associated with tango more than any other style for over a hundred years. This urban music with rural roots appeared in the late 19th century, when Buenos Aires became Argentina's capital city, but it's also experienced a thrilling revival of late, brushing thighs with dance beats and electronica.

❶ MI BUENOS AIRES QUERIDO CARLOS GARDEL
from **BUENOS AIRES BY NIGHT**
The most famous tango singer ever became a global phenomenon for his operatic style during tango's golden age in the 1920s and 30s. Then he died in a plane crash, ensuring immortality.

❷ LA CUMPARSITA JUAN D'ARIENZO Y SU ORQUESTA TIPICA from **100 AÑOS EN 100 TANGOS**
The most popular instrumental tango of all time. Much covered (you'll recognize it!) the first recording of it dates from 1916, but this 1937 version is superbly atmospheric.

❸ RESPONSO ANÍBAL TROILO from **100 AÑOS EN 100 TANGOS**
One of the stars of the 1940s, accordionist and composer Troilo gave Piazzolla his first break. Here he shows off his skills as a soloist on an intense, cinematic instrumental.

❹ SOBRE EL PUCHO TITA MERELLO from **WOMEN OF TANGO**
A gloriously dramatic, almost camp, number from 1964 by this little known artiste. Despite the music's chauvinism, there have been plenty of excellent female tango singers.

❺ VUELVO AL SUR ROBERTO GOYENECHE from **CAFÉ ARGENTINA**
Goyeneche was hugely respected by generations of younger *tangueros*, and by the Argentinean public for his *garganta con arena* (throat with sand) .

6 MILONGA DEL ANGEL ASTOR PIAZZOLLA from **LUNA**

Like watching gravity hold its breath, this ghostly, drifting masterpiece by the Einstein of tango was recorded during his last ever concert on July 26, 1989.

7 CADA VEZ QUE ME RECUERDES ADRIANA VARELA from **CORAZONES PERVERSOS**

There is no other contemporary female tango singer who can touch Varela for sheer style and sultriness. This early 90s piece is a highlight in a career still going strong.

8 SANTA MARIA (DEL BUEN AYRE) GOTAN PROJECT from **GOTAN PROJECT**

Tango moves effortlessly into club lounge class with this imaginative piece of tango electronica. Grace Jones would be proud of it, having herself tackled Piazzolla.

9 MULETA DE BORRACHO DANIEL MELINGO from **SANTA MILONGA**

A heavenly choir and a voice that sounds like it's been through hell make for a winning combination on this recent recording by an icon of tango's contemporary avant-garde.

10 AY, DI MÍ CRISTÓBAL REPETTO from **CRISTÓBAL REPETTO**

A dazzling new vocal talent, whose take on this 1941 song is as old school as 21st century tango gets. Repetto has also worked with electronic *tangueros* Bajofondo Tango Club.

Jon Lusk

James Taylor

JT created the template for the sensitive singer-songwriter and has found no need to depart from it in almost forty years.

1 SOMETHING IN THE WAY SHE MOVES from **JAMES TAYLOR**

From his debut 1968 album on The Beatles' Apple label, and the song that inspired George Harrison's Something.

2 CAROLINA IN MY MIND from **JAMES TAYLOR**

Taylor at his sunniest – although before we get too carried away the song does include the line, "Ain't it just like a friend of mine to hit me from behind."

3 SWEET BABY JAMES from **SWEET BABY JAMES**

A lilting lullaby for his young nephew and the title track of the most perfectly sensitive singer-songwriter album of its time.

4 FIRE AND RAIN from **SWEET BABY JAMES**

Was there ever a more heartbreaking opening line than "Just yesterday morning they let me know you were gone"?

5 YOU'VE GOT A FRIEND from **MUD SLIDE SLIM AND THE BLUE HORIZON**

Written by Carole King and with Joni Mitchell singing backing vocals, all the ladies wanted to be James's special friend.

6 MUD SLIDE SLIM AND THE BLUE HORIZON from **MUD SLIDE SLIM AND THE BLUE HORIZON**

On which he gets a little funky with guitarist Danny Kortchmar and a top-notch band.

7 DON'T LET ME BE LONELY TONIGHT from **ONE MAN DOG**

And a thousand broken hearts in bedsitter-land sung along.

8 SHOWER THE PEOPLE from **IN THE POCKET**

Tender sentiments with his then-wife Carly Simon on backing vocals.

9 SECRET O'LIFE from **JT**

Words of wisdom from a 1977 album, made just as his own life was about to go off the rails into addiction and divorce.

10 COPPERLINE from **NEW MOON SHINE**

It's perhaps unfair that this 1991 track is the only representation of Taylor's post-70s output, for he's continued to make quality albums throughout his long career.

Nigel Williamson

The Teardrop Explodes

Brass-flavoured acid depravity and pop songs of searing, everlasting perfection from Julian Cope and his posse. The Teardrops took psychedelia back to the schoolkids, knowing they could be trusted to fry their own brains when the time came. Stardom wasn't to Julian's taste and he turned first odd, then solo (for more on which, see his individual playlist).

❶ BENT OUT OF SHAPE from THE COLLECTION
Spooky beats and deceptively jaunty brass introduce the Teardrops' unique mix of over-awing pop and nervous, inquisitive lyrics.

❷ BOUNCING BABIES from THE COLLECTION
Desperate sounding yet still undeniably sweet and appealing, Baby Julian must have been a dear. He grew up to be a bouncing bomb, so he says here.

❸ COLOURS FLY AWAY from THE COLLECTION
Julian's skilled weave of strange yet compelling imagery instantly promoted him to the premier league of psychedelic explorers. This ream of slightly threatening nonsense hasn't dated in the least.

❹ KILIMANJARO from THE COLLECTION
Spinning around in a daze booted rhythmically in the rear by the band's most rock solid beat, Julian pumps out the psychedelia like a man who's taken some kind of a drug.

❺ LIKE LEILA KHALED SAID from THE COLLECTION
Ms Khaled hijacked her first airliner in the late 60s and became a revolutionary pin-up for frustrated guerrillas all over the world – even in Julian's bedroom. The song has little to do with her life but it's good to know who she was.

❻ PASSIONATE FRIEND SAINTS & SINNERS MIX BY LIQUID Single
Long before he was openly championing the lost majesty of Scott Walker, Julian was doing a fair impression of the man. This is pure 80s but could so easily have been 20 years previous. The Liquid remix of this already heavenly soulful tune lays on even more of the diva vocals.

❼ REWARD from THE COLLECTION
Horns blare, keyboard lines wiggle up and down the keyboard like snakes on your spine then Julian lets rip "Bless my cotton socks! I'm in the news!". This song is a rush.

❽ SEVEN VIEWS OF JERUSALEM from THE COLLECTION
The Teardrop Explodes, it must be remembered, was a band – not simply Julian and a set of session musicians. This is keyboards-man Dave Balfe's highest achievement, an infinitely repeatable progression teased from nowhere.

❾ THE GREAT DOMINIONS from THE COLLECTION
Saint Julian's most glorious awesome sunset of melancholy.

❿ TREASON (IT'S JUST A STORY) from THE COLLECTION
Julian hides his poison in the sweet-smelling bouquet assembled and attractively wrapped by the band as an ensemble.

Al Spicer

Techno

The robots are taking over! Dance music for a machine world. All tracks are singles, but they appear on various compilations, such as the *Hardest Hits* and *New Wave Club Class-X* series.

❶ WARM LEATHERETTE THE NORMAL single
This 1978 B-side could have been released into clubs today… though the lyrics (inspired by J.G. Ballard's automobile-erotic novel *Crash*) aren't exactly uplifting.

❷ FUTURE MODEL 500 single
"The future is here": so says the robotic voice on Juan Atkin's cold, metallic techno manifesto from 1985.

❸ ONE NIGHT IN NEW YORK CITY
THE HORRORIST single
Eerie music-box bells and a nauseating squelchy bassline underpin this twisted techno lullaby, telling the story of a sleazy night out.

❹ INNER CITY JUNKIES
KEKTEX/SARCOBLAST single
An anti-anthem of the nihilistic London squat techno scene, with its vocal cataloguing every conceivable drug abuse. Also, a typical example of London techno: fast and relentless.

❺ ENERGY FLASH JOEY BELTRAM single
Representing the backlash to the second Summer of Love, this is a dark, uneasy blend of subtly filtered synths and handclaps, along with the famous "ecstasy…" vocal samples.

❻ DOMINATOR HUMAN RESOURCE single
Notable for its effective early use of the "hoover" noise, which was later appropriated by a million terrible hard house tunes.

❼ THE BELLS JEFF MILLS single
With its remixes still causing mayhem in clubs now, The Bells boasts the most instantly recognizable hook in techno.

❽ MUTATE AND SURVIVE OLIVER HO single
Weirdly looped backwards vocals gradually emerge over a backing of densely layered percussion. The blend is sweatily euphoric.

❾ SOMETIMES LEO LAKER single
A perfect example of how minimal techno should be done… warm and hypnotic, repetitive but never boring.

❿ SPASTIK PLASTIKMAN single
A flurry of syncopated snare rolls, an insistent kick drum, and not much more. Richie Hawtin's finest moment.

Dan May

Television

Arty, poetic and capable of some of the most elegant and beautifully flowing guitar lines in rock, Television still get lumped in with primeval New York punk rockers like the Ramones. Tom Verlaine probably finds that slightly irritating.

❶ LITTLE JOHNNY JEWEL from THE BLOW-UP
Kicking off the list with a fifteen-minute guitar virtuoso performance that makes strong male guitar players fall down on their knees and weep, and a lyric of four-word three-chord dumbness. The ultimate art-punk interface.

❷ PROVE IT from MARQUEE MOON
Laid-back New York swagger of a tune, with a cool Spanish strolling guitar riff that leads you unsuspecting into a Verlaine ambush around the corner down the alley in the chorus.

❸ GUIDING LIGHT from MARQUEE MOON
So trippy and hallucinatory that the band, and finally you too, lose your place in this real world and float off to the land of Tom Verlaine's elegant solo from paradise.

❹ TORN CURTAIN from MARQUEE MOON
Darkest of Television's epic ballad-expeditions to the core of inner space and one of Verlaine's most melodramatic moments. It's not surprising the rest of the band left him soon after.

❺ VENUS DE MILO from THE BLOW-UP
One of the best guitar riffs to come from the CBGB's scene and a perfect example of the band's psychedelic/jazz/punk/soul grooves.

❻ ELEVATION from THE BLOW-UP
The live take of this classic is the one to hold out for; it's dramatic and heart-wrenchingly gorgeous.

❼ MARQUEE MOON from MARQUEE MOON
Nine minutes long (the Ramones would be halfway through their set in that time), this has enough confidence to stretch out forever and

beyond, only kicking in with the full-on majesty when everybody's comfortable.

❽ FRICTION from **MARQUEE MOON**
Staccato guitar from Lloyd, like he's trying to machine gun the first three rows of the crowd, making way for one of Verlaine's balletic whirls up and down the neck of his guitar.

Al Spicer

The Temptations

Motown's most versatile vocal group, blessed with several fine lead singers and the ability to handle both smooth ballads and socially conscious funk-psychedelia.

❶ SINCE I LOST MY BABY
from **THE ULTIMATE COLLECTION**
A classy early Smokey Robinson production, the strings and call-response vocals dripping with reflective sorrow.

❷ AIN'T TOO PROUD TO BEG
from **THE ULTIMATE COLLECTION**
A rough'n'ready David Ruffin vocal, and another example of how The Temptations could growl as well as purr.

❸ MY GIRL from **THE ULTIMATE COLLECTION**
An unforgettable upward-curling guitar lick, one of Smokey Robinson's best lyrics, and a magnificent uplifting chorus. What else do you need?

❹ (I KNOW) I'M LOSING YOU
from **THE ULTIMATE COLLECTION**
Few other Motown productions emanate such angst, from both the foreboding piano riff and David Ruffin's straining lead vocal.

❺ THE WAY YOU DO THE THINGS YOU DO
from **THE ULTIMATE COLLECTION**
The Temps' first hit was a mega-catchy mid-tempo groove, with a strutting swing quite impossible to resist.

❻ GET READY from **THE ULTIMATE COLLECTION**
Underrated mid-charting 1966 single had both a compulsive funky riff and a superb Eddie Kendricks falsetto lead vocal.

❼ I CAN'T GET NEXT TO YOU
from **THE ULTIMATE COLLECTION**
Wonderful tag-team lead vocal tradeoffs on this lusty 1969 American #1, as well as a surprise instrumental drum break.

❽ PAPA WAS A ROLLING STONE
from **THE ULTIMATE COLLECTION**
Post-60s gloom hits soul music with a vengeance on the grim percolating funk of this tale of a shiftless patriarch.

❾ CLOUD NINE from **THE ULTIMATE COLLECTION**
Psychedelia hits soul music on this late-60s hit, both in the waves of wah-wah guitar and the drug-alluding lyric.

❿ PSYCHEDELIC SHACK
from **THE UNIVERSAL MASTERS COLLECTION**
Gimmicky but fun hit from the peak of the group's psychedelic excursions, with some positively searing guitar and electronic squeals on the chorus.

Richie Unterberger

Texas singer-songwriters

Despite its great expanse and a spate of regional differences, Texas produced a tight community of singer-songwriters who shared a loyal if not stadium-filling fan base. Dylan had already proven that you didn't have to be a good singer to write good songs and, voice-wise, the Texas group is hit and miss. The talent, though, is rich and they offer up a bit of everything: high plains and backland prairies, country and rock, western and folk, gypsy music and Mexicali blues.

① PANCHO AND LEFTY TOWNES VAN ZANDT
from **THE LATE GREAT TOWNES VAN ZANDT**
Now that Van Zandt is gone, it's hard to see a show in which his cohorts don't cover at least one of his tunes. Recognized in his time as the great poet and lyricist he was, his songs made the rounds even then. Pancho and Lefty, a hit for country outlaws Willie Nelson (Texan!) and Merle Haggard, was a favourite.

② DALLAS FLATLANDERS
from **MORE A LEGEND THAN A BAND**
Jimmie Dale Gilmore, Joe Ely and Butch Hancock, each of whom could have a number of songs on this list, came together for one great if initially unacclaimed album in 1972. Their spirited partnership, now renewed, brings out the best in each of them: Hancock's deft writing, Ely's imagery and Gilmore's ghostly quaver, which is at once chilling and warm.

③ STAR IN MY HEART BILLY JOE SHAVER from **THE EARTH ROLLS ON**
One of the lesser known of the Texans, cowboy-poet Shaver wears his rough life on his sleeve and in his music. Teamed here with his son Eddy just before Eddy's death in 2000, this glimpse of lost potential adds a raw ache to a song about unconditional love.

④ GRINGO HONEYMOON ROBERT EARL KEEN
from **LIVE NO. 2**
With a rough-hewn, almost monotone voice, Keen tells stories as much as sings them. Evocative details – hot sand and an old gut-string guitar – paint a tale of love on the border.

⑤ LA FREEWAY GUY CLARK from **OLD NO. 1**
A gifted songwriter, Clark's LA Freeway was a hit for adopted Texan Jerry Jeff Walker. Here, native Clark gives it his own craggy treatment as he sings about disillusion and alienation.

⑥ MR BOJANGLES JERRY JEFF WALKER
from **MR. BOJANGLES**
Born a New Yorker but a committed member of the Texas music scene, Walker made countless albums but is best known for this gentlest of songs, written about a former cellmate.

⑦ LOVE AT THE FIVE AND DIME NANCI
GRIFFITH from **LAST OF THE TRUE BELIEVERS**
Finally, a song by a woman. Sounding more like a folk singer than some of her category-defying counterparts, Griffith has a pure, eternally youthful voice that graces this melodic tale about love in a small town and on the road.

⑧ YOUR'RE STILL STANDING THERE STEVE
EARLE WITH LUCINDA WILLIAMS from **I FEEL ARIGHT**
Another hard-living Texan with the songs to show for it. Here, Earle and Williams (Louisiana born but a big part of the 70s Austin scene) bring their voices and baggage together.

⑨ HER FIRST MISTAKE LYLE LOVETT
from **ROAD TO ENSENADA**
With one of the better singing voices of the Texas men, Lovett also has a sharp, self-deprecating wit that blows through his lyrics like a prairie wind. That's evident here, along with his strong sense of regionalism and of people.

⑩ I NEVER CARED FOR YOU WILLIE NELSON
from **TEATRO**
It's hard to know where to put Willie Nelson. Labelled "outlaw country," he predates Van Zandt and company by a few years. He can fill stadiums. But he's always been supportive of his fellow Texans, covering their songs, dueting with Lovett. In I Never Cared for You he toys with the beat, singing in front or behind his guitar, yet somehow keeping in time with backup vocalist Emmylou Harris.

Madelyn Rosenberg

Tex-mex

The music of the Mexico-Texas border, known to Anglos as Tex-Mex and to Mexicans as Conjunto (literally "group") is all about accordion-led dance music. Ain't nothing better for beer'n'chilli parties.

① MAL HOMBRE LYDIA MENDOZA
from **MAL HOMBRE**
The first Mexican-American star, Lydia sang

and played a 12-string guitar, and began recording in San Antonio in 1934. This was her first hit and remains a Tex-Mex classic.

❷ LA CHULADA NARCISO MARTINEZ from **15 REGIONAL MUSIC CLASSICS OF MEXICO**
Narciso combined bajo sexto (12-string bass) with his accordion playing in the 1930s so pioneering the sound now called Conjunto. Thus "the father of conjunto music".

❸ MI ROSITA ISIDRO LOPEZ from **EL INDIO**
This lush ballad helped establish Isidro as the pioneer of Tejano (the Texan music that blended big bands and conjuntos) and the Mexican-American Sinatra.

❹ VALENTE QUINTERO SANTIAGO JIMENEZ JR from **CORRIDOS DE LA FRONTERA**
This is a classic "hard times" corrido from the son of the master accordionist (Santiago Sr) and brother of Flaco Jimenez.

❺ JUAREZ FLACO JIMENEZ from **AY TE DEJO EN SAN ANTONIO**
Flaco became the world's most famous Tex-Mex musician after his Arhoolie recordings lead him into Ry Cooder's band. Here he pumps out a lovely danzon on his button accordion.

❻ OAXACA STEVE JORDAN from **EL HURRACAN**
The one-eyed, accordion-pumping Texan wild-man cooks up the musical chilli peppers here.

❼ UNA MAS CERVERZA THE TEXAS TORNADOES from **THE BEST OF**
Late, great Texan rocker Doug Sahm blended conjunto into his sound for this anthem to beer. Formed The Texas Tornadoes with Flaco Jimez, organ blaster Augie Meyers and Chicano country singer Freddy Fender.

❽ SI UNA VEZ SELENA from **12 SUPER EXITOS**
Huge hit from the Tex-Mex Madonna. Her synthesized conjunto-pop is an acquired taste but huge fun. Shot to death by the former president of her fan club in 1995.

❾ WAVE ALEJANDRO ESCOVEDO from **A MAN UNDER THE INFLUENCE**
Lyrical reflection on how Mexicans arrived in Texas and kept moving by the legendary Chicano rocker.

Garth Cartwright

Richard Thompson

Thompson's sinuous, Celtic-influenced guitar sound has become the trademark of his long, prolific career – that and the lashings of burnt sugar he tends to pour over his love songs.

❶ WHEN I GET TO THE BORDER from **I WANT TO SEE THE BRIGHT LIGHTS TONIGHT**
A short encyclopedia of musical styles, this hymn-like march bristles with mandolin solos, bursts of electric guitar, and has a delightfully shouty chorus.

❷ BEESWING from **MIRROR BLUE**
So delicately fingerpicked, this sweet folk number about innocence and love transports you to places usually only depicted in soap commercials.

❸ WALKING ON A WIRE from **SHOOT OUT THE LIGHTS (RICHARD AND LINDA THOMPSON)**
You can almost hear Richard and Linda's marriage dissolving in the background, as she resignedly delivers the hammer blows; the tension is nearly unbearable, the up-and-down guitar soloing unimpeachable.

❹ NOBODY'S WEDDING from **HENRY THE HUMAN FLY**
Cheeky and folky, this seems casually tossed off, especially when it breaks into rockin' its little jigs, but it manages to dig deeper, thanks largely to his earnest, almost shy vocals.

"In late 1999, I was asked for a list of the greatest songs of the Millennium," Richard Thompson recalls. "Hah! I thought, they don't mean millennium, they mean the last twenty years. I'll call their bluff and do a real thousand-year selection." The magazine declined to print his list – so he turned it into a live show. Here are ten from down the centuries you might hear him cover on a good night…

❶ SUMER IS ICUMEN IN TRAD

❷ KING HENRY V'S CONQUEST OF FRANCE TRAD

❸ WHEN I AM LAID IN EARTH HENRY PURCELL

❹ SHENANDOAH TRAD

❺ THERE IS BEAUTY… GILBERT & SULLIVAN

❻ OLD ROCKING CHAIR'S GOT ME HOAGY CARMICHAEL from HOAGY SINGS CARMICHAEL

❼ DRINKING WINE SPO-DEE-O-DEE STICKS MCGHEE from ATLANTIC RHYTHM AND BLUES, 47–74

❽ KISS PRINCE from PARADE

❾ MONEY, MONEY, MONEY ABBA from GOLD

❿ IT WON'T BE LONG THE BEATLES from WITH THE BEATLES

❺ SO BEN MI CA BON TEMPO from 1000 YEARS OF POPULAR MUSIC
Thompson's transforms this sixteenth-century Italian trifle (translated: "I know a lucky fellow") into a hypnotic, nearly religious incantation; the whole album, in which he covers the highlights of Western music from 1068 AD on, including Britney Spears, is priceless.

❻ NIGHT COMES IN from POUR DOWN LIKE SILVER
The last three minutes of this spellbinding epic could be the closest he's ever sounded to Pink Floyd.

❼ I MISUNDERSTOOD from RUMOUR AND SIGH
The coolly detached delivery works almost too well – though the lyric is about being taken by surprise by a lover's departure.

❽ WHEN THE SPELL IS BROKEN from ACROSS A CROWDED ROOM
In between the snaking, ominous guitar opening and the final, repeated warning that "you can't cry if you don't know how", comes a punchy, acerbic take on a relationship, with surprising doo-wop female harmonies.

❾ JEALOUS WORDS from THE OLD KIT BAG
This recent song lunges at you with bluesy brio. New female foil Judith Owen adds a harmonic touch, while the barely controlled solos kick off the tune, then erupt after each chorus.

❿ WALL OF DEATH from SHOOT OUT THE LIGHTS
The best thrill-ride-as-metaphor-for-life song ever penned; certain doom never sounded so good.

Andrew Rosenberg

Thrash Metal

Take some straight-ahead heavy metal and inject a lethal dose of speed and brutality. Headbang to this list and you'll end up in a neckbrace…

❶ AS THE WORLD BURNS KREATOR from **TERRIBLE CERTAINTY**

There's nothing quite like a global apocalypse to fan the flames of thrash. This is efficient, deadly and to-the-point.

❷ BLOOD OF THE SCRIBE LAMB OF GOD from **ASHES OF THE WAKE**

Intelligent, twisted and technical, this abrasive monster of a song displays both speed and virtuosity in equal measure.

❸ DISASTERPIECE SLIPKNOT from **IOWA**

Extreme thrash given a brutal and downtuned nu-metal twist, this sounds like it's raining anvils pure and simple. Not for wimps.

❹ I AM THE LAW ANTHRAX from **AMONG THE LIVING**

2000AD's harsh but fair lawman Judge Dredd gets all thrashed up. Mosh-friendly verses and a megafast mid-song break make this a thrash classic.

❺ LEGIONS OF THE DEAD TESTAMENT from **THE GATHERING**

Vocalist Chuck Billy sounds like his soul is being ripped apart. A heads-down, no messing speedfest from start to finish.

❻ PEACE SELLS MEGADETH from **PEACE SELLS...BUT WHO'S BUYING?**

One of the crunchiest, chewiest riffs in mid 80s thrash. An awesome chugging opening leads to a frenzied dash for the finishing line.

❼ RAINING BLOOD SLAYER from **REIGN IN BLOOD**

So scary this will have you crying for your mummy. Thunder rolls and a riff forged by Satan himself bludgeons you into submission.

❽ RATAMAHATTA SEPULTURA from **ROOTS**

The band's Brazilian heritage takes them beyond the realms of mere brutality to create a cool amalgam of world music and crushing metal.

❾ REVELATION THE HAUNTED from **THE HAUNTED MADE ME DO IT**

Can you stand the pace? Intense, savage and extremely violent this lot cram an entire song into one and a half minutes.

❿ THE STORM WITCHERY from **SYMPHONY FOR THE DEVIL**

A title that promises exactly what the band delivers. Tornado-scale riffs and licks whip around you with flesh-ripping intensity.

Essi Berelian

Tindersticks

Nottingham's kings of soul-tinged, booze-drenched melancholy.

❶ A MARRIAGE MADE IN HEAVEN from **DONKEYS**

Stuart crooning with Isabella Rossellini like they were Nancy & Lee. The original Rough Trade single is even better, if you can find it.

❷ RENTED ROOMS (SWING VERSION) from **THE RENTED ROOMS SINGLE**

A track with more sleaze, feathers and swinging brass than your average night out in Soho.

❸ KATHLEEN from **LIVE IN AMSTERDAM**

An amazing take on the Townes Van Zandt classic. Just when you thought the song couldn't get any better.

❹ HER from **TINDERSTICKS (THE FIRST ALBUM)**

A quick flourish of Spanish guitar and a dollop of self-loathing add up to a live favourite. It's the scraped strings. They get you every time.

❺ TINY TEARS from **TINDERSTICKS (THE SECOND ALBUM)**

A kitchen sink drama of a song, it might just be the perfect early Tindersticks track. It swoons.

❻ SHE'S GONE from **TINDERSTICKS (THE SECOND ALBUM)**

You could never accuse the first couple of albums of lacking melancholy but this ode to missing your daughter is as poignant as they come.

❼ PATCHWORK
from **TINDERSTICKS (THE FIRST ALBUM)**
Wonky glockenspiel with a tapped tambourine could only hint at what was to come on this early, and glorious, single.

❽ CAN WE START AGAIN from **SIMPLE PLEASURE**
Out went the suits and the indie miserablism. In came some heartbroken soul and some serious yearning. With handclaps.

❾ PEOPLE KEEP COMIN' AROUND
from **CAN OUR LOVE**
The transformation into a bruised soul band is almost complete with the merest hint of funky bass, female backing singers and less crooning.

❿ TRAVELLING LIGHT from **TINDERSTICKS (THE FIRST ALBUM)**
More from the Nancy and Lee school of brooding male vocal and wry and infuriated female response. Topped off with a trumpet. What more do you need?

Gavin McNamara

Toasters

Rather than "deejays" in today's accepted sense of the word, these are old school, pre-1980 toasters whose primary job was to big up whatever sound system they were working on at the time. This was done live to whatever record the selector was spinning, so lyrical dexterity and a nimble train of thought was a given. These records reflect such qualities, and the ability to turn nonsense into a dancefloor delight.

❶ WEAR YOU TO THE BALL U-ROY
from **VERSION GALORE**
Classic, old school rocksteady toasting, with U-Roy whooping, yelping and talking nonsense on top of The Paragons' immaculate harmonising.

❷ NUMBER ONE STATION DENNIS ALCAPONE
from **GUNS DON'T ARGUE: THE ANTHOLOGY 70–77**
Fabulous illustration of the glorious self-servingness of early toasting: Alcapone's sprightly, musical tones do little other than celebrate his environment and the assembled company.

❸ COOL BREEZE BIG YOUTH from **RIDE LIKE LIGHTNING: THE BEST OF 1972–1976**
On top of a dub cut of Keith & Tex's Stop That Train, Big Youth swings wildly between a yearning love song and a tribute to the blaxploitation hero of the title, before tying up the two.

❹ UNDER HEAVY MANNERS PRINCE FAR-I from **UNDER HEAVY MANNERS**
Deep roots steppers' beat and Far-I warning mankind in a voice that sounds like a bear abruptly woken up from hibernation at the back of a very deep cave.

❺ THREE PIECE SUIT AND THING TRINITY from **LOVE OF THE COMMON PEOPLE (JOE GIBBS)**
Mad toast detailing what it takes to be a ladies man – "diamond socks and t'ing" – over the top of a dub of I'm Still In Love With You, the tune that also became Uptown Ranking.

❻ COCAINE IN MY BRAIN DILLINGER from **COCAINE IN MY BRAIN**
Maybe the maddest reggae record ever made: built on the central riff from the Philly funk classic Do It Any Way You Wanna, the hardest working lyric is "A knife, a fork, a bottle and a cork/That's how you spell New York". Draw your own conclusions.

❼ WELDING I-ROY
from **THE CHANNEL ONE STORY – VARIOUS**
Back on more familiar turf with a lazily phrased piece of slackness, as I-Roy rides a classic rub-a-dub rhythm as he sorts out the battle of the sexes aided only by his "welding iron."

❽ MR HARRY SKANK PRINCE JAZZBO from **GLEN BROWN & FRIENDS: RHYTHM MASTER VOLUME ONE**
The portentous dread of the backing beat – heavy heavy bass and drum spiked with a scary sax – Jazzbo's delicate delivery and hymn

to a sound system operator make the perfect counterpoint.

⑨ DRAW YOUR BRAKES SCOTTY from THE BEST OF SCOTTY
Coming very close to singing, and with a remarkably cogent narrative, Scotty delivers the smooooovest of lyrical laments over the original Stop That Train.

⑩ JACK OF MY TRADE SIR LORD COMIC from LOVE OF THE COMMON PEOPLE (JOE GIBBS)
Simple, totally infectious old-time reggae groove, complementing Comic's easy action stream-of-consciousness good naturedness.

Lloyd Bradley

Toots & The Maytals

Frederick "Toots" Hibbert remains one of reggae's most compelling performers, almost four decades after the string of dance hits that made his name.

① SIX AND SEVEN BOOKS OF MOSES from TIME TOUGH THE ANTHOLOGY
The first Toots classic, recorded at Studio One in 1963.

② DO THE REGGAY from TIME TOUGH
The first record to mention the word "reggae", from 1968.

③ 54-46 WAS MY NUMBER from TIME TOUGH
Inspired by his incarceration for marijuana possession, this guaranteed floor-filler from 1968 has to be Toots' finest hour.

④ PRESSURE DROP from TIME TOUGH
A sophisticated rock steady number from 1969, which builds to a frenzied climax and was later covered by The Clash.

⑤ MONKEY MAN from TIME TOUGH
A quintessential Maytals romp from 1969.

⑥ FUNKY KINGSTON from TIME TOUGH
By 1973, Toots was achieving global success, hard on the heels of Bob Marley.

⑦ REGGAE GOT SOUL from TIME TOUGH
Evidence from 1975 of Toots' ongoing fascination with fusing reggae with American soul music.

⑧ (I'VE GOT) DREAMS TO REMEMBER from TIME TOUGH
A sublime tribute to Otis Redding, from 1988's *Toots In Memphis* album.

Greg Ward

Top shelf

Music for lovers, shall we say? Tunes for those private moments? Bedroom ballads? Oh, you know what we're driving at…

① LET'S GET IT ON MARVIN GAYE from THE VERY BEST OF

② STRAY CAT BLUES THE ROLLING STONES from BEGGAR'S BANQUET

③ LET'S STAY TOGETHER AL GREEN from THE VERY BEST OF

④ BLACK CHERRY GOLDFRAPP from BLACK CHERRY

⑤ SEXUAL HEALING MARVIN GAYE from THE VERY BEST OF

⑥ LOVE HANGOVER DIANA ROSS from DIANA

⑦ WOMEN RESPOND TO BASS RENEGADE SOUNDWAVE from RENEGADE SOUNDWAVE 1987-1995

⑧ BABY WANTS TO RIDE FRANKIE KNUCKLES from FRANKIE KNUCKLES PRESENTS

⑨ LOVE TO LOVE YOU BABY (ALBUM VERSION) DONNA SUMMER from LOVE TO LOVE YOU BABY

⑩ DIRTY EPIC UNDERWORLD from DUBNOBASSWITHMYHEADMAN

Al Spicer

Trains

Oddly, the best songs about trains make no reference whatsoever to Thomas the Tank Engine. Mind you, tots should like a decent number of these, all the same.

❶ LAST TRAIN TO CLARKSVILLE THE MONKEES from **BEST OF THE MONKEES**
Some deft song writing (by Boyce & Hart; not by any actual Monkees) and nice packaging made this an easy hit for the band.

❷ MONKEY AND THE ENGINEER GRATEFUL DEAD from **RECKONING**
A monkey jumps in the driver's seat of a train and drives off at 90 miles per hour. The original comes from blues man Jesse Fuller; the Grateful Dead remake speeds it up and smooths it out.

❸ MYSTERY TRAIN ELVIS PRESLEY from **THE KING OF ROCK'N'ROLL: THE COMPLETE 50S MASTERS**
From a quick chug to the long, sweeping toot of a train whistle, Presley varies the lengths of his notes to great effect in this fast blues recorded for Sun in 1955.

❹ NEW RIVER TRAIN BILL MONROE from **THE ESSENTIAL**
The New River is said to be the world's second oldest. This song dates, too, back to the turn of the last century. In this speedy version, Monroe and company give it a bluegrass treatment, with mandolin chops instead of chugs.

❺ NIGHT TRAIN JAMES BROWN from **NIGHT TRAIN**
"HELLO, BOISE!" Some performers shout out the name of the city they're performing in. The Godfather of Soul namechecks all of the major cities on the East Coast, plus New Orleans, with soulful hollers that constitute singing and a groove that doesn't stop.

❻ ORANGE BLOSSOM SPECIAL JOHNNY CASH from **ORANGE BLOSSOM SPECIAL**
Written about a real, Miami-to-New York train and recorded as a bluegrass song in the 1940s (and probably every year since), Cash's 1965

version became one of the best known. He makes the song less about the fiddle and more about voice – though his own sounds a little drunk during the exchange between the third and fourth verse.

❼ LAST OF THE STEAM-POWERED TRAINS THE KINKS from **THE KINKS ARE THE VILLAGE GREEN PRESERVATION SOCIETY**
Good hooks and harmonies with a riff that would have been a favourite among plugged-in teens had the song received any radio play.

❽ THE TRAIN IS COMING KEN BOOTHE from **A MAN AND HIS HITS**
A reggae classic from 1966, Boothe's melodic voice is full of both yearning and comfort.

❾ TRAIN KEPT A ROLLIN TINY BRADSHAW from **THE GREAT COMPOSER**
The Yardbirds recorded it. So did Aerosmith. But Bradshaw did it first and better with throaty vocals, a big band, and a swinging blast of sax.

❿ WABASH CANNONBALL DAN ZANES WITH BOB WEIR from **HOUSE PARTY**
There must be a thousand versions of this song, first made popular by the Carter Family in the early days of recorded music. Former Del Fuego Dan Zanes put it on his perfect-formula kids' record with vocal help from Weir.

Madelyn Rosenberg

T Rex

Marc Bolan sold his soul and all his hippie threads for the chance of three years in the spotlight as the prettiest star in UK pop history – where Tyrannosaurus Rex had dallied in sun dappled glades, T Rex stomped in the spotlight. Primarily a singles band, the best of their material is always available on whichever Best Of collection is at your local store.

❶ 20TH CENTURY BOY

from THE ESSENTIAL COLLECTION

Stomping all over London like some cocaine-crazed killer reptile from before the dawn of history, with Flo & Eddie providing bad influences and soprano-pitch backing vocals.

❷ KING OF THE RUMBLING SPIRES from THE ESSENTIAL COLLECTION

One of the earliest T Rex (as opposed to Tyrannosaurus) tracks, and one where Marc still had to completely ditch his Tolkien fantasies. Very dark, bass-heavy and stardust-sprinkled.

❸ SOLID GOLD EASY ACTION from THE ESSENTIAL COLLECTION

Easy action is a technical term that describes the closeness of guitar strings in relation to the neck of the instrument. Of course, with Bolan at the helm, it turned into a fast-paced song about fucking.

❹ METAL GURU from THE ESSENTIAL COLLECTION

The bopping elf of the 60s had traded in his fairy cloak for teen superstardom, T Rextasy in the newspapers and fame so unassailable that he could knock out rubbishy lyrics like this and still take them to the top of the charts. Magnificent nonsense.

❺ CHILDREN OF THE REVOLUTION

from THE ESSENTIAL COLLECTION

"You won't fool the children of the revolution! No Way! Hey!" Oh the powers that be must have quaked at this powerful polemic. Great riff though, great solo too.

❻ HOT LOVE from THE ESSENTIAL COLLECTION

Bolan and the band never surpassed this early bopping classic, a standard twelve-bar blues stripped down for the pre-teen audience. Hot love, indeed!

❼ JEEPSTER from THE ESSENTIAL COLLECTION

The jury is still out on what exactly Bolan meant by Jeepster, but when he claims to be "A vampire for your love" all the little girls understand.

❽ RIDE A WHITE SWAN

from THE ESSENTIAL COLLECTION

Another transitional tune from the late hippy-early glam period, and another dead simple tune suitable for someone like Marc, new to the electric instrument. If he'd lived long enough to write a guitar tutor manual, this would have been on page one.

❾ TELEGRAM SAM from THE ESSENTIAL COLLECTION

Sam, according to legend, was a dealer; a man who delivered drugs to the stars. Bolan apparently "wrote" this in the lift at the BBC, on his way to record a Peel session.

❿ GET IT ON from THE ESSENTIAL COLLECTION

Three chords, a sympathetic photographer and a winning, pants-melting smile will get a boy a long way in the music business. This song was banned in America because of the "bang a gong" line. Evidently percussion is still frowned on over there.

Al Spicer

Trojan reggae

From the late 1960s onwards, via compilation albums like the legendary *Tighten Up* series, the Trojan record label was largely responsible for introducing reggae to British audiences. Countless CD re-releases have ensured that timeless rock-steady classics like those listed below remain widely available.

❶ DREADER THAN DREAD HONEY BOY MARTIN from THE TROJAN STORY

Heavy-duty "rude boy" bragging from the mid-60s.

❷ FAT MAN DERRICK MORGAN from TROJAN JAMAICAN HITS BOX

Yet more proof of how much early reggae drew from New Orleans R&B.

K T Tunstall
Takes 12

Part-Chinese, part Scottish, K.T.Tunstall sung with Oi-Va-Voi before releasing her debut solo album *Eye To The Telescope* at the end of 2004. Hailed as one of the most exciting new British singer-songwriters in many a year, the album has gone platinum and gained a Mercury nomination. "I know there's 12 on this list, but I really can't live without any of them," she insists.

❶ INNER MEET ME THE BETA BAND from THE 3 EPS

❷ FOLSOM PRISON BLUES JOHNNY CASH from JOHNNY CASH AT FOLSOM PRISON

❸ COUNTRY CASSETTE HALFCOUSIN from THE FUNCTION ROOM

❹ J'BULLITT: MAIN TITLE THEME LALO SHIFRIN from BULLITT SOUNDTRACK

❺ BE MY HUSBAND NINA SIMONE from PASTEL BLUES/LET IT ALL OUT

❻ ROOT DOWN BEASTIE BOYS from ANTHOLOGY

❼ LOST CAUSE BECK from SEA CHANGE

❽ JIMMY T DAVID AXELROD from DAVID AXELROD

❾ PATIENCE MICAH P HINSON from AND THE GOSPEL OF PROGRESS

❿ WHO ARE YOU TOM WAITS from BONE MACHINE

⓫ PERFECT DAY ELISE PJ HARVEY from IS THIS DESIRE?

⓬ SEGA RY COODER & ALI FARKA TOURE from TALKING TIMBUKTU

❸ EVERY NIGHT JOE WHITE & CHUCK from TROJAN JAMAICAN HITS BOX
A fascinating hybrid of reggae and country – a cruelly underexploited genre, if ever there was one.

❹ HOLD THEM ROY SHIRLEY from TROJAN JAMAICAN HITS BOX
A lovely little shuffle from Joe Gibbs' studio, just as reggae was finding its feet.

❺ ISRAELITES DESMOND DEKKER from BEST OF
A worldwide #1 from an often neglected artist who really deserves a playlist all his own.

❻ JOHNNY TOO BAD THE SLICKERS from TROJAN RUDE BOY BOX SET
This indictment of youthful lawlessness is most familiar from the wonderful *The Harder They Come* soundtrack.

❼ LONG SHOT KICK DE BUCKET THE PIONEERS FROM TIGHTEN UP VOL 2
The best of many such topical 1960s hits, relating the saga of a death at the races.

❽ RUDY A MESSAGE TO YOU DANDY LIVINGSTONE from TROJAN RUDE BOY BOX SET
Dandy's Jamaican hit was later admirably covered by The Specials.

❾ SOUL LIMBO BYRON LEE from TROJAN RUDE BOY BOX SET
This much-loved MGs cover was for many years the theme music to *Test Match Special* on the BBC.

❿ VIETNAM JIMMY CLIFF from REGGAE GREATS
Hailed by Bob Dylan as the finest protest song to emerge from the Vietnam era.

Greg Ward

Ike & Tina Turner

Ike Turner releases the "first" rock'n'roll record with Rocket 88 in 1950, marries Annie Mae Bullock and transforms her into Tina Turner, discovers cocaine and becomes Mr Nasty. Still, they cut some fine tunes before Tina fled for superstardom.

❶ RIVER DEEP MOUNTAIN HIGH from RIVER DEEP MOUNTAIN HIGH
Phil Spector throws the proverbial sink in for this epic blast of orchestrated pop.

❷ NUTBUSH CITY LIMITS from NUTBUSH CITY LIMITS
Fuzz guitar, funk keyboard, sleazy horns and Tina in a rage over small town life. Didn't they just rock so hard?

❸ I THINK IT'S GONNA WORK OUT FINE from IKE & TINA TURNER
Stomping slice of soulful optimism. Hear this and you can believe they loved one another back in 1961.

❹ PROUD MARY from IKE & TINA TURNER
The Creedence tune gets slowed down, given some soul flavour, then builds into a R&B hurricane.

❺ FUNKIER THAN A MOSQUITA'S TWEETER from WORKIN' TOGETHER
Tina dismisses a sleazy admirer: "you got a mouth like a head o' bo-wevils". Go git 'em, girl!

❻ I'VE BEEN LOVING YOU TOO LONG from WHAT YOU SEE IS WHAT YOU GET
Extraordinary live version of the Otis Redding song. Tina sucks Ike. Ike eats Tina. Or so they strongly hint.

❼ A FOOL IN LOVE from THE SOUL OF IKE AND TINA TURNER
Their first single. This 1960 tune is tough Southern soul, steeped in blues and grits.

❽ BABY – GET IT ON from ACID QUEEN
Ike and Tina engage in another mutual bout of lust – this is 1975, hard to believe they still shagged each other – with this tough, sexy disco-flavoured rocker.

❾ SWEET RHODE ISLAND RED from SWEET RHODE ISLAND RED
Tina recycles the Nutbush riff to tell this semi-autobiographical tale of being a very hot, young mulatto woman.

❿ UP IN HEAH from IKE & TINA TURNER
Tina sings in the voice of a girl who left her church background to become a "daughter of evil". Cut in 1972 when Ike was coked up and strung out, this has to be a cry for help.

Garth Cartwright

U2

Pious Irish godbotherers turned anthemic political campaigners turned fly hipsters turned anthemic godbothering hipsters again. No wonder U2 have *Vertigo*. Still setting the standard for the biggest band in the world: pretenders beware.

❶ SUNDAY BLOODY SUNDAY from **WAR**
Not a rebel song, said Bono famously, but the flagbearer for the militant pacifism of *War*, set to a martial drum tattoo.

❷ NEW YEAR'S DAY from **WAR**
A bleak piano figure drips like an icicle through the angular post-punk funk of this concert favourite.

❸ PARTY GIRL from **UNDER A BLOOD-RED SKY**
Under A Blood-Red Sky, a live mini-album recorded in the aftermath of a Colorado rainstorm, is the perfect distillation of the early, utterly sincere U2. Party Girl, a jerky B-side, is here reimagined as an autumnal elegy for misspent youth.

❹ PRIDE (IN THE NAME OF LOVE) from **THE UNFORGETTABLE FIRE**
All right, so they got the time of day of Martin Luther King's assassination completely wrong. (To their credit, they resisted any temptation silently to fix it: as their mentor Eno said, honour your mistakes.) And you can hear the grinding gear change in the chorus. But what a chorus.

❺ IN GOD'S COUNTRY from **THE JOSHUA TREE**
The Joshua Tree was where U2 hit the big time. Side 1 has all the hit singles, side 2 all the best songs, including this furiously strummed slice of American mythology.

❻ UNTIL THE END OF THE WORLD from **ACHTUNG BABY**
Achtung Baby was a swerve towards Bowie's soundtrack for *Christiane F*. U2 made pretty convincing children of Zoo Station, never more so than on this title-tune from Wim Wenders's messy futuristic picaresque ramble of a film. Listen closely, and this is the Garden of Gethsemane from Judas's point of view.

❼ ZOOROPA from **ZOOROPA**
It's Mitteleuropan pomp and circumstance all the way in this majestic opener from a dodgy album, knocked together on tour.

❽ IF YOU WEAR THAT VELVET DRESS TONIGHT from **POP**
Pop was a stinker. But if it can be redeemed, this carnal whisper over a stuttering drum machine loop is the song to do it.

❾ BEAUTIFUL DAY from **ALL THAT YOU CAN'T LEAVE BEHIND**
By the end of the 90s most people thought U2 were fogged in the incense of their own pretentions. But this perfect single, whose chorus goes off like dynamite, proved them wrong.

❿ SILVER AND GOLD from **SUN CITY (ARTISTS UNITED AGAINST APARTHEID)**
An early shot at setting the world to rights, from a polemical anti-Apartheid benefit album. This dry-as-dust version is Bono and The Edge with Ron Wood; the full band version on *Rattle And Hum* is overblown by comparison.

David Honigmann

Uncle Tupelo

Alt.country's own Lennon & McCartney, Jeff Tweedy and Jar Farrar, with drummer Mike Heidhorn, wedded traditional country themes – depression, drinking, God, and manual labour – to punk vitriol, energy and anger. The results were revolutionary.

❶ NO DEPRESSION from **NO DEPRESSION**
This update of the 30s Carter Family classic was the song that kick-started alt.country. "Depression" here meaning something else.

❷ SCREEN DOOR from **NO DEPRESSION**
A laid-back early track; you can hear the youth in Tweedy's voice as he sings "sometimes it snows, but when it does it doesn't last long".

❸ FALL DOWN EASY from **STILL FEEL GONE**
On Tupelo's more punky second album, this rant against "the moral stare of Big Brother" is driven by Mike Heidorn's martial drumming.

❹ STILL BE AROUND from **STILL FEEL GONE**
Sung by Jay Farrar, this is a gentle, acoustically strummed number in which "the Bible is a bottle and the hardwood floor is home".

❺ SAUGET WIND from **89/93: AN ANTHOLOGY**
With its towering, wailing build-up, it's amazing this song was never properly released until the *Anthology*. A cathartic epic.

❻ CRIMINALS from **MARCH 16–20, 1992**
On *March*, Tupelo pulled a reverse-Dylan and went acoustic, baiting George Bush Sr with the line "they want us kinder and gentler… at their feet."

❼ MOONSHINER from **MARCH 16–20, 1992**
An old standard lamenting the hard-luck life of a moonshiner, in good company on back-to-basics *March*; Dylan's version is also fantastic.

❽ NEW MADRID from **ANODYNE**
Tweedy began to come into his own on Tupelo's last album, showing hints here of the surrealist imagery he'd later use to such success in Wilco.

❾ WE'VE BEEN HAD from **ANODYNE**
This explosive rocker careens from the "Marshall stack," stopping to indict "Republicans and Democrats" and shout about how "we've been had."

❿ STEAL THE CRUMBS from **ANODYNE**
A career-ending track as fitting as the Beatles' "The End," as Jay and Jeff harmonise the heartbreaking lines, "No more, no more will I see you."

Hunter Slaton

Stevie Ray Vaughan

He had the chops, for sure, but it was Stevie Ray's soulfulness that marked him out from the crowd. Then he was cut off in his prime by an air crash after beating the addictions that nearly killed him. Asked the secret of his success he said "Use heavy strings, tune low, play hard and floor it."

❶ PRIDE AND JOY from **TEXAS FLOOD**
From the first album – overseen by the legendary John Hammond. This signature tune is a statement of intent, and a great solo displays all Stevie Ray's warmth, attack and tone.

❷ TEXAS FLOOD from **TEXAS FLOOD**
Another song Stevie Ray made his own. Nothing better demonstrates the rich, full-bodied tone he pulled out of "Number One", his battered old 1959 Sunburst Stratocaster guitar.

❹ THINGS THAT I USED TO DO from **COULDN'T STAND THE WEATHER**
There's fierce competition, but when it comes down to it, this wins the vote for best slow blues from Stevie Ray. Thrilling.

❸ COULDN'T STAND THE WEATHER from **COULDN'T STAND THE WEATHER**
The genuinely funky title-track of the second album. Tight and loose, it's a showcase for his razor-sharp rhythm guitar playing.

❺ CHANGE IT from **SOUL TO SOUL**
This stinging, often overlooked track is as tough as sun-baked saddle leather. It's from an album that is grossly underrated.

❻ LIFE WITHOUT YOU from **SOUL TO SOUL**
As well as thick slabs of rich, crying guitar over the coda, this displays the sweetness and soul in Stevie Ray's singing that most peers and rivals lacked. Curse the fade-out on this studio recording then go looking for the live versions.

❼ CROSSFIRE from **IN STEP**
Cleaning up can do terrible things to a musician. But an unstoppable low down groove embellished with steely Albert King-style fills puts those worries to rest.

❽ TIGHTROPE from **IN STEP**
And if you thought that was good, wait until you hear the solo on this.

❾ LOVE ME DARLIN' from **IN STEP**
Wonderfully exuberant cover of an old Howlin' Wolf track. Wolf's original may be hard to beat, but Stevie Ray is on exhilarating, joyful form.

❿ LITTLE WING from **THE SKY IS CRYING**
Hendrix was such a unique talent that there aren't many who can get away with covering his music, let alone make his songs sing and soar like this one does.

Rowland White

The Velvet Underground

Blasting out a furious counterpoint to the complacencies of the hippy era, The Velvet Underground burned themselves out in a few short years at the end of the 1960s. But they still sound contemporary.

❶ HEROIN from **THE VELVET UNDERGROUND & NICO**
It's the sheer tender wistfulness of Lou Reed's hymn to the joys of heroin – "it's my wife, and

it's my life" – that makes the original version so much more shocking than his histrionic 1970s renditions .

❷ I'LL BE YOUR MIRROR from THE VELVET UNDERGROUND & NICO

Somehow, the fact that Teutonic ice maiden Nico is at her most dispassionate only serves to heighten the power of one of Reed's most beautiful love songs.

❸ SISTER RAY from WHITE LIGHT/ WHITE HEAT

The Velvets at their most unrelenting; a 17-minute duel between Cale on organ and Reed on guitar that only Cale's ultimate departure from the band could resolve.

❹ SWEET JANE from LOADED

On their last true album, the Velvets sounded much more like other rock bands of the era – but this carefully crafted Reed classic ranks among their finest moments.

❺ THE BLACK ANGEL'S DEATH SONG
from THE VELVET UNDERGROUND & NICO

Lou Reed intones darkly portentous lyrics atop the cacophonous barrage of John Cale's electric viola; exactly the sound for which the Velvets were born.

❻ WHAT GOES ON? from LIVE 1969 VOL 1

By the time of this live album, Cale's viola had been replaced by what sounds very like a fairground calliope – and weirdly, it works, to superbly hypnotic effect.

❼ I'M STICKING WITH YOU from VU

This frivolous but affectingly romantic little song languished in the vaults for years, until the Velvet's so-called "lost" fourth MGM album was finally released.

❽ PALE BLUE EYES
from THE VELVET UNDERGROUND

The Velvet's third album came as an oasis of calm after the storm of their first two, and never more so than on this sublime, gentle love song.

❾ WHITE LIGHT/ WHITE HEAT
from WHITE LIGHT/ WHITE HEAT

For once, the original Velvets manage to cram all their power and ferocity into less than three minutes, though as a paean to heavy drug use it was never going to make the pop charts.

❿ VENUS IN FURS from THE VELVET UNDERGROUND & NICO

It may turn up in TV ads these days, but this S&M epic had an erotic, fetishistic charge that emphasized just how far removed Andy Warhol's New York really was from the West Coast's Summer of Love.

Greg Ward

Rufus Wainwright

Is there a better singer-songwriter right now? That's a purely rhetorical question. Rufus Wainwright writes and sings with a daring that takes your breath away. His albums are modern treasures, laden with songs that could grace the classic American songbook.

❶ CIGARETTES AND CHOCOLATE MILK
from **POSES**
Start here for an enduring love affair. Great tune, hint of a lisp, and an enticing sense of excess and danger ("everything it seems I like is a little bit harmful for me").

❷ APRIL FOOLS from **RUFUS WAINWRIGHT**
A story-song that could almost be prime Lennon/McCartney, this was promoted with a wonderful pop video of Rufus racing round town to rescue fallen opera divas.

❸ IMAGINARY LOVE from **RUFUS WAINWRIGHT**
"Every kind of love, or at least my kind of love, must be an imaginary love to start with": now what kind of miracle of an opening line is that?

❹ POSES from **POSES**
Rufus, accompanying himself at the piano, sings of "wearing flip-flops on Fifth Avenue". You will it to go on forever.

❺ ACROSS THE UNIVERSE from **I AM SAM**
This was always one of the most beautiful Beatles songs. Rufus plays it fairly straight – in his own terms – and lets that wonderful nonsense "jai guru deva om" shine through.

❻ DINNER AT EIGHT from **WANT ONE**
"No matter how strong I'm going to take you down with one little song… see what you're really worth to me." A song about his dad, Loudon, that delivers its promised knock-out, dwarfing Wainwright Sr's entire ouevre.

❼ 11:11 from **WANT ONE**
Nobody else has managed it – a 9/11 song of real substance, celebrating domestic life in New York, lamenting all the hours wasted.

❽ OH WHAT A WORLD from **WANT ONE**
The audacity of it! A beautiful lyric about life's passing beauty, with an arrangement that begins as monkish hum and escalates to a full-blown orchestral rendition of Ravel's Bolero.

❾ NATASHA from **WANT ONE**
You want an exquisite, simple love song, just voice and vibes, a few strings? This is the one.

❿ OLD WHORE'S DIET from **WANT TWO**
Virtuoso singing from Rufus and androgynous pal Anthony (of Anthony & The Johnsons), on this anthemic gay wake-up call. Rufus's sister Martha helps them rock out.

Mark Ellingham

Tom Waits

He can be sentimental and he can be fiercely avant-garde but to call Tom Waits a singer-songwriter has never seemed a remotely adequate description.

❶ OL' 55 from **CLOSING TIME**
The Eagles covered it but ol' Tom's was the definitive version.

2 TOM TRAUBERT'S BLUES from **SMALL CHANGE**
Another song famously covered, this time by
Rod Stewart. But the peerless, tormented
original was again the best.

3 PIANO HAS BEEN DRINKING NOT ME
from **SMALL CHANGE**
Louis Armstrong meets Jack Kerouac in a
twilight world of late-night whisky bars.

4 SOMEWHERE from **BLUE VALENTINE**
Improbably brilliant reinvention of Bernstein's
West Side Story standard.

5 THIS ONE'S FROM THE HEART
from **ONE FROM THE HEART**
An oil-and-water duet with Crystal Gayle (of
Don't You Make My Brown Eyes Blue fame),
written and recorded for Coppola's 1982 film.

6 SHORE LEAVE from **SWORDFISHTROMBONES**
Surrreal soundscapes played by a junkyard
orchestra on this sailor's tale.

7 DOWNTOWN TRAIN from **RAIN DOGS**
Rod Stewart knew a good song when he heard
one and he covered this too. But once again he
couldn't match the grit and honesty of Waits'
intuitive original.

8 WHAT'S HE BUILDING from **MULE VARIATIONS**
In which Tom wittily ventriloquises conserva-
tive small town paranoia in the face of introspective kookiness.

9 ALL THE WORLD IS GREEN
from **BLOOD MONEY**
Even as his later music grew ever more angular
and dissonant, Waits remained capable of
bittersweet serenades of haunting beauty
such as this.

10 LONG WAY HOME from **BIG BAD LOVE**
A little-known and understated masterpiece
from the soundtrack of Arliss Howard's 2001
film, recently covered by Norah Jones.

Nigel Williamson

Tom Waits
For No Man

**A typically eclectic ten from TOM WAITS,
one of rock's most singular figures.**

**1 IN THE WEE SMALL HOURS OF THE
MORNING FRANK SINATRA** from **IN THE WEE
SMALL HOURS**

**2 DEE'S DINER COLONEL LES CLAYPOOL'S
FEARLESS FLYING FROG BRIGADE** from **PURPLE
ONION**

**3 THE DELIVERY MAN ELVIS COSTELLO AND
THE IMPOSTERS** from **THE DELIVERY MAN**

4 I SHOULD CARE THELONIOUS MONK
from **SOLO MONK**

**5 I JUST WANT TO SEE HIS FACE ROLLING
STONES** from **EXILE ON MAIN STREET**

6 JESUS BLOOD GAVIN BRYARS
from **THE SINKING OF THE TITANIC**

7 DIRTY OLD TOWN THE POGUES
from **RUM SODOMY AND THE LASH**

8 LUCILLE LITTLE RICHARD
from **THE SPECIALTY SESSIONS**

9 CIRCLING PIGEONS WALTZ TEXAS-CZECH
from **BOHEMIAN-MORAVIAN BANDS**

**10 NESSUN DORMA FRANCO CORELLI WITH THE
ROME OPERA THEATRE ORCHESTRA & CHORUS**

Scott Walker/ Walker Brothers

The golden-throated Walker's journey from quality MOR pop-rock (with the Walker Brothers) to darkly theatrical singer-songwriterisms, and out-there electronic landscapes, is unique in popular music.

WALKER BROTHERS

❶ MAKE IT EASY ON YOURSELF from TAKE IT EASY WITH THE WALKER BROTHERS
Walker was once a master at delivering relatively big pop numbers, as this 1965 chart-topping Bacharach/David cover proves.

❷ AFTER THE LIGHTS GO OUT from PORTRAIT
Flip the British #1 smash The Sun Ain't Gonna Shine Anymore to find this stellar B-side, the Spectorian production bringing to mind a moodier Righteous Brothers.

❸ IN MY ROOM from PORTRAIT
No relation to The Beach Boys classic of the same name, with a grand mock-classical opening theme leading into heart-rending operatic crescendos on this opus of isolation.

❹ ORPHEUS from IMAGES
An early indicator of the artier pop Scott would sing in his solo career, with its swirling pseudo-classical air.

SCOTT WALKER

❺ PLASTIC PALACE PEOPLE from SCOTT 2
Swimming strings waver between dreamland and reality, Walker observing his fellow men and women with a wry inside-the-fishbowl detachment.

❻ TIME OPERATOR from TIL THE BAND COMES IN
Desperate for romantic connection, Scott croons his come-on to a telephone operator. She doesn't listen, just keeps announcing the time. Beyond creepy.

❼ THE OLD MAN'S BACK AGAIN from SCOTT 4
"Dedicated to the Neo-Stalinist Regime," this is almighty gothic obscurity from the King of Brood, accented by Aeolian chanting.

❽ THE SEVENTH SEAL from SCOTT 4
The inspiration from the classic Ingmar Bergman film might be transparent, but the sweeping intimation of oncoming calamity in this melodramatic song is entirely Walker.

❾ THE ROPE AND THE COLT
from IN FIVE EASY PIECES
Riveting extract from an obscure French movie that ranks as the best Ennio Morricone spaghetti western-styled theme not penned by Morricone himself.

❿ MATHILDE from SCOTT
Walker tucks into this lively Jacques Brel tune – one of many he'd cover – with the exultant elan of a starving man at the banquet table.

Richie Unterberger

Dionne Warwick

Let's get this straight: Dionne Warwick may no longer make great records, nor thrill in concert. But in her heyday, debuting a string of Bacharach/David compositions, she was sensational. Download these old recordings from a good compilation such as *Walk On By: The Definitive Dionne Warwick Collection*; beware of remixed, modern or medley versions.

❶ WALK ON BY from WALK ON BY
Possibly Bacharach/David's greatest song, and certainly Dionne's most iconic. Who could be unmoved by the quiver, the mix of strength and despair, as Dionne instructs her former lover to walk on by as she starts to cry?

❷ SOMEWHERE from THE WINDOWS OF THE WORLD
There's a place for us. Okay, the Tom Waits ver-

James Walsh's
Barbecue songs

JAMES WALSH's band Starsailor burst on to the scene in 2002 with their debut album *Love Is Here*. Clearly owing a debt to such 70s troubadours as Tim Buckley (one of whose albums gave the band their name) and Van Morrison, the band marked a return to pre-Britpop indie values.

The sun must have been shining in Ireland where Walsh lives, for the list he supplied was headed "best songs for a summer barbecue".

❶ A DAY IN THE LIFE THE BEATLES from SGT PEPPER'S LONELY HEARTS CLUB BAND

❷ LAST GOODBYE JEFF BUCKLEY from GRACE

❸ WHERE THE STREETS HAVE NO NAME U2 from THE JOSHUA TREE

❹ SYMPATHY FOR THE DEVIL THE ROLLING STONES from BEGGAR'S BANQUET

❺ RING OF FIRE JOHNNY CASH from RING OF FIRE

❻ RIVERMAN NICK DRAKE from FIVES LEAVES LEFT

❼ JUST WHEN YOU'RE THINKIN' THINGS OVER THE CHARLATANS from THE CHARLATANS

❽ THE NIGHT THEY DROVE OLD DIXIE DOWN THE BAND from THE BAND

❾ THE BUCKET KINGS OF LEON from AHA SHAKE HEARTBREAK

❿ TINY DANCER ELTON JOHN from MADMAN ACROSS THE WATER

sion runs it close, but this is a gorgeous, near definitive take on the West Side Story number.

❸ DO YOU KNOW THE WAY TO SAN JOSÉ from WALK ON BY
Another Bacharach/David gem – and a perfect vehicle for Dionne, breathing the romance of the great big LA freeway.

❹ ALFIE from WALK ON BY
Dionne sung this first, then Cilla Black copied her intonation note by note for a #1 hit. But there really was no comparison.

❺ THERE'S ALWAYS SOMETHING THERE TO REMIND ME from WALK ON BY
Big voice, big horns, great song.

❻ HASBROOK HEIGHTS from DIONNE
One of Dionne's last Bacharach/David songs, from 1972, combining delicacy, spring and

poignancy. Dionne's magic is made clear if you hear Burt ballsing it up on his own box set.

❼ I JUST DON'T KNOW WHAT TO DO WITH MYSELF from WALK ON BY
A Bacharach/David lament which builds into a triumphant barrage of melancholy.

❽ YOU'VE LOST THAT LOVIN' FEELIN' from SOULFUL
Soulful was a great Dionne album, taking a new R&B direction, and as the drum shuffle gives way on this number, Dionne lets rip.

❾ THEN CAME YOU from THEN CAME YOU
In 1973 Dionne's sound was again nicely updated, this time by The Detroit Spinners and a spot of funk guitar.

❿ TRACK OF THE CAT
Alas, 1974's *Track of the Cat* album was the last

time Dionne got a sympathetic make-over. Tigers roar, flutes purr, as Thom Bell lays on the Philly sound on an irresistible track.

Mark Ellingham

Muddy Waters

The Rolling Stones famously took their name from one of his songs – and many others copped a whole lot of attitude from his pioneering Chicago electric blues.

❶ I JUST WANT TO MAKE LOVE TO YOU
from **HIS BEST 1947 TO 1955**

What doesn't Muddy want you to do, other than make love? Hear him count the ways on this elemental bump-and-grinder.

❷ I'M YOUR HOOCHIE COOCHIE MAN
from **HIS BEST 1947 TO 1955**

Another classic that seals Muddy's status as both a wholly uninhibited love-man and a genius messenger of the blues start-stop rhythm.

❸ GOT MY MOJO WORKING
from **HIS BEST 1956 TO 1964**

It's one of the most overdone bar band staples by now, but Muddy was the one who popularized this incessantly motoring, cocky (in all senses of the word) blues standard.

❹ I CAN'T BE SATISFIED
from **HIS BEST 1947 TO 1955**

Breathtaking slide guitar and agile bass were the only instruments Waters needed to get his point across on this breakthrough late-40s single.

❺ I WANT TO BE LOVED from **THE ANTHOLOGY**

I Just Want To Make Love To You from the reverse viewpoint, with a defy-you-not-to-dance funky groove, mischievous vocals, and just-right dots of harmonica.

❻ TIGER IN YOUR TANK from **ONE MORE MILE**

Not far short of Got My Mojo Working if you want some quick rollin'n'honking Waters R&B, penned by ace blues songwriter Willie Dixon.

❼ YOU NEED LOVE from **HIS BEST 1956 TO 1964**

An atypical organ is added to Waters's usual guitar-bass-drums combo on this pounder, (in)famously adapted by Led Zeppelin for Whole Lotta Love.

❽ WALKIN' THRU THE PARK
from **HIS BEST 1956 TO 1964**

Shows how Muddy's 1950s bands electrified down-home blues with unbelievably guileless ease, the harmonica, piano, and guitar becoming more than the sum of their parts.

❾ I'M READY from **HIS BEST 1947 TO 1955**

Waters in a devious mood that leaves no doubt what he's ready for, with fine harmonica by fellow Chi-town blues giant Little Walter.

❿ TROUBLE NO MORE
from **HIS BEST 1947 TO 1955**

Celebratory promise of revenge that's more good-humored than mean-spirited, ducking in and out of time like a light-on-his-feet boxer.

Richie Unterberger

Watersons

The Watersons – the first family of British folk music – have dominated the trad music scene for 40 years and remain as prolific as ever, both solo and in various combinations. Our list includes classic tracks from the Watersons and Waterson-Carthy, the group which superceded them, plus various off-shoots and solo outings from Norma Waterson, Martin Carthy and their exuberant daughter and number one folk babe, Eliza Carthy.

❶ JOHN BARLEYCORN from **FROST AND FIRE**

Sung by Mike, this arrangement was later covered by Steve Winwood and Traffic.

❷ THE WHITE COCKADE
from **A YORKSHIRE GARLAND**
Immaculate harmony singing from Lal, Mike, Norma and John Harrison.

❸ SOUND SOUND YOUR INSTRUMENTS OF JOY from **SOUND SOUND YOUR INSTRUMENTS OF JOY**
With Martin Carthy now a fully paid-up member of the family group, has folk music ever sounded more vibrant than on this stirring rendition of the trad hymn?

❹ I BID YOU GOODNIGHT from **OUT ON THE ROLLING SEA**
The Joseph Spence song recorded by the Watersons and friends under the name Blue Murder.

❺ BLACK MUDDY RIVER from **NORMA WATERSON**
An improbable Grateful Dead cover from the solo album that saw Norma nominated for the Mercury Music Prize. She came second behind Pulp.

❻ BRIGHT PHOEBUS from **BRIGHT PHOEBUS**
The magnificent title track from a great album by Mike and the late-lamented Lal Waterson.

❼ THE GREY COCK from **WATERSON:CARTHY**
An early showcase for Eliza from the first album she made with the family.

❽ WORCESTER CITY from **ANGLICANA**
The stand-out performance on Eliza's 2002 album that won her four BBC Radio 2 Folk Awards.

❾ HEARTBREAK HOTEL from **SIGNS OF LIFE**
Anything is a folk song in Martin Carthy's hands, as he proved with this remarkable cover from a 1998 solo album.

❿ AIN'T NO MAN WORTH THE SALT OF MY TEARS from **MIGHTY RIVER OF SONG**
Norma sang this on her first solo album, but there's an even better a cappella version by her and Eliza, that long remained unreleased until it saw the light of day in 2004 on a Watersons' four disc career retrospective box set.

David Honigmann

Weather news

In daily conversation, the weather's what you talk about when there's nothing left to say. In music, the weather's what you sing about when your true love's broken your heart or blown you away. Or when there's nothing left to say.

❶ PORTLAND WATER MICHAEL HURLEY
from **LONG JOURNEY**
From the fringes of folk comes the rough and ragged Michael Hurley, with a song that comforts like soft flannel on a gray day.

❷ BLACK SHEETS OF RAIN BOB MOULD from **BLACK SHEETS OF RAIN**
Mould's voice is too high to compare to thunder, but there's a storm of guitar and emotion.

❸ A HARD RAIN'S A-GONNA FALL BOB DYLAN
from **THE FREE WHEELIN' BOB DYLAN**
Anointed spokesman for a generation, Dylan's keen observations are captured here as always: with poetry and precision.

❹ BLUE EYES CRYING IN THE RAIN
WILLIE NELSON from **REDHEADED STRANGER**
With a whiskey-warm voice that is as distinctive as the songwriter himself, Nelson has the power to bring rain or sun, joy or sadness.

❺ GOOD DAY SUNSHINE THE BEATLES
from **REVOLVER**
The sort of mood-enhancing music you wish you could bottle, no prescription necessary.

❻ COLD RAIN AND SNOW THE GRATEFUL DEAD
from **THE GRATEFUL DEAD**
Hardly recognizable as a traditional piece: more reminiscent of surf than mountain music. The weather apart.

❼ BIG RED SUN BLUES LUCINDA WILLIAMS
from **LUCINDA WILLIAMS**
The emotion behind Williams' voice comes through raw and uncut under the sun.

❽ WHO LOVES THE SUN VELVET UNDERGROUND from **LOADED**

A boppy, poppy – sunny – chorus makes Lou Reed sound all the more worn and woeful.

❾ WALKING ON SUNSHINE KATRINA AND THE WAVES from **WALKING ON SUNSHINE**

Nothing says 1980s like an infectious pop tune. Here's one that could get cynics to roll down the car windows and sing.

❿ LIKE A HURRICANE NEIL YOUNG from **AMERICAN STARS 'N' BARS**

A reedy voice that bends with emotion and an extended, wailing guitar solo make this song the obvious finale for a Neil Young show and of course for this weather set.

Madelyn Rosenberg

Easy does it: Jimmy Webb

Jimmy Webb achieved fame as a songwriter in his teens but never matched it as a performer. He has often been compared to Burt Bacharach (his hero), and if you want to extend the simile into metaphor, then his Dionne Warwick was Glen Campbell.

❶ MACARTHUR PARK RICHARD HARRIS from **TUNESMITH: THE SONGS OF JIMMY WEBB**

What's it all about? There are a thousand theories for this way-over-the-top classic. Notably covered by Donna Summer.

❷ UP, UP AND AWAY FIFTH DIMENSION from **TUNESMITH: THE SONGS OF JIMMY WEBB**

Cheese didn't come much riper than this in the 1960s: you know the one, "…in my beautiful, my beautiful, ball–oooon" (cue horns).

❸ EASY FOR YOU TO SAY LINDA RONSTADT 'GET CLOSER from **ASYLUM**

Linda Ronstadt was in top form with this beautiful bitter ballad.

❹ THE MOON'S A HARSH MISTRESS JOE COCKER from **I CAN STAND A LITTLE RAIN**

This is probably Cocker's best album and his voice is put to amazing effect here.

❺ MET HER ON A PLANE IAN MATTHEWS from **TUNESMITH: THE SONGS OF JIMMY WEBB**

Fairly hard to find, but this version is gorgeous and haunting.

❻ WHEN CAN BROWN BEGIN? JIMMY WEBB from **LETTERS**

Regarded as Webb's finest album and this track has many of the elements of his greatest work with Richard Harris. Scott Walker did a cool version, too.

❼ CRYING IN MY SLEEP ART GARFUNKEL from **WATERMARK**

From an album entirely of Jimmy Webb songs. Nearly a hit but a damn fine miss.

❽ HIGHWAYMAN THE HIGHWAYMEN from **TUNESMITH: THE SONGS OF JIMMY WEBB**

This track topped the country charts for a fine ensemble consisting of Waylon Jennings, Johnny Cash, Willie Nelson and Kris Kristopherson.

Dave Atkinson

Weird but great cover versions

Metal meets country, pop meets industrial, Tuvans take on Joy Division: whatever the clash there's nothing quite like a bizarre cover version that leaves you slack-jawed with amazement.

❶ ACE OF SPADES HAYSEED DIXIE from **LET THERE BE ROCKGRASS**

Motörhead's classic hymn to fast living gets the bluegrass treatment complete with screeching fiddles and some fast'n'furious banjo mayhem.

❷ LOVE WILL TEAR US APART ALBERT KUVEZIN AND YAT-KHA from RE-COVERS

Tuvan throat singer Kuvezin and his band take on Manc misery, and pull it off royally. They also do a cracking version of Led Zep's When The Levee Breaks on the same disc.

❸ CHEERS THE WILDHEARTS from COUPLED WITH

The sentimental and nostalgic piano-led theme tune is turned into a pedal to the metal, honest-to-goodness punk'n'roll romp.

❹ COMMON PEOPLE WILLIAM SHATNER from HAS BEEN

Captain Kirk back in *Transformed Man* territory only this time with Joe Jackson, Ben Folds and an entire choir helping out. Quite astonishing.

❺ (I CAN'T GET NO) SATISFACTION DEVO from Q: ARE WE NOT MEN? A: WE ARE DEVO!

A (new) wave of nerdy ebullience permeates the Ohio quintet's revamped Rolling Stones standard, the shards of which get aurally rebuilt as if trundling down a production line.

❻ RAINING BLOOD TORI AMOS from STRANGE LITTLE GIRLS

Only a singular talent such as Tori Amos could take an evil mother of a thrash metal song and transform it into something so menacingly ghostly.

❼ SWEET DREAMS (ARE MADE OF THIS) MARILYN MANSON from LEST WE FORGET

Some of them want to abuse you, indeed. The Eurythmics' electro-pop hit gets metalized with an industrial-sized boot up the backside.

❽ DON'T STOP MOVIN' THE BEAUTIFUL SOUTH from GOLDDIGGAS, HEADNODDERS & PHOLK SONGS

Ever imagined how the S Club would sound if they'd started drinking pints of bitter, smoking tabs and then headed off to the Working Mens Club? Wonder no more...

❾ LIVE IS LIFE LAIBACH from OPUS DEI

This brooding Balkan collective stepped out from relative obscurity to rework Opus's crowd-friendly anthem. The Austrians' original was a life-affirming singalong, but Laibach mutated it into a growled set of directives, backed by a pounding drum beat.

❿ APACHE MICHAEL VINER'S INCREDIBLE BONGO BAND from DJ POGO PRESENTS THE BREAKS

Just imagine The Shadows trying to do their crazy leg dance to this version of their hit. Sampled by every rap artist – proving that, unbelievably, Cliff Richard helped spawn hip-hop.

Essi Berelian/Neil Way

Barry White

Affectionately known as the " Walrus of Love", Barry White rose from South Central LA's gangs to become a soul star, sex symbol and pop culture icon.

❶ WALKING IN THE RAIN WITH THE ONE YOU LOVE from LOVE SONGS

Barry's first hit found him lending his deep voice to female vocal trio Love Unlimited's tune. If Phil Spector had possessed a sexier voice he might have done this kind of thing with The Ronettes.

❷ I'M GONNA LOVE YOU JUST A LITTLE BIT MORE BABY from I'VE GOT SO MUCH TO GIVE

Blending Isaac Hayes' husky voice and Al Green's gentle seductiveness, Barry emerges as the cuddliest of all 70s soul stars.

❸ NEVER GONNA GIVE YA UP from STONE GON'

Opens with hi-hat and strings – very Temptations – then Barry's deep breathing comes in and everything goes to disco wonderland.

❹ CAN'T GET ENOUGH OF YOUR LOVE from CAN'T GET ENOUGH

Considering Barry's girth a more honest title may have been Can't Get Enough Fried Chicken. But, hey, that's not likely to go down too well on Ally McBeal.

❺ YOU'RE THE FIRST, THE LAST, MY EVERYTHING from CAN'T GET ENOUGH

Barry takes the most clichéd romantic couplets

and inflates them until they're convincing. There's a certain genius in that.

❻ WHAT AM I GONNA DO WITH YOU
from **JUST ANOTHER WAY TO SAY I LOVE YOU**
If you listen to Barry's original early-70s albums you will get to hear his sex raps where the great man murmurs "take off that brassiere" and "I don't wanna see no panties".

❼ YOUR SWEETNESS IS MY WEAKNESS
from **THE MAN**
In Barry World everything is love'n'lust and ecstasy is easily achieved. Which, I guess, makes him the black Barbara Cartland.

❽ PUT ME IN YOUR MIX from **PUT ME IN YOUR MIX**
Barry returns sounding slicker than ever: from disco to hip-hop he could do no wrong.
Garth Cartwright

White punks on dub

The stories of Don Letts playing reggae to the punks before there were any punk records to play are legendary, and have given rise to a fine album. But what those impressionable kids did with the ideas they heard have been literally floor shaking.

❶ ARMAGIDEON TIME THE CLASH
from **CLASH ON BROADWAY.**
The first inkling of white people playing slower reggae beats, and still stronger in the original than the proper Justice Tonight/Kick It Over dub version.

❷ BABY, I LOVE YOU SO COLOURBOX
from **COLOURBOX**
A true dub ska classic given a rock overhaul and film samples.

❸ JU87 PRIMAL SCREAM from **ECHO DEK**
The standout track on The Scream's dub album – weird effects and the voice of Prince Far-I.

❹ JAH WAR THE RUTS from **SOMETHING THAT I SAID**
Another of the early punk/dub crossovers, with a killer bassline. Their later dub album is good but lacks the focus of this one track.

❺ VISIONS OF YOU JAH WOBBLE'S INVADERS OF THE HEART from **VISIONS OF YOU**
There are two mixes of this on the CD single, which highlight the talents of Adrian Sherwood and Andrew Weatherall, both working with a punk bass legend.

❻ DARKHEART (SABRES OF PARADISE MAIN MIX) BOMB THE BASS from **DARKHEART**
The collision of two talents into one mighty slab of sound.

❼ TOWERS OF DUB THE ORB from **UFORB**
Yes, they noodle about and can lose direction but here is a quarter of an hour of music that shakes the soul and never gets dull.

❽ BELA LUGOSI'S DEAD BAUHAUS from **CRACKLE**
Riding a very sparse beat with plenty of echo and effect, one of the more commercial outings of dub style.
Steve Birt

The White Stripes

Garage rock revivalists Jack & Meg White have what few other "The" bands can claim: real talent, a massive sound, and Dylan-esque inscrutability.

❶ SEVEN NATION ARMY from **ELEPHANT**
Opening the Stripes' post-big-break album, Seven Nation Army kicks things off confidently with a caveman-heavy rock'n'roll call to arms.

❷ HAND SPRINGS from **WHITE BLOOD CELLS (JAPANESE IMPORT VERSION)**
A 1950s garage rock fight-song that sees Jack buy his girl a Coke before putting a bowling ball through the glass of a rival's pinball game.

❸ HELLO OPERATOR from DE STIJL

Classic Stripes blues-stomp, with wailing amplified harmonica and squawking guitar, as Jack tries to get the phone operator into bed.

❹ WHY CAN'T YOU BE NICER TO ME?
from DE STIJL

With a bump-bump-BUMP beat that harks back to Jimi's "Foxy Lady," Jack shows his sensitive side, wildly begging the song's title.

❺ JOLENE from BLACKPOOL DELUXE (LIVE)

Covering Dolly, Jack turns a plaintive cry for mercy into something from the depths of fear and jealousy.

❻ BALL AND A BISCUIT from ELEPHANT

A dirty, slow-burn rave-up that sees Jack spouting blues-myth lines like "It's a fact that I'm the seventh son." Best Stripes guitar solo to date.

❼ FELL IN LOVE WITH A GIRL
from WHITE BLOOD CELLS

Like Robert Johnson played by The Ramones, weighing in under-two-minutes.

❽ HOTEL YORBA from WHITE BLOOD CELLS

Jaunty, stomp-along front porch number, among the Stripes' catchiest. In many ways the track that broke them to the world.

❾ FOREVER FOR HER (IS OVER FOR ME)
from GET BEHIND ME SATAN

A big departure for the peppermint twins, flush with marimba, xylophone, egg shakers and a restraint not previously noted.

❿ I'M LONELY (BUT I AIN'T THAT LONELY YET) from GET BEHIND ME SATAN

Over an old blues melody, Jack sings sweetly about missing his sister so bad – but incestuously implies that he "ain't that lonely yet."

Hunter Slaton

The Who

Power chords, aggressive rebellion, a wicked sense of humour, an underrated facility for both pop tunes and whimsical spirituality – and the most energetic stage show of their generation.

❶ MY GENERATION from MY GENERATION

From Roger Daltrey's defiantly sputtering vocal to the crazed climax of feedback and splashing drums, it was always going to be The Who's definitive statement.

❷ I CAN SEE FOR MILES from THE WHO SELL OUT

Both threat and the joy of revenge hang over this track like thunder splitting dark clouds, the crackling drums and bee-buzz guitar announcing the Day of Judgement come.

❸ SUBSTITUTE from THE ULTIMATE COLLECTION

Power pop's greatest moment, especially in the opening declarative guitar chords. Its lyrics depicting confused identity and willful illusion are great, too.

❹ UNDERTURE from TOMMY

Ten-minute instrumental from *Tommy* whose pseudo-classical sweep has a grandeur seldom achieved by rock, underscored by wondrous guitar riffs and characteristically maniacally urgent drums.

❺ ANYWAY, ANYHOW, ANYWHERE
from THE ULTIMATE COLLECTION

A riot of feedback in the instrumental break, but a solid proto-power-pop tune underneath, delivered with appealing bluster by Daltrey.

❻ THE KIDS ARE ALRIGHT from MY GENERATION

The power-chord youth anthem to beat all youth anthems, and an early hint of a sensitive heart beneath the group's pillhead toughness.

❼ THE REAL ME from QUADROPHENIA

Quadrophenia's dynamic curtain-raiser launched this rock opera as surely as a mod kick-starts his scooter.

❽ PICTURES OF LILY from THE ULTIMATE COLLECTION

Another great single from The Who's early career, one whose catchy tune and bouncy story-song masks penetrating tragicomedy.

9 I CAN'T REACH YOU from **THE WHO SELL OUT**

A relatively obscure album track, but one of Pete Townshend's most tender expressions of vulnerability and spiritual hunger.

10 I'M FREE from **TOMMY**

Ecstatic midtempo riff-driven rocker that works just as well removed from the context of the group's famous rock opera.

Richie Unterberger

Wilco

Having morphed from Uncle Tupelo also-rans to become the US Radiohead, Wilco's art-damaged Americana continues to dazzle, delight and confound.

1 CASINO QUEEN from **A.M.**

Jeff Tweedy still managed to have a great time while burning out the last vestiges of Uncle Tupelo; this rollicking, reckless song is proof.

2 MISUNDERSTOOD from **BEING THERE**

Announcing loud his new vision, Tweedy hollers "nothing" over the noise in this cathartic kick-off to the double album *Being There*.

3 SUNKEN TREASURE from **BEING THERE**

A sweet, sad ballad where Tweedy laments being "so out of tune with you," before the song collapses into squawking feedback.

4 A SHOT IN THE ARM from **SUMMERTEETH**

Wilco's third album is shot through with songs like this: irresistible technicolor pop juxtaposed with addict lyrics.

5 I AM TRYING TO BREAK YOUR HEART from **YANKEE HOTEL FOXTROT**

The first song by Tweedy the surrealist poet, with lyrics like "I assassin down the avenue" over a neo-tribal drumbeat.

6 ASHES OF AMERICAN FLAGS from **YANKEE HOTEL FOXTROT**

A hymn to and a jeremiad against autumnal America, alongside a noisy self-immolation of one whose "lies are always wishes."

7 SPIDERS (KIDSMOKE) from **A GHOST IS BORN**

Thrill as the bar-band guitar heroes from Chicago fight the Krautrock spiders from Michigan for eleven epic minutes!

8 KICKING TELEVISION from **A GHOST IS BORN BONUS EP**

Whether it's a snotty throwaway rocker or the smart way forward for Wilco, this tongue-in-cheek anti-consumer rant still kicks.

9 THE LATE GREATS from **A GHOST IS BORN**

Happily ending the masterful *A Ghost Is Born*, Wilco returns to its roots with this fence-straddling, winking bit of self-parody – or is it?

10 BOB DYLAN'S 49TH BEARD from **THE MORE LIKE THE MOON EP**

Tossed-off but touching, a simple slice of odd, strummed-guitar genius, laced through with spacey, dreamlike, underwater murmurs.

Hunter Slaton

Hank Williams

The heart and soul of country music, Hank Williams burnt out young but left a vital and admired – and much covered – legacy.

1 MOVE IT ON OVER from **HANK WILLIAMS: 40 GREATEST HITS**

The first Williams single is classic honky tonk with great words – and classic backing vocals.

2 LOVESICK BLUES from **HANK WILLIAMS: 40 GREATEST HITS**

The song that made Hank Willliams respectable enough to be invited to take the stage at the Grand Ol Opry.

3 LONG GONE LONESOME BLUES from **HANK WILLIAMS: 40 GREATEST HITS**

Nihilistic yodel heaven.

❹ YOUR CHEATIN' HEART from **HANK WILLIAMS: 40 GREATEST HITS**
One of his most famous and covered songs, written just after he had divorced his wife, Audrey Mae Sheppard.

❺ LOST HIGHWAY from **HANK WILLIAMS: 40 GREATEST HITS**
The song that best embodies the rootless, drifting lifestyle that helped to kill Williams at the age of 29.

❻ COLD COLD HEART from **HANK WILLIAMS: 40 GREATEST HITS**
Feel Hank's pain.

❼ JAMBALAYA
from **HANK WILLIAMS: 40 GREATEST HITS**
Popularised by The Carpenters of course, but the original is the real deal.

❽ YOU'RE GONNA CHANGE from **HANK WILLIAMS: 40 GREATEST HITS**
Band and voice in perfect harmony.

❾ MANSION ON THE HILL from **HANK WILLIAMS: 40 GREATEST HITS**
Money and fame can't buy you happiness, as Hank knew better than anyone.

❿ SAW THE LIGHT from **HANK WILLIAMS: 40 GREATEST HITS**
Hank gets religion.

Martin Dunford

Lucinda Williams

"It's my belief that Lucinda Williams is the closest living counterpart to Hank Williams when it comes to writing from the heart with absolute economy," Elvis Costello reckons. "And it's a bonus that her rock'n'roll vocal style will shake up any band in a fashion that I can only compare to Keith Richards' guitar playing."

❶ LAFAYETTE from **HAPPY WOMAN BLUES**
Lucinda goes Cajun on this early composition from 1980.

❷ PINEOLA from **SWEET OLD WORLD**
Knockout, literate southern story-telling in the Flannery O'Connor tradition.

❸ CAR WHEELS ON A GRAVEL ROAD from **CAR WHEELS ON A GRAVEL ROAD**
After a six years silence following *Sweet Old World*, we'd just about forgotten her. Then she showed up in Nashville and came out with this 1998 masterpiece.

❹ CONCRETE AND BARBED WIRE from **CAR WHEELS ON A GRAVEL ROAD**
Blissful acoustic guitars embellished with , mandolin, slide and Steve Earle's harmonies on one of Williams' most perfect songs.

❺ LAKE CHARLES
from **CAR WHEELS ON A GRAVEL ROAD**
Another exquisitely evocative Southern vignette from an album that really deserves to be heard in its entirety as an indivisible mood piece.

❻ GET RIGHT WITH GOD from **ESSENCE**
A drop of country-gospel fervour that was one of the highlights of a fine 2001 album.

❼ AMERICAN DREAM
from **WORLD WITHOUT TEARS**
Williams turned 50 in 2003 and marked the occasion with the best album of her career, which included this coruscating alternative state-of-the-nation address.

❽ OVERTIME from **WORLD WITHOUT TEARS**
Classic heartbreak like a latter-day Patsy Cline, with a touch of Patti Smith thrown in.

❾ RIGHTEOUSLY from **WORLD WITHOUT TEARS**
You can get horny just listening to her moan her way through this.

Lucinda Williams
On a roll

She's more country than almost anything out of modern Nashville and she's funkier than a mosquito's tweeter. What's more, LUCINDA WILLIAMS started making the best music of her life in her mid-40s with the release of 1998's classic *Car Wheels On A Gravel Road* and has been on a roll ever since. She does a list pretty good, too…

❶ IT MAKES NO DIFFERENCE THE BAND from NORTHERN LIGHTS SOUTHERN CROSS

❷ GOOD DAY PAUL WESTERBERG from EVENTUALLY

❸ MARY PATTY GRIFFIN from FLAMING RED

❹ THESE DAYS GREG ALLMAN from LAID BACK

❺ FAMOUS BLUE RAINCOAT LEONARD COHEN from SONGS OF LOVE AND HATE

❻ SYLVIA PLATH RYAN ADAMS from GOLD

❼ MY FUNNY VALENTINE CHET BAKER from MY FUNNY VALENTINE

❽ DON'T EXPLAIN NINA SIMONE from LET IT ALL OUT

❾ TEARS ARE IN YOUR EYES YO LA TENGO from AND THEN NOTHING TURNED ITSELF INSIDE-OUT

❿ NO OTHER LOVE CHUCK PROPHET from NO OTHER LOVE

❿ REAL LIVE BLEEDING FINGERS & BROKEN GUITAR STRINGS from LIVE AT THE FILLMORE
The rocking studio version on *World Without Tears* is blistering – but this live take is nuclear.
Nigel Willamson

Steve Winwood & Traffic

Just fifteen when he started singing with the Spencer Davis Group, Steve Winwood's genius was some kind of freak of nature. His voice had barely broken but he sounded like a veteran soul singer and he could play organ, lead guitar, bass and drums with equal virtuosity. When he tired of playing R&B every night, he explored psychedelia with Traffic, formed the world's first "super-group", with Eric Clapton, and later reinvented himself for the dancefloor.

SPENCER DAVIS GROUP

❶ GIMME SOME LOVING from BEST OF THE SPENCER DAVIS GROUP
A searing, soul-drenched vocal and one of the killer rhythms of all time, only the Beach Boys' Good Vibrations kept it from number one.

❷ I'M A MAN from BEST OF THE SPENCER DAVIS GROUP
He was a 16-year-old boy, but he sounded like Ray Charles.

BLIND FAITH

❸ CAN'T FIND MY WAY HOME from BLIND FAITH
Blind Faith could never sustain the weight of expectation that the supergroup tag imposed, but Winwood contributed three brilliant songs to their sole album, of which this is the best.

TRAFFIC

❹ DEAR MR FANTASY from MR FANTASY
The spirit of 67 personified in the lead track from Traffic's stellar debut.

❺ NO FACE, NO NAME, NO NUMBER
from **MR FANTASY**
Traffic invented the notion of "getting it together in the country" and this vulnerable, melancholic ballad was one of the finer results of Steve's rural idyll.

❻ JOHN BARLEYCORN from **JOHN BARLEYCORN MUST DIE**
Having tired of being the white Ray Charles, he then turned into a more soulful Martin Carthy on this magnificent and mysterious rendition of the old folk ballad.

❼ LOW SPARK OF HIGH-HEELED BOYS from **LOW SPARK OF HIGH-HEELED BOYS**
Twelve minutes of inspired improvisation over a jazz-tinged groove, Traffic had never sounded more fluid than they did on this.

SOLO

❽ VALERIE from **TALKING BACK TO THE NIGHT**
A tune so memorable that 22 years after its release, Eric Prydz borrowed it for his 2004 number one single, Call On Me.

❾ HIGHER LOVE from **BACK IN THE HIGH LIFE**
Not even the horribly dated synths and programming can ruin this irresistible dance groove that ruled the airwaves in 1986.

❿ ROLL WITH IT from **ROLL WITH IT**
Backed by the Memphis Horns, Winwood paid tribute to the Motown beat on a song that rolled back the years and sounded as if it could have come from his Spencer Davis years.

Nigel Williamson

Wire

One of the quirkier and more interesting bands to emerge from the late 70s British punk scene, Wire were largely ignored at the time but have consistently referenced since, by bands as diverse as Elastica and Franz Ferdinand.

❶ MANNEQUIN from **PINK FLAG**
Chosen as a single for its pop tune and harmonies, its chunky chords and vicious lyrics belie the rosy exterior in sinister fashion.

❷ OUTDOOR MINER from **CHAIRS MISSING**
It takes genius to squeeze such a delicious pot pourri of melodic hooks into 1:45. Lyrics like "Face worker, a serpentine miner, a roof falls, an underliner, of leaf structure the egg timer" defy criticism.

❸ I SHOULD HAVE KNOWN BETTER from **154**
Staccato bell effects and downbeat spoken lyrics help issue the salutary warning intended.

❹ LOWDOWN from **PINK FLAG**
The Stooges' guitar pauses for Newman's punk musings.

❺ MAROONED from **CHAIRS MISSING**
Sporadic bass rumbles and ice cool guitar stabs summon up the plight of being stranded on a melting iceberg. Newman remains stoic throughout the ordeal.

❻ 15TH from **154**
The poppiest cut on the album could almost be a precursor of The Cure.

❼ FEELING CALLED LOVE from **PINK FLAG**
A brief blast of garage with dashes of Louie Louie and angelic harmonies thrown in.

❽ ANOTHER THE LETTER from **CHAIRS MISSING**
Frenetic flight of the bumblebee synth and staccato drop-tone vocals show where the lines between Colin Newman and Gary Numan occasionally got blurred.

❾ ON RETURNING from **154**
A Buzzcocks-like jaunt. Punk of the first order with chopped guitars, runaway synth and furious vocals.

❿ MR MARX'S TABLE from **SEND**
In this effort from their recent reformation, Newman sounds incongruously tuneful over a wall of sound that could be Spacemen 3.

Nick Edwards

Bill Withers

Navy vet Withers brought a very adult understanding to 1970s soul music. His beautifully literate songs were informed with a singer-songwriter's perspective and several have become standards.

❶ AINT NO SUNSHINE from **JUST AS I AM**
One of the most perfect songs ever written. Dig it when Bill goes into his mantra "I-know-I-know-I-know-I-know-I-know."

❷ USE ME from **STILL BILL**
One of the few truly smart songs about sexual pleasure that our sex-obsessed culture has ever produced.

❸ GRANDMA'S HANDS from **JUST AS I AM**
A meditation on his Grandma whose hands "would sometimes ache and swell." Who else in popular music has written with such natural observation?

❹ WHO IS HE (AND WHAT IS HE TO YOU?) from **THE BEST OF BILL WITHERS**
Bill gets a little uneasy when he and his partner pass a man who tries to stare Bill down. The confusion grows and the paranoia builds.

❺ LEAN ON ME from **STILL BILL**
Songwriting rarely gets better than this hymn to solidarity amongst friends and lovers. Bill obviously paid attention at church.

❻ I CAN'T WRITE LEFTHANDED from **BILL WITHERS LIVE AT CARNEGIE HALL**
Bill sings from the perspective of a Vietnam veteran who has lost his right arm and is struggling to fit back into society.

❼ HARLEM/COLD BALONEY from **BILL WITHERS LIVE AT CARNEGIE HALL**
Bill's encore is a slice of social reality that's quietly understated yet builds until its absolutely devastating.

❽ LOVELY DAY from **MENAGERIE**
A hymn to the simple pleasures of enjoying a day with the one you love.

❾ JUST THE TWO OF US from **THE BEST OF BILL WITHERS**
Bill teams up with saxophonist Grover Washington Jr in 1981 for a US #2 pop hit and R&B Grammy.

❿ BETTER OFF DEAD from **JUST AS I AM**
Bill adopts the voice of a suicidal alcoholic whose wife has left taking the children. As good as a Raymond Carver short story.

Garth Cartwright

Bobby Womack

A master singer-songwriter-guitarist, Bobby Womack started out as a teenage protégé of Sam Cooke (whose widow he married), eased into shaping 70s soul, and wrote classic songs for The Rolling Stones (It's All Over Now) and Wilson Pickett (I'm A Midnight Mover). Plus he plays all over Sly Stone's *There's A Riot Going On*. Respect is the word.

❶ THAT'S THE WAY I FEEL ABOUT CHA from **THE VERY BEST OF**
This was Womack's first big hit – an early 70s number that sounds like it came straight out of Memphis soul. It's hard to get another of this.

❷ FLY ME TO THE MOON from **THE VERY BEST OF**
Nobody makes a cover version their own quite like Bobby Womack. He adds a jazz sensibility to other folks' songs and here, on this delicate flight of soul, he disregards both lyric and tune.

❸ CALIFORNIA DREAMING from **THE VERY BEST OF**
Lush, beautifully evocative reading of The Mamas & The Papas hit. Gave Womack a surprise 2004 UK hit when it served as soundtrack for a car ad.

❹ ACROSS 110TH ST from ACROSS 110TH ST

Womack scored the extremely tough blax-ploitation flick and his brooding title tune is heavy with ghetto claustrophobia. So much so Tarantino re-employed it for *Jackie Brown*.

❺ HARRY HIPPIE from UNDERSTANDING

Laidback soul hit with Bobby casting a cold eye at panhandlers. Features some of Womack's most beautifully fluid guitar playing.

❻ WOMAN'S GOTTA HAVE IT
from UNDERSTANDING

His biggest US R&B hit is a gorgeous hymn to loving and listening to your woman.

❼ I'M A MIDNIGHT MOVER
from THE MIDNIGHT MOVER

Bobby was a notorious party animal so this anthem to sleeping all day and raising hell all night is possibly autobiographical.

❽ IT'S ALL OVER NOW from THE MIDNIGHT MOVER

Originally penned by the teenage Womack for his group The Valentinos, it gave The Rolling Stones their first #1. This 70s remake is a funky feast.

❾ IF YOU THINK YOU'RE LONELY NOW
from THE POET

1981 comeback hit that proves Womack is amongst the greatest of soul men.

❿ LOVE HAS FINALLY COME AT LAST
from THE POET II

Bobby teams up with Patti LaBelle and they sing their asses off.

Garth Cartwright

Stevie Wonder

Born blind, Steveland Morris was signed to Motown aged 12 and named "Little Stevie Wonder" by Berry Gordy. That's foresight: Wonder developed into Motown's most talented and consistently successful artist. But his true genius was revealed in the groundbreaking albums he made in the early 1970s, from *Talking Book* through to *Songs in the Key of Life* – records on which he played just about everything himself.

❶ FINGERTIPS from THE DEFINITIVE COLLECTION

Little Stevie was just 13 when this came out: a blast of harmonica so exuberant, it still gets you standing to applaud.

❷ YESTER-ME, YESTER-YOU, YESTERDAY from THE DEFINITIVE COLLECTION

1969 hit that finds the mature –nineteen-year-old – Stevie delivering a gorgeous love song.

❸ SUPERSTITION from TALKING BOOK

The toughest groove, the most ferocious atmosphere: launched in 1972 and still keeping heads ringin'. Hats off to Jeff Beck, too, for whom Stevie initially wrote the song, and who puts in brilliant guest guitar on the album.

❹ YOU ARE THE SUNSHINE OF MY LIFE from TALKING BOOK

Whatever Stevie sang he did with such heart-felt appreciation it wins you over. But this was also the launch of the definitive Stevie Wonder rhythm, one he returned to time and again.

❺ LIVING FOR THE CITY FROM INNERVISIONS

"A boy is born in hard time Mississippi" begins the song and Stevie leads us through a tale of poverty and desperation as shaped by white American racism.

❻ VISIONS from INNERVISIONS

"I know that leaves are green/They only turn to brown when autumn comes around" sings a blind man as he demands Dr King's vision of equality be made real.

❼ SIR DUKE from SONGS IN THE KEY OF LIFE

Duke Ellington and co' are celebrated in this joyous hornfest. One of the highlights of an album part genius, part just a little too kitsch.

❽ HAPPY BIRTHDAY from **HOTTER THAN JULY**
Stevie's constant campaigning helped get Dr Martin Luther King's birthday made a national holiday. This was the campaign's glorious soundtrack.

❾ MASTERBLASTER (JAMMIN')
from
HOTTER THAN JULY
Stevie acknowledges Bob Marley as a contemporary giant and the funky reggae groove sizzles.

❿ I JUST CALLED TO SAY I LOVE YOU from **THE DEFINITIVE COLLECTION**
Sentimental. Catchy as hell. Hugely popular. Agreed. Now what's your problem?

Garth Cartwright

World jazz

The landscape of jazz music is changing dramatically as musicians from every corner of the globe adopt it, adding in elements of their own folk roots.

❶ FUSIC TOUFFIC FARROUKH from **DRAB ZEEN**
Lebanese sax man Farroukh has blended jazz and Arabic old and new together seamlessly, grooving all the way to the Kasbah.

❷ FUNK RAI NGUYEN LE from **MAGREB & FRIENDS**
Born in Paris to Vietnamese parents, Le has fast become one of world's premier jazz guitarists. Funk Rai opens doors from Saïda to Vienna, Algiers to France, Hanoi to Sardinia and beyond.

❸ ENTRE CONTINENTES RENAUD GARCIA-FONS from **ENTREMUNDO**
When it comes to the acoustic bass, Garcia-Fons is in a class by himself. On Entremundo he fuses together brilliant jazz bass and the fiery heat of Flamenco.

❹ LA ABUELITA AQUILES BAEZ from **REFLEJANDO EL DORADO**
Aquiles Baez is a national treasure in his homeland of Venezuela. It's easy to see, or rather hear, why. A brilliant guitarist, he brings together local traditions with jazz freedom.

❺ NEKEMTENEMMUTOGATOL ORO BESH 'O DROM from **CAN'T MAKE ME**
Besh 'o Drom from Budapest take the folk driven Balkan Brass sound and makes it as jazz-filled as anything you've ever heard. Jazz cimbalom? Yessir!!

❻ WHITEWASH JASPER VAN'T HOF'S PILI PILI from **HOTEL BABO**
Pili Pili span 20 years of world jazz music. Dutch jazz pianist Van't Hof built this band with musicians from all over Africa – Mali, Senegal, Congo, South Africa, Guinea – and discovered Angelique Kidjo, who performs on this track.

❼ BIEL ANNA MARIA JOPEK WITH PAT METHANY from **UPOJENIE**
With one of the most beautiful jazz voices of our time, Polish jazz vocalist Anna Maria Jopek teamed up with guitarist Pat Metheny to create this extraordinary album. Who cares if the vocals aren't in English?

❽ JUNGLE ME MUNGLE FREE WINDS from **INDIAN AIR**
German sax player Heinrich Von Kalnein recorded two alums with Indian Air, this being the most special. It features Kanjira master V. Selvaganesh along with tabla master Jatinder Thakur and the blend of modern jazz and Indian rhythms is utterly intoxicating.

❾ THE HAPPY SHEIK RABIH ABOU-KHALIL from **THE SULTAN'S PICNIC**
Oud master Rabih Abou-Khalil adapts traditional folk melodies to great jazz effect.

❿ VOL DE NUIT HADOUK TRIO from **LIVE A' FIP**
Literally a world-jazz super-group with Didier Malherbe, Steve Shehan and Loy Erlich, the trio creates something entirely fresh and new in the jazz realm. The trio takes its name from the two primary instruments used in these record-

393

Songlines'
World music landmarks

Nobody likes the term much, but "world music" has a rapidly growing audience, dozens of labels and a cluster of magazines (not to mention a two-volume Rough Guide). Here SIMON BROUGHTON, editor of *SONGLINES* magazine, picks some of world music's landmark hits – from African pop to Sufi soul.

❶ SINA SALIF KEITA from SORO
A great track from Keita's seminal 1987 album, which brought African music to a new international audience. The incantatory opening immediately evokes Mali's vibrant musical world.

❷ KALIMANKOU VOIX BULGARES from LE MYSTÈRE DES VOIX BULGARES
Bulgaria's Radio-TV choir had a surprise global hit with this recording. Yanka Rupkina's solo voice carries a beautifully ornamented melody through dangerous harmonic waters.

❸ MUSTT MUSTT NUSRAT FATEH ALI KHAN from MUSTT MUSTT
Nusrat, who died in 1997, was simply a phenomenon. Who'd have thought that a devotional song to a Pakistani Sufi saint could turn into such a worldwide hit? Who'd have thought religious music could be so funky?

❹ UTRUS HORAS ORCHESTRA BAOBAB from PIRATES CHOICE
With its spacey guitar and mellow sax, this is the 1982 signature track from one of Africa's greatest bands.

❺ MARIA LISBOA MARIZA from FADO EM MIM
With her debut recording in 2002, Mariza became the new voice of Portugal's bluesy fado music. This is wonderful version of an old fado classic.

❻ DIDI KHALED from KHALED
This storming track opened the Algerian *rai* star's first international release – and it's a song that he's been performing ever since.

❼ BALADA CONDUCATORULUI TARAF DE HAIDOUKS from MUSIQUE DES TZIGANES DE ROUMANIE
An extraordinary success story: poor Romanian Gypsies become ambassadors of their music round the world. This track tells of the fall of the dictator Ceausescu in 1989.

❽ LI MA WEESU YOUSSOU N'DOUR from NOTHING'S IN VAIN
Probably the biggest name in African music now and this is one of his catchiest recent songs from 2002.

❾ CHAN CHAN BUENA VISTA SOCIAL CLUB from BUENA VISTA SOCIAL CLUB
You only have to hear the first chord to know what's coming. The catchiest track from world music's greatest success story. Sublime music from Eliades Ochoa and Compay Segundo.

❿ CLANDESTINO MANU CHAO from CLANDESTINO
A great melody, snatches of conversation, street sounds and a whiff of subculture – this is distinctively Manu Chao, drawn from his groudbreaking 1998 album.

ings, the doudouk and the hajouj.

Geoff Colquitt

Robert Wyatt

Robert Wyatt proclaims himself a true minimalist ("I really don't do a lot"), an assertion that flies in the face of a constantly inventive 30-year solo career since leaving Soft Machine in 1974. His is a unique voice that has integrity and heart, at the fore as much in his personal compositions as in a memorable series of political songs and off-kilter covers.

❶ SEA SONG from **ROCK BOTTOM**

Rock Bottom is Wyatt's great work, recorded in recovery from the accident that left him paralysed and wheelchair bound. It's not really an album to excerpt, but this marine opener is a good way in, with his trademark wordless voice as primary instrument, set above a wonderful swirl of guitar from Mike Oldfield.

❷ AT LAST I AM FREE from **NOTHING CAN STOP US**

This was pretty special as a disco number by Chic. Wyatt slows it to a beat you couldn't even tap a foot to, and lets the words soar. Magic.

❸ INSENSATEZ from **CUCKOOLAND**

Wyatt has an unerring instinct for the heart of a song, and Tom Jobim's lovely bossa nova suits him perfectly.

❹ TE RECUERDO AMANDA from **MID-EIGHTIES**

Victor Jara, the Chilean songwriter murdered by Pinochet's regime, wrote this most tender love song. Wyatt's treatment, almost funereal, and in the original Spanish, renders it a song as much for Jara, as for itself.

❺ LEFT ON MAN from **DONDESTAN**

Wyatt is a great percussionist: here his urgent beats and rhythm-chorus of "simplify, reduce, oversimplify" underpin a stark political message: "What we call freedom in the north is just freedom to use you…"

❻ MARYAN from **SCHLEEP**

A dreamy highlight of this mid-90s album, recalling Rock Bottom in mood, and with exquisite guitar work from Philip Catherine.

❼ THE WIND OF CHANGE from **FLOTSAM JETSAM**

Long before African music grew popular in the West, and when Mozambique was a forgotten war zone, Wyatt enlisted the SWAPO singers, and a London big band, to assert a buoyant message of hope and liberation.

❽ I'M A BELIEVER from **GOING BACK A BIT**

You have to grin as Wyatt launches into The Monkees' love-affirming number. An oddball UK hit, it even got him onto *Top of the Pops*.

❾ O CAROLINE from **MATCHING MOLE**

An affecting song of lost love, recorded with Wyatt's post-Soft Machine band.

❿ SHIPBUILDING from **NOTHING CAN STOP US**

Elvis Costello wrote this marvellous, subtle political song for Wyatt as the Falklands war gathered momentum. "Diving for dear life, when we could be diving for pearls," is the chorus, but really it is perfect from start to finish.

Mark Ellingham

Robert Wyatt's
Records de France

"What this list's about," wrote ROBERT WYATT, "is the French take on a non-European culture during my lifetime: from exiled black American jazz musicians after the war to North African influenced music. Europe beyond Europe. It's inadequately explained but from the heart."

He broke the key rule of this book by specifying albums rather than individual songs, but, hey, someone's allowed to do things different and Wyatt's the man.

❶ BOHEMIA AFTER DARK EDDY LOUISS
This – and the three choices below – are all on the wonderful French jazz label, Gitanes. So nostalgic! Louiss plays Hammond organ, in the style of Jimmy Smith or Shirley Scott.

❷ JAZZ SUR SEINE BARNEY WILEN
A French tenor sax player, accompanied by a group which is basically the (black American) rhythm section of the Modern Jazz Quartet.

❸ JOUE BUD POWELL RENÉ UTREGER
Utreger is a pianist who worked a lot with Bud Powell, after he made his home in Paris. The French treated Black American musicians as real artists, not just entertainers. Americans couldn't play in Britain at the time because of our Musicians Union restrictions, which was maybe why all the guitar bands took over.

❹ JEUX DE QUARTES BOBBY JASPAR
Jaspar was actually Belgian. He played sax and flute – with a very light touch, each of his notes was very good.

❺ LUCKY IN PARIS MARTIAL SOLAL
A great session, featuring drummer Gerard Pochonet and sax player Lucky Thompson. But it's the Algiers-born pianist, Solal, who makes such a fresh sound. A master at work.

❻ POULINA ORCHESTRE NATIONAL DE BARBES
I love this. It's a big band of North Africans from Barbes, the Paris suburb.

❼ HADOUK DIDIER MALHERBE
Didier plays every wind instrument under the sun. He recorded this with Maghrebi players.

❽ LES RUES DE LA NUIT HELÈNE DELAVAUT
Totally French. She's a very sexy 1930s French opera singer, and this is just her and a pianist.

❾ PORTRAIT-ROBOT BERTRAND BURGALAT
He's a French pop producer who does this home-made easy music. But he's used some of Alfie's (Alfreda Benge, Robert's wife) lyrics on this one. So he's in!

❿ CHANSONS JOHN GREAVES & ÉLISE CARON
John lives in Paris, so this is a proper French record. He's a wonderful bass player, and songwriter. I did a very discreet bit on the album.

X-ray Spex

The greatest talent to rise up from a genuinely street background in the London punk scene, Poly Styrene was wise enough to step away from fame when she found it not to her taste. Before that though, she knocked out one brilliant album and a bunch of superb, spirit-of-the-age singles.

❶ I AM A CLICHÉ from **GERM FREE ADOLESCENTS**
Classic punk tune from Poly and the band – played loud, played fast with one verse, one chorus, one repeat and a fade.

❷ THE DAY THE WORLD TURNED DAY-GLO from **GERM FREE ADOLESCENTS**
Apocalyptic in a streetwise manner that Patti Smith could only sigh at wistfully, Poly trips out on the sheer number of plastics, additives and E-numbers in her life.

❸ IDENTITY from **GERM FREE ADOLESCENTS**
Forget about identity fraud, Poly's talking about total identity crisis and personality breakdown. Punk rock of the highest quality, provoking thought and questioning the status quo.

❹ I AM A POSEUR from **GERM FREE ADOLESCENTS**
A charming piece of swagger that captures the sheer fun of shocking the straight world.

❺ GENETIC ENGINEERING from **GERM FREE ADOLESCENTS**
Way back before cloning, in a time when even photocopiers were still regarded as magic, Poly wrote this prophetic little nightmare of a bleak future still to come. A perspective on Aldous Huxley's *Brave New World*, as observed from the Worlds End in Chelsea.

❻ ART-I-FICIAL from **GERM FREE ADOLESCENTS**
Excellent meditation on the role of make-up, messed-up education and enforced reliance on the domestic appliance in a woman's world. And you can dance to it too!

❼ I LIVE OFF YOU from **GERM FREE ADOLESCENTS**
Cats live off rats in Poly's world, where pimps beat whores and Freddie will try to strangle you with your own plastic popper beads. Life sucks.

❽ GERM FREE ADOLESCENTS from **GERM FREE ADOLESCENTS**
The ultimate Western teenage love song, in which one's entire romantic life depends on the state of one's skin.

❾ OH BONDAGE! UP YOURS! from **GERM FREE ADOLESCENTS**
The band's anthem, and still unfortunately necessary as a rallying cry for the oppressed 51 percent.

Al Spicer

XTC

British pop's answer to Mr Pooter in *The Diary Of A Nobody*, the work of XTC shines a friendly light onto the niceties of British culture. Starting as thoughtful punks they progressed to a stately middle age of epigrams and anecdotes.

❶ SCIENCE FRICTION from **FOSSIL FUEL**
This song can be dated to the end of the 70s just by listening to the angular guitar lines and tinny keyboards. A charming piece of harmless

British New Wave perked up beyond jollity by Andy Partridge's super-clipped vocal delivery and the sheer joy of the twitchingly urgent tune itself.

❷ TOWERS OF LONDON from **BLACK SEA**

Deliciously twangy guitar and sloppy-sounding drumming are the instant hooks of this rather unusual musing on the city's long and distinguished pedigree.

❸ GENERALS AND MAJORS from **BLACK SEA**

This is as near as XTC ever got to a downbeat comment on the gloom of the cold war and the militarised political scene of the 1980s; of course, being one of Andy Partridge's compositions, it bops and bounces along as if it had just won a prize at a kid's birthday party

❹ STATUE OF LIBERTY from **WHITE MUSIC**

A silly lyrical love song in tribute to New York's best known attraction. Neatly sums up the emotional reaction of more than four million annual tourists to the big lass who stands on the island.

❺ SGT ROCK (IS GOING TO HELP ME) from **BLACK SEA**

Daytime radio favourite – and one of Andy's chirpiest, fruitiest tunes – this is a classic "coming of age" tune for boys in the vein of the Who's "Pictures of Lily".

❻ LOVE ON A FARMBOY'S WAGES from **MUMMER**

A far more mature look at the world of romance from a chap having to make do on a cult musician's wages.

❼ BALL AND CHAIN from **ENGLISH SETTLEMENT**

Exuberantly anti-development singalong from one of the band's best albums. Lyrics are reduced almost to simple slogans as Andy lets the repetitive beat of chisel on masonry do the talking for him.

❽ MAKING PLANS FOR NIGEL from **DRUMS AND WIRES**

XTC's biggest chart hit was so successful that management at British Steel (damned by faint praise in the lyric) rounded up all the Nigels they could find on the payroll and paraded them, show-trial style, in front of the cameras to say just how happy they were to be in the industry.

❾ SENSES WORKING OVERTIME from **ENGLISH SETTLEMENT**

Delightful British psychedelia from a man who might not even need LSD to see the hidden charms in rainy old Swindon, Wiltshire.

❿ THIS IS POP? from **WHITE MUSIC**

Dating back to XTC's days of punkish attitude, this champions the band's own musical taste in the face of abuse from the normals. Snotty, teenage rebel music, but polite – Andy Partridge is nothing if not well brought up.

Al Spicer

Y

Yes

Yes were always the most atmospheric, adventurous and loopily strange of prog acts. If they often lost sight of reality, they rarely lost sight of melody.

❶ STARSHIP TROOPER from THE YES ALBUM
Epitomising the excitement of classic Yes, this three-part space-rock suite soars ever upward, from its arpeggiated opening to acoustic middle to sinister fade.

❷ LONG DISTANCE RUN AROUND from FRAGILE
Yes at their most direct and poppy: guitar and bass syncopate snappily around Jon Anderson's keening falsetto.

❸ GOING FOR THE ONE from GOING FOR THE ONE
Charging heavy rock lifted skyward by lightning steel guitar from Steve Howe and Anderson's jaw-droppingly dramatic vocal.

❹ HEART OF THE SUNRISE from BUFFALO 66
As featured in *Buffalo 66*, it's proto trip-hop with a huge bass riff and ambient synth washes. Only Anderson's bonkers lyric ("SHARP, distance") belongs firmly in prog.

❺ YOUR MOVE from THE YES ALBUM
Another simple, early Yes song: a lapping wave of acoustic beauty that is a modest precursor to the more pompous And You And I.

❻ CLOSE TO THE EDGE from CLOSE TO THE EDGE
Twenty-minute pastoral epic that opens and closes with birdsong but in between it pulls and pushes with equal parts excitement and beauty.

❼ ROUNDABOUT from FRAGILE
Take a simple R&B riff, add classical flourish courtesy of new boy Rick Wakeman, add a chorus classic rock fans could hum and – bingo! – an American breakthrough.

❽ GATES OF DELIRIUM from RELAYER
Late epic from a neglected album: an anti-war song that goes from nippy opening to combative middle before ending in swooning serenity.

Toby Manning

Yo La Tengo

An indie rock institution, Yo La Tengo have been around for over 20 years, and have rarely repeated themselves, feedback and folk being equal staples of their sound.

❶ BLUE LINE SWINGER from ELECTR-O-PURA
Yo La Tengo at their My Bloody Valentine-esque best: indistinguishable male/female vocals, a simple, nagging hook and layer upon howling layer of feedback.

❷ SHADOWS
from I CAN HEAR THE HEART BEATING AS ONE
YLT at their most delicate: drummer Georgia Hubley's wounded bird whisper makes you want to hug her as she approaches the high notes.

❸ ALYDA from PRESIDENT YO LA TENGO
An early, folk-rock mid-pacer, the first to feature Hubley's gorgeous backing vocals alongside Ira Kaplan's (Lou) reedy tones.

❹ TOM COURTENAY from ELECTR-O-PURA
Perfect pop, YLT style, with noisy guitars and oodles of "ba ba bas". Extra points for name-checking Julie Christie and Eleanor Bron.

❺ I HEARD YOU LOOKING from PAINFUL
Instrumental feedback freakout that keeps looping back to its original, cyclical catchy riff.

⑥ BY THE TIME IT GETS DARK from **LITTLE HONDA SINGLE**

Hubley and Kaplan duet deliciously on this Sandy Denny ballad, like the Velvet Underground doing folk.

⑦ YOU CAN HAVE IT ALL from **AND THEN NOTHING TURNED ITSELF INSIDE OUT**

An old disco cut milked both for campness and melancholy, Hubley's shy vocal wooed by the boys' ebullient "da-ba-das".

⑧ FIVE-CORNERED DRONE (CRISPY DUCK) from **MAY I SING WITH ME**

One of many culinary titles from these notorious foodies: a rich repast of poppy melody and chiming guitars, plus eruptions of feedback.

Toby Manning

Neil Young

Part sensitive singer-songwriter, part guitar-thrashing axeman, Neil Young has been consistently releasing great records ever since he left Canada forty years ago. All his best work is characterized by the raw honesty that unites the two sides of his personality.

① MR SOUL from **DECADE**

This Buffalo Springfield hit shows Young's views on the record industry were already fully formed by 1967.

② CINNAMON GIRL from **EVERYBODY KNOWS THIS IS NOWHERE**

Backed by Crazy Horse on his second solo album in 1969, Neil Young perfected the technique of writing haunting love songs that also allowed space for over-amped guitar wig-outs.

③ DOWN BY THE RIVER from **EVERYBODY KNOWS THIS IS NOWHERE**

Quite why Neil shot his baby when he seemed to like her so much is rendered no clearer by nine minutes of musical mayhem.

④ ONLY LOVE CAN BREAK YOUR HEART from **AFTER THE GOLDRUSH**

A typically simple but damnably catchy song of the kind that brought Young-as-lonesome-troubadour his greatest commercial success.

⑤ OLD MAN from **HARVEST**

Back in 1972, when being 24 seemed pretty old, Neil's willingness to admit his similarity to his father was both radical and touching.

⑥ ON THE BEACH from **ON THE BEACH**

The title track from Young's bleakest album revealed that even worldwide acclaim had turned sour by 1974.

⑦ TONIGHT'S THE NIGHT FROM **TONIGHT'S THE NIGHT**

A desolate 1975 lament for the way drugs had destroyed a generation.

⑧ LIKE A HURRICANE from **AMERICAN STARS'N'BARS**

The rest of the album it's from is no great shakes, but this gloriously churning riff has been a live mainstay ever since.

⑨ CRIME IN THE CITY from **FREEDOM**

The energy and intensity of this 1989 album made Neil Young seem relevant again for at least another decade.

⑩ FARMER JOHN from **RAGGED GLORY**

Neil has never sounded happier than when reunited with Crazy Horse for this raucous 1990 singalong.

Greg Ward

Townes van Zandt

Before there was alt.country there was Townes van Zandt (1944–1997), self-effacing poet, songwriter and chronicler of lives. Once a military academy drop-out and latterly a recluse, he never had anything approaching a hit, but the list of country and folk stars who have recorded his troubadour's truthful songs is long and still growing.

❶ PONCHO AND LEFTY from **THE LATE, GREAT TOWNES VAN ZANDT**
It was Emmylou Harris' 1977 cover of this portrait of two ageing Mexican bandits – one dead, the other living in a cheap hotel – that brought van Zandt his first real recognition.

❷ TECUMSEH VALLEY
from **OUR MOTHER THE MOUNTAIN**
A miner's daughter finds a job in hard times, tending bar for Gypsy Sally but finds she can never go home again – an early sad story but poignant truth rather than country hard corn.

❸ MR MUDD & MR GOLD
from **HIGH, LOW AND IN BETWEEN**
Gripping, well-worked tale of playing cards conspiring to bring a gambler down – until the Queen of Diamonds is reminded of her lost son and starts to pray.

❹ LORETTA from **FLYIN' SHOES**
A travelling man finally acknowledges his undeclared love for his barroom goodtime girl – "Keep your dancing slippers on/keep me on your mind a while/I'm coming home".

❺ MARIE from **NO DEEPER BLUE**
From near the end of his career, a very different and deeply affecting monologue: of love on the welfare line, between a homeless drifter "with no one left to call" and his pregnant girl.

❻ TWO GIRLS from **LIVE AT THE OLD QUARTER**
"One's in heaven, one's below/One I love with all my heart and one I do not know." A typically intense, demanding portrait of a disturbed man wrapped up in his own world.

❼ I'LL BE HERE IN THE MORNING
from **TOWNES VAN ZANDT**
Like Gentle On My Mind in style, but the reverse in content: a drifter declares his lover more important to him than his travelling – a gentle, charming, upbeat song of devotion.

❽ FRATERNITY BLUES from **LIVE AT THE OLD QUARTER**
Droll, talking-blues satire of the American college fraternity system, with barbed asides: "Besides, I figured if you want good friends, you gotta pay for them."

❾ WAITING AROUND TO DIE
from **TOWNES VAN ZANDT**
This wry collection of sad attempts to escape aimless lives of low expectations – and the hopeless alternatives – packs a powerful message: make the most of your opportunities.

❿ TWO HANDS
from **HIGH, LOW AND IN BETWEEN**
Delightful, uplifting Carter Family–style spiritual: a modest pastiche but its gospel style simple avowal of faith – "I ain't gonna think about trouble any more" – hit the spot.

Ian Cranna

Frank Zappa

BARRY MILES has written key books on 60s culture as well as biographies of such figures as Burroughs, Ginsberg and Paul McCartney. He knew Frank Zappa, attending many of his recording sessions and, in 1994, writing his biography. Selecting a playlist proved a challenge: "Zappa composed in a wide variety of styles, from post-Varesian sound clusters to retro doo-wop, from novelty ditties to jazz-inspired rockouts, protest music to spoken-word collages. With more than 70 CDs in print, many of them doubles, to choose just ten tracks would not even cover all his styles, let alone rank his output. There were certain melodies that he re-worked time and time again, and some other tracks that jump out for attention, so, in no particular order, here are ten great Zappa tracks."

❶ PEACHES EN REGALIA from HOT RATS

A beautiful instrumental number described by Zappa as "probably the ultimate across the board Frank Zappa song of all time. It's the only thing I've never heard anybody say they didn't like."

❷ UNCLE MEAT from UNCLE MEAT

Another instrumental, a favourite for string quartets and ensembles to cover. Zappa recorded it many times but the original Uncle Meat album has the best version.

❸ WILLIE THE PIMP from HOT RATS

Another Hot Rats track, this a vocal sung by Captain Beefheart; it combines classy vocals, a classic example of Zappa's weird lyrics and terrific musicianship.

❹ THE JAZZ DISCHARGE PARTY HATS from THE MAN FROM UTOPIA

Zappa regarded this as one of his best. He described it as coming "close to Schoenberg, with its jazz accompaniment and a "Sprechgesang" text presentation." Many people find the lyrics deeply offensive.

❺ BROWN SHOES DON'T MAKE IT from ABSOLUTELY FREE

Recorded by the original Mothers line-up, this shows exactly why Zappa got such a following in the first place.

❻ WATERMELON IN EASTER HAY from FRANK ZAPPA PLAYS THE MUSIC OF FRANK ZAPPA

Recorded many times. Frank Zappa Plays… has two versions, including the original from Joe's Garage. One of his most beautiful compositions, beautifully played.

❼ BLACK NAPKINS from FRANK ZAPPA PLAYS THE MUSIC OF FRANK ZAPPA

Another superb composition, also present on Frank Zappa Plays… alongside the original recording on the Zoot Allures album.

❽ VALLEY GIRL from VALLEY GIRL SOUNDTRACK

One of Zappa's few hits, and a song that shows his anthropological approach to pop culture, in this case the teenage girls of the San Fernando Valley, whose accents are wonderfully imitated by his daughter Moon Unit, then 14 years old.

❾ VALARIE' (SIC) from BURNT WEENIE SANDWICH

A cover version of Jackie and the Starlite's Doo-wop original that shows how deep Zappa's roots were in West Coast R&B.

❿ G-SPOT TORNADOS from THE YELLOW SHARK

Another of Zappa's favourite tracks. This stark Ensemble Modern version is perhaps the most unusual and interesting.

Zimbabwe

Pungwe! In Zimbabwe, licensing laws do not apply. The music goes on all night, as loudly as possible. The arrival of Western instruments in the 1960s and 1970s saw such pioneers as Thomas Mapfumo and Oliver Mtukudzi combine the traditional patterns of drum and mbira with soul and reggae to create styles like jit, chimurenga and sungura: music for drinking, dancing and easing troubled minds.

❶ CHITIMA NDITAKURE THOMAS MAPFUMO from CHAMUNORWA

"Train, take me away". Hypnotic and heavy on the mbira, this is as rootsy as it gets.

❷ NDIMA NDAPEDZA OLIVER MTUKUDZI from TUKU MUSIC

The most beautiful moment on a beautiful album – the perfect Tuku blend of soul and groove.

❸ KUROJA CHETE THE BHUNDU BOYS from SHABINI

Even the struggle to pay the rent sounds like a cause for celebration!

❹ MISORODZI DUMISANI MARAIRE from THE AFRICAN MBIRA

Pure mbira tradition. All the sorrow of Africa.

❺ AMAI VARUBHI ALICK MACHESO from SIMBARADZO

The biggest hit from the biggest-selling Zimbabwean album ever. Macheso urges dialogue between wives and husbands over an unstoppable sungura beat.

❻ MAPIYEMANA STELLA CHIWESHE from KUMUSHA

Mbira, voice, clapping, drums and hosho hand-rattle – you don't get much more trance-inducing than this.

❼ TORNADOS VS. DYNAMOES (3-3) REAL SOUNDS from VENDE ZOKO

An epic piece of rumba. Zimbabwe meets the Congo in the greatest football clash in African music history.

❽ KULELIYANI'ZWE LOVEMORE MAJAIVANA from THE BEST OF LOVEMORE MAJAIVANA

The biggest star of the minority Ndebele tribe (an offshoot of the Zulu), steeped in South African mbaqanga.

❾ NDIVUMBAMIREIWO FOUR BROTHERS from ROOTS ROCK GUITAR PARTY

Awesome, no-messing-about Shona guitar pop from the 1980s Golden Age.

❿ KUMAKORODZI MBIRA DZE NHARIRA from RINEMANYANGA HARIPUTIRWE

Probably Zimbabwe's best new band of the past few years, Mbira dze Nharira play stripped-down, ethereal mbira music.

Tom Bullough

A DIGITAL MUSIC GUIDE FOR MAC & PC

MENU

THE ROUGH GUIDE TO

iPods

iTunes & music online

▶ ‖

2ND EDITION: COVERS IPOD PHOTO & SHUFFLE

Another lovely book you might enjoy